The Book of Water

The Book of Water

Healing, Regeneration and Recovery

by Steven Forrest

Seven Paws Press, Inc.
Borrego Springs, CA

Published in 2020 by Seven Paws Press, Inc.
PO Box 82
Borrego Springs, CA 92004
www.sevenpaws.com

ISBN 978-1-939510-09-9

Cover art by Diren Yardimli

Printed in the United States of America
LCCN 2020947324

ACKNOWLEDGEMENTS

Yet again, I want to express my gratitude to my manager and friend, Tony Howard. He still plays a pivotal role in supporting my outreach to the wider world, even as he supports so many other fine astrologers with his online Astrology University.

The Book of Water, like its three predecessors, was written rather than transcribed from talks. Still, it was an enormous help to be able to refer to a transcript of my original "Water" program – "Healers and Regenerators" – offered back in November 2016 at my bi-annual Apprenticeship Program meeting in Alpine, California. For the painstaking, tedious work of producing that transcript, I once again thank my student, JoAnn Anderson.

My gratitude also to my editor Shelley Madsen for her meticulous attention to my typos, misspellings, and other sins against the majesty of the English language.

I want to thank Thomas Miller for creating the audio versions of these Elements books. His voice conveys the spirit of my work as well as the content.

A profound *gracias* to the people who have run my various Apprenticeship Programs around the world over the years. The workload has often been crushing and I would have long ago either given up or committed homicide. Even though all but one of those programs are currently on hiatus in order to make time for me to write these Elements books and get my school fired up, I can affirm that teaching astrology in that rigorous, intensive way, and facing the intelligent questions and existential realities of around two thousand students over the years, has made me the astrologer I am today. Here, in no particular order, are the names of the brave souls who have led these programs over the past couple of decades. In southern California: Ingrid Coffin and her team at the Blue Sky Ranch Fellowship, with special thanks there to Cristina Smith, Jonathan Sacks, Paula Wansley, and Carey Nash. In China: Felicia Jiang and David Railey, along with the amazing NoDoor team. In North Carolina: Kathy Hallen and her able assistants, Carol McLauren and Tricia Mickleberry. In Nelson Bay, Australia, and various places around Europe: the indomitable Mercurial Connections team, Lisa Jones and Christine Murfitt. Finally, in northern California, I thank Joyce Van Horn, Kathy Jacobson, and Deni Mateer. My Apprenticeship Programs have come and gone, as have the people who have made them possible. Thanks, *emeritus*, to Karen Davis, Vinessa Nevala, Barbara King, and the late David Friedman.

I would like to offer special gratitude to two dear friends and colleagues, Dr. Catie Cadge and Jeff Parrett, with whom I am currently working hard to create the Forrest Center for Evolutionary Astrology – more about that project at the end of this book.

Finally my gratitude to the following people who were actively engaged with me in various ways during the writing process: Scott Ainslie and Barbara Ackerman, Lynn Bell, Virginia Bell, Cheryl Benedict, Chris Brennan, Lonnie and Josh Busic, Matt Cohen, Chip Conley, Cui "Chloe" Ying – my intrepid Chinese translator, Carol and Mike Czeczot, Rona Elliot and Roger Brossy, Michael Faith, Basil Fearrington, Hadley Fitzgerald, Rishi Giovanni Gatti, Stormie Grace, Robert and Diana Griffin, Eileen Grimes, the Grossenbacher clan: John, Tracy, and Ryan, Pamela Hoback, Susie and Mark Hodge, Sylvia Hsiao, Bariş İlhan, Bill Janis, Sherry Jayne, Kelly Jean, Mark Jones, Kathy King, Peter and Ingrid Kondos, Lisa Kostova, Kate, Alex, and Paisley Laird, Jackie Larsen, Rick Levine, Laurie Lindgren, Elizabeth Long, Ralph MacIntyre, Barbara Matson, Juliana McCarthy, Mary Ann McGuire, Kym and Scott McNabb, Cristin McVey, Randy Meeks, Thomas Miller, Linnea Mirron and Ricky Williams, Marley Willilams, Dominic Miller, Elizabeth Motyka, Jim Mullaney, Rafael Nasser, Brian O'Flynn, Annette O'Neill, Marie O'Neill, Nina Ortega and Miguel Bracho, Carol Peebles, Joey Paynter, Nicholas Polimenakos, Steven Poster and Susan Williams, Aminah Raheem and Fritz Smith, Claire Rauwel, Dusty Recor and "Indian Joe" Stewart, Ray Ristorcelli, Evelyn Roberts, Paige Ruane and Jack McDonald, Dr. Mamta Singhvi, Fran Slavich, Katie Sloan, Debbie and Scott Steingraber, Sting and Trudie Sumner-Styler, Kay Taylor, Elaine and Mark Thomas, Julia Trawick, Jaan Uhelszki, Dick and Artemisa Walker, Cindy Wyatt, Scotty Young and Diane Colie Swan, and Helen Zou.

TABLE OF CONTENTS

PART THREE: THE MOON, PLUTO, MARS, JUPITER
AND NEPTUNE THROUGH THE TWELVE SIGNS
AND HOUSES

PART FOUR: SEEING FUTURES

This one is for my Watery friend, Ingrid Coffin. For a quarter of a century, each one of us has been trying to trick the other one into being the Teacher. So far, the results are about even.

INTRODUCTION

I grew up speaking astrology as a second language. Both my mom and aunt were armchair astrologers. My aunt even wrote a series of fictional books using made-up astrological charts to develop the personalities and plots of the characters in her books. I remember thinking that was pretty groovy!

As a teenager in the 1970's, I gained some popularity from writing a monthly astrology column for the high school newspaper. But way before that, I have vivid memories of my best friend Susie and I lying together on my mom's king-size bed, pouring over her astrology books that were strewn all over the bed. Her mission was to look up the astrological charts of boys she thought were cute in order to determine if they were her 'soulmates,' destined for marriage. I poured through the same astrology cookbooks trying to understand why my life was so hard and why I felt things more deeply than anyone else I knew.

Of course, we didn't have Steven's Forrest's *Element Series* – or even the thought of evolutionary astrology – back then. The two books I remember were by Linda Goodman, her *Sun Signs* book and her *Love Signs: A New Approach to the Human Heart*. I can still remember the cover of that book – it was bright red with hearts and stars and a lion cuddling a ram.

If I had had *The Book of Water*, I would have felt deep comfort from understanding that I have a packed eighth house with my Sun, Pluto and Jupiter residing there. Even understanding my Mars in Pisces and my Saturn in Scorpio, from Steven's evolutionary astrology perspective, I would have understood that I was in for a life of actively healing past life wounds and facing hard truths. What a difference that would have made in how I saw myself and interpreted my life's experiences.

What makes Steven's approach to astrology so dramatically different from everything I grew up with is that it does not just describe your personality or predict your love life, but instead wrestles with the fact that life hurts us all and that astrology can help us actively heal ourselves from the "slings and arrows of outrageous fortune." Steven's evolutionary astrology approach is "prescriptive" rather than "descriptive." *The Book of Water* meets you where you are and guides you into viewing the classroom you're in and all the pathways available to you. We get to choose the high road or the low road, or any of the pathways in between.

I first met Steven Forrest in 1997 when I attended his *Introduction to Astrology* program that was held prior to the Northwest Astrological Conference (NORWAC) in Seattle. I remember calling my friend David Freidman, exclaiming with excitement and joy, "I can speak astrology again. I understand it." In that course, Steve walked us through the basic language and symbols and it was as if lifetimes of astrological knowing reawakened in me again. David and I talked about approaching him to see if he would create an Apprenticeship Program where neophyte astrologers like us could learn to approach astrology the way he did. That was the birth of the first Apprenticeship Program to be held in Southern California in 1998.

After that program, I signed up to get a couple of readings from Steven, both a birthchart analysis and a transits and progressions. I still have those cassette tapes. Every time I got one in the mail, I would sign up for an update. The time between each reading grew steadily longer and longer as his fame and popularity grew.

In those readings, Steven helped me deepen my understanding of my packed eighth house, with all of its Scorpionic overtones. When I understood that "the underlying evolutionary motivation of Scorpio is the urge, even compulsion, to face the truth squarely and courageously, I felt that I had had an epiphany – that I could heal the wounds of my painful childhood, and open up again to the miraculous.

In *The Book of Water,* Steven describes miracles as the "wondrous events *which we cannot understand or foresee."* He adds that, "Miracles make us think of the Higher Powers in the universe."

He writes:

When you were brokenhearted, you saw no hope. Maybe you said you would never love again. But you did. Like a miracle. How did you do that? How exactly did you heal? What mechanism regenerated you? How did you recover? That is the active side of the Water element. There will always be some things we do not understand about it. Water seeps down deeply into us, linking our awareness to our souls, our instincts, and our unconscious minds. Much of what happens at those interior levels is out of the reach of any kind of conscious analysis. And yet, we can learn to cooperate with those healing forces. We can make an alliance with them, as if they were invisible friends.

It is Steven's wisdom and guidance that inspired me to do my deeper healing work. As my progressed Sun moved into Scorpio, a series of synchronistic events transpired which engaged me in my own depths. I participated in Jean Houston's Mystery School for several years and hired a Jungian Analyst to help me look my wounds straight in the eye with unflinching honesty. I discovered a shamanic call and engaged in a three-year shamanic practitioner training. It was there that I found an even deeper calling for working as a *psychopomp* – which meant helping to escort newly-deceased souls from Earth to the afterlife. If that seems exotic to you, have a look at chapter four of this book, where Steven explores what has often been called "the Occult" in a way that integrates seamlessly with the larger processes of healing, regeneration, and recovery.

As Steven writes in this book, "We live in an enchanted universe, and it lives inside of us. If we experience the impact of conscious, choice-centered astrology – *and if we think about the implications of what we are experiencing* – the ground shifts beneath our feet. We are luminous creatures on a mysterious, meaningful journey." Thanks to Steve, that is what my life has become.

In 2019, I felt a call to finally write a book. I entitled it, *The Wisdom of Transition: Navigating Change at Work.* I struggled during the first two months, because it felt like I was writing two books. One was a deeply intimate, spiritual and personal book about transitions from that Scorpionic eighth-house perspective. The second book emerging was tamer – a book that would fit the worldview of the clients that I serve in my day job as a leadership consultant and executive coach. I went with the second book and it was published in early 2020. The only way I could find balance with that choice was to speak of Steven's work and ask him to write the jacket endorsement, which he did. He wrote "*Entire forests have been converted to self-help books in the past two generations and yet I've never before seen one so brilliantly and helpfully focused on this single, nearly universal zone of stress and opportunity – professional change. Cheryl Benedict has given all of us who work for a living a genuine treasure.*"

In complete candor, I think it means more to me to have Steven's endorsement than it means to have published a book. That is how important he has been to me as a mentor and guide throughout the past twenty-three years of my life.

Three weeks after I published the book on Amazon, my husband Paul rushed me to the hospital for emergency surgery – where I was told that I almost died on the table. I had a near-death experience where I basked in God's presence and felt radiant unconditional Love. All of the eighth house work with shamanism, which Steven had "prophesied" so many years before, really supported my ability to leave my body and journey to the light. When I got home and began the recovery process, I wrote to him to let him know what had transpired. He wrote, *"This is so classic "Transiting Pluto Trine Your Sun! Truth time, for sure – and Pluto is still Pluto, so you saw Death up close, but it's giving you wisdom about what's important and what is not, and that is precious."*

When I first began working with Steven, I was in my late thirties. Even then, based on my astrological configuration, he was preparing me to become a wise woman – an elder of my tribe – and to face aging with dignity and grace. He said to me pretty much exactly what is written in *The Book of Water:* 'You are, ultimately, a wise woman. Every tribe since the human world began has had a few of them. You are, at least potentially, part of that precious lineage. That is what you signed up for in this life. Or, more precisely, you signed up with *an evolutionary intention and soul-capability of attaining that level of sheer naked presence."*

Clinging to those wise words in the center of my being – I knew that I had to face the truth squarely and courageously and face the frightening, edgy truth that Scorpio encourages us to bravely contemplate. I was armed and prepared, as Steven wrote, "to commit to a path of stark naked, undefended *realness.* With success comes real wisdom, the kind that does not fail when the chips are all down."

Those truths allowed me to almost die and still come out on the other side to write this foreword for my dear friend, mentor and modern day Merlin.

Thank you Steven for the gift you are in all of our lives.

– Cheryl Benedict
Evergreen, Colorado

1

HEALING, REGENERATION, AND RECOVERY

An old woman dances alone in the moonlight on a windswept beach. Only she can hear the music that moves through her soul and animates her body. Her eyes are closed; she moves by faith and by instinct.

She's been dancing for eighty years. She used to want someone watching her. She would practice her steps in front of a mirror, checking out her moves.

Not anymore. It took her eighty years for her to learn how to forget herself. Her reasons for dancing now are not anything she could easily explain to a young person.

Every line on the old dancer's face tells a story. Many of those stories are sad ones: the husband she loved for fifty-two years, and buried twelve years ago. The dear friend who died suddenly of a brain aneurysm when they were both young mothers. The son who slipped away, overdosed on Oxycontin. The daughter who could have been a poet, but married a cretin who flatlined her delicate spirit.

And yet, we are confronted with this inexplicable miracle on that moonlit beach: the old woman still dances.

Of all of life's mysteries, is there a deeper one? Not that terrible things happen, *but that we dance anyway.* That we can recover. That spirit *regenerates.*

This woman is not a saint – that word is too narrow, too exclusive, too otherworldly. Using it would make her different from the rest of us. That is a mistake. She is as human as you or me.

Even better, that resilient old woman lives inside every one of us, if only we can find our way back to her.

Finding our way back to that dancer is what this book is about. Let's meet the good medicine of the Water signs – the guardians of the sacred mysteries of healing, regeneration, and recovery.

CAN WE CALL WATER "THE FEELING ELEMENT?"

Ask any astrologer. Water is about *emotions*. Fire *acts*, Earth *plans*, Air *thinks*, and Water . . . well, Water *feels*. That single word – *feeling* – covers a lot of bases: joy, sorrow, *ennui*, ecstasy, good moods, bad moods, and every other emotional state in between them.

All of them are in Water's domain.

Astrologers who equate the Water element with feelings are correct – Cancer, Scorpio, and Pisces do resonate with your emotional body. Without Water, we would all become inhuman, just walking microchips – flat, cold and mechanical, devoid of heart and soul, and probably with no particular reason to live. We read about the link between Water and feeling states everywhere in the literature of our craft. Our argument in these pages will not be that this equation of the Water element and our moods is incorrect, only that it leaves out too much of the magic.

In *Planets in Youth*, the great Robert Hand writes, "Water is the element of soul, feeling, emotion, and compassion." Liz Green, in *Relating*, adds, "Water has all the blessings of the feeling type – sensitivity to atmosphere, subtlety, charm and insight, a strong sense of values in human relationships, and the capacity to bring individuals together and instinctually understand their needs." Ronald C. Davison, in *Astrology,* writes, "Water is a personalizing element, adding emotional content to that which was hitherto only existing as a mental concept." More recently, April Elliot Kent, in *The Essential Guide to Practical Astrology*, describes the Water signs as "empathetic and sensitive" and warns that they might be "ruled by emotion, lack objectivity" – and possibly be "too defensive to get close to other people."

These are all fine astrologers, and every word they write here is correct, no argument.

But what does any of that have to do with an old woman dancing in the wind and the moonlight? How did she get there? What gives her the strength to defy the despair that threatens to drag her down into that fathomless well of sorrow?

That is the question I want to explore in these pages.

ONE DAY AT SCHOOL

Years ago when I was still living in North Carolina, I was offered a chance to teach a short astrology program at the local Society of Friend's School – the Quakers, as they are commonly known. The kids were perhaps eight years old, so I knew that my usual "talking head" approach would not hold their attention. I decided to try a more active experiential approach. I divided the children up by the element families of their Sun signs and assigned each group the same task. Their job was to try to get all of the children in each tribe to fit themselves inside an eighteen-inch circle. No one's feet could be outside it or they would fail. Each group had five or six kids in it. That meant that on the face of it the task was impossible. There just was not enough space in that circle to hold all of those tiny feet.

What happened next was pure astrology in action.

The Air kids sat down and discussed various possible solutions. In classic "committee" fashion, they accomplished absolutely nothing, but at least everyone had his or her say. Theories and ideas abounded. Nobody actually did anything.

The Earth kids got right down to the task and attempted a very logical solution. Earth-fashion, they tried to *build a structure*, with a couple of the larger boys forming the foundation, and stacking the lighter kids on top.

A great, practical idea – but it failed. They fell down.

The Water kids sat glumly in a circle, lost in their emotional reactions, and grumbled about feeling defeated by impossibility – and we will return to their dilemma in a moment.

The Fire kids won the prize. They all held hands in a circle and spun faster and faster in classic *Ring-Around-the-Rosie* fashion, leaning outward, letting centrifugal force hang their bodies away from the center, while their feet were all two-stepping inside that eighteen-inch circle.

All hail the gods of Fire! They got the laurels that day.

But we explored those gods back in the first book of this series.

On the face of it, the Water kids came off the worst of the four groups. *They didn't even try.* Instead, they wallowed in their misery – in their *feelings* – and did nothing.

As we will soon see, that defeated emotional attitude does not define the limits of the Water element. Its higher potentials will put tears of joy in your eyes. But every front has a back – and the low expression of Water is indeed that kind of befuddled inability actually *to do anything.* We have all been laid low by a mood, rendered unable to lift a finger even to make simple, helpful changes. That is the soul-cage that Water can represent.

My anecdote about the children at the Friends' school illustrates one of the ways we unfairly cripple Cancer, Scorpio, and Pisces when we think of the Water element simply in terms of feeling states. *Feeling states, in and of themselves, tend to go nowhere.* They can become morbidly self-contained and passively auto-referential. They can become paralyzed by the hypnotic spell of their own all-encompassing moodiness. They can be too depressed even to turn on the lights as afternoon fades to evening.

Here's a quick real-life illustration of that principle expressed in a broader way: we have all come to dead ends in intimate negotiations when someone cuts off all discussion and any chance of genuine resolution by deploying the nuclear option: *"That's just the way I feel."*

End of story.

There will be no more progress in that relationship. The door is now closed. Water has doused the Fire, drowned the Air, and left Earth stuck in the mud.

And none of that has anything whatsoever to do with healing, regeneration, or recovery.

MORE THAN A FEELING

Water must be understood as something beyond the source of human affect and moodiness. Thinking about it in those limited ways quickly leads us to these kinds of dead ends. If that is all there is to Water, then all the Cancerians, Scorpios, and Pisceans would just stay home in bed. That *deification of our moods* is a pitfall we must all learn to avoid. We escape it, not by avoiding Watery states, but by letting them open like flowers into realms of magic, transcendence, and healing insight.

Remember that old woman dancing on the beach. She has a lot to teach us, and it is not only about feelings. It is also about the wellsprings of our *spiritual resilience.*

Thinking of Water simply as if it were a moody, undisciplined child who needs tolerance, indulgence and correction leaves out something utterly simple and obvious – and something lucidly, brilliantly revealing – about the nature and purpose of *literal* water as it comes out of a faucet or a mountain spring.

Specifically that . . .

WATER NURTURES LIFE

Three days without a drop of it and you are dead. That is the rule of thumb in the Search and Rescue community, although it is subject to many modifying factors. Under optimal conditions, you might survive dehydration for as long as a week. In a hot desert, you might not make it for one day.

Water is far more important than food. Mohandas Gandhi fasted for three weeks. Jesus fasted for forty days. But without water we are all quickly doomed.

And of course, in this absolute need for water, we are not alone. All life as we understand it requires water to survive: asparagus, penguins – you name the life-form, in every case, *thirst kills.*

That statement is literal, but it is also symbolic. There is water that comes from faucets or mountain springs – *and there is another Water,* something that serves our souls the same way that those molecules of oxygen and hydrogen serve the cells of our physical bodies.

Finding that sacred well inside ourselves and *learning how to drink from it* is what we will be exploring in everything that follows.

THE ACTIVE SIDE OF WATER

The heart of the matter is that the astrological tradition in general has done a good job of mapping the *passive* dimension of the Water element: all of the moods, feelings, and affective states that arise naturally in the psyche and which color our inner lives. Usually these states are animated by our underlying *needs* and *appetites*, along with the emotions which arise automatically in response to them being satisfied or left wanting.

That is all helpful, relevant insight. Any counseling astrologer needs to understand those passive, descriptive, parts of the astrological tradition regarding the Water element.

What gets systematically left out however is the *active* side of Water.

Here is what that word means: maybe you get divorced or go through a hard breakup. Maybe someone you love dies suddenly. You are sad. You experience grief. Those passive, reactive processes are necessary and they deserve respect and understanding. *But five years later, you are fine.* You can love again. You can have faith in life.

What happened to create that miracle?

"Miracle" is the right word too. Miracles are wondrous events *which we cannot understand or foresee.* Miracles make us think of the Higher Powers in the universe.

When you were brokenhearted, you saw no hope. Maybe you said you would never love again.

But you did.

Like a miracle.

How did you do that? How exactly did you heal? What mechanism regenerated you? How did you recover?

Those are the *active* sides of the Water element.

There will always be some things that we do not understand about those processes. Water seeps down deeply into us, linking our conscious awareness to our souls, to our instincts, and to our unconscious minds. Much of what happens at those interior levels is beyond the reach of any kind of conscious analysis.

And yet, we can learn to *cooperate* with those healing forces. We can *make an alliance with them,* as if they were invisible friends. Maybe they *are* invisible friends – and in fact in many cultures throughout human history they were seen that way, as angels, saints, and benevolent daemons.

Whatever we might call these Watery forces of healing and regeneration, if we fail in creating alliance with them, miseries accumulate in us like bad credit card debts with compounded interest.

Succeed, and you'll be dancing on beaches in the moonlight when you are ninety years old with an enigmatic smile on your wrinkled face.

A HARD PASSAGE

Please bear with me for the next couple of hundred words. They will be unfashionably dark and painful to read – but I promise that they lead us directly to what is perhaps the greatest treasure we can ever find in this world.

What follows is the truth, but not the whole truth – it leaves out friendship and starry nights and flowers being beautiful for no reason and birds singing in the morning.

We will soon get to those good things, but first, fasten your seatbelts. We've got to get over a bumpy patch on the highway of life.

Human existence can be absolutely awful. How much heartbreak have you known in your life? How many tragic deaths have you witnessed? How many cancers and heart attacks have struck down people you loved – and maybe struck them down before their time?

How many failed relationships can a person endure? How many losses? How many broken dreams and broken hearts?

How many promising kids have you witnessed falling into bitterness, empty materialism, or addiction? How often has someone else's suicide taken a bite out of your soul?

How many of your best aspirations have gone poof?

What about the daily onslaught of the news headlines – mutilated bodies in mass graves, creatures driven to extinction, melting ice caps, along with scoundrels in high places, ruling, raping, and robbing this fallen world?

While we are at it, how does your physical body feel? Any aches or pains?

And what about your own personal moral and spiritual failures? Think for a moment about the worst things you have ever done in your life – your lowest, most shameful moments. We all have them. Guilt may not get us anywhere spiritually, but it is hard to shake free of its grip unless you are either perfect or have no conscience at all – and the former is a rarer condition than the latter.

How can we take it? How can we endure the fierce, relentless onslaught of pain and disappointment that we call human life?

But we do.

There is a sacred mechanism inside of each one of us – a mechanism that triggers our miraculous, inexplicable capacity for healing, regeneration, and recovery.

I can guarantee that you know exactly what I am talking about. That is because you have lived it. I can affirm that with confidence.

Otherwise you would be too defeated or depressed to be reading this book.

ON THE ROAD TO RECOVERY

Cancer, Scorpio, and Pisces – the three Water signs – offer us a map of certain specific healing processes hardwired into human consciousness. These processes can restore us to vibrancy, no matter what kinds of body-blows we have experienced.

Literal water always seeks the lowest level, and in a sense, that is what these three zodiacal processes do too. *They lead us down into the interior realms of the psyche, guiding us through a labyrinth of defenses and emotional scar tissue, down to where the hurts and the wounds actually lie.* Once there, they reveal a three-staged process of active healing, one that can render you whole again, just as surely – and just as mysteriously – as your skinned knee healed up after you fell off your bicycle when you were nine years old.

In *The Book of Fire*, we looked at a set of mechanisms that can help sustain our vitality and give us a reason to live. Those are sacred processes too – but in a sense they simply give us the pluck to keep on keeping on. The Fire Family helps us to "drink out of the full half of the cup," while effectively blocking out the pain of its empty half. Fire offers the kind of toughness and ability to bounce back that comes from simply having faith in life.

In a nutshell, the Fire Family puts a bandage on our pain, offers us a stiff drink or a cup of tea, followed by an encouraging pat on the back.

That is all precious and we are grateful for it – but Water works differently. With the active side of the three Water processes, we actually *go down into the dark*. We face everything hidden or buried there. *We dare to feel it.* We let ourselves be vulnerable. Water sometimes invites us to try to keep our hearts open in hell-worlds – that is how fierce it can be.

For all our talk about its sensitivity to inner states, *there is nothing weak about Water.*

If we fear tears, we fail Water's test.

If we try to live in our heads, it will tear our heads off our shoulders.

To navigate these healing Water-worlds, we need a map. That map is what I will try to offer you in the rest of these pages. Read on, and fasten your seatbelts.

2

THE INTERDEPENDENCY OF THE THREE WATER SIGNS

Cancer, Scorpio, and Pisces – these three signs *need* each other a lot more than they actually *like* each other. Over the years, rumors of their harmony have been grievously exaggerated. We learn that they "understand each other," that they "have a lot in common," that Cancers should marry Scorpios or Pisceans – in essence, that you could lock the three of them up in a tiny New York studio apartment and they would proceed to live happily ever after in a merry *ménage à trois*.

Most of that amorous take on the three Water signs is nothing more than the triumph of astrological herd instinct and endless repetition over the actual realities of human experience. Astrologers are no more immune to it than anyone else.

Let's look at these three signs with fresh eyes, while thinking carefully about the actual nature of their interactions. Each one of them represents a very deep well of meaning. Each one plays a critical, but very distinct, role in the processes of healing, regeneration, and recovery – a role that is not always welcomed by the other two. Over the next three chapters, we will lower our buckets down the shafts of each one of those wells and put the water we collect under a microscope.

For now, let's just take a quick peek at all three of them, trying to get a fix on the big picture.

ENDPOINTS

Ultimately, all twelve signs of the zodiac can be understood individually simply as an *ideal*. You might even call them "ideas in the mind of God." That is true of every sign, not just the three Water signs. Every sign represents a unique *evolutionary endpoint* – and that means a lofty spiritual goal toward which we can aspire, but which we can never really attain, not any more than the sailor sailing north expects to arrive at Polaris.

In spelling out these endpoints, the impulse to employ the caps key is irresistible. Try these three, for example – a Fire sign, an Air sign, and an Earth sign:

- *Perfect Courage* (Aries)
- *Perfect Openness* (Gemini)
- *Perfect Self-Discipline* (Capricorn)

No one, of course, is ever that impeccable. There are plenty of cowardly Arians, dogmatic Geminis, and even the occasional lazy Capricorn. Again, these are *ideals*, not "personality profiles." We are delving far deeper into the purpose of life than that. Our aims lie in the *mysteries of regeneration*, not in the trivial ego-aggrandizements of marketplace astrology.

When we start thinking of the twelve signs *aspirationally*, we have taken a giant step closer to what I believe to be the true purpose of astrology. We have left the banal and uninspiring realm of mere *astrological description*, where "all the Geminis talk too much" and "all the Arians are hotheads." We are no longer reducing anyone's chart – or anyone's life – to a litany of silly personality traits.

Take that giant step, and you have arrived squarely in the world of evolutionary astrology, where we simply acknowledge that each and every soul is evolving – or *trying* to evolve, or at least *needing* to evolve – in the general direction of those lofty endpoints.

We are offering *prescription rather than description*.

That dogmatic Gemini could use a dose of "perfect openness." That lazy Capricorn needs to quit playing video games and get an actual job.

That cowardly Aries needs to stop blustering, and actually stand up for something.

In my first book, *The Inner Sky,* I introduced a formal schema which underlies our interpretation of each one of the signs. In that model, each sign of the zodiac represents:
- An *Endpoint* – that lofty spiritual goal.
- A *Strategy* for actually getting there.
- A set of inborn *Resources* that are the essential tools for the job.
- And finally, a *Shadow* expression of the energies – one in which the tools are misused and the endpoint forgotten.

That schema applies to the Fire, Earth, and Air signs, and it is true of the Water signs as well. Even now, thirty-six years after *The Inner Sky* was published, I still think of the zodiac in exactly the same way: the signs represent twelve *pathways* – not just twelve pre-programmed behavioral microchips stuck into our skulls at the moment of birth.

What about Cancer, Scorpio, and Pisces? What ideals and aspirations do they symbolize?
- Cancer's Endpoint is *Perfect Sensitivity and Self-Nurture.*
- Scorpio's Endpoint is *Perfect Transparent Honesty.*
- Pisces' Endpoint is *Perfect Transcendence and Release.*

It hurts my heart to reduce each sign to a single word or two that way. Each Water sign deserves and demands many pages – read on, that is what the rest of this book is about. But for now, let's take these simple "starter kit" ideas about the specific Endpoints of the three Water signs and use them to question the hoary astrological *shibboleth* that "all the Cancers should marry Scorpios or Pisceans."

A SCENE FROM A MARRIAGE

Scorpio: (gazing penetratingly) "I notice that you've put on a few pounds lately. You're starting to look a little porky. What's wrong? Is there something that we need to talk about?"

Cancer: (in tears) You don't love me anymore . . .

Inevitably, in writing those last few words, I'm reducing human beings to cartoon characters. Scorpio and Cancer *people* are rarely that simple. For one thing, they have Moons and Mercuries and so on. Charts are complicated – just like human beings. Further, each sign is like an educational track in which we have people in spiritual kindergarten and people in spiritual PhD programs. The *evolutionary level* at which someone is operating is not really visible in the birthchart. The person's level of consciousness naturally has a profound impact on how he or she acts. There are high, conscious Scorpios and Cancers, and goofy ones too.

- Still, Scorpio's truthfulness can sting – hence the "scorpion" symbolism.
- And Cancer is the Latin word for *crab* – a creature with a shell, and if that shell is penetrated, the crab is doomed. Crabs understand that, and so they are cautious

One look at Scorpio and Cancer begins to tremble. A marriage made in heaven? *And yet . . . and yet . . . might Cancer actually benefit from hearing some of that Scorpionic truth?*

And might Scorpio learn something from Cancer about gentleness and patience?

A SECOND SCENE FROM A MARRIAGE

Scorpio: Why are you laughing? Can't you see that I'm trying to be serious?

Pisces: (giggling) I'm sorry – I know this is important to you, I really do. But it's just that you look so funny when you're all frothy with intensity like that. I wish you could see yourself!

Scorpio: "I am trying to work on our relationship. There is something we really need to talk about here . . .

Pisces: (looking heavenward) Why can't you just drop all the drama for once? I give up . . . OK, whatever . . . talk all you want.

Go ahead, be the judge and the jury – in that little Scorpio-Pisces disagreement, who is right and who is wrong? Honest intimate processes can be difficult, but resolving those difficulties is what makes truly bonded relationships different from mere hook-ups. Scorpio knows that and is the custodian of that particular piece of human wisdom.

On the other hand, *what happens to people who can never laugh at themselves?* And, more pointedly, would you ever want to live with one?

Or, worse, to *be* one?

Scorpio can learn a lot about "getting the joke" from Pisces . . . that is, if it can get over itself enough to listen to a broader, more forgiving – and probably more humorous point of view.

Meanwhile, Pisces can sometimes be summoned back from *la-la land* by one penetrating Scorpionic insight.

On yet another hand, let's be careful not to put a halo on Pisces . . .
Cancer: "You never wanted children!"
Pisces: "It wasn't that I didn't want them . . . I . . . *I just forgot.*"

ANOTHER SCENE FROM A MARRIAGE

Here is another story with the ring of high Pisces as it balances Scorpio and Cancer. It is a true story this time, and one which will carry us beyond the cartoonish illustrations that I have been creating so far and directly into the human world.

I used to do a lot of ongoing counseling. Two women in a relationship were having some trouble getting along. They came to me for help. We would meet every two or three weeks and try to sort through their various psychological dilemmas. One of their visits happened to fall on the first truly perfect Spring day in Chapel Hill, North Carolina, where I lived for many years – and, at least on that one day, there is no better place to be in this world. The azaleas are blooming, the birds are singing in the trees, and there is perfume in the air. To grasp that perfection, you might cue native son, James Taylor, singing, *Carolina On My Mind.*

Naturally, the three of us loudly lamented having to go inside on a perfect day like that. In those days, I lived by the edge of a forest. I suggested that we take a stroll down a woodland path and do our session there instead of in my office. I knew a secluded spot where we could sit on a granite outcrop beside a gurgling brook. It was only a quick walk of three or four minutes.

They happily agreed.

We soon sat down on those rocks, under the towering evergreens, by the whispering water. I picked up where we had left off in my office a couple of weeks earlier. "You were saying that you feel that Meg has unresolved issues with her mother which she sometimes projects onto you. Is that a fair summary?"

We took it from there.

"Meg" naturally had a different perspective.

Inside of ten minutes, the three of us were laughing out loud. Under those pines, sitting on that ancient granite, that kind of Scorpionic psychology became almost comically irrelevant. Nature's overwhelming beauty that day had put us in a Piscean framework – a framework of *transcendence.*

We ended our session early. I still remember following these two women back up the path to my house. They were holding hands as we left the forest. All of that psychological stuff just seemed silly to them now. They let it go – and just decided to love each other despite everything.

The family that prays together stays together.

If we give that last line some cultural breathing room, it quickly becomes quintessential Pisces – "praying together" is not just about a billboard in Mississippi or even saying grace before a meal. There are lots of ways to pray. One of them is to sit in a forest and to feel eternity flowing through your bloodstream – and to turn to your partner and see her or him in that violet light of wisdom and radical Piscean acceptance.

- What we have in this little anecdote is an illustration of how Piscean transcendence can balance, correct, and heal the go-for-the-jugular psychological qualities of Scorpio – not to mention the potentially defensive self-absorption of Cancer.

My underlying aim in every one of these "scenes from marriages" is to illustrate what will be the backbone of this final book in the Elements series: *that it is not harmony, but rather interdependency, which unites Cancer, Scorpio, and Pisces.* As we saw at the beginning of this chapter, they need each other a lot more than they like each other.

In summary:

- Cancer can teach Scorpio about the healing powers of *kindness, forgiveness, unambiguous commitment,* and *patience,* while teaching Pisces how to remain *grounded in the heart of self-accepting, authentic, 100% human, naked emotional need.*
- Scorpio can teach Cancer about how *courageous emotional honesty* can be the ultimate healing tool, cutting straight to the actual

sources of what actually creates pain and fear in our lives. Meanwhile, Scorpio can teach Pisces about how *unresolved, or unconscious, woundedness* can *block our ascent* on the evolutionary path.

- Pisces can teach Cancer that the Vastness that surrounds us all has a benign, welcoming face, rather than a threatening one, and that *we need not fear it.* Meanwhile, Pisces can teach Scorpio that *our wounds are no match for compassion, forgiveness, and a gentler and more humorous perspective on life.*

ELEVEN WORDS

As with the previous three volumes in this Elements series, we are not looking only at the trio of Water signs. We will also explore their three associated houses – the fourth house, which corresponds to Cancer, along with the very Scorpionic eighth house and the Piscean realms of the twelfth house. Houses and signs are not interchangeable quantities, but they are closely related. We will pursue the distinctions carefully in the pages that follow. In a nutshell, the houses are external *behavioral expressions* of the interior *motivations and values* symbolized by the signs. We *feel* the signs inwardly and we actually *do something* about those feelings in the houses.

Three signs and three houses: that makes six words that we need to learn in our attempt to master the vocabulary of Water. But we are not yet done. We need to add planets to the mixture.

The Moon rules Cancer. That is straightforward enough, and "Moon" is our seventh word.

What planet rules Scorpio? Traditionally the answer was Mars, and in my opinion, that connection is still completely valid. But when Pluto was discovered in 1930, many astrologers quickly saw that it also very clearly resonated with Scorpio. Some astrologers replaced Mars with Pluto as Scorpio's ruler, while others resisted the change, seeing many good reasons why Mars should continue to rule the sign

It remains a contentious area.

In my opinion, *both* planets rule Scorpio – and, looking at it a little more deeply, the problem stems more from the *dominator* term "rulership" than with any true dilemma. Despite the notion of "ruling," neither planet "bosses Scorpio around" – that would be dangerous business, even for toughies such as Mars and Pluto.

Bottom line, we can now add two more words to our Water vocabulary: *Mars* and *Pluto*.

A similar dual-rulership situation exists with Pisces. Its historical ruler is Jupiter, and that resonance remains valid despite the 1846 discovery of Neptune. In my view, both planets rule Pisces, while each one expresses a different dimension of the sign.

That makes a total of eleven words: *Cancer, Scorpio, Pisces, houses four, eight, and twelve, plus the Moon, Mars, Pluto, Jupiter and Neptune.*

Learn the meaning of each one and you will have mastered astrology's Waterworld.

We learned a lot about Mars and Jupiter in *The Book of Fire*, so we will downplay them somewhat here in *The Book of Water*. But we will not ignore them – that would be misleading, and it would leave giant holes in our understanding. I focus less attention on Mars and Jupiter only to avoid too much repetition from that earlier volume – and also to leave plenty of room in these pages for some brand new territory: Neptune, Pluto, and the Moon.

I MUST REALLY LIKE ALL THREE OF THE WATER SIGNS . . .

. . . since I've already written books about three of their ruling planets.

A decade into my writing career, now defunct ASC Publications commissioned me to write *The Book of Pluto*, which came out in 1994. Many years later, in 2010, I wrote *The Book of the Moon* and published it through our own Seven Paws Press. And in 2016, I brought out *The Book of Neptune*. All three volumes are available at www.forrestastrology.com.

Some of you undoubtedly already own at least one of those books – and thank you for that. Inevitably, there will be some overlap between those three works and what you will read in the forthcoming pages. The Moon remains the Moon, of course, and even though all of the writing here will be new, most of the underlying concepts remain the same.

Here are the differences:

- Here in *The Book of Water*, we will follow the format of the earlier Elements volumes. We will delve into the three Water houses – something we did not explore nearly as deeply in those earlier books.
- We will tie the overriding theory to the traditional rulers of Scorpio and Pisces: Mars and Jupiter. And I've never written *The Book of Mars* or *The Book of Jupiter*, so I am glad to have the opportunity to explore them in this series.
- We will catalog each one of the various possible house, sign, and aspect placements of those five Water planets individually and in "cookbook" fashion, along with taking a deeper look at how all eleven of these Water syllables interact with each other.
- We will consider the Moon, Neptune, and Pluto in a broader, more astrologically integrated way than we did in those earlier planet-focused books.
- We will also do a better job of holding the hands of readers who may just be starting their study of astrology.

Still, not to ignore the obvious: an entire book devoted specifically to the Moon, Neptune, or Pluto can penetrate the symbol a lot more deeply than a chapter or two in a volume with a wider scope. Especially if you are new to astrology, I would recommend starting here with *The Book of Water*, then delving into those previous volumes if you find your curiosity piqued.

PART ONE

THE THREE WATER CLANS

Over the next three chapters, we dive into three deep oceans of astrological meaning – the "clans" of Cancer, Scorpio, and Pisces. I use the word "clan" because these three signs do not operate in a vacuum – they are hardwired to certain planets and certain houses. Cancer is ruled by the Moon and has a natural resonance with the fourth house. Those three symbols are not interchangeable, but they are closely related, interactive, and interdependent in meaning. Together, they form the "Cancer clan" and it makes sense to see them working in symbolic unity.

It is the same with Scorpio and Pisces, along with their associated houses and ruling planets.

Our immediate aim here in Part One is to become familiar with the root evolutionary meanings of these "eleven words" in our Water vocabulary, specifically as they operate in a natal chart. Over the next three chapters, we explore each clan in an extended essay.

Later, in Part Four, we will set them dancing in the form of transits, progressions, and solar arcs.

3

THE CANCER CLAN

To simply feel what I actually feel, uncensored and unedited and without interpretation . . . to surrender to my own heart . . . to experience my inner life in a self-accepting way, with no judgment and nothing rejected.

Imagine that you approach someone who knows nothing at all about astrology. You say, *"You're a real Cancer, aren't you?"* The results might not be pretty. Modern people hear the word "cancer" and their first reflex is to think of the disease rather than a sign of the zodiac. Outside of astrology conferences, calling someone "a cancer" might get you a dirty look, or worse.

Poor Cancer has a serious public relations problem. I remember back when I was a kid there was a Sun Sign column in *The Daily Argus*, our local newspaper, that went, "Aries, Taurus, Gemini, *Moon Children*, Leo, Virgo . . ."

And the Moon does actually rule Cancer, so between that legitimate astrological fact and not wanting to sow the seeds of despair, maybe the author of that column made the right call. Moon Children they were.

Loudly and clearly, let me say that being born in the month following the northern Summer Solstice does not up your cancer risks. There are slight statistical "season of birth" variations in cancer rates, with some specific forms of the disease linked to certain seasons, while other forms of cancer are linked to different seasons. The distribution is all over the map, in other words, and the variations are small anyway.

Bottom line, all of you astrological Cancers can breathe a sigh of relief.

But why do we use the same word for the sign and the disease? The answer goes back to the "Father of Medicine," Hippocrates. In Greece, around 400 B.C., it is claimed that he named masses of cancerous cells *karkinos*, which is the Greek word for crab. No one knows for sure, but he allegedly gave it that name because the hardened mass of an advanced tumor felt like a crab's shell to him. Around 47 A.D., a Greco-Roman philosopher, Celsus, wrote an encyclopedia of medicine in which he translated the Greek word *karkinos* into its Latin equivalent: *cancer.*

And we have been stuck with the mess ever since.

SYNCHRONICITY STRIKES AGAIN

In writing the last three or four hundred words, I've had both an overt and a covert agenda. At the obvious level, I have been exploring the etymology of the word we use for the zodiac's fourth sign. But at a more deviously Scorpionic level, I have been trying to work with the magic of synchronicity. *I have been trying to give you an experience that triggered a Cancerian reaction in you.*

Let's see if I succeeded . . .

My words have been about astrology, *but also about a terrible disease.* I am sure that you understood the astrological point of the opening words of this chapter – but I suspect that more was going on inside of you than that, at least subliminally. I brought up something nightmarish. The disease we call cancer is a dreadful beast. Maybe you've lost someone to it. Maybe you've faced it directly yourself. My mentioning cancer, even indirectly, very likely catalyzed a subterranean emotional reaction in you – a deeply human event not found in the abstract domain of Air, but rather in the vulnerable, emotional heart of the three Water signs.

As you scanned my opening words, I speculate about two possible interior reactions you might have had:

- Perhaps you felt the tender, nurturing, and protective energies that naturally arise in any of us toward a loved one who has just received such a disheartening medical diagnosis.
- Perhaps you recoiled in horror from this terrible imagery, wondering why I choose to make you contemplate such a thing. Might there not have been a *nicer* way in which I could have opened this chapter?

My point with all of this is simply that both of those emotional responses represent active dimensions of this first Water sign.

Cancer is both nurturing of others and, at the same time, self-protective.

Cancer reaches out toward the suffering of other beings. Simultaneously, *it is acutely aware of the possibility of getting hurt itself* – and profoundly motivated to avoid that pain at all costs.

That is why Crabs have shells.

Getting one chapter ahead of myself, while I have written about the *disease* we call cancer in order to trigger a direct experience of the *sign* Cancer in you, my *sneaky-for-a-good-cause* way of doing it is a pretty fair illustration of the way Scorpio works. But more about that second Water sign later on. First we need to grasp this *Cardinal* expression of the Water element. Cancer represents the *root manifestation* of this whole family of symbols. Cancer is raw, direct emotion served up with an extra box of handkerchiefs, straight, no chaser – and no second-guessing about the uncontested primacy of what we *actually feel.* At this point, we do not care what it means or why we feel it. We simply feel it directly, as it is.

And right there, with our vulnerable humanity queued up on center stage, we have the Cancerian *foundation* of all healing, all regeneration, and all possibility of recovery. That is where it must always begin. If you cannot feel your hurts and your needs honestly and authentically, then your Water Family rocket ship just blew up on the launching pad.

CRABS AND THEIR SHELLS

A crab, snug and safe inside its shell, snuffles around on the seabed, scrounging up a meal. Along comes a hungry eel, looking to perhaps dine on crab this evening. Too bad for the eel – that crab is well-defended. That shell is tough.

Knock, knock says the eel. Forget about it, says the crab. The eel swims off, and the crab proceeds nonchalantly to its own seabed buffet.

And therein lies the problem: as the crab eats, it grows.

And its shell does not.

Maybe you are young. Maybe your feet are size 6, going on size 7. You are growing, but your shoes are not. You probably remember how it felt. Your toes are pinched.

The crab feels the same way.

The creature has only one good choice: *it must shed its shell* – and as quickly as possible grow another, larger one. For a shaky moment, it is *a soft-shelled crab* – spying it, that eel's culinary ambitions would take a more optimistic turn.

Eat and grow, eat and grow – if you are a crab, sooner or later eating gets you into trouble.

Ditto for a human Cancerian, except the issue is not narrowly about food. *It is about the food of the soul, which is experience.* As a result of experience, Cancer sooner or later finds itself having "outgrown its shell."

The trouble is that Cancer has also *outgrown the safety* that shell provided.

The crab in nature, faced with this perilous transition, chooses the time and place for that shell-shedding with care: it happens in a sunken spare tire, under the pier at midnight . . . with no Moon in the sky, if you please.

A human Cancerian is wise to do approximately the same thing – to risk vulnerability, but *to do so carefully and judiciously.* He or she must be cautious about who gets past the wall of that shell. This process of cautious discernment, as we will see, is right at the core of any possibilities of healing.

This *shedding of the shell of safety* is always Cancer's first step. It does not happen without risk – which leads to a dark temptation: *choosing not to shed the shell at all.*

CANCER IS NOT WEAK

When a client comes to sit with me for the first time and I see Cancer symbolism prominent in his or her chart, there is a line I often use: *when you were born, the universe turned the volume up to maximum on your ability to feel.*

It's true too. As the first of the three Water signs, Cancer epitomizes the capacity to respond to life primarily through the heart. It is, above all, *sensitive.*

Let's think about that word "sensitive" for a moment. Every term in the English language – and probably every other language too – has a halo of secondary meanings around it. If we are not careful, those nuances can muddy the water without our knowing it.

If I meet someone socially and I comment that he or she seems to be "a very sensitive person," the inevitable response is "thank you." We tend to view sensitivity as a virtue. And it *is* a virtue, of course. But built into that compliment is a potential barb. To understand Cancer, we need to dispel an unspoken error that comes packaged with the word "sensitive." Implying that someone is "sensitive" might be understood to mean that we must walk on eggshells around him or her, being wary of giving offence or triggering a dramatic crying jag.

Believing that Cancer's sensitivity implies weakness is an error.

Nature itself corrects us there, if we stop and reflect for a moment. *The crab's shell works just fine.* Crabs are not an endangered species. Cancer people can generally take care of themselves quite effectively – often with enough energy left in reserve to take care of you as well.

DEFENSIVENESS

I get a giggle out of this – maybe you will too. *Perhaps the single most reliable way of triggering a psychologically defensive response from any halfway-educated person is to suggest that he or she is "being defensive."*

People hate to hear that. They feel attacked. Claws come out. *"Who the hell do you think you are, my psychologist?"*

Perhaps we encounter a crab on the beach. Perhaps we say, "Mr. or Ms. Crab, I hope you don't mind if I give you some personal feedback. *You come across as if you have this shell around you . . .*" And of course the crab scuttles away, probably cursing the plague of paperback psychology books.

An absolute key in understanding the psychodynamics of Cancer is to recognize a fundamental law of nature: *that sensitivity must defend itself.* Or it dies.

Still, the crab in nature must eventually shed its shell, or it dies a different kind of death: a morbid, changeless condition of *spiritual stasis.* We might even call it dying of sheer *boredom.* This tension between the *exigencies of evolution* and the natural impulse toward *safety* and *self-preservation* is absolutely pivotal in our understanding of the Cancer clan.

Crabs figured out how to blend these two countervailing drives countless millennia ago – the bottom line for any crab is that while you must shed the shell, you need to do it *carefully.*

We have now come face-to-face with Cancer's core evolutionary paradigm: *grow while living inside the safety of a shell, then judiciously shed the shell, then grow another, larger one, then safely grow inside it some more, then shed it again . . . and ever onward.*

For an Enlightened Being who is a Cancer, I suspect the entire universe is included inside the shell, and there is no longer anything to fear at all.

But that is the end of a very long and winding road – one with a long trail of shed shells strewn behind it.

HIDING UNDER THE KITCHEN TABLE

I recall a birthchart session years ago with a woman who was very Cancerian, with lots of fourth house planets too. As we began, I described the typical "first shell" of the Crab to her – a shell we often see in youth: *shyness*. It is as if Cancers are saying, *"Reality, I don't like you very much and you don't like me very much. Tell you what, let's make a deal: you leave me alone and I will leave you alone."* Such shyness is common, especially in younger Cancerians.

My client lit up and responded right away. Her words were, "I spent the first five years of my life hiding under the kitchen table."

Voilà: shyness.

Let's take that story deeper. Say we ask a literal-minded individual if that little girl is in fact *alone* under that kitchen table. He marches over, lifts the edge of the tablecloth, and reports that she is indeed all by herself.

Now we ask Carl Gustav Jung the same question. He chortles sagaciously and, without even needing to look, says *"of course not."*

Jung knows that the girl is accompanied by imaginary friends. He also knows that she is far from bored. She is swimming in an ocean of stories and adventures. Shockingly, it would not greatly surprise Dr. Jung that the stories and characters in the little girl's mind are, for one example, the motifs of Persian folktales from the fourth century, B.C.

The girl does not know about those folktales, of course – she's never even heard of Persia. Still, she is *mapping consciousness* in the most ancient – and perhaps the most effective – way ever devised: through *myth, fable, and story.* Following her Cancerian instincts, she is immersed in her inner world – and her inner world is, in turn, immersed in what Carl Jung called the *collective unconsciousness.*

Mapping consciousness that way is what Cancer is all about. If you have even one planet there, we can say that you are at least "minoring in psychology" in this lifetime.

Here is the heart of the matter: *inner work is inseparably bound to healing*. Without immersing ourselves in our subjective interior realms, without feeling – but also without fantasy and dreaming and daydreaming – no one can recover from anything.

In fact, no one would even know what they needed to recover *from*.

Everything – every possibility of regeneration – begins when we are willing to look inward in an undefended way *and simply feel.*

THIRTY YEARS LATER . . .

A five-year-old who withdraws from strangers by hiding under the kitchen table does not really concern us. Children are often shy. They usually turn out all right – and of course introversion is not a psychological disorder.

A thirty-five-year-old person still hiding under the kitchen table triggers a less benign prognosis.

But we do not actually see thirty-five-year-olds doing that very often. Many pressures, both social and evolutionary, soon begin to make themselves felt as we grow up. Those forces impact shy kids too. Around puberty, sexual fascinations begin to stir, for example. Suddenly youngsters begin to feel driven by an instinctual urge to go out and meet other people. Teenagers feel a compelling – and ultimately healthy – need to separate themselves from their parents and to begin to take their independent place among their peers. Eventually, almost all of us become part of society.

Children grow up and eventually they engage with their communities and rule the world. As novelist Kurt Vonnegut memorably put it, "True terror is to wake up one morning and realize that your high school class is running the country."

And it always works that way. Life goes on.

Radical "under the kitchen table" shyness simply does not usually survive those forces.

This natural pattern of social development which carries us beyond *obvious* shyness creates an illusion: that Cancerians somehow *automatically* shed their shell. For Cancer Clan people, that is not necessarily the case. *All that happens automatically is that a veneer of social adaptation forms over the core of self-defending reticence. We might not still be shy at a party – but we can still be "shy" about life.*

To keep perspective, let's recall once again that introversion is not a psychiatric disorder, nor is introversion quite the same as shyness. Here is how this kind of "shyness about life" might actually look:

- A man marries at age twenty. Eighteen months later, the last meaningful conversation that will ever happen in that relationship sputters out in irresolution and guarded silences. Half a century later, he and his partner celebrate their fiftieth wedding anniversary.
- A woman takes a job straight out of college. It is not what she really wants to do with her life, but she "has to eat." At age sixty-five, she retires from that same career.
- A man sits in church, not relating to anything he hears. Ten years later, he still does not relate to any of it – but he is now a Deacon.

Each of these people might be quite functional socially. They can meet people and behave in reasonable, unremarkable ways. They seem comfortable in the world. They might even tell a joke at a party. No one would call them "shy." But, again, the point is that they are *shy about life.* They are hiding. They found a comfortable shell and decided, rather than shedding it, to spend their lives lurking inside it.

As we think about this shadowy, fearful, overly self-protective side of the Cancer archetype, we need to keep the clear eye of compassion engaged. In this world, being sensitive is not always an advantage. People are sometimes less than perfectly kind to each other. Sensitivity *must* defend itself or "eels will eat it."

Shyness is often an effective defense against those hungry eels – and we quickly saw that criticizing a crab for having a shell would be a comical error.

Crabs need their shells or they die.

Another line from a few paragraphs back: "We have come face-to-face with Cancer's core evolutionary paradigm: grow inside the safety of a shell, then judiciously shed the shell, then grow another, larger one, then safely grow inside it, then shed it again . . . and ever onward."

We do not curse or condemn the shell – but we need to be careful not to get totally hooked on having one either.

HOME AT LAST

You have a rotten day. At work, the boss was mean to you. Traffic was terrible. You have had a lingering headache since this morning. You know that you will forget about all of these indignities soon enough – but right now, you feel like a horse that has been "ridden hard and put away wet."

Finally, blessedly, you arrive home. Key in the lock, cross the threshold, shut the door, lock the door behind you and . . . . *ahhhhh.*

Home at last.

Your psychic deflector shields have been red lined for the past nine hours. *Now the walls of your home can take over.* They can become your shell for a while. You can relax and begin to heal from the day's difficulties. You are safe at last. You've survived. You pour a glass of wine. You consider a bubble bath. You give some thought to dinner.

I suspect that we can all relate to this little scenario. We may not all be Cancers or even have any planets there. We may not even have anything in the fourth house. But we surely have a Moon in our chart – and that Moon alone is enough Cancer symbolism that we can all feel the comfort of those familiar walls holding the big, nasty world at bay.

All along, we have been talking about how the Crab needs a shell. We have spoken about shyness as an early form of Cancerian shell, but we know we do not want to get stuck there. "Shedding shells" has been a consistent metaphor for the healing evolutionary process here – *but what kinds of shells can eventually replace the shell of shyness?* The Crab cannot simply stand naked and shell-less in the world. Sensitivity like that, as we saw, *must defend itself* or it dies.

Remember that sigh of relief when you stepped through your door? That moment leads us to another Cancerian strategy of regeneration: *creating a safe and restorative home.*

In all the astrological traditions, Cancer is related to *where we live* and the *people with whom we share our lives* in an ongoing way. Could we ever soothe our beleaguered souls without either one of them? *Home* is a wide-spectrum word, embracing much that lies beyond the realm of architecture. Famously, "a house is not a home."

A little later in this chapter when we get to the Moon itself, as well as to the fourth house, we will explore the intimate and familial dimensions of the Cancer clan more deeply. They can play an enormously critical role in our processes of recovery. All that is equally true of the sign Cancer. We will just see it all a bit more concretely when we get to the fourth house and the Moon. For our initial purposes right now, let's keep it simple: *the walls of your home can take over from your psychic defenses,* and give you a chance to catch your breath.

The success of that strategy depends mightily upon *there being peace in the home.* Said simply, there are people who have bad days such as the one I just described – and when they get home, things are even worse. At this point in our explorations, let us just say that, for anyone in the Cancer clan, finding or creating *a safe place to live* is a fundamental regenerative strategy. The walls of the home can serve as a shell too, and reduce the pressures of this clanging, banging world.

THE BRIDGE TO UNDERSTANDING THE CRAB'S SECOND MAJOR SHELL

Rather than just cutting to the chase, let's cross into this next territory by crossing the bridge of theory. The process will deepen our understanding of Cancer and it only takes a few moments.

At its earliest developmental stages, Cancer gazes in abject horror at a world populated by *givers of pain.* They may be people or they may be situations, but they all can potentially hurt us. Being protective of its own sensitivity, Cancer recoils and constructs its ramparts and watchtowers. Inside its fortress walls, the Crab is safe.

There is nothing weak or unduly vulnerable about Cancer at that point. The shell of that "shyness" works well and allows the wheels of the inner emotional processes which are the engine of the Crab's evolution to turn.

Then from the relative safety of that fortress perspective, Cancer begins to consider the world from a less cautious perspective. That happens because its self-protective and self-preserving needs have been satisfied. That safety liberates the Crab's intelligence and curiosity. It begins to take a broader view of the world.

Here I insert an Indian proverb about perception which I already employed extensively in *The Book of Air* – it works well with Cancer too.

When the pickpocket meets the saint, he sees pockets. The point is simple: we all see the world according to our interests and natures. The "pockets" which Cancer now sees are *other givers of pain* – equally real and hurtful, but lying at a safer, non-threatening distance. Those givers of pain are preying upon other vulnerable beings *with whom Cancer now identifies psychologically.*

As Cancer's first impulse is self-protection, its second impulse is the pro-tection of other vulnerable beings with whom it feels a natural identification.* Thus we find the *nurturing, caring, and protective* qualities that characterize many of the higher expressions of this sign. We now encounter the arche-types of the *Healer* and of the *Great Mother* – two subjects into which we will dive deeply later on in this chapter as we explore the role of the Moon.

Naturally, we celebrate nurturing, caring, and kindness as virtues. We will not simply pathologize them as Cancer's "second shell," as if they were only a hiding place. Still, if you want to hide out emotionally, *nurturing, caring, and kindness can provide a very effective cover*, which leads us directly to . . .

HIDING BEHIND CANCER'S SECOND SHELL

A Cancer clan woman falls in love. At first, she and her new lover with-draw into the secret world of pair-bonding – in other words, her friends don't see much of her for a while. But after a few weeks, she decides to introduce her partner to her intimate circle. She decides to throw a huge party – at least huge for a true Cancer type: *six of her friends are invited to her house for dinner.*

At the party, her lover seems awkwardly quiet. She would naturally prefer for him to shine a little in front of her friends. She gives him a meaningful look; he gets the message – and immediately launches into a funny, if somewhat embarrassing, story *about her.*

Everyone laughs. She laughs too. But then he clams up again – until he embarks on a second embarrassing story about her.

She doesn't laugh as loudly this time.

The evening unfolds that way, with him teasing and vaguely dimin-ishing her with almost everything he says. She notices her friends catching each other's eyes. The unspoken ambient sentiment is clear: *"If this is Mister Right, I'm glad she didn't invite Mister Wrong . . ."*

The guests have all departed by ten o'clock. Our protagonist sits down with her lover and says, "You humiliated me in front of my friends tonight. I should throw you out the door." Maybe there is a tear in her eye. Then she adds, "But if I don't have this conversation with you now, I'll be having it with you in my head for the rest of the night . . ."

He looks at her blankly and perhaps a little defensively.

She goes on to explain that she knows about how his mother failed him, and how his first wife was the lying, betraying clone of his mother.

She references her friend Jenny who was at the party, and adds, "Jenny could be your ex's sister. They looked totally alike" She adds, *"I think that when Jenny walked through the door, all of your buttons were pushed."*

His jaw drops.

She goes on, *"Sometimes you are going to look at me and see me for what I am, and it will be great between us. But other times, because of what's happened to you, you'll see mother, traitorous ex-wife – woman . . . kill."* She says, "I think that was what was really going on tonight."

She rests her case.

In the heavens above, his guardian angels are nodding their heads with tears in their eyes. They know she is right. They know how wounded he is.

The blood has drained from her lover's face. He responds, "My god . . .thank you . . .I don't deserve you . . . I feel like such a rat."

Feebly he adds, "Will you help me work on this?"

Like the All-Forgiving Great Mother, our Cancerian agrees. "Of course I will. That's what love is all about, right?"

He says, "I don't know how to make it up to you . . . can I take you out for some Black Bottom Pie?"

"Sure," she says.

And off they go, arm in arm, to eat something sweet, if not particularly nutritious.

What is wrong with this picture?

Many "spiritual people" would say that, given his crappy behavior at the dinner party, that she has acted nobly, "beyond the call of duty." She is forgiving. She is insightful. Like a good Cancerian, she has seen past her own hurt into his hurt. She has understood that his immature conduct had its origin, not in any inherent evil, but rather in his unhealed woundedness. She has quickly moved past rage into forgiveness and understanding.

Call the Vatican. What's not to admire?

Here's the answer: *she is hiding her heart behind Cancer's second shell – that of the Great Mother.* The least controversial phrases in the English language are: "I know you are doing your best . . . I forgive you . . . No worry, it doesn't matter . . . we can just let it go."

Words of forgiveness: *what an excellent hiding place they make for a heart that does not want to face the fires.* And those fires can be hot. To a Cancer, they can look like a hungry, marauding eel. Time to withdraw into a convenient shell, and being forgiving, patient, and understanding can provide it.

AN ALTERNATIVE ENDING

"Get out of here right now." She shows her lover the door, not even five minutes after the last perplexed guest has left. *"You humiliated me tonight."*

"But, but, but . . ." says he.

Says she: *"Just get your sorry ass out of my house. I am going to cry and I don't want you anywhere near me when I do. After tonight, I don't trust you enough even to cry in front of you anymore."*

He goes, protesting. He had been anticipating sex, not this. Maybe she never hears from him again. Good riddance. That way, she's traded some brief tears for the avoidance of a major heartbreak, or possibly even a failed marriage.

That is a bargain.

On the other hand, maybe the next morning he phones her. "Can't we at least talk about this . . .?" She suggests lunch on Friday. He protests, *"Friday?* This is Sunday . . ."

Her response boils down to take it or leave it. She still needs some time to think.

Friday finally comes around. Each of them has had an awful week. Breaking up is hard to do. They meet for lunch. He has had five or six days to *meditate upon the cost of his irresponsible, childish conduct toward her* – not to mention five or six days to meditate upon the pain of losing her. He realizes that earning her forgiveness is going to cost him a lot more than the price of a slice of Black Bottom Pie.

She did none of this in order to manipulate him. She just chose a path of honest emotional nakedness – and she avoided the temptation of taking refuge behind Cancer's second shell: the shell of the all-forgiving Mother Goddess.

Here's an easy question: in which one of these two versions of this archetypal Cancerian love story is the couple more likely to "live happily ever after?"

A ROGUE'S GALLERY OF FAILED CANCERIAN RESPONSES

- A woman in her twenties would love to spend a long weekend visiting her best friend in another state, but her poor cat would miss her too much if she did that, so she can't even think about making the trip.
- A man of nearly forty lives with his mother. He has no job. He passes his time playing video games. His mother feels that he never got over his father abandoning them. She can't imagine putting him out on the street.
- A married man puts up with his wife's chronic infidelity because he understands that she was sexually abused as a child and now has difficulty setting boundaries.
- A sixth-grader intentionally botches tests at school because he doesn't want his best friend to feel badly about himself for his own low scores. There is a kind of loyal solidarity in their shared failure.
- A family keeps grandpa in a vegetative state on life support for three years because they love him too much to let him go.

Turn any of these five scenarios around, and you have an instant Angel's Gallery of conscious evolutionary steps for any member of the Cancer clan. That cat will be fine for a long weekend alone. Our video gamer needs a job – and maybe a life. A little motivation, and that straying wife might learn actually to set some grown-up boundaries. Our sixth-grader's friend might rise to a bit of boyish academic competition. And poor grandpa's consciousness is not as extinguished as his family imagines; he hears grandma calling him from the Other Side and he knows that he has no business left here in this world anymore. It's time to let his soul move on.

Cancer wisdom: *kindness is truly a virtue – but sometimes it must engage in conversation with harder truths and broader perspectives or it can become limiting and dangerous.*

Another way to say exactly the same thing is that Cancer's kindness can do a lot of unintentional damage *unless it takes some cues from Scorpio and Pisces.* Like the Fire, Earth and Air clans, the Water clan is a team. Each member needs the other two or it simply becomes dysfunctional.

HEALING BEGINS WITH FEELING

We have all had the experience of struggling through a hard day only to be too tense to sleep when it was finally over. Or maybe we stand our ground under fire all day, then find tears in our eyes when we finally lie down and turn out the lights. It is natural, and nothing to be lamented: when we are in "combat mode" – or survival mode – feelings can come with a dangerous price tag. We can get too scared, angry, or overwrought to function effectively – or we might behave impulsively in ways that are not in our own best interest. We might, for example, say things we wish that we had not said.

Mother Nature has endowed us all with the capacity to *suppress emotion* in order to deal with reality in a practical way. We need that capacity, or life quickly trends toward catastrophe. The astrological symbol for that kind of self-control is Capricorn – which is the sign opposite Cancer. That only means that Cancer represents the other side of the coin – *that no pain is ever addressed unless it is first felt.* And pains that go unaddressed tend to become increasingly dangerous.

So we lie down, but we cannot sleep. We can no longer suppress the accumulated tensions of the day. *Maybe we need to reflect on them.*

Or we turn out the lights and are surprised by tears. Why do they surprise us? They come from your soul. *How could you have become so estranged from your own soul that it surprises you?*

In both cases, we are now in Cancer paradise: we are in a place where we sense that we are safe enough to feel.

As the first sign in the Water Family, Cancer's role is to create an environment in which creating that kind of safety is prioritized. Nothing needs to be understood or analyzed – understandings and analysis can be wrong. They can be distorted by our various defense mechanisms. Sometimes it is better simply to feel, and not to think too much.

Imagine trying to explain tears to an alien stepping out of a UFO. "You humans make water come out of your eyes, and that makes you feel better? I don't get it. *Why do you do that? How does that work?*"

But crying works. Grief works.

Maybe you think you are crying "for no reason" – which seems to imply that there is something wrong with you. But possibly some complex is surfacing from truly deep waters inside of you. Maybe, for one fanciful illustration, in a prior life you were in the mustard gas trenches of World War One. Maybe you saw things you were just not ready to remember. Maybe that past life is the reason that you are crying now. Maybe you are *years away from remembering* those nightmare trenches in any literal fashion. Maybe you never will remember them.

But you aren't crazy.

And maybe because *grief actually works,* those inexplicable tears are part of your healing process from that prior life trauma, even though you do not understand them.

Healing begins with feeling. And that is what Cancer is all about – making ourselves feel so safe that we can let those moods flow up from the interiors of our hearts.

Later, in the Scorpio clan, we become more questioning and analytical about the *origins* and *true nature* of those emotional states. That might sound like higher ground – *but we could never get there if we were not standing on the foundation of direct emotional truth which Cancer provides.*

Even later, after Scorpio weaves its spell, we will have to break its hypnotic gaze and let the Piscean angels kiss our hurt away. We still have many pages to go in the book of healing, regeneration, and recovery, in other words. But never forget that the whole process starts with Cancer.

It starts with simply letting ourselves feel.

LET'S GO TO THE MOON

Go to any astrological gathering. Pretend you are a beginner and that you have forgotten what the Moon means. There is a near-certain chance that you will quickly hear the word "feelings."

And it is true: like the rest of the Water Family, the Moon resonates powerfully with everyone's emotional body – but it does so in its own signature ways, depending on its astrological context. The way a Gemini Moon feels is quite distinct from the way a Moon in Scorpio or Aquarius experiences emotion, and so forth through the houses and the aspects.

Still, in all cases, *the Moon is simply your mood averaged over a lifetime.* Here is what that means. We all have good days and bad days – moods come in lots of flavors, in other words. Smooth out that emotional ebb and flow and you have an effective working definition of the Moon.

- Maybe you've got a friend who is almost always really serious – that seriousness is her mood "averaged" over all the years that you have known her.
- Maybe you have another friend who turns everything into a joke no matter how serious it is.
- Maybe you have a third friend who tends toward gloom.
- Maybe you have a fourth one who is so reflexively optimistic that if he caught the flu, he would immediately welcome it as a chance to lie in bed and read.

That is what I mean when I call the Moon "your mood averaged over a lifetime." Here is another quick definition, just as fundamental: *the Moon is your cruising attitude* – and by "cruising," I again mean to smooth out the emotional bumps and instead to take in the big, long-term picture.

"Attitude" might not seem so different from mood, but I add it to our list for good reason. When we think of feelings, we tend to think of *inner states.* True enough – but feelings usually express themselves outwardly as well. That is where "attitude" comes into play. A depressed stranger walks into the cafe where you are having a cup of coffee. One look, and you sense that black cloud around her.

Was that some kind of psychic perception on your part? I am wide-open to that possibility, but I'd also point out that you could see that depression in her physical posture, facial expression, and gait – her *behaviors*, in other words. *Attitude flavors everyone's actions and is revealed in them.*

Placing the Moon in a little box labeled "my inner life" is, in other words, a big mistake.

Our take-away: *the Moon is not strictly private and internal.* Attitude almost always leaks out, even if we are trying to hide it.

REALITY AS WE EXPERIENCE IT

The Moon defines reality as we experience it.

To many astrologers, given the Moon's correlation with subjective matters, my linking it to "reality" might seem odd. But a large part of what we see "out there" is actually more reflective of our attitudes, fears, and desires than of any objective analysis of physical facts. The pessimist's attitude that "nothing will ever work out" *manifests behaviorally* as an unwillingness to take risks. Tell him that "you've got to play the game if you ever want to win," and you get a blank, defeated look. He *could* win – that is of course possible. In his fearful negativity, he thinks he is seeing reality. In fact, he is seeing his own mind.

The optimist's attitude, on the other hand, might lead her to trust the wrong people, to think that there is "plenty of time" before the flight boards, and to believe that the tax people would never have any interest in small-fry such as herself.

We might say that "half of reality is in your head" – but perhaps an even better way to phrase it would be that *half of reality is in your heart.* Attitude is inseparable from how we see what we believe to be "really" out there.

Later in the book, we will go through the Moon sign by sign and house by house. For now, let's just say that someone with a Capricorn Moon might well see a reality defined by *tasks, risks to avoid, and lists of things that require doing.* Meanwhile someone with a Sagittarian Moon *living in the same physical reality* is presented with possibilities, opportunities, and adventures.

In Woody Allen's masterpiece, *Annie Hall,* there is a memorable scene that beautifully illustrates the point I am making. Woody and Diane Keaton are having troubles in their relationship. Each of them is in psychotherapy. Woody Allen's shrink asks him how often he and Diane have sex. He answers, "*Hardly ever,* maybe three times a week." Cut to another shrink in another office. Diane Keaton is asked the same question. Her famous answer is, "*Constantly.* I'd say three times a week."

Here is a silly question: which one of them is right?

So far, all of these perspectives on the Moon have been simply descriptive. Let's make them active. How do they tie in with the processes of healing, regeneration, and recovery?

The attitude indicated by your Moon is *right for you* – at least if you respond in a conscious way to the lunar messages. The person with that Capricorn Moon, for example, *in accomplishing Great Works* gains dignity and self-respect. Someone with the Moon in Sagittarius *in immersing herself in adventure and risk* gains confidence that the universe is a safe place for her to be.

Your Moon's position is purposeful, in other words. It says something about *what needs to be healed and regenerated in you*, along with exactly how to do it.

HEART AND SOUL: THE MOON IN LOVE

Those are two gold-plated Moon words – *heart* and *soul* – at least as the terms are used on the street. We are not talking about the organ that pumps your blood nor are we discussing the immortal principle of consciousness. "Heart" means what you might see scrawled on a city wall with initials inside it and an arrow running through it. "Soul" is why we use a term like "soul mates." Forget sexual passion for a moment and just think of true love, minus the hormones – and don't worry: if you are a hormone fan, the next chapter of this book is for you. When love is truly "true," people are simply *comfortable* in each other's energy fields. *That particular kind of domestic comfort is Moon territory.* Such people, unlike new lovers, relax together easily. They express needs and tastes and opinions spontaneously in the expectation that their natures will be accepted without major editorial intervention.

Earlier, when we linked Cancer to the feeling of being "home at last," we touched on the idea that home is not just a piece of architecture. It is connected to *relationships* too. Desire and passion are not so central here – those energies are more in the domain of the Scorpio clan.

What we are looking at here is the ability to actually *live together* . . .

UNDER ONE ROOF

New lovers cannot be trusted alone in a room together. They'll soon be in each other's arms. If you need their attention, knock first.

We will look deeply and carefully at that kind of body heat in the following chapter. Here, in talking about the Moon and Cancer, we follow that kissing magic a little further down the timeline. Instead of *grand mal* purple passion, let's think of another stage in the trajectory of intimacy – one that is of absolutely primary lunar significance. Our passionate lovers have now known each other for a while. Maybe not very long, maybe it's just weeks – but it is long enough that we encounter another scene: the first time they go to bed together and, by mutual agreement, "nothing happens." No sexual expression, at least not in the narrow sense of the term. They simply *go to sleep* together.

Let's frost the lunar cake by adding that they go to sleep in each other's arms.

For any couple, this is a classic Moon initiation. The ones who pass the test might very well remain together for a lifetime.

The couples who fail it almost never do.

A client once told me that for her, sleeping together – taking the words literally – was a more intimate act than sex. I could see her point. In sleep, we surrender our defenses. Falling asleep together is a profoundly vulnerable interaction. It takes a lot of Moon-trust between two people for it to happen. In "merely" sleeping together, it is as if we have regressed temporarily to a *pre-sexual state* – something more akin to infancy, with all of its characteristic vulnerabilities. That state is very lunar. Therapists sometimes say that "an adult is a child who survived." *Falling asleep in each other's arms – what kind of primary instinctual trust does it take to allow your inner child to let down his or her guard to that extreme degree?*

As astrologers, we can answer that question quite concisely. It requires a *Moon-bond.* This is one reason why Cancer clan synastry interactions are so common among long-term couples.

If our Moons feel easy with each other, then maybe we can live together.

And if they don't, we probably can't.

Look to Mars and Venus for pure sexual energy – but for *domestic relationships*, it is the Moon's domain. We might or might not want to defend the idea that sleeping together is "deeper" than sex. Perhaps it would be more accurate to say that it is simply different, and that the difference has a lot to do with the ego's defenses being abandoned.

People can hide behind their sexual *personas*. Most couples do, at least at first. Those illusions are so delicious that few people ever feel moved to challenge them. When, however, sex needs a moment to catch its breath, the Moon peeks through the storm clouds – and the truth about whether we can actually *get along with each other domestically* is revealed.

Revealing the Moon can therefore be understood as the primordial act of human trust. For our larger purposes, here is the crux of the matter: *such trusting, domestic relationships are healing practices*. It is commonly observed that married people outlive single people – although let's quickly acknowledge that there are many complexities with that idea, especially in the modern world, starting with what do we mean by "married." Rather than focus on that narrow notion, just ask your heart one question: *is feeling lovingly connected to other people whom you trust profoundly good for your health?*

I doubt we would have too many dissenters.

DIFFERENT STROKES . . .

Everyone has a Moon in his or her chart. At the same time, not everyone is cut out for long-term lunar commitments. The truth of all that is in your birthchart. The personal astrology of intimacy is a big subject, too big to rehash here. We've reflected on it a lot in the previous three volumes of this series under the banners of Mars, Venus, Libra, and the seventh house. In this volume, we will complete the picture, both here in this Cancer clan chapter and in the next Scorpionic one.

Suffice to say that having the Moon in your chart does not mean that you are required to spend your life with one other person. But if you *want* to spend your life with one other person, my prayer for you is that your lunar moods and attitudes are compatible. That is the key to keeping those famous intimacy-induced homicidal tendencies away from your front door – and from your back door too.

Moon connections really come down to simply *liking* each other, and to having domestic rhythms and instincts that work together in relative harmony.

MOTHER MOON

A woman's fertility cycle and the Moon's phases: there's a matched set – and very probably the primordial astrological observation as well . . . where the whole system began, in other words: twenty-nine days between successive Full Moons and very nearly that same rhythm for ovulation and menstruation. Of all the various celestial/terrestrial correlations, could any of them be more obvious?

I suspect that our female ancestors back in the Olduvai Gorge in Africa figured that one out long before history was recorded. *I also suspect that this correlation gives us a reason to believe that the first astrologer was a woman.* Women feel the Moon in their bodies in ways that men can only imagine. To this day, about three quarters of my clients and students are female. I would like to see more balance in the ratio, but I do not imagine that I will. Women are simply wired to "get it" about astrology in ways that men are not. That is a gift their Moon-tuned bodies give them.

Moon as the *Great Mother* – that is another closely-related piece of astrological insight. It is a short step from the lunar phase/ovulation cycle to seeing the Moon as the fertile, feminine face of God.

We have to be careful though – men have Moons! The astrological Great Mother reflects a *nurturing, healing, protective* instinct – and there are many men who embody those impulses, while there are many women who do not. Still, "Moon" and "Mother" are inseparable archetypes, and that has led astrologers to both a lot of insight and a fair amount of confusion too. Much of the confusion boils down to making the mistake of believing that *the Moon describes your mother*. It doesn't – or if it does, the description is only indirect and imprecise. Proving that point is easy – siblings often have different Moons, but the same mom. The natal Moon does not describe your mother; it describes your *experience* of your mother. The distinction is mission-critical. Again a simple proof: adult siblings talking about their childhood experience of family tend to remember their mothers differently.

GOOD MOM, BAD MOM ... AND A SORE THROAT

Mothers come in both flavors, good and bad, as well as many flavors in between. There is a wide spectrum, running from maternal skill and tenderness down to flagrant child abuse and criminal neglect.

With a bit more subtlety, we can also recognize that sometimes there happens to be a good soul-fit between a mother and her child – as years go by, they become friends. Other times, two decent, sane, people are just not wired to get along with each other. Their parent-child relationship remains formal and diplomatic, or it loudly crashes and burns.

Those treasures and toxins can have complex origins. They might lie more in the child's subjective experience of the mother than in her actual nature. A mother naturally feels *protective* toward her child. The Cancer child probably appreciates that quality, while the Arian child might find it smothering.

However we look at it, one point is constant: for good or for ill, *the mother-experience becomes our inner template of nurturing behavior, both toward ourselves and toward others.* As we advance into adult life, Mother Moon lingers inside us, *shaping how we care for ourselves and others* – or fail to care. A positive experience of the mother tends to support *mindful kindness towards ourselves and others* throughout life, while a negative one tends in the opposite direction.

A man wakes up one rainy Thursday with a slightly sore throat . . .

- If he has a healthy relationship with Mother Moon, he takes his temperature. It's a fraction of a degree above normal. His body is fighting something. He calls in sick to work, casually adding that he "doesn't want anyone else to catch it."
- If he has an unhealthy relationship with Mother Moon, he kicks his butt out of bed and goes to work. Three days later, he is even sicker – and five co-workers have caught his bug as well.

Note that in the healthy version of this tale, *the man's gentle treatment of himself is reflected in his caring behavior toward his fellow workers.* He treats them as he is treating himself. Meanwhile, the second man is not intentionally harmful; there is no malice in him toward anyone. He is simply treating others the same way he is treating himself: *uncaringly.*

Did the first man have a good childhood experience of his mother and the second man a lousy one? That is certainly one possibility. Psychologists long ago figured out that if you were beaten as a kid, you are a candidate for abusing your own kids. Love and poison are both contagious.

Still, none of this is ever black and white, nor quite so deterministic . . .

HEALING AND REGENERATION

The Moon is the great healer. People recover from horrendous experiences, both in childhood and in adult life. I began this book with an image of an old woman dancing on a moonlit beach. As we saw, every line on her face told a story, and many of them are sad. Yet she still dances. That *miracle of regeneration* is our central theme throughout these pages. The Water element has many expressions – the Scorpio clan and the Pisces clan are part of it too, and they still lie ahead.

Yet in many ways, Mother Moon is the heart of the matter.

Take care of it, trust its whimsies, and you will be glad that you are alive – no matter what blows you have sustained and failures you have endured. And when those blows strike you down, you will know how to recover. Your healing instincts will be sound. You will be wise and patient with yourself in those regenerative processes.

And when you wake up with a sore throat, you'll stay home, take care of yourself – and not unwittingly spread those germs around town.

LUNAR PHASE

Looking at the Moon in the sky, what could be more obvious than its phases? And yet the subject is, if not ignored, typically underplayed in astrological circles. The reasons for that go deep into the heart of our modern culture, how we got here, and what we have lost in the process. It is a subject close to my heart, and I dived into it as deeply as I could in my 2010 volume, *The Book of the Moon*. Here in this introductory chapter about the Cancer clan, I want to give you just a brief summary of the phases of the Moon and the role they play in the birthchart.

Let me start by saying that there is nothing subtle about lunar phase. Once you learn to look for it, that Sun-Moon angle in the birthchart stands out like the nose on a person's face. It is about as evident as a person's Sun Sign or a planet conjunct his or her Ascendant: loud and clear, in other words.

Here are a few core points about it:

- The darker two weeks of the Moon's cycle of phases correlates with the *inner subjective world*, while the brighter two weeks is linked to the realm of *manifestation*. We swing out into the realm of light and concrete expression, then we swing back into the realm of darkness, mystery, and interior reflection.

- With the Moon in its darker (less than a half-Moon) phases, people tend to be more self-contained, mysterious – and often beguilingly charismatic, as if they "know something." With the Moon in its brighter phases – the week before and the week after the Full Moon – there is much emphasis on outward experience, relationship, and collective endeavors. They get things done.

- The *waxing half* of the Moon's cycle has a natural resonance with the spirit of youth: *energy, enthusiasm* – and a certain propensity for headstrong idiocy.

- The *waning half* of the Moon's cycle has a natural resonance with the spirit of the second half of life, from mid-life onward: *reflectiveness, more subtle, nuanced judgments* – and vulnerability to *resignation* and *despair*.

- Try as might, I just cannot make a system of twelve phases sing. In the end, I went with Dane Rudhyar's *schema* of eight phases, although my take on them varies from his in a few significant areas.

Here are the eight phases of the Moon as I understand them, reduced to an evocative image and a few words of explanation. Once again, for a full treatment, please have a look at *The Book of the Moon* – and remember that since we are talking about the Moon, aligning one's behavior with the spirit of one's lunar birth phase is one of the paving stones on the road to happiness and wellbeing.

1. NEW MOON – *The Teacher*
(The Moon 0°-45° ahead of the Sun)
Sweetness. Nurturing. Leadership. Guidance. Charismatic presence. Becoming symbolic to others; making others into symbols. A bringer of gifts to the community.

2. WAXING CRESCENT – *The Extremist*
(The Moon 45°-90° ahead of the Sun)
Drive to accomplish and experience. Hunger. Imbalance. Success – and its costs. Radiant, infectious hope in the face of darkness. Pluck.

3. FIRST QUARTER – *The Crusader*
(The Moon 90°-135° ahead of the Sun)
Tension between self and group. Concern with justice. Battles which need to be fought – and battles which do not, but are fought anyway. Group efforts; organizations. Sacrifice for the tribe.

4. WAXING GIBBOUS – *The Helper; The Lover*
(The Moon 135°-180° ahead of the Sun)
Service. Identification with group ideals. Sexual energy. Support offered to a person or to a principle. Generosity. Cooperation. Teamwork. Shared creativity; mutual inspiration.

5. FULL MOON – *The Human Being*
(The Moon 180°-225° ahead of the Sun)
Caregiving. Familial complexities; divorce. Art and creativity made manifest. Nurturing. Outward expression of light and dark. All the karma on the table. Standing naked.

6. WANING GIBBOUS – *The Shaman*
(The Moon 225°- 270° ahead of the Sun)
Deep inner work. Psychic intervention in other people's lives and transformations. Offering assistance around death, dying, and crisis. Attunement to "primitive" wisdoms. Death and rebirth. Gratitude.

7. LAST QUARTER – *The Pilgrim*
(The Moon 270°-315° ahead of the Sun)
Searching for home. Sweet sorrow. Romantic tragedy. Solitude. Forgiveness. Karmic debts paid and received. Art as an inner, spiritual search. Service. Theater; Ritual. A poignant sense of the transitoriness of life.

8. WANING CRESCENT – *The Mystic Wanderer*
(The Moon 315°-360° ahead of the Sun)
Deep psychic sensitivity; possible mental imbalance. Ghosts and spirit visitations. Creative, visionary imagination. Sensitivity to ancestors and to the dead. The veil between the worlds grows thin and transparent.

THE FOURTH HOUSE

Cancer is the fourth zodiacal sign and so it has a natural resonance with the fourth house, while the Moon rules over them both. There are many parallels among the three, but as ever, we must be mindful of the distinction between signs and houses. Signs give us *values, desires, interests, and motivations.* Houses, meanwhile, offer us *behavioral avenues* for the expression of those same energies. In the houses, we turn *impulse to action.* Here, in a quick list, is a way to see both the "parallels and the perpendiculars" between Cancer and the fourth house.

- Cancer is the *need* to crawl inside our shells from time to time; in the fourth house we see you actually getting into your bed with a good book and your cell phone turned off.
- Cancer is the *emotional attunement* to the fact that you are hungry and stressed; in the fourth house we see you cooking your favorite comfort food.
- Cancer is the *longing* for the company of your soul-tribe; in the fourth house, we see you turning down the lights, lighting the fire in the fireplace, pouring the wine, and settling in for a long, soulful talk with two or three people whom you really love.
- Cancer is *feeling sad or crazy;* in the fourth house, we see you finding someone to talk to about it.
- Cancer is the *motivation* to nurture something; in the fourth house, we see you having a baby – or rescuing a kitten from the pound.
- Cancer is *feeling battered* by the events of the day; in the fourth house, we see you asking someone you love for a hug.
- Cancer is the *need* for a safe space; in the fourth house, we see you moving to a new home or a better neighborhood.

- Cancer is the *longing* for a sense of roots; in the fourth house, we see you researching your genealogy or visiting the land in which your ancestors' bones are buried.
- Cancer is *feeling tired* after a long, hard day; in the fourth house, we see you going to bed early.

BONDED RELATIONSHIPS

Somewhere long ago, I encountered the term *bonded relationships*. For me, those two words capture something absolutely central to our understanding of the fourth house. I've Googled around to see if I could once again find the provenance of the term, but I get nowhere. After four or five off-the-mark hits, I am quickly led to ways I can "Meet Hot Singles in Borrego Springs, California."

And that's not the kind of "bonded relationship" I am talking about.

As I dimly recall from encountering the term long ago, it dates back to Medieval Europe. It was, I believe, a legal designation as well as an astrological one. In essence, *a bonded relationship referred to any human connection that could be broken only by death* – the bonds, for example, between a parent and a child, bonds of marriage, and bonds of kinship.

With all other kinds of relationships, Medieval Europeans apparently had considerable latitude for treachery. But the bonded ones were for a lifetime, come hell or high water.

We still see this principle clearly enough in the modern world. One place is our understanding of the natural relationship between parents and children. Everyone's expectation is that such a bond will remain active until one of them passes away, hopefully the parent rather than the child. Of course, life does not always work out that way. We have all seen situations where people have to "divorce their toxic parents." Or where an adult child drifts off into oblivion and the parents have no idea anymore where he or she might be. In such situations, even if they are psychologically necessary, most of us sense that some kind of unresolved karma has been created. There is something unnatural about parents and kids losing touch with each other.

It is different from the way friends might drift apart after one of them moves to another state or marries someone insufferable.

I am quite sure that those same kinds of family schisms happened in Medieval Europe, just as they do today. With bonded relationships, we are rather obviously talking about an *ideal* – and as with most ideals, falling short of God's Glory is not unusual. Yet it is fair to say that even today, kids and their parents generally remain in touch for a lifetime, *whether or not they like each other very much.* This particular fourth house instinct remains a real force in the world.

Here is the essential point: while there are many forms of human connection, the fourth house deals with one very specific subset of all the possibilities – *a relationship which is mutually anticipated to last for a lifetime.*

What about marriage? That used to be on the list of bonded relationships. Is it still? There's an essay question. Maybe we attend a wedding. Our hearts are full of good will toward the happy couple – but of course somewhere deep down inside we're thinking that their chances of remaining together "unto the grave" are about fifty-fifty. We may not include that commentary in our champagne toast, but we all understand that marriage is not quite the stable institution that it once was.

And that is a complicated subject. Suffice it to say that something has been lost and something has been gained.

Still, even today in this shaky world, the *ideal* of marriage is widely recognized to include life-long commitment: specifically, *growing old together under one roof.* Despite changing customs, marriage still remains a prime example of a bonded relationship – perhaps second only to the parent-child bond.

Let's add some modern perspective: saying that "the two have become one" seems a little off in today's more Aquarian world. But consider this scenario: you are standing in line at a ticket counter. People approach the agent one at a time, taking their turns. In front of you is a couple. Their turn comes, *and they approach the agent together.*

No one bats an eye. Even today, that is customary social behavior. They are *a couple*; "the two have become one" – and everybody knows it, understands it, and is not troubled by it. Bonded relationships, in other words, are not something out of a museum of medieval artifacts; they are alive and well in the modern world, even if they are somewhat rarer than they once were. A sense of the special status of bonded relationships is hardwired into the human psyche. They will always exist in some form, as surely as there will always be an astrological house squeezed in between the third one and the fifth one.

That "bond" is what distinguishes a fourth house relationship from every other kind. One dimension of such a partnership is *a sense of mutual obligation.* That burden may be so light that you barely notice it, or so heavy that it eats up your life – but it will always be there, "until death do us part."

How does all of this relate to healing, regeneration, and recovery?

One underlying principle is that these kinds of committed connections between people are fundamental to human sanity. People are different, but it is rare to find an *isolated* man or woman – someone without any kinds of lasting bonds at all – who is in good mental health. Bonded relationships, in some sense of the word, are therefore quite elemental when it comes to the processes we are exploring.

They are a slippery subject though . . .

THE FLUID DEFINITION OF FAMILY

Bonded relationships may be an eternal principle, but they are always in a state of cultural flux. They do not always mean "family" in the conventional sense of the word. In times past, you really *knew* your cousins. They probably lived close by. Very likely, you were involved in each others' lives.

With even more confidence, we could assume that you were intimately involved with your parents and your siblings, along with any children your siblings might have. Simply said, for a very long time, *most of us were farmers* – and "we Smiths have always raised sheep in this valley." That world of *active familial kinship* is not entirely gone, but it has significantly dissipated. Nowadays, people move around a lot. They cross a continent to take a new job. They move a thousand miles away to go to college. When that happens, *the familiarity engendered by daily contact disappears.* Nowadays, kinship relationships, at least as they are understood by the old definitions, tend to become more formal than active.

Still, while the fourth house changes its form of expression, it will never disappear. It is an archetype and all archetypes are eternal.

Your phone rings. It's your second cousin twice removed whom you barely remember. He is wondering about borrowing $10,000 from you.

How do you react?

Your phone rings. It's your dearest friend in the world. Her husband left her a month ago, and today she was suddenly fired from her job. She's in psychological trouble. She tells you that she is scared to be alone. She wonders if she can sleep on your sofa for a few weeks until she gets back on her feet. You tell her to *come over right away and stay as long as she needs to.*

After all, she is your best friend.

In the modern world, that kind of "best friendship" is more of a bonded relationship than the one you have with your second cousin, twice removed.

- Human society is moving away from an experience of bonded family relationships based on shared DNA and formal ties of marriage and toward one based on choice, affinity, and volunteerism.
- Therefore, modern astrologers must adjust their understanding of the fourth house to conform with current cultural realities.

A SCENE FROM TODAY

Your best friend accepts a job in a distant city. It is a good professional move for her. She of course has your blessing – that goes without saying. You will always love each other, but naturally you accept the sad fact that you will no longer be having a cup of coffee with her and catching up with each other every few days. Still, you are a modern human being. You are realistic about such matters, and supportive of your friend. You would never dream of standing between her and this incredible career opportunity.

A SCENE FROM TWO HUNDRED YEARS IN THE FUTURE

Your best friend is offered a job in a distant city. The position is attractive to her – but she takes the fact that you two are best friends seriously, as is the custom. Two hundred years from now, the world's culture has changed. Marriage is not as common as it was two or three centuries ago. But such a *friendship* is now understood to be a *bonded relationship*, with certain mutual obligations – obligations that did not exist back in the harsh, lonely days of the twenty-first century. *Now, everyone understands that disruptions in these kinds of fourth house connections can create psychological damage for all concerned.* Entering into "best friendship" with someone is 100% voluntary – but once that line is crossed, the bond entails serious mutual commitment. Your friend sits down with you to wrestle with the knotty question of her staying or going. If she wants to leave and take the job, *she asks for your permission and your blessing before she commits to the move* – that is how seriously she now takes being in a fourth house "friendship" with you.

In a nutshell, in this view of *Tomorrowland,* such deeper friendships have taken the place formerly occupied by kinship, or perhaps even to some extent by marriage.

A SCENE FROM FIVE HUNDRED YEARS AGO

A woman is offered a meaningful, remunerative position in a prestigious household in a distant city many miles from the village where her extended family has lived for centuries. She decides to take the position. *No one can believe what a cold-hearted monster she is.* She is leaving her own people to move among *strangers* – for what? *For money! For power!* Her sister is five months pregnant – and she won't be there for the birth or to be a good aunt to her new niece. Her parents are getting old; they are already *in their fifties.* What if they need her? What if they simply miss her? *How will they deal emotionally with her vicious betrayal?* How could she be so icy in the face of normal human obligations that everyone understands?

EVERLASTING AND EVER-CHANGING

Everything changes. The fourth house is eternal, but the form it takes is always evolving. I doubt many of us would want to live in that stultifying scene from five hundred years ago. Family can obviously be oppressive, even today – and yet there is something in that faraway scene worth considering: *that people once took their bonded relationships more seriously, and that something precious has been lost.*

The scene I described from today seems quite normal – who would even consider "forbidding" a friend from taking a new job, even if it were somewhere far away? Trying to enforce such a restriction on a friend's career would seem completely inappropriate – today.

And yet, might we be wrong? *There are seven billion of us, but still we have a worldwide plague of loneliness.* Have we sacrificed something in pursuing our zeal for Aquarian autonomy? Could freedom really be "just another word for nothing left to lose?"

And what will fourth house relationships look like two hundred years from now? The *Tomorrowland* anecdote I presented is probably not correct. I don't have a crystal ball. But I do feel that the fourth house represents a very basic human need for reliable, long-lasting bonds. I know that its *form of expression* is mutable over historic scales of time – but I know that it will not go away.

Our basic fourth house needs are currently on a starvation diet in this crowded, but weirdly lonely world. Perhaps that is why there are so many self-help books, so many psychotherapists, and still such coldness in the air.

Bottom line, healing, regeneration, and recovery are tough without this kind of loving support and without this sense of being connected, reliably and for life, to a few other souls upon whom we can always count.

YOUR NATURAL HOME

Undoubtedly, there is a career-oriented person living thirty stories up in a furnished high-rise apartment in a city to which his work brought him a year ago, and which he knows he will probably leave in another year or two.

No judgment: he might be a sensitive, evolved being whose path in life simply reflects a tenth house focus on work and career.

But if a fourth house person finds himself in that situation, he will suffer grievously. Such people need a real home.

In the fourth house, we experience a kind of *soul-resonance with the ground under our feet.* Our wellbeing is very directly linked to where we live – and "where we live" is a full-spectrum question. There are many ways to define it, and we need to be sensitive to all of them. "Home" can refer literally to our house or our apartment – but it can also mean our neighborhood, our town, or our region – and, really, to the *daemon* of the land itself.

Ask anyone with a fourth house focus: *there are geographical places that feed her a steady diet of good energy and there are places that drain her of it.* With such a chart, if you are *not living in your soul's natural home,* you can still grow and learn and evolve – but that evolutionary staircase is a lot steeper and the air you breathe is a lot thinner.

- Neptune in the fourth house? Maybe you need to live near the sea or some body of water.
- Mercury? Stimulus is helpful – city life?

- Venus? You can count on peace, quiet, and beauty feeding something inside of you. Life in some beautiful, natural landscape?

Those are obviously quick sketches, but I hope you get the idea. With a planet in the fourth house, your home can help regenerate you – or drain you if you are living in the wrong place.

Lacking a planet there, the question recedes in importance – although planets in Cancer or a very charged Moon do echo some of these same themes.

THE INNER WORLD

Older forms of astrology tend to be concrete and biographical, while modern forms trend in a more psychological direction. Evolutionary astrology straddles both worlds. It is certainly psychological in tone – but we also pay a lot of attention to the way synchronicity creates outward, experiential circumstances which reflect the inner work we need to do. Wherever we go, we meet what we are needing to learn, in other words.

As the Buddhists suggest, "take what arises as the path." The view in evolutionary astrology is essentially the same: no event is seen as random or meaningless.

In what I have written so far in this section, I have been trying to underscore the outward, behavioral dimensions of the fourth house.

- We have appreciated the enormous role in our healing journeys of *the long story we share* with a few other human beings.
- We have cultivated sensitivity toward the importance of finding our right physical place in the world.
- We have considered the maturing impact of familial obligations and commitments upon us.

But the fourth house also relates very directly to the world inside us. In a nutshell, it is *the house where psychology happens.* Like the Moon, the fourth house resonates with our emotional body, reflecting our needs, our fears, and our feelings.

The final doorway through which I want to take us helps us flesh out that inward psychological dimension of the fourth house. It involves a reflection upon the interdependency of the fourth and tenth houses. The tenth of course lies directly opposite the fourth, which links them in eternal synergy.

Conventionally, the tenth is the house of career, although I prefer to think of it as the house of our *mission* in the world. What kind of job might you have that *actively enhances your own regeneration* rather than just exhausting you or giving you a paycheck? To succeed in finding such a place in the world, *the underlying archetypes of your fourth house must inform your outward mission in the community.* That synergy is how you reach the Holy Grail of the tenth house, which is *to figure out a way to get paid for being yourself.*

That last line might sound silly, but if you get that right, you have found a big piece of "the secret of eternal happiness." Of course we immediately see the Cancer clan signature – *healing* and *self-nurture* can arise directly from feeling that you have found a meaningful role in your community. That can only be good for you, body, mind, and soul.

Here is a quick personal illustration: I have Pisces on the cusp of my fourth house and Virgo on my Midheaven. *My "inner mystic" (Pisces) needed to find a "craft of service" (Virgo) that reflected its mystical nature* – that is Pisces again. Evolutionary astrology fits the bill perfectly: its outward appearance is of a technical craft that serves people, but its roots are inseparable from my Piscean inner life.

That's just me. There would naturally be many other possible expressions of this Pisces/Virgo dyad – one might for example have *a rich fantasy life* and *learn the craft of writing fiction.* Or *love the sea* and become *the navigator on a merchant ship.* Or be *fascinated with dreams* and become *a Jungian analyst.* The range of meaning with any astrological symbolism is truly vast. But there is a consistent principle active here: in the fourth house, *you encounter your own soul* – and if you immerse yourself in that transrational realm, if you fully surrender to it, then you have put down some profound roots.

Out of those roots, a flower might bloom, visible in this material world. That flower might be so obvious that even the tax man will detect it.

4

THE SCORPIO CLAN

To cut straight through any rationalizations or defenses down to the raw, uncomfortable, emotionally threatening, realities which lie behind what I am feeling . . . to be brave enough to ask myself hard questions . . . and never to unduly fear the naked truth.

Scorpio the *scorpion* – one word, and we are immediately aware that our astrological ancestors were not trying to comfort us when they named this sign. Scorpions make us think of pain and death. In doing so, they confront us with our ultimate fragility. They compel us to reflect upon the temporary quality of mortal existence.

None of those are likely gambits for lighthearted cocktail party banter.

Breaking *taboos* such as these – both within ourselves and in terms of social "politeness" and "appropriateness" – is the essence of Scorpio. *The underlying evolutionary motivation of this sign is the urge to face all emotionally-charged truths squarely and courageously.*

Some of those edgy truths engage everyone universally: death, disease, and ageing, for a few quick examples. Some of them are purely personal – one person is terrified of heights, while another one climbs mountains. One person shudders at the sight of a snake, while another has a pet boa constrictor slithering around his torso. I am so unnaturally terrified of anything touching my eyes that I am incapable of wearing contact lenses. The only time I ever actually felt a cold sweat was when a gentle eye doctor tried to fit me with a pair.

Naturally, individual Scorpionic human beings do not always succeed in being quite so steadfast in the face of their own fears and phobias. The highest expression of Scorpio, just as with the rest of the signs, is something toward which we can aspire. The road to achieving it can be a long one, but it is worth the journey.

In common with the rest of the signs, Scorpio has a shadow. There are many ways to get Scorpio wrong, and we will catalog most of them in the pages that follow. But we should never lose sight of Scorpio's North Star: *the brave, honest contemplation of the raw reality of life and of our absolute, ultimate vulnerability within it.*

Any planet in Scorpio, if it is to be functional, must be committed to a path of stark, undefended *realness*. With success comes real wisdom – the kind that does not fail when the chips are all down, which is to say when we are faced with death or some other grievous loss. If we fail on the Scorpionic path, we fall into morbidity and darkness.

As you can see, the stakes in this sign are very high.

THE URBAN POLICY STUDY

Many years ago, before I found that astrology could pay the bills, I worked for a few years for the United States government. In my middle twenties, I was a go-fer on a big sociological research project called the Urban Policy Study. It was funded by the National Institute of Mental Health through North Carolina State University.

As the "cast-of-thousands" data-gathering phase of the project wound down and reports needed to be written, I was retained by the project bosses because they had seen that I was able to write well and clearly. I was also doing some of the computer work, having learned to operate a system called the Statistical Package for the Social Sciences. This was back in the days of mainframe computers and punch cards, by the way – sometime just after the end of the late Pleistocene era.

My connection to the data-processing side of the project put me in an excellent position to commit a minor crime and to get away with it. We had a million dollars' worth of psychological and sociological data regarding a random sample of human beings in the Triangle Area of central North Carolina.

And we had their birth dates.

You probably see where this is going. It was not difficult for me to compare our data with our respondents' Sun Signs. I couldn't go any deeper than that astrologically without getting into trouble, but that was deep enough to yield some interesting – and statistically significant – results.

One of the psychological dimensions we were exploring (and comparing with various social behaviors, such as voting and civic engagement) was *depression*. In a "twenty questions" sort of way, we had a fairly complex scale to measure it. People who, for example, claimed to be happy all the time, but who suffered from chronic headaches and sleep issues, lost a few points.

Before I write another word, let me quote some very relevant ancient wisdom – "there are lies, there are damned lies, and there are statistics." No individual human is ever simply a statistic. Emphatically, what I am about to report here does not define the existence of any individual Sun Sign Scorpio person.

Message received? I pray so, or everything I believe about how astrology really works erodes.

Based on the rigorous data from the Urban Policy Study, people born with the Sun in Scorpio emerged in a statistically significant way as the most miserable sign-cohort of the zodiac.

My project bosses – Karl and Alden – liked me, and *vice versa*. They tolerated my interest in astrology with a manly spirit of *bonhomie*, basically expressing their amusement about it. I was the "flaky hippie" who believed in astrology. When I showed them the Scorpio data, they thought that I had cooked it up as a playful way of pulling their legs. I had not. The numbers clearly showed that being a Scorpio was about as good a predictor of existential misery as was being a poor black female – at least in the North Carolina of 1973.

Once again, there are lies, damned lies, and statistics. I am sure there were happy Scorpios back then, not to mention some happy poor black females.

But the *pattern* was real.

These are truths, but they are dangerous ones – and even that phrase itself puts us squarely in the realm of the eighth sign. Scorpio reflects many "dangerous truths" – things that are real even though we might prefer otherwise. They always involve areas where we might be tempted into denial and rationalization.

Emphatically, the takeaway is not that "Scorpio means depression," but rather that *when we give a large number of people this much access to unconscious, repressed, or taboo material, a number of them are going to wind up with a bad case of the blues.*

Others, as we will see, will become very wise.

And I suspect you already sense which way the wind is blowing: facing the truth of our woundedness, wrestling with our Shadow, reckoning with the *true* story of our lives – all of that has a lot to do with healing, regeneration, and recovery.

A FRIEND IN NEED

Let's say you are significantly resonant with Scorpio. Maybe, for example, it is the sign of your Sun, your Moon, or your Ascendant. *(By the way, as we get a little further into the stew of the Scorpio clan, we will see how a packed eighth house can have similar effects, as can a strongly placed Pluto.)* Mars is part of this clan too, but that planet would have less connection with the tale I am about to spin.

A friend texts you, saying that something very serious has come up. She would rather not talk about it on the phone. Is there any way that you could possibly meet her really soon – say, this afternoon – for a cup of coffee? You sense her urgency and you trust her. She is no drama queen. With some difficulty, you clear your schedule and you make a plan to meet in a local cafe at 5:30.

After a quick hug, she cuts right to the chase. She had a routine physical examination. The doctors called her back with bad news. Pancreatic cancer. She's probably got three months to live. She tells you all of that, then she looks you straight in the eye and she says, *"How the hell am I going to tell Jerry and the boys?"*

That's the kind of woman she is. Her first thoughts are not for herself, but for her husband and her children. She knows that her death is going to explode like a hydrogen bomb in their lives.

And you were the first person she told.

That last line is the point of the story. You are a Scorpionic type; one of the things that astrological fact signifies is that *you know in your bones that everyone dies.* You are not "comfortable" with it – who is? But your friend senses, correctly, that you will not collapse into hopeless, useless tears – or far worse, descend into a litany of religious platitudes – in the face of her hard news. *She knows that you are someone to whom she can talk.*

She recognizes that you are, ultimately, a wise woman or a wise man.

Every tribe since the human world began has had a few of them. With Scorpio clan influences prominent in your chart, you are, *at least potentially*, part of that precious lineage. That is what you signed up *to become* in this life. Or more precisely, you signed up with *an evolutionary intention and soul-capability of attaining that level of sheer naked presence.*

You can do it. The question is, will you do it? To get there, there are steps and methods you must employ. There are initiations to endure. And there are pitfalls and dead ends.

Read on; you will learn about them.

SHADOWS AND LIGHT

Here is another line from a moment ago: "Any planet in Scorpio, if it is to be functional, must be committed to a path of stark, vulnerable *realness*. If it succeeds, that planet becomes very wise. If it fails, it falls into morbidity and darkness."

If you are working with Scorpionic energy in this lifetime, here is our question: will you become the kind of person to whom your friend would reach out in the face of a grim diagnosis? Or will you wind up like one of the statistics in the Urban Policy Study?

It is not a question of pressing your favorite button. To land heads up, there is a Scorpionic evolutionary path you need to follow. As you probably sense already, it is not a path for the faint-hearted. Still, you can draw honest inspiration from one golden guarantee that is hardwired into your chart: *if you commit to a path of honest self-examination, if you open your mind and heart to human reality as it actually is, if you are willing to live in the presence of your own death and draw counsel from it, then when you are gone, you will be remembered as a person of estimable, even shamanic, wisdom.*

And if you get it wrong . . . well, here I think of a saying I learned from one of my psychotherapist friends: "you work on your stuff, or your stuff works on you." If "your stuff works on you," the bottom line is that you will be miserable – and, worse, you will learn nothing from it.

High stakes – but never forget that you can win. *No one is born with an evolutionary challenge – that is to say, a birthchart – at which they cannot succeed.* You are ready for this, and there are souls in the world who are counting on you to rise to this level because *they are going to need you* when the raw enormity of life strikes them.

And it strikes everyone, sooner or later. Scorpio clan planets link you synchronistically to some life-and-death dramas. Some are your own, and some are those of other people who will someday need you to be there for them in this powerful, decisive way.

AS YOU ARE LOOKING DEEPLY INTO YOURSELF . . .

. . . *similarly, you are looking deeply into everyone else.* That is a line I often use with my Scorpionic clients. Some people find that quality of focused intensity that is so characteristic of Scorpio people unsettling. Others find it attractive, even comforting.

All in all, that signature intensity is always a bit of an "ink blot test" for the observer – people uncomfortable with psychological truth are generally uncomfortable around Scorpio types as well.

Here is another line I use in building a bridge to Scorpionic people: "I sense that you are not looking *at* my eyes, but rather that you are looking *into* them."

And there is nothing subtle about that "at" *vs.* "in" distinction.

Once more, some people *like* that intensity and others do not. Either way, that *penetrating quality of eye contact* and its *longer-than-average duration* are classic markers of Scorpio clan components in anyone's birthchart.

You can recognize them that way. It rarely fails.

WHAT A BABE

Imagine a pretty woman who really *works hard at being a pretty woman.* You know the type – she can't go around the corner for a quart of milk without first spending fifteen minutes in front of the mirror. Other women often feel intimidated by her beauty – or competitive with her, while heterosexual men can be relied upon to go through a hideous transformation in her presence.

Say you are Scorpionic. You take one look at this gal and *you see through her* as clearly as the cold blue winter sky. You immediately sense that underneath all of her cosmetic stagecraft, the poor thing is basically insecure.

You are not even judging her; you are *discerning* – and there is a big difference. Perhaps you even feel a little sorry for her. *Compassion and unflinching insight merge at the highest levels of Scorpionic evolution.*

Our point is that *this woman cannot get away from you fast enough.*

Her whole hyper-sexual gender routine is designed as a hiding place. It is only a "blind" for her insecurities – and she senses that you are in a position to blow her cover. That may not be your desire, but it is indeed your capability. The old Soviet Union built missiles because America was building missiles because the old Soviet Union was building missiles because . . .

This little anecdote brings us to Scorpionic bedrock: *people who are afraid to face themselves will also be afraid to face you.* This energetic reality will account for some bizarre and paranoid social reactions you will encounter in this world. There will be those who turn away from you in fear, seemingly for no reason.

As a member of the Scorpio clan, you were born under a Water sign. That means that the energy is turned up on the *feeling function* in you. That tells us that these paranoid social reactions will probably hurt you. Cold comfort – but do realize that such reactions say more about the state of the person perceiving you than they do about you yourself. That realization is perhaps of some comfort, but there is another compensation. As we have already established, you can function as a wise man or wise woman, helping people in tough situations, making a real difference in their lives. That work may not be a trip to Disneyland, but it can be profoundly meaningful.

And it beats wasting your time at an endless cocktail party.

Going one step deeper, there is another side to this Scorpionic intensity that radiates from you. Some people will be frightened of you, but others will feel compelled to . . .

MAKE THEIR CONFESSIONS

If the Scorpio clan is a big part of your energetic signature, here are some lines that you are going to hear a great number of times before you are gone from this world:

- *I've never said this to anyone before, but . . .*
- *I know it seems as if we don't know each other very well, but I feel I can tell you this . . .*
- *Please don't judge me, but . . .*
- *I really don't know why I am telling you all this . . .*
- *Promise you'll tell no one, but . . .*

In each case, what follows is some kind of confession. Such confessions can take many forms, from the trivial to the extreme. Everyone has done a thing or two that they would rather not have posted on Facebook – the stolen kiss, the petty revenge, the lost temper: life's familiar list of predictable *peccadilloes.* Human folly is almost universal – but here is another nearly universal truth: in "the great cocktail party of the world," *everyone pretends that none of those things are true of them personally.* As a result, most people carry some burden of guilt – a burden they are eager to offload, provided that they can find someone who lives close enough to his or her own shadow that the confession will not lead to judgment and condemnation.

And if you are Scorpionic, that means you.

This "hearing confessions" piece is quite fundamental to our understanding of Scorpio. For many non-Scorpionic people, it might seem burdensome. But remember: Scorpio thrives on real truth – and real truth is often in short supply in the social world. These kinds of conversations can actually energize natives of this sign more than they drain it. Eye-to-eye truth-telling is one of Scorpio's regenerative strategies.

Let's add a couple more dimensions to the picture.

PHONY GUILT

There are religions that have made a lot of money by tricking people into feeling guilty about their sexuality, while offering some kind of ever-receding "cure" for their sinful natures. This is an example of phony, futile, toxic guilt, and it has done untold damage to the human spirit. Still, a man or woman might be bamboozled by such a religion into feeling awful about themselves because of having feelings that *in fact arise naturally in pretty much everyone.*

Their guilt is real in their own minds, even if its basis is false.

Like everyone else, they benefit from getting it off their chest – and maybe being offered a clearer perspective on it.

Enter a member of the Scorpio clan as their "confessor" and counselor.

REAL GUILT

Some confessions, on the other hand, involve *genuine darkness.* People do truly terrible things, and then they have to live with the consequences of their actions. If you carry the mark of the Scorpio clan, a young man who did military service in the Middle East might get very shaky one day and tell you how he "emptied his M-16 into a house once just to shut them up." That is murder most foul, of course – but if you are doing well on your Scorpionic path, you will be living close enough to your own shadow to know that anyone could collapse morally under the strain, endless tragedy, and sheer exhaustion of combat.

Your first reaction will probably not be *"this murderer,"* but rather *"this poor young man."* You understand that he now has to live with this wound on his soul for lifetimes. In the words of the good Christians, if you are doing well on the Scorpio path, you can "separate the sin from the sinner." You know that there, but for fortune, go I.

And, for Scorpio, *that compassionate relationship with the dark side of life* is the Holy of Holies, while meditating on it is one of the main incubators of meaningful spiritual evolution.

THE DARK SIDE OF THE FORCE

We saw earlier how, when a large segment of the human population is given this much access to the unconscious mind, a significant number of them simply become miserable. That *moody, brooding quality* is probably the main expression of Scorpio's dark side – but it is not its most spectacular one. Down that depressive road, most of the harm done is directed inward. The person making this kind of weak response to Scorpio's evolutionary challenges does most of the suffering himself or herself.

Sometimes, however, the shoe is on the other foot. Sometimes we see real viciousness in this sign – a kind of viciousness rendered thermonuclear because it is augmented with genuine insight into the wounded places in another person. Here is what I mean by that. One manifestation of this bleak side of Scorpio might sound this way: in a situation where many of us, fed up with another person's rotten conduct, might invite him to "go to hell," a Scorpionic person might instead say, *your mother never really wanted you, did she?"*

That line makes high grades for sheer nastiness – *but what if it is actually true?* Like most medicines, truth, when misapplied or linked to a dark purpose, is diabolically poisonous.

Why would anyone want to shatter another human being that way?

In the opening sentence of this section, we spoke of people being "given this much access to the unconscious mind." Perhaps a better way of saying it is that the unconscious mind has this much access to *them*. It is of course a two-way street.

Inner rage – and its close cousin, inner pain – can leak out into the world.

PROJECTION

Material becomes unconscious in the first place because it is threatening to the ego. Maybe it is just too painful to bear. Maybe it is so dark that we would risk losing all faith in life were we to engage with it. Maybe the energies it contains could trigger behaviors in us so self-destructive or sociopathic that the psyche arranges for them to remain buried.

And maybe, in this imperfect world, that *repression* is more a good thing than a bad one.

Our pivotal concept here is that the conscious mind *hates and fears this charged material*. It tries to drive it out of existence – or at least out of mind. The former is impossible, but the latter is commonplace.

Because of the essential violence of this repressive process, whenever we see anything in the world that resembles the thing we fear in ourselves, we treat it precisely the same way that we are treating that part of ourselves.

Once again, our aim is to drive it out of existence. Psychologists have labelled this phenomenon *projection* – and when a Scorpionic person starts projecting, you had better be wearing a Kevlar vest.

Please remember that none of this is intended as an attack upon people who have the Sun in Scorpio. We all have the energy of this sign in us somewhere – and of course we will soon need to extend our thinking about the Scorpio clan to include the eighth house, Mars, and especially Pluto. All of them deal with our relationship to the unconscious mind, one way or another. For all of them, that courageous inward road can be a pathway to healing, regeneration, and recovery.

But if the dark material begins to surface, and the conscious mind rejects it, those venoms do not dissipate. All that happens is that instead of seeing them inside ourselves, we see them in the world – and, like a cat trying to pounce on the beam of a flashlight, we try to blot them out of existence.

Here is our rogue's gallery of Scorpionic projections:

- The rabidly homophobic man who is terrified of the inherent ambiguity in his own actual sexual orientation.
- Nazis who felt that Jewish people were "materialistic and hellbent on world domination."
- The white lynch mob fearing that "negros" are disposed to be violent and dangerous,
- The big game hunter, so out of touch with his own instinctual side that he shoots animals for sport.
- The raging feminist who feels that "all men are insensitive pigs incapable of seeing women a human beings."
- The abusive husband symbolically attacking his own weakness and helplessly low stature in the world by berating, shaming, and even hitting his beleaguered wife.
- The person hooked on pornography and simultaneously ashamed of his (or her) own body.
- The atheist who attacks anyone with a religion; the religious person who merrily consigns all atheists to hellfire.

In every one of these cases, people travelling the dark Scorpio road are doing to others pretty much exactly what they are doing to themselves.

Perhaps there is some ultimate justice in that . . . but then there is the body count.

REMEMBER...

The Water family is ultimately about healing, regeneration and recovery. Some of the territory we have just been traversing seems to only be about darkness. *Making the unconscious mind conscious* is not a process for the faint-hearted – but it is an essential part of any true psychological healing that we might ever do. *That is because unless we face these benighted parts of ourselves, they rule our lives.*

These healings are initiations through which we must pass. Getting through them makes us worthy of being that wise man or woman who "hears confessions" or who can be there for other people in their darkest hours. Most of these initiations revolve around some manner of profoundly honest confrontation with ourselves, which is always the essence of Scorpionic territory.

- We have a hard conversation with someone we love. It is exhausting – and yet when it is over, we both agree that we are "glad we talked about it." That is an example of Scorpionic *healing*.
- A woman's body-image and gender dignity is damaged by bad religion – she learns that "Eve gave Adam the apple" – (and I think we can all figure out what that "apple" was.) She goes through a cathartic, painful split with her former church congregation. It is very hard for her – and totally worth it. She gets past that shame. And she learns to dance as if no one were watching. That is an example of Scorpionic *regeneration*.
- A soldier just returned from the nightmare of war endures three hard years of confrontive psychotherapy. Once or twice during the process, thoughts of suicide cross his mind. In the end, he reclaims his faith in life and his ability to feel. The process was awful, but totally worth it. That is an example of Scorpionic *recovery*.

SEXY SCORPIO

In pop astrology, Scorpio is generally viewed as the sexy sign. There is actually some truth in that assertion, but it is helpful to keep perspective. I have run a careful survey and I have learned that sex is in fact popular with the other eleven signs. Clearly, Scorpio has not cornered the market on that very elemental human activity.

Still, there are many sexy clues for us to understand and absorb here.

At the most obvious level, Scorpio is about dealing with taboo material. And, "dirty jokes" and sexual innuendos aside, in social interactions sex remains a very controlled subject. Tell a sexy joke and chances are that everyone laughs. But start asking them graphic questions about their desires and their actual experiences, and you will soon encounter evidence of a boundary that few people dare to cross.

Try, for example, getting everyone's attention at a party, and saying, "Let's go around the room and share how many sexual partners we've had . . ." Or, over the champagne toast, try asking the couple celebrating their twenty-fifth wedding anniversary if they have really been *totally faithful to each other for twenty-five years . . .?"*

I could get a lot more concrete here, but I am aware that kids might get their hands on this book. The point is that, for all of our social posturing around being sophisticated human beings, when it comes to sexuality, people are generally about one question deep before you collide with their defenses. Other than perhaps death itself, there is probably no subject as hedged about with taboos as human sexuality. For that reason alone, *we can in fact say that Scorpio is the sign of sex.* That is not because sex has nothing to do with Gemini or Cancer; it is because as soon as you begin to talk about sex in anything except a humorous or medical way, you have crossed the line into taboo territory.

And that means that you have entered the Scorpionic realm.

A MAN AND A WOMAN ALONE ON A MOONLIT BEACH . . .

They stand there in the luminous dark, waves surging and receding just beyond them, as if the ocean itself were panting. They gaze soulfully into each other's eyes, their noses only ten inches apart, speaking softly, intimately. They touch; from time to time, one takes the hand of the other. Once, they hug, holding each other close for a while, then resuming their whispered, urgent conversation.

How would you read the nature of their relationship?

Come on, we all know what you are thinking . . .

But they are actually a mother and her beloved son. Or two truly dear friends. Or a brother and a sister.

Scorpio, at its best, is about that kind of intense intimate communion. As our little vignette demonstrates, when we see evidence of that kind of connection between two people, *we tend to interpret it romantically.*

And that can be a mistake.

The deepest kinds of sexual experience do have that same Scorpionic energetic signature – but *we can be close to another person in a tender way without any kind of erotic exchange or sexual feelings.*

Critically, let us also acknowledge that in actual reality, sexual intercourse often occurs between people without that kind of deep soul-contact.

How many couples only "do it" with the lights out?

How many treat sex as if it were a game or a joke?

How many avoid each other's eyes during sex?

How many spur-of-the-moment sexual "adventures" do you suppose have happened somewhere in the world ever since you read the first words of this chapter?

No judgment – my aim is only to focus on the *specifically Scorpionic face* of the far wider world of human sexual expression. A line from earlier bears repetition: "as you are looking deeply into yourself, similarly you are looking deeply into everyone else." For a healthy Scorpio clan person, no other kind of sexual interaction is worth the effort of going through with it.

For such an individual, the eyes are the most erogenous zone of the body.

The calculatedly sexy, posturing Scorpio *femme fatale* or *playboy* of street astrology are actually perversions of this evolutionary path. They may be sexy, but they are not deep – and "deep" is what Scorpio is actually about. That depth is about a lot more than tight clothes and eye shadow.

When Scorpio goes sour, it can slip into projection. It can become cruel and hurtful. Link those dark projections to sexuality, and we have a formula for some of the bleakest storylines that have ever played out on the face of the Earth. Sadism in all its forms, the chronic heartbreaker, rape and sexual aggression, anyone proud of "conquests" – all of that is Scorpionic poison. That is all horribly true and real – but never forget to file that kind of misery under the right heading: that is Scorpionic *dysfunction.* That is the ancient darkness.

Seeking – and facing – truth is the healing path of the Scorpion. That may hurt, but it is never about hurting people.

Let's bring all of this into a sharper *behavioral* focus by turning our attention to . . .

THE EIGHTH HOUSE

Scorpio is the eighth sign of the zodiac, so it has a natural resonance with the eighth house. The language we use in speaking of one overlaps with the language we use in speaking of the other. In practice, they are sometimes hard to distinguish. Still, confusing Scorpio with the eighth house is a source of imprecision in our work – and keeping them as separate in your mind as possible increases the clarity of your language.

As ever, our key insight is that *we are our signs and we do our houses.* Signs are *motivational,* while houses are *behavioral.* With Scorpio, our *motivation* – at least when we are on the right track – is to deal as honestly and authentically as possible with life's more frightening or threatening realities, and thereby to reclaim parts of ourselves that have been hurt or damaged.

That process leads us directly into three arenas of human *behavior* which lie at the very heart of the eighth house, and which are *outward expressions* of Scorpionic interests, instincts, and values.

SEX, DEATH, AND THE OCCULT

Death and the occult are two subjects which have a long history of scaring people – but what about sex? The majority of humans are enthusiastic in that department – *that is, until you invite them to be honest about it.* You may recall, in speaking of Scorpio, we entertained committing the *faux pas* of asking people at a party to reveal how many sexual partners they have had. *Can we start with you please, ma'am . . .?*

You can quickly see where that would go.

Equally, you might walk into that same gathering, tap your spoon on the side of glass and announce, "We are all going to die."

In either case, the next time those people have a party, your name is not on the guest list.

There we have sex and death: taboo subjects, either one of which will get you banned from polite society.

What about the occult?

How would you honestly feel if you were suddenly to see a ghost? Even a *nice* ghost would probably raise the hairs on the back of your neck. What about being all alone in a tumbledown Victorian mansion on a dark and stormy night – and suddenly feeling a truly malevolent spirit slipping into the bed with you?

People are generally so frightened of that stuff that many of them have agreed to pretend that it is not even true.

The eighth house is indeed scary. In fact, a good working definition of it is that *the eighth house embraces everything in life that invokes feelings of fear in us – or fear's first cousin: denial.*

That goes way beyond sex, death, and the occult, but those three provide a good starting point.

SEX

To label the eighth house the house of sex is useful, so long as we use that famously multidimensional word in the inclusive way we just used it while discussing Scorpio. Mating behavior in general is the heart of it, not just the physical act. Graphically speaking, a person's style in bed is actually revealed more clearly in the fifth house, along with his or her Mars and Venus placements. The eighth house is about the alchemical cauldron of *true intimacy,* body, mind, and spirit *In the eighth house context, "sex" refers to everything across the entire spectrum of what makes a committed coupling bond different from any other kind of human partnership.*

With clients, one of my favorite ways to quickly introduce this dimension of the eighth house is to say, *"two people have now been lovers for somewhere between six and eight consecutive weekends . . ."* Everyone smiles – but they also immediately understand. That situation represents "early days" in any relationship. No one really knows what reefs and shoals lie ahead for the nascent couple. *But the point is that we all know that such a relationship is starting to get serious.* Even if they are committed to their fling being "casual" or "no strings attached," it is never going to remain that simple. Even six or eight weeks of repeated sexual exposure is enough to trigger an ancient mammal program buried deep in everyone's brain stem – *mating.* That is a process with many subterranean elements, and one that is inextricably bound to eighth house symbolism.

Such a relationship may be the greatest treasure available to anyone on this earth – or it may be a psychiatric catastrophe. Either way, a kind of *Crazy Glue* oozes up out of the psychic depths and creates psychic interdependency between the partners. That "crazy glue" is symbolized by the eighth house.

Everyone knows that the mating relationship *feels fundamentally different* from simple friendship. Hopefully, such a bond *includes* friendship – but that is not always the case. Purple passion devolving into homicidal ideation over a period of just a few months is not a rare storyline. "I realize now that I never even really *liked* him . . ."

How does all of this fit into our Scorpionic schema of healing, regeneration, and recovery? That leads me to one of my favorite questions: *why did God make love?*

I hope you enjoy the *double entendre* as much as I do.

DIGGING IN THE DIRT

Nothing brings the actual reality of our psychic wounds nakedly to the surface as quickly or as effectively as sexual intimacy. And those words are virtually the definition of the healing processes embodied in this second phase of the Water Family. It does not matter what the wounds are, or what their origin was. In every case, committed sexual intimacy will reliably reveal them – at least after "six to eight consecutive weekends."

The brilliant English composer, Peter Gabriel, absolutely nailed it in his song, *Digging in the Dirt*, when he sang this utterly Scorpionic verse . . .

> *The more I look, the more I find.*
> *As I close on in, I get so blind.*
> *I feel it in my head, I feel it in my toes.*
> *I feel it in my sex, that's the place it goes*

Tellingly, a little earlier in the same song, he added this tender, painfully honest, quatrain:

> *Stay with me, I need support.*
> *I'm digging in the dirt*
> *To find the places I got hurt,*
> *Open up the places I got hurt*

Gabriel's lyrics really say it all, but let's delve a little deeper into these eighth house mysteries.

Say, for example, that I was abandoned by my mother when I was a little kid. She ran off with the milkman and I never saw her again. (Not really true – thanks, mom!) Anyone would then assume that I probably had some "abandonment issues." Fair enough. *But I could have male buddies and never fear that they were about to abandon me.* I could even have respectful, pleasurable sexual arrangements with various women – note the plural – and still feel emotionally secure enough in those relationships.

But let me start to bond with one woman and inside of six weeks, as sure as the rain will fall, I would fear that she was going to abandon me.

If we love anyone with our body, we invite the unconscious mind and all of its dark materials to the table – and to the bed. Here is how it might go:

Crazy Steve: I saw the way you were flirting with that guy at the party . . .

My Poor Partner (innocently): *What guy?*

From that juncture, our story could go down two roads. One is the disastrous face of the eighth house – the one that puts the "crazy" in the crazy glue. The other is a holy path that weaves our grown-up sexuality into our soul's journey in a kind of ancient, even pagan, sacrament of healing, regeneration, and recovery.

- Storyline #1: Crazy Steve yells, "Don't give me that *what guy* crap! You know who I am talking about!" From there, my poor girlfriend and I move into one of those hellish intimate arguments that goes nowhere and leaves everyone bloody in mind, and perhaps even in body. No relationship can survive many of those kinds of dispiriting interactions. Intimate trust is fragile. Perhaps my own madness has just destroyed it.

- In Storyline #2, my partner points out that *what I am experiencing is actually the resurrection of my unresolved hurts regarding my mother's abandonment of me.* It probably takes me a while to see the situation that way. Maybe I am defensive at first. Maybe she loves me enough to hang in there while I work through my surfacing wounds. Maybe I love her enough to humble myself before her and eventually own my craziness. Maybe I apologize. Maybe we hug each other. Maybe we live happily – and more importantly, *deeply* – ever after.

Two stories, with two possible endings. The second one is the high evolutionary method implicit in the sexual face of the eighth house. It is the path of healing, regeneration, and recovery. Remember: *this is the house of everything that scares us.* And little is more frightening to us than the raw experience of our own wounds.

What specific eighth house configurations could suggest a storyline such as the one I just described? One possibility is that I have the planet Uranus there – a planet that can correlate with literal abandonment – and perhaps it opposes Mother Moon. There are many other possible configurations we could name. An Aquarian Moon might also underscore "distant" mother symbolism. Mars would put the spotlight on anger. Saturn would put the focus on my fear of trusting anyone. Link them up in any combination, and you might have a storyline of abandonment, such as the one I just told.

There is no one simple astrological formula, in other words. What we have is something even better: *in any eighth house configuration, we encounter an astrological message which brings us directly to the heart of the personal issue we must resolve if we are ever to experience intimate joy.*

At the same time, this eighth house structure also gives us a second gift: insight into the qualities of anyone whom we might call our *natural mate* – a person designated by the universe to help us address these exact wounds. That means someone destined to play a pivotal role in our own healing, regeneration, and recovery.

Later in the book, we go through each planet individually in terms of how it functions in the eighth house, how it defines the wound, the healing process, and who might help us with the process. Right now, in this early chapter, we are just trying to grasp the basic astrological principles.

Eighth house sexuality is the heaven-and-hell process of living in energetic intimacy with another person. It is a *physical yoga* – a yoga which includes sex in the simple sense of the word – but it is also a *mental and spiritual discipline* which demands everything from us and *pays us back double* if we succeed at it.

This coupling path is literally not for everyone – there are other evolutionary methods, and there are people who are not wired to be partnered at all. We must honor them too.

For those of us doing the yoga of committed intimacy, we will surely sooner or later be required to "dig in the dirt," as Peter Gabriel put it. But there is an energizing, ecstatic side to the process too. We should never forget that rewarding piece of the puzzle. *Love can give us the energy we need to endure the rigors of the very healing processes it triggers.*

Here, to shine a light on the brighter side of the eighth house coin, are some lines from *Sacred Love*, a song by my friend Sting. He understands what I am writing about here – he and his wonderful wife, Trudie Styler, who was kind enough to offer the cover endorsement for *The Book of Air*, have been together for four decades or so. I smile when I hear him sing this lyric and at the same time think of the way I have seen him look at Trudie. I also giggle a little when I recall a warning that my ex-wife Jodie and I got when we first were invited to visit them in England, back in 1993. A family member, knowing that Sting was a "rock star," gravely warned us about how we would surely be pressed into participating in an orgy as soon as we got there. In reality, what we found was a happy couple and house full of children.

The spirit moves on the water
She takes the shape of this heavenly daughter
She's rising up like a river in flood
The word got made into flesh and blood
The sky grew dark, and the earth she shook
Just like a prophecy in the Holy Book
Thou shalt not covet, thou shalt not steal
Thou shalt not doubt that this love is real
So I got down on my knees and I prayed to the skies
When I looked up could I trust my eyes?
All the saints and angels and the stars up above
They all bowed down to the flower of creation
Every man, every woman, every race every nation
It all comes down to this sacred love

DEATH

There are traditions in astrology that purport to predict the length of your life. These traditions all share a tragic flaw: in my experience, they don't work.

That objection is definitive, but let's add another question: would you really want to know when you would die? And would we really be helping anyone if we told them what day to mark on their calendar?

Or to stop buying calendars?

All through history, there have been human beings who have lived into their nineties or beyond. But there is simply a much higher percentage of them now. Since astrological cycles are effectively invariable in length over historical time scales, it follows that even if these death-predictions were *ever* reliable, many of us would simply be outliving them today.

I believe that it is safe to say that your chart does not reveal the day that you will die. That said, let's add that we do generally die under some kind of astrological stress; no surprise there. But astrological stress is not rare. You could probably circle 10% of the days on your calendar and have a 90% certainty that one of those dates "has your name on it."

There are some deeper astrological techniques around predicting death and they do involve the eighth house. One's birthchart does in fact give broadly impressionistic information about the *nature* of one's most probable death, for example. There are also certain transitory astrological conditions that are generally present around death, but those techniques are too nebulous to be of any use in telling someone in his or her twenties that death will arrive on December 7, 2094. These conditions come and go; they are not rare. They quickly bring us back to circling "10% of the dates on the calendar."

As common sense evidence mounts that death is looming on the immediate horizon – *grandpa is in the hospital and at this point the doctors are only trying to make him comfortable* – there are some methods for focusing the timing of death on the calendar with reasonable accuracy.

The human reality is that even this kind of astrology is very charged psychologically. Just to be totally transparent, I've promised myself only to teach these techniques to my more advanced students. I've encouraged them not to go public with them – only to use them judiciously with trusted clients. "First do no harm," in other words. So I am not going to write any more about those techniques here. That's a hard decision, but it feels like the ethical path. My apologies. Please understand. If you were to feel the need for that kind of astrological perspective, I'd encourage you to contact one of my more advanced students. They are listed in the Directory on my website.

THE MIRROR OF OTHER PEOPLE'S CHARTS

Many of us have lost parents. The majority of us have lost dear friends. When someone close to us passes away, it is obviously a big event in our own lives. It follows that we will see astrological correlates of that death reflected in our own charts.

In fact, it is a commonplace teaching among astrologers that the best place to look for evidence of one person's death is in the charts of that person's nearest and dearest.

How could it be otherwise? Astrology works, and a major bereavement is typically a major turning point in anyone's life. Astrology must reflect its timing as well as its meaning. When we love someone, we are *identified with them* psychologically. When they die, in a sense we die too. Our "death" does not occur literally – but there is a vicarious experience of passing from this world on the coattails of our friend. It can be an experience of agonizing grief.

Or an experience of magic.

TY STEPHENS

I was probably about twenty years old, working as a clerk in a music store in Chapel Hill, North Carolina, earning money so I could stay in college. Near closing time, a man named Ty Stephens walked into the shop and pulled down a guitar. One look and I knew he wasn't buying, but he sure could play that instrument.

Business was slow. After a while, I pulled a bass guitar off the wall and joined him. Our eyes met. We had musical chemistry. A couple of nights later, we played together again, this time at my house with a couple of friends of mine, Tommy the drummer and Jim, the lead guitarist. Magic happened again. We were as loud as Led Zeppelin, but my Siamese cat fell asleep curled up on the base of Ty's microphone stand.

A week later, really after only that one rehearsal, we played our first gig at a fraternity house.

Ty was a total Aquarian "original." He had played in the halcyon days of the Greenwich Village folk music scene in New York City. I'm tempted to tell his story, but let's suffice to say that he was somewhere between a

1950's "Jack Kerouac" bohemian and a genuine "Johnny Cash" Country and Western outlaw.

Our band, Brotherhood, turned out to be pretty successful in a local kind of way – we must have played a hundred gigs and we had a big following of fans, including an edgy motorcycle gang called the Storm Troopers – that relationship taught me a lot about diplomacy. A few of them were soon in prison for murder.

After a couple of years, life ran its course. The band broke up amicably. Ty and I drifted apart.

Fifteen years down the road, I got a call from a friend. Ty was dying. He was in the Veteran's Administration hospital in Durham, North Carolina, and did not have much time left to live. I got in my car and shot over there right away, only to be met by sad faces and the news that he had lapsed into a coma. He was unresponsive and not expected to survive for many more days.

I sat down quietly by his bedside to say a little prayer of blessing and gratitude for my friend – and, truth said, my mentor.

And against all reason and contrary to all medical understanding, Ty's eyes opened. He recognized me. He said, "*hey, man . . .*"

And then his eyes closed again.

I returned the next morning.

His hospital bed was empty. He had died that night.

What about the astrology behind that miracle story?

I have Gemini on the cusp of my eighth house, so Mercury rules it. *That means that Mercury will always be a personal death-significator for me.* If you have a planet in the eighth house, it carries death symbolism for you too. And naturally you have a sign on the cusp of your eighth house. What planet rules it? There's another bit of your personal death symbolism – something about the face that death will show you when it arrives.

As Ty Stephens lay there dying, my progressed Mercury was making a station and about to turn direct. That put a major Mercury signature on that period of time, and, strictly for me personally, that Mercury signature added a vector of encounters with death.

I wrote about my Mercury station in *The Book of Earth*. Briefly, it coincided with "finding my voice" – the beginning of my public work, publishing books, and so on.

But Ty Stephens gave me an essential gift that afternoon when he miraculously returned from a comatose state just to say "hey, man" to me. *Any cultural conditioning that remained in me about how we humans are merely flesh and blood went poof in that moment and has never plagued me again.* Had any of those kinds of doubts remained active in me, they would have corrupted my teaching. I would not have been able to write the books that I have written.

So here's to my old friend, Ty. I have much to thank him for – but those last two words of his were maybe his greatest gift to me.

We are so conditioned to think of death in tragic terms. Simple compassion dictates that such an attitude must be honored in anyone experiencing such a loss. But death is not always simply a tragedy to be endured. It is also potentially a doorway into some very fundamental wisdom. When that wisdom comes knocking, something is surely happening in your astrological eighth house, or with aspects to any planet you might have there natally, or with the planet that rules its cusp.

Whatever form the event takes, and even if it takes a toll, it has the power to regenerate your elemental faith in life.

The sages of history all agree: there is no counsellor in this world as efficacious as death.

THE OCCULT

The word "occult" carries a whole different halo of meaning than sex or even death. "Occultism" sounds spooky – and to some people, maybe it sounds worse than that. For individuals raised in conservative religious environments, "occultism" implies the dark face of witchcraft, pacts with Satan, demonology, and so on.

The Merriam-Webster dictionary defines the occult simply as "belief in or study of the action or influence of supernatural or supernormal powers."

I think that definition is about right.

But keep on reading: this is not nearly as weird as it is probably beginning to sound. Remember: *everyone has an eighth house.* Having one is your human birthright, and you do not have to sell your soul to the devil in the bargain in order to keep it – although our next few sentences might make you think that we are trending in that perilous direction.

Witches are reputed to have "familiar spirits" who do their bidding. Magicians "learn the name of a demon" and thereby gain some measure of control over it. Faust sold his soul to the devil Mephistopheles in exchange for knowledge. A thousand years ago, Pope Sylvester II was reputed to have had a relationship with a female demon named Meridiana who opened the road to the papacy to him. More recently, American blues legend, Robert Johnson, allegedly "went down to the crossroads," where he sold his soul to Satan in exchange for mastery of the guitar.

Listening to his recordings today, you've got to wonder . . .

Ask any Sunday School teacher – all of this makes it sound as if we are treading on distinctly shaky theological ground.

Picture a healer – one of those people who pray over you, lay their hands on you, and cure you of whatever ails you. Charlatans abound of course, but there are also many stories of that nature which are hard to explain away as mere trickery.

Maybe you are the one being healed. After throwing away your crutches, you offer heartfelt gratitude to the healer – and almost undoubtedly he or she says, *"Don't thank me. Thank God. God healed you, not me."*

You can almost hear the healer say those words. They are that familiar. Let's take them at face value – and consider them in the light of what we have just been reading about occultists "having relationships with demons."

The occultist connects with an empowering spirit and works in cooperation with it.

So does the healer.

In both cases, a *relationship* lies at the heart of the particular personal empowerment. Do you perhaps already begin to hear some echoes here of the sexual dimensions of the eighth house? There too, we are *empowered by a relationship with another being,* the only difference being that in the sexual framework, this other being has a physical body, unlike "the demon"– or unlike God, for that matter.

- "An evil sorcerer" sees an undesirable condition in the world: a happy family with a cow that gives them sweet milk. With the help of a demon, he curses the cow, and the milk goes sour. He is cheered by their misfortune.

- "A healer" sees an undesirable condition in the world: a person suffering from some malady. He or she, with the help of some higher power, cures the disease. He is cheered by that person's recovery.

There is a huge difference between these two phenomena, *but the difference is 100% a moral one.* Otherwise, they are identical.

Both scenarios – dark magic and healing magic – arise in symbolism of the eighth house. If you have such powers, they are indicated there. So is the path to claiming them and activating them.

All of this still admittedly sounds pretty exotic. So let me bring it down to earth with a quick personal reflection.

LADIES AND GENTLEMAN . . . STEVEN FORREST

In my teaching programs, I often lecture for four or five days. I generally do it without notes. I know the material; I have a supply of metaphors and stories ready to go. Over the years, I have built a library of ideas and word-structures to convey them. There are full paragraphs that I am certain that I have said at least a thousand times, word-for-word.

But sometimes I have no idea whatsoever what I am going to say next. I just open my mouth in a spirit of faith that something meaningful will come out of it.

And it usually does.

I've had students tell me that they think I am "channeling this stuff." I'm not comfortable with that word. I take personal responsibility for what I am teaching – and my experience is surely not that of some spirit doing all the work while I sit there waiting for a paycheck.

But what do we really mean by "channeling?" Where does such inspiration actually come from? We have all had the experience of something brilliant just popping out of our mouths. Expressing surprise, maybe we even say, "I didn't know I knew that."

However we might answer those questions, one point is clear: *we are talking about a process that is happening beyond the reach of the conscious, logical mind.* I am more complicated than what is happening in the top two inches of my head.

So are you.

In the eighth house, we can potentially enter into cooperative rapport with something – or some entity – beyond our rational comprehension, and thereby become more powerful than we could ever be without that assistance.

As I mentioned earlier, writing about Ty Stephens, I've got Gemini in my eighth house, with Uranus there as well. Mercury rules Gemini, and it lies on the cusp of my third house – language again. Taken all together, that Geminian eighth house symbolism suggests that my personal "super-power" is *linguistic.*

I am using myself as an example here, but not in order to make any special claims about myself. You have an eighth house too. What is the shape of your own "superpower?"

Here's how to answer that question:

What sign rules your eighth house cusp? Where is that ruling planet located? Do you have any planets in your eighth house? Those are the sym-bols which describe your own potential superpowers. Perhaps more help-fully, they let you know what methods you can use to activate them, not to mention what wounds might be draining their batteries – and how to heal those wounds so that you can eventually access these higher energies.

THREE TALES OF DAEMONS

Astronaut Neil Armstrong had two such eighth house "demons" – and from now on, I am going to spell it *daemon* just to put some distance be-tween us and Lord Voldemort's crowd. Armstrong needed both daemons back in 1969 when he was landing on the Moon. Apollo 11 had overshot its intended landing area by many miles and was descending disastrously into dangerously rocky terrain. And with only seconds of fuel remaining, the onboard computers froze.

History records that Armstrong took over and just *flew* that capsule down to the surface by the seat of his pants. When they landed, they had only 25 seconds of fuel left.

Neil Armstrong had a natal Sagittarian Moon on the cusp of his eighth house and Saturn in Capricorn a little deeper into it. For our pur-poses, I think it is safe to say that the "daemon" Saturn gave him the cool-headed, calculating *sang froid* he needed if he was going to survive at all, while the "daemon" of that Sagittarian Moon gave him the sheer "cowboy" instincts so evident in his impulse to throw out the manual, ignore instructions, and just grab the controls.

Chess genius Bobby Fischer had Mercury in Aquarius in the eighth house conjunct his lunar south node. What "daemon" whispered shocking Aquarian chess strategies in his ear as he was defeating Boris Spassky for the World Championship?

In Astrodatabank, the chart given for the great ballerina Margot Fonteyn is "dirty data," with much uncertainty around her time of birth. Despite the need for caution with shaky birth times, I like the tentative chart they suggest. It shows an empty eighth house – but with artistic Libra on its cusp. That makes Venus her "daemon" planet, wherever it might lie. Her Venus is in Cancer, conjunct Jupiter and Pluto, *in her fifth house* (performance).

When she leapt, how could she account for the grace that animated every molecule in her physical body? "Ms. Fonteyn, would you please explain the calculations of momentum and inertia that go into your *pirouettes* and how you adjust them for slight variations in your weight, atmospheric pressure, geographic variations in earth's gravity, and so on?"

Of course she could not answer those questions in words. But she could answer them with her body and her soul. What helped her do that? What gave her that inexplicable superpower?

When I speak of the "occult" dimensions of the eighth house with a client, there's a line I sometimes use. *"I hope I am not getting too weird for you – but I hope I am getting weird enough."* Everyone laughs, but generally people have understood. There are bodiless powers in this universe that cannot really be explained logically. Some of them are benign, some are not. It probably does not matter whether we think of them as daemons – as independent, non-physical, *conscious beings* with whom we can cooperate, in other words – or simply as "powers" without any independent volition of their own. Even in thinking of them simply as neutral powers, we are left with another unanswerable question: *do these powers reside inside us as "unconscious complexes" such as a psychoanalyst might describe – or are they something far stranger than that?*

In any case, just as a healthy committed relationship with another human being is for most of us a precious treasure that makes us stronger, happier, and wiser, in similar fashion we can establish, *via* our eighth houses, an intimate, empowering link to mysteries which lie beyond ourselves, mysteries which make us stronger than we could ever be if we were simply "our personalities" and nothing more.

That empowerment is *healing* and *regenerative*. No one who has experienced it would ever doubt that.

PLUTO AND MARS: CO-RULERS OF SCORPIO

For centuries, astrologers called Mars the ruling planet of Scorpio. I still believe that is correct. Perhaps the most obvious reason is the quality of *passionate intensity* that characterizes both the sign and the planet. Seeing that sense of *a communality of energy* is always the basic signature of any sign rulership as we have seen many times before. Verbal Mercury's link to communicative Gemini leaps out, as does Jupiter's expansiveness with Sagittarian verve and openness to life.

Mars rules Scorpio, always has, always will.

But then in 1930, along came Pluto. As ever, the mirror of synchronicity linked the discovery of the planet with the climate of the times. In a nutshell, Pluto's discovery marked the *collective discovery of the unconscious mind.* Psychology had existed for a few decades already, but 1930 is a plausible "epicenter" for its integration into the collective mind. And the world *needed* some psychotherapy around then too, as we were on the verge of the descent into Plutonian madness we call World War II.

Any astrologer, in my opinion, who resists seeing the obvious connection between Pluto and Scorpio is as blind as any other kind of Fundamentalist, and for similar reasons.

Pluto rules Scorpio too, and it shares that role equally with Mars.

We explored Mars thoroughly in *The Book of Fire*. We will have a brief look at it again later in this chapter, focusing on its more Scorpionic qualities. But Pluto is new territory, and so let's delve into it and see how "the Lord of the Underworld" can be made to play a pivotal role in our processes of healing, regeneration, and recovery.

PLUTO, THE GOD OF HELL

The Greeks called this same god Hades, a word which eventually came to refer to a place rather than to a personage. The Romans had essentially the same god and called him Pluto, Lord of the Underworld. The Norse had a goddess rather than a god who presided over the underworld. She was named *Hel*, and you would not relish meeting her either. That is where we get our modern word, Hell.

Translating Pluto into "the God of Hell" is not a major stretch, so let's begin our explorations right there. Say we find ourselves at a little church in the countryside. We ask the pastor to tell us about hell. He says that there are three things that we need to know about it: *hell is hot, it's buried under the ground, and you really don't want to go there.* Those three statements might sound naïve, but they are actually helpful. Almost every culture that has ever existed on Earth has had some concept of hell. That proves beyond the shadow of a doubt that hell is part of the human mind. If it were otherwise, we would not project it willy-nilly onto the fabric of the universe. *So, is there a place, found universally in the human mind, that is so hot that we bury it and we really don't want to go there?*

Framing the question that way takes us quickly to the essence of hell – and therefore of Pluto. From these folklore words, we can see that hell at least overlaps significantly with the idea of the unconscious mind and may be identical with it. The unconscious mind is where we bury things that are so hot we cannot face them. It too is a place where we "do not want to go."

You, speaking to a friend who has just been abandoned by her partner: "How are you doing about Chris and all of that lately?" Your friend, tearing up and suddenly looking stricken and vulnerable, blurts out, *"thanks . . . but I really can't go there today, OK?* Of course you immediately understand: she is not doing very well about "Chris and all of that." She is afraid that she will start weeping out loud right there in *Starbucks* if she tries to talk about it. She appreciates your support, but she is not yet ready to talk about the situation.

You nod, and deftly switch to a safer topic. That is the path of kindness.

But you also understand that regarding "Chris and all that," your friend is going to "have to go there someday" – that, or she will just meet another Chris. That is a Plutonian insight.

We all have to make occasional excursions down into the underworld. And hell – Pluto's realm – is essentially the place where we keep all of our pain and hurt, all of our woundedness, all of our shame and humiliation, every sin we have committed, every lie we have heard, every parental failure, and every betrayal we have ever endured.

MAKING AN "A" IN PLUTO UNIVERSITY

Back to the coffee shop. You are sitting with another dear friend, having a conversation. Unbeknownst to you, the thread of the talk has led you to stumble into a danger zone. *Your friend knows something that is guaranteed to upset you.* You've unwittingly slid into it, and that twist in the conversation has put her in a bad spot – she does not want to hurt you, but she is too close a friend to lie to you either.

This is not an unfamiliar human situation. People have often found themselves there. A kind of ritual social procedure is available for your friend. She buys time by saying, *"I don't know if I should tell you something that you don't want to hear . . ."*

If you are marked astrologically by a strongly-placed Pluto, or a lot of Scorpio or major eighth house energy, your immediate reflex is to look her straight in the eye and say, *"What is it?"*

She tells you, and you are depressed for a week.

We could debate the wisdom of "always wanting to know everything" – but if you are a Plutonian type, the debate will not help. You will *still* want to know everything. That is your path.

Always "wanting to know everything" is how you make an A.

Now let's go for an A+, with honors and a gold star.

You are pouring your heart out to a friend, talking about a tough situation in a primary relationship of yours. Your friend listens reflectively. When you are done, she seems hesitant. Finally she says, with some tentativeness, *"I think there's something that you're not dealing with here . . ."* With those fateful words on the table, she awaits some body-language version of a green light from you. You understand the implicit warning: if she were a rattlesnake, she would have just rattled. But she is not a rattlesnake; she is one of your true eighth house friends. The contract between you is "truth above all." Your eyes widen and you nod your head slightly. You have indicated that she has your blessing for going forward and saying what she actually thinks. She proceeds to offer you an entirely different interpretation of that tough situation you are facing – *an interpretation in which you are a lot more culpable,* and much less the hapless victim, than in your own version of the situation.

Immediately you feel defensiveness rise in your gullet. You are ready to "pop her one." Then you reflect for a moment, seeing the situation through her eyes. Looking humbled and vulnerable, you quietly say, *"Oh my God . . . you might be right."*

Maybe after another moment, still looking right at her, you add, *"Thank you. You're such a good friend."*

That is how you make an A+ with honors and a gold star with Pluto. You felt defensive – but you resisted the reflex to let defensiveness define your actual behavior. You were willing to go to Hell. You knew it would be good for you.

WHERE PLUTO LIES, WE HAVE A WOUND

A couple of decades ago, I did some seminars and wrote the two volumes of *Measuring The Night* with astrologer, Jeffrey Wolf Green. In his system of evolutionary astrology, Pluto represents the *soul.* That principle is a major linchpin in his work.

I never really agreed with that idea – in my system, Pluto is the w*ound,* not the soul.

Jeff and I wanted to work together, but that difference in our approaches seemed as if it could present an insurmountable stumbling block. Jeff solved the problem with one simple insight. His exact words were, *"Under the patriarchy, all souls are wounded."*

I agreed, and we went forward from there. That was enough agreement to bridge our two very distinct systems of interpretation. We did some good work together.

I still feel that the soul is manifest through *all* of the planetary symbolism, not just through Pluto, and that ultimately the soul is something beyond it all.

If your natal Pluto represents a wounded place in the psyche, we recognize that this wound *must have its origin in the mystery of who you were before you were born.* To understand it, I use the language of reincarnation

– although translations into genetic heredity or "how God made you" can be made to fit as well.

This quickly enters complex territory, with many interacting factors. The short version is that there is a powerful interplay between Pluto's position in your birthchart and the whole lunar nodal complex in the chart – territory I explore in my book, *Yesterday's Sky*.

For our purposes here, let's stay focused on Pluto itself. Later, we will look at it in the various signs and houses in "cookbook" fashion. For now, let's lay out a few quick sketches at random to give you the basic idea of how it all works.

- Pluto in the second house? The "house of money?" Perhaps in a prior life you were poor. Perhaps you starved to death. Perhaps, alternatively, you were wealthy – and never forget that great wealth can wound a person in many ways too.
- Pluto in Virgo? Perhaps in a prior life you were *shamed*. Perhaps you were *enslaved* in some sense. Perhaps you were crushed under a burden of *terrible responsibilities*.
- Pluto in aspect to Mars? Maybe in a prior life you were a *victim of violence* – or you *perpetrated violence*. Perhaps you were impacted by the nightmares of war. Perhaps you carry a wound of *anger* – or, alternatively, one of *fear*.
- Pluto in the seventh house? Perhaps in a prior life you were *betrayed in an intimate context*. Perhaps someone lied to you. Perhaps you experienced a *tragic bereavement*.
- Pluto in Scorpio? Terrible things happen in life – events so dispiriting or disgusting that we can barely stand to think of them. Perhaps in a prior life you actually had such a *nightmarish experience*. Perhaps you were born into this life bitter and shell-shocked because of it.
- Pluto in aspect to Mercury? Perhaps in a prior life you were punished for your ideas or for your speech. Perhaps you were prevented from accessing education in some sense of the word – or perhaps you were damaged by distorting *miseducation*.

In each one of these sketches, I commit the cardinal interpretive sin of ignoring the larger context of the chart, and especially of ignoring the nodal structure. Each example also leaves out two out of the following three ingredients: a sign, a house, or aspects. All of them also ignore the question of how central a role Pluto plays in the chart – is it conjunct the Ascendant or hiding out quietly in a corner somewhere?

All of those issues are critical – but I hope you are starting to get the basic idea of how Pluto manifests as a wound. That is half of what we need to understand. The other half brings us to the happier territory of healing, regeneration, and recovery.

Pluto holds those keys as well.

A FRIEND SUFFERING FROM THE BALEFUL EFFECTS OF PSYCHOTHERAPY

You run into a friend on the street. He looks awful – shaken and vulnerable. Redness around his eyes suggests that he was crying not too long ago. You're close, so you don't stand on the usual boundaries and formalities. Without preamble, you ask him what's wrong.

He says, "I just had a really tough session with my shrink . . ."

Now let's imagine that you are ten times dumber than you actually are. You say, *"So why do you bother to go there then? It doesn't sound like it's any fun . . ."*

You are not that dumb, or you wouldn't be reading this book. You know why your friend is in psychotherapy. He does too. *He anticipates that as a result of that intentional descent into hell, he will be happier in the future.* He understands that the aim of the psychotherapeutic process is to root out *underlying causes* of unhappiness or dysfunction in his life.

It often works too.

Quickly, let's add that the vast majority of people who do well with Pluto challenges do so without seeing psychologists. I am not shilling for that industry, even though I have great respect for its wiser, more skillful, practitioners. But "psychotherapy"– *soul healing* in the original Greek – is the essence of any strong response to Pluto. Where Pluto lies, we all need a long, hard talk with ourselves – and we will not like what we learn, at least not at first.

Your friend is right: if he sticks with therapy, he is indeed very likely to get better and be happier.

A little while ago, I listed six examples of Plutonian woundedness. Let's turn each one of them around and let them illustrate Plutonian healing.

- Pluto in the second house? You can do some deep work around your wounding issues about poverty or opulence and thereby develop a sense of spiritual security and psychological safety in life. Establishing a healthy relationship with money is likely to be a significant practical part of that healing process.

- Pluto in Virgo? You can delve into the origins of your internalized shame and thereby develop self-love and self-respect. You can learn to be discerning about what criticisms can help you and which ones are only other people's toxic projections. You can find work that is meaningful to you, and gain dignity from it.

- Pluto in aspect to Mars? You can probe into the roots of your anger and your fears. After dancing with them, you might eventually come to a state of forgiveness – but don't rush it, or it will be phony, and you absolutely do not want anything that is phony to be part of your life at this point.

- Pluto in the seventh house? You can do some honest work around your intimate hurts and recover your ability to discern other people whom you can trust again – but only if they themselves are honest, only if they are willing to work as hard at being as emotionally naked as you are.

- Pluto in Scorpio? You can embark upon some healing around the seemingly unforgivable events in your karmic past and thereby recover a sense of life's other side: its sweetness and its beauty. With effort, you can learn to feel safe among other humans again and grateful to be alive.

- Pluto in aspect to Mercury? You can do some brave work about the price you have paid for speaking out truthfully and thus recover a sense of confidence in your voice and the value and legitimacy of your views. You have something profound to share with us – and this time, many of us are ready to hear it. We will benefit, and so will you.

HIT THE KIDS AND MARRY A DRUNK

What's not to like, right?

None of you reading those opening words are likely to think that either of those behaviors are desirable. And yet, among you, I am sure that there are some who have succumbed to at least one of those existential pitfalls.

Why? We all *know better*, in principle – and yet "knowing better" and how *we actually act* do not always line up.

In the old days, when we did something that we were not proud of having done, one expression was that "the devil made me do it." That anachronistic line makes people smile today, but it does ring one bell in reality – *some force external and alien to my conscious mind and my values temporarily took over control of my life.* Substitute "the unconscious mind" for "the devil," and we are squarely in Plutonian territory. Unhealed wounds in the psyche may have their *origin* in the distant past, but they live on today. In a perverse way, they are the gift that keeps on giving.

- A statistical predictor that you will hit your children is that you yourself were abused that way when you were a child.
- Why did you marry a drunk? Your mother or father were active alcoholics, and you are still trying to get blood from that same stone.

Again, *you work on your stuff or your stuff works on you.* Wounds from the past play out in the present. Perhaps the single most ungrounded optimistic statement ever made is, "once burned, twice smart." *Often it is once burned, burned again and again and again.*

Furthermore, when children are hit, they learn two things. The first, obviously enough, is how to endure being a victim, even to expect it. The second is *how to be a victimizer* themselves. How to hit their own kids.

People who break these toxic patterns are Plutonian heroes.

Where Pluto lies in your chart, there is a wound. That is guaranteed; that is already water under the bridge. There is no guarantee that you will actually heal that wound in this lifetime.

There is only a guarantee that you can.

And that process is almost the definition of healing, regeneration, and recovery. We just have to remember that without the basic *attunement to the heart* symbolized by the Moon, we would simply have nothing on which to work. We would not even know what we were feeling. And of course, the *release* and *forgiveness* symbolized by Jupiter and Neptune still lie ahead. The Scorpio clan is the middle step, the one that bridges Cancer and Pisces.

The Water Family, like the rest of the Elements, is one interdependent system.

PLUTO PAY DAY

It takes a lot of energy to be crazy. That might sound like a throwaway line, but if we pursue those words, they lead us to a golden city. Here is the short version: when you are no longer squandering your life-force, bleeding it out through your wounded behavior, what can you do with all that energy you have now saved?

Whatever you please.

It is, after all, your own energy.

Dad was a drunk, and he loved you in his own drunken, maudlin way. He loved you – but he consistently failed you. He made promises, forgot them, apologized, and made more promises only to break them too. He was doing his best, only his best wasn't very good.

Still, kids need their parents' love. You struggled to squeeze a drop of life-giving parental blood from that unyielding stone.

Early experiences become archetypal templates of experience. Thirty years down the road, you are still trying to get blood from that same stone. Father may be dead and gone – but let anyone show up *who has your father's energetic signature*, and deeply ingrained reflexes take over. Pretty soon you are trying – and failing – to get a drop of blood from that new stone too.

Wedding bells: you've now married a drunk. Or an addict. Or a compulsive escapist of any stripe.

Thanks again, dad.

How much energy can you waste playing out that same dead-end pattern? How many "drunks" can you marry? It is like Einstein's famous definition of insanity: doing the same thing over and over again, each time hoping for a different result.

But what happens if you figure this out? What happens if you get to the bottom of it – and not just intellectually, but energetically too. Maybe that futile, groundless *faith* in your father – a faith that drives this terrible repeating pattern of "marrying drunks" – gives way to more authentic emotions and insights, however raw they might be.

What was that child actually feeling deep down inside toward that failed father – *but afraid to feel consciously?* Rage? Resentment? Contempt?

Whatever the true feelings were, *eventually they need to surface.* And when they do, a psychic logjam is broken. That is obviously good news: the unconscious mechanism that has led you to "marry drunks" loses its ability to control you.

But *how much energy was locked up in holding those feelings of rage, resentment, and contempt out of the conscious mind?* A lot, obviously – even though you were unaware of the suppression at the time. And now that the dam has broken, now that this energy is truly yours again, liquid and unfrozen, what will you do with it? Again, *whatever you please.* It is your energy. That life-force blossoms into creativity, libido, intelligence, and zest. It enlivens you. It's like going from burning wood to burning high octane fuel.

It can carry you into spaces that you previously could not even have imagined.

I love writing about this *healing, regenerative* side of Pluto. So often, astrologers leave their clients with the feeling that they should fear Pluto, or at best, sort of righteously endure it. The planet can indeed be scary – but if that is all we have conveyed about Pluto, we have not done a good job of offering counsel. We have left out the good news.

Psychological astrologers often emphasize the virtues and moral rewards that derive from honest self-scrutiny. Do well with Pluto, and you will at least earn some kind of psychological Merit Badge. That's true too.

But the real point is that after your "descent into hell," you get to "sit on the right hand of God the Father Almighty." You win a prize of sheer energy.

And you can do anything you want to do with it.

It was yours all along – and you have just stolen it back from the devil. Talk about healing, regeneration, and recovery.

WHAT ABOUT MARS?

Fight – and fright: those two adrenal words capture much of the spirit of Mars. Both energies can leave us shaking – such is the visceral power of these passions as they course through our minds, not to mention our bloodstreams. Without stretching our imaginations, we can easily see fight and fright figuring in full-blown life-and-death situations. And wherever the scent of death is in the air, we are in a Scorpionic landscape.

I want to feed you a stimulus, one that will bring us face to face with Mars' rulership of Scorpio: *do you have anyone in your life for whom you would willingly die?*

If not, I am sorry for you.

Now, a *desire* to die for anyone is just the ancient blood-myth, and one of the most fundamental sources of human depravity. That kind of wish for glorious martyrdom is part of the dark face of all of this Scorpionic symbolism, not its higher purpose. But Scorpio is indeed about *ties that bind* – and so is Cancer, as we saw in the previous chapter. The only difference is that with Scorpio, there is more of a focus on *eye-to-eye life-bonds* between equals, while Cancer generalizes a bit more to *family*. Either way, these two Water signs are what *glue people together*.

When it comes to healing and regeneration, loving relationships have an obvious role to play for virtually all of us. As we reflect on the specific role that Mars plays in these kinds of bonds, one of its faces is *do-or-die loyalty*. If we don't feel that kind of *radical commitment,* we may still be in a loving relationship – but not one that passes the Cancer or Scorpio tests. We are talking about people *for whom you would die.*

There are many people whom we *like*, but we could live without them. And there are people who, if we were to lose them, *we might feel as if we could not go on.* Even if we *do* go on, those desolate feelings of bereavement arise with terrible authority.

When we reflect on people for whom we would potentially *give our lives,* our children naturally come to mind. But if we have a life-partner, someone with whom we have entered into the *mysterium tremendum* of committed eighth house sexual intimacy – *and then we imagine some situation in which we would give our life so that this person could live* – we have come to the heart of why Mars and Scorpio are such a natural match.

In a Mars-bond . . .

- We would be *willing to die* for that person – if that is not true, we have not truly surrendered.
- We would do anything – pay any price – to *protect* him or her. We would face a mad dog or stand up to a knife-wielding mugger.

- We feel confident that this man or woman feels *a reciprocal level of commitment to us.* His or her betrayal would shock us. Its possibility does not enter our minds.
- We *trust our relationship* with that person enough to express anger and resentment when those kinds of emotions raise their heads.
- We face the *fear of our own vulnerability* enough to broach difficult subjects with that person, at least when doing so is necessary to the maintenance of the bond.
- Our working assumption, even though we hate to think about it, is that *one of us will have to go to the other one's funeral.*
- We probably hope that we *die second* in order to protect the beloved from enduring the bitter experience of losing us.

You may note that in each of these statements, there is a single underlying emotional common denominator: *we have crossed the line into uncomfortable emotional territory.* To many people's ears, it might sound as if in writing these words, I have become too heavy or too serious.

Welcome to the Scorpio clan, of course – that kind of drama and psychological resistance is in its nature. The passions implicit in these lines carry the very strong signature of Mars the Warrior and they thus demonstrate its role in this Scorpionic terrain.

This is why Mars continues to be the ruler of Scorpio, sharing that crown – without any conflict at all – with Lord Pluto. If our eyes and our hearts are open, we can see both rulerships clearly and unmistakably.

5

THE PISCES CLAN

To find refuge and perspective in the realm of transcendence . . . to genuinely release, forgive, and let things go . . . to take whatever arises in your life as your homeward path.

We jumped from a crab to a scorpion, and now we come to a fish. And what a magical fish it is. Pisces is the *fish of awareness* diving deeply into the *ocean of consciousness*. Perhaps it seeks the seabed, but never fear: that bottom will never be found. The ocean of consciousness, unlike mere puddles such as the Pacific or the Atlantic, is infinitely deep.

With every stroke of its fins, every new depth it reaches, the Piscean fish draws more energy into itself. It becomes at once both more luminous and yet more transparent to the sea which it is fathoming. For any planet or point conditioned by Pisces, the underlying motivation lies simply in diving, diving, diving. It is becoming one with that vastness, more and more translucent, less resistant, more accepting.

Every surrender is a victory.

And that brings us back full circle – what a blessing it is that this sea of awareness has no bottom. If it had one, the very process of diving which sustains a Piscean planet would come to an end and simply burn out. There would no longer be any purpose to its existence.

As we begin to try to find words for the Piscean evolutionary goal – *which lies in becoming identical to the profoundest depths of this ocean of consciousness* – our language inevitably becomes mystical, even religious. Pisces aims for Cosmic Consciousness, Enlightenment, *Satori,* Christ Consciousness, *Ridā,* Heaven, *Moksha,* Salvation, *Hózhó,* Liberation . . .

. . . put your offering in whatever theological plate strikes your fancy.

THE MAP

The tools Pisces brings to this final – and in many ways highest – task in the zodiac are concentrated primarily in one fundamental Piscean quality: in this sign, *ego simply has a lighter hold* than we might see in less "fishy" people. To that quality of undefended openness, we might add *sensitivity,* both emotional and psychic. And *visionary imagination.* And a *fascination with trance states.* And a *compassionate attitude,* aided by a warm *sense of humor* – as distinct from judgment – about human vanity, delusion, and arrogance.

These sensitive qualities can potentially become overwhelming for anyone who has them, which leads us directly to understanding the Piscean shadow – *escapism* in all of its myriad forms and disguises. This level of sensitivity can be frightening and a corresponding urge to turn away from it can naturally arise.

It all boils down to the picture of a fish diving deeper and deeper into an ocean that has no bottom, and glowing more numinously with every downward stroke.

Let's map that ocean right from its surface down as deep as we can manage to go. If you have a planet in Pisces, this is the map you need to follow. And the more you follow it, the more transparent to the universe you become.

We will start at the beginning – on the chaotic surface of this bottomless sea.

BREAKING WAVES

Picture shore-break on a wild and windy day. Seagulls are screaming overhead. Whitecaps extend outward halfway toward the horizon. Salty mist fills the air. Closer in, the waves are breaking and foaming as they feel the bottom. They are backlit by afternoon sunshine in a way that makes them flash into transparency just before they curl and crash – *and in those lucid moments, you can see schools of mullet struggling to get traction there in the translucent, turbulent water.*

The surface of the Piscean ocean, just like any other ocean, can be wildly chaotic. The poor fish are tossed in those waves as if they were paper cups. Some might even be tossed up on the shore, where the seagulls make short work of them.

We must start mapping Pisces by remembering that it is a Water sign – and all across the board, Water is about our *emotional lives,* among other less obvious inner potentials. In Pisces, just as with Scorpio and Cancer, *the volume is turned up to maximum on the ability to feel.* But here in Pisces, that basic emotional sensitivity is complicated by the presence of an additional layer of psychic sensitivity. *A Piscean planet is not just dealing with its own emotional life; it is dealing with all of the ambient psychic energies around it as well. It can become caught in those frothing waves and either panic or seek numbness.* Such a planet can look like a fish tossed in the breaking waves of a stormy sea, in other words. Pisces can founder in the intensity of its own emotional life.

Some of those mullets and mackerels might really prefer to make for the relative peace and stability of deeper waters, *but just watch them as they try to get their fins to achieve some traction in all that tossing foam . . .*

There are solutions to this dilemma and we will be looking at them, but let's continue mapping our descent into the Piscean sea.

What have we learned so far? *That for Pisces the first evolutionary step lies in not becoming so hypnotized and traumatized by its own sensitivity that it remains trapped on the surface of its psyche, lost in mere feeling, tossed on turbulent seas of emotion, simply remaining wide-eyed and overwhelmed from cradle to grave.*

A DIVERSITY OF FISHES

Let's continue to map our dive into the watery labyrinths of consciousness. Just a little deeper in the ocean, beneath all those whitecaps, we find schools of fish. These fish represent all the teeming people in the world and all the twisted and intertwined storylines of their lives. We encounter a realm of *overwhelming diversity.* We are still a long way away from Piscean transcendence, in other words. We are in the thick of life.

Watching that *kaleidoscope of humanity* can also mesmerize our diving fish. But the difference is that now the fish of awareness is gazing "beyond its own navel," into the lives of other people. Good news: some degree of *selflessness* is born, along with the beginnings of *compassion*.

There is bad news too. Imagine having the television news on twenty-four hours a day, with the volume turned up. *A house burned down in Peoria, Illinois! A man in Chengdu, China, decided he had always really been a woman! His wife is angry with him! A dog is lost in Texas! An ageing rock star is touring again! The stock market is unchanged from yesterday! An asteroid is heading for Brussels and expected to impact tomorrow afternoon! There is a chocolate shortage! Purple is the new black!*

You get the picture. Even once we begin to get our own emotions shuffled into some kind of perspective, the noise and complexity of the world can press us towards numbness – or, once again, a kind of hypnosis. One form which that hypnosis can take lies in *a fascination with other fish:* the endless, compelling, repetitive dramas of sex, power, money, and so forth.

Bottom line, our Piscean fish can be tricked into stopping its evolutionary dive, either entranced or overwhelmed by the glitter, fear, and noise of this crazy world. It stares, wide-eyed, at a wrap-around television with the volume up and no "off" button.

It may also begin to discover that "a few beers" can take some of that edge off.

Remember: *Pisces draws its energy from the intensity of its downward dive in the moment.* It is helpful to think that the deeper it goes, the stronger it becomes. That is valid – but we need to add the other side of the coin: that becoming stuck and complacent at any level of the dive quickly drains the Piscean battery.

The fish needs to keep diving. The hypnotic trance of this world must be broken. There is a lot more depth to this soul-healing map.

A DEGREE IN PSYCHOLOGY

Perhaps there are better ways than beer to take some of the edge off all of that psychic tension. As our Piscean fish dives deeper into the sea of awareness, a curiosity arises in it about *inner work and the perspective it promises.* Pisces begins to recognize *underlying patterns* in those myriad human storylines it observed a little while ago when it was closer to the surface – swimming in more shallow, more social, waters, so to speak.

At this point, Piscean people begin to recognize *predictable patterns* in how people tie their lives in knots. The married man in midlife falls in love with a twenty-two-year-old – how will that storyline play out? The brilliant physicist decides that she is smart enough to avoid the perils of addiction, so she begins to experiment with cocaine. The young man still living at home decides he will look for a job "next month," but for now he'll smoke marijuana and play video games.

If its dive is to continue unabated past this point, our fish must react to all of that *meshugas* with warm-hearted humor rather than judgment – and that *quality of humor about the human drama* allows compassion to flavor its perception of the patterns. *"Getting the joke" about human life is a major step in the Piscean dive.* This is far from the belief that life itself *is* a joke. It is sweeter than that. Critically, this Piscean humor has a big-spirited quality of *forgiveness* woven into it, along with a sense that all of us are in the same boat. The fish begins to realize that most people are doing their best most of the time, even though sometimes their best is not very good, as they are buffeted by their own fears and their appetites.

Pisces begins to smile at the world the way we might smile at a child with its knickers in a knot. Transcendence? Perhaps not quite yet, but humor – at least when it is spiced with compassion – is a step in the right direction.

Our fish can take another big step here at this very psychological stage in its dive: it can begin to *recognize itself* mirrored in those common behavioral patterns and scripts. Psychological wisdom and insight arise.

In its light *our Piscean fish begins to self-correct.*

This is clearly a major, positive step – and along with this "degree in psychology" there arises a terrible trap, one that might stall the fish's dive for a lifetime: *Pisces can become addicted to the power of psychological thought.* We can begin to believe that, with these insights, we have reached the bottom of the ocean. The reality is that our dive is still only beginning.

Think of someone with a PhD in psychology who is "too grounded" to believe that mystical spirituality is anything more than an emotional crutch for people too wounded to face reality as it actually is. There's a stuck fish for you, *hypnotized by the endlessly ramifying kaleidoscope of psychological insights.*

A FISH NAMED CARL

As we dive deeper into the Piscean sea of the psyche, the fish get larger and there are fewer of them. Eventually we encounter a fish named Carl Gustav Jung.

Saying it that way pleases me; I feel that no modern form of astrology could exist without our "Uncle Carl." We all owe him an enormous debt. Still, speaking of "a fish named Carl" is just a way of framing a larger point. Jung's great contribution was his introduction of the notion of *archetypes* into the human conversation. Essentially, Jung recognized that beneath those exploding patterns we recognized closer to the surface back when we were getting our "degree in psychology," there are a few patterns of a far more fundamental nature. Here are Jung's own words, taken from his 1951 essay, *The Psychological Aspects of the Kore.*

> *For years I have been observing and investigating the products of the unconscious in the widest sense of the word, namely dreams, fantasies, visions, and delusions of the insane. I have not been able to avoid recognizing certain regularities . . . There are types of situations and types of figures that repeat themselves frequently and have a corresponding meaning . . . Thus there are not only typical dreams but typical motifs in dreams. . . . (These) can be arranged under a series of archetypes, the chief of them being . . . the shadow, the wise old man, the child (including the child hero), the mother . . . and her counterpart the maiden, and lastly the anima in man and the animus in woman.*

At this deeper level of the fish's dive into the sea of awareness, we have left the fractal confusion of the human world and come to calmer, clearer waters. The wild, frothing waves of the surface are far behind us now. Just as behind your computer screen there lies a realm of *machine language* which is the wellspring of the digital words and images you see, similarly, there is a "machine language" behind life: *the realm of archetypal patterns.*

Since the beginning of time, it has "always looked bad for the good guys, but here comes the hero."

Since the beginning of time, the young lovers find each other against all the odds.

Since the beginning of time, Gandalf has guided and counseled Frodo, Dumbledore has guided and counseled Harry Potter, and Merlin has guided and counseled Arthur.

At this depth of the Piscean sea, there often arises a pressing hunger to share these archetypes with other human beings – remember, compassion has already arisen, and it drives a compelling desire to be *helpful*.

This fascination with the archetypal realm is the great engine of *visionary imagination* that drives all art worthy of attention. We can honor that *artist's path* as an effective Piscean spiritual practice at this stage too. The mind learns to receive inspiration. We realize that creativity is another form of trance work.

Again, as the fish reaches these depths there arises a familiar danger. Just like our psychologist up closer to the surface, with this archetypal understanding, *we can believe that we have found the bottom of the sea.* Laziness can hide itself in pride, while pride puts on the mask of all-knowing understanding.

There are wise and helpful Jungians, but an air of arrogance and psychological superiority is not unknown among them – nor among those smaller fish puffed up with their "degrees in psychology."

Even art can be a trap. Cut from similar cloth, artists of all stripes who radiate the smug superiority of "coolness" are not rare creatures.

Our dive is not over. There are far deeper waters waiting in the darkness beneath us. We are perhaps finally beginning to sniff a whiff of something . . . truly *transcendent*.

A FISH NAMED ASTROLOGY

Call me prejudiced, but I believe that beneath the relative diversity of the Jungian archetypes there are *twelve more archetypes* which are even more fundamental to the fabric of the universe. Every possible human story and every potential human situation can be related to Aries, Taurus, Gemini, and the rest. Taken together, we might call the signs of the zodiac the *Primal Twelveness* of the cosmos.

And since the signs of the zodiac themselves spring from Fire, Earth, Air, and Water, that can bring us down to the *Primal Fourness* of the cosmos.

Still in the realm of astrology, but perhaps a little closer to the surface of the ocean, we of course find all of astrology's technicalities: houses, aspects, asteroids – and naturally the planets themselves. They are all part of the system too.

The real point here is that astrology can be understood as "the machine language behind the machine language" we encountered in the realm of archetypal psychology. It is a little bit deeper. And as things get deeper on this soul-healing journey, they tend to become simpler – and as they become simpler, they become more mysterious.

When we think of the Piscean dive arriving at this astrological level, it is important to remind ourselves that we are not talking about a mere intellectual or technical knowledge of astrology. That is a noble thing and an honorable achievement, but mere academic engagement with astrology would be more naturally placed under earning "a degree in psychology"– a far earlier stage in the Piscean dive. In these deeper waters, we are looking at the *direct experience* of the astrological archetypes. This process has more in common with meditation than with any astrology class.

With astrology, *practiced with a spiritual intention and as a form of mind-training*, we have crossed into a Piscean realm that we can perhaps begin to call transcendent.

Once more, as we come to this stage, we encounter the soul-stalling beast of ego-driven stasis: we can get stuck here too, so illuminated by the brilliant light of astrological consciousness that we imagine we have reached the bottom of the sea.

A FISH NAMED PARAMAHANSA YOGANANDA

As with "A Fish Named Carl," my reference to the great Hindu saint and teacher, Paramahansa Yogananda, is intended at least somewhat metaphorically. I will let him represent any and all of humanity's spiritual guides and lighthouses: saints, gurus, and other inspiring figures whom we might strive to emulate.

In framing this paragraph, I was tempted to name the fish Ram Dass, who just passed away as I write these words. He would have fit in here too – and we will indeed visit him in the penultimate chapter of this book.

One might say that at this "Yogananda" stage of our Piscean dive, we have entered *religious territory*. Fair enough – but it is helpful to recognize that we are really talking about human beings who were (or are) somehow in a state *beyond religion*. I get the feeling, for example, that Yogananda would have felt an instant *simpatico* with the great Roman Catholic figure,

Saint Francis. I do not think that doctrinal differences would have prevented either one of them from looking into the other's eyes and smiling.

This level of the Piscean sea is about mysticism, not theology.

At these depths, meditation practice becomes compelling and effective. And *transcendence* begins to be quite obvious and pressing. This
physical world starts to become transparent. It begins to resemble a dream.
Space and time become elastic and fluid.

Fish such as Paramahansa Yogananda are truly vast and incompre-
hensible creatures. They are precious treasures. These are human beings
who have attained something that can only be witnessed, never understood
or fully described. Their presence inspires us and strengthens us. They show
us how we might get there ourselves if we dedicate ourselves to the goal.
Like a tuning fork, their consciousness transfers resonance to our own.

Simply meditating on their enormous *presence* helps our fish to dive
even deeper.

THE JESUS FISH, THE BUDDHA FISH

Two confessions before I go an inch further. First, we are now officially
and fully "transcendent" – and that means that I am now officially out of
my own depth, so please take what I say with caution and correct it with
your own intuitions.

Second, I am confident that I am about to get into trouble. Where I
am now going, people tend to be extremely partisan.

I now believe that I am discerning a fish named Jesus Christ and a
fish named Gautama the Buddha. There may be a few others at this level
of the sea – but not many. Mohammed? I am wide-open to that idea, but
unlike the two I've just named, I have had only minor direct experience
of inner contact with Islam. The energy of the Blue Mosque in Istanbul
knocked me out as did the sheer *ju-ju* of the Whirling Dervishes I saw
there. In saying that I intend no disrespect, only a confession of ignorance.

Similarly, hats off to Quetzacoatl and Lao Tse and Zoroaster and
Cernan of the Beasts.

The point here, as we reach this extreme depth of the Piscean ocean,
is that there have occasionally been beings on Earth who seem to have
become completely transparent to the cosmos – *one with God*, so to speak.

Rather than the winds of their own karma compelling them into incarnation, they seem to be here by something more akin to their own choice, motivated by compassion for our own self-inflicted suffering.

For Pisces, devoted meditation upon such figures is evolutionary dynamite. They are a direct route to the transcendent realms.

THE PRIMAL ONENESS OF THE UNIVERSE

Again, I am aware of my peril here – but can we go even deeper than Jesus or the Buddha? I think that what I am really asking here is, can we go deeper than a meditation upon their outward images? To whatever depth we might descend from here, Jesus and Buddha are already there – just not wearing any recognizable human form any longer

Earlier, we saw astrology mirroring what we called "the Primal Twelveness" of the universe. Mystics speak of a *Primal Oneness* that underlies everything and everyone. That Primal Oneness is part of the Piscean sea as well – and that is the depth we have now attained in our imaginary, visionary journey.

At these ineffable depths, Pisces can become *the raindrop landing in the sea*, somehow merging its own awareness with an absolute non-resistance to all that is or all that might ever be.

THE PRIMAL ZERO-NESS OF THE UNIVERSE

Can we go deeper yet? The Buddhists, whose theology I have always found to be most compelling, speak of the fundamental *emptiness* of all phenomena. This gets into very abstruse theological territory. To a Buddhist, emptiness does not signify pointlessness, or even exactly *non-existence* – but rather a sense that it is the mind itself that creates the illusion of the universe, along with the illusion that it is a separate self.

At some level of evolutionary progress, consciousness can go beyond all of that, entering what Buddhists call *nirvana*.

We might speak of our arrival at the Primal Zero-ness of the Universe.

TERRA INCOGNITA

At this juncture, I feel like a cocker spaniel sitting at the feet of a saint – I don't understand what I am talking about anymore, in other words. But of one point I feel quite certain, and that is that this Piscean ocean has no bottom.

What lies beyond the primal zero-ness?

I do not know.

Let's call it *Terra Incognita* – the unknown land. If we are patient, we will all visit it someday. Everything is ultimately impermanent, even the fact that you are not enlightened.

THAT'S THE MAP . . .

There's our Piscean map. A few points in quick summary before we move on to consider its *behavioral expressions* in the twelfth house.

- The underlying motivation of Pisces lies in the *exploration of consciousness*. To succeed in that exploration, the fish follows, more-or-less, the step-by-step map we have just outlined.
- The main tool Pisces which brings to bear upon this task is *sensitivity*, both emotionally and psychically.
- With that tool comes the danger of *escapism* – seeking numbness and stasis, rather than conscious evolution, as a means for dealing with pain.
- For Pisces, the deeper it dives, the more energized it becomes. Balancing that reality is another one: if Pisces fails to make continued effort to dive deeper, no matter what level it has attained, malaise arises. The wind goes out of Pisces' sails at a time when what it desperately needs is more wind.

HOW ALL THIS FITS INTO OUR GRAND SCHEME

There is so much in life that we ultimately have to let go. That release lies at the end of a long process – and as we have seen, we cannot arrive at that state of transcendent grace by skipping Cancer and Scorpio. If we do that, it is *phony transcendence*, which is just another form of Piscean escapism.

We need to *acknowledge our hurt* – that is why the Universe gave you a Moon.

And you need to deal honestly with the *effects* of that hurt – which means a lot more than pointing a Scorpionic finger at the guilty parties, however truly guilty they may be. You also need to look into the mirror and take responsibility for what you see there. No one else will do it for you. Truth can heal you, if you are brave enough to endure it. That is why the universe gave you Mars and Pluto.

Get those first two Watery steps right, and you are ready to start that long Piscean dive into a sea with no seabed. Get them wrong, and you may start, but you will not get very far before your unresolved wounds stall your descent.

Family life – that classic evolutionary test – can be challenging. It provides a fine example of the Watery process. People fail each other, sometimes in grievous ways. Basic needs go unmet. Resentments fester. Eyes roll. Teasing slips into meanness.

Faced with that kind of hurt, Cancer can go hide inside its shell. Scorpio can deploy its famous stinger.

And, while sometimes we do need simply to protect ourselves and sometimes we do need to express our rage, *neither of those strategies actually ever resolves anything.*

Sometimes for the family to stay together, everyone needs to rise up to that higher Piscean place in themselves – a place where we see that everyone is struggling to get traction in their own foaming shorebreak.

There, sitting high up in our inner cathedral, we "get the joke"– *and we realize that we are part of it.* We find compassion, perspective, and forgiveness. We let things go. We get over ourselves.

Faced with the genuine hurts of life, *what would Jesus actually do?* What would Gautama do? What would any of those beings who have dived a little deeper into the sea do?

This holy sacrament of Piscean transcendence, release, and forgiveness completes our Watery triad, and allows us to achieve a pinnacle of healing, regeneration, and recovery.

Without that gift, we would spend our lives caught up in a labyrinth of fractal psychological insights, imagining it to be the universe.

THE TWELFTH HOUSE

If you want a direct experience of a higher or more transcendent state of consciousness, what do you actually have to *do*? That is the question which brings us to the twelfth house. As ever, houses are about our actual choices and behaviors. *What concrete experiences might we seek if our inward motivations are oriented toward reaching spiritual goals?*

The twelfth house has lower meanings too, and we will get to them.

What if a person does not have any conscious desire at all for higher states of awareness? What if he or she does not even believe in them? What if, in their judgment, it is all just *woo-woo* silliness? Add one more ingredient to our three questions – this person has a planet or two in the twelfth house.

That situation is not rare.

Here is how it can play out. Planets are energy, and energy can be neither created nor destroyed, only changed in form. That is an immutable astrological principle. Regardless of a person's philosophy or beliefs, with planets in the twelfth house, *the soul needs experiences which can potentially lead to those higher states.* It does not matter greatly if the person's conscious mind is unaware of that reality or feels unmotivated by it. It remains true anyway.

So what happens when someone fails to cooperate with those intentions? Under the eternal laws and principles of synchronicity, *something* has to happen. What can it be? Can spirituality be forced on a person?

Well, no . . . not exactly.

We will answer those questions, but to do that we need to map the full range of twelfth house possibilities. As always with all astrological symbolism, it will not be inherently good or bad, but rather it will contain both of those possibilities, and many shades of gray in between.

Let's be patient, and start with the higher ground.

TRANSCENDING THE EGO

That is a loaded phrase and in many ways a dangerous one – but it is difficult to go very far into twelfth house theory without encountering it. To keep us from throwing out the baby with the bath water, it is helpful to remember that the human ego is only a vehicle through which spirit gathers experience. Without an ego, we would simply stare blankly into space. If you are an advanced yogi in a Himalayan cave, that staring might be a helpful practice. But for the rest of us, we need to learn from actually living our lives – experiencing and digesting our relationships, our work, our adventures and our misadventures.

Ego is not the enemy, in other words, unless we descend into "egoism"– which is to say, into the kind of *prideful aggression that separates us from the human family* and from all possibilities of love and tenderness.

Rather than beating up our poor egos or wasting time defending them, I prefer to avoid the word entirely. I would like to replace it with the far less loaded term, *personality*. Life would be dull if no one had a personality, or was embarrassed at any sign of one. Changing ego to personality quickly leads us to a trio of mission-critical understandings:

- The central Piscean *motivation* can be understood as the *separation of consciousness from personality*.
- Therefore any effective twelfth house *behavior* is one that involves our becoming more identified with the larger framework of awareness and less "busy being our personalities."
- This reframing of our identity in a more transcendent way can be achieved consciously and intentionally – or it can be thrust upon us unwillingly by synchronistic circumstances.

This *consciousness vs personality* perspective is one way of interpreting the tradition of representing Pisces as *two* fish, each one heading a different direction, rather than as one single fish. One of those fish is your personality – or your ego, if you want – and the other fish is your consciousness. We can respect each of these fish, but we are mindful of the fact that we merely "do" the personality, all the while remembering what we truly "are," which is the vastness of awareness itself.

If you want to achieve this separation of consciousness from personality, what do you actually do? *You start by getting away from anything that entangles you in the world of ego.* That means that to escape the sticky hold of personality, one optimal twelfth house behavior lies in simply *getting away from people*. Mystics have always loved those Himalayan caves. Monks inhabit cloisters and cells.

Everyone has a twelfth house; everyone needs some time alone. With planets there, you simply need more of it. Solitude is a component of your spiritual path. You can evolve without it, but why try? Why do it the hard way? As comedian Steven Wright said, "Everywhere is within walking distance if you have the time." With planets in the twelfth house, having time alone is your Boeing 777.

You could walk if you wanted to, but that jet will get you there a lot faster.

EVERYWHERE I GO . . .

. . . people expect me to do Steven Forrest impressions. Here is an example of my fate: often people take one look at me and reflexively they say, *"In my chart . . ."* Fair enough – in this lifetime, my *personality* has crystallized around the role of astrologer. I can do that work; I feel good doing it; I feel as if I am sincerely being myself when I read a chart. And people expect me to do it, and they would be surprised if I didn't.

It is all OK. The system works. It's called human life. But in the final analysis, *am I really Steven Forrest?* In parallel fashion, are you really "you?" I mean, are you truly and finally, your "name, rank, and serial number?"

Or are we all something far vaster, more ancient, and more mysterious?

You know the answer or you would not be reading a book like this one. At some more nearly ultimate level, *you are the thing that is looking out through your eyes.*

Still, as soon as you encounter another human being, a necessity arises to interact through your personality. How else could we communicate? And good things happen when personalities interact – friendship is healthy. Most of us share our daily lives with co-workers. Maybe we have a lover or a partner. Even our rivals and our antagonists can teach us enormous spiritual lessons. Despite the toxic teachings of some religions, there is no inherent shame connected with being in a body or being human. In eleven out of the twelve astrological houses, "being human," one way or another, is what it is all about.

But in the twelfth house, we return to something far more fundamental. *We lose our identification with our identity* – and that is a sentence worth reading twice. We lose the *human form*, so deeply ingrained in our habitual consciousness. In any healthy response to the twelfth house, we can become something much more like *the part of ourselves that actually reincarnates* – which is of course not the personality, but something far more fluid.

After all, when you are reborn, you will have a different astrological chart – and that is another line worth a second reading.

Merely *being by yourself* teaches us nothing about any of this, at least not automatically. But it does create conditions that are supportive of our reaching this particular higher ground.

At the risk of sounding too harsh, we might say that *all human interactions are based on ego*. That line of course smacks of claiming that everyone is out for himself and it's a dog-eat-dog world, but that is not really what I mean.

Again, "ego" is not a dirty word. It really just means personality.

With a planet or two in the twelfth house, the bottom line is only that you need more time alone than most other people do. Some solitude is positively good for you – and, if you don't get enough of it, you become vulnerable to some of the Piscean and twelfth house dysfunctions we have already considered: escapism, an attraction to numbness, feeling like a ghost.

Earlier we raised a question: what happens to a person with twelfth house planets who has no interest in the evolution of consciousness? Don't worry, we haven't forgotten about it. We are just building a framework in which we can understand the answer.

INEXPLICABLE EXPERIENCE

Everything in astrology is inextricably linked to synchronicity, but that fact is particularly clear with the astrological houses. The reason is simple: houses *represent that which is obvious*. They correlate with *actions* and *events* – things that anyone can see.

The mind is a deep and mysterious place. Anyone who closes her eyes can experience that reality directly, but it is quite possible that someone sitting next to her would have no idea that anything magical had happened. Sensing that vastness directly is a *Piscean* experience – a *sign* experience, in other words – while having some *visible expression* of that Great Mystery enter your material life unexpected, unbidden, and miraculous, is a twelfth house event. It is an *outward manifestation* of that same energy.

- Rummaging through a collection of photographs from twenty years ago, you dwell for a moment on the face of an old friend with whom you have lost touch. The next day, she sends you a Friend request on Facebook, along with a message renewing your friendship.
- A book inexplicably falls from a bookshelf and lands on your toes. You pick it up and open it to a sentence you *really need to read* right at that moment.
- Your phone buzzes. A friend's face enters your mind. You pick up the phone. That's who it is.
- You are playing a game with dice. Just before you roll, you suddenly *know* that you are going to roll a twelve. And there it is two seconds later: *boxcars!*
- Something makes you hesitate before walking down the block; moments later, a loud fight breaks out.

With a strong twelfth house emphasis in your chart, these kinds of *outward mystical experiences* arise naturally in your life. Nothing you learned in high school science class can explain them, and yet life is demonstrating them to you.

Why is that happening?

Individually, these experiences perhaps do not carry much meaning. We shrug our shoulders and move on. But there is a deeper synchronistic perspective: with these kinds of events, life is leading you in a twelfth house direction – into the very enigmas of consciousness that you were born to explore. These are the "breadcrumbs" that can lead you into a deep, dark forest of mystery and mysticism.

The only question is, will you follow them?

MEDITATION

Sitting in meditation is the quintessential twelfth house behavior. *In any such practice, we are actively attempting to experience consciousness as something separate from our personalities.* That is what the twelfth house is all about and there is no more efficient pathway to the heart of it than meditation practice. The trouble with the word "meditation" is that it comes slathered in cultural salad dressing. As soon as we hear that people meditate, we might make a lot of assumptions about them, many of which will probably prove accurate for purely social and tribal reasons. We might, for one example, assume that they are vegetarians – or at least vegetarian sympathizers. We might assume that they wear bluejeans, vote progressively, are open to Eastern religious perspectives, use words such as "karma" and "cool," and so forth.

We will often be correct in those assumptions – but the deeper truth is that they ultimately have nothing to do with meditation.

Meditation can be understood simply as a *brain-state* – or a *mind-state*, if you prefer. I think "mind" is the better word, but there are definite correlates of meditation in the physical brain. Theta waves tend to predominate, for example. That quickly gets into a complex territory that is not really our subject here.

Suffice to say that actively choosing to enter the trance-states that are characteristic of meditation is the purest expression of positive twelfth house behavior.

Getting past all that "cultural salad dressing" is critical though. People of all faiths and persuasions can trigger this transcendent condition in themselves, and with planets in the twelfth house, they need to. They often do not even call it meditation, so let's not set up any linguistic roadblocks for them. I want to be careful of getting pulled into my own cultural ghetto as I write these words, so under the banner of the word meditation, let's include:

- Prayer
- The creative trance all artists experience when they open themselves to inspiration
- Chanting
- Singing hymns
- Trance-dancing
- Conscious psychedelic experience
- Mantra
- Mindful yoga and *tai chi*
- Stargazing; gazing at beautiful scenery
- Gazing into a candle flame
- Playing music – or listening to it deeply.

All of these are effective, positive twelfth house behaviors. That's because all of them – if they are practiced consciously, consistently, and diligently – can trigger the separation of consciousness from personality. All of these behaviors lead the mind to become *identified with its own spaciousness* rather than with the more narrow "personality perspectives" necessitated by the realities of our daily monkey-lives.

YOUR INNER GURU

Here is a little trick that I have found to be very helpful, both for myself and for getting the reality of twelfth house planets across to my clients: *I think of any planet in that house as your guru.* I immediately emphasize that I am not referring to a Hindu gentleman with a long white beard – a planet in the twelfth house, like any other planet in your chart, is part of *you*, not anyone else. But, like a true spiritual master, a planet in that position *stands between you and a higher state of consciousness – not as an obstacle, but rather as a bridge.*

Just as with a flesh-and-blood guru, the relationship is personal. That planet knows you well. It understands the specific blockages that are slowing down your evolution. It also has some perfect tailor-made remedies to heal those problems. Again, just as with a true spiritual master, you may not always like what you hear – but you really do need to hear it.

In chapter eight, we will dive in some detail into how to integrate any specific planet with the archetypal field represented by the twelfth house. Here, let me just offer a few quick images to give you the general idea.

- Venus is, among other things, connected with the *perception of beauty*. With Venus in the twelfth house, *losing oneself in aesthetic ecstasy* is a particularly effective meditation practice.
- Mercury is, among other things, connected with *study and mind-training*. With Mercury in the twelfth house, I hope you have a stack of metaphysical books on your bedside table.
- The Moon is, among other things, connected with *devotion and adoration*. With the Moon in the twelfth house, *losing yourself in loving, even tearful, appreciation of some sacred figure* is a particularly efficacious spiritual practice.

Again, a planet in the twelfth house is not an external figure – it is simply the part of you that is positioned to guide you toward the quickest, easiest path to the separation of awareness from ego. That is what happens if you get it right.

As ever, there is always a darker option. That twelfth house planet can also represent a *spiritual blockage*. In fact, the two ideas are inseparable – a weak response to the planet is the problem and a strong one is the solution.

Mars there? You need to develop a very specific kind of *mystical courage* – the ability to *maintain one-pointed steadiness* even when faced with potentially frightening inner experiences: precognitions, out-of-body experiences, and so forth. Willingly doing almost anything that frightens you, *and doing it more than once,* will guide you toward that Martial sweet spot. I have been told, for example, that the first time you do a parachute jump, it is absolutely terrifying. By the tenth time, you are looking forward to it. You have found Martial *steadiness in the face of massive stimulus.* Mars in the twelfth house? *Maybe you should take up skydiving as an adjunct to your meditation practice.* I am aware of how crazy that sounds, but it could really help. In a nutshell, you are learning to work with the impact of fear on your consciousness. That is the optimal path for you. Your "inner guru" is a *spiritual warrior.*

On the other hand, with Mars in the twelfth house, if you make a weak response to it, very likely your path is blocked by your own unresolved fears, angers, and resentments. Because of synchronicity, you probably draw experiences of accidents or even victimization to yourself. We have to keep one eye on the dark side, as ever. Fair enough – but with equal accuracy, and perhaps a more encouraging attitude, we can also call that twelfth house planet the part of yourself that is potentially so wise that it can lead the rest of you to the higher ground.

Follow that twelfth house planet and you can be your own guru, in other words.

LOSS AND NON-ATTACHMENT

Dr. Walter Gorn Old, who went by the pen name "Sepharial," was a prominent Theosophical astrologer in Britain a century ago. In his book, *The Manual of Astrology*, he characterized the twelfth house with the following cheery list of words: *"Confinement, restraint, bondage, exile; secret enemies, ambushes, and plots."*

When I was learning astrology, I often saw the twelfth house defined as the "house of troubles," its baleful symbolism prophetic of a pattern of loss, failure, and tragedy in one's life.

While these negative appraisals of the twelfth house seem antiquated and unnecessarily depressing nowadays, as we will soon see there is still truth in them – truth of the most dangerous sort, because while it is indeed real, it is also incomplete and lacks any evolutionary framework.

Modern astrologers have generally been kinder to the twelfth house. I quote my colleague, Greg Bogart, in his book, *Astrology and Spiritual Awakening*. Just a few pages into that helpful volume, he uses a very different set of words than Sepharial to define the twelfth house: *"Solitude, retreat, introspection, altruistic activity, awareness of karmic forces and the collective unconscious, and inner exploration through meditation, dreams, fantasy, and astrology."*

Obviously, Greg Bogart's language is closer to the spirit of what we have been exploring in this chapter.

Still, no two ways about it – loss can be a powerful teacher . . .

In the East, we often hear that the greatest enemy of spiritual progress is *attachment*. We can get stuck on how important – or unimportant – we are. We can get attached to our looks, to our money, even to our spirituality. *All of these attachments feed energy into ego rather than consciousness,* and thus stall the soul in its evolutionary journey.

In the Judeo-Christian tradition, the First Commandment of the Big Ten is, "Thou shalt have no other gods before me." When you boil away the Bronze Age language, that commandment is really the same exhortation: *let nothing become more important to you than your own spirituality.* We can even read that First Commandment as a lawyer might, noting that there is nothing in it about having no other gods *after* me. I think that is actually a legitimate interpretation. It is fine to love your partner or your cat or your house – just remember what comes first.

Here in seven words is the key to putting all of this together in one unified field of symbolism: *the twelfth house is ultimately about non-attachment.* And because planetary energy can be neither created nor destroyed, when you have a planet in the twelfth house, *you are going to get some lessons in non-attachment.* That much is simply fated. There is no escaping it. Your freedom lies in how you choose to experience that lesson. You can "go for it," using the kinds of methods we have been exploring throughout this chapter. Or you can invite it to come and get you.

In reflecting on that last point, we can finally answer the question I posed right at the outset of this section: *what if a person with planets in the twelfth house couldn't care less about spiritual matters?* What happens then? Seven more words: *in the twelfth house, attachment triggers loss.*

Here is a Rogue's Gallery of failed responses to twelfth house planets:

- You buy a new car. You get attached to it to the point that you begin to neglect your inner life, or you never had one in the first place. You step out of the grocery store only to discover that someone has put a dent in it.
- You fall in love. You get so attached to your new partner that you neglect your own previous spiritual practices, or never had them in the first place. The universe introduces your partner to someone cute and seductive.
- You get attached to your beauty. You get zits and warts, or inexplicably put on lots of weight.
- You get attached to your money. Your company fails.
- You get attached to fame; people forget about you. Styles change. You are yesterday's news and today's cheap joke.

As you reflect on all of this, you can see why the old astrologers took such a dim view of the twelfth house. It can indeed correlate with "having more than one's fair share of bad luck."

The deeper insight is that these *unwanted lessons in non-attachment* are not something that we must expect or predict when we see planets in the twelfth house. They are only realities that necessarily arise if we are missing the deeper evolutionary point. They are not even "punishment;" they are only expressions of *natural law* moving in its eternal, impersonal, non-judgmental ways.

Eat enough junk food and you'll look like *Porky Pig.* That is natural law too. Actions have results, and there is nothing in your chart that can ever simply go away and have no effect upon you. It is the *nature of the effect* that is under your control, or at least under your influence.

"DRUNKENNESS"

Even with the universe trying to "help us along spiritually" with these kinds of unwanted losses, there is still no guarantee that we will learn anything at all. Evolution is always voluntary; it never happens by default. It is easy to see how a person making a weak response to his or her twelfth house might begin to feel jinxed, as if that life has singled him out for misfortune.

When I think of someone making a weak response to the twelfth house, an old blues lyric comes to mind. It is variously attributed to Lightnin' Slim, William Bell, and Albert King:

> *Born under a bad sign, been down since I began to crawl*
> *If it wasn't for bad luck, I wouldn't have no luck at all.*

Listening to the blues can be therapeutic. Singing about sadness often paradoxically makes people feel happier. There's a core twelfth house lesson in that observation: remember, transcendence is the ultimate point in the Piscean clan. Without slipping into denial or rationalization, we humans can simply *get bigger than our problems* and help to keep them in perspective that way. The sons and daughters of the African diaspora who brought us the blues and gospel music have offered us many Piscean lessons about how to live with terrible burdens and still not be utterly defined by them.

Still, feeling as if we have been personally targeted for misfortune and unfairness does not always bring out the best in a person. It does not always bring out transcendence. Sometimes all it brings out is a hunger for oblivion.

The abuse of alcohol is a classic avenue for the expression of that hunger to escape – but it is a short step from there to thinking about other chemical interventions in the human nervous system. Anything which dampens our emotional response to life can become a road to oblivion. A broader way to say it is that *anything that is pleasurable and repeatable can be used in an escapist fashion.* We can escape into eating. We can escape into sexual release. We can escape into work, or exercise, or the thrill of dangerous adventures. Many people nowadays escape into their cell phones or their "devices," using them nervously, the way people in the 1950s would light up cigarettes.

The list of such escape hatches is long, and constantly growing.

Under natural law, any weak response to a twelfth house planet triggers loss. Loss is painful and leads quickly to a desire for the hurt to stop. And in the twelfth house, *that pain can be stopped in healthy ways* – but only by traveling the higher path, at least if we want to keep the price tag on stopping the pain under control.

If we do not see our way to that higher path, then *anything that stops the pain becomes compellingly attractive.* We go like the moth to the flame. These escapist methods quickly lead to more pain – and the deadly twelfth house downward spiral begins to suck one's soul into stasis.

On top of all of this, let's refresh a point that we have already explored under the banner of Pisces. It applies to twelfth house planets too. These are all *psychically-sensitive* symbols. And so, to our personal pain, we add *an attunement to the collective undercurrents of energy of the suffering world.*

Will it drive us to Spirit in its compassionate face – or to "spirits?" There's the eternal question.

FLYING AA

To all of this, I would add an affirmation that, unless a person is suffering from the disease we call alcoholism, I would not begrudge anyone a cocktail or two. I don't want to become attached to puritanical attitudes which are probably just as much of soul-cage as are hedonistic ones. Life is hard. Compassion is inseparable from the spiritual path – and that includes having some compassion for ourselves. Taking some comfort here and there is not something we should condemn in ourselves or in anyone else.

It comes down to that ancient and famously tricky question: being mindful of the *difference between use and abuse*, between creature comfort and the search for oblivion.

There is a middle path. The trick for finding it is more Scorpionic than Piscean. You need to be willing to ask yourself hard questions – and listen to the honest answers.

APATHY

Ego fills us with desires and aversions – I want this, I hate that. Those wants and fears derive rather logically from the vivid delusion that we are separate from everything else, locked in competition with other beings, and engaged in an endless, hungry battle for survival. The spiritual literature of almost all traditions warns us about getting caught up in that passion play. Still, it is difficult to avoid. Again, such drives emanate directly from the nature of the human ego, and we are all born with one.

So what happens when ego's hold on us begins to loosen its grip? That is what Pisces and the twelfth house are all about – "transcending the ego." That is true of Neptune too, as we are about to see.

If we have any of these Pisces clan symbols wired into our charts in central ways, are we less susceptible to that kind of ego-driven madness? In a word, are we simply more advanced spiritually?

Well, that is a possibility . . . but we have to be careful here. We have to remember that every front has a back. There are lower possibilities too.

Let's start with the higher ground: a solar Aries and a solar Pisces are stuck in an endless, stop-and-start traffic jam. Everything else being equal, *which one of the two are you going to bet on for maintaining a lofty perspective?*

That is a cartoon illustration, but you probably already see which way the wind is blowing. Aires, being a Fire sign, tends to be less patient. Aries, ruled by Mars the Warrior, is more likely to be pounding the steering wheel and uttering maledictions.

Meanwhile, what is Pisces doing? Try this: Pisces is thinking, *"what will this matter in five hundred years?"*

So far, so good. That more transcendent attitude works well in traffic jams. With ego having less of a grip on our consciousness, faced with a jammed freeway at 5:30 in the afternoon, I would rather be a Pisces than an Aries.

That's the front. What about the back?

There is a fine line between transcendence and *apathy*. Think of a teenager rolling her eyes at "yet another pointless parental demand or restriction." She feels outgunned. Mom and dad may be "dumb, clueless, and unfair," but they hold all of the aces. The teenager has given up on ever really being heard or on any prospect of justice. She glances heavenward and acquiesces with one despairing word: *"Whatever . . ."*

That is apathy – and yet another Pisces clan method for simply turning life off.

Ego can certainly get us into trouble. Don't forget that it can get us out of trouble too. Sometimes we need to make a stand. Sometimes we need to set boundaries. Sometimes we need to insist. Sometimes we need simply to say no. *Sometimes thinking "what will this matter in five hundred years" is a formula for passivity, spiritual failure, and misery.* Those are risks a soul takes when it is working with this family of astrological symbols.

- My marriage has been nothing but empty ritual for the past ten years, *but what will that matter in five hundred years?*
- My body is falling apart with neglect, *but what will that matter in five hundred years?*
- My job pays me nothing but money, *but what will that matter in five hundred years?*
- I know I should meditate more, *but what will that matter in five hundred years?*
- My country is going to hell in a handbasket and I know I should register to vote, *but what will that matter in five hundred years?*

With just a little reflection, I think it is easy to see that this Piscean or twelfth house *apathy* is second cousin to drunkenness. It is just another way to turn off our connection with difficulties and pain. The trouble is that, in so doing, we also turn off any opportunity to grow and evolve. I would label this condition *transcendence abuse* and cite it as one more fundamental spiritual disorder in the Piscean clan, right up there with passing out on cheap wine in the alley behind the dumpster.

NEPTUNE AND JUPITER

The dual planetary rulership of Pisces is controversial among astrologers, as are all of the other dual rulerships. I advocate the use of both rulers and I have a simple, experiential way of making a case for that approach. My premise is simple: *that there are two kinds of Pisces people – Jupiter ones and Neptunian ones.* They are very different, and the distinction is easily observed if we simply look for it. In seeing it, we get the message that the fishes indeed have two fundamentally different faces.

- The *Jupiter cohort* of Pisceans is composed of the sorts of big-hearted people for whom the world is full of friends they have not yet met. They are expansive and generous. They laugh easily and tend to "party hearty." Physically, they are often fleshy. They enjoy food and drink, as well as uninhibited company. In their spiritual lives – which can be profound – they are drawn to ritual and collective observation. Religion often works well for them, although they tend to emphasize *agape* over doctrine. These are Piscean people – but you can easily discern Jupiter's DNA in everything about them. They are the embodiment of that famously eternal spiritual rocket fuel: *unconditional love for all people.*

- The *Neptunian cohort* of Pisceans is composed of more otherworldly, mystical types. They radiate sensitivity, sometimes to the point of seeming fragile, even ghostly. They report psychic experiences. They are easily startled. Crowds do not attract them. Loud sound repels them, unless it is musical. Often they are artistic. They relate best to people one at a time rather than in groups. They "give things up" easily – even perhaps things that they should not give up. Religious ritual often feels empty and pointless to them; their spiritual lives are deep, but tend toward being private and internal. Again, these are Piscean people – but they are the embodiment of Neptunian energy, values, instincts, and behaviors. They represent a different pathway up the spiritual mountain: *insight, psychic experience, and meditative trance.*

Naturally, Pisceans who display Jupiter qualities tend to have Jupiter placed more prominently in their natal charts than Neptune – and obviously it is *vice versa* for our more "Neptunian" Pisceans. That is just astrology at work.

To me, this simple human observation is strong verification that there are two sides to Pisces, and that it is appropriate to consider both Jupiter and Neptune its natural rulers.

As with Mars and Pluto in the previous chapter, my approach in the remaining pages of this chapter will be to focus more deeply on Neptune and to spend less time on Jupiter. That is only because we explored Jupiter in detail in *The Book of Fire.* If you need a refresher, please have a look at that earlier volume.

As many of you know, I also published *The Book of Neptune* back in 2016. If you are drawn to delve more deeply into that mysterious planet, allow me to recommend those pages too. In that book, I cover many dimensions of Neptune that go beyond what we will be considering here.

NEPTUNE AS YOUR UNIQUE SPIRITUAL PATH

Religious fanatics, almost by definition, want you to believe as they believe. They are an annoying group, of course – and since you are reading an astrology book, I speculate that you have had at least one of these people try to "correct" your interest in the subject, assailing you with Dantesque warnings about hellfire and damnation.

Our next realization is difficult, but it's as good for you as an organic apple: *maybe such a fire-breathing, judgmental religious fanatic has actually found a path that works for him.* Let's grant him that joy, and bless him on his journey – but please don't let him dissuade you from continuing to expand your shelf-space for the Collected Works of Steven Forrest, *et al.*

You have your path; he has his. It is tempting to add, "and never the twain shall meet." But perhaps they will someday. My favorite book title ever is from the southern writer, Flannery O'Connor. She called a collection of her short stories, *Everything That Rises Must Converge.* Remember that as we neared the end of our dive into the Piscean ocean, we found Oneness, not separation and division. You and that judgmental Fundamentalist are heading for the same mountaintop. You are just doing it via different pathways.

If you can open your heart that wide, you have found the marriage of Jupiter and Neptune.

Still, it is fair to acknowledge that, while all the pathways might lead to the same mountaintop, *souls have reached different levels in their ascent.* That's true too – but not really our concern. Our concern is only to concentrate on *where we are going to put our foot next* in that long climb. That question of our next footstep brings us face to face with the position of Neptune in the natal chart in terms of its sign, house and aspects.

Once we understand that, we know what to do with our feet.

In chapters eleven and fourteen, we will look in cookbook fashion at Neptune in each of the twelve signs and houses, and in chapter seven and eight we'll go into more detail about how to grasp their synthesis. Here, just to ground our reflections, let's consider a few quick examples of how Neptune can guide us toward the best route up the mountain.

Our underlying premise is that you are in a specific spiritual predicament, *with certain steps potentially acting as highly efficient triggers for the expansion of your consciousness.* What works for me might not work for you – and that is where our Fundamentalist made his big mistake. What worked – perhaps quite authentically – for him will not necessarily be of any use to another person.

Imagine, for example, a person with *Neptune in the ninth house*. That covers a lot of possibilities, but one of them is the helpfulness of *spiritual adventures*. She has come to a place in life where, for example, *pilgrimage* might be a powerful spiritual catalyst for her – she might need to travel to a holy place. Similarly, she might benefit from taking metaphysical classes, exposure to spiritual teachers, traveling in order to study mystical topics. Contact with *other cultures* and *alien spiritual perspectives* can be effective catalysts for her.

Now, by contrast, let's consider a man with Neptune in Virgo and the sixth house. Those two symbols – Virgo and the sixth house – are quite parallel in meaning. They both underscore the ideas of *humility* and *service*. Virgo is the urge and the sixth house is the resultant behavior. *Making another person's needs more compelling to you than your own needs* is a classic spiritual method. For this man, *a life of service* is just the ticket. Nothing will advance him on the path more dramatically than such a commitment simply to getting over himself and being helpful to other people.

Note how different these two Neptunian evolutionary methods are.

My hope is, that as you read these words, you have no trouble respecting both of these people. If you need to "fix" either of them, you are clinging to a view of the Piscean path that is too narrow.

Another hope of mine is that these two people can respect each other. But of course in these scenarios the woman in the first vignette might view the man in the second one as "missing the whole adventure" and "wasting his life on endless drone work."

And naturally, the man might judge the woman as "hopelessly self-indulgent and insensitive to anyone's needs except her own."

There are many comments we could make about either of these attitudes, but the main one is simply *what a waste of energy.*

For all of us, there are certain Piscean principles that can fairly be viewed as "one size fits all." *Refraining from harming other beings* is one such guideline. Not *stealing*, not *lying*, not *pressing ourselves sexually on anyone* – these are similarly universal behavioral principles. *Quiet time alone* helps us all.

Beyond all that, we enter highly individual terrain. Each soul has distinct evolutionary needs – and specific blockages that need to be undone.

The position that Neptune occupies in the birthchart illuminates all of those more personal perspectives. Religions are pretty good at describing the general moral guidelines that speed our journeys – or at least help us to not create unnecessary impediments and complications for ourselves.

After that, Neptune kicks in. It agrees with "all of the above," then it tells you – and you *personally* – where your foot needs to go next.

MYSTICS DON'T DATE MUCH

Celibacy is not everyone's path. You might, for example, have Neptune in the eighth house. For you, the experience of *sacred sexuality* is potentially a major catalyst for your evolution. God kicked you out of heaven, saying "and don't you dare come back here a virgin!"

Still, in the cross-cultural history of human spirituality there is a distinct theme of aspirants and saints avoiding sex.

And that is a lot to give up.

Similarly, mystics have often avoided wealth, or even taken vows of poverty.

They often dress simply, frequently wearing robes that obscure any physical charms they might possess, and almost always choosing clothing which eclipses their individuality.

Mystics often fast. And that is hard too.

They have been known even literally to give up their lives for the sake of some higher principle. You may, for example, have heard the story of Jesus. Or of Obi-Wan Kenobi in *Star Wars*, for that matter. It is not a rare theme.

Mystics giving things up – if you look for it, you will find it. Such abstinence is an unmistakable pattern in the study of comparative religion. And it is not particularly hard to understand why. As we saw earlier, *attachment is the main obstacle to the separation of consciousness from personality*. For that reason alone, *an intentional practice of non-attachment* is a classic spiritual pathway. Such *asceticism* goes right to the heart of the matter. The higher will gradually asserts its dominance over our appetites and our general predilection for all the variations of human monkey business.

Once, back when I was maybe thirty years old, I had lunch with a man just a little older than myself who was a monk in a mystical Christian order. We liked each other right away; there was no barrier of formality separating us. Intrigued, I asked him the obvious guy-question, at least from the perspective of my being a hormone-addled thirty-year-old male: *how could he live without sex?*

He told me that it was indeed difficult at first, but that after a while he found he just wasn't thinking about it anymore.

I had great respect for this monk – but I hope that he didn't have Neptune in the eighth house or even aspecting his Venus. If he did, he would have then given up something that he actually needed for his path. Sex can surely become one of life's ultimate attachments – but it can be a *path* too.

The "big religions" have not been very adept at honoring that reality. The old pagans were pretty good at it.

There is a general principle here. Each planet correlates with an archetypal energy that can manifest as a virtue or a vice. Mars, for example, is about courage – *and we can be courageous in thoroughly stupid actions.* Venus is about giving ourselves in love – *and we can love the wrong people for the wrong reasons, and suffer pointless agonies of the heart.* Jupiter is about having faith in ourselves – *and we can misplace such faith as ego inflates and chases after glitter.*

Similarly, Neptune is about the practice of non-attachment – *and we can give up things that we actually, legitimately, need for our soul's journey.*

Giving things up is simply a *behavior*, nothing more, nothing less. There is nothing inherently virtuous about it at all, *unless it is allied with conscious intention.* In the same way, conventional people might believe that a person who goes to church has a spiritual life. Maybe yes, maybe no. In reality, going to church only means sitting in a certain building at a certain time. What is going on in that person's soul? We cannot tell from the outside.

No judgment, no praise.

Where Neptune lies in your chart, there is always something that you need to *actively claim* in order to truly follow your most efficient evolutionary path. Our woman with Neptune in the ninth house might *need* a pilgrimage. Our man with Neptune in Virgo needs to find a path of *meaningful service.* "Giving up" those things would only be a waste – and worse, a form of spiritual self-sabotage.

Paradoxically, *getting Neptune right requires ego strength.* You have to be able to say, "this, but not that." You have to stand up for yourself. You have to claim your right to your own unique path – even if other people are handing you *Hare Krishna* literature, warning you of God's wrath, or explaining to you that there is no scientific basis to astrology.

LET'S NOT FORGET JUPITER

As I mentioned earlier, for a full exploration of the glories of Jupiter, please refer back to *The Book of Fire.* There, we deal with the "king of the gods" in the full fashion the biggest planet in the solar system deserves.

Here, in the Piscean context, I just want to quickly underscore a couple of points that have particular relevance to Jupiter's connection with mystical pathways and the evolutionary skills which support them.

FAITH

Faith is a classic Jupiter word – and it is of course also one that we often encounter in spiritual and religious contexts. In putting faith in the spotlight, I want to de-emphasize the notion of simply talking ourselves into believing things for which we have no personal evidence. That kind of "faith" may indeed sometimes serve an authentic spiritual purpose – as for example, when a primitive soul decides to try on the notion that if I am kind to others, perhaps they will be kinder to me.

Hey, it's worth a try.

And just maybe by tentatively "having faith" in that unproven hypothesis, this soul learns something useful. He may have even gotten this idea from a priest – and priests can be shepherds, helpfully guiding us to have faith in principles of which we are not yet totally convinced by our own experience. Sometimes that works out copacetically. Instead of killing somebody, the thug helps an old lady cross the street.

Such priestly guidance can be in Jupiter's domain – but it really pertains more clearly to the Sagittarian side of Jupiter's equations. On the Piscean side, we are centered much more on *true mysticism* – which is to say, on the *direct experience of the Divine.*

Compared to Sagittarius, faith – at least in the sense of believing things that we have not known directly – is far less relevant in the framework of Pisces and the twelfth house. Here, faith manifests as something more akin to *tolerating risk* and being willing to take chances for spiritual purposes. It is not a *theological* faith so much as *a feeling that things will work out* – that I will be protected and that what I need will be provided.

As we saw earlier, a woman with Neptune in the ninth house might benefit from going on a pilgrimage. Once she starts to really think seriously about doing it, she probably gets scared. She will be far from home among foreigners. Bad things could happen. She could be uncomfortable. Hiking the pilgrim road, she might be physically strained or otherwise out of her depth. There are no guarantees that the experience will work out positively.

But she packs her bags for the Pilgrim Road anyway. That's faith. Her Neptune is in the ninth house – but maybe her natal Jupiter is conjunct Mars in Aries. And if both planets were cats, they would be purring.

Here are her questions. They are all legitimate.
- Will I be safe?
- Where will the money come from?
- Am I going to look stupid or flaky?
- Will I go to hell for doing this?
- Will I go crazy?
- Will I get hurt?

The great god Jupiter hears all that and says, don't worry. You can trust me. I will take care of you. Have faith. I control the manifestation in the universe of what people call "dumb luck." Trust me . . .

And you can.

The question, as ever, is, will you?

LOSS

There is a tendency among astrologers to think of Jupiter as a lucky planet. That is a perspective that often stands up to scrutiny. In most situations of simple "dumb luck," there is Jupiter involvement. Still, the notion that Jupiter is lucky is incomplete. I only want to point out that this equation of Jupiter with good fortune derives very strongly from its rulership of Sagittarius. Meanwhile, Neptune's clear and obvious resonance with Pisces has had the unfortunate effect – at least in the context of modern astrology –

of eclipsing Jupiter's own natural association with Pisces and the twelfth house. That has subtracted some poignant dimensions from our current understanding of Jupiter.

Pisces, as we have seen, is very much about non-attachment. And the twelfth house, under certain conditions, can correlate with loss. It follows that Jupiter must also sometimes ring those same bells.

And it does.

"Losing that (fill in the blank) *was the best thing that ever happened to me."*

That is surely a line that you have heard before. I suspect that you have had occasion to use it yourself. It reflects one of those basic templates of human experience – one that is connected astrologically with Pisces, the twelfth house . . . and somewhat counter-intuitively with Jupiter as well. At least it is "counter-intuitively" only if we have forgotten about Jupiter's traditional rulership of two signs, not just one.

- A person with Jupiter in the second house experiences bankruptcy – and walks away free to start a new and more satisfying life.
- A person with Jupiter conjunct Venus experiences a heartbreaking, ego-shattering divorce – and three years later meets a true soul mate.
- Someone with Jupiter in Sagittarius misses a flight to Sydney – and that plane was diverted to the Aleutian Islands with mechanical troubles, where it remained for three cold, rainy days.

You get the picture. Where Jupiter lies in your chart, you may experience some significant losses – losses which, in retrospect, *benefit you.*

You will figure that out sooner or later. Why not enjoy it sooner?

To do that, *all you need is a little faith.*

6

THE HANDOUT

In November 2016, I presented a four-day seminar on the Water Family to my southern California Astrological Apprenticeship Program. I called it "Nurturing the Roots." In preparing and presenting that material, I laid much of the foundation for this book, even though in these pages we take the material down many new pathways.

To support my students in that program, I made a one-page handout. I want to share it here, with only a few minor modifications. I hope that it will serve the same purpose in this book as it served in that class: simply as an aid-to-memory. A single page cannot substitute for a book or a class – but for someone who has actually read the book or attended the class, perhaps a word or a phrase might bring some helpful recollections back to the surface.

NURTURING THE ROOTS:
KNOWING THE WATER FAMILY

All creatures great and small seek happiness and well-being. But how many actually find them? Joy is famously elusive. Many paths toward it are advertised. Most are fraught with illusions, marketing ploys, mirages, and misleading temptations.

Jesus said, "Man shall not live by bread alone." But tell that to someone who is starving. Well-being is, at least in part, connected with having our basic material needs met. Healthy food and reasonable shelter are obvious requirements. But what about having a hundred pairs of shoes? What about a billion dollars?

Why do soul-cages such as those promise so much and yet deliver so little? *The Upanishads declare, "attachment to sense objects is bondage." Great—but how do we overcome something so hardwired into our heads?*

Knowing ourselves, truly knowing our own souls and effectively caring for them – and thus finding an actual foundation for happiness – is the task of the Water family: Cancer, Scorpio, and Pisces, along with their associated houses, and the planets that rule them. These symbols correlate with everything that supports the endless, moment-to-moment process of self-regeneration. Without that kind of Water in our lives, we dry up and blow away.

To Embrace the Heart Without Pre-conditions . . .

CANCER AND THE MOON

Antagonists: Logic and Stoicism. That which would silence your uncensored, spontaneous, child-like attunement to your own needs, hurts, and desires. Any vice – or any virtue – which stands between you and your heart.

Key Concepts: Heart and soul. The mood is the message. The need for roots, home, and safety. Necessary walls and boundaries. Family feelings. Pregnancy, fertility, and child care. Reliable intimate commitment. Sweetness. Kindness. Instinct. The reigning needs of the psyche and the organism. The inner Mother. Attitude. Assumptions – including ones that blind us. Intimate surrender. Self-care. The energy, values, and disposition of a Healer. Uncritical immersion in emotional states. Re-generation.

> *"It isn't normal to know what we want. It is a rare and difficult psychological achievement."*
> - Abraham H. Maslow

To Bravely See What We Do Not Really Want To See . . .

SCORPIO AND MARS/PLUTO

Antagonists: Denial; Rationalization; Compartmentalization. Social training around "taboo subjects". The automatic tyranny of the unconscious mind. Timidity. Primness. Crippling "positiveness;" the "flight into light." Ostracism for truth-telling. The way we are trained to lie about how we really feel.

Key Concepts: Honesty. Penetrating psychoanalytic insight. Hard questions. Eye contact. Intensity. Acting out. "Possession" by "evil spirits." Psychopathology and sociopathy. Looking into others as deeply as you are looking into yourself. Breaking taboo. Being ready to face the truth. Digging in the dirt. Passion. Sexuality. Being real. Magick. Wrestling with power. "Staring at the Gorgon Medusa." Becoming a person to whom it is difficult to lie.

> *"Digging in the dirt. Stay with me, I need support. I'm digging in the dirt to find the places I got hurt. Open up the places I got hurt. The more I look, the more I find. As I close on in, I get so blind."*
>
> - Peter Gabriel

To Surrender in Faith to the Higher Powers . . .

PISCES AND JUPITER/NEPTUNE

Antagonists: Egocentricity. The need for control. Cultural indoctrination in modern materialism. Bad religion. judgments and divisions. Having nothing in life that is more important than one's self. Cynicism. Materialism. Allowing fears and desires to make our decisions. The veil of opinion which stands between us and reality.

Key Concepts: Consciousness itself. Spirituality. Dreams. Meditation and trance. Psychic phenomena. Miracles. Mysticism. Interfacing with other dimensions. Ghosts, angels, and guiding spirits. Escapism. Ungrounded thinking. Amorphous identity and values. Art and creativity as spiritual paths. Surrender, in both the good and bad sense. Addiction. Voices in your head. Compassion. "What will this matter in five hundred years?"

> *The sea refuses no river.*
>
> - Pete Townshend

PART TWO

MASTERING THE ALCHEMICAL MARRIAGE OF SIGN, HOUSE, AND PLANET

If someone asks you what potatoes taste like, you can make a stab at answering. The same could be said for the taste of carrots or garlic or onions. But lift a piece of any one of those vegetables out of a stew where they have been bubbling away together for a few hours, and almost everything you just said about their taste is wrong. In a stew, ingredients flavor each other. Each one becomes different than it was originally – more complex, and much more difficult to describe.

In exactly the same fashion, your natal chart is a stew of dozens of astrological symbols. We can speak helpfully, for example, about the Moon as a general concept – but a Moon in Gemini in the ninth house is a very different beast than a Moon in Cancer in the eighth house. And what if either one of those Moons are squared by Venus and opposed by Saturn? It may still be delicious – but it is not "your grandmother's" Moon in Gemini or Cancer any longer.

In the foregoing chapters, we have been describing "potatoes" and "onions" as if they were sitting on the shelves of a grocery store – pristine and unalloyed by contact with the rest of the vegetables. Now it is time to let them interact and flavor each other in the cauldrons of life.

Just as chefs need to learn the basic ingredients of cooking, to become as-trologers, we must learn the core vocabulary. That is what we have been doing in these pages so far. To go further, we need to learn to let the symbols marinate and bubble in the heat of consciousness. We must master the art of synthesis. Let's learn how to make a stew out of the solar system.

7

SYNTHESIS I: PUTTING A WATER PLANET IN A SIGN

S igns animate planets. Understanding that interactive mechanism pre-cisely is mission-critical to any success in astrology. In developing that skill set, we have a real asset – even though there are a great many symbols in astrology and a nearly infinite set of possible combinations, there are some simple general principles which overshadow everything. We can let these principles guide us step-by-step in this process of synthesis.

Let's illustrate how they work with a specific example. We will start by putting the Moon in a sign.

Learning how to take care of the Moon, as we have seen, boils down to learning the secret of happiness. In thinking actively about anyone's Moon, that idea is a good, practical starting point. *How can we help such a person to be happy?*

What if the Moon lies in Virgo? Virgo is the archetype of the Servant. Then, *being good at something that helps another person* is a major source of joy in one's life. Lying on a beach, "wasting away again in Margaritaville," might have occasional appeal for a Virgo Moon person, but *as a lifestyle* it would devolve quickly into emptiness. People with Virgo Moons might not want to admit this out loud, but *getting back to work on Monday morn-*

ing after a two-week vacation would probably feel pretty good – especially if they are fortunate enough *to have a job that pays them more than money*.

Another person might have the Moon in Gemini, which is an entirely different beast. What supports happiness now? In order to maintain a consistent sense of wellbeing, he or she needs lots of *sensory and mental stimulation*. Life must maintain a quality of sheer *eventfulness*. For such a man or woman, *boredom kills the spirit*. We might wonder, does anyone actually *like* to be bored? Not too many people would agree to that. The key is to realize that boredom slips into people's lives hidden inside the Trojan Horse of *practicality, stability, maturity*, and so on – *and those are not bad things!* Lots of people accept boredom, and even appreciate it, when it comes wrapped in that kind of packaging. But for anyone with a Gemini Moon, they're just anthrax with cyanide sauce. Too much of them, and such a person is robbed of happiness.

Those are two very simple examples. In the "stew" of an actual chart, we would doubtless see many modifying and complicating factors. But the underlying principle is that, while the Moon is always the Moon, the sign it occupies has an enormous impact on how it expresses itself. What makes the Virgo Moon happy might make the Gemini Moon miserable, and *vice versa*.

Everyone has a *mood*; everyone has *reigning needs*. Meet them, and a state of wellbeing arises automatically. That's the Moon in action. But what is the *nature* of that mood? *How can we list those reigning needs specifically?*

Don't ask the Moon itself – ask the sign it occupies.

THE VIEW FROM THE MOUNTAIN TOP

Our underlying principle in a nutshell is that each of the Water planets has an intrinsic nature. That is what we have been exploring in the last few chapters. But that intrinsic nature is animated by a unique set of *values* and *motivations*, based on the sign it occupies.

* Pluto, for example, *always seeks the heart of the matter* – but in Sagittarius, it is looking for *what life really means*, while in Cancer it might ask *what I really need* or *what really frightens me*. It is a different orientation; "the heart of the matter" has one meaning for Sagittarius and another meaning for Cancer.

- Neptune is attuned to the *higher mysteries,* but in Gemini it *wants to learn about them cognitively,* while in Taurus, it *wants to feel them viscerally in its physical body.* Gemini might read about them, while Taurus dances about them.

- A thriving Mars wants to *face challenges* worthy of its warrior-nature. In Scorpio, those challenges might be in *the psychological category* – facing the sheer intensity of complex inner or intimate truths. Put Mars in Leo, and the challenges take on the tonality of *true self-expression* and the sense of *scary vulnerability* that usually goes along with stepping out on a stage, one way or another.

- A healthy Jupiter questions how it has been *underestimating itself* or *settling for too little* in life. In Libra, those questions revolve around *grace,* both in human partnerships and the *aesthetic dimensions* of our existence – how have I sold myself short in terms of the qualities of *mutual respectful attentiveness* in my most significant relationships. In Pisces, Jupiter's motivations become more *creative, visionary,* and *spiritual* – how have I underestimated myself in those arenas? How have I sold myself short?

Those are our five Water planets. Each of them can occupy any one of twelve zodiacal signs – although because of the long orbital periods of Neptune and Pluto, for some possible sign placements, there will be no living representatives. For example, the last group of babies to be born with Pluto in Aries took their first breath a very long time ago – on February 13, 1853. As I write these words, they have just had to blow out 167 candles on their birthday cakes.

None of them are likely to knock on your door with astrological questions.

The next crop of children to be born with Pluto in Aries are due to arrive on April 8, 2067. The majority of their *parents* have not yet been born.

Still, this basic interpretive principle – *that a sign adds specific motivations and values to a planet* – is always reliable across the board no matter what century we are in. Signs make planets come alive. They make them human rather than abstract.

Master this technique of synthesis, and you can basically have dinner with Wolfgang Amadeus Mozart, Queen Elizabeth the First, and Julius Caesar – just don't get in an argument with Elizabeth. She had Mars in

Gemini opposite Jupiter in Sagittarius, so she was "right about everything" even when she wasn't.

THE COOKBOOK SECTIONS

Spread through the pages of this series of four volumes, you will find detailed thumbnail sketches of every possible planet/sign combination. I hope those word-pictures are helpful, but please remember that they are only a starting point. Everything in astrology always draws its fuller meaning from *context*. Remember our "stew" metaphor. Onions flavor the potatoes – and Queen Elizabeth the First's Jupiter flavors her Mars . . . while her Sun was in Virgo . . . while she had a Saturn-Uranus conjunction in Cancer in her seventh house, and so on.

Eternally, the deepest message of astrology lies in absorbing the full, integrated picture. Learning to read the basic unit of *a planet in a sign* is the step we are taking in this chapter. Our next move in that direction is to go more deeply into a few examples in order to illustrate our approach. As we take that step, three underlying principles will guide us:

- A sign gives a planet a set of *reigning needs* and *motives*. It *flavors* a planet with tastes, interests, and values, giving it a particular sense of purpose and direction.
- Every planet/sign combination has a *high spiritual, evolutionary purpose*, along with a set of tools to accomplish the job.
- Every planet/sign combination has a *dark, dysfunctional side*. It is not our "fate" to fall into any of those unfortunate dead-end traps – but it is our fate as humans to have to wrestle with them if we want to avoid becoming ensnared by them.

THE MOON IN SCORPIO

Everything else being equal, the Moon is inherently kind and gentle. It is, after all, the symbol of the Great Mother. But Scorpio is a scorpion – not a creature we normally associate with nurturing instincts. Who can look down and see a scorpion scurrying across his foot without shuddering?

Still, a scorpion can sometimes be a good teacher, and even bring us a rich gift or two. Imagine, for example, that you are hiking in the desert with a dear friend. You stop to gaze across a beautiful arid landscape. Suddenly, your friend exclaims, "ouch." She looks down and sees a scorpion on her sandal. *She's just been stung.* Moments later the neurotoxins strike; she's experiencing convulsions and serious difficulty in breathing.

One minute earlier, she was fine. Now it is possible that she might be facing death right before your eyes, and you both know it.

She pulls through.

But that is how fragile and uncertain our lives are in these physical bodies. That scorpion just reminded you both of that taboo reality.

I am tempted to say that no one would call this little adventure in neurotoxicology "positive." The horror is obvious. But as your friend was convulsing, as she stood there at death's door, you were *absolutely present* for her. She had your full attention. You did what you could for her practically, but that was not much. The critical point is that *spiritually, you did not fail her.* You will never forget the look in her eyes, nor will she forget the look in yours, in those terrible, centuries-long, minutes.

She is your friend; you have always loved her. *But the shared experience of her brush with death has forged something deeper between you.* There is no nakedness to compare with such a stark moment. Neither of you will ever lose track of that memory.

From that moment forward, that Scorpionic episode will be the defining, if unspoken, metaphor of your relationship.

Even if you have the Moon in Scorpio, no one would suggest that you "enjoyed" your little adventure in the Wild Kingdom. *But it fed something in you,* and that is the point. That naked moment *healed* you from the effects of the endless, enforced superficiality of daily social life. It helped you *recover* from its draining effects. Your deeper communion with your friend's soul, not to mention with your own, *regenerated* something vital in you.

Remember: the Moon represents a fundamental need that must be met if we are going to be happy in life. And for you, with your natal Moon in Scorpio, what you need above all is *something real.* That episode in the desert might have been a bit of an overdose, but no one could deny that it was an experience of naked reality. You walked your friend to death's door, and you walked her back again.

Conversely, if you have a Scorpio Moon, and *if I wanted to leach all life out of you,* if I wanted to fill your soul with emptiness, I would put you at a dress-up cocktail party full of name-droppers – a cocktail party that lasted forever. Again, that "cocktail party" is an over-the-top image – but try this: the world often resembles that kind of vacuous social ritual. People chit-chat. Everything inherently lightweight is treated as if it were significant – what the latest starlet wore at the Emmys, who she is sleeping with this month. Meanwhile everything truly serious is treated as if it were radioactive. Just for example, next time you find yourself at a gathering like that, try bringing up the possibility of some kind of environmental Armageddon. Try asking people how they think they will die. Share a few cancer statistics.

Next time those people have a party, your name will not appear on the guest list.

Underlying everything that I have just written is one unifying principle: *we are seeing what happens when the Moon's intrinsic nature is conditioned by Scorpionic needs, values, and motivations.* I am only using dramatic imagery in order to spotlight the heart of the matter. To say it more simply, *the Scorpio Moon is hungry for some honest reality and authenticity of human connection.* No need to be stung by a scorpion. If we would prefer to avoid that unpleasant possibility, we can sometimes just say those portentous words, *"Honey, there is something we need to talk about . . ."*

That will do it – provided that you have found the right "honey."

THE SCORPIO MOON AND INTIMACY

Let's go further. The Moon is connected with our *domestic environment* and what we need there if we are going to be happy. It is about the physical home, but also about the kinds of relationships that happen "under one roof." Truly to *bond* with another human being – *to make a home*, in other words – is fundamentally a lunar transaction. With the Moon in Scorpio, any such committed relationship if it is going to be a happy one must be characterized by a high level of *genuine honest emotional connection* – with the added understanding that any truly Scorpionic connection is not always about sweetness and light. *The depths of the soul* are what Scorpio is all about, and those depths can often be stormy. Not everyone feels comfortable sharing them – but no one with a Scorpio Moon can feel truly close to another person unless each one is the guardian of at least a few of the other person's secrets.

As we learned in chapter three, the Moon is *your mood averaged over a lifetime.* With the Moon in Scorpio, that mood is penetrating and deep.

From the outside, such a mood might even seem to be suspicious, dark, or "too psychological." The point is that anyone who makes those kinds of judgments about someone with the Moon in Scorpio is simply not a good candidate for any kind of deeper connection.

Mister Wrong: You're too intense.

Madame Scorpio: Too intense *for who?*

Socially, *truth is a controlled substance*, and anyone who breaks the rules aimed at containing it tends to be punished with ostracism, criticism, and isolation. Kids with Scorpio Moons learn that lesson early in their lives.

Little Johnny: Grandpa is really old. He's going to die soon, isn't he?

Mom and Dad: That's a terrible thing to say! Grandpa is just fine!

And a year later, grandpa is dead. But no one remembers what Johnny said. *What Johnny himself remembers is that death is one of the subjects that he is not allowed to mention.* He soon learns that there are many others.

- Once he references *how grandma smells* – and gets a dirty look for it.
- He talks explicitly about *bodily functions* and is shamed for it.
- In front of a group of family friends, he anxiously shares how scary it was when his mother and father had a big fight over somebody named Suzy.
- He recounts how *grandpa's ghost* visited him.

In every case, he experiences *negative reinforcement* for being truthful about specifically Scorpionic subjects. Another time, and with equal candor, Johnny says that dinner tastes very good tonight, mommy. He expresses gratitude for a birthday present he really likes. He says he loves Jesus. Maybe all those statements are true too. But they are *positively reinforced.* People smile at him when he says them, unlike his more Scorpionic comments.

Johnny begins to *compile a map*, figuring out exactly where the boundaries around "taboo material" lie. He begins to *edit* himself, trying not to cross those lines. Like the rest of us, he tries to avoid punishment.

Pretty soon, Johnny has learned the rules that govern the great cocktail party of the world.

All of this learning would be harmless except for one thing that we have seen over and over again: *taking care of the Moon is the secret of happi-*

ness. As we have been emphasizing, for anyone with the Moon in Scorpio, that happiness depends upon *sharing something real* – and typically, these *real* subjects are the very things that lie on the "wrong side" of that border we draw around everything taboo. A line I used earlier applies to Johnny: "If I wanted to leach all life out of you, if I wanted to fill your soul with misery and emptiness, I would put you at a dress-up cocktail party full of name-droppers – a cocktail party that lasted forever."

This is a pathway to the Shadow.

The world is hellbent on training Johnny to "behave himself" at that endless cocktail party. He shouldn't learn those lessons, but he could. Down that road, anyone with a Scorpio Moon gradually descends into a *brooding, isolated state,* cut off from the kinds of souls who could actually offer real support.

Back in chapter four, we explored the correlation between Scorpio and depression. This sense of emotional isolation is how you get there.

What is the alternative? Learning to say, "Too intense . . . *for who?*" Learning who your real friends are, in other words. Diving into the living heart of life – tragedy, darkness, and all. Finding a few people who can *share that deep dive* with you, and cherishing them, while comparing notes with them. Learning to let an awareness of your own mortality guide you as you sort out what is worth experiencing from what would only waste your precious time.

And never forgetting that life, although brief, is full of music, kittens, and rainbows. They are real too – and it is ultimately only *what is real* that sustains your deep, turbulent spirit.

You need accept the whole package, and leave nothing out – including the music, kittens, and rainbows. Do that, and your Scorpio Moon leads you up a path of healing, regeneration, and recovery.

That is what the Moon looks like when it is conditioned by Scorpio. Were it in Capricorn or Pisces, our language would be very different. In chapter nine, you will see a telegraphic paragraph about the Moon in each sign. My hope here, with this more rambling exploration of the Moon in Scorpio, is that you get a feeling for how a planet and a sign can learn to dance together.

PLUTO IN LIBRA

I'm going to concentrate on Pluto rather than on Mars in this chapter since we explored Mars thoroughly back in *The Book of Fire*. Our broad aim in this chapter is to illustrate how any one of the Water planets interacts with the archetypal field of any astrological sign. That synthesis is our main subject, and Pluto can serve our purposes as well as Mars – and maybe in the bargain move us toward deeper understanding of a planet that has not appeared on as many pages in this series yet.

One reason that I have chosen to explore Pluto in Libra specifically is that it will be directly relevant to many of you. Pluto entered Libra in 1972 and remained there until 1984, with some retrograde ins and outs at both ends of the period. As I write, the oldest members of this Pluto-in-Libra generation are nearing the age of fifty, while the youngest are in their mid-thirties – all of you are currently in the thick of life's middle passage, in other words.

By the way, Pluto's last visit to Libra happened between 1724 and 1737, while its next passage through that sign does not begin until November 5, 2217.

Plutonian people in general love the intensity that is fostered by stretching into realms of honesty that might feel threatening to anyone else. If you read the earlier pages of this chapter, those words probably ring bells. Because Pluto is the modern ruler of Scorpio, some of what I write here will already be familiar since we were just looking at the Moon in that same sign. It is worth risking some repetitiveness because now the shoe is on the other foot – instead of Scorpionic energy conditioning the Moon, we now see Libran energy conditioning a planet with a Scorpionic flavor.

Pluto may indeed reflect the psychological spirit of Scorpio – but the sign Libra is ruled by peacemaking Venus, and so those *Venusian motivations* add a very weird and alien note to "the Lord of the Underworld."

Pluto and Libra, in other words, are not exactly "a marriage made in heaven." Let me quickly add that there is nothing wrong with having Pluto in that sign – only that, in order to grasp it, we are going to have to dance with some paradoxes. Pluto would be described technically as being "in detriment" if it were in the sign opposite Scorpio, which is Taurus. Libra is not Taurus – but both signs are ruled by Venus, so there is some common ground.

As with any so-called "detriment" situation, we are attempting to marry two energies that seem to be pulling in radically different directions.

- Pluto wants eye-to-eye truth time. Pluto might say, "I am going to tell you something you might not want to hear."
- Venus – and thus Libra – would hesitate to be so gracelessly and indelicately intrusive.

Libra chimes in, adding diplomatic, harmony-building *values* and *motivations* to Pluto, as signs always do. Libra therefore encourages Pluto to "be nice" – a notion which could veer quickly into a joke when it comes to Pluto.

Pluto is, after all, "the god of hell."

And yet, *synthesis and integration are always our aim when we are putting a planet in a sign. The sign's nature must be made to animate the behavior of the planet – and do that without eclipsing the planet.* How can we possibly succeed at such a synthesis with Pluto in Libra? I am reminded of a quote often erroneously attributed to Winston Churchill. Someone – and it is unclear who actually said this first – once defined diplomacy as "the art of telling a person to go to hell in such a way that he asks you for directions."

With diplomatic Libra on its side, Pluto might actually be able pull that stunt off.

In the midst of a reading for a longtime client of mine, he said, "Steve, you can say the *damnedest* things to me and make them sound all right." Pluto rules my Ascendant, but I have Venus in the first house.

He nailed me.

Let's dive into our analysis of Pluto in Libra in a more formal, step-by-step way. Our aim is to learn the principles behind merging a planet and a sign – and thereby creating something a bit different from either one of them. I hope that an orderly procedure will help us see the underlying principles behind any such synthesis.

Pluto, no matter what sign it is in, is always connected to *how we relate to our psychological and karmic wounds.* We can face them actively, in a healing way – that is the higher ground. Or we can let them control our lives, thereby hurting ourselves and usually hurting other people too. Songwriter Randy Newman (born with Pluto opposing his eighth house south node) wrote a painfully honest tune about his guilt over leaving his wife and kids. He takes just eighteen words to tell the sad side of the whole Plutonian story of the world:

> *I just want you to hurt like I do.*
> *Honest I do, honest I do, honest I do.*

The point is that much bad human behavior comes out of pain and woundedness. It is spiritually healthy, even if very difficult sometimes, to look at everyone through this clear eye of compassionate understanding – even if they have trashed us. Few people get out of bed in the morning wondering what evil they might accomplish by sunset. Still, there is no shortage of darkness in the world. Those people *just want you to hurt like they do.*

People who succeed at the healing work of Pluto are heroes. They break long chains of bitterness. They declare that the chain of darkness stops right here and now, with them. They remind me of Chief Joseph of the Nez Perce when he said, *"From where the Sun now stands, I will fight no more forever."*

Perhaps with no other planet is the contrast between its moral highs and its demonic lows more dramatic than with Pluto.

- You can trust your high Plutonian friends with your deepest secrets. You do that without a second thought that they might betray you or fail you or violate your confidence. Deep down, you know that they would die first.
- If, on the other hand, you have the grievous misfortune of trusting a low Plutonian, you will be used, lied to, and spat out like mold on a piece of cheese, without any sign of regret or remorse.
- Your closest, trusted Plutonian contacts *will tell you the truth as they see it,* even if their words are not designed to please you.
- Those low Plutonians can manipulate you as if you were *Silly Putty.* That is because they have mapped every weakness, every delusion, and every errant desire that you have. They have done so accurately, always thinking of their long-term advantages. As liars, the skill of a low Plutonian is consummate.

You may notice that in the images I have just invoked for Pluto, I have been using *human relationships* as the backdrop. As many of you have probably already realized, that is no accident. We are talking about Pluto in Libra – and arguably, Libra's single most fundamental *motivation* and *value* is the establishment of intimacy and cooperative partnership. With Pluto in Libra, the basis of all such connections – if they are to be healthy – must be truthful.

In many cultures, relationships are ritually sealed through the exchange of gifts. With Pluto in Libra, the parallel structure lies in the *exchange of secrets*. I share my fears, failures, and embarrassing moments with you – and if you reciprocate, we begin to forge a bond of mutual trust.

I mentioned that Pluto was in Libra from 1972 through 1984. Children born in those years are the group to whom I am speaking most personally now. But the passage of an outer planet through a sign does not only leave its mark on the people who are born then. It also leaves a mark on the *times themselves*. My older readers probably remember the sexual free-for-all of the 1970s. Some of you have scars to prove it. As synchronicity would have it, there was a period of about two decades that fell between the invention of birth control pills, on one hand, and, on the other hand, the AIDS crisis. It was a wild time – *and unsurprisingly, it was very hard on the institution of marriage*. When Pluto was in Libra, divorce rates skyrocketed. The psychological body count was very high.

Conservative people might view that period as reflective of a general decline in public morality. *But let's not forget that everything that happens in the sky is meant to serve an evolutionary purpose down here on the earth.* What was happening between 1972 and 1984 was that the *Plutonian values of honesty, passion, and intensity were trying to integrate with the very Libran institution of polite, stable marriage.*

That was not an easy synthesis.

Out of the blue, there dawned on the collective mind *a brand new reason for getting divorced* – one that in a single flash of insight suddenly began to seem perfectly reasonable to almost everyone. For the first time perhaps in history, a person had a natural right to leave a marriage simply because *something was missing.*

And what was that "something?" The answer was not simply sex, even though many dimmer bulbs interpreted it that way. *It was Plutonian honesty, passion, and intensity.* (And if they were missing, sex soon went missing too, giving those dimmer bulbs a leg to stand on.)

What dawned on people a lot more slowly was the realization that finding those passionate qualities was *not just a question of locating the "right person."* It also involved a lot of *work on oneself* – something that became a lot clearer when Pluto finally entered Scorpio in 1984.

The point of all of this is that the children born with Pluto in Libra carry inside themselves a little hologram of those times. What their parents struggled toward, often blindly, sometimes even tragically, this generation is tasked with actually accomplishing. *Their collective destiny lies in recreating marriage – or something like it – in the age of Plutonian psychology.*

The only maps they have, apart from astrology, are the ones with which they were born.

I want to take these observations two steps further. One step is modern psychology. The other one is ancient metaphysics. Evolutionary astrology lies at their intersection, and could not exist without both of them.

From the psychological perspective . . . in essence, we now reflect upon the impact of childhood experience on adult personality. That form of analysis is what many psychologists spend their lives doing, and it can be revelatory. As a group, it is fair to say that the Pluto-in-Libra generation are "the children of divorce."

What exactly happened to these kids while their mothers and fathers were learning, or trying to learn, how to forge some kind of *detente* between their souls and their genitals? For these children, marriage was not the safe – if stultifying – haven in which their own parents had likely grown up, and from which those parents were trying to escape. For these kids, marriage was unstable, unreliable, treacherous terrain. As a group, they were badly hurt by it.

- Some became stronger because of the hurt, learning a kind of *stoicism* in the face of intimate uncertainty – something which we can still see evident in many of them today.
- Some became *bitter or cynical,* horrified at the thought of ever trusting another human being. These are now either tragic romantics or simply the walking wounded.
- A few became *vessels of a kind of pagan wisdom* about love, sex, and gender that I believe will echo down through the next two thousand years.

From the metaphysical perspective . . . even though much of what I just wrote from a psychological angle makes sense as we contemplate the Pluto-in-Libra generation, it presents us with a fundamental logical problem. We have been using these people's childhood experiences as a way of understanding their birthcharts.

That puts the cart before the horse. The reason is simple: they had their birthcharts *before* they had their childhoods. Effects follow causes, not the other way around.

So why did this particular cohort of human beings wind up being born with Pluto in Libra? Was it just life's random roulette wheel? I do not believe that, and I suspect that you don't believe it either.

What was happening to them *before they were born* in order to make it *meaningful* for them to be born with this configuration? If we think about it in metaphysical terms, the answer leaps out. As usual, all it takes is asking the right question.

In prior lifetimes, people born with Pluto in Libra have been wounded in love.

That wounding could have taken many forms: *betrayal, bereavement, arranged marriages, tragic affairs, too-youthful marriages, enforced separations, sexual crudity or exploitation, "date rape," abandonment,* even just the grinding down of the human spirit that comes with *stable, empty domesticity.*

Many things can go wrong in love – and this soul-tribe of human beings has seen it all. *They have Libran wounds which they need to heal* – that is to say, wounds connected with knowing *who* to trust and *how* to trust. Some are defined by those wounds, not having recovered from them. Some are reenacting those old dramas. Some are afraid to love or to let themselves be loved.

The ones who find their way back to love have given themselves a great gift: love itself. But they also present a gift to the rest of us. *They are showing us how intimacy can work in the age of psychology, individuality, and far looser rules about how each gender should behave.*

If marriage has a future, they hold the key to it. They are the alchemical cauldron in which life is experimenting with post-patriarchal, post-heteronormative, definitions of the meaning of human intimacy and commitment.

NEPTUNE IN PISCES

We are not ignoring Jupiter's natural association with Pisces, but for our purposes here in this chapter, let's use Neptune as our example instead. We got to know Jupiter in detail back in *The Book of Fire*. I want to make sure that by the time we reach the end of these four volumes, we will have achieved a balanced perspective, and Neptune could use a little more air time.

Neptune loves being in Pisces, of course. That is basically the meaning of the term "rulership" – it is really just about a *natural affinity* between a planet and a sign. It is a synergy, something which works the same way that romance gets along with flowers or peanut butter is in love with strawberry jelly. When Neptune is in Pisces, *both energies are strengthened*. They reinforce each other, and waste not a single volt of energy on disagreement.

At first blush, everything that I just wrote probably sounds good. What's not to like about harmony and agreement? Let's answer that question by going back for a moment to our previous exploration of the much less harmonious marriage of Pluto and Libra. *As we saw there, a little dose of Libran sensitivity and diplomacy can take some of the edge off Pluto's bluntness, while some Plutonian directness and honesty can cut through any Libran tendency toward flowery obfuscations aimed at avoiding necessary conflict.*

All of the so-called planetary "detriments" and "falls" work that way. Mercury is incompatible with Sagittarius? *The Sagittarian instinct for seeing the big picture can actually balance Mercury's tendency to get lost in a sea of facts.* Saturn is in detriment in Cancer? *Cancerian instincts for self-care can balance Saturn's tendency to overwork and assume too much responsibility.*

Symbols that don't like each other very much can be very good for each other, in other words. That, as we saw, is how it works with Pluto and Libra. But what about Neptune and Pisces? *They love each other.* They agree about everything. They are like Romeo and Juliette or Friday night and a paycheck, all rolled up in one happy, harmonious burrito.

That means that If Neptune decides it wants to make an ass of itself, Pisces says let's go.

In writing these words, I really don't want to make Neptune in Pisces seem like something negative. There is really no such thing as an astrological configuration that is simply "bad" – or one that is simply "good," for that matter. There are fundamental laws of nature that forbid that from ever happening. I write in cautionary fashion about Neptune in Pisces only in an effort to balance the misleading idea that it is automatically "good" for a planet to be in a sign that it rules.

It's not bad; it's just *complicated*.

Bottom line, the energy of Neptune in Pisces can be very strong and direct, but it could use some corrective glasses.

2011 - 2026

As I write, Neptune is currently in Pisces. It entered that sign back in 2011 and 2012, crisscrossing in and out of Aquarius over several months *via* retrograde motion. It hits the cusp of Aries in early 2025, drifts back into Pisces again that October, then finally enters Aries solidly on January 26, 2026.

People born with this configuration are, in other words, the world's current crop of little children. And there are more of them on their way. By eternal law, they will be a diverse group. That is always true. Librans, Capricorns, Aquarians will naturally all abound among them – and they will be as distinct from each other as they have always been. But every one of these children will sustain one note loudly and in unison: *a pure clarion pulse of Neptunian energy.*

For some of them – those born with the Sun, Moon, or Ascendant in Pisces, for example – this Neptunian signature will be the central feature of their characters and destinies. For others, Neptune will seem to be hiding in a corner, *but only compared to the rest of their cohort.* Compared to the way humans have been *throughout history,* even these less-Piscean people will be "Neptunian." They just won't stand out from the crowd any more than a yellow *Frisbee* would stand out in a field of dandelions. For every one of them, the volume is turned up on *visionary imagination.* All of them will experience an abundance of *inexplicable psychic events* – things that they know without knowing exactly *how* they know them. For all of them, there is at least the potential of genuine *mystical experience.*

And for every one of them, we must add a big dollop of *psychic sensitivity to the ambient energies that surround them.* If they do some inner work, they will be able to surf that energetic wave. If they do not do the work, then they will be overwhelmed by their own sensitivity. Many in that latter group will seek numbness.

Between 2011 and 2026, Earth is receiving back into its arms . . .

- A precious, ancient family of *saints, lamas, shamans, priests* and *priestesses* – treasured beings whom we sorely need to see again. There is even the possibility of some kind of *genuine messiah* taking birth.
- Souls blessed with *visionary imaginations* in every category, from the arts through new social and economic structures.
- Reincarnate *monks, nuns,* and *disciples,* back on Earth to reunite with their teachers.
- *Town drunks* and *drug addicts* galore.
- *Lost souls,* all of them dazed and confused – and quite ambivalent about being back here at all. Some of them have literally been *ghosts,* lost on the *bardo,* who have finally found their way back into embodiment.
- *Skillful fakers, deceivers,* and *con artists.*
- Enough *brilliant actors* to create a golden age of film and theater.
- *Geniuses of the art of escapism* creating previously unimagined new pathways to help us avoid the reality of embodied life – virtual reality, anyone?

You get the picture. This is a diverse group. All of these different kinds of people, from the lowest to the highest, reflect an elevated centrality of Neptunian and Piscean energies in their birthcharts. As ever, *how they express those qualities* depends upon how their consciousness interacts with these hyper-Neptunian archetypal fields of possibility.

Some of the categories of response that I have listed here might give pause to anyone contemplating having a child before 2026. I cannot take back what I have written, but I can offer some practical advice. A mysterious resonance draws a reincarnating soul into a particular womb, with a particular mother and a particular father. If you would prefer to give birth to a saint rather than to a con artist, just remember two key ideas: *meditate more, while abstaining from swindling money from your neighbors, during the time you are trying to get pregnant.*

That'll take care of it. You can always trust the laws of spiritual magnetism and resonance.

We need to remember that all of these reincarnating souls, from the most advanced to the most deluded, are making a bid for a major evolutionary breakthrough in consciousness. That is why they have taken birth with this Neptunian signature so central and so powerful in their natures.

As with everyone else, whatever our soul's intentions might be, the question is not *can they do it?* The answer to that question is always the same: yes, they can do it. They are capable. No one is ever born with a chart at which they are guaranteed to fail. That is not how the universe works. That is not the mechanism that underlies the mysteries of rebirth, nor its intimately related mysteries of astrology.

Their question, as ever, is not can they do it – it is will they do it?

I know that I have made that point more than once already in this book. You may hear it again too. It bears repetition.

8

SYNTHESIS II:
PUTTING A WATER PLANET
IN A HOUSE

Water always seeks the lowest level. That's a powerful symbolic statement, so long as we are careful not to think of the lowest *moral* level or the lowest kind of humor. Water seeks the *roots* and it *nourishes* them. Astrologically, the Water element always sends its tendrils down into the interior world. It tunes into the messages that arise from the depths of the psyche and which underlie the actual choices that we make in the physical world. Compared to Fire, Earth, and Air, Water is simply more psychological, subjective, and, at least potentially, more spiritual.

Exactly that same interior orientation pervades the Water houses – numbers four, eight, and twelve. For practical reasons, astrologers tend to avoid the term "Water houses," simply because it could get confusing – but the connection is a valid one.

As we have seen all along, houses are the *behavioral expressions* of the *psychological motivations* represented by the astrological signs. Thus, the *urge to experience the transcendent* that characterizes Piscean motivation finds *biographical manifestation* in the behaviors of meditation, visionary creativity, and perhaps even the choice of monastic life.

Water-sign needs and drives are expressed in three-dimensional, human terms, visible to anyone, in the three watery houses.

My obvious next comment here might seem to be, "so don't confuse houses and signs. They are different." And I do believe that – however, let me express it with a bit more subtlety this time: don't confuse signs and houses *too much*. Confusing them *a little* probably means that you are understanding them very well.

I did not want to say that in the first three books of this Elements series. But, hey, this is the last one – we are in graduate school now.

I know that saying "confuse them a little" sounds like gobbledy-gook, but it really is not. Signs are *being*, while houses are *doing* – and those two poles of our existence interact like watercolor paints. For example, psychological research has revealed that if you smile, you will feel happier. We often think of it the other way around – that if you are happy, you will smile. That works too. But the act of putting a smile on your face, even if you are feeling blue, lifts the spirit.

In that case, *doing* triggers *being*.

A bad novelist might write, "Annie was shy." A better novelist might write, "Annie went reluctantly to the party. She entered the room with her eyes downcast, and surreptitiously scanned the crowd for a familiar face."

In that case, "doing" reveals the reality of Annie's "being."

And that is how life works. That is how humans actually get to know each other. We may *be* our signs – but houses are how we reveal ourselves to each other.

All that is practical astrology. I'd happily stand by the principle that signs and houses are distinct and that confusing them is a rampant source of error in modern astrological practice – but let me add that the boundaries between signs and houses are even fuzzier with houses four, eight, and twelve than they are with other nine houses. *That is because these three Water houses symbolize the behavior of interacting with our inner worlds.* What does a person do when she is actively exploring memories of her childhood? Maybe she is turning the pages of an old album of family photos. That is the *factual face* of her behavior – but of course that observation is trivial and secondary compared to her inner behavior of realizing that her father was in reality a twenty-one-year-old *boy*.

Being and doing are always somewhat interactive, but that is never so obvious as it is with the three "Water houses."

- In the *fourth house*, we *interact uncritically with our emotional world.* The particular *behaviors* which trigger, support, and enhance that process are connected with having quiet time, along with some kind of domestic, familial life. Creating material conditions which help us relax and feel safe is essential.

- In the *eighth house*, we penetrate down into *what is behind our psychological states.* We ask ourselves the hard questions and face scary material. We acknowledge our woundedness. The particular *behaviors* which trigger, support, and enhance that process are inseparable from what we learn about ourselves in the deepest forms of human intimacy. Encounters with death are significant here too, along with encounters with anything that we might call "spooky."

- In the *twelfth house*, we open to the transcendent. We surrender. We release and we forgive. We experience the presence of benign higher powers. The particular *behaviors* which trigger, support, and enhance that process are, most obviously, prayer and meditation. The behavior of *social withdrawal* is helpful – simply having some restorative time alone.

These three Water houses naturally have dark sides too. In the fourth house, we might just "hide out" forever. In the eighth, we can become moody and lost in a labyrinth of psychodrama. In the twelfth, we can feel overcome by the world and slip into the ghost-world of escapism.

What determines how we respond to these three houses, be it well or poorly? First and foremost, the answer lies in our own choices. As ever, your chart is not your "fate," it is your path. It is the *road to the higher ground* – and you were born to travel that road, fully capable of succeeding there. It does require effort, however. Consciousness is never generated unintentionally. It is always the fruit of an intentional process. *But you can do it.* That is always true. And if you are not doing it, blaming this planet, or that square, or this opposition for your failure is just a cheap trick. Consciousness and high intentions come first. That is fundamental.

Once we have accepted that reality, we then begin to put planets in these houses and signs on the cusps, and so on. We learn about the tools and the techniques. In the toolbox, *planets are the active ingredients.* You can think of them as Teachers.

When a planet is in a Water house, it is your guide through that existential terrain. It holds the lantern over the path you need to follow into that particular cavern of the inner realms.

Learning to integrate the spirit of a particular planet with the behavioral arena of a house is another fundamental astrological skill, every bit as significant as learning how to put a planet in a sign. That process was our subject in the previous chapter. Here, let's work with some examples of how to put planets in houses.

We are aiming for the grand prize, which is learning how to read the elemental *quantum unit* of astrological symbolism: the *triad* of a planet conditioned by a sign and expressing itself through a house.

THE MOON IN THE EIGHTH HOUSE

When I was a kid way back in the 1950s, I saw a television program in which post- World War II Europeans who had spent time in America were interviewed about their impressions of my country. The interviewer was baiting them to praise us for our enviable material prosperity – our big cars, our movie industry, our blenders and our washing machines.

I will always remember a dure young Norwegian woman sitting on a park bench in Oslo, with a scarf around her neck. Her response sunk into me like a stone. She said, *"I liked America . . . but everyone there feels that they have to be happy all the time."*

Hearing her words was liberating for my own nascent Capricorn-Scorpio self. It felt oddly comforting to hear that at least for some people, "being happy all the time" was not a requirement. *The key concept here – and one which hits the bull's eye of an eighth house Moon – is that there are many positive states of consciousness which are not exactly characterized by feeling "happy,"* at least not in any simple sense of the word.

- How do you feel, for example, when you are in the midst of a difficult but necessary talk with an intimate partner – a talk that is conducted respectfully and bi-laterally, aimed at finding solutions and understandings that work for both of you?

Talks such as that one are tough. No one "feels happy" during them – but we probably feel good about ourselves and good about the relationship. They are constructive, and they are very close to the soul of the eighth house.

- Perhaps you have a deathbed talk with a beloved parent. You are holding hands. You say "I love you" – and you know that you are also saying goodbye.

Are you *happy* as you watch your mother's last breath? The question itself sounds insensitive. But I guarantee that you will treasure the memory of those moments in a sacred place in your heart for the rest of your days. Once again, we see that there are "positive states of awareness" that are not characterized by jump-up-and-down happiness.

As we have seen many times, taking good care of the Moon is the secret of happiness – and so with the Moon in the eighth house, our well-being depends upon *intense encounters with reality*, either within ourselves or between ourselves and someone whom we love. Let's reflect on that latter theme – eighth house *intimacy*. It is absolutely central to our understanding of the Moon in this house.

In the previous chapter, I spoke of the Moon in Scorpio, which is the eighth sign of the zodiac. The repetitiveness of my now introducing the Moon in the eighth house is intentional. The two overlap somewhat in meaning – as we saw a few paragraphs ago, *being* and *doing* are interactive, and therefore so are signs and their corresponding houses. My aim here is to clarify the distinction between Scorpio and the eighth house, without artificially exaggerating it.

The *impulse* to connect deeply with another human being is Scorpionic; the *act* of connecting that way is an eighth house behavior.

Sex can be a major vector here, provided we are careful to emphasize the psychospiritual dimensions of a relatively long-term sexual partnership rather than the simple graphics of erotic contact. Friendship is a welcome part of it too – but no one would mistake being lovers with someone for simple friendship. Here is a quick formula: *subtract friendship from the energy that binds a contented couple together. What remains is the core of the eighth house.*

Passion? Chemistry? Some ancient mammal-brain bond?

Part of that core is so naked and raw that it can be very difficult. That is why lovers tend to quarrel. If as a child I felt that one of my parents did not respect me, I will sometimes *project* that resentment onto my partner. She may not deserve that projection; she may be innocent of disrespecting me. If one of my parents ruled the family with fear, I will sometimes be *afraid of my partner*. If one of my parents was touchy and defensive, I will sometimes be *unnecessarily cautious* around my partner.

Note that in all of these scenarios, we are talking about the *actual situation* of being in relatively committed sexual intimacy – not the impulse, not the theory, not the hunger, but the actual act. The *behavior*. That act is *house* material, not sign material. Such intimacy *is a behavior that deploys basic Scorpionic drives into the three-dimensional world of biography.*

With the Moon in the eighth house, in order to experience a state of regenerative wellbeing, you need to bring your own woundedness to the surface and to feel that you are dealing with it effectively. There are many ways of doing that, but one that is tried and true lies in staying in a committed bodily relationship with a partner for more than a year or so.

In that kind of bond, there is typically nowhere to run and nowhere to hide. That is why it works so well.

Let's quickly expand our eighth house horizon. Loudly and clearly, let me say that one does need to experience committed sexual interchange with another human being in order to enter into this kind of transformative, evocative intimacy. It helps, that's all. Certain deep friendships can count too – but their earmark is a similar willingness to *risk the relationship for the sake of keeping it honest.* Maybe you have a friend or two with whom you can genuinely "say anything." If you have an eighth house Moon, even if you are celibate, those friendships mean that you are taking good care of yourself.

So far, much of what I have been saying revolves more around the eighth house than around the Moon. Having the Moon there simply *turns the eighth house on* in a major way. But the Moon adds its own needs and energetic signatures to the mixture. The result is distinct from having the Sun or Mercury or Jupiter in that house. The Moon *bonds very deeply* – remember its natural alignment with the fourth house and the sign Cancer. It is the "Great Mother," and the connections it forges resemble the lifelong commitments we generally expect between parent and child. With the Moon in the eighth house, for such relationships to be the spiritual catalysts they are intended to be, they must be *deeply committed.* That level of commitment which parallels the parent-child bond is the lunar signature. Such relationships do not "have to last forever." It is more accurate to say that each person is *open* to the idea that "this person" and "my home" are becoming inseparable concepts – and by "open," I mean that we are already at least halfway there. That level of emotional investment and trust are in the mix.

Without that kind of *familial* commitment, we may be in a fine relationship, but it is not a lunar one. The Moon mates for life. Of course, life is tricky and full of surprises. If you have an eighth house, it does not mean that you are immune to divorce. It means that you are wired for it.

With a client who has this Moon signature, I often say, "you have one bullet in your mating gun. Aim carefully."

NOBODY GETS OUT OF HERE ALIVE

The Moon is about happiness and the eighth house, historically, was the House of Death. There's a strange juxtaposition! Mortality is not the first thought that most people have when they think of happiness. Here's the connection: death helps you know what is important and what is not.

We may be wasting our lives worrying about money or status or the shape of our nose. A dear friend announces that she has a terminal disease, *and all of those trivial pursuits instantly go poof.* That strong medicine works well with a friend – and it works even better if it is you who is diagnosed that way.

Houses tend to be synchronistic – that is to say, things always "just happen to happen" in ways that reflect the conditions of our astrological houses. People with planets in the eighth house – and the Moon would be a major example – often have more than their fair share of encounters with death. That statement has several meanings.

- Such individuals may very well experience "near-miss" accidents – accidents which leave them unharmed, but mightily impressed with the brevity, fragility, and uncertainty of life.
- The sudden and untimely loss of parents, other family members, partners, or friends is common.
- A scary medical diagnosis – or misdiagnosis – proves pivotal, even if it turns out to be a false alarm.

Again, I would not feel comfortable "predicting" such losses or events just because a client had the Moon in the eighth house. I might bring it up as a possibility – and underscore the *meaning* of any such events: *that you are being reminded of your mortality.* When it comes to being happy, there is no counselor as wise or eloquent as death. Death helps you sort out what is ultimately important from everything that distracts you from concentrating on it.

TWO TRUE STORIES

Imagine being beautiful, wealthy, and thirty-four years old. You go for a ride in a convertible with your handsome, powerful husband. Imagine his head exploding right next to you as a bullet entered it. Poor Jackie Kennedy – that was her experience on November 22, 1963.

Jacqueline Kennedy Onassis was born with both Venus and Pluto in her eighth house.

Imagine finding your lover dead of a heroin overdose and lying in a bathtub in a foreign country. That is how Pamela Courson found Jim Morrison of The Doors on July 3, 1971. Courson's chart shows a conjunction of Jupiter and Venus in Scorpio in her eighth house, both of them squared by Pluto. Less than three years later, she was dead too – of a heroin overdose, like her partner. They never married, but on her gravestone, she is Pamela Susan Morrison, which seems fitting.

WHAT ABOUT THE OCCULT?

"Occult" experiences are not rare among people with eighth house Moons. Often they are closely related to death. The ageing parent appears mistily in a dream and says, *"I'm fine, but I am going on a long journey."* The phone rings at dawn with the news that dad passed away peacefully, if unexpectedly, in his sleep during the wee hours.

If you have the Moon in the eighth house and you quietly share with me that ever since your father died, you have been feeling his presence from time to time in your bedroom at night, I would let you know that I take that experience of yours quite literally.

This universe has more dimensions than we learned about in school. The eighth house is a portal to many of them. Meanwhile, the Moon is the part of you that is sensitive to everything that slips through the nets of rational, quantitative analysis. With the Moon in the eighth house, you will have some strange experiences. I'd advise you to tell your astrologer and your dearest friends – but maybe don't mention them to a psychiatrist, who might offer you a prescription.

Eighth house fashion, you and I can keep those experiences as our little secret. Let's trust each other that way.

PLUTO IN THE FOURTH HOUSE

Peel away the layers of someone's onion, delving deeper and deeper into the secret world of intimacy with him or her. Sleep with someone for ten years or so, and thus *begin* to get to know him or her. Move under one roof together, dealing with each others' families, along with the bills, where to set the thermostat, and life's inevitable episodes of boredom,

Welcome to the fourth house, the symbol of our most fundamental root connections with the human world. This is where the Sun is found right around astronomical midnight – buried eight thousand miles deep, in other words, on the other side of the world. In parallel fashion, the fourth house resonates with the most deeply-buried roots of our interior labyrinths.

We reveal those roots slowly, if at all – and that revelation is the primal act of intimate surrender. When such surrender happens *mutually*, we have a sweet, comfortable sense of *arriving home* with someone. After that initiation – and many couples do not survive it – we can live together in relative peace, under one roof. We can achieve that fourth house Holy Grail: we can become *family*.

But what if you have Pluto in the fourth house in your natal chart? *The god of hell in the house of the home?*

Don't worry – it can be a lot better than it sounds.

For starters, with Pluto right down there near the midnight point of your chart, we immediately know for sure that deep inside you are a truly Plutonian character, even if other people do not know that about you. You *think psychologically* – and very likely you look at other people with penetrating insight, reflecting on what *underlies* their behaviors and their attitudes. You have canny instincts around human foibles and people's darker motivations. Very simply, as a Plutonian, you *look beneath the surface* – and doing that has not always led to victories in the local popularity contexts.

But no worry: you learned about that reality early in your youth, probably back in your family of origin. This leads us to echo two points about Pluto in the fourth house: number one, you are very Plutonian, and number two, *your Pluto is buried very deeply.*

All of that brings us to the heart of the matter: *for you to experience a sense of arriving home with anyone, your Pluto must be revealed and feel accepted.*

That revelation is fundamental to the meaning of *any* planet in the fourth house – whatever it is, when it is revealed and accepted by another person, we feel connected and safe with him or her. That means that with Pluto there, *anyone who is right for you will never think that you are "too intense."* They will view you as "refreshingly honest" rather than "unnecessarily confrontive." Parity is a requirement: that other person must also reveal her or his Plutonian side to you. Whenever Pluto is involved, the *sharing of secrets* shapes the foundation of any healthy fourth house relationship.

Each one of you will die the faithful custodian of a few of the other one's fears, humiliations, and *peccadillos*.

DAMAGE CONTROL

In the course of my career, I have cleaned up after a lot of astrologers who hurt their clients who had Pluto in the fourth house. The mistake these astrologers made was to miss the brighter side of the planet. It is easy to get caught up in "god of hell" narratives, and therefore to pull out all the nightmare stops as we try to describe the person's early family life.

Astrologer: "You were raised by Satanists who compelled you to perform unnatural acts with animals, right?"

Baffled client: "Uh . . . no. My mom and dad were actually very nice."

Astrologer, thinking to himself: (This person is obviously not ready to deal with the truth.)

That is the cartoon version, of course. But still the assumption that there must have been terrible family secrets, sexual abuse, raging alcoholism, violence, parental infidelities, and so forth is a common theme here, at least in the astrologers accounts. *All of that can be true.* I am not exactly saying the opposite. In fact, I am confident that if we took a random sample of people born with Pluto in the fourth house, we would see a statistical bump in terms of those kinds of horrors.

There are other possibilities though – and leaving them out not only opens the astrologer to making a technical error. *It also puts the astrologer in the ethically dubious position of pointing the finger of guilt at people who are innocent.* As we all know, that is a serious moral lapse, with unpleasant karmic consequences. Even the Bible warns us about "bearing false witness."

Going a little further down this Plutonian road, one of the cheapest tricks in low-rent psychotherapy is to get the client to blame all of his or her personal problems on "bad parenting." Hours can be spent critiquing parental failures without any progress made at all towards taking personal responsibility for the present realities of one's life and thus making any real changes.

If you have Pluto in the fourth house and you were not "raised by Satanists on a goat farm," be wary of such a psychotherapist or such an astrologer.

Again, I do not mean to be insensitive to the genuine reality of damage done to children by awful, failed parents. That is a reality – and as I've said, it is in my experience a little more common to see it among people born with Pluto in the fourth house.

Let's just dial back the drama a bit. What other experiential possibilities might exist with this configuration?

With Pluto in the fourth, as we indicated right at the outset of this section, if we strip away the layers of your onion, we see a person with a very Plutonian interior life. Let's focus that point with a helpful question: *compared to who?* Implicit in all such statements is a comparison to other people. We place them on the human spectrum, in other words. We humans are fast runners *compared to snails*, but not compared to giraffes and cheetahs.

The point is that, with Pluto in the fourth house, there is an excellent chance that you were simply *more Plutonian than the rest of the members of your family.* That makes no one right and no one wrong. That just means that people are different. And there are psychological consequences to that reality for you, even if your mom and dad were sweethearts.

Back in the previous chapter, to illustrate the Moon in Scorpio, I invoked a little scene in the family car. I use it a second time here because it works with Pluto in the fourth house just as well:

Little Johnny: Grandpa is really old. He's going to die soon.

Mom and Dad: That's a terrible thing to say! Grandpa is just fine!

And a year later, grandpa is dead. But no one remembers what Johnny said. *What Johnny himself remembers is that death is one subject that he is not allowed to mention.*

Johnny might have Pluto in the fourth house. *He told the truth as he saw it.* He was not trying to be mean or hurtful. Death simply felt like an important subject to him – fancy that! *But his parents were not ready to deal with it.* Perhaps grandpa is the father of Johnny's father. Perhaps Johnny's father has a plethora of unresolved resentments toward his own dad – and perhaps he even knows that, but he is simply not yet ready to have that conversation.

Johnny just unwittingly hit the tripwire on his father's defenses.

Johnny didn't know he was doing that – he is, after all, only five years old. He certainly did not want to upset anyone. He just asked his parents a question about life. And let's grant Johnny's father some respect too – many of us have issues with our parents that we are just not ready or willing to discuss with them. Maybe our parents are not ready yet either. Maybe they will die before those beasties are put on the table.

Maybe that is just the way of this imperfect human world.

We are condemning no one here, in other words – but we recognize that Johnny, *being the most Plutonian one in his family,* quickly learned that he needed to keep his mouth shut about certain subjects. *When it comes to any positive prospects for future intimacies in his life, this is a wound that must first be healed.* Otherwise part of Johnny will always feel that it must remain hidden. He will not know why, but he will "just know it." His isolation is sealed behind this wall of unresolved trauma, no matter how wise and open his future partner might be.

And imagine that partner's experience. Such a person will constantly feel – correctly – that "Johnny is hiding something, that he is holding something back. In an intimate relationship, can such a perception breed serpents? That is an easy question.

Will Johnny heal this wound? Again, we do not know. All we know for sure is that he can – and much of what he needs in order to accomplish that is help and support coming from someone who "doesn't think he is too intense."

PLUTO IN GLORY

Let's take Pluto in the fourth house down a final road. This one is in the Department of *This Is As Good As It Gets.* And sometimes, in real life, it does actually get this good.

Imagine a family characterized by a high degree of honesty and mutual acceptance. No members are ever shamed for being who they actually are or for expressing themselves honestly. Everyone's place in the family is securely assured – and is not contingent upon living up to anyone else's standards. People feel safe to be themselves. Plutonian honesty pervades every relationship. Hypocrisy is never rewarded, even if that hypocrisy makes someone look like Saint Francis of Assisi. The kids discover their sexuality in an environment that honors and celebrates it. When a younger person is angry at an older person in the family, expressing that anger is accepted – and if appropriate, the older person is willing to apologize.

Pluto in the fourth house can also symbolize growing up in that kind of psychologically honest and supportive domestic environment. If any wounds arise from such a sweet family-of-origin experience, they are probably of the nature of imagining the rest of the world to be the same way. It isn't, of course – and such a child's reflexive honesty will doubtless lead to a few "learning experiences."

My point here is that *families which are Plutonian in a healthy way* also exist. It is a mistake for an astrologer to exclude that possibility and to concentrate exclusively on negative assumptions. Lest I sound ungrounded with these happy assumptions, let me close this section with two true stories.

A very Plutonian friend of mine once told me that he "had heard that people often had trouble raising teenagers." He said that he had experienced no such trouble at all – and he had raised a few. Here was his policy. He told his teenagers that "they could do anything that they wanted to do – but if they did something that he didn't like, *they had to look him straight in the eye and tell him why they were doing it.*"

Brilliant!

He simply called them to their own best Plutonian truth, in other words. He understood that if they were doing something that was truly wrong, that *they would know it too.* Looking him in the eye, there would be no way at all for them to hide that knowledge.

And he let his kids be different than himself.

Here's a second sweet, sad, and ultimately very beautiful story. It is about a client of mine from my North Carolina days. She had Pluto in her fourth house. When her beloved father died, she came to me for counsel. There were no rusty razor blades between them, nothing psychological for us to try to resolve. She just needed some help with her grief. I asked her to tell me a good story about her father. Here is what she told me:

"The first time I menstruated, I guess my mother told him. Thank God he didn't say a single word about it, *but he brought me a dozen red roses.*"

The power of her words hung in the air between us like an angel of light. We just looked at each other. I could not think of a single word to say.

We both soon had tears in our eyes.

That's the signature of a high, healthy Pluto functioning in a family situation. Grace, but no secrets and no place for shame.

NEPTUNE IN THE THIRD HOUSE

With our previous two examples, my aim was to put a Watery planet in a Watery house, just to maximize our in-depth coverage of astrological "wetness." With our next example, let's get a bit more "dehydrated." We will stick with the Water planet, Neptune – but let's place it in the Airy third house. At first blush, this probably sounds like a strange combination of energies. Neptune is mystical and visionary, while the third house tends to be rational and cognitive. How can they ever merge in any kind of harmony and mutual support?

Let's start to unravel this mystery by blowing some of that apparent strangeness out of the sky. Someone is asking you for information about a woman you know. Everything is friendly and there are no ethical boundaries to concern you, so you feel comfortable speaking freely. The person inquires, *"So, would you describe her as a rational, grounded type or kind of . . . you know . . . mystical and flaky about things?"*

The true horror underlying that little anecdote is that in this present world, such a question might sound completely reasonable to a lot of people. "Rational" and "mystical" are often perceived as opposites. Never the twain shall meet. That at least is a common belief.

But of course it is completely incorrect.

For one proof, it has become commonplace lately to point out that science and spirituality seem to be converging. Quantum Mechanics and Relativity sound an awful lot like Vajrayana Buddhism. *The idea that the three-dimensional reality that we perceive equals Reality Itself has completely collapsed in the realm of physics over the past century or so* – and of course such an attitude never existed in metaphysics in the first place, almost by definition. The late, great Carl Sagan – who was Mister Science down to his toes – wrote these words in his book, *The Demon Haunted World*:

> *At the time of writing there are three claims in the ESP field which, in my opinion, deserve serious study: (1) that by thought alone humans can*

(barely) affect random number generators in computers, (2) that people un-
der mild sensory deprivation can receive thoughts or images "projected" at
them, and (3) that young children sometimes report the details of a previ-
ous life, which upon checking turns out to be accurate and which they could
not have known about in any other way than reincarnation.

So is your friend "rational and grounded" or "mystical" – and therefore
presumed to be "flaky?" *The question itself is irrational,* not to mention kind
of unconsciously offensive. It is like asking if someone is a mathematician
or a woman, or a man or someone who can cook and clean a house? Those
questions reflect an antiquated set of assumptions about gender, while the
question on which we are focusing here reflects an equally antiquated set
of assumptions about the universe.

Mysticism is rational.

And that little sermon finally positions us to understand the meaning
of Neptune in the third house. Conversely, if we never achieved that wider
perspective, we could never understand this configuration. With Neptune
in the third house, *a person is born to look at the world through the eyes of*
a mystic. There are lower possibilities too and we will explore them. But
mystical (Neptune) *perception* (the third house) is the essence of the matter.

In conventional astrological practice, the third house is related to *commu-*
nication. It is about language skills and our style of speaking. Back in *The Book*
of Air, we presented a more rigorous three-layered model of the third house.
In a nutshell, *speech must rest upon the foundation of thought, while thought must*
rest upon the foundation of perception. It is really pretty simple: if we never perceive anything, we would have nothing to think about and therefore nothing
to say. And if I say something to you, you might perceive it, think about it,
and respond – and I in turn perceive your response, and soon we are painting
that quintessential third house masterpiece: a good *conversation.*

Underlying all of this is one critical notion: *that perception, rather than*
speech, is the true heart of the third house. Any planet there shapes how we
look at the world. (The same can be said for the sign on the cusp of the third
house, and of course we must consider the sign position of any planet there
too. And where is Mercury? All of that is beyond the scope of this chapter).

A bully scans a crowd of people, looking for the weaker and more vulnerable ones whom he can possibly dominate. Someone of a more saintly
disposition scans the same crowd looking for people in need or in pain.

Meanwhile, someone in the business of selling luxury automobiles sorts out the more prosperous people from those of the working class. Someone hungry for sex edits the crowd for those who are desirable, discounting those who are deemed irrelevant. The psychoanalyst sees walking complexes. Personally, I tend to see "a walking Jupiter" or "the Moon goddess". *And we are all looking at the same crowd.*

We all see the world, not as it is, but rather according to our natures. As Anaïs Nin wrote in her 1961 autobiographical novel, *The Seduction of the Minotaur*, "We don't see things as they are; we see them as we are." (I have been told that the phrase actually has its origins in the Talmud). Saying it that way makes it sound as if this were a problem to be solved. I do not think that is really true. I think you have exactly the chart you need to have, and that includes your third house. *You are wired to pay attention to certain things that you need to see, while filtering out the rest.* That is what planets there naturally do. If you have Neptune in the third house, *what you need to perceive is the ample evidence that this world is more akin to a dream than to a mechanical clock.* With Neptune in the third house . . .

- You think of a friend whom you have not seen for a few years. A week later, he makes contact with you. *You notice that happening; it becomes part of your understanding of how the world actually works.*

- A book falls off a shelf and lands on your foot. You pick it up, open to a passage that you really need to read. *You notice that; it becomes part of your understanding of how the world actually works.*

- You have a lucid dream – you are dreaming, but you know that you are dreaming. *You notice that; it becomes part of your understanding of how the world actually works.*

- You are pretty sure that you just saw a ghost. *You notice that; it becomes part of your understanding of how the world actually works.*

- You attend a lecture. The speaker seems to be surrounded in a halo of light. You do not judge your perception. You just let it be. *You notice that; it becomes part of your understanding of how the world actually works.*

- A Tarot card reading comes true. *You notice that; it becomes part of your understanding of how the world actually works.*

- Sitting in meditation, you experience a transcendent state. *You notice that; it becomes part of your understanding of how the world actually works.*

- You visit a foreign city. It seems inexplicably familiar to you. *You notice that; it becomes part of your understanding of how the world actually works.*
- A psychic tells you that you died in World War One. A year earlier, you had dreamed the same thing. *You notice that; it becomes part of your understanding of how the world actually works.*

Note that in each one of these images, a *perception* arises that supports your *thinking* about the world in a mystical, metaphysical, or transcendent way. That is Neptune's action in the third house. Each such perception presses you toward questioning any merely mechanical, "logical" interpretation of reality – although the word "logical" gets a bit of comical twist here. Much of what is defined as "logical" in this materialistic, existentialist society is just as bogus as taking it as "obvious common sense" that Earth is as flat as a frying pan – even though, hey, it does in fact *look* that way . . .

With Neptune in the third house, the laws of synchronicity demand that these kinds of perceptions will abound in your life. That is not the question; *the question is whether or not you will acknowledge them.* In every one of the little sketches we just listed, there is enormous herd-pressure on you to dismiss your experience as "coincidence" or to otherwise rationalize it away, ignoring its implications.

You wouldn't want to sound flaky, would you?

Maybe the halo around that speaker was just an after-image on your retina. Maybe you saw that foreign city in a movie once. It was just a dream . . . it was only a chance happening . . . the Tarot card reader must have Googled you.

Neptune has a tendency to give things up. Our exhortation here, if you have Neptune in the third house, is simply that y*ou do not give up having faith in the message of your own senses and paranormal experience.*

We have spoken here of two out of the three layers in our third house model: perception and thought. What about *speech*, which finally rests upon those two foundations?

One active expression of third house speech is *teaching*. Add Neptune to the recipe, and we come directly to the idea of the *spiritual* (Neptune) *teacher* (third house). And that role is indeed a high expression of this configuration. Ram Dass had Neptune in the third house. So does the

Dalai Lama. Immediately, let's give the notion that "you were born to be a spiritual teacher" some room to breathe. That role has many legitimate expressions. They range from the obvious (teaching meditation, metaphysics, evolutionary astrology, Bible studies, and so on) down through any use of *communication skills* which draws other people's attention toward anything uplifting. Novels, for example, can lead us to reflect on life's big questions – even trashy novels. So can certain films. Deep psychoanalytic work can do the same thing. So can poetry.

Bottom line, while it is fair and accurate to say that, if you have Neptune in the third house, *you are here on Earth with a soul-intention of becoming a spiritual teacher,* we have to be careful to keep our definition of that term as fluid as possible. We are not all here to be Sunday School teachers – but let's bless them too.

I again think of musician Peter Gabriel, who was also born with Neptune in the third house. I often quote his thoughtful lyrics. Here's a verse from his song, *Solsbury Hill,* which I suspect is significantly autobiographical:

> *Climbing up on Solsbury Hill*
> *I could see the city light.*
> *Wind was blowing, time stood still.*
> *Eagle flew out of the night.*
> *He was something to observe.*
> *Came in close, I heard a voice.*
> *Standing, stretching every nerve*
> *Had to listen, had no choice.*
> *I did not believe the information.*
> *Just had to trust imagination.*

Gabriel did not "believe the information" of his own senses – but instead of rejecting it, he decided that he just had to "trust his imagination." That sounds like a spiritual teaching to me, not to mention a fine summary of his personal experience of Neptune in the third house.

LANGUAGE

Neptune is our interface with the sheer vastness of consciousness itself. That sounds great, but it also presents an enormous practical problem: *trying to find words to describe all of that.*

We have all met academic people who just seemed to be "talking heads" – articulate, even intellectual, but somehow disembodied. It is easy to tune them out. They are like robot voices.

Neptune in the third house presents the opposite problem. Let's get at it with a thought experiment. You are with a congenial group of people who are mostly strangers. The subject of astrology comes up. Someone mentions that you are an astrologer. You get a few skeptical glances and a few glances that are simply curious. Somebody breaks the ice by asking, *"So, you actually believe in that stuff?"*

Where do you even begin? The subject of astrology is vast. Its reality undercuts half of what we are all taught to believe before we leave grammar school. These people who are looking at you for an answer are open-minded, but you are in a social situation. They do not want a two-hour lecture. They probably don't want a lecture at all.

What they want is a simple answer to a question that is not simple.

With Neptune in the third house, dozens of possible answers – many of them very good answers – are suddenly all swimming around in your head, trying to surface in the form of comprehensible speech. Neptune is our interface with the sheer vastness of consciousness itself – and that can create big problems when it comes to streamlining ideas down into plain English. Be careful that you don't say this:

"Uh . . . where to begin? Uh . . . well, astrology just works . . . well, it works for me at least . . . once for example when Neptune was transiting my Ascendant. . . . no, that's too complicated to talk about . . . uh . . . anyway, astrology works because of synchronicity . . . you know, Carl Jung and all of that . . . but it's really old . . . and, uh . . . actually there's different kinds of it . . . and it's not really about the stars . . . except for some kinds of it . . . and the Moon . . . the Moon is a big part of it . . . you have to know the Moon, it's not just about the Sun . . . you know that if you are a Gemini, that means that was where the Sun was, right? . . . People say there's no scientific evidence for it, but that's not really true either . . .

Anyway, I hope all of this is clear. Astrology's actually kind of a big subject."

I had fun writing that mess, but there is a serious point underlying it. *People with Neptune in the third house can actually sound that way.* For them, a great deal of multidimensional, even *inter-dimensional,* material is right there near the surface of consciousness all the time. It can become confusing – and not only for the person speaking, but also for his or her unfortunate listeners.

Each one of the poorly, tentatively expressed, ideas in that chaotic speech *contained the germ of a serious point.* Any single one of them could have been molded into a socially-appropriate and effective response to anyone questioning astrology. But, with Neptune in the third house, *thoughts* (which lie midway between perception and actual speech) are like a bunch of goldfish swimming around in a tank that is getting hotter and hotter by the second. That means that those goldfish are swimming faster and faster. With Neptune in the third house, you really need to learn how to pick a particular fish, catch it, and get it out there in some kind of linear, sensible fashion. This confusion is not a trap from which Neptunian people can never escape – that perpetual state of mental discombobulation is just a weak expression of the archetype. Trying to capture Neptunian reality in words is not an easy thing to do. Obviously, in our little tale here, our astrologer did not win any converts.

Spiritual teachers are always in a similar bind; they need to explain something that in truth can never be understood academically, only *witnessed* and *experienced.*

Let us all bow our heads in gratitude for the handful of lucid teachers who have graced human history from time to time.

Their love was so strong that they did not let the impossible stop them.

PART THREE

THE MOON, PLUTO, MARS, JUPITER, AND NEPTUNE IN THE TWELVE SIGNS AND HOUSES

If we took a strand of your DNA and cloned it, might we create a second you? The verdict is still out on that question, both practically and ethically. My guess is that we could create a physical body that bore a distinct resemblance to yours – but would it actually be "you"? I doubt it. You are more than your chromosomes; you are the sum of your experiences and your influences. Everyone you have ever loved is part of you too.

DNA is just chemistry; you are chemistry with a soul. There is a difference.

Planets, signs, and houses work like chromosomes. They are the "building blocks of life," but they are not life itself. They are not even human. To bring them truly alive, they need to bubble and gurgle together in your head, while something eternal and beyond the realm of astrology animates them.

On its own, Pluto is not meaningless – we have already said much about it that was meaningful. But to give Pluto human meaning, we need to enliven it with a sign and let it express itself through a house. Then we have to let it dance with the rest of the planets, and finally, we need to hand the whole seething mechanism over to you and see what you can do with it.

There are five "Water" planets, along with twelve signs, and twelve houses – that represents a lot of possible combinations. In the previous chapters, we have explored the process of how we tie a planet to a specific sign or house. In the next few chapters, I am hoping to support that integrative process further by spelling out, one by one, the core ideas that underlie each one of these possible configurations.

My prayer is that these paragraphs provide you with an interpretive jump-start rather than short-circuiting your own creativity. They are, in essence, the foundational thoughts and ideas that arise in my own mind when I first see any of these configurations in anyone's chart. I have, for example, a sense of what it means for someone to have the Sun in Gemini or the Moon in the twelfth house. But what if the Moon squares that person's Gemini Sun?

Figuring that out is where the fun – and the art – begins . . .

Some of the material in the next six chapters appears in exactly the same form in The Book of Fire. *That is because Mars and Jupiter rule Fire signs as well as two of the Water signs that we are investigating in this volume. What I wrote in that first book about Mars in Gemini , for example, remains the same and equally relevant in this volume. Once again, I apologize for "making you buy the same pages twice" – but it would feel even worse to leave* The Book of Water *incomplete.*

Chapters ten and thirteen contain fresh, never-before-seen, material about Pluto in each sign and house. The same goes for Neptune in chapters eleven and fourteen. Our next step is a fresh one as well – let's fly ourselves to the Moon.

9

THE MOON IN THE TWELVE SIGNS

THE MOON IN ARIES

The Evolutionary Goal: In this lifetime, I resolve to press toward a point where I never allow fearful reflexes to stand between me and any experience that I believe might feed my soul. I may be afraid, but I will not panic – that at least is my goal.

My Instinctual Tools: I am cogent and clear under pressure. I can make good decisions when the chips are down. I know how to survive. I can improvise. I have a relative immunity to panicking. I can do battle if I have to; I may not want to, but I am capable.

The Secret of Happiness: To be happy, I need to feel that I am pushing myself towards the far limits of my own excellence. I need to feel the dignity of the Warrior archetype in myself – that I am defending those I love, that I am living in an honorable way, that I am doing something worth doing with my life. I need to feel a high degree of autonomy and independence. I do not appreciate being told what to do. It helps me to feel as if I am "the best" at something.

The Mood of My Life: I have a sense of constant urgency, even of emergency – it is not fear exactly, but rather something more like a feeling of constantly needing to rise to a challenge. While I do not revel in defeating anyone, I do aim to win. An underlying sense of stress is my constant companion.

The Attitudinal Dead End: I can wallow in resentments. I can harbor anger internally – or vent it destructively and unfairly. I can turn rage on myself. I can interpret the world in a fearful, paranoid, overly competitive fashion.

THE MOON IN TAURUS

The Evolutionary Goal: I resolve to try to calm down and to remain quietly, serenely centered no matter what happens. I will not sweat the small stuff. I resolve to fully inhabit my physical body and avail myself of the wisdom of all of its built-in instincts. I will learn to trust my guts. I aim to find inner silence in this lifetime – and to listen to it very carefully.

My Instinctual Tools: I can quickly and accurately detect insincerity, phoniness, and heart-numbing mental hyperactivity in anyone. I can smell a liar or a con artist a mile away. I can cut through a haze of words straight into the human essentials of any situation. I can stay grounded when others are tying themselves in knots.

The Secret of Happiness: To be happy, it helps me enormously to find time to work with my hands using physical materials that come from the earth. I also benefit a lot from quiet time. *Dolce far niente*, as the Italians say – sometimes it is sweet just to do nothing. Music makes me happy; time spent in nature makes me happy; good food shared with familiar faces makes me happy. As it says in the old hymn, it is a gift to be simple – I really understand that, and I strive to live that way.

The Mood of My Life: Let's keep everything as grounded and as simple as possible. Let's stay real and authentic in the moment. I am wary of fads and hyperbole. I prepare in practical ways for life's eventualities, but I do not add unnecessary worry to the mix. I relax and I try to live in the here and now. In general, my mood is patient – but I am impatient with the yackety-yack of people's overheated theories, especially when they are irreconcilable with obvious, simple truths.

The Attitudinal Dead End: I can be stubborn and set in my ways to the point of being closed-minded and impervious to evolutionary possibilities. I can find it unbelievable that another person might be right when I myself was wrong. I can become predictable.

THE MOON IN GEMINI

The Evolutionary Goal: I resolve to keep a youthful, open-minded, and curious attitude toward life until the end. I will even view my death as "interesting" and see it as a chance to learn something new. I resolve to accept the fact that whatever I see or know, the truth is beyond my current understanding. I resolve to learn how to express the contents of my heart in clarion-clear language. Rather than blaming other people for not grasping what I am saying, I resolve to take personal responsibility for people understanding me; I will develop the communicative skills which support it.

My Instinctual Tools: I can learn anything if I apply myself, and I experience joy in applying myself to tasks of learning that way. I adapt easily to surprise and to the unexpected. I can multitask. I am blessed with language skills and I am also a good listener. Without even trying, I know how to get people to open up verbally to me.

The Secret of Happiness: To be happy, I need lots of variety and mental stimulation in my life. Boredom is not good for me, even if it sneaks up on me disguised as maturity or responsibility or some other virtue. It is a great support for me to be surrounded by interesting people who can speak from their hearts and who themselves are interested in life.

The Mood of My Life: My reflexive emotional attitude is one of curiosity and engagement with whatever arises, especially if it is fresh and new. I feel as if I am trying to pack the experience of several lifetimes into one life. I am restless, and I do not have a problem with that.

The Attitudinal Dead End: I can hide from hard truths behind a wall of words, rationalizing and dancing away from realities whose existence I do not want to admit. I can work myself up into a lather of nervous agitation and activity, all as a way of escaping the scary places in my own heart.

THE MOON IN CANCER

The Evolutionary Goal: I resolve to feel whatever I feel without defenses, rationalizations, or editing. I will nurture myself, recognizing the nature of my own woundedness. In that self-healing process, I will be patient and gentle with myself. I do not need to explain myself. I will practice kindness toward all other beings, human, animal, or in spirit-form. I resolve to approach the pinnacle of compassionate engagement with all life.

My Instinctual Tools: I can quickly sense the presence and nature of hurt in myself and others. I have the instincts of a healer – and a healer not just of bodies, but of minds and hearts as well. I know how to nurture. I know how to offer genuine comfort. I am a good friend.

The Secret of Happiness: To be happy, I need quiet time to myself, away from the noise and distraction of the world. It really helps me to have a home I love and in which I feel safe and secure. Similarly, it helps me to have "a family", at least in some sense of that word – that means other beings upon whom I can count completely, whether they have two feet or four.

The Mood of My Life: My reflexive emotional attitude is one of slightly worried caring and concern – and a little worry only means that I am paying attention to where life's jagged edges and emotional minefields might lie. I know that they are real; I guard and nurture my sensitivity skillfully by being wary of them.

The Attitudinal Dead End: I can be excessively self-protective, to the point that I am only halfway here in this world. Risk can never be entirely avoided unless I entirely avoid life. In the same way, I can be protective of others whom I love to the point that I suffocate them or stand between them and lessons which they really need to learn.

THE MOON IN LEO

The Evolutionary Goal: I resolve to conquer my fear of being emotionally vulnerable or of looking silly. Others probably do not see that frightened part of me, but I acknowledge it and resolve to get past it by risking the full expression of my heart and soul and letting the chips fall where they may when I do that.

My Instinctual Tools: I am an inherently creative person, at least in some sense of the word. By instinct, I can perform and hold people's attention – maybe or maybe not literally in front of an audience, but in some fashion. I will identify that tool and I will employ it. Before I die, others will know what I hold to be beautiful or sacred. I will have expressed it.

The Secret of Happiness: To be happy, I need applause and appreciation. That is not out of any kind of insecurity or egoism, but rather because it completes a healing loop in my heart. Here is the map of that loop: I risk self-expression; others respond positively; my feeling of "risk" is lessened; vulnerable self-expression becomes easier – and I am happier for it.

The Mood of My Life: My reflexive emotional attitude is one of constantly living as if I were on the wings of the stage and about to step out in front of a huge crowd. I feel like I have butterflies in my stomach, but I appear to be supernaturally confident anyway. I feel as if I need to prove myself that way again and again.

The Attitudinal Dead End: I can be self-protective to the point of crippling my own evolution, keeping up appearances rather than being sincere and truly present. When I slip into that error, I take on an authoritarian "royal" vibration of stability and false well-being that belies the fearful insecurity which I am actually feeling.

THE MOON IN VIRGO

The Evolutionary Goal: I resolve to find a way to be of meaningful service toward other people in this lifetime, and thus attain the dignity of a job well done. I will polish and develop my inborn skills, constantly pressing them in the direction of perfection. Similarly, I resolve to work on myself, always acknowledging the humble realities of my evolutionary predicament, but never slipping into the sinkhole of losing faith in myself or crippling myself with self-criticism.

My Instinctual Tools: I was born with the seeds of a specific talent which can make a difference in other people's lives. I have a good instinct for how to identify that skill set and bring it fully online. I can recognize my teachers and mentors, and I am humble enough to know how to receive their gifts. I am precise. I can think critically without descending into reflexive negativity.

The Secret of Happiness: To be happy, I must find work that truly matters. On that road, I find joy in the company of people who can guide me because they are a few steps ahead of me. I will judge myself – but never against the standard of perfection, only against the standard of the intensity of my own evolutionary effort.

The Mood of My Life: My reflexive emotional attitude is one of an insecurity-driven concern over details and practical worries. That is not because I am neurotic; it is because I am careful and responsible. I ask a lot of myself. I do not rest on my laurels, but instead I feel moved toward fresh efforts. I am, above all, realistic.

The Attitudinal Dead End: I can be overly hard on myself to the point that I lose faith in myself. If that happens, I run out of steam in my own journey – and I quickly begin to project my own self-criticism onto other people. I become picky and chronically dissatisfied.

THE MOON IN LIBRA

The Evolutionary Goal: I resolve to prioritize the peacefulness of my soul above all other motivations in this lifetime. I recognize that serenity of spirit is equal in evolutionary value to any kind of intellectual insight. I choose my relationships, my beliefs, and my environment in the light of that priority. Grace is my goal.

My Instinctual Tools: I can immerse my senses in beauty, whether it is the beauty of nature or the beauty that human beings create. I can surrender to it in such a way that I breathe out my accumulated tensions. I can recognize my soul-friends and I know how to take comfort in their presence. I see other people as they are, which is to say, as different from me. I don't say, "if I were you . . ." because I know that I am not. By instinct, I see both sides of every question.

The Secret of Happiness: To be happy, I need gracefulness in my life. That means aesthetic experience and a harmonious environment – but above all, it means companionable people with whom I share affection, mutual respect, and appreciation. Time spent with them is fundamental to my happiness and well-being.

The Mood of My Life: My reflexive emotional attitude is that of an artist, even if I am not actively creative . . . although I may be that too. Taste, balance, and beauty mean a lot to me. My attitude is live and let live. One might call my mood "diplomatic," so long as that word does not imply phoniness or insincerity, but rather respect and a genuine desire to meet people in the middle.

The Attitudinal Dead End: I can be so intent on maintaining harmony in my various relationships that my own soul somehow gets lost in the mix. My actual needs and my own edgy places do not always please other people. I must remember to make sure that a commitment to grace does not eclipse my authenticity.

THE MOON IN SCORPIO

The Evolutionary Goal: I resolve to be true to my own heart no matter where it leads me. I will let myself feel anything and everything, no matter how dark or taboo it might be, so long as it rises up naturally within me. I sometimes choose to edit my *behavior* – but I resolve never to silence my own inner dialog with my authentic emotional states, perceptions, and needs.

My Instinctual Tools: I can face any kind of truth within myself without fainting or slipping into denial and rationalization. I am skillful at looking beneath the surface of other people's behavior. I can see the true story behind their "official" story in very much the same way as a good psychoanalyst does. I have the skills and instincts of a skillful detective. I am good to have around in any kind of emotional crisis; I can handle it when people express strong emotions.

The Secret of Happiness: To be happy, I need a feeling of authenticity and realness in my primary relationships. I need to feel connected in a naked, heart-to-heart kind of way with other people. It feels good to me to be connected with the invisible realms – spirits, God, higher powers, angels, whatever I might call them. To do that successfully, I need time alone. One secret of happiness for me is the realization that I am not required to be happy all the time.

The Mood of My Life: My reflexive emotional attitude is intense, psychological, even suspicious – and suspicion only means that I am profoundly aware that everyone has secrets and everyone has a darker side. What people do not understand about me is that my suspicious mood is not really judgmental or negative. It is simply that I see a lot of truth which other people often do not accept – truths which often make people so nervous that they deny the reality of what is actually going on.

The Attitudinal Dead End: I can do a tailspin down into psychological and emotional depths from which I do not know how to escape. Lacking deeper, balancing connections with a handful of soul-friends, I could lose balance. I could get deeper a lot faster than I could handle, slipping into isolation and brooding moodiness.

THE MOON IN SAGITTARIUS

The Evolutionary Goal: I resolve to devote my life to a quest for meaning and higher purpose. I resolve to deepen my understanding of the laws of the universe and try to align my behavior as best I can with those principles. I resolve to live a life in which I positively believe, trusting my own path – and trusting the higher powers that are watching over me.

My Instinctual Tools: I can adapt to alien cultures and new environments. I can connect the dots of experience and weave them into broad principles of understanding – I am, in other words, an instinctual philosopher. The wider my experience, the wiser I will become.

The Secret of Happiness: To be happy, my life must be adventurous. Thrills alone are not the point – the point is richness and variety of experience itself, which is evolutionary dynamite for me. I learn from living. To be happy, I cannot be afraid of life. Feeling that I am walking my talk gives me a sense of sustained wellbeing. It boils down to knowing that I am on the right path and that I have not let mere practicality get in the way of learning what my life is really all about.

The Mood of My Life: My reflexive emotional attitude is one of damn-the-torpedoes enthusiasm for experience. "Yes" comes more easily to me than "no." I am not afraid of making mistakes; I embrace them without shame or fear, knowing that everything I do, whether it turns out well or poorly, is ultimately grist for the mill of my own evolution – so long as what I do is aligned with my highest principles.

The Attitudinal Dead End: I can be opinionated. My need to be right – or to not be "made wrong" by anyone – can block me from learning anything new. In my zeal to defend my freedom, I can fail to commit to paths in life that could teach me what I have actually incarnated in order to learn.

THE MOON IN CAPRICORN

The Evolutionary Goal: I resolve to achieve some Great Work in this lifetime. When it is complete, it will probably be visible to other people, although it is possible that it might be purely an internal, spiritual accomplishment. If it is the latter, then I myself will be the Great Work and that is what will be visible. I will reach the far limits of what I am capable of doing. I will attain excellence in some area of life that is meaningful and engaging to me. I will make myself proud as I look back on my years in this world and on what I have accomplished.

My Instinctual Tools: I can put emotions, fears, and questions aside and simply bear down on a task. I can be self-sustaining too – I do not need applause or cheerleaders. I have the instincts of an Elder, whatever my current age. Solitude does not frighten me; in fact, it feeds me. I can persist where others have given up. If I have to, I can make one can of beans last for a week.

The Secret of Happiness: To be happy, I need to undertake projects that are actually worthy of me. I need to always be making an effort, accomplishing something which I deem to be worthwhile. Having a vivid sense of *compelling purpose* in my life is essential to my feeling good. At a simpler level, I also benefit from having quiet time to myself, away from everybody.

The Mood of My Life: My reflexive emotional attitude is one of endless effort, endless responsibility, and interminable lists of things that must be done. I am not "out of touch with my feelings." I just refuse to allow feelings to run my life. An attitude of quiet self-sufficiency and endless productivity permeates my days.

The Attitudinal Dead End: I can be time-serving and long-suffering in such a way that I live a life of pointless drudgery. I can hang from a cross when I do not have to. I can accept responsibilities that are not truly mine. Even with people around me, I can cast a spell of loneliness on my life by holding the expression of my own heart in check.

THE MOON IN AQUARIUS

The Evolutionary Goal: I resolve to align my biographical life with the authentic promptings of my own heart, even if that makes me look weird or threatening to other people. I will free myself from the monkey-need to be accepted and approved of by everyone. I resolve to truly *lead* my own life, following my soul wherever it guides me. I do not need anyone to tell me that I am on my correct path; I know it myself when I see it.

My Instinctual Tools: I recognize the pitfalls of "group think" even when no one else can. I have an instinctive suspicion of the herd instinct. I do not follow leaders. I sense that much of what is taken to be evidence of sanity and normalcy in this world is in fact insane. I question what "everybody knows." I question authority. When someone tells me to turn right, my eyes turn instinctively to the left.

The Secret of Happiness: To be happy, I need to follow my heart wherever it leads me, even when everyone is hellbent on correcting me or saving me from myself. When people imply that my feelings "are not working right," I need to realize that what they are saying is simply that my heart is not following their familiar script. That script may be fine and natural for them – but for me, to follow it would be a disaster.

The Mood of My Life: My reflexive emotional attitude is independent, irreverent of authority, even rebellious. Others can live as they want – I have no problem with that. Just don't try to tell me how to live my life. Your judgment of me does not concern me; your opinion of me is none of my business.

The Attitudinal Dead End: I can become detached and aloof, even cynical, as a way of coping with the social realities of the world. The problem with that defense is that it costs me the right actually to live the life I was born to live. Instead of following my heart, I look heavenward and mutter, "*whatever . . .*"

THE MOON IN PISCES

The Evolutionary Goal: I resolve simply to prioritize the advancement of my spiritual life over all other concerns in this lifetime. I can love other people; I can live my outward life competently – but nothing will stand between me and what I know is of ultimate centrality, and that is what I will take with me when I leave this world. My soul has priority over everything else.

My Instinctual Tools: I have a natural sensitivity to the presence of other dimensions; I can actually feel them. Some people might call that "faith," but for me it is something closer to direct experience. When I close my eyes, I am in a world that feels deeper and vaster than this material one. Call it spirituality, call it visionary imagination – but whatever we call it, those kinds of perceptions open up naturally in me, by instinct.

The Secret of Happiness: To be happy, I need some quiet time alone every day – time in which I let go of my habitual identity and directly experience the natural spaciousness which is the deeper essence of my being. To be happy, I need to feel that I am actively advancing in this spiritual way, feeding my soul's journey.

The Mood of My Life: My reflexive emotional attitude is one of exaggerated sensitivity at every level. It is not that I exaggerate anything intentionally. This level of sensitivity arises spontaneously in me. It is my responsibility to protect it, nurture it and care for it. Much of the mood of my life derives from that overriding necessity. One of the qualities that arises from it is a sense of compassion for everyone else's sensitivity. Another quality is a mood of *humor* – of "getting the joke" about the various trivial pursuits that animate most people's lives.

The Attitudinal Dead End: If I fail to take care of my soul, I can become spacey, vague, and unformed. An attitude of passivity and resignation can replace the natural drive toward active evolution in me. I can prioritize achieving numbness over the exploration of the pathways my own sensitivity has opened up before me.

10

PLUTO AND MARS IN THE TWELVE SIGNS

*F*or the sake of completeness, I want to look at Pluto in all twelve signs de-spite its two and a half century orbital path. There are no living examples of some of these configurations, but we can of course do some fact-checking with historical examples. Thinking of Pluto in Aries for example brings us to George Armstrong Custer and Sitting Bull, both born with Pluto in that sign. As you read about that configuration, think of the Battle of Little Big Horn, the mas-sive Native American victory that day, its consequences for all concerned, and the karmic residue all of that nightmarish bloodshed left in its wake. All that is one possibility for what happens when "the god of hell" sits in the sign of the warrior. Read on; you will see that there are other possibilities too.

PLUTO IN ARIES

The Intended Evolutionary Breakthrough: I resolve to liberate myself from the distorting grip of fear and rage. I resolve to reclaim the courage to live my life as if I were safe in this world, so I could do as I please and trust my whims without constantly looking over my shoulder for dangers and antagonists.

The Wounding Truth That Must Be Faced – And Felt: I recognize and accept the fact that in prior lifetimes I was subjected to extraordinary levels of stress. Contact with warfare is at least a good illustration, and maybe even literally true. My soul has been brutalized or terrorized, and I acknowledge that I am in recovery from that trauma. Because of that wound, I will wrestle with pulses of rage or fear which I do not understand. I resolve to be careful about confusing the past with the present.

The Prize: If I succeed in this healing process, I recover my passion for being alive. I become genuinely happy to be in this body and in this world. My libido increases and becomes more aligned with my soul, as does my ability to relax and to accept loving support. I feel less stress – and far less as if I were always alone and on my own.

The Price of Failure: I am scared for no visible reason or angry in the face of no visible provocation. I act on those feelings in ways that are self-destructive as well as harmful to others. I create unnecessary trouble and conflict. I pick fights – or run away from people who only want to help me.

PLUTO IN TAURUS

The Intended Evolutionary Breakthrough: I resolve to liberate myself from the distorting grip of social conformity, predictability, and the kind of enforced tedium which arises from cultural rigidity and judgment. I will learn to trust the messages of my physical body. Examples: a "bad feeling in my stomach" about a choice I am about to make, someone who "just does not smell right" to me, sexual attractions or their opposite. I am recovering my relationship with my instinctual self.

The Wounding Truth That Must Be Faced – And Felt: I recognize and accept the fact that in prior lifetimes I was pressed into being part of a social herd, compelled to be "normal" in a situation where that kind of normalcy made my life meaningless and mechanical. For that reason, I was born into this life ready to explode. I meditate upon the difference between a bomb and a rocket: the only real distinction is that the rocket has a sense of direction. I resolve to become that rocket.

The Prize: If I succeed in this healing process, I experience a kind of freedom and personal empowerment that shocks me with its physical energy. My body feels stronger. My horizons of possibility in life widen exponentially. I feel like a healthy wild animal set free, finally, from a cage in a zoo where it had paced back and forth for years.

The Price of Failure: I volunteer for slavery. I do not think of it that way, nor do I realize that I am doing it. As I look at my life, I realize that very little in it arose from any real choice, desire, or soul-intention on my part. I have only played an assigned role.

PLUTO IN GEMINI

The Intended Evolutionary Breakthrough: I resolve to liberate myself from the distorting grip of "polite" societal controls on my speech and my thoughts. In this lifetime, I will first deepen my ability to look at the edgy truths of human existence clearly and honestly. Secondly, I resolve to claim my right to say what I see. I will learn to speak truthfully and directly, and I will do so without slipping into unnecessary destructiveness.

The Wounding Truth That Must Be Faced – And Felt: I recognize and accept the fact that in prior lifetimes I was simply silenced. This silencing may have been brutal, even lethal. But it may have taken a second form: religious and social training, which conditioned me to interpret life according to a dogma rather than trusting my own senses – and thus finding my own natural voice.

The Prize: If I succeed in this healing process, I become a truth-teller. I turn into an honest witness to life's reality, and I become increasingly incisive and penetrating in my speech – and helpful to those who are ready to hear about what is actually real and what is actually happening.

The Price of Failure: I find myself defending things in which I do not actually believe. I may not even know that I am doing that. Unresolved anger at having been silenced leads me to silence others. My tongue becomes unnecessarily sharp. Sarcasm corrupts my compassion. Perhaps I become a master of the kind of humor that makes some people laugh, while leaving others bleeding.

PLUTO IN CANCER

The Intended Evolutionary Breakthrough: I resolve to liberate myself from the suffocating grip of family pressures. I will see my life as an independent, internal psychological quest, and thereby define it according to the promptings of my own soul rather than by the standards of whose child I am, or whose mate, or whose parent. I do not reject family ties or demonize them – I simply resolve not to be steam-rollered by those kinds of external roles and expectations.

The Wounding Truth That Must Be Faced – And Felt: I recognize and accept the fact that in prior lifetimes my freedom was somehow trodden under foot by family dynamics. I may, for one example, have just been "junior" or just been "mom." Equally, I may have been the head of a family facing some harsh reality – and my life was consumed by the moral imperative to keep my people protected and alive. Either way, my own soul was eclipsed from expression. My life had nothing to do with me.

The Prize: If I succeed in this healing process, I sense how to create meaningful, vibrant family ties – ties which enhance my life rather than subtracting from it. Honesty and soul-transparency are shared in the context of unconditional family support – support which flows in all directions, not just from myself toward others. I re-vivify my sense of the potential joy that comes from life-long, committed relationships.

The Price of Failure: I am blunted in my self-expression and my spiritual explorations in this life by letting myself become entangled in a spiderweb of other people's needs and projections. I gaze longingly out of my window, looking at streets I will never wander, wondering where they might lead me, if only I were free . . .

PLUTO IN LEO

The Intended Evolutionary Breakthrough: I resolve to liberate myself from the distorting grip of public acclaim or the need to maintain "a certain appearance." I will learn to stand naked, revealing myself emotionally, as I actually am, without shame or self-consciousness. I will reclaim my ability to be imperfect and fully human, without being limited by concern regarding my vanishing need to impress anyone else with my "status" in terms of spirituality, finances, social position, "coolness," or whatever.

The Wounding Truth That Must Be Faced – And Felt: I recognize and accept the fact that in prior lifetimes I often found myself in a social position which others interpreted as advantaged. They projected some manner of "star quality" or "luck" or "power" onto me. Meanwhile, deep inside of myself, I felt frightened, unworthy, and in danger of losing my privileges if I ever once allowed my mask to slip.

The Prize: If I succeed in this healing process, I can actually just relax and be myself. People who say they love me will love me for who I actually am. There is nothing that I need to prove, no one whom I need to impress with my performance. I liberate myself from the need to be known, to be on center stage, or to position myself above anyone else.

The Price of Failure: I live a fake life. I keep one eye on the audience at all times, adjusting my behaviors according to their reactions. I live for reviews. I hunger after some golden city on the hill, which does not actually exist, and so I never get there. I cannot walk past a mirror without checking myself out.

PLUTO IN VIRGO

The Intended Evolutionary Breakthrough: I resolve to liberate myself from the distorting grip of self-judgment, shame, and humiliation. In this lifetime, I will learn to truly love myself unconditionally. This does not mean that I will become lazy or unmotivated – only that from now on, I will judge myself only by the standard of my effort, not by anyone else's standards, and certainly not against the unreachable standard of perfection. Reflecting this advancing self-acceptance, I resolve to find work that truly matters to me and is worthy of me.

The Wounding Truth That Must Be Faced – And Felt: I recognize and accept the fact that in prior lifetimes I was wounded by a society or situation in which I was viewed with contempt or simply treated dismissively. Shame was thrust upon me. I internalized that unfair humiliation and was reborn carrying it within myself.

The Prize: If I succeed in this healing process, I walk this earth like a king or a queen. I will not become haughty, but I will feel confident of my own worth and nourish an expectation that I will be treated accordingly. I will be valued and honored for my skill in some area that is meaningful to me. I will be comfortable in my physical body – not vain, but reflexively self-accepting of my physical form, however I might look.

The Price of Failure: If I fail, I will fall far short of fulfilling my actual potential in this life. I will sabotage myself psychologically, intimately, and professionally. I will hurt myself; perhaps I will hurt my own body in some way, as I unconsciously and compulsively act out the poison which others fed me lifetimes ago.

PLUTO IN LIBRA

The Intended Evolutionary Breakthrough: I resolve to liberate myself from the distorting grip of deeply embedded, unspoken cultural assumptions about the way human partnerships are meant to work. If I choose to establish that kind of commitment with another human being, it will be our own independent masterpiece and it will reflect our own values. I resolve never to let any serious relationship of mine slip into "sleepy niceness," but instead to remain naked and alive to each other, whatever emotional perils such a promise might create.

The Wounding Truth That Must Be Faced – And Felt: I recognize and accept the fact that in prior lifetimes I was damaged by conventional assumptions about intimacy and marriage. Perhaps I was constrained from honest self-expression by traditional gender roles or patriarchal beliefs. One way or another, I became adapted to being lonely even though I appeared to be in a relationship.

The Prize: If I succeed in this healing process, I can experience a vibrant, active, lasting sense of genuine connection with another human being or two. I learn the secrets of *sustainable passion.* I create a working balance between naked truthfulness and the need for kindness, support, and tenderness. I do not need to choose between those two poles; I can learn to walk that tightrope, and have both of them.

The Price of Failure: If I fail, my life will be shaped by an unconscious fear of being trapped in a dysfunctional relationship. That fear can manifest in either of two ways. The first is that I develop an aversion to the kinds of people who could actually be good for me; I barely even notice them, and thus guarantee a life of intimate frustration and hurt. The second possibility is that I simply, once again, find myself caught up in an unsatisfying bond, and see no way to escape it.

PLUTO IN SCORPIO

The Intended Evolutionary Breakthrough: I resolve to liberate myself from the distorting grip of the polite denial of almost everything that is actually real and true in life. I reject the package of lies that we are taught to recite almost from birth – lies about how we actually feel, lies about sex, lies about family love. I will not be afraid to "look the devil straight in the eye" in this lifetime. My ideal is to never have to lie about anything ever again.

The Wounding Truth That Must Be Faced – And Felt: I recognize and accept the fact that in prior lifetimes I experienced some of the darkest possibilities that human existence has to offer. I was wounded by unthinkable nightmares. I have experienced human depravity. I learned the hard way that "the good guys do not always win." The heart of the matter – the truth that I must face squarely – is that I am still wounded by those bitter poisons.

The Prize: If I succeed in this healing process, I recover lightness in my being. I learn again how to trust life's sweetness and beauty. Bitterness and resentment no longer flavor my understanding of everything I see and everyone I meet.

The Price of Failure: As I age, I am increasingly defined by a dark or tragic interpretation of human existence. My negativity repels people, especially younger ones. They avoid me; soon I become brooding and isolated, while my spirit becomes inextricably fused with a bleak ego that cannot see beyond itself.

PLUTO IN SAGITTARIUS

The Intended Evolutionary Breakthrough: I resolve to liberate myself from the distorting grip of the culture into which I was born. I will break the stranglehold of my socialization. I do not need to condemn my roots – only to recognize that my aim is to experience life through a far wider and more universal lens, freed from the parochial, arbitrary, or religious interpretations in which I was trained. I resolve to liberate myself from the gravitational field of believing "what everybody knows." I will move beyond the deadening framework of consensual reality. My life will be a quest for the truth that lies beyond anyone's sermons about the nature of truth.

The Wounding Truth That Must Be Faced – And Felt: I recognize and accept the fact that in prior lifetimes I was hurt by other people's dogma. Opinions were fed to me; perhaps I was bamboozled into believing them, or perhaps I was beaten down into acquiescence. Either way, my freedom of thought was severely constrained. In this lifetime, let me be free from the grip of rigid thinking and any kind of orthodoxy, be it religious, social, or political.

The Prize: If I succeed in this healing process, my life becomes a genuine quest for truth. It will probably carry me into many adventures that involve me immersing myself in other cultures, other communities, and therefore in some radically different perspectives on life. Under these cross-cultural stresses, my sense of what is right and what is wrong will mature. I will become a "universal earthling" rather than a representative of my tribal roots.

The Price of Failure: If I fail, I slip unknowingly into a rigid, narrow interpretation of reality – one that, without my understanding of what was happening to me, was fed to me by other people before I was old enough to see what was happening. I become fearful and judgmental regarding any people or ideas that diverge too far from my narrow comfort zone. Annoyingly, I feel compelled to make converts to my own view of things, be those views philosophical, political or aesthetic – and thus unwittingly reveal my underlying insecurity about that view.

PLUTO IN CAPRICORN

The Intended Evolutionary Breakthrough: I resolve to liberate myself from the distorting grip of anyone's arbitrary sense of morality, especially when such people attempt to enforce their rules and values on me. I will live a life of which I am proud and I will strive to walk my talk – but I refuse to allow other people's judgments to grab the moral steering wheel of my life. I reject responsibilities that others try to thrust upon me. I do not let them get in the way of the Great Work of finding and fulfilling my own path. I choose my own responsibilities and I reject the rest.

The Wounding Truth That Must Be Faced – And Felt: I recognize and accept the fact that in prior lifetimes I was so defined by duty that it damaged me. Perhaps these duties were quite real, and it reflected virtue in me that I did not shirk them – I took care of my family, for example, or I died for my country. Perhaps these duties were toxic, but I had been tricked into internalizing them – "God has chosen you to charge these machine guns." Under that kind of pressure, I got too good at not listening to my own heart or taking my own needs, instincts, and sense of self-preservation seriously.

The Prize: If I succeed in this healing process, I free my energy from wasteful, fruitless paths pressed on me by conventional social assumptions about what is right and what is wrong. I use that energy instead to achieve acts of heroic self-discipline which I have chosen freely based on the promptings of my own soul. Perhaps I feed hungry children somewhere.

Perhaps I write a novel of which I am proud. Perhaps I use this energy to learn how to play the piano. The point is that I use as I please, according to my own values.

The Price of Failure: I effectively become a slave. I may not look that way; I may appear to be successful or prosperous, even righteous. But in my heart I am faced with the reality of living a life for which other people wrote the script. There is no sweetness in my tiredness at the end of a day, and no real sense of accomplishment.

PLUTO IN AQUARIUS

The Intended Evolutionary Breakthrough: I resolve to liberate myself from the distorting grip of social conditioning and consensual reality. I become skillful at recognizing – and dodging – people who have a plan for me, even ones who sincerely believe that they only want what is best for me. I realize that I alone truly know where my path lies. I resolve to clear away the cultural debris that stands between me and the recognition of that path, and then I resolve to unswervingly follow it regardless of anyone else's judgments, fears, or exhortations.

The Wounding Truth That Must Be Faced – And Felt: I recognize and accept the fact that in prior lifetimes I was constrained – in a sense, *tricked* – into giving up my natural right to autonomy and thinking for myself. Before I knew what was happening, I had been painted into a corner, hedged about by social expectations and customs. To survive that situation, I became somewhat dissociated and aloof, watching the train wreck of my life from a "safe distance" – except it wasn't safe. In this lifetime, I resolve to regain my ability to be fully present and to do as I please.

The Prize: If I succeed in this healing process, a certain quality of genius arises in me – and not only genius, but also the passion to pursue it. Genius, in this sense, does not mean that I will be remembered in future history books; only that I am capable of creating some truly unique insights and perspectives. As I do that, pursuing their expression brings me fully back into the human world, finally revealed in my true nature.

The Price of Failure: I become fixed in a state of cold distance from society. At some fundamental level, I cease to care about anyone or anything very deeply. I am impregnably defended against hurt – but that means that I am defended against life as well.

PLUTO IN PISCES

The Intended Evolutionary Breakthrough: I resolve to liberate myself from the distorting grip of an overdose of "white light" on my spiritual path – and by "white light," I mean the denial of darkness and shadow. I will do my inner psychological work in a spirit of humility and radical honesty with myself. I will not flinch from frightening or embarrassing realizations. I promise myself that I will not "enter Enlightenment" until the entirety of my psyche is ready to come along for the ride. I will not compartmentalize myself, in other words. In this lifetime, I resolve to achieve a fusion of true spirituality and hard-hitting psychological insight.

The Wounding Truth That Must Be Faced – And Felt: I recognize and accept the fact that in prior lifetimes I was impacted by religious or spiritual teachings characterized by the avoidance of anything that was threatening, dark, or "too human." There was too much emphasis on "avoiding sin," and not enough emphasis on truthfulness and self-acceptance. Very likely, my sexuality was constrained, whitewashed, or even demonized. Lip service was paid to truth – but being truthful about my needs and feelings was viewed as evidence of a lower state of evolution. Some of these reflexes still exist in me; I resolve to free myself of them.

The Prize: If I succeed in this healing process, I experience a monumental evolutionary breakthrough. It is as if I have been unwittingly dragging a heavy weight behind me – a weight composed of all of the parts of myself that I was pressured into condemning or denying: needs, natural human hungers, understandable resentments. As I welcome those parts of myself back into the light of my awareness, that which was once heavy becomes light. I soar.

The Price of Failure: I begin to lose evolutionary momentum as something inside of me that I do not understand holds me back. Frustrated by a palpable lack of effective progress, I begin to feel a hunger for oblivion – anything to turn off the emptiness. Perhaps I find it. Perhaps I slip into a kind of soul-tiredness in which I turn away from everything, myself included.

From here, we move on to present a similar quick sketch of Mars in each one of the twelve signs. This material is taken word-for-word from The Book of Fire, *where it appeared originally.*

MARS IN ARIES

Underlying Agenda: I resolve that fear will never grab the steering wheel of my life. That is not to say that I will never be afraid; it is that I will not allow fear to stand between me and doing what I feel is right for myself. I resolve to accept the fact that life entails risk, and that no one gets out of here alive. I will protect myself and those I love.

Strategy: I commit to doing things that frighten me. Some of these brave actions will be physical; I understand and accept that putting my body on the line is one method for my full engagement in this particular evolutionary effort. I also understand and accept that this process unfolds on levels other than those requiring physical courage; I will be truthful about expressing my emotional needs and my feelings, even when that might lead to conflict in my relationships.

Tools: Into this world I bring a reflex of courage under fire. Compared to most people, I have a relative immunity to panic, even though it might take the right circumstances for me to become aware of this steady quality in myself. My nature is honest and direct, and I am fiercely loyal to those whom I love.

Dealing with the Shadow: I resolve to be wary of my temper. I will not pretend that my anger and resentments are always "righteous indignation." I will reflect on the possibility that at times forgiveness or even surrender might be the right course.

MARS IN TAURUS

Underlying Agenda: I accept the fundamental paradox of my life: that I must constantly fight for peace. I am not weak, but I choose solace; I prioritize serenity above everything else. I understand that battles lie ahead of me on my way toward those safe and natural harbors. I will courageously face those battles, fearing nothing and no one – and simultaneously I will scrupulously avoid being sucker-punched into battles I do not need to fight.

Strategy: I resolve to establish a reasonable level of physical security in my life, understanding that peace cannot arise if I feel constantly embattled or under practical stress. I will enter the natural world in a spirit of adventure and I will derive solace from it. I will be fiercely loyal to any animal companions that join me in my journey. I will take comfort in music.

I will carefully monitor the feedback I receive from my own physical body, and thus keep my stress levels down to reasonable levels.

Tools: I have come into this world with a no-nonsense set of instincts about what is truly important and what is simply excess. I will prioritize that which is essential to my survival and well-being, while distancing myself from the mirages of mindless materialism and vain display. My body speaks loudly, clearly, and eloquently to me. I value it and I listen to it.

Dealing with the Shadow: I resolve to be wary of lassitude and sloth. I affirm that happiness derives more from wanting what I have than from getting what I want. I do not pretend that I am without desires, but I recognize that every desire comes with a price tag, in that every moment spent chasing after it can erode my serenity. I make those choices mindfully.

MARS IN GEMINI

Underlying Agenda: I resolve that I will never let fear silence my voice. I am becoming brave enough to claim my right to be heard. I recognize that while courage is the critical ingredient here, it is not the only one – to find my voice, I must first have something to say. And I resolve to discover the worthy content of my voice through a commitment to wide experience and endless learning. I bravely pursue whatever triggers my curiosity or my interests, no matter what perils such a journey entails.

Strategy: When adventure calls, I answer. That applies to mental adventures too. I resolve to cultivate an open mind. When I feel intellectually intimidated, I dive into my studies and thus develop confidence in my knowledge. When reasonable fear stands between me and an experience that appeals to me, I never give fear the final vote. When I feel afraid to speak, I take that as a signal that it is time for me to speak. I will become confident in argument.

Tools: I have been blessed with a penetrating mind, capable of cutting right to the heart of any matter. I can quickly and intuitively grasp the essentials in any situation. I am formidable in argument. I can convey not only information to people, but also enthusiasm and passion about that information.

Dealing with the Shadow: I am aware that I can win arguments even if I am wrong. I can be unintentionally abrasive. When I set out to be verbally defensive, I can effectively defend myself against growth or the possibility of ever learning anything. I can express myself with too much vehemence, to the point that no one wants to listen to me even if they agree with me. I resolve to be conscious of these qualities and to try to minimize their hold upon my behavior.

MARS IN CANCER

Underlying Agenda: I resolve to cultivate the courage to heal my inner wounds. Some people behave bravely by distancing themselves from their feelings of fear or insecurity; I will never do that. I will let my heart speak and I will be vulnerable, always, to its message, no matter how threatening that message might be. Like a warrior, I will face the reality of my own heart.

Strategy: I recognize that I need time alone, in silence and safety. I resolve to make space in my outer life for my inner life. I defend those necessary borders fiercely. I recognize that nothing so reveals the reality of my heart as committed relationships: this means partnership – but it also means my family in the larger sense of the word. I claim the enormous courage that is necessary for committed "no exit" love and friendship.

Tools: I have a passion for inner work. My heart speaks loudly to me; I cannot help but listen to it. There is no warrior in the forest like a mama bear when she feels that her cubs are threatened; I am like a mama bear. I defend my home, my hearth, and my clan. I have no desire to die for them, but I would do that if necessary, without a moment's hesitation. That is the quality of the love I offer.

Dealing with the Shadow: I accept the fact that life is inherently dangerous; there are limits to how effectively I can defend myself. I accept that fact. I recognize that my innate caution can grab the steering wheel of my life, robbing me of vitality in the name of security. This creates a paradox: in my zeal to be safe and secure, it is possible that I might fail to live. I will not let that happen.

MARS IN LEO

Underlying Agenda: I resolve that I will not exit this world before I have left in its hands some evidence of my inner life. I will somehow express my values concretely – my sense of what is beautiful, what is sacred, what is worth living for. I am not afraid to roar like a lion. I will impact the community around me; people will know I was here. They will be touched by me. I am not afraid to be seen.

Strategy: I seek avenues of creative, personal expression. These creative avenues might take the form of art, but they are not limited to art. I will leave the stamp of my soul upon institutions, events, and people whom I meet. Even when I am frightened, I step out on the stage of life and I sing my heart out. Vulnerability does not scare me.

Tools: I have flair; I have charisma and presence. My passionate engagement with life radiates magnetically from me. I can perform. I can step out on the stage. I have the ability to trigger in other people an identification with me. I can ask for what I want. I am not afraid to shine.

Dealing with the Shadow: I am aware that I am not the center of the world. I cultivate fascination with other people and sensitivity towards them. I can as easily be a good audience as I can be the performer who is the focus of everyone's attention. I accept the fact that the critical ingredient in my self-expression must always be the authentic baring of my soul. It must always entail that kind of vulnerability, and I resolve that it will never descend into mere posturing. I will not become a dancing monkey calculating how to create the response of applause; I will not fear the risk of being nakedly honest even if people don't like it.

MARS IN VIRGO

Underlying Agenda: My spiritual survival depends upon my finding some kind of work that matters. Whether or not I am paid for this work is not the issue; what matters is that in the end I can honestly know that I polished and fully expressed the skills and abilities with which I was born. I understand that my pursuit of these crafts entails facing my own fears and insecurities. I will not let them stop me. I am a warrior in service to my community.

Strategy: I will allow nothing to stand between me and the training I need in order to fully develop and express my potential. "Training" in this context might refer to school, but the intention is broader: life itself can educate me, so long as I engage with it bravely. I understand that my particular path through this world entails encounters with *masters* of various sorts. I am part of a lineage; I will receive guidance from those who have gone before me – and I will repay the debt by passing on these skills to those who come after me.

Tools: I am not afraid of hard work; I understand self-discipline; I can focus; I can sustain concentration over long periods of time. I am not intimidated by complexity or detail. I can hammer away long after others, who might perhaps be more talented than me, have given up and gone home.

Dealing with the Shadow: I understand that sometimes "perfect" is the enemy of "good enough." I can accept that I have done well, declare victory and go home to my bed and sleep. I know that I am a worrier; I understand that worry can sap my energy, robbing me of the juice that I need in order to live my life as I want to live it. I carefully distinguish natural, healthy *concern* from needless, vitiating worry. Simultaneously, I resolve gracefully to accept the imperfections I accurately perceive in others.

MARS IN LIBRA

Underlying Agenda: I accept that my major aim in life is to achieve genuine intimacy – and "intimacy" here refers to all close human relationships, not only to the ones based on sexuality. I accept the fact that such authenticity of connection is inherently frightening. To be honest – and to create the space for a partner also to be genuinely honest – is true warrior work. I understand that conflict is not the opposite of love; it is part of authentic love, woven into the very DNA of genuine intimacy.

Strategy: I resolve to cultivate the skills of the intimate warrior. As I learn to express my needs and any pain I might feel in a relationship, I will not lose sight of my compassionate, respectful, three-dimensional *perception* of my partner. I do not fight to win; I fight to achieve fairness. Diplomacy in service of loving honesty is the craft I am developing.

Tools: I have an innate sense of how other people are different from me. I celebrate that reality, I am not surprised by it; I expect those differences. To intimacy I bring an open-minded sense of discovery. Without being foolish or ungrounded about it, I am a romantic. I accept that fact about myself, and I do not apologize for it. Love is important to me; I am willing to bravely commit to it and to do the work of sustaining it.

Dealing with the Shadow: I will never let diplomacy eclipse my honesty; instead, I express my honesty diplomatically. I resolve to be aware of this critical distinction. Harmony in relationships is valuable to me, but I will not participate in creating a false harmony that derives from my hiding who I am, what I need, and what I genuinely feel.

MARS IN SCORPIO

Underlying Agenda: Mars – which is to say, passionate intensity – is maximally powerful here, being the classical ruler of Scorpio. Therefore, I came into this world with my heart on fire. I came into this world, saying, "give me some truth." I am looking for a naked, unvarnished relationship with my own stormy heart. Once I have established that, I can seek similarly deep connections with a few other equally brave souls in this world.

Strategy: When something smells bad, people naturally turn away from it. My instinct, however, is to go toward the smell. What that means is that I am doing deep Shadow work in this lifetime. I trust my fascination with everything taboo; I may edit my behavior, but never my actual consciousness. I think anything, feel anything. Above all, I am true to my sexuality, knowing that its instinctual, mysterious compass needle points me unerringly to my path.

Tools: I can smell a lie from ten miles away. I can look anyone straight in the eye. I can handle intensity and drama. I understand that life is short and uncertain; this gives me an impatience with game-playing and superficiality. There is heat in my blood; people who cannot accept that tend to be afraid of me and go away. Let's celebrate their departures rather than lamenting them.

Dealing with the Shadow: Even without my intending it, my honesty, bluntness, and directness can hurt people. Because of that, when I was young, I was probably punished or criticized for those very qualities. Paradoxically, this could lead me to hide my honesty, bluntness, and directness. Internalizing those energies only hurts me; I could become isolated, resentful, and depressed. I resolve to not let that happen: I seek alliances with people who celebrate my intensity.

MARS IN SAGITTARIUS

Underlying Agenda: I resolve never to let fear compromise my fidelity to my gypsy soul. I seek wide experience and I resolve to live my life passionately. I am not afraid to make mistakes nor to learn things the hard way, if that is the deepest way to learn them. I hurl myself into experience in a spirit of faith and adventure. I am on a quest for *meaning* in life; I will not sacrifice that search on the altar of "practicality" – or of anyone else's agenda for me.

When I come to the end of my life, I will have few regrets. I will not look back and say that I missed my chance to live.

Strategy: I will travel and be open to cross-cultural experiences. I learn from people who are different from me, socially or culturally. I live to stretch my horizons in every way possible – I accept the fact that this kind of stretching includes physical adventures, but also opportunities to learn and to immerse myself in anything I have never seen before.

Tools: I am fascinated with everything foreign or alien; I trust that feeling and let it motivate me. I am plucky. I bounce back from adversity. My faith in life is bulletproof. By reflex, I say yes rather than no. I express myself straightforwardly and directly. People will know who I am; they are free to make their own decisions about whether to like me or not.

Dealing with the Shadow: I am wary of how I can be blinded by my own passionate opinions. I know I can be wrong, even when I feel I am right. I temper my spontaneity with an awareness of other people's sensitivities or wounded places. My good-hearted desire not to do harm to anyone must be enhanced by constant mindfulness of my own Fiery nature.

MARS IN CAPRICORN

Underlying Agenda: Half fish, half mountain goat – Capricorn is a strange piece of biological engineering. But in the world of symbolism, it represents absolute mastery: the ability to swim the widest ocean and climb the highest mountain. With my Mars in Capricorn, I resolve to do exactly the same thing: with my courage married to my innate relentlessness and self-discipline, I have come into this world to accomplish Great Works. I seek only mountains worthy of my strengths, my values, and my highest aspirations.

Strategy: Looking at the astrological house in which my Mars lies and taking into account the aspects it makes, I perceive and define the exact nature of those "worthy mountains." Perhaps one is a professional accomplishment; just as easily, another could take the form of some inner work, creativity, or the perfection of an intimate relationship. With single-pointed focus, an absolute commitment to integrity, and monumental self-discipline, I ascend the peaks.

Tools: I was born with the ability to steel my nerves in the face of daunting circumstances. I am blessed with focus and a capacity for sustained concentration. I am efficient; I can sense priorities correctly and organize effective strategies for attaining them. I can put my ego and my insecurities aside and focus one-pointedly upon the goal. I am at my best in situations where other people are giving up.

Dealing with the Shadow: I resolve to be mindful of life's softer side, both in myself and in other people. When I am tired I will sleep. When I am hungry I will eat. I will take time to treat my own needs and the needs of others with tenderness and respect. I recognize that the blinders which allow me to maintain my focus might also blind me to life's unexpected wonders and sweet compensations. I resolve not to fall into that cold trap.

MARS IN AQUARIUS

Underlying Agenda: I accept that I must fight to be free. No one has granted me a right to express my individuality; instead, I must assert myself and claim that right. The experiences that actually nourish my inner warrior are experiences which others might try to forbid me to have. My distorted social training began early in life, so brave inner work is required as I sift my real desires from what is merely internalized social conditioning. I resolve to heed my inner voice, to follow its guidance – and to face down anyone who tries to make me wrong for being true to myself.

Strategy: Setting boundaries is not enough; I must learn to *defend* those boundaries as well. I will undoubtedly attract petty tyrants into my life – people with plans for me, and even if they are well intended, these are plans that would render my life meaningless. Faced with them, I resolve to stand my ground. I will question authority. I will doubt the "received wisdoms" of my generation and my society. I bow to no one unless they have proven themselves worthy of my submission.

Tools: I have been blessed with an ability to think outside the box. If we understand "genius" as the ability to ask questions no one before has even thought to ask, then I acknowledge I possess a certain genius. I have a warrior's instinct to defend minority viewpoints and the rights of those whose voices are not heard. I can argue effectively; I have the ability to pry open closed minds.

Dealing with the Shadow: I affirm that life is multidimensional, full of paradox, and inhabited by other human beings with hearts and souls as deep and authentic as my own. I will not become lost in abstraction; I will not turn people into symbols. I cultivate kindness and forgiveness in myself. I always remember to laugh and to love. I honor tenderness.

MARS IN PISCES

Underlying Agenda: I recognize that the thinnest of barriers stands between me and a fundamental breakthrough in the depth of my consciousness and my spirituality. I recognize that the exact nature of that barrier is fear. The divine mystery is not "safe" in some churchy sense of the word. I have reached a stage in my evolutionary journey in which the next steps will launch me upon some stormy – and rather shamanic – seas. I boldly surrender to the Mysteries.

Strategy: I am learning to steady my nerves in the face of psychological and spiritual experiences that frighten me. While the ultimate application of this skill lies in my inner work, I can strengthen it by facing almost any kind of scary adventure. Riding a roller coaster can thus be understood, for me, as a spiritual discipline. Walking past the graveyard alone after midnight can be even more effective. In a nutshell, I face my fears – and especially those fears that derived from the opening of my psychic faculties.

Tools: I was born with a natural attunement to the edgy dimensions of the psychic realms and astral worlds. The archetype of the spiritual warrior arises naturally in me; I understand it intuitively, even if no one has ever explained it to me. When I tune into my deep self, I quickly connect with the part of my consciousness that has no fear of death – the part of me that knows that my consciousness will survive it. The more I meditate upon that place in myself, the more fearless I become.

Dealing with the Shadow: I fight passivity. I am cautious about the "transcendent" parts of myself – which are also the parts of me that could let life slip through my fingers. "What will this matter in five hundred years" is a wise statement – but also a dangerous attitude when contemplating a committed relationship, or a decision to pursue a career, or choosing to embrace a system of beliefs. I will not become a ghost in my own life.

11

NEPTUNE AND JUPITER IN THE TWELVE SIGNS

NEPTUNE IN ARIES

The Next Step on My Ascending Path: I have reached a point in the evolutionary journey of my soul in which, in order to maintain forward momentum, I must move in the direction of more boldness in pursuit of the soul-feeding, embodied experiences that I need. Higher levels of consciousness can sometimes be scary and disorienting. I must steady my reactivity to such strangeness. I must learn to just let fear be what it is, and observe it with emotional neutrality, never losing my stability in the face of whatever extreme or "psychedelic" experiences might arise. My soul-aim here is ancient, classic Warrior material: it is that I become genuinely "ready to die at any moment." I will fight to live – but when that moment comes, I resolve that I will be prepared to not fear it. I will have spent my life preparing for it.

The Skillful Means for Attaining It: In order to achieve this breakthrough, I need to face fears, including physical ones. For me, there is a spiritual purpose in zip-lining, scuba diving, and sailing across an ocean. Fears I might face in those kinds of endeavors teach my mind steadiness under stress. That steadiness translates directly into my ability to remain one-pointed in meditation, no matter what arises in my consciousness. I am on the path of the *spiritual warrior.*

The Energy Squandered: If I waste this evolutionary opportunity, the energy dissipates in the form of ungrounded, passionate beliefs and crusades. War is always wasteful, and pointless war – where the battle is really a projection of some argument that I am having with myself – is even more wasteful. I resolve not to squander this evolutionary opportunity by attacking ghosts in my own mind.

NEPTUNE IN TAURUS

The Next Step on My Ascending Path: I have reached a point in the evolutionary journey of my soul in which, in order to maintain forward momentum, I must move in the direction of a simpler, less analytic, form of inner experience. I need to calm down and become more grounded in my animal body. In meditation, I resolve to cease expecting "visions and miracles" to sweep me away. Perhaps *nothing* will happen next. Perhaps here and now, this breath and the next one, is all I have – and all I need. At this moment, I am already there. It is ultimately as simple as that, if only I can realize it.

The Skillful Means for Attaining It: In order to achieve this breakthrough, I benefit enormously from immersing myself in silence. Outward silence helps me to become silent inwardly, which is my actual aim. As I try to stop the endless inner dialog, even simply becoming aware of its constant chatter is a helpful step forward. My body can guide my next steps: yoga benefits me, as does Tai Chi, rhythmic music, and conscious dance. Every moment I spend in Mother Nature advances me. Contemplating the wordless consciousness of animals helps me attune myself to my goal, which is in many ways quite similar.

The Energy Squandered: If I waste this evolutionary opportunity, the energy dissipates in the form of lassitude. I become predictable and repetitive. My life and my consciousness are numbed by a lack of any apparent *need* for alertness. I become a creature as dominated by habit as any mouse or rabbit in the fields. I learn nothing.

NEPTUNE IN GEMINI

The Next Step on My Ascending Path: I have reached a point in the evolutionary journey of my soul in which, in order to maintain forward momentum, I must move in the direction of more precise cognitive insight and understanding regarding the nature of consciousness itself. There is a missing component in my grasp of the true nature of experienced reality – that missing component triggers a critical, cascading error in how I *think* about spirituality. To sort it out, I must cultivate humble, curious open-mindedness. I must be willing to learn. I must find the pure innocence of the true beginner's mind, and, in a sense, start my path over again, freshly.

The Skillful Means for Attaining It: In order to achieve this break-through, I benefit enormously from immersing myself in the spiritual literature of the world. Even erroneous or flawed teachings can help me in that they teach me how to spot errors and how to think critically. Direct contact with spiritual teachers of all stripes is a breakthrough catalyst for me. Words themselves can trigger such breakthroughs – I will hear phrases in this lifetime which I will remember a thousand years from now. Extrasensory phenomena abound for me; the question is whether I notice them, and accept them as they are – or rationalize them away in order to avoid threatening some more conventional description of reality in which I have been indoctrinated.

The Energy Squandered: If I waste this evolutionary opportunity, the energy dissipates in the form of mere mental gymnastics. It is as if I prefer a discussion group about enlightenment over the possibility of enlightenment itself. I put more energy into appearing wise to others than I do into actually attaining greater wisdom. I would rather be seen as right than to learn anything.

NEPTUNE IN CANCER

The Next Step on My Ascending Path: I have reached a point in the evolutionary journey of my soul in which, in order to maintain forward momentum, I must take steps in the direction of opening my heart to other human beings to a point where my level of vulnerability frightens me. I am aiming to align my soul with the spirit of the Great Mother – that feminine face of the Divine, the part which is compassionately attuned to the needs and the endless suffering of all embodied life-forms. Dissolving in that sea of love, forgiving all beings, blessing the good, the bad, and the ugly – it is a tall order, but I am ready to begin that noble work. I am ready to forgive the universe.

The Skillful Means for Attaining It: In order to achieve this break-through, I can start right at home, working with the people in my own life:

my family, my closest friends – blessing them, forgiving them, exercising the patience and unconditional acceptance of them which we might expect to see arising naturally in a mother toward her child. Meditation upon the Great Mother is a powerful practice for me – visualizing Mother Mary, Kwan Yin, Gaia, Green Tara, and so on. Time spent feeding people and otherwise serving them is a significant catalyst for my evolution.

The Energy Squandered: If I waste this evolutionary opportunity, the energy dissipates in the form of excessive self-protection and worry about getting hurt. I become a ghost, going through the motions of life. I may be "feeding and serving" other people, but the reality is that I am hiding my heart. Keeping my heart open right up to that point where it begins to become scary is really the point.

NEPTUNE IN LEO

The Next Step on My Ascending Path: I have reached a point in the evolutionary journey of my soul in which, in order to maintain forward momentum, I must move in the direction of making a gift to the world of all that I myself have been given spiritually. This has nothing to do with self-aggrandizement or spiritual advertising; it is all about the triggering impact on my being that comes from cultivating unguarded *generosity* and *vulnerability.* I need to keep my ego out of it, and just give of myself without holding back, always with my focus on how I might help others spiritually rather than how I might look as a result of helping them that way. As I speak from my soul, my sense of vulnerability is enormous. I resolve to take that risk.

The Skillful Means for Attaining It: In order to achieve this breakthrough, I need to walk a tightrope. On one hand, the heart of the matter lies in my humble, grateful surrender to that transcendent spark of the Divine that burns within me – I can never lose sight of the fact that none of this is really about "me" in any narrow sense of the word. On the other hand, I do need to learn some stage craft. There are some theatrical skills connected with conveying these gifts to others; otherwise, no one pays me any attention and no one benefits. I need to build a bridge between my soul and the world. If no one benefits directly from my generosity, my heart might be in a good place, but I have not learned what I need to learn.

The Energy Squandered: If I waste this evolutionary opportunity, the energy dissipates in the form of mere theatricality. Ego, driven by insecurity, holds my soul back. I slip into needing personal attention instead of paying compassionate, engaged attention to others. I spend too much time in front of mirrors.

NEPTUNE IN VIRGO

The Next Step on My Ascending Path: I have reached a point in the evolutionary journey of my soul in which, in order to maintain forward momentum, I must move in the direction of three virtuous wisdoms. First, I commit to *cultivating humility.* Second, I resolve to *serve others.* Third, I aim to *recognize my teachers* and submit to them. In all of these virtues, I discern one common thread: a commitment to seeing my own karmic predicament as clearly as possible, and in so doing, to realize all of my dilemmas boil down to my own ego fighting for its turf. Each of these three paths directly challenges my excessive focus on myself

The Skillful Means for Attaining It: In order to achieve this breakthrough, I apply each one of those three remedies. I humbly thank the universe for giving me the gift of being able to receive direct transmission from men and women who have advanced further than me on the path. As I immerse myself in their energy fields, I can by-pass slower, more painful ways of learning exactly the same lessons. As I do that, my gratitude toward these teachers increases and naturally seeks expression in the form of my wanting to help others – and the mystery is that then I too become capable of offering these transmissions, just as I myself received them. Thus, I take my place in a soul lineage.

The Energy Squandered: If I waste this evolutionary opportunity, the energy dissipates in the form of my undervaluing my own level of evolution and becoming enmeshed in a dither of unworthiness. Down that road, I resign myself to endless drudgery far beneath what I am actually capable of delivering to anyone. I turn away from my spirituality, imagining myself to be "more practical than that," missing the point of my life and holding back my best gifts from the world.

NEPTUNE IN LIBRA

The Next Step on My Ascending Path: I have reached a point in the evolutionary journey of my soul in which, in order to maintain forward momentum, I must move in the direction of *shared evolution* and interdependency
with wisely-chosen *spiritual friends.* I need to learn how to internalize the
catalyst of another person's consciousness, and to do so in a spirit of mutual
surrender. Opening my heart to aesthetic rapture also triggers evolutionary
breakthroughs for me – that means letting myself be lifted up by music, art,
and the natural beauty of the physical world.

The Skillful Means for Attaining It: In order to achieve this breakthrough, I must practice relentless discernment in choosing those with
whom I interact intimately. Without true soul-recognition, relationships
are just the usual monkey-business – with the added peril of my greatly enhanced psychic vulnerability. Truly receiving another's soul into my heart
lifts me up. Time spent letting myself be moved and uplifted by aesthetic
experience is a more effective spiritual practice than academic study or any
"more obviously spiritual" practices of austerity or self-denial.

The Energy Squandered: If I waste this evolutionary opportunity, my
energy dissipates in the form of endless intimate and sexual drama, as
ghost projects its desires upon ghost, and no true contact of souls is made.
The path of the *tragic romantic* leeches life out of everyone who travels it,
and soon leads to weakness in the face of every temptation.

NEPTUNE IN SCORPIO

The Next Step on My Ascending Path: I have reached a point in the evolutionary journey of my soul in which, in order to maintain forward momentum,
I must move in the direction of becoming wide open to everything that
I really do not want to face in myself. I am ready for it. I resolve to integrate my personal psychological work with my higher spiritual intentions,
realizing that inner stones left unturned only hold me back. As I begin to
succeed in that honest and very human effort, something unexpected and
extraordinary happens: what can only be called *powers* begin to arise in me,
powers that have a shamanic or magical feeling. I begin to cooperate with
them, thereby cultivating an ability to interact in intense, but helpful ways
with the journeys of other people.

The Skillful Means for Attaining It: In order to achieve this breakthrough, I must resolve above all to be honest with myself about any lingering anger, bleeding wounds, hungers, or resentments inside of myself. I must inventory my memories, seeing them as objectively as I can, through the eyes of wisdom. Poisons which I allow to persist inside of me can interact explosively with the massive visitation of energy that looms for me in this lifetime. I must be steady and clear in order to receive it without it creating instabilities in my psyche.

The Energy Squandered: If I waste this evolutionary opportunity, the energy dissipates in the form of a vulnerability to moody depression and general negativity. I may feel as if I am "doing my psychological work," but the reality is more like I am just stewing in it. A longing – which is actually my longing for a higher level of consciousness – begins to take on shades of morbid sexual and romantic desires. No human being can ever satisfy it, which leads either to despair or to endless unproductive intimate entanglements.

NEPTUNE IN SAGITTARIUS

The Next Step on My Ascending Path: I have reached a point in the evolutionary journey of my soul in which, in order to maintain forward momentum, I must move in the direction of packing several lifetimes of spiritual experience into one single lifetime. I am on a soul quest; I commit to the worldly adventures such a quest entails – and I trust angels to help me out as I audaciously accept the risk and uncertainties of this path. My view of reality now requires some shock treatment, especially the kinds of shocks that come from seeing life from different cultural perspectives. If I grew up with a religion, I do not need to reject it – but I do need to watch what happens when it collides with other, equally powerful and authentic belief-systems.

The Skillful Means for Attaining It: In order to achieve this breakthrough, I must prioritize what the world will certainly call "impractical" choices. I reflect on the brevity and uncertainty of life, and focus on using my minutes here on Earth as boldly and as consciously as I can. I will travel; I will undertake *pilgrimage* – and it is up to me to determine where my own "holy lands" lie. I resolve to immerse myself in philosophy and metaphysics – and if I begin to think that I have found "the answer," I keep myself honest by letting it encounter other answers.

The Energy Squandered: If I waste this evolutionary opportunity, the energy dissipates in the form of ungrounded dogmatism. I make a religion of my preexisting beliefs and defend it against all possibilities of growth or evolution with the zeal of the Spanish Inquisition or any other kind of fundamentalism. Those preexisting beliefs might not even be in obvious religious categories. They can be political or social, even something as trivial as the notion that Honda is better than Ford. Whatever form the squandering takes, the evolutionary possibilities are dissipated.

NEPTUNE IN CAPRICORN

The Next Step on My Ascending Path: I have reached a point in the evolutionary journey of my soul in which, in order to maintain forward momentum, I must move in the direction of an enormous outpouring of sustained, focused discipline. The spiritual mountain has grown steep before me; I resolve to continue climbing it anyway. I can learn to do without certain comforts and distractions. I accept that some austerities benefit me. Winter breeds strength. I willingly take on some Great Work that involves bringing what exists inside me into outward manifestation. This project may not look "spiritual" in obvious ways – it could be a work of creativity or some effort directed at social transformation. In all cases, these great works are about bringing something of the spirit-world into manifestation in the physical one.

The Skillful Means for Attaining It: In order to achieve this breakthrough, I resolve to be undaunted and relentless. Resistance only makes my resolution stronger. My eye does not stray from the prize. I do not indulge in pointless self-pity. I benefit from regular meditation and from it I draw the strength to continue on my path. My integrity is precious to me – I never compromise it. Something inside of me is nourished by solitary time – I do not need to be a hermit, but I am a better friend or partner if I have some uncontested privacy a few times per week. Wasted time leeches life out of me. I need mountains to climb.

The Energy Squandered: If I waste this evolutionary opportunity, the energy dissipates in the form of feelings of defeat, as if everything were arrayed unfairly against me and that there was never any possibility of my winning. I grow cold and tired, my spirit broken. I become a time-server and I begin to envision the world around me as a prison. Eventually even fantasies of escape lose their *mojo.* I give up.

NEPTUNE IN AQUARIUS

The Next Step on My Ascending Path: I have reached a point in the evolutionary journey of my soul in which, in order to maintain forward momentum, I must move in the direction of questioning everything I have ever been taught about human spirituality. It is not that everything I have learned or heard is wrong – it is just that everything has been distorted by history, bigotry, gender fascism, and so forth. The only way I can learn where those flaws actually lie is by questioning everything, with nothing sacred until it is proven sacred. I resolve never to fear the truth. If the truth of the universe is that when we die, that is the end of it all, I will face that truth squarely. (But first I will contemplate the compelling evidence for some other, more Neptunian perspectives . . .)

The Skillful Means for Attaining It: In order to achieve this breakthrough, I resolve militantly to trust my own senses and the realities of my own experience. I can listen to spiritual teachers and consider what they are saying with an open mind, but I bow down before no one unless they have truly earned that kind of devotion. Nothing – and no one – is so sacred that I cannot question it. I am wide-open to fresh, historically unprecedented, evolutionary pathways opening up for me, perhaps as a result of technology or biochemistry. Spirituality may be eternal, but for me, the future is not a mirror of the past. I acknowledge that I am part of the future of human spirituality.

The Energy Squandered: If I waste this evolutionary opportunity, the energy dissipates in the form of mere intellectual contrariness – the need to make everyone else's beliefs wrong. I develop a knee-jerk reaction against faith, magic, and miracles. I slip into the illusion that I am somehow above the spiritual path, watching it as a commentator rather than walking it myself in a fragile body that came with an expiration date.

NEPTUNE IN PISCES

The Next Step on My Ascending Path: I have reached a point in the evolutionary journey in which, in order to maintain forward momentum, I must move in the direction of total immersion in the life of my soul. I am ready to prioritize it that way, no matter what other people might think or how crazy I might look. I am opening up psychically at a rapid rate – that sounds good, but I need to learn how to handle it day by day, lest my increasing sensitivity destabilizes me. Religion might help me, but this process is not ultimately about religion at all – it is far more direct than that.

The Skillful Means for Attaining It: In order to achieve this breakthrough, I benefit enormously from some kind of regular spiritual practice, formal or informal. It boils down to my having time, ideally each day, to let go of my personality and experience myself as a kind of luminous spaciousness. That process might look like meditation or it might just look like me staring out a window. It might take the form of some creative work I do. People's opinions and labels for it do not matter. Appearances do not matter. The entire point is that I am going beyond the world of labels and appearances. A doorway is opening in me which leads into something higher than all of that.

The Energy Squandered: If I waste this evolutionary opportunity, the energy dissipates in the form of my becoming overwhelmed and confused by my own expanding consciousness. I become passive. I stare into space. I seem to "not care." Eventually I begin to find some refuge from life. The standard warnings are about alcohol and drugs, although I could just as easily escape into fantasy literature, video games, endless television – anything that distracts me from the scary miracle trying to happen in my own consciousness.

Neptune is not the only ruler of the third Water sign, Pisces. Jupiter rules it too, and leaving Jupiter out of consideration when we think about Pisces always creates a blind spot in any astrologer's work. Since Jupiter also rules Sagittarius, we explored it in depth back in The Book of Fire. *To keep balance in this series, in this volume we have been concentrating more attention on Neptune, which did not make an appearance in the previous books.*

Ignoring Jupiter's connection to Pisces would be a blunder, and for the sake of completeness and easy reference, in the rest of this chapter I include verbatim the material about Jupiter through the twelve signs which appeared already in The Book of Fire.

JUPITER IN ARIES

The Prize: To achieve meaningful victory – and "meaningful" is the key word here. Aries energy is the astrological equivalent of nuclear power; when allied with the expansive qualities of Jupiter, it is essential to maintain some restraint and clarity of intention, lest we leave a trail of blood behind us. Self-knowledge about *what is actually good for you* must underlie your decisions. With this configuration, there is a good chance that you will get what you want.

Never Underestimate . . . your courage under pressure. Your ability to snatch victory from the jaws of defeat. Your ability to bounce back from adversity. Your resilience. Your ability to improvise strategy and tactics in the face of unforeseen circumstances.

Beware of Inflation . . . arising from the marriage of ego and anger. The intoxication of winning and the single-minded fixation upon victory can blind you to their costs. Make sure the victory is one that is worthy of you – and worth its costs.

Your Gift From the Gods: Pluck and resilience.

Helpful Wisdom: Wise old karate masters tell us that sometimes the most effective strategy is simply to walk away from the fight.

JUPITER IN TAURUS

The Prize: What is more precious than a serene heart? Your wisest aim in life is the achievement of an abundance of peace. To relax. To know that enough is enough – and to recognize "enough" when you see it. Silence is precious. So is a healthy relationship with your physical body. Real friends, natural beauty, a freedom from trivial distraction, and above all, time to immerse yourself in them – these are the true prizes.

Never Underestimate . . . the therapeutic impact on your soul of quiet, of physical touch, and of listening carefully to the promptings of your physical body. Never underestimate the wisdom of your instincts. Trust your animal friends: they have something important to teach you.

Beware of Inflation . . . regarding the hyped, empty promises of this commercialized world – glamour, money, fame, and so forth. They promise far more peace than they ever actually deliver.

Your Gift From the Gods: If you are truly quiet and listen carefully to the still, small voice within, you have utterly reliable instincts.

Helpful wisdom: 'Tis a Gift To Be Simple.

JUPITER IN GEMINI

The Prize: A life of endless fascination, a life in which you are never bored, a life of wonder and miracles – that is the prize. Endless learning is pivotal; but do not confuse that with dry academic pedagogy. This is about intellectual passion. It is about the mental appetite that we call curiosity curating a feast of epic proportions.

Never Underestimate . . . the simple fact that you have something important to say in this world. Never underestimate the benefit of education in the broadest sense of the word. Never underestimate your powers of persuasion; you can convey not only information, but contagious enthusiasm for that information.

Beware of Inflation . . . regarding your estimate of other people's fascination with your opinions, along with your certainty about the veracity of those opinions. Mark Twain wrote a windy letter to a friend that began with an apology: "I am sorry this letter is so long. I didn't have time to write a short one." Remember that sometimes it is best to "write the short one."

Your Gift From the Gods: Curiosity. Persuasiveness. Skill with language. Educability – you can learn anything.

Helpful wisdom: Never fail to take full advantage of an opportunity to keep your mouth shut.

JUPITER IN CANCER

The Prize: Home Sweet Home – and that familiar phrase has many levels of meaning, all of which can potentially constitute an enormous source of joy for you. Any planet in Cancer reflects an inward agenda of self-healing, and, pursuant of that, a pleasant, quiet, safe place to live is always helpful in that process. But a house is not a home; domestic love is a critical ingredient here – but that love need not take a traditional form. It is about people upon whom you can count, people who share the road of life with you in a spirit of commitment. Framing these human treasures as the grand prize in life, and valuing them above all other distractions, is the right use of this energy.

Never Underestimate . . . the healing, deepening impact on you of quiet time in a safe place with people you love. Recognize that much good comes to your soul while you are sleeping, so make sure you get enough of it.

Sleep heals more than the physical body. Never underestimate the healing impact your faith has on people around you.

Beware of Inflation . . . regarding other people's definitions of your duties and responsibilities toward them. Beware of the endless insatiability of family; do not allow yourself to be devoured by them. Beware of defending yourself too much against life.

Your Gift From the Gods: Sensitivity. A big, generous, nurturing heart. A full-time guardian angel watching over your domestic environment. Luck finding a good place to live.

Helpful wisdom: As Leonard Cohen said, "Put your hat on your headache and dance."

JUPITER IN LEO

The Prize: Spontaneity. A feeling of being at ease with your own vulnerability; expressing it without hesitation under the assumption that you will be appreciated. You are here learning to walk like a king or a queen in this world, confident, with your head held high, and comfortable with your valued place in the human family. To attain the prize, you must offer a rich gift: leaving some sincere evidence of your inner life in the hands of your community.

Never Underestimate . . . your creativity, your capacity to perform, and your personal magnetism, especially when you are taking chances regarding self-revelation. Trust your sense of drama and your ability to hold the attention of an audience, small or large – and never underestimate the charm of your sense of humor.

Beware of Inflation . . . regarding your own capacity to endlessly fascinate people. Other people's appreciative attention can be intoxicating; enjoy a glass or two – but not three or four.

Your Gift From the Gods: Star-quality.

Helpful wisdom: Less is more, at least sometimes. A short, punchy dramatic moment can be more impactful and memorable than a sermon. Leave your audience – even if it is just one person – wanting more, not less. Trust that half the message lies simply in your quality of presence.

JUPITER IN VIRGO

The Prize: In the long run, is there any prize more worthy of pursuit than feeling that we actually made a difference in the world? Your prize, in a nutshell, is to find work and responsibilities that truly matter. You revel in skill and competence; you shine when you are appreciated for your well-honed skills.

Never Underestimate . . . what you are capable of achieving in terms of prestige in your field – not that prestige itself is the point, only that prestige arises naturally when you spread your wings and truly claim the highest levels of your potential skill set. You are capable of more than you imagine.

Beware of Inflation . . . regarding other people's ever-expanding definitions of your alleged duties and responsibilities. You are here to help people; but you are not a public utility. We are talking about *self-expression through service*, not having your life defined by other people's whining.

Your Gift From the Gods: The ability to master complex skills; the ability to harness your intelligence and press it toward the far limits of its potential development.

Helpful wisdom: Your prayer: God grant that today I do work that matters.

JUPITER IN LIBRA

The Prize: A life of grace and elegance, for sure – but, to keep perspective, immediately contemplate the graceful elegance of a gazelle, and compare it with crass, tasteless ostentation, especially when it is fueled by wealth. Go for the gazelle, in other words! This is about a single rose in a vase on your kitchen table. This is about poetry and music, and the company of the sorts of friends who appreciate them. You claim your true prize when that external grace and elegance sink into the marrow of your bones. That is more likely to happen if you are not seeking to keep up with anyone or trying to impress anyone.

Never Underestimate . . . your aesthetic instincts; they unerringly lead you to the creation of an environment that soothes your spirit. Trust your creative impulses and invest generously in their development. Never underestimate the benefit to you of the company of people who can be moved to tears by a sunset or a fading rose or a piece of haunting music.

Beware of Inflation . . . regarding the generation of the outward appearance of position, prosperity, beauty, or personal importance. Be as beautiful as you can be; enjoy that. But be wary of vanity, both physically and socially.

Your Gift From the Gods: The ability to harmonize colors, shapes, contradictory ideas, and different kinds of people. The ability to present yourself attractively to many different sorts of people.

Helpful wisdom: As the Navajos say, "May you walk in beauty."

JUPITER IN SCORPIO

The Prize: Imagine, on one hand, the fiercest, most psychologically threatening truths you can muster – and on the other hand, meeting them with joy and faith. That marriage of apparent opposites is the prize here. We are talking about looking "the devil in the eye" – and smiling, even laughing. In this configuration, we see evidence of a soul finding itself on the cusp of achieving victory over an ancient wound – dancing triumphantly on its own grave from a past life.

Never Underestimate . . . the ultimate power of truth to liberate you from despair. And never underestimate the strength that enters the human spirit when we let humor be one of our tools. Laughter is a healing force. Eventually on this path, you can even learn to laugh at the feebleness of death itself.

Beware of Inflation . . . regarding the dramatic gravity of your own wounds and issues, and your "Tell-All" narrative about them. Even when they are real and legitimate and you are facing them honestly, recognize that they can hypnotize you. You have a real capacity for psychological penetration – but do guard your sense of perspective. Be wary of a subtle, creeping vanity in regard to your own depth.

Your Gift From the Gods: The ability to maintain faith, humor, and spiritedness in the face of life's genuine darkness.

Helpful wisdom: Some people say angels can fly because they have wings, but angels fly because they take themselves lightly.

JUPITER IN SAGITTARIUS

The Prize: A complete commitment to living your life as a Quest, and doing so unabashedly, enthusiastically, and without shame. This involves a deep integration of the idea that there are ultimately no mistakes, only experiences to be digested. We are talking about faith, but not in a narrowly religious sense – it is more like faith in the fundamental goodness of embodied existence, and an enthusiastic willingness to dive into it. Your basic goodness is being forged into wisdom in the cauldrons of experience.

Never Underestimate . . . your luck. Here is another way to express that idea: you have a guardian angel who has vowed to protect you so long as you maintain your commitment to being fully alive. Not comfortable with the idea of angels? Then let's say the same thing a third way: you are plugged into the synchronistic fabric of the universe in a way that favors risk and audacity.

Beware of Inflation . . . regarding "being right" all the time. In your enthusiasm for understanding, you can jump to conclusions. And about that fabled "luck" of yours – it operates in service of your Quest, not in service of greed or stupidity.

Your Gift From the Gods: A primal enthusiasm for life; an ability to find meaning in chaos.

Helpful wisdom: Experience brings wisdom; a lack of wisdom brings experience.

JUPITER IN CAPRICORN

The Prize: The dignity, self-respect, and personal *gravitas* that arise from genuine accomplishment. It is as if the universe has challenged you, "Show us excellence.

Show us the Great Work of a lifetime. Make something that outlasts you. Leave some substantial evidence of your existence, your vision, and your integrity behind you in this world."

Never Underestimate . . . your capacity for sustained discipline and focused concentration over long periods of time. Never underestimate the fruits of persistence. Like the tortoise and the hare, slow and steady wins the race.

Beware of Inflation . . . regarding your own self-importance. Be hesitant and generous in your judgment of others: not all those who wander are lost. Cultivate sensitivity to your own needs; learn to sleep when you are tired, to eat when you are hungry – and to play in the mud when you are becoming too "adult" for your own good.

Your Gift From the Gods: You can keep your eye on the prize long after others have become distracted. You are hardwired for the accomplishment of great works.

Helpful wisdom: Moral values and integrity are everything; take care to define them for yourself rather than accepting external, conventional definitions of them. Harness your strength to your own heart, not to the values of strangers.

JUPITER IN AQUARIUS

The Prize: A magnificent life that is truly your own; a free-spirited existence guided by your own stars; a unique story that has never been lived before by anyone else. To have enough faith in your own perceptions that you need no one else's validation, agreement, or approval. To breathe deeply in the intoxicating stratosphere of true individuality and genuine freedom.

Never Underestimate . . . the validity of your own perceptions, even if no one else shares them. There is an element of genius in your makeup; never doubt that. Never underestimate the soul-crushing power of any vestige in you of a need for other people's approval – and never underestimate your ability to resist that deadening force.

Beware of Inflation . . . regarding the sanctity of your quirks. You have a natural right to be different, but those differences do not make other people wrong. Do not be afraid to learn from others: you can spend a long time reinventing the wheel, only to find out that it was already done a few thousand years ago.

Your Gift From the Gods: an ability to think outside the box; an ability to see possibilities that no one else has ever imagined.

Helpful wisdom: As Oscar Wilde said, "I put all my genius into my life; I put only my talent into my works."

JUPITER IN PISCES

The Prize: There are prizes we must forfeit at the moment of death and there are prizes that, once we have won them, remain ours for eternity. Your prize is in the second category: it is nothing less than a breakthrough in consciousness. It is a major step in the direction of wisdom, even the potential attainment of something akin to sainthood. Only with spiritual discernment can anyone even recognize this precious prize – learn to pursue what your soul truly values.

Never Underestimate . . . your evolutionary potential. You have already earned the right to a spiritual breakthrough. Take heart from that fact, and go about your life expecting miracles. In this lifetime, you will be kissed by an angel. Do not fail to notice it.

Beware of Inflation . . . regarding your spiritual and psychic accomplishments. Recognize that these developments are not happening in your ego; they are happening because your ego is becoming transparent to your larger self. Do not allow mere pride to debase this gift.

Your Gift From the Gods: Psychic sensitivity. No matter what path you take through life, you will feel the presence of higher powers – of God, of angels, of energies: the words do not matter; it is the experience itself that is the gift from the gods. The world might call this perceptual phenomenon "faith," but it is more direct than that.

Helpful wisdom: Earth is not the most prestigious address in the galaxy.

12

THE MOON IN THE TWELVE HOUSES

THE MOON IN THE FIRST HOUSE

The Healing I Seek: In this lifetime, I resolve to experience the feeling that I am living my life however I *choose* to live it – that I am actually *leading* my life rather than having life happen to me. I am warm and loving, but I am also an autonomous, independent being, and those free-spirited qualities are what I need to emphasize in myself. When I care for someone else, it is because I have chosen to do so, not because I feel that I must. My will, my whimsies, and my own desires are what give shape to my life. I am free to make my own mistakes and I take full responsibility for the outcome of my path.

The Tools I Have Been Given: Good immediate instincts about what to do when I am faced with uncertain forks in the road of life. I need to trust those instincts. My intuition guides me well, even when facts and accurate information are scarce.

If I Want to Be Happy, I Must Prioritize . . . healing my sense that I have a fundamental right to freedom and autonomy. I do not always need to put myself first, but I always have a natural *right* to do that if I want to. It is my own decision. To be happy, I have to prioritize the attainment and main-tenance of a state of *enlightened selfishness* – not meanness or coldness, but a sense of respect for my own right to choose my own course through life.

What Gets Me Down: Realizing that I have let an opportunity for an experience that I might have cherished slip through my fingers. Giving away my power. Seeing my own hesitation or my fear of other people's judgment stopping me from jumping when I should have jumped. Regretting what I have *not* done rather than what I *have* done.

A Bad Attitude That Could Sabotage Me: The sense that I am on Earth simply to take care of everyone else – that I am destined to forever be a kind of public utility. The belief that inner experience is "all that really matters" – a belief which would rob me of the kind of bold, vibrant outer life I was actually born to live and which feeds my soul.

THE MOON IN THE SECOND HOUSE

The Healing I Seek: In this lifetime, I aim to restore a sense of my own legitimacy, dignity, and full self-confidence to my life. I resolve to reach that goal not by simply patting myself on the back, but by impressing myself with my own very real accomplishments. I will *earn* this dignity, in other words. No "path of least resistance" can ever offer me lasting faith in myself – I recognize that reality and I do not fall into the snares of those kinds of "comfort zones." Through my own hard work on myself and by developing my own competence, I will gain a deepened sense of my own worth. Creating some degree of financial success and self-sufficiency can be part of this healing process for me; I am not apologetic about that. Creating a meaningful sense of home and family in my life is an even more pivotal piece of the puzzle.

The Tools I Have Been Given: Drive. Industry. Hunger. An immunity to resting on my own laurels. Good instincts around money and resources. An abhorrence of waste.

If I Want to Be Happy, I Must Prioritize . . . healing my fear that I somehow just don't have what it takes. I will not let hesitation or personal insecurity stand between me and the bold moves that I know I need to make. For some people, lying on a beach might make them happy – and I might enjoy that too for a while. But for me, wrestling with my own limits, and pushing myself beyond them, is my real source of lasting happiness. This is not a "resting life." I am here to get things done.

What Gets Me Down: Looking back on my life and seeing that it is a story of missed opportunities, crippling hesitation, and the price paid for simply not trusting myself – seeing that my fear of losing or failing prevented me from taking a shot at winning.

A Bad Attitude That Could Sabotage Me: The sense that I am always somehow faking it. The feeling that others are better, more worthy, or more skillful than me, or that I have bitten off more than I can chew. Wallowing in hesitation and caution rather than rolling the dice, trusting myself, and just seeing what happens.

THE MOON IN THE THIRD HOUSE

The Healing I Seek: In this lifetime, I resolve to find my natural voice and to make sure it is heard. I can be silent if I choose to be – but I will not "be silenced" by anyone. I will speak from my heart and I will learn to be skillful in finding vocabulary that conveys what I am actually feeling into the awareness of my listeners. Only in this way will I *feel heard.* I am learning to speak clearly from my heart. Balancing active speech, I resolve to *listen well* to other people as well. There will be healing power in the words I say – but also healing in the silences I share with others.

The Tools I Have Been Given: Good listening skills. A love of language. Curiosity. The ability to put soul-power into my verbal self-expression. I convey the weather of my heart as well as information.

If I Want to Be Happy, I Must Prioritize . . . healing my faith in my own ability to express myself clearly. For starters, I resolve to trust my native intelligence – but I will also further support its development with education in some sense of the word: books, classes, conversations with interesting people. I will polish my vocabulary; I will become more articulate; words will be my friend. I will learn to look at the world through the eyes of a healer – that is to say, as a kind, caring person would see it, oriented to what people need rather than to how I might come across as being "right."

What Gets Me Down: Realizing that "I should have said that" – which is to say, letting myself miss chances to speak up or to offer an insight or some act of verbal kindness. Dithering or brooding instead of "writing my book" – and "my book" might take some other form, but it always includes my leaving my mark upon the lives of other people through words I say, teachings I offer, or stories that I might tell.

A Bad Attitude That Could Sabotage Me: Two dark roads lie before me: one is the sense that no one would ever be interested in my thoughts or ruminations anyway, so I might as well not bother articulating them. The second is the opposite: the belief that everyone will find my cataloging my every mood swing, opinion, or rambling free-associative speculation fascinating.

THE MOON IN THE FOURTH HOUSE

The Healing I Seek: In this lifetime, I resolve to find my *natural home.* The healing which arises there comes from a right energetic fit between my soul and the physical place where I live – and that "place" can mean the literal roof over my head, but it can also range up to the town, region, or even the country in which I make my home. Another part of my healing derives from the old observation that "a house is not a home" – much of the process of finding my natural home revolves around finding the actual people who are my true soul-family and drawing comfort from them.

The Tools I Have Been Given: Psychic attunement to the land and to the spirit of a place. The capacity to form deep, lasting soul-bonds with other people.

If I Want to Be Happy, I Must Prioritize . . . a willingness to sacrifice all other concerns – career, money, status, and so on – if they stand between me and actually finding my natural home. Where I live and with whom I share the unfolding story of my life are far more mission-critical to my sense of wellbeing than any other more worldly areas of focus.

What Gets Me Down: Realizing that I am not feeling viscerally connected to the land beneath my feet, whether it is the city in which I live or forty acres on a mountaintop. Realizing that the people in my life have little idea who I actually am – the sad realization being that it is not difficult to imagine a time when they have forgotten about me and I have forgotten about them, and no one is worse for it.

A Bad Attitude That Could Sabotage Me: The sense that I am invisible and that I might as well get accustomed to it. A sense that isolation and alienation are simply the human condition – something we must all simply accept as mature adults in a cold, lonely, existentialist universe.

THE MOON IN THE FIFTH HOUSE

The Healing I Seek: In this lifetime, I need to recover a genuine sense that I am glad to be here, in this world and in this physical body. I resolve to escape from unnecessary constraint, inhibition, and self-consciousness. I will enjoy my life; I will not be afraid to revel in it. I do not demonize pleasure. I will use the word "sin" sparingly, and only in the context of hurting someone. I will learn to express myself spontaneously. I will claim a creative outlet. I will act as if I expect applause rather than criticism. I will become more skillful at the selection of partners and friends.

The Tools I Have Been Given: Presence and style. The ability to "dance as if no one is looking." Creative talent. An appreciation of the present moment. The ability to "be here now."

If I Want to Be Happy, I Must Prioritize . . . healing my sense that I am in fact *safe* in this world. I must salve an ancient wound of pain, inhibition, and despair which arose due to some horror in a prior lifetime; I may not remember the facts of that lifetime, but I do remember the pain. It is still with me. Establishing a right relationship with the pleasures of the physical body is essential – I affirm that it is now safe to be in the flesh. It is greatly beneficial to me to balance physical pleasures with the more mental, emotional, and spiritual pleasures of creative self-expression.

What Gets Me Down: Realizing that I have been afraid to say yes to myself, afraid to give myself permission to sing and dance, and to give myself a chance to be truly joyful. Feeling that I have held myself back too much, given too much power to rules and appearances, and not enough power to simple pagan ecstasy.

A Bad Attitude That Could Sabotage Me: Too much attachment to the belief that pain is a spiritual teacher and that pleasure is only a temptation that leads us away from the spiritual path. Pain *can* be a teacher – that is certain. But no one ever complains of having too *little* pain in life – that side of the equation takes care of itself. For me, as I heal my old karmic wound, it is pleasure, not pain, that restores my gut sense that I am truly glad to be alive.

THE MOON IN THE SIXTH HOUSE

The Healing I Seek: In this lifetime, I need to feel that the efforts I am making in my daily life really matter to the world somehow – that I am making a genuine difference in other people's lives, and that I am doing so by expressing some part of the best of myself. *Meaningful* responsibilities – as opposed to merely "working" – are what lead me to the higher ground. To achieve this goal, I need to contact teachers and mentors who resonate with my spirit and impart the necessary skills to me, whether they are practical or spiritual skills, or both.

The Tools I Have Been Given: Competence. The urge to be good at something. A capacity for hard work and serious application. An ability to recognize my natural mentors and to receive psychic transmissions from them, as well as more obvious lessons and teachings.

If I Want to Be Happy, I Must Prioritize . . . healing my sense of my own native ability to have a positive, healing impact on other people. I must recognize that finding the *right work* is central to my happiness. This path is not narrowly about money and it is not about career status; those are only secondary issues. It is about being good at something that truly makes a difference in the negative or limiting conditions which I encounter.

What Gets Me Down: The realization that I have a job that pays me only money. Realizing that I have learned nothing and accomplished nothing that makes me feel genuinely proud at the end of the day. Feeling like a gear in someone else's machinery.

A Bad Attitude That Could Sabotage Me: The sense that acquiescing to a feeling of daily slavery is simply realistic – that such abdication of my own higher potentials is part of becoming "grounded and mature." A willingness to "suck it up" and not complain or make any changes in my life. Stoic acceptance of the *status quo.* Despair – or a kind of quiet arrogance – that prevents me from seeking my natural teachers and mentors.

THE MOON IN THE SEVENTH HOUSE

The Healing I Seek: In this lifetime, I will recover my ability to recognize people who are truly worthy of my trust, and then to learn actively to trust them in ways where we both benefit psychologically and spiritually. At the same time, I resolve to develop the kinds of discernment I need in order to ferret out the sorts of people into whose hands I should never place my heart, perhaps because of their unreliable moral qualities or for reasons of simple incompatibility. I am healing my ability to trust human love and the skills which support my finding it.

The Tools I Have Been Given: Empathy. The ability to connect with people. Bridge-building skills. Diplomacy. All of the qualities that make a good counsellor.

If I Want to Be Happy, I Must Prioritize . . . healing my faith in the idea that it is safe to experience deep human commitment and the inherent vulnerability that goes along with it – that there are in fact trustworthy, decent men and women out there, and that at least one of them is looking for me. I must prioritize relationships that have what it takes to endure the test of time.

What Gets Me Down: Realizing that I have been the creator of my own loneliness through bad choices about who to trust, or as a result of ancient fears – fears which inhibit me from trusting decent, worthy people who are actually in my life.

A Bad Attitude That Could Sabotage Me: The sense that most other people are crazier and more needy than myself, and that it is my fate always to be taking care of them, all the while surrounded by people who either cannot or will not come through for me in a consistent, effective way when it is my turn to need them.

THE MOON IN THE EIGHTH HOUSE

The Healing I Seek: In this lifetime, I will be unafraid to face and accept the stormy depths of my own psyche. I will refrain from rationalizing or compartmentalizing any threatening realizations, even under the banner of trying to be "positive" or "spiritual." For me, truth always comes first. I resolve to seek intimacy with people who understand and support these kinds of affirmations, and to seek it *only* with such people. That is especially true in situations of sexual intimacy, where I am especially open psychically. Death will always be my most trusted counsellor, and death will whisper "tick, tock, tick, tock" in my ear whenever I am wasting my time.

The Tools I Have Been Given: A relatively fearless attitude toward the unconscious mind. Steadiness in the face of life's darkness and difficulties. Knowledge of my own mortality. The ability to engage with other people, one at a time, with enormous psychic nakedness, flowing in both directions.

If I Want to Be Happy, I Must Prioritize . . . first and foremost, healing my capacity to be genuinely, unguardedly intimate with my own mind without any censorship or any repressive imposition of "goodness" on my thoughts. With that radically honest personal inner attunement achieved, I can establish similar connections with a few other souls of similar depth.

What Gets Me Down: The realization that life is appallingly short and that much of our time here boils down to hours wasted on the pressing, but ultimately trivial, concerns of simple survival: going to work, paying the bills, and so forth. I resolve to fight letting this sense of waste get to me. I succeed at that by using the remaining time with as much mindfulness, intensity, and wisdom as I can muster.

A Bad Attitude That Could Sabotage Me: A sense that "life is a bitch, and then you die." A feeling of existential pointlessness, even bitterness. I must recognize how that cynical feeling might don the clever disguise of "worldly wisdom." I will not fall into the grips of such a dead-end attitude. I will not give myself up to mere moodiness.

THE MOON IN THE NINTH HOUSE

The Healing I Seek: In this lifetime, I resolve to let my heart lead me on a grand adventure. I will prioritize the mysterious soul-benefits that come from travel, guided by my intuition about where I need to go. I will learn things simply because they fascinate me. I am healing my sense that the universe is safe, interesting, and inviting rather than a place to be feared – that it is a friendly schoolhouse for me, full of classes I need to take. I can therefore risk stretching my boundaries, packing as much experience as possible into this lifetime.

The Tools I Have Been Given: Skill in pattern-recognition: connecting the dots of experience in a way that gives me genuine insight into the underlying natural laws of mind and nature. Good cross-cultural instincts. A strong moral compass.

If I Want to Be Happy, I Must Prioritize . . . healing my faith that it is safe for me to be alive and to take calculated risks. I am aligning my heart with the notion that my life is a quest for meaning rather than a futile effort simply to stave off death and difficulty for as long as I can. I enter alien cultures and I learn from them. I immerse myself in philosophy and the human search for understanding. To be happy, I must feel that I am living in a way that aligns with my higher values. I must live a life in which I positively believe – and that means more than just refraining from bad behavior.

What Gets Me Down: Realizing that I have drifted into predictable routines. Seeing that a year has gone by and that I have learned nothing or that I have seen nothing that I had not seen before. To lie on my deathbed realizing that I never saw the sun rise over Machu Picchu or wandered past Stonehenge while it was bathed in moonlight. To do anything that gives me material advantage at the price of feeling ashamed of myself deep down inside.

A Bad Attitude That Could Sabotage Me: The sense that "I should be more practical" – when in reality, what could actually be more practical than using every moment of life to solve the puzzle of life? "Practicality" is a dangerous word for me if, beneath its clever disguise, it really means a life of boredom, predictability, and slavery to routine.

THE MOON IN THE TENTH HOUSE

The Healing I Seek: In this lifetime, I resolve to turn myself into a positive gift to my community. I will naturally have my own personal life, separate from my life in the world – but I will also find a way for my heart and soul to express themselves in the form of some larger mission that touches the wider circle around me. I resolve to positively impact the lives of people whom I do not know personally. I do not need to be famous – I only need to leave a mark beyond the immediate framework of my friends and family.

The Tools I Have Been Given: First and foremost, I simply have a mission. I recognize that. There is a genuine need out there in the community which I was born to meet. I have the ability to have a healing impact upon the bodies, minds, or spirits of people whom I do not know in an intimate, two-way-street sort of way.

If I Want to Be Happy, I Must Prioritize . . . healing my reflexive urge toward self-protection in the face of the world's various insensitivities. I cannot let those kinds of cautions blind me to my mission. I must prioritize figuring out a way to "get paid" for having a heart and an inner life. Money is not really the issue, but "getting paid" means being recognized and appreciated for giving something to the community which also feels personally meaningful to me. That gift must reflect Mother Moon's human touch, and not just be some robotic skill set which I have been trained to perform.

What Gets Me Down: Realizing that I could have made a real difference in terms of alleviating some degree of suffering somewhere in the world, but that I let fear, self-protection, or simple moodiness prevent me from doing it.

A Bad Attitude That Could Sabotage Me: The sense that the best anyone can ever actually do is merely to survive. The sense that the world's condition is irredeemable and that all I can do is to keep my head down and try not to get hurt.

THE MOON IN THE ELEVENTH HOUSE

The Healing I Seek: In this lifetime, I resolve to strengthen my belief that I am actively shaping my own future rather than simply waiting passively to see what happens to me. I am learning that setting an intention is a magical act. I am learning to have faith in that power. I will succeed in realizing this goal by making plans and never failing strategically to follow through on them, always keeping my eye on the prize. I resolve to *seek alliances* with people who can help me achieve these goals – and to avoid squandering my time with people who only distract me from where I choose to go and what I choose to become.

The Tools I Have Been Given: A strong, instinctive feeling for strategy. The ability to recognize allies. The capacity to be a team-player.

If I Want to Be Happy, I Must Prioritize . . . anything connected with specifically *lunar* needs and values: home, family, and self-care, along with reliable friendships that pass the test of time. Attaining material or financial success can be a priority too, but only insofar as they support those kinds of lunar aspirations, while never exacting too high a price from them. One example would be placing family over career. Another would be elevating self-care over material productivity.

What Gets Me Down: The realization that I have somehow lost the thread of my life, having become "all tactics, but no strategy." Not having an overriding, long-term life-plan that excites me. Feeling as if I am going nowhere fast – or nowhere slowly, for that matter. Wasting time with people who also seem to be going nowhere.

A Bad Attitude That Could Sabotage Me: A sense that life simply happens to people, myself included, "while they are making other plans." A feeling of powerlessness – of my only being a cog in some mindless, purposeless machine. Surrendering to the herd instinct, to being swept along by the crowd – my life shaped by the trivialities of custom, social obligations, fashion, and so forth. Too much belief in the idea of "fate."

THE MOON IN THE TWELFTH HOUSE

The Healing I Seek: In this lifetime, I resolve to deepen my direct conscious contact with Divinity. I am healing my capacity to be open to dimensions which lie beyond this one. I resolve that what the world calls "faith" will become stronger in me, not because of religion, but rather due to the accumulated direct evidence of my own experience.

The Tools I Have Been Given: Psychic sensitivity. A sense of the presence of invisible energies, other dimensions, and spirit-beings. An instinct that this physical world is a dream from which we will all someday awaken.

If I Want to Be Happy, I Must Prioritize . . . healing my capacity for meditation and prayer, by whatever name I call those intentional inner states. I must prioritize subjective and transrational experience over academic rigor and critical thinking. A particularly efficient evolutionary path forward for me lies in engaging my heart in the contemplation of the universe's *loving, nurturing generosity* toward me – what has often in religious history been seen as the feminine face of God: Mother Mary, Kwan Yin, Green Tara, and others. As I meditate upon those energies, my heart opens like a flower.

What Gets Me Down: Realizing that I have wasted my time on lassitude, distraction, or escapism when I could have been sitting awe-struck in the presence of life's transcendent mysteries. Getting pulled away from my inner life by the whining demands of others who would be better off learning to take care of themselves rather than pressing my nurturing, protective buttons.

A Bad Attitude That Could Sabotage Me: A feeling that I exist only to care for others. A willingness to surrender my potential for leaps forward in consciousness on the altar of family roles, requirements, and expectations. A belief that I have no right to stand up for myself – that such "selfishness" is "sinful." A fear of looking silly, flaky, or self-indulgent as a result of following my rightful and necessary spiritual path.

13

PLUTO AND MARS IN THE TWELVE HOUSES

PLUTO IN THE FIRST HOUSE

Where I Confront My Soul-Wounds: The hurt places in me tend to manifest in bad decisions I make at critical existential crossroads. The pressure is on, and sometimes my wounds make the call rather than my soul. It is not that I am more wounded than other people; rather it is that I tend, often unwittingly, to put my "stuff" on the table rather than keeping it secret. I am capable of behaving self-destructively, but sometimes those wounds involve my creating pain for other people through what I say or do to them. When I am in the grips of my hurt places, I can seem cruel or unnecessarily confrontive.

How They Originated: In a prior lifetime, I was in a position of leadership and responsibility in a dark situation in which there were no good, morally acceptable answers. My long-ago adaptation to those circumstances left me with scars that I am trying to heal in this present lifetime.

How I Can Heal: I must seek companionship with people who are strong enough psychologically that they can accept my raw truthfulness without flinching. With them, I can recover my lost spontaneity. I can stop editing myself or "walking on eggshells." I will "learn by doing" in this lifetime – and what I am learning is how to move with dignity and self-respect through morally-complex questions where there is often no clear right path.

The Prize: A feeling of empowerment that does not go straight to my ego, but rather feels like I am simply being myself. If I succeed, I become a leader or a role model for others who are ready to face life's true complexity. I feel loved and appreciated. I feel natural. I feel good about myself.

The Price of Failure: I slip into a mixture of dark moodiness and over-bearing imperiousness. Wherever I go, I leave a trail of blood behind me, emotionally speaking.

PLUTO IN THE SECOND HOUSE

Where I Confront My Soul-Wounds: The hurt places in me manifest as feelings of self-doubt, illegitimacy, and insecurity. They may not show in any obvious sense, but they systematically undercut my ability to reach my highest potentials – potentials I truly have, but which no one suspects because they remain so well-hidden. An exaggerated attention to money or physical security can become the arena in which these unconscious insecurities express themselves.

How They Originated: In a prior lifetime, I was impacted by some nightmarish kind of material lack that threatened my survival or the survival of those whom I loved. Perhaps poverty was a factor. Perhaps it was famine or plague. Perhaps I had money – and was attacked for it, and lacked the ability to defend myself.

How I Can Heal: I must prove myself to myself by gaining faith, through experience, in my ability to be honest and direct about my needs without fearing punishment for doing so. I must learn to ask for what I need, demanding it if necessary. I will establish reasonable physical and financial security in this world, without falling into an impossible, neurotic fugue of trying to become "perfectly secure." No amount of money can do that for anyone.

The Prize: A feeling of finally being able to relax, feeling that I am as safe as anyone can be in this world and in these fragile bodies of ours. I am gaining the psychospiritual strength that will allow me to die in a spirit of faith and psychic ease when my time finally comes.

The Price of Failure: I slip into a kind of insecure desperation, constantly fearful of threats that mostly never actually manifest. I give too much power to money. I worry about it, and compromise myself to acquire it. I value physical security to the point that I am afraid to live. Perhaps I become a hoarder.

PLUTO IN THE THIRD HOUSE

Where I Confront My Soul-Wounds: The hurt places in me are rooted in my deepest cognitive patterns, where I am oriented to be especially alert to lies, darkness, and distortions. I do not "make those things up" either – they are quite real. That "suspicious" orientation of my mind finally manifests in my speech, where I can seem dark and even hurtful, even though I usually do not intend it. But even truth can be used as an anti-personnel weapon – and if I am angry with someone, I know where to stick the needles. Paranoia, along with negative interpretations of other people's behavior and motivations, can arise, creating a distorted view of life in me. In this lifetime, I have sometimes been punished for seeing more deeply than people wanted me to see – and my *overreaction to that punishment* mirrors the effects of my wounds.

How They Originated: In a prior lifetime, I was simply punished for telling the truth. Perhaps I was even martyred for it. Alternatively, in a prior lifetime, in order to avoid punishment I learned to lie skillfully to people who had power over me. I always saw more than I dared to say.

How I Can Heal: I must tell my story and hold nothing back. I must find my voice, knowing that it is the voice of a shaman or a psychoanalyst or a detective – the voice of a truthsayer, in other words. That means it will sound confrontive to many people. I must therefore choose my audience carefully. Keeping a hidden journal can help me make a start on my healing process. So can being open and revealing in psychotherapy – provided that the therapist is accepting, courageous, and flawless at keeping confidentiality.

The Prize: A feeling of not being at all self-conscious about what I say. A feeling of looseness and uncalculated spontaneity in my speech. Truthfulness becomes a reflex. Perhaps I experience empowerment as a writer or a teacher.

The Price of Failure: I slip into verbal nastiness and argumentativeness. I drive people away from me with my dark attitudes and pronouncements. My words do damage to people who do not deserve it. I fervently believe that I am telling the truth when in reality I am only telling half-truths.

PLUTO IN THE FOURTH HOUSE

Where I Confront My Soul-Wounds: The hurt places in me show up most directly in domestic or intimate situations – family dynamics, issues around my physical home, and relations with my dearest friends. I can feel lonely and misunderstood. I can feel isolated, even with people around me. I can become identified with my secret self to the point that I become an alien in my own home.

How They Originated: In a prior lifetime, I was abused in a family situation from which I could not readily escape. I learned to protect myself by going inward – the less I was seen, the safer I became. I saw everyone with crystalline clarity, but I knew better than to say what I saw.

How I Can Heal: I must establish a domestic life based on genuine, authentic intimacy – and by "domestic life," let's include my deepest, longest friendships as well "family" in the more obvious sense. I heal in a situation where I feel seen and accepted for who I am, no matter how edgy or "psychological" I become. I also heal in a situation where I am equally accepting of those with whom I am sharing life. We become two mirrors of truth, facing each other.

The Prize: A feeling of finally having found my true home. The liberating empowerment of sure and certain love. Unabashed, confident spontaneity in a domestic situation.

The Price of Failure: I slip into brooding self-absorption, feeling like a spy in my own life and my own home, gathering dark data – data that I will never be able to report.

PLUTO IN THE FIFTH HOUSE

Where I Confront My Soul-Wounds: The hurt places in me manifest in my complicated relationship with pleasure. I can be prim, self-punitive, and judging there – or I can line up to buy First Class tickets for the oblivion express. There are many such railroads, but they all boil down to over-doing what people naturally do for joy and release. My own issues might possibly be echoed in the lives and natures of my children, if I have any. They can also be reflected in poor sexual or romantic choices I make – trusting people who are not worthy of my trust.

How They Originated: In a prior lifetime, something normally pleasurable became cruelly distorted. Did I experience rape or prostitution? Did I fall in with self-destructive hell-raisers? Did I experience addiction? Did I fall in love with the wrong person – not just someone with whom things did not work out, but rather someone truly poisonous? Did I binge and purge?

How I Can Heal: I must re-establish a right and healthy relationship with the normal appetites of my body. I cannot win this battle by avoiding them. Sex must be linked to soul-intimacy, even if it does not last. Fun and release must be decoupled from a hunger for oblivion – and positively linked to actually connecting with other people.

The Prize: A feeling of my spirit being buoyed up by life's little innocent joys – a glass of wine or a fine meal shared with a dear friend, for example. A stable, comfortable, non-destructive relationship to my human appetites. A return to childlike playfulness free of any feelings of compulsion, shame, or dread.

The Price of Failure: I slip into morbid and compulsive patterns of behavior in relation to anything that is alleged to provide joy or pleasure, but which in fact does the opposite once the initial stimulation has worn off. That, or I retreat from these issues by becoming too restrictive or judgmental regarding my own natural animal appetites.

PLUTO IN THE SIXTH HOUSE

Where I Confront My Soul-Wounds: The hurt places in me show up in terms of the kinds of responsibilities I allow myself to accept in my life. Maybe they are work-related, maybe not. I resolve to define my own ethics and duties. No one else has any right to define them for me. When I was younger, I may have been damaged by dark role models, or simply by the absence of good ones. These hurts can easily *somatize*, which is to say, they might show up in my physical body as illnesses.

How They Originated: In a prior lifetime, I was something very much like a slave. Literal slavery might possibly be the actual truth – but more broadly it means that I was somehow under someone else's orders. I found those orders odious, but I could not escape them. Someone or something that felt evil to me was in power over me.

How I Can Heal: I must establish truly meaningful work in my life, and I must have the subjective experience of undertaking that work freely and of my own volition. My work absolutely must not feel like slavery in this lifetime. It is enormously helpful for me to seek mentors who are characterized by honesty and candor. These mentors do not ever lie to me, and they help me to become more skillful in expressing my own honesty. They honor my freedom and thus they willingly grant me the right to make my own mistakes, and to learn from them.

The Prize: A feeling of being deeply resonant with the work I am called to do. A sense of having a genuine, meaningful mission in life. An appreciation for my teachers, whose words come out of my own mouth from time to time. Contact with those teachers leads me directly later in my life to the satisfaction of feeling that I have interacted helpfully with people who are younger than myself – the feeling that I have passed along the gift that I myself received from my own guides and teachers.

The Price of Failure: I slip into the time-serving hopelessness of a slave. I avoid even thinking of escape since its apparent impossibility makes escape too painful to contemplate. I give up, my spirit broken.

PLUTO IN THE SEVENTH HOUSE

Where I Confront My Soul-Wounds: The hurt places in me manifest in my intimate life, and that includes my friendships as well as mating bonds or romantic relationships. I can be attracted to people who harm me, either through their own unresolved craziness or perhaps through darker motives. Who has hurt me? Who has lied to me? Who has used me? And more to the point, *who chose to trust them?* The answer, of course, is me. Taking full responsibility for those choices rather than blaming those who have hurt me is where I directly confront my own wounds – and thus create the possibility of healing them, and not repeating them.

How They Originated: In a prior lifetime, I was damaged by a marriage or a marriage-like situation. I was shackled to someone who might have simply been dark, even evil. At the very least, he or she had power over me and used the power in cruel ways. I was lied to. I was treated as disposable. It sunk in.

How I Can Heal: I must, above all, hear truth spoken out loud in any relationship worth pursuing. Truth will heal me – and to be worthy of it, I must become the kind of person who can *hear* truth too, even if I do not like what I hear. My healing is not *simply* a "search for an honest man or woman" – it also involves searching for that honest person *inside of myself*. That is how I become worthy of someone who is worthy of me in this life. That is how I recover.

The Prize: A feeling that my ability to love and to trust is being restored. A return to the life-giving warmth of healthy intimacy. Naked, reliable closeness with another human being.

The Price of Failure: I slip into patterns of experience which confirm my worst fears about human nature. I develop an "attitude about men" or an "attitude about women" – and unwittingly, unconsciously, seek experiences which reinforce it.

PLUTO IN THE EIGHTH HOUSE

Where I Confront My Soul-Wounds: The hurt places in me tend to show up specifically in my sexuality, both in terms of my actual relationships and in terms of my desires and fantasies. More broadly, I experience exaggerated, moody reactions in relationships – reactions which upon reflection seem out of proportion to my actual experiences. I may very well encounter extreme life-and-death circumstances in life – major dramas which too are manifestations of my soul-wounds, echoing past-life events.

How They Originated: In a prior lifetime, I was confronted by truly dark and nightmarish situations – the worst that humanity has to offer. I saw grim and unnatural death up close. I may have been hurt sexually too. I looked the devil right in the eye.

How I Can Heal: I must dive into these wounded places. Confronting them directly is the only way I can heal them. Turning my back on them only makes them stronger. Sharing my impressions of these inward encounters with one other brave and psychologically-steady person is enormously helpful. That person might be a dear friend, or a trusted mate, or a counsellor of some sort.

The Prize: A feeling of liberation from an old ghost which had been haunting me and sucking life out of me. Release from an underlying mood of darkness. A return of libido and sexual energy. The possibility of healthy intimacy. A sense that death is the natural, even sometimes welcome, end of life rather than a tragic nightmare that is always gaining on us.

The Price of Failure: I slip into a grim attitude toward life, always prepared for tragedy and feeling perpetually on the edge of impending darkness. I experience compulsive attractions to vampiric people who are not good for me – both the users and the walking wounded.

PLUTO IN THE NINTH HOUSE

Where I Confront My Soul-Wounds: The hurt places in me are most likely to manifest in the areas of religion and education. "Moral" values – which are inconsistent with the actual path of my soul – are pressed upon me. If I internalize them, I cripple myself. I am likely to receive "education" which actually hampers my ability to see the very truths that I need to see. One illustration would be learning that "astrology is a superstition" when it is my destiny to become a working astrologer. In one more very concrete area, I encounter my soul-wounds – that is in *travel*. In this lifetime, without intending it or knowing it, I will visit places where I was hurt in prior lifetimes. I will experience goosebumps of recognition when I get there.

How They Originated: In a prior lifetime, I was force-fed shaming religious dogma. My spirit was damaged in the "Holy Name of God." My entire sense of reality was toxified by beliefs that were antithetical to what should actually have been my path. The shaming of the normal expression of human sexuality is a prime illustration of this wound.

How I Can Heal: I must not turn away from religion and philosophy; instead I must question them. No heresy is taboo, no question is too charged to ask. Similarly, education is beneficial to me, so long as I doubt everything I am taught until it passes the test of my own direct experience. I will travel, and unwittingly I will return to the physical scenes of certain prior-life traumas. Seeing them from my present perspective of consciousness will be liberating and energizing.

The Prize: A feeling of aligning myself with the actual truth of my own experience rather than "passing anybody else's theological examination." I do not need to worry about the Holy Inquisition. I can think for myself and frame my own moral compass without fear.

The Price of Failure: I either slip into some sort of morbid Fundamentalism or into a kind of cynical avoidance of all of life's larger questions. My view of the world becomes dark, bitter, and dog-eat-dog.

PLUTO IN THE TENTH HOUSE

Where I Confront My Soul-Wounds: The hurt places in me manifest in an inexplicable fear of the "big world" in which I find myself. I fear government, law, Imperial power, or bad guys in positions of authority – even when there is no immediate evidence of their truly being a personal threat to me. My urge to hold my gifts back from the world and to "keep my head down" are direct manifestations of this wound in my soul. Another possibility lies in my aligning myself with those darker social forces – if I can't beat them, I join them.

How They Originated: In a prior lifetime, I was hounded and persecuted, and perhaps worse, by corrupt public powers or by grievous social inequity. The obvious suspects are racism, sexism, homophobia, religious bias, fascism, ethnic cleansing, and so on. Human history displays no shortage of these kinds of toxins. If I was once on the receiving end of any of them, Pluto in the tenth house might well be the karmic result.

How I Can Heal: I must claim my power in the world. My aim is not to become mean, corrupt or oppressive myself, but rather to become *indispensable* – so good at something which is meaningful to my community that I am surrounded by natural allies. I need to feel that I *can* be dangerous if I am attacked – that I have that capability and that some of that power to defend myself comes from my allies. If someone wants to harm me, it will be their mistake. My hope is to never need to use that retaliatory capacity.

The Prize: A feeling of empowerment and of being in a safe, even valued, position in society at large. Deep professional work that actually helps to give a sense of meaning to my life. Freedom from an old anxiety that pervaded my insecure attitude toward becoming visible in this world.

The Price of Failure: I slip into a delusional place where my public role always feels strangely furtive. Unconsciously, I feel as if my actual identity must be kept secret, and that maintaining that secrecy about who I truly am is the key to my survival. I don a clever disguise in the world, making sure that the life I am living offers no clues about my soul's actual nature. I therefore live and die as a spy.

PLUTO IN THE ELEVENTH HOUSE

Where I Confront My Soul-Wounds: The hurt places in me are connected with the kinds of madness that are particularly characteristic of groups of people operating together – tribes, armies, lynch mobs. As Sting once sang, "Men go crazy in congregations, but they only get better one by one." I confront my soul-wounds directly by bravely contemplating the sea of faces around me. Why am I with these people? Why do I waste my time with them? Why have I made these choices? *And where is my true soul-tribe?*

How They Originated: In a prior lifetime, I was swept along by some kind of mass movement. It could have taken many forms, and some of them might even have looked fairly benign. But the problem was that I lost my own way; I was defined by the group rather than by the nature of my own soul. Hive-mind replaced internal guidance; group-think replaced my own conscience.

How I Can Heal: I must choose the people with whom I associate consciously, intentionally, and carefully. Avoiding group entanglements entirely might tempt me, but that will not really help – I need to face this wound more squarely. I do so by learning to recognize my own soul-family. How? Simple: these are people who help me to go where I would have been going anyway – they just support me in getting there faster. In a nutshell, we share common values.

The Prize: A feeling of healthy *membership*; a feeling of having my own direction in life – and the added bonus of a team of friends, allies, and associates who can support me in that evolutionary process and whose company gives me energy.

The Price of Failure: I slip into herd instinct, my life defined by social expectations. Increasingly, a moral abyss opens between my soul and the groups of people with whom I have formed associations. I do not believe in them or approve of them, but I am still with them and I do not know why.

PLUTO IN THE TWELFTH HOUSE

Where I Confront My Soul-Wounds: The hurt places in me reveal themselves in the ways that I set myself up for failure and loss, or perhaps even for tragedy. I can be my own worst enemy, and not even know that I am doing it until afterwards when I am picking up the broken pieces. I can experience a spooky sense of the presence of something we might call "evil spirits" or just "bad *ju-ju*." Unfocused, ill-defined fears can pervade my experience.

How They Originated: In a prior lifetime, perhaps I was subjected to some extreme form of mystical initiation – a process for which I was simply not ready. I was taught to refute my body and to view this world with distaste. Those toxic initiations sunk into my bones – and made me inclined to undercut my own successes or desires. They also simply scared me. In a more general way, in a prior lifetime I very likely encountered some kind of "total loss" or unimaginable tragedy from which I have not yet healed. Maybe it was no one's fault, like an earthquake or a plague. In any case, the wound is still with me.

How I Can Heal: I must find an inward path which does not separate my spirituality from my journey of psychological development and healing. Everything must be kept grounded and real, and be taken at my own pace. I have a natural right to doubt everything I am taught about human spirituality until it has proven its worth to me.

The Prize: A feeling of absolute honesty and psychological authenticity in my spiritual path. I take nothing simply "on faith" because I have been told to believe it. I only believe what I have genuinely experienced myself with my own mind and senses. That is enough for me.

The Price of Failure: I slip into a mixture of denial or avoidance regarding any contact with the spirit world, along with a kind of spooky "whistling past the graveyard" superstitious nervousness. And I continue to magnetize patterns of loss into my life. At some level I am still "angry at God."

Mars shares the rulership of Scorpio with Pluto. It is a blunder to forget the reality of that primal astrological connection. The house positions of Mars carry that same unmistakable Scorpionic stamp as surely as Pluto's house positions. Here, in The Book of Water, we are concentrating more heavily on Pluto, not because it is more important than Mars, but simply because it is fresh material. We already went into depth with Mars back in The Book of Fire. *For the sake of completeness and easy reference, I include that same house-by-house analysis of Mars here, word for word, as it appeared in the first book of this series.*

MARS IN THE FIRST HOUSE

Battlefield: Forks in the road of life; fateful choices that require a lot of courage. Assertiveness training. Critical decision points, which are often characterized by insufficient information. Binding vows made in an imperfect world. Painful choices. Leadership, in situations where others who are incapable of defending themselves are counting on you. Meeting resistance with appropriate force.

Strategy: To accept the challenge. To recognize that "fear is the mind killer." To avoid panic. To be willing to burn bridges behind you. To use sufficient force – but no more than necessary. To protect that which is worthy of protection – and sacrifice the rest.

Objective: To truly *lead* a life rather than have it happen to you. To recognize that fear – and only fear – blocks your path. To find your inner warrior.

The Shape of Failure: Cowardice. Allowing yourself to become the designated victim. To let fear make your decisions. To surrender your freedom to the will of petty tyrants. Alternatively, to become cruel and tyrannical yourself. To let anger rule your life.

MARS IN THE SECOND HOUSE

Battlefield: Challenges that afford you an opportunity to prove yourself to yourself and to others. Winning despite limited resources. Financial stress: either too little money – or too much. Gaining confidence in your inner warrior and his or her ability to come out on top despite the odds.

Strategy: Feel the fear, but do it anyway. Rise to challenges. Prove yourself to yourself by facing people and situations that intimidate you. Be willing to bet on yourself financially, taking money risks in order to fulfill your dreams and aspirations. Be willing to "die with your boots on." Accept the risks entailed in claiming the resources and tools that you need for your journey.

Objective: A fundamental, elevating transformation in your level of self-confidence and warrior dignity.

The Shape of Failure: Being afraid to follow the path with heart. Looking back on the life you did not live. Giving your need for material security too much power in shaping your decisions. Attracting a pattern of financial stress.

MARS IN THE THIRD HOUSE

Battlefield: Finding your voice. Expressing your passion. Standing up to intellectual intimidation. Trusting your own perceptions even if others tell you they are incorrect or heretical. Claiming your right to an education in every sense of that word. Learning to be effective in argument.

Strategy: Speaking up. Expressing yourself with passion and convincing vehemence. Trusting your curiosity. Seizing experience that has been forbidden to you. Not allowing yourself to be silenced. Recognizing that you do some of your most penetrating thinking while in physical motion – that is, while walking, driving, or traveling.

Objective: To claim your right and your ability to speak passionately, confidently, and persuasively on any topic, even in the face of judgment or intimidation.

The Shape of Failure: Allowing yourself to be silenced, your voice shut down by others whom you have allowed to overpower or overshadow you. To betray your own best truths by leaving them unsaid. Alternatively, to become compulsively argumentative, defensive, bitter, and damagingly sarcastic.

MARS IN THE FOURTH HOUSE

Battlefield: First and foremost, this configuration is about developing the emotional courage necessary for all inner work – facing the truth of our own souls is frightening. Psychological wounds are often connected to family dynamics, and these kinds of issues figure prominently here. Anger, resentments and repression linked to domestic life arise and require resolution.

Strategy: Contemplation of the Warrior archetype, leading to the integration of the inner warrior into the shape of the outward biographical life. Bringing your fierceness, passion, and heat to the surface where others can see it. Finding the strength and courage to claim one's natural home and to protect it against any assault.

Objective: A passionate *soul* is not enough; the aim here is a passionate *life*, lived in the right location and shared with the right people.

The Shape of Failure: To harbor seething resentments or frustrations without a ripple on the surface. The bomb detonating inside the steel room. Domestic or familial conflict endlessly repeating and never resolving.

MARS IN THE FIFTH HOUSE

Battlefield: Stepping onto the stage of life and belting out your song, whatever that means for you. The courage to express yourself honestly and creatively. The courage to be sincere to the point of genuine vulnerability. Performance. Facing stage fright. Feeling confident and legitimate in the behavioral expression of your sexuality. Passionate love affairs, with the ghost of unresolved karma hovering over them.

Strategy: Finding your natural instrument of self-expression and polishing your skills with it. Committing yourself to a life of creativity and taking the emotional risks that path entails. Using sports to gain confidence in your warrior-body. Trusting your lust – but first, making sure that it is trustworthy.

Objective: Total unselfconscious self-expression at every level.

The Shape of Failure: Being ruled by your inhibitions and your fear of ridicule. Turning away from your passion; allowing others to shame your sexuality. Remaining in unresolved, karmically-based relationships with people who hurt you.

MARS IN THE SIXTH HOUSE

Battlefield: Finding the right work. Independently defining your own responsibilities and executing them decisively. Seeking mentors who embody courage and who show you the right use of force. Learning to compete mindfully. Protecting those who legitimately depend on you. Forcefully defending your right to self-care.

Strategy: Letting no one and nothing stand between you and the path that leads to meaningful work – and being brave enough to strike out on your own independent career or vocation. Seeking teachers who instantly fill you with respect for them. Finding a place for competitiveness in your life, one that does not leave a trail of blood behind you. Defending your right to take care of your health at every level.

Objective: Mastery. Finding the right vocation. Developing the skills that underlie meaningful victory. Seeking your teachers – and later defending your students.

The Shape of Failure: Working for a boss who was "Attila the Hun" in a prior lifetime. Accepting abuse, internalizing shame that derives from the niggling criticism of minor tyrants. Stress-related disorders, both physical and mental.

MARS IN THE SEVENTH HOUSE

Battlefield: Intimacy in all senses: marriage, friendship, partnership. Passionate connections. Difficult relationships – including those that are worth the trouble. Accepting the fact that some element of conflict is endemic to all human interdependency, along with the development of mindful skills for dealing with it. Facing the seductive, slippery dangers of numbing familiarity and mechanical ritual in long-term relationships; defeating those dangers.

Strategy: Learning the art of intimate conflict resolution. Being direct and truthful rather than harboring tensions under the banners of tolerance or forgiveness. Most critically, learning to discern and select partners *who would immediately understand the previous sentence.*

Objective: The maintenance of genuine passion in long-term intimacy.

The Shape of Failure: A chronic attraction to people whom you do not actually like or respect. Endless drama – or endless therapy – that goes nowhere. Fights that are not about what they appear to be about; mere venting and needless, pointless emotional bloodshed.

MARS IN THE EIGHTH HOUSE

Battlefield: The behaviors that arise from all of the complex emotions, instincts, and issues that are triggered by the process of coupling or mating. Unresolved psychological wounds and how we deal with them – or how they deal with us. The unconscious mind manifesting in our intimate behavior. Human mortality – that is to say, our psychological and spiritual relationship to our own deaths and to the deaths of people with whom we share life.

Strategy: Above all, honesty – the inner behavior of truthful self-examination, along with the outward behavior of penetrating interactions with people with whom we have deep bonds. Committed sexuality as one path of the spiritual warrior. Lifelong preparation for the spiritual adventure of death.

Objective: Making death our counselor – which is to say that in the light of our mortality, much becomes very clear. We then understand what is important and what is not important. Bringing that wisdom to bear upon the entire length of life. The wasteful futility of lying to ourselves or lying to anyone with whom we are pretending to be intimate. Our objective is to live each day as if it were our last and to love with that kind of transparency, intensity, and nakedness.

The Shape of Failure: Belief in the illusion of a "magical partner" with whom we can remain in a fairyland of passion forever without making any evolutionary effort; the inevitable cycle of disappointments that follow from such an erroneous belief. Acting as if we think that we will live forever.

MARS IN THE NINTH HOUSE

Battlefield: The endless, passionate search for meaning and understanding in life. Adventures of all sorts. Travel that requires courage; cross-cultural experience. Education, both in the formal and the experiential sense. Robust religion and philosophy tempered and deepened by a willingness to hurl oneself bravely into life.

Strategy: Going where we are drawn to go but afraid to go. That includes travel, but also crossing cultural or social boundaries closer to home. Assertively claiming our right to learn or to achieve education. Testing our beliefs against reality and being willing to renounce the ones that fail the test, all the while accepting the social consequences of walking that talk.

Objective: A warrior's path of endless stretching and adventure that leads to a personally convincing and utterly honest sense of the meaning of life. A feeling of having been set free in the world, able to move confidently through various cultures, social strata, and exotic places.

The Shape of Failure: The armchair adventurer eating potato chips in front of a television. Angry religious or philosophical fanaticism and dogmatism impervious to information. Preaching. The need to convince others of that which, in truth, we do not fully believe ourselves. Willful ignorance.

MARS IN THE TENTH HOUSE

Battlefield: Your mission in the world. An independent, adventurous career. A colorful reputation. Bravely affecting the myths and symbols of your community. Forcefully making a difference in the world. Standing up publicly and being counted. Enemies and competitors. Two dogs and one bone. Public conflicts where compromise is not available or possible.

Strategy: To be willing to pay the price and face the stress of accepting your legitimate public mission in the world. To cultivate autonomy and independence as you shape your lifestyle. To recognize that others' fates are dependent upon your being courageous. To accept that it is your path to protect entities – that is to say, people, ideas, even creatures – which are incapable of protecting themselves.

Objective: To have a mission in life so passionately meaningful and so transcendently important to you that you would die for it – not that you are eager to die for it, but that you would if you had to. Waking up each morning with that kind of vitality. A fire in your belly to go to work in the morning.

The Shape of Failure: Endless stress in meaningless work or social situations, typically characterized by oppressive, unfair, or angry authorities above you. Being defined as the natural victim or scapegoat – everyone's favorite punch.

MARS IN THE ELEVENTH HOUSE

Battlefield: The search for your natural tribe. Networking; teamwork – often with difficult people. "Herding cats." Soul-clans characterized by stressful karma – enemies, class struggle, social conflict. Meaningful aims involving experiences that can only be attained via cooperation with other people. Passionate devotion to long-term goals and projects. Battles in the second half of life; the "call of destiny" coming in maturity.

Strategy: Setting goals which require courage – and accepting them and committing to them long-term. Relentless devotion, with the eye on the prize. Once such goals are set – and only then – the seeking of the team or the human network necessary for reaching them.

Objective: To devote the first half of life to embodying a warrior-spirit worthy of the mission that emerges in the second half of life; to assemble the network of allies who allow you to fulfill that mission. To keep the faith that you have something important to contribute to your community despite the slow emergence of the circumstances that call for it.

The Shape of Failure: Empty, pointless alliances. Stressful, fruitless social over-extension. Gossip; petty wars and rivalries; "court intrigue." Endless interpersonal politics. Exhausting inner tension or frustration boiling over in the second half of life, often taking the form of an existential explosion – or a depressive surrender to exhaustion.

MARS IN THE TWELFTH HOUSE

Battlefield: Consciousness itself; the psychic realms; the spiritual path. What stands between you and a major breakthrough in those categories is simply *fear*. You have reached the stage in the evolutionary journey where you will either make a breakthrough or you will break down. Thus you attract everything scary, from apparitions of the lower astral planes to brushes with physical danger in this world.

Strategy: You are training your nerves to remain unflappable and steady in the face of strange, unsettling, or weird psychic stimuli. Facing specific fears of any sort, even physical ones – repeatedly, over time – *desensitizes your response to panic.* Thus, for example, you might contemplate the possible spiritual benefits of skydiving, spelunking, or mountaineering – or if you are an old woman in a walker, contemplate the possible spiritual benefit of walking across the street.

Objective: Staying centered no matter what happens. An absolute, self-possessed sense of presence in the eternal now, no matter what manner of stimulus arises. Spiritual courage. Alignment with the archetype of the spiritual warrior.

The Shape of Failure: Accidents and misfortunes arising as the law of synchronicity presents you with frightening growth opportunities from which you turn away – in other words, it is better to embrace those scary experiences rather than fleeing them and thus forcing them to manifest in a more negative way. Spiritual stasis; being stalled on the cusp of evolutionary breakthrough. Vague, unspecified fears and free-floating anxiety; the specter of madness.

14

NEPTUNE AND JUPITER IN THE TWELVE HOUSES

*T*he *Book of Neptune* goes into chapter-length detail about Neptune in each one of the twelve houses. We do not have space for that kind of granularity here. You might want to have a look at that earlier volume, especially if Neptune plays a prominent role in your own astrological journey. Here, as with our previous "cookbook" examples, my intention is just to telegraph some initial impressions about Neptune's action in each house as a starting point for some deeper thoughts involving its sign and any aspects it might make. What follows are the seed notions that enter my mind whenever I first look at Neptune's house position in anyone's birthchart.

NEPTUNE IN THE FIRST HOUSE

The Focal Point of My Spiritual Evolution: Learning to enlist my ego in the service of my soul, and eliminating any feeling that the two are opposites. I resolve to make the hard – and sometimes unpopular – decisions which are necessary if I am going to have experiences in this lifetime which actually feed my evolution. I will *make a stand* for my spirituality and I will defend that stand if necessary.

My Most Skillful Means For Achieving It: Getting past the misleading notion that sometimes being willful and setting boundaries are antithetical to the soul's evolution. I resolve to be decisive, even fierce, in claiming my right to follow my path wherever and however it leads me. My journey this time is not about meekness and humility – it is about claiming spiritual adventures even if other people judge, block, or even try to forbid them.

The Angels' Gift: I have been given a strong motivation to explore consciousness. I attract magical, inexplicable experiences into my life which enhance and stimulate that motivation. When I am decisive regarding my higher inner commitments, I am supported by invisible forces. Doors to consciousness-triggering experience open before me.

Wasted And Dissipated: I drift; I feel like a ghost in my own life. I feel as if I am constantly playing a role in a movie that does not spark any emotional engagement in me.

NEPTUNE IN THE SECOND HOUSE

The Focal Point of My Spiritual Evolution: Learning to accurately assess my actual level of soul evolution in order that I employ evolutionary methods which are actually effective and appropriate for me – matched to the true level of my needs, in other words. Some people need to sing hymns on Sunday morning, while others need to meditate in Himalayan caves. I need to find my rightful place on that spectrum. It comes down to my having faith in myself – and just *enough* spiritual pride that I challenge myself in meaningful, soul-triggering ways.

My Most Skillful Means For Achieving It: Being willing to bet on myself spiritually. Pushing my limits. Acting as if I were a few steps ahead of where I think I am spiritually – heading for that "Himalayan cave," in other words. Money can become a symbolic focal point in my spiritual journey. Here is how – do I invest in that week-long meditation program? It is not free. Do I buy the physical object of devotion that attracts me – the crystal, the icon, the holy book? If not, then I must ask myself: am I denying myself because I truly cannot afford it – or is it because I do not think that I am worth it?

The Angels' Gift: I have been given humility, which is a precious treasure spiritually. I just need to be careful not to overdo it. I have also been given a pressing hunger to evolve – and to succeed, my humility must not slip into self-limitation.

Wasted And Dissipated: I drift into a state of *spiritual lassitude* simply because I am under-stimulated, under-fed, and uninspired. Spiritually, it feels as if I am endlessly repeating the sixth grade – and that I have no idea that the seventh grade exists.

NEPTUNE IN THE THIRD HOUSE

The Focal Point of My Spiritual Evolution: Learning to trust my senses as the bandwidth of my awareness begins to expand into the psychic and astral realms. Learning to let language flow out of my mouth straight from my larger self, trusting that the right words will come. Learning to question "common sense," and instead immersing myself in an entirely different and far more mystical description of reality. Contingent on my success in those areas, I can potentially be worthy of serving others as a spiritual teacher..

My Most Skillful Means for Achieving It: Immersing myself in "alternative education" – which is to say, *unlearning* the conventional assumptions about what is "obviously true." One example would be letting go of the common beliefs that the universe is three-dimensional and time-bound, that we ourselves are only material objects, and that mind and brain mean the same thing. I actively question all limiting materialist assumptions.

The Angels' Gift: I have been given a natural attunement to other realms and other dimensions. My senses are less constrained by conventional assumptions than are most people's. I find myself saying helpful things without knowing that I knew them.

Wasted And Dissipated: I drift into a weird state of alienation from myself in which I do not trust my own thoughts or perceptions. Caught in this limbo, I become confused – and my speech quickly reflects that disorder. Half the time, people do not know what I am talking about, and neither do I.

NEPTUNE IN THE FOURTH HOUSE

The Focal Point of My Spiritual Evolution: Learning to attune to the vibrations of the land, and drawing strength from the Earth. Consciously inhabiting my dream body. Connecting with ancestral spirits. Merging the spiritual and the psychoanalytical without getting too tangled up in a narrowly academic framework or the navel-gazing ego-worship of purely conventional psychology. Family dynamics as an incubator of soul growth.

My Most Skillful Means For Achieving It: Quiet inward time free of worldly entanglements is critical for me now. Sitting alone in silence in nature. Establishing a dedicated sacred space in my home, and using it regularly. Surrounding myself with spiritual reminders in my home – icons, images, crystals, and so on. Finding my natural home – which is to say, a place that feeds and supports my soul. Living there if possible.

The Angels' Gift: I have been given sensitivity to the spirits of places – I can find the right rock in the forest or the right park bench to sit on. I can also recognize the wrong ones, the ones which suck energy out of me. Ancestors in spirit form are on my side, guiding and protecting me. I acknowledge them with gratitude. Faith in the continuity of consciousness through death and beyond it arises naturally in my heart.

Wasted And Dissipated: I drift into a sleepy state of daydreaming and wool-gathering as if I had no direction and no real motivational foundation. I sacrifice myself to family, losing my personal identity in the roles they prescribe for me.

NEPTUNE IN THE FIFTH HOUSE

The Focal Point of My Spiritual Evolution: Learning to harness the evolutionary power of ecstasy. Integrating spontaneous joy into my inner path. Art and creativity as pathways to self-discovery. The soul-triggering impact of close, brief, meaningful encounters with people who seem strangely familiar. Performance – literally in front of an audience – as a method of "getting over myself," losing or reducing my self-consciousness.

My Most Skillful Means For Achieving It: Celebrating life like a pagan – dancing, drumming, singing. Enjoying and affirming my physical body. Discovering and cultivating my creative talents to the point that they can flow through me unimpeded by self-consciousness – thus transcending "effort" and entering "flow." Embracing and acting on the fact that joy opens my heart to Divinity far more effectively than duty and suffering ever can.

The Angels' Gift: I have been given creative talent and imagination as a kind of "starter kit" for my inner work in this lifetime. I know how to forget myself and have a good time. I am not over-burdened by an exaggerated sense of sin or guilt. I feel that "God loves me" whatever I do, so long as I am not hurting anyone else.

Wasted And Dissipated: I drift into pointless dissipation, mistaking ecstasy for enlightenment and bacchanalia for insight. I unwittingly trivialize the mysteries of higher consciousness by reducing them to various forms of escapism. Alternatively, I simply "hang on the cross," having given up joy.

NEPTUNE IN THE SIXTH HOUSE

The Focal Point of My Spiritual Evolution: Learning to correctly identify my true spiritual teachers. Creating regular habits of spiritual discipline; making them as natural and instinctive to me as brushing my teeth in the morning. Losing my self-importance by devoting time to service and to acts of charity and kindness towards others. With success in all these areas, I will eventually pass on the gifts I have received to people younger than myself. Being a link in that chain of spiritual gifts spanning generations is fundamental to my fulfilling my evolutionary intentions in this lifetime.

My Most Skillful Means For Achieving It: Willingly exposing myself to a variety of teachers and discerning and dissecting their impact upon me. Did something more than words enter me? Is there a human resonance between us? Is this teacher the real deal? Committing to routine, discipline, and regularity in whatever spiritual practices attract me – I choose them freely, but once chosen, I then unfailingly submit to them as part of the routine structure of my daily life.

The Angels' Gift: I have been given the "receptor cells" for receiving transmission from certain men and women who are ahead of me on the path. My karma is such that these lofty beings are disposed to help me. All I have to add to the mixture is humility, gratitude, and appreciation – and a willingness to pass the gift onward once the wisdom has ripened in me with time.

Wasted And Dissipated: I drift into slavery, taking orders from unworthy figures of authority. In my work, I feel like a phantom – invisible and ignored. I become a drone; I dissolve into the mechanical execution of my assigned duties.

NEPTUNE IN THE SEVENTH HOUSE

The Focal Point of My Spiritual Evolution: Learning to recognize my true "spiritual friends" – and while that term can include lovers and life-partners, it also includes other kinds of soul-companions as well. These are people with whom *shared experiences of the transcendent* will naturally arise. These experiences can be as simple as the same thought forming in each of us at the same moment – or as weird as our seeing a ghost together or independently remembering the same shared past life. In all cases, their *corroboration* of my own psychic perceptions strengthens my confidence in those perceptions. I cannot advance efficiently without such soul-intimacy and such corroboration.

My Most Skillful Means For Achieving It: I must ensure that any relationship which I allow to achieve importance in my life always has a spiritual basis. I do not squander my time on any other kind of bond. We do not need to share a religion, but before trusting people in a deep way, I need to see them spontaneously offering me evidence that they have an inner life which is important to them – and that they cannot explain life to themselves without reference to some larger framework of purpose.

The Angels' Gift: I have been given an ironclad promise that I am not alone in the world. Some old soulmates have chosen to incarnate along with me. The laws of the universe guarantee that we will meet. What I need to guarantee *myself* is that I will have done enough inner work in advance to be able to recognize these people. I also understand that finding soulmates does not mean that we effortlessly "live happily ever after." There is always a higher purpose in these encounters, and fulfilling it demands some stretching on my part. With their help, I can do that.

Wasted And Dissipated: I drift into relationships and friendships with people weaker than myself. Inevitably, they fail me in various ways. In response to the chronic hurt, something in me gives up on the idea of spiritual intimacy. That vacuum slowly fills with sadness.

NEPTUNE IN THE EIGHTH HOUSE

The Focal Point of My Spiritual Evolution: Learning to integrate deep, sometimes even confrontive, psychological work on myself with my spiritual path. The two – psychology and spirituality – are inseparable. There are interior emotional wounds in me that I must face and heal, or they will stymie my spiritual growth. Sexual intimacy is always an area where these wounds will become visible. Because of that fact, I embrace my sexuality wherever it leads me. Death is a powerful teacher for me too. I will encounter it in many of its forms and faces. Much of my life is a preparation for my own passing, which will be a monumental evolutionary opportunity for me, if I have prepared myself for it correctly.

My Most Skillful Means For Achieving It: Nothing brings me face to face with the inner healing I need to do faster than human sexual intimacy. Committed physical relationship, so long as it has a spiritual basis, is an effective evolutionary method for me – but it is not the only one: I also have an affinity for shamanic work. I have a natural attunement to disembodied beings and energies that can assist me in helping others – and with such invisible help, I can cultivate "spiritual powers" such as reading symbols, interpreting dreams, and various forms of energetic healing. Following these paths assists me in resolving my own psychic wounds.

The Angels' Gift: I am not alone. In this lifetime, a few deep soul-friends will appear in my life, holding the mirror of truth before me. Our relationships will unfold on many planes simultaneously and we will be aware of it happening that way, even if we cannot explain it. I have help from "the other side" as well. As my own journey unfolds, certain mysterious powers will manifest in me, or pass through me. I will receive several precious gifts of magic and mystery around the passing of people I love.

Wasted And Dissipated: I drift into a state of chronic longing for something that I either cannot define or which I misunderstand as a kind of unrequited romantic hunger. Moodiness grips me, along with morbid, hungry ideation. I am easily spooked; there is a haunted look in my eyes.

NEPTUNE IN THE NINTH HOUSE

The Focal Point of My Spiritual Evolution: Learning to correct flaws and errors in my understanding of consciousness and its relationship to the universe. That sounds like a tall order, but here is the essence of it – wise humans have been offering us all a map for this homeward path for a very long time. It is the treasure of the world's spiritual literature and the living legacy of teachers who carry it consciously in themselves today. The more I understand that map, the less time I waste on misleading views of what is ultimately going on. Simply said, I have come to a point in the soul's journey in which the study of metaphysics is enormously beneficial. I am ready to understand some of life's most fundamental mysteries. I need *mind training*. And I need to challenge and eliminate errors in my own inner map. My description of reality may be flawed – but it is correctable.

My Most Skillful Means For Achieving It: Studying holy books, seeking teachers and teachings – these are necessary and helpful. But first the groundwork must be laid. Certain shocks must be applied to my existing assumptions – *and they will be*. For one example, cross-cultural experience is a powerful catalyst: the Navajo has much to teach the Benedictine, the Buddhist lama has much to teach the Mullah and the shaman. All wisdom starts with questions; all learning starts with an open mind – or a mind which has been blasted open.

The Angels' Gift: I have been given an instinctual sense of life as a spiritual quest, along with an ability to connect the dots of many diverse mystical experiences in a coherent way. The more I immerse myself in a diversity of spiritual perspectives, the more I find their common core – a common core that can be witnessed more than it can be understood. That core is what I must experience.

Wasted And Dissipated: I drift in a sea of disembodied theories which contradict each other, searching for meaning – as if meaning itself were an idea rather than a visceral, intuitive experience. Eventually, tiring of this lost feeling, I might escape in unwitting desperation into some dogmatic religious "certainty" which only locks me in limbo and evolutionary stasis.

NEPTUNE IN THE TENTH HOUSE

The Focal Point of My Spiritual Evolution: Learning to execute a *spiritual mission* in my community, to be a kind of "lighthouse of consciousness" for people whom I do not know in an intimate way, with my life reminding them of the higher ground. Emphatically, this does not have to put me in "priestly garb" – artists can lift people up that way, as does anyone whose life is devoted to service or acts of kindness and grace.

My Most Skillful Means For Achieving It: If anyone has "Spiritual Giant" printed on his or her business card, we are wise to be suspicious. We cannot teach what we do not know. Spirituality always has something to do with becoming less identified with "the little self." That is the paradox which I am navigating: to play the role of a spiritual lighthouse, *I must not have any ego-driven need to be seen that way*. I must turn away from any trace of spiritual self-importance. If I succeed in that, I will be *called* to my path. I do not need to create it or advertise for it. It will come to me, naturally and without effort.

The Angels' Gift: I have been given a mission. There is a genuine need for what I can offer in my community. That is a great gift. I am the answer to a pressing, life-changing question that is really out there, embodied in the lives of people whom I do not know. To say it more precisely, I have the *potential* to meet that need. To rise to it, to be *worthy* of this mission, I must first become comfortable with being "nobody special." Everything starts with my inner spiritual work and my effort to become transparent to the Divine, so the light can shine through.

Wasted And Dissipated: I drift into some ghost-role in my community. It might be a "prestigious position" which feels increasingly like a joke to me as years go by. Or it may be that I come to symbolize some kind of escapism or failure: everyone knows me as the wastrel, the philanderer, or the town drunk.

NEPTUNE IN THE ELEVENTH HOUSE

The Focal Point of My Spiritual Evolution: Learning to recognize my soul-tribe. I have come to a point in the journey where it is enormously helpful for me to be part of some kind of spiritual fellowship: a congregation, a *sangha*, a group of kindred souls. When I fall down, they lift me up – and when they fall, I return the favor. We compare notes, and keep each other psyched up about the path we are on. It is an ancient spiritual symbiosis. Keeping my eye on the prize is critical here: setting my own soul's evolution as the central priority of my life, and making choices which reflect that precise long-term value. I promise myself to grow a little bit closer to the Great Mystery every day, step by step, forever.

My Most Skillful Means For Achieving It: As I create a more intentional spiritual orientation in my own life, I naturally lose interest in all social activities and relationships which are irrelevant to it. Simultaneously, I am naturally drawn to groups of people who share my orientation and direction. Once the seeds of my commitment to prioritizing the evolution of my own consciousness have germinated, the rest takes care of itself. I meet my tribe.

The Angels' Gift: I have taken birth with a spiritual clan of souls with whom I have been traveling for a long time. We recognize each other. The laws of synchronicity guarantee that we will meet. Some may come and some may go; these tribes are always a revolving door. But I will always have spiritual support, so long as I am open to it, willing to reach out, and willing to support others in return.

Wasted And Dissipated: I drift into a maze of pointless, purposeless social entanglements and obligations. Energy drains from me as I go through motions that are dictated by the stultifying norms, customs, and expectations of the group – which could range anywhere from wealthy drunks at the country club to bohemian artists congratulating themselves for being cool, or even that most deadening of possibilities: people "on the spiritual path," foolish and arrogant enough to imagine that there is actually any alternative.

NEPTUNE IN THE TWELFTH HOUSE

The Focal Point of My Spiritual Evolution: Learning to loosen the tight shoes of my ego. Learning truly to let go of the need for anyone else to think of me as a very spiritual person – to see that as just another form of pride, which leads only to divisions. All that matters to me now, if I get this right, is the reality of my own direct experience of the Divine. *I am learning how to be alone in its presence.* I am becoming identified with the parts of me which are eternal and indestructible rather than the parts which will die when my heart stops beating. I now know how to find those places in myself. I just have to make the time to do that.

My Most Skillful Means For Achieving It: I do not need to become a hermit, but *spending time alone* is critical for me now. I am beginning to understand why mystics favor caves and mountaintops and solitary huts in the wilderness: to become less identified with my ego, I need to get away from anything which entangles me in it – and people are right at the top of the list. I resolve to "log hours" in transcendent states, away from worldly entanglements.

The Angels' Gift: I have been given a direct line of communication with the Infinite. I can simply close my eyes and go there. All I have to do is to *remember to do that* – and having just a little bit of quiet, solitary time each day is enough to trigger it. I am on the cusp of a monumental breakthrough in consciousness. I am grateful for that.

Wasted And Dissipated: I drift into a wide-eyed state of feeling overwhelmed by life. Because I have not taken the time to learn to work with them, my considerable psychic sensitivities wash away my defenses, leaving me vulnerable and vaguely frightened of things that I cannot easily name.

This unfortunate condition soon drives me into a quest for some kind of numbness. Such quests tend to be successful.

Here, as we explore the planetary rulers of our third clan in the Water Family, we have put our primary focus on Neptune. Modern astrologers are acutely aware of the natural resonance between Neptune and Pisces. That resonance is unmistakable to any astrologer who reflects on the question with an open mind rather than being blinded by fealty to historical forms of astrology. Still, as we saw back in chapter five, it is an equally benighted mistake to ignore the traditional ruler of Pisces, which is Jupiter.

Since we explored Jupiter deeply in The Book of Fire, *we are soft-pedaling it here in* The Book of Water, *but we cannot ignore it. What follows is a quick look at Jupiter through the twelve houses. It is taken verbatim from that earlier volume.*

JUPITER IN THE FIRST HOUSE

Above All, Believe . . . that it is your destiny to be some kind of leader and to have a positive impact on the lives of other people. That leadership can take many forms, starting with simply being an influence on others. From there, it runs right up to a substantial capacity to shape the future of your community or your profession.

Never Underestimate . . . your impact on other people, even when you simply walk into the room. Trust your charisma and your "star-quality." Never underestimate the magnetic charm invoked by your sense of humor and your generosity of spirit.

Your Gift From the Gods: In a word, magic. The power of your Will is not only strong in obvious ways, but it also possesses a subtle higher harmonic: what you intend or desire often tends to crystallize before your eyes. That is especially true when your benign intentions are aimed at impacting other people – when you are in a position of leadership, in other words. People probably think you are "lucky." Whatever that word actually means, it is fair to say that they are not wrong.

When Ego Grabs the Steering Wheel: You can become haughty, seemingly expecting to be treated as rock-star royalty. You might not even intend that effect or feel that way, but that appearance arises and creates bad reactions in other people. You might lose your sense of humor about yourself – but don't worry: if you fall into that trap, others will supply the humor behind your back.

JUPITER IN THE SECOND HOUSE

Above All, Believe . . . in yourself. You have set the bar of success quite high in this lifetime. The conventional standards by which people generally define a successful life are not sufficient for you. You have been born to accomplish something of greater significance. Exactly what? The answer to that pressing question lies in the larger logic of your birthchart as a whole.

Never Underestimate . . . your resourcefulness nor your capacity for relentless effort once you have your eye on the prize. Never underestimate your ability to attract the resources you need in order to fulfill your destiny: allies, tools, and sufficient financial fortune to do what you are here to do.

Your Gift From the Gods: A destiny that, if you choose to accept it, will give meaning to your life until the end of your days – and probably beyond them. All that – plus the gods have made you a promise: no matter what path you take, you will always have rice in your bowl. You are protected financially and materially.

When Ego Grabs the Steering Wheel: You turn away from your best self and your higher calling, and instead chase after mere glitz: money, prestige, the enthusiastic support of shallow people. Your magic is such that you can have those things too, if you are crazy enough to want them. They promise abundance and deliver emptiness.

JUPITER IN THE THIRD HOUSE

Above All, Believe . . . that you have something important to say to this world. You bear a much-needed message of encouragement – perhaps of spiritual encouragement – that many people need to hear. You have the ability to express it compellingly; they are depending on you to deliver it.

Never Underestimate . . . your powers of persuasion. You are capable of conveying not only information, but also enthusiasm for the information. Never underestimate your potential for developing these communicative skills. If you are thinking of whispering, that probably means you need to shout. If you're thinking of a short story, that probably means you have a novel in you.

Your Gift From the Gods: Some degree of eloquence. The ability to convey ideas appealingly, so listeners enjoy *hearing* you – or perhaps they enjoy *reading* your words. You have the gift of gab; you have the gift of humor. You can get behind people's defenses. You can convince skeptics. You can learn anything.

When Ego Grabs the Steering Wheel: You talk too much. You become enamored of your own voice and your own opinions, overestimating their appeal to your listeners. You can jump to conclusions; you can fail to see real obstacles and genuine problems. Positive thinking potentially has a dark side: it can blind you to uncomfortable truths, especially ones about yourself.

JUPITER IN THE FOURTH HOUSE

Above All, Believe . . . in the power of your big heart to attract the sweetness of a rich inner life to you, along with the gift of a happy home. A major evolutionary focus in your life lies not with the larger world, but rather with the people in your intimate circle – those with whom you share life's long story. You are here to make a real difference in their lives. Your generosity of spirit plays a pivotal and encouraging role in their journeys.

Never Underestimate . . . the long-term transformative power of your sustained faith in the people whom you love. Never underestimate the spiritual significance of a life that the larger world ignores or about which it never even knows. Not all soul-victories are for public consumption. Never underestimate your ability to recover from loss or adversity; you are resilient.

Your Gift From the Gods: A certain magic when it comes to finding the perfect place to live. Angels seem to watch over you in that department. Family is another gift from the gods – but here, although we might be thinking conventionally of your kinship group, we are actually referring more reliably to the great blessing in your life of your soul-family. Celebrate them – and thank the gods and goddesses for them by prioritizing time spent in their company.

When Ego Grabs the Steering Wheel: You can experience an inflated desire for an impressive physical home. You might become too attached to your family name, your ancestry, or your social circle. It is better to impress yourself than to impress everyone else.

JUPITER IN THE FIFTH HOUSE

Above All, Believe . . . in your creative capacities. Quite probably, you were born with some genuine artistic or performance talent – but we intend the word "creativity" more broadly than that. You have the ability to leave the stamp of your soul upon people, events, materials – or even businesses. Believe, above all, in your profound capacity to engage people's attention and to capture their imaginations.

Never Underestimate . . . how contagious your spontaneity and humor can be. When you are brave enough to step out on the stage without a master plan, magic happens. Never underestimate how a good performance or a skillfully-wrought work of art can sneak behind people's defenses and take root in their hearts.

Your Gift From the Gods: Creativity – and along with it, the capacity to trigger in other people a psychological identification with you. Thus, you can invoke cathartic experience in any audience. When you are brave enough to shine, people feel what you are feeling and think what you are thinking.

When Ego Grabs the Steering Wheel: Your personal life becomes the stage of a soap opera and you find yourself cast in a silly role which embarrasses you. Your soul is better than that, and you know it. Down that road, you succumb to various excesses – too much food or alcohol, a vast collection of shoes you never wear . . .

JUPITER IN THE SIXTH HOUSE

Above All, Believe . . . that you have the ability to become superlatively proficient at some skill that makes a real difference in the lives of others. What skill? The shape of the answer lies in the context of the larger, integrated interpretation of your birthchart. It will have something to do with offering encouragement, support, and blessing to those who partake of your gifts.

Never Underestimate . . . your potential impact on other people's lives. You are part of a *lineage*; trust your teachers and your mentors, and seek them out. Never underestimate your ability to master difficult talents, procedures, and tools. Never doubt that your destiny lies on the path of service.

Your Gift From the Gods: With your skills, you are capable not only of helping people in concrete ways, but also of restoring their damaged faith in life itself. Your faith brings them faith. You are blessed with role models: men and women who have gone before you on a road similar to the one you are traveling. They care about you; their example and teaching are one of your gifts from the gods.

When Ego Grabs the Steering Wheel: You find yourself drowning in a sea of ever-expanding, meaningless responsibilities. You have bitten off more than you can chew. The demands on your time and energy outpace your human limits; people seem to think of you as a public utility.

JUPITER IN THE SEVENTH HOUSE

Above All, Believe . . . in the uplifting, transformative impact of love – and here we use the word "love" in an inclusive sense: marriage and similar partnerships are on the list, but so are deep, long-lasting friendships. You are not alone; other familiar souls have accompanied you into this world. Some of them "owe you one" and are eager to repay the debt; accept their help without feeling like you have to offer anything in return – this frees them as well as supports you.

Never Underestimate . . . your own level of spiritual and psychological sophistication. This is a critical point, because if you do underestimate yourself, that error will manifest as destructive intimate choices – specifically, you might give yourself to people who are unworthy of you.

Your Gift From the Gods: Friends who believe in you more than you believe in yourself. Their faith in you triggers your ability to reach for the higher ground and the far limits of your human potential. The humor, affection, and support of these soul-allies are your gift from the gods.

When Ego Grabs the Steering Wheel: You choose partners and associates based on their appearance or status, without listening to your own heart. The "decorative" lover or the prestigious "close personal friend" are a sugar diet; they only nourish the ego, not the soul.

JUPITER IN THE EIGHTH HOUSE

Above All, Believe . . . in your insights. Have faith in your X-ray ability to see into your own wounds, and above all, have faith in your ability to triumph over them in this lifetime. Trust your insights into other people as well, even when faced with resistance, denial, or anger. Believe in the mutual healing impact of honest intimacy. Believe that by the end of this lifetime, if you follow the path of your destiny, you will laugh at the illusion we call death.

Never Underestimate . . . yourself regarding your choice of an intimate partner. You need someone who is worthy of you – and that worthiness proves itself by his or her ability to hold the helpful mirror of truth before you in a spirit of love. Never doubt the insights that are arising in you regarding the lessons – and the fierce blessings – deriving from human mortality. Death is your guru.

Your Gift From the Gods: The ability to maintain a plucky, positive spirit in the face of life's fiercest truths. You have no need to take refuge in any metaphysical or "spiritual" fantasyland; you can look life's darkness straight in the eye and still smile. You know that you are bigger than it is. Your faith can digest life's harder truths.

When Ego Grabs the Steering Wheel: You become uncritically governed by your own passionate nature; you begin to take too much pride in your intensity and your honesty, to the point that you lose sight of humility, a sense of humor about yourself, and your ability to surrender to the kinds of people who are actually good for you.

JUPITER IN THE NINTH HOUSE

Above All, Believe . . . that the ultimate purpose of your life is a quest for meaning. Everything else is secondary. You were born with the seeds of genuine philosophical wisdom. Never lose sight of the fact that if you boldly follow the adventurous path of your destiny, by the end of this lifetime your wisdom will be seven times deeper.

Never Underestimate . . . the triggering impact on your consciousness of contact with other cultures and other systems of belief. The expansion of your wisdom in this incarnation depends on encounters with exotic thoughts and ideas, along with exotic societies and people who represent alien perspectives. These experiences nourish you. Predictability does not.

Your Gift From the Gods: You intuitively and quickly figure out how to build bridges across cultural divides. You are a good traveler. You have a genuine enthusiasm for learning; you enjoy it and are motivated to live a life of endless education. Life offers you these opportunities; they seem to fall out of the clear blue sky into your lap.

When Ego Grabs the Steering Wheel: You become convinced of the absolute validity of your own opinions. You become, in your own mind, an expert. In place of intellectual expansion, you experience intellectual stasis. Behind your back, people warn each other, "Don't get him (or her) started . . ."

JUPITER IN THE TENTH HOUSE

Above All, Believe . . . that you were born with a larger mission in this world. If you follow the path of destiny, you will energize and illuminate the lives of people whom you do not know or with whom you do not have personal karma to work out. You are here to do something big – do not doubt that. Many souls are depending on your getting this right.

Never Underestimate . . . what you are on this earth to accomplish, nor your ability to accomplish it. Humility is a virtue, but you need to be wary of it: if you are unwilling to "think big" about your mission, your imagination will fail to encompass it correctly.

Your Gift From the Gods: The capacity to plausibly play the role of the "star" or the hero, and thus embody some principle in which you believe on the public stage – and to embody it in a way that inspires enthusiasm for that principle in anyone watching you. Your magic can open doors for you. You can gain the ear – and the trust – of people in positions of power.

When Ego Grabs the Steering Wheel: You succumb to the cotton-candy temptations of power, position, or fame. The gratification of your ego becomes more compelling to you than the mission itself. One way of saying this is that "the devil" fears the good you will accomplish if you rise to your actual mission, and so he is inclined to "make you an offer too good to refuse . . ."

JUPITER IN THE ELEVENTH HOUSE

Above All, Believe . . . that the great work of this lifetime for you is not the work of a young person. If you are young, you must keep the faith – and pursue the experiences that lead you toward the bright future in mid-life and beyond for which you were born. If you are older, it is time to step up to the plate and find some way to make a gift to the world of your hard-earned wisdom. Above all, believe that you play a pivotal role in a soul-tribe and that its members recognize you and are counting on you.

Never Underestimate . . . the sweet fruits of faith, persistence, and of keeping your eye on the prize over the long haul. Never underestimate the power of a noble dream. Furthermore, never doubt that you have *help* in all of this – that you are not alone; others, who believe in you, have accompanied you into this world. Never mistrust your feelings when you have that sense of recognition; you know the members of your own soul-clan when you see them.

Your Gift From the Gods: An ability to dream big, uplifting, long-term dreams. You also have the ability to generate strategies for making those dreams real. You can absorb the big picture and see the subtle shapes unfolding in the present – shapes that prophesy the nature of the future. And you are gifted with a soul-tribe, here to support you in fulfilling those big dreams.

When Ego Grabs the Steering Wheel: You find yourself mired in social overextension, dealing with tedious, draining relationships that seem to offer you very little in return except possibly glitter. As you enter the second half of your life, while you may have the outward appearances of success, you have the feeling that somehow you have lost the thread of any real existential purpose – and you have.

JUPITER IN THE TWELFTH HOUSE

Above All, Believe . . . that you are poised for a major breakthrough in consciousness in this lifetime. You have earned it; meritorious actions in prior lifetimes have put you in this position today. All that is required to trigger this breakthrough is that you place a big bet on yourself in terms of some audacious bid for spiritual catharsis.

Never Underestimate . . . the impact of a single bold move. Do you quit your job to go on a year-long spiritual retreat? Do you do a vision quest or a pilgrimage? Do you actively seek a spiritual teacher? *Ask and ye shall receive* – all you need in order to pick the lock on this spiritual treasure chest is absolute faith in those words.

Your Gift From the Gods: There are many ways to translate the following idea, but here is one wording: *you have a Guardian Angel.* Something or someone is watching out for you in this lifetime, making it safer for you to take the spiritual risks you need to take. All you have to do is to supply the audacity.

When Ego Grabs the Steering Wheel: You become spiritually compla-cent, even arrogant, to the point that you fail to make the bold moves that precipitate the spiritual breakthrough you have incarnated in order to expe-rience. Down that road, you detour into a familiar *cul-de-sac:* spiritual pride.

15

ASTROLOGICAL ASPECTS: KEEPING PERSPECTIVE

In every birthchart, there is a web of aspects which tie everything together. Just like neurons in your brain, they form an overwhelmingly complicated system of cross-referencing among the planets and other sensitive points. If we count the minor aspects, every chart has literally hundreds of these geometrical interconnections. The whole picture is beyond comprehension – and I mean *literally* beyond comprehension. There are simply too many aspects in every chart for any astrologer to take them all in. Nobody's brain is big enough to do that.

So don't feel bad if your own brain is not big enough to hold them all either.

In the earlier volumes of this series, we studied many of the aspects individually, as well as a few *aspect patterns*. We have learned their individual characteristics, both in the natal chart and by transit, progression, or solar arc. No one can really be an astrologer without that body of knowledge. In this chapter, my aim is to fly over aspect theory at 100,000 feet, taking in the bigger picture.

Above all, I want to give you permission to *throw most of the aspects out the window*. I know that sounds strange, but in truth, it is only realistic. There are too many of them for any other strategy to be humanly feasible. If our aim is to present an integrated, "big picture" analysis to a client, the trick is to know which aspects to dump and which ones to keep.

(And if you are lecturing other astrologers rather than sitting with a client, go ahead and dive into that bi-quintile between Mars and the midpoint of two asteroids – it does actually have meaning, just not *enough* meaning to eclipse other, more important aspects.)

In the practical world of astrological counsel, some of those decisions about what aspects to keep and which ones to ignore can be made in a fairly rote way. Here, briefly, are the four major guidelines underlying smart choices about which aspects deserve attention:

- Major aspects (conjunctions, sextiles, squares, trine, and oppositions) are generally more evocative and pressing than the minor ones – semi-sextiles, bi-noviles, quintiles, and so on.
- The "poker hand" of aspectual power goes something like this, in descending order: conjunctions, oppositions, squares, trines, sextiles, quincunxes, sesquiquadrates . . . (The order gets fuzzy after that, but by then we have descended into the realm of minutia, and unless you can juggle seventeen balls while balancing a crystal goblet on your head, you are probably not going to be very concerned with these minor aspects.
- Tighter aspects are more active than loose ones.
- Aspects made to the more important planets and points (the natal Sun, Moon, or Ascendant, for example) deserve more of your attention than the rest.

Those kinds of decisions are simple. They could even be made by a computer. With a little astrological experience, they become so reflexive you hardly realize that you are making them.

Beyond that stage, these judgments become something closer to an art.

It is that art that I want to try to convey in this chapter. That is what I meant when I wrote about "flying over aspect theory at 100,000 feet.

PERSPECTIVE IS EVERYTHING

Let's imagine that there is a woman whose astrological makeup reflects considerable self-sufficiency and independence. Without going into detail, let's just say that the primary components of her chart are Aquarian, Arian, and Sagittarian. She's a free spirit, in other words, and she's been happily single for much of her life.

Ask her angels: she is doing just fine. In this incarnation, she is definitely not "majoring in relationships." But of course she is still human – people are important to her. Like the rest of us, she exchanges love with others, as surely as she breathes air. She has sexual and romantic impulses. Hardly anyone lives in a true vacuum, or would want to.

Even though she prefers autonomy as a lifestyle, she has Neptune in Sagittarius in her seventh house. Reflecting that configuration, the deeper intimate connections that she has made – at least the successful ones – have all been with people with *active inner lives*. If I tell her that the only kind of relationship that will ever work for her is one with a spiritual basis, she might very well nod her head in agreement. That is the most straightforward way of describing Neptunians – and with Neptune in her seventh house, she is rightfully drawn to them. They are her soul mates.

By the way, if the word "spiritual" did not work for her, I might try *visionary* or *imaginative* or *artistic*. I might try *sensitive*. At least one of those words is likely to ring her bells – and as astrologers, our task is to find the right ones.

Those are all positive words of course. Let's not forget the negative side of Neptune. She may have fallen in love with a *drunk* or an *addict* as well – but with all that Aquarian, Arian, and Sagittarian energy, she is resilient. She soon got over it.

Getting to aspects, let's now add another planet to the picture.

In this woman's twelfth house, in Taurus, we find Jupiter. It forms a *quincunx* to her seventh house Neptune, thus flavoring it. The quincunx always brings a need for some *stretching* and *adjusting*; it challenges any part of us that is set in its ways. Seventh house planets spotlight the kinds of people whom we are destined to meet. Any planet *in aspect* to a seventh house planet adds a little spice of its own meaning to the intimate picture.

- Neptune in the seventh: the primary message is about relationships with that "spiritual basis" we just described.
- Jupiter adds another descriptive hint. "Jovial" people, ones with a *simple, earthy* (Taurus) kind of *spirituality* (twelfth house) might come into our subject's life. When they do, they will surely "stir her pot," and offer her an evolutionary opportunity to stretch her perspective on herself – that's the effect of the quincunx.

Let's say that our Aquarian woman is a Buddhist – and quite *opinionated* (Sagittarius!) about it. Cutting to the chase, she meets a man; they become involved. *And he is an earthy farm boy from Indiana and a devout Christian.* He is not dogmatic about his religion. For him, it is a private thing. He does not criticize her Buddhist path. But, in the words of the old gospel song, "Jesus is just alright" with him. He has no problem with her religion – but *she* has a big problem with his Christianity. Try as she will in her Sagittarian way, she cannot shake his faith – he is solidly Taurean about it, and he doesn't even want to argue, let alone try to convert her. He thinks fighting about God is silly. He figures that our fighting about it doesn't affect God at all anyway.

Into the life of our protagonist, he has brought the *useful vexation* which is so characteristic of the quincunx aspect. *He is one manifestation of that Jupiter-Neptune quincunx in her chart.* Probably there will be others.

Now, we finally get to the question of how we keep perspective on aspects, knowing which ones to study and which ones to ignore. Remember our initial point – this woman is not "majoring in relationships" in this life. In the light of that reality, two observations jump out:

- We can clearly see the action of her quincunx in her relationship with our Christian man from that farm in Indiana. The aspect "works." It is real. There are never any non-functional aspects in anyone's chart.
- *But how important is it?*

If you had two hours to sit with this woman to offer her an interpretation of her birthchart, would this quincunx even merit comment? Is it worth the minutes it would take to do it?

Maybe not. My main aim in this chapter boils down to this: *I want to legitimize and support that attitude in you.*

In *The Book of Fire* and *The Book of Earth*, we introduced aspect theory from both natal and moving perspectives. In *The Book of Air*, we dived into three aspect patterns: the Grand Trine, The Grand Cross, and the Yod.

Here in *The Book of Water*, let's build on those foundations. Let's think strategically and integratively about aspects.

And let's start by directly confronting the main problem: *there are just too many of them.*

WELCOME TO TASMANIA

This morning, I recorded a natal chart interpretation for a woman "down under" in Tasmania. In my usual fashion, I employed the familiar complement of planets out through Pluto, plus Chiron. I was interested in the aspects they formed, but I also always put the Ascendant and the Midheaven on the aspect grid, along with the lunar north node – which of course helps me see aspects to the south node as well.

As indicated a few paragraphs ago, I tend to focus most of my attention on the major aspects – the conjunction, the sextile, the square, the trine, and the opposition. But I always run a fuller complement of aspects, including the minor ones – the semi-sextile, the semi-square, the quintile, the sesquiquadrate, the bi-quintile, and the mighty quincunx.

There are other aspects – noviles, septiles, and more. But the eleven I just mentioned are enough to put me on the borderline of madness, so in my own practice I always stop with having my computer only calculate the ones I mentioned. I also assume that most of the time, I will only be working with the major ones – I add the others only because they might possibly prove interesting and my computer can print them without effort.

Boiling the whole aspect map down in the personal way I just outlined, and using only the major aspects, I am *always confronted with fourteen sensitive natal points, each one of them capable of interacting with the others in eleven possible ways.*

My Tasmanian client today is fairly representative of the human family. In her aspect grid, there were forty-nine such aspects. I could vary that number by employing tighter or looser orbs, but you get the picture: *too many aspects.*

I felt like I was in Tasmania, hanging upside down by my toes.

You would too!

My recorded readings run about two hours in length. If I wanted to talk about each one of those forty-nine aspects individually, I would have only had *about two minutes* for each one – and of course no time left over for talking about more important things, such as what sign her Sun was in, and so forth. Worse, *if I had chosen to talk about all of her aspects, I would have had no time left for the high art of any competent astrologer: tying everything together integratively and clearly in a way that connected with her heart.*

That's why some aspects just have to go. There is just no way around it. There is just not enough time in the real world of the counseling room to use them all.

YOUR PRECIOUS INTUITION

Once we accept the inescapable strictures I just explored with you, we realize that we always have to leave most of the aspects out of a consultation – but which ones? Below are some more guidelines, but first there is a cardinal principle: *Guard your intuitive function as if the fate of everyone and everything that you love hinged upon it.*

When you are trying to think logically about too many things at once, your intuitive function gets killed. Your brow wrinkles; you get uptight – and you are no longer a very good astrologer. At some point, astrology simply becomes too complicated for anyone. It is a humbling realization, but a necessary one. The more experience you have, the more balls you can juggle at once – but don't turn that juggling act into trying out for the Mensa Olympics or you will crash and burn – and your flames will smell just like those of the most boring, pedantic professor you ever had.

- *When you feel yourself starting to struggle to stay on top of the web-work of aspects, just throttle everything back a bit.*
- *Simplicity preserves your intuition; straining to work with too much detail does the opposite.*

The key to mastering this critical interpretive strategy lies in having a clear *hierarchy of importance* in your mind regarding aspects. Every astrologer sooner or later needs to "throttle back."

But which direction exactly is "back?"

We answered that question in a few dozen words with our four guidelines at the outset of this chapter. Let's take a deeper look at those initial principles.

THE POKER HAND OF ASPECTS

In the game of Poker, a Royal Flush beats a Full House. In astrology, a conjunction beats a square – usually. It can sometimes get tricky, and some judgment calls need to be made. A conjunction to Mercury might not prove as pivotal as a tight square to the Sun. Going further, one astrologer's "third most important aspect in the chart" might be another astrologer's "fifth most important one." They really don't need to argue about it. Once again, what they do need to do is to guard their precious intuitions – if their brows start to wrinkle around aspect number four, they should just forget about aspect number five and work with what they are feeling in their hearts about those first three or four aspects.

Maybe after they have done that, they will find that they have some intuitive energy left over to work on aspect number five. Will they ever get to aspect number seventeen? Probably not – and that is all right.

As I have mentioned, in my own practice, I primarily work with the major aspects, and only rarely find myself paying attention to the minor ones. Within the major aspects, in my experience ("everything else being equal," and it rarely is . . .) *the conjunction beats the opposition, which beats the square, which beats the trine, which beats the sextile.*

What that means is that "everything else being equal," don't fuss with interpreting that sextile *if the price is that you shortchange a conjunction.*

Remember our Aquarian woman from the beginning of this chapter? Certainly don't put twenty minutes into explaining her Jupiter-Neptune quincunx, only to discover you have five minutes left to cover her Moon-Uranus opposition. *She let go of her farm-boy from Indiana two years ago without a second thought – but she is still struggling with the ongoing rift between herself and her mother, which dates back to her childhood.*

ORBS

A square means a 90° angle between two planets or points – but no astrologer would ignore a 95° angle. That is close enough to count as a square. What if the "orb" were ten degrees instead of five? Would that count as a square too? That is where the fist fights break out in the local astrological society. When astrologers fuss over orbs, my favorite rejoinder is, *exactly when does a kitten turn into a cat?* No one can answer that question rigidly without looking silly. It is the same with aspectual orbs.

But one point is certain about them: *the closer the aspect is to perfection, the more powerful it is.*

Should we make sure to discuss that sextile between Neptune and Pluto? If the orb is one degree, maybe the answer is yes.

If it is five or six degrees, maybe not.

I keep repeating the words "everything else being equal." Here's why: planets themselves vary enormously in their centrality and power in a person's chart. They are never "equal." And while it is a good general rule to assume that the Moon is more important than Mercury, for a Gemini with Gemini rising and Mercury in Gemini conjunct the Ascendant, you might want to modify that attitude.

We are left with a rather obvious principle, but one which throws a monkey wrench into any attempts to over-simplify how we think of the hierarchy of importance with aspects: *the more critical the role of the planet, the more attention its aspects deserve.*

Applying that last guideline starts with an easy idea, one which you can apply at a glance. Experience has taught us all to pay a lot of attention to the Sun, Moon, and Ascendant. Aspects formed by planets to those three "Primal Triad" points tend to be very obvious in their impact. I cannot, for example, imagine doing a consultation and ignoring a conjunction of any planet to my client's Sun, Moon, or Ascendant.

What about a sextile to any one of those three pivotal points? I might ignore it – that decision would depend on "the strength of the competition." Some charts have a lot of major league aspects; others have fewer.

- Remember: we are setting up this hierarchy of aspectual importance primarily so that we can determine which ones to leave out.
- Never beat yourself up for leaving out less important aspects.

LOOSE ENDS

The *planet that rules the Ascendant* – commonly called "the ruler of the chart" – is always of elevated importance, and therefore so are its aspects. We will look at that issue carefully in chapter twenty-five, by the way.

The *planet that rules the sign in which we find the Sun* – the Sun's *dispositor* – is similarly enhanced in significance. We are simply very sensitive to it since it is so resonant with the core of our nature.

In evolutionary astrology, the *lunar nodes* play a central role. Planets in aspect to the nodes – especially conjunctions, oppositions, and squares

– always make themselves felt in a palpable biographical fashion. I dive deeply into them in *Yesterday's Sky*, which is mission-critical reading material for anyone practicing the deeper forms of evolutionary astrology.

Those nodal aspects are not just about past lives – unresolved issues from prior lives reincarnated right along with you, and along with your clients too. *In your present life, you will again experience situations that are echoes of past life dilemmas, as if you have asked the universe to give you another chance to work on them.* Pay attention to those prior-life clues! And the same goes for the clues built into any hard aspect to the ruler (or rulers) of the south node. Keep an eye on them too.

As you are doubtless sensing by now, what I am advocating in working with aspects is a balancing act. You have to make judgment calls, and it is never as if there were only one right answer. Even though "oppositions beat squares" in the poker hand, that very tight square of Neptune to the Sun might be more pressing in significance than that wide opposition to it from Jupiter . . . oh but, wait a minute, Sagittarius is the Ascendant, so that Jupiter rules the chart . . .

You get the picture: lots of balancing, lots of judgment calls.

Still, these are the systematic principles which underlie all of those judgments, at least if you make them wisely. Reduced to fit in a pistachio nut shell, here is the entire idea: *Tight, hard aspects to really important points take precedence over softer, looser aspects involving less important points.*

As with so much in astrology, practice leads to skill and confidence – and to finding your own style.

THE MAJOR AND MINOR ASPECTS: THE TABLE

For easy reference, here is our table of aspects as it has appeared in previous volumes of this series.

Aspect	Separation	Action
Conjunction	0°	Fusion; formation of one "meta-planet"
Semi-sextile	30°	Clash; annoyance. Waning: Letting go.

Semi-square	45°	Fighting for freedom; endings, awkward transitions.
Sextile	60°	Mutual excitation and stimulus
Quintile	72°	Creativity; inspiration
Square	90°	Blocking; challenge; contradiction
Trine	120°	Mutual enhancement; support
Sesquiquadrate	135°	Tension; breakthrough or breakdown; sacrifice
Bi-quintile	144°	Demands toward transcendence; "the Call"
Quincunx	150°	Adjustment; shared creativity; romance
Opposition	180°	Polarization or Complementarity

PART FOUR

SEEING FUTURES

For every one of us, there come times when the universe prompts us to admit to ourselves that something is wrong. The message may be drastic – "my life isn't working anymore." Or it might be subtle, as if monotony were now all that was left in life. The news might come to us encoded in sad evolutions in a relationship: we are drifting apart and we don't know why. It might come as a feeling of professional or spiritual malaise. It could show up in the form of bodily disease, or just a chronic tightness in our guts.

In every case, the success of our continuing soul-journey depends upon our heeding that Watery counsel. As hard as it is, we need to welcome it in the same preemptive way we might welcome the early detection of some physical problem. Even though the signals are unpleasant and we have a natural desire to push them aside, they actually contain an encouraging note. It is time to surrender to the mysteries of healing, regeneration, and recovery. And those mysteries can work miracles.

Sometimes we resist these promptings. Sometimes, for reasons of pride, worldly responsibility or just plain habit, we do not want to acknowledge these little warnings and corrections. No worry; they are patient and persistent. They might start out by whispering in our ears as we surrender to sleep. They might waft a few unsettling vapors into our meditations or daydreams. If we continue to resist their message, they can become considerably more fierce.

The crowning paradox is that, while nobody feels good at such a time, the hidden reality is that we are on the cusp of a personal renaissance, at least potentially. It does not feel that way, but it is that way.

At such times, when the inner world is calling out for attention and support, a member of the Water Family is always activated. That is the signal. That is their job.

No matter your astrological makeup, you will pass through such Watery times. Navigating them gracefully is the subject of the rest of this book.

What marks the arrival of these opportunities for healing, regeneration, and recovery? Against the backdrop of your natal chart, there is a constant flow of moving transits, progressions, and solar arcs. Any planet can move through Water signs or houses, announcing the impending arrival of messages from the deep wells of the psyche. Sometimes they form aspects with the Moon, Mars, Pluto, Jupiter or Neptune – the Watery planets.

Within that celestial flow, there is another set of motions: those five Water planets are also moving through your natal chart, triggering it through their own transits, progressions and solar arcs.

Always at such times your soul is clamoring for a few moments of attention. There is something that you need, perhaps more desperately than you realize. You lack a critical "vitamin" – but your teeth have not started falling out yet. Depression has been sighted at the edge of your radar screen – but right now, you just feel a little out of sorts from time to time, no big deal.

Like most things that can go wrong in life, catching them early is your best shot at heading them off.

In what follows, we toss out the astrologers' traditional crystal ball. We are not "making predictions," at least not in any concrete or deterministic way. We will use the same techniques that astrologers have used to "see the future"– but seeing the future in explicit or fatalistic terms is not our aim. Instead, we use these Watery events to counsel ourselves about the exact natures of our wounds and the remedies that can bind them and heal them.

If we are wise, we cherish these "early warnings." We want to know the remedies we can apply here and now, and thus avoid darker troubles down the road.

You have many possible futures. Astrology can describe them all, along with their consequences. It can help you to navigate wisely among them. It lays the map of all of those possible futures before you.

The road you choose to travel is your own decision.

16

THE WATER FAMILY
AND ASTROLOGY'S
CRYSTAL BALL

"**F**ate" is a popular word with some astrologers, but I rarely use it. Personally I have always found it to be too depressing and limiting, and actually kind of a specious concept. In my own work, I will typically use the word only once: *"it is your fate to now be facing certain questions and certain possibilities."* After that I make a point of never using the word again. Said simply, I value human freedom – and its corollary of personal responsibility – far too much to succumb to fatalistic views of anything.

For ethical reasons, I like to beat that drum really hard.

Casting a colder eye on reality, I can perhaps give the question a little more room to breathe, and maybe beat the drum with a little less *brio*.

Here's how:

A baby has just been born. Give me five minutes with her birthchart, and I can say with a high degree of confidence that "in mid-2047, she will be wrestling with the balance between love and freedom in an important relationship."

(Uranus will then be transiting through a conjunction with her natal Venus).

If I were around then to counsel her, I could probably help her out too. Here is what I would say:

"Just try to be as real and honest as you can be, and let the intimate chips fall where they may. Don't fake anything, or you'll only wind up in a fake relationship. Trust the possibility that your partner might actually love the person whom you really are. Don't be afraid to learn the answer. Be yourself and see what happens."

I would run out of fingers and toes counting the times I have had to clean up after one of my more fatalistic colleagues who has told someone who was currently experiencing contentment in a relationship that that Uranus transiting over Venus spelled an impending breakup. Divorce is indeed *one of the possibilities* that such a transit can portend – and let's add that some divorces are necessary and benefit all concerned. But to say such an event in the sky *means divorce* is to misunderstand something absolutely bedrock basic about human existence and how astrology fits into it: *what actually happens in your life occurs at the interface of your consciousness and the vast archetypal fields the planetary symbols represent.* Knowing what is going on in a chart is only half of the equation. The other half is what is going on in the person's head and heart – how he or she is responding to the "questions and possibilities" the astrological configurations represent.

Fate – in the sense that there is one single "choice" that you are inescapably, deterministically, doomed to make – is simply an erroneous concept. In my view, in this age of quantum theory and relativity, astrologers simply need to dump the term, at least if they are using it in that sense. Goodbye and good riddance. We are not marionettes dangling from strings that the planets pull.

We are more powerful than that by far.

One more blow against the falling empire before I get down from the pulpit: I have noticed a pattern of "Monday morning quarterbacking" among my more fatalistic colleagues. In retrospect, they can pronounce that something that *has already happened* was "fated to happen." *After the event has transpired,* they can see it clearly in the chart, as if it had always been inevitable – but only after it has already happened.

Seeing the past has always been a much easier trick than seeing the future. In fact, I believe that we cannot see the future for exactly the same reason that we cannot see unicorns: *the future does not exist* – at least not yet. That is because we still have not created it.

Again, we simply cannot leave human consciousness out of the equations.

With all that said, let's acknowledge that there is indeed a long tradition of astrological predictions that came true. I would not argue against that fact. In the 17th Century, astrologer William Lilly apparently predicted the Great Fire of London fourteen years in advance – and nearly went to jail for it, as if he had set the fire himself. A generation ago, the great American astrologer Robert Hand effectively predicted the terrorist attacks of September 11, 2001.

Astrological prediction works – sometimes. Similarly, predicting divorce based on transiting Uranus forming a conjunction with someone's natal Venus is a dirty game, but it often works too.

What pains me is the knowledge that a marriage *that might have made it through a difficult evolutionary passage* was pushed over the cliff by the astrologer's baleful prediction.

The client is already experiencing some unsettled feelings about her or his relationship. What happens when the astrologer says that divorce is "written in the stars?"

A QUICK PERSONAL TALE

Seeing the future is a real superpower, and the human ego loves that kind of stuff. With my clients, I only "predict questions" and I am good about keeping strictly to that philosophy. Of course with my own life, I cannot resist the temptation of gazing into the crystal ball from time to time. Like most people, usually I am far better at seeing my wishes and my fears than I am at actually seeing the future.

Even when I do "see the future," I am usually at least somewhat wrong about it.

Here's a story which illustrates my point:

My then-wife and I moved west in the summer of 2008. I saw Pluto bearing down on a square to my fourth house Moon, and so I expected some kind of Plutonian trouble in connection with my family and home. I was already moving from North Carolina, where I had lived for forty-two years, but I sensed there was going to be more to this transit. My "prediction" – which I kept to myself – was that my mother would probably die. She was in her late eighties, and reasonably healthy, but at that age, her passing was of course always a possibility. Mom and I were close emotionally – but, with her living in Maine, we were about as far apart geographically as two people could be and still be living in the continental United States. I was so convinced that she would pass away as Pluto made its transiting square to my Moon that I actually cleared time in my work schedule in anticipation of wanting to be with her.

Here's what actually happened: Mom was fine – she lived another nine years. But my wife left me.

If I wanted to defend the idea of astrological prediction, I could make a case that I had accurately foreseen that in 2009 and 2010, there would be "some kind of Plutonian trouble in connection with my family." I was right about that – but totally wrong about the nature of the trouble.

Here's the deeper take-away from this tale of woe:

It was indeed "my fate" to interact at that time with a difficult field of Plutonian archetypal potential in connection with my family. That prediction functioned like clockwork. My error was to underestimate the breadth and depth of that archetypal field. I picked out one possibility from a field of many, then I became attached to my prediction – and that attachment blinded me to the bigger picture.

I forgot a cardinal principle in astrology, *that symbolism is not literalism.* I thought that Pluto squaring my Moon could mean only one thing when in fact it could have meant dozens of different things.

What actually happens in our lives is always reflected in astrological events. *Astrology never fails* – I feel that I can honestly be that dogmatic about it. In retrospect, we can always clearly see the fingerprints of these archetypal fields on the shape of the events which actually took place. That is why specific prediction always works so terrifically – *so long as we remember to only do it backwards.* Retrospectively, in other words.

But what will actually happen as a result of a transit, a progression, or a solar arc?

Admitting that we cannot know the answer in specific terms is a beginning.

Here are some more inspiring statements:

- That we are not powerless and that we actually have something to say in the matter.

- That the human will is not an illusion, but in fact a powerful, even magical, force.
- That the stories of our lives unfold at the interface of our consciousness and the incomprehensibly vast archetypal fields of possibility that constitute astrology.

MARIAN STARNES

My first true spiritual teacher was a woman from Sandpointe, Idaho, named Marian Starnes. She was a Cancer, born in 1926. I've mentioned her a few times in this series of books and I dedicated *The Book of Fire* to her memory. Like any true teacher, she said many things to me that sunk like stones deep down into the roots of my consciousness. Of all of them, here is the one that probably shaped my work more than anything else that she ever told me:

The ambition of every prophet is to be proven wrong.

For obvious reasons, my first reaction was that her words made my head spin. One might imagine that a prophet would enjoy being proven *right* from time to time. That's true, but that is also just the ego talking. Marian understood how the universe worked – how we are all at least partly responsible for the shapes of the futures we create for ourselves. Marian also understood that any future worth living does not arise automatically without positive efforts on our part. She understood that laziness, willful ignorance, and fear are forces too strong to discount.

In the light of all that, Marian knew that a "prophet" might see some dark potential on the horizon, and *warn us of it* in the hope that we might awaken in time to avert it.

Transiting Uranus is approaching your natal Venus – If you were my client, I probably would not use these exact words, but here in essence is how I might present my interpretation:

"I see divorce looming on your horizon . . . *prove me wrong.*"

YOU ARE HERE

We come to a familiar crossroads in our *mappa mundi*. In the parallel chapters of the previous three volumes of this series, I presented some general introductory material about how to look at astrology developmentally over time. That boils down to the craft of working technically with transits, progressions, and solar arcs. Once again, at this same crossroads, I now face my familiar dilemma: do I bore diligent readers by repeating all that material – or do I abandon the Cancer, Scorpio, and Pisces readers who picked up this last book of the series first?

Sometimes the best we can do is to find a middle path. Sometimes that is as good as it gets. What follows, in honor of any new readers, is a very short *verbatim* lift from earlier in this series, simply defining what we mean by transits, progressions, and solar arcs. After that, I want to telegraph "in bullets" a few critical points about working with these predictive methods. Those lines are intended as brief aids-to-memory for those of you who have been following along with this whole series. For any beginners, I am hoping that you will be inspired to delve into the earlier books in order to get a deeper perspective on the bullet points which follow. They are only brief summaries of more nuanced ideas.

Finally, I want to look at the specific *orbital characteristics* of our five Water Family planets in order to get a feeling for how they operate in their unique and particular fashions by transit, progression, and solar arc.

That is all new material.

SOME QUICK DEFINITIONS

There are several different techniques for moving planets and points against the backdrop of the natal chart. In my own practice, I use three of them:

- *Transits* are the actual motions of planets in the sky. If, for example, Venus is currently in Pisces by transit, that is true for everyone. Transits, in other words, are *external factors*. They are like weather. Everyone shares them. We just each respond to them in our own way, just like some people find a gray drizzly day gloomy while others may find it poignant and romantic.

- *Progressions* work more like an *internal biological clock*. Your progressions are unique to you. While your progressed Mercury is moving through Virgo, my Mercury might be progressing through Aries. The theory behind progressions sounds strange, but they work reliably: *days are set symbolically equal to years*. If you want to know the positions of your progressed planets on your fortieth birthday, look at where those same planets were in the sky (that is, by transit) literally forty *days* after your birth. *Voilà:* those are your progressed planetary positions.

- *Solar arcs* are a subset of progressions. We note the distance in degrees that the Sun has progressed according to the methods we just described. Then we add exactly that same "arc" to every one of the rest of the planets and points, equally. In other words, all solar arcs move at *exactly the same speed.* With small variations, the Sun progresses approximately 1° for every year of your life, so when you turn thirty, it has moved about 30° ahead of where it was located when you were born. To calculate your solar arcs on your thirtieth birthday, we would then add *that same 30°* to your Moon, your Mercury, your Ascendant, and all the rest. (One quick technical note: Earth's orbit around the Sun is elliptical. The effect is that we are moving more slowly during the northern hemisphere summer and more quickly six months later. *So if you were born with the Sun in Capricorn, your solar arcs move slightly faster than someone born with the Sun in Cancer.* The idea that Solar arcs move 1° per year is a useful approximation, in other words. Yours will vary slightly. The average annual motion of the progressed Sun is 59'08".)

- Since solar arcs are *slaved to the Sun,* they reflect the Sun's nature – which is to say they tend, like the Sun, to be more *biographical and outward* in their manifestations. Meanwhile, progressions are more sensitive to evolutions occurring beyond the boundaries of the human ego and the conscious, rational mind. Most of us have had the mysterious experience of waking up one morning and suddenly everything looks very different to us, even though we cannot put our finger on exactly why. Somehow our attitude has shifted. Progressions are more likely to mirror those kinds of deep psychic events than are solar arcs. They are not, in other words, quite as tied to the reasoning parts of our conscious "solar" minds. At the same time, let's give your poor ego a break. You need it and it needs you, and solar arcs are its astrological reflecting pool.

THE ENTIRE THEORY OF ASTROLOGICAL PREDICTION IN 250 WORDS

- The natal chart is the *root prediction*. Transits, progressions, and solar arcs simply put the developmental spotlight on its underlying potentials. Looking for example at a progressed planet making an aspect to a transiting one is not taboo – but it is always a better practice to prioritize the impact of moving points on the natal chart itself. Those developmental events represent the heart of the matter.

- The transits of the Sun, the Moon, Mercury, Venus, and Mars are quick; they therefore do not have much time to develop *depth and complexity of meaning*. Instead, they tend to operate as *precipitating triggers* for events whose deeper significance is reflected in slower-moving cycles.

- All progressions and all solar arcs, plus the transits of Jupiter, Saturn, Uranus, Neptune, and Pluto move slowly enough to sink deeply into our bones. They are the basic tools we employ in holding a *thematic mirror* before anyone's life.

- Astrology is so complex that no one can deal with everything at once. To guard your precious intuition, you need to set priorities, making hard decisions about what to consider and what to put aside. In making such editorial decisions, in general it is helpful to remember that hard aspects are more dynamic than soft ones, and that anything impacting the Sun, Moon, or Ascendant is always going to be particularly pivotal.

- If you see something "bad" – before you open your mouth, make sure you have figured out its higher meaning and potential. If you see something "good" – reflect on how it might be misused. All of those possibilities always exist. Consciousness is always part of the equations.

THE RHYTHMS OF THE WATER PLANETS

Because of the dual rulerships of Scorpio and Pisces, fully five out of the ten major planets have Watery qualities. That is a striking realization, of course. I think it says something significant about the intentions of the higher intelligence of the universe for us. Half of why we are here seems to be about our healing, regeneration, and recovery.

The fact that this focus on Watery processes might seem less obvious with Mars and Jupiter than it does with the Moon, Pluto, and Neptune really says more about the current culture of astrology than it does about the actual natures of those two planets. Jupiter is inseparable from the experience of *faith* – and it would be hard to come up with a more Watery concept than that one. And Mars is *passionate* – there is a Water-word if ever there was one.

Five planets is half of them – a lot, in other words. That means that as we move into the realms of Watery transits, progressions, and solar arcs, we have a lot of balls to juggle. Our intention to keep our intuitions engaged through *strategic simplification* will therefore be tested in the Water Family, especially now as we move into developmental astrology. A birthchart alone is complicated enough – but now we add legions of moving points to the mixture, far more than we have had to face with the families of Fire, Earth, and Air.

In subsequent chapters, we wrestle with the *meaning* of these many specific kinds of Watery periods. For starters, let's have a look at their *rhythms*, starting with the easiest step: their solar arcs.

WATER PLANETS BY SOLAR ARC

How far has your Sun progressed since you took your first breath? By solar arc, all the rest of your planets, nodes, Angles, and so on, have covered exactly that same distance. The number of degrees they have advanced should be equal, more or less, to your age in years.

That quick "years equal degrees" trick will often be a little bit off, especially as you get older – but if it is far off, you made a mistake in your calculations.

The solar arcs of the Moon, Mars, Pluto, Jupiter, and Neptune are all powerful and significant. Exactly how significant they are for you personally depends partly on the tone of your birthchart in general – but the essential point is that the solar arcs of the Water planets are all quite central to everything we will be exploring in the remainder of this book.

As we move into the realm of transits and progressions, everything gets a lot more complicated. By those methods, we have a huge range of possible motions, from the jitterbug motions of the transiting Moon to the languorous, iguana-like crawl of your progressed Pluto.

With transits and progressions, we have to consider the motions of each one of these planets individually.

THE MOON

Earth's major satellite takes 27.3216609 days to complete a single orbit – that is for it to return to an alignment with any fixed point on the ecliptic, such as conjuncting a certain star. That period works out to twenty-seven days, seven hours, and about forty-three minutes.

During the course of that cycle, the Moon's speed actually varies considerably. A good way to visualize it is to think of a car accelerating from 45 mph to 60 mph, then slowing back down to 45 mph. Because of that variation in velocity, we cannot nail down exactly how long the Moon is going to take to get through a sign, but the average figure is about two days, six hours.

With a similar amount of flex, a good rule of thumb is to say that *the Moon takes about two hours to move through one degree.*

Cutting to the practical angle, if we allow an orb of six degrees on either side of an exact aspect, the transiting Moon will, for one example, form a conjunction with your natal Saturn for about one full day out of each month. That does not give it much time at all to develop "depth and complexity of meaning." You may perhaps feel a little blue that day, or perhaps driven to industry – those are Saturn-signatures on your mood, and mood is the Moon's domain. But such lunar transits are not a big deal. They are not life-changing.

The Moon is a very interesting beast astrologically, full of paradoxes. We all know how profoundly significant it is in a natal chart. No interpretation would be complete without including it. And yet, by transit, the Moon wimps out. It simply moves too fast to be a major player – at least not in the kind of developmental astrology I like to practice. You can definitely feel it; it leaves a mark on you – but only for a day.

It is by *progression* that the Moon really steps onto center stage. I don't believe that I have ever done a current reading for anyone without mentioning the progressed Moon.

- The progressed Moon defines the *emotional chapters* of our lives.

- The progressed Moon casts light on *where your heart is* at a given time.
- The progressed Moon reflects your current area of *emotional attention* – which can mean concern or worry, or excitement and engagement.

We will explore all that in detail in the next couple of chapters. Right now, our purpose is only to get a feeling for the Moon's rhythm.

By progression, days become years. So the transiting Moon's 27.3216609 *day* cycle turns into 27.3216609 *years* – or just slightly under twenty-seven years, four months. Once again, by progression the Moon's speed varies. In average terms it takes the Moon about twenty-seven months to pass through a sign. Given a six-degree orb, *we are looking at progressed Moon aspects unfolding over a period of about a year.* Thus, unlike the Moon's transits, they have plenty of time to develop depth and complexity.

Welcome to the progressed Moon: one of astrology's most reliable workhorses. For a counseling astrologer, there is nothing so encouraging as to feel that you know what a client is likely to be concerned about before he or she walks through your door.

Learn about the progressed Moon; it will give you that kind of vision.

MARS

The red planet correlates with *stress*, among other things. That linkage manifests right down to the technical headaches it often provides astrologers. By *transit*, Mars is generally too fast to operate at the symphonic level of progressions, solar arcs, and the transits of the outer planets – but it is *sometimes* slow enough for it to be too dangerous to ignore, the way we might safely ignore the transits of Mercury or Venus.

More about all that in a moment.

Mars takes 686.971 days to get around the Sun. That works out to one year and around ten and a half months. But there are many complicating factors. One of them is that Mars's orbit is quite *eccentric*, which is to say, its distance from the Sun varies quite a lot. Enter Johannes Kepler, who showed us that a planet's forward speed in its orbit falls off as it gets further from the Sun's accelerating gravity, while quickening as it gets closer.

That means that when Mars is further away from the Sun – at *aphelion* – it is moving a lot more slowly than when it reaches *perihelion.*

That is true of all the planets, but *because of the extreme eccentricity of Mars's orbit, it is simply more true of Mars.* In average terms, the planet advances about one-half a degree per day – but don't count on that in specific cases. You really have to look it up.

Mars is the next planet out from Earth. That means that we are moving faster. When Mars is at *opposition* – which means that Earth is directly between Mars and the Sun, things get interesting. We sort of zip past Mars, as if we were passing another car in the slow lane of the highway. As you know from driving, the visual effect is that the car we are passing seems to be moving backwards. We know better, but that is what it looks like.

It works the same way with Mars. When it reaches opposition, from Earth's perspective, Mars looks like it is moving backwards. It is then in *retrograde* motion.

Be careful – because of the planet's vexing orbital eccentricity, everything I am about to write is subject to quite a lot of variation. Let's just start by trying to get an overview, in hopes of staving off those Martian headaches.

About five or six weeks before it reaches opposition, Mars makes a station and turns retrograde. After the exact Mars-Sun opposition, it takes another five or six weeks for Mars to station again and turn direct.

Here's the hook: *during that entire retrograde period of perhaps as long as three months, Mars will have only retreated somewhere between ten and twenty degrees.*

Still with me? I know this stuff can be tedious, but understanding it makes you a better astrologer – not because you have to pass some kind of high school test, but because these are the actual rhythms of the cosmos. This is how the solar system breathes.

I complained about the headaches Mars can give us. Here's an aspirin:

- Slow planets give us the big picture. Any planet remaining within the orbs of an aspect for long enough to develop depth and complexity of meaning is mission-critical to understanding anyone's life.
- When Mars is near opposition, *it passes that test* – as we just saw, it might *stay within the same ten to twenty-degree range for ten or*

twelve weeks. That is a lot of time for us to ponder the same energies and thoughts, especially if the figure is closer to ten degrees.

- In the most extreme situation, that means that transiting Mars
  can remain within the orbs of an aspect for three months – long
  enough to turn your life upside down.
- If Mars happens to be aligned with your Sun or your Moon during
  that time, you are going to learn a lot about the sort of "depth and
  complexity" that Mars can provide.
- Bottom line, when Mars slows down near opposition, it metamorphoses into a major astrological player.
- At other times, when it is moving more quickly, Mars tends to
  operate more like a "trigger planet," such as transiting Mercury.

Sun-Mars oppositions last for many weeks. One effect is that inevitably more children are born under a Sun-Mars opposition than at other
points in the planet's cycle of solar aspects. *Sun-Mars oppositions are therefore a whole lot more common in the general population than Sun-Mars conjunctions, sextiles, or squares, for example.* That astronomical fact has fooled more
than one would-be statistical researcher. You can easily prove, for example,
that more murderers have the Sun-Mars opposition than the conjunction.

More saints as well. And more pastry cooks.

More everyone.

All of this so far has been about *transiting* Mars – but it naturally
translates into a lot of parallel variability in terms of how Mars operates by
progression as well. Remember: with progressions, days turn into years. By
transit, as we just saw, Mars remains in retrograde motion for many weeks.
By *progression,* those ten or twelve weeks can turn into a big chunk of your
lifetime. If you were born on the very day that Mars turns retrograde, you
might be in your eighties before it stations again and turns direct. In your
whole life, the planet might progress less than twenty degrees. That means
that, if you were born near a Mars station, any progressed aspects which
Mars forms will be in effect for decades, and thus very difficult to apply
astrologically.

On the other hand, maybe you were born near a Sun-Mars conjunction. Relatively speaking, your Mars is then a speed demon. As an illustration, I see there is a Mars-Sun conjunction on October 8, 2021. If a baby

born on that day makes it to his ninetieth birthday, his progressed Mars will have swung through almost exactly *sixty degrees* and formed *nineteen* major aspects.

Bottom line, look it up. With Mars, it is hard to generalize. And saying that its average motion is a half a degree per day (or per year, by progression) is one of those truths that can get into a world of trouble if you do not understand its flexible context.

PLUTO

The Lord of the Underworld is a real slow boat, currently taking 247.94 years to get around the Sun – which works out to about three weeks short of 248 years. Call it a quarter of a millennium and you strike the right emotional note.

Transiting Pluto is not a bus for which you want to wait.

By progression, don't even think about it. For Pluto to progress all the way around your chart would require about 90,520 years – that progression translates into the stately pace of about a quarter of a millennium *per degree*.

Pluto's orbit is fairly eccentric, so like Mars, it speeds up and slows down, although not so dramatically. In broad terms, Pluto is farthest from the Sun when it is passing through Taurus and closest when it is in Scorpio. A passage through Taurus takes over three decades, while a quick zip through Scorpio only takes Pluto about a dozen years.

Like Mars, Pluto turns retrograde around its oppositions, but since Pluto is so much further out in space, the visual effects are very different. Basically Pluto remains retrograde for just under six months, then is direct for just over six months. It loses an inch, then it gains an inch – plus a cat's whisker.

In working with Pluto's transits, it is helpful to pay particular attention to those stationary times. In common with the rest of the planets, Pluto's "amperage" then goes through the roof. Pluto might, for example, make a station a couple of degrees *beyond* a sensitive point in your chart – and that might very well be the most dramatic moment of the whole event.

Missing those stationary aspects that are still tight – but just beyond the "hits" shown on the computer screen – is a classic neophyte's mistake.

JUPITER

Jupiter needs only 11.862 years to orbit the Sun, giving it a neat one year, on average, to get through each sign. It advances for about nine months, stations, and then remains retrograde for about four months. Since Jupiter is relatively fast-moving, its four-month retrograde periods swing it through a fairly wide arc, averaging about ten degrees. Once it gets into its nine months of direct motion, it will advance forty or forty-five degrees, covering about four or five degrees per month.

There is an essential astrological technique lurking in those numbers. We know that when a planet stations anywhere near a sensitive degree, it is going to hit a lot harder than if it is moving fast – you may recall our line about "developing depth and complexity of meaning."

- Jupiter may zoom through a trine to your natal Sun, but it is there and gone again in two or three weeks. *There is a good chance that you will hardly notice it.*
- On the other hand, Jupiter may make a station in that same trine aspect to your Sun. *That means that it is time to start planning what you are going to do with those millions you are about to win in the lottery (just don't forget to enter the contest . . .)*

By progression, Jupiter is so slow that I tend to ignore it. A full cycle around your chart by progression would require over four millennia. Still, since Jupiter's speed is quite variable, some of you who were born during the quicker parts of its cycle might find some use for its progressions. I am open to that possibility, but somewhat skeptical too. As I write these words, I am seventy-one years old. During that whole time, my own Jupiter has only progressed about fifteen degrees. It has made just three major aspects, and each one lasted for such a long time that while I can make some sense of them, the reality is that I would need to generalize about periods of my life lasting a decade or two. I can do that, and even do it with some authenticity – but it smacks of vagueness. Astrology works well enough that there is no need for us to play those kinds of head-games with ourselves.

And, hey, isn't astrology complicated enough for you already? As we have seen, the most perilous enemy of our precious intuition is the sort of intellectual complexity which wrinkles our brows, while drowning out the messages of the heart. Anytime we can consciously and strategically leave something out, that helps our cause.

That's why I ignore the progressions of Jupiter – not to mention the progressions of Saturn, Uranus, Neptune, and Pluto.

NEPTUNE

Pluto and Neptune are locked in a 3:2 orbital resonance. That means for every three orbits of Neptune, Pluto orbits the Sun twice, more or less. Neptune's "year" takes exactly 164.8 of our years to complete. With its fairly regular orbit, Neptune spends fourteen or fifteen years in each sign, advancing for about seven months, then retrograding for about five.

Neptune's average daily motion is tiny – only about 21 arc-seconds per day, which is a tiny fraction of a degree. And of course, as ever, be wary when you see that word "average." Like the rest of the planets, Neptune speeds up, slows down, stops, goes backwards, stops, and starts up again.

Again, you really have to look it up.

YOUR GOLD STAR

Congratulations, you have survived one of the more tedious chapters of the book. You have seen lots of numbers, and not much in the way of human astrological meaning assigned to them. We are about to improve our track record in that department.

Obviously, these are all technical points that we need to understand if we are going to practice the craft of astrology, but I do believe that this kind of material serves a deeper purpose as well. As I wrote earlier, understanding it makes you a better astrologer – not because you have to pass some kind of high school test, but because these are the actual rhythms of the cosmos.

This is how the Water planets breathe. To understand them, you need to learn to breathe in synchrony with them.

17

CELESTIAL NAVIGATION I: MOON TIMES, CANCER TIMES

An Australian airline pilot once texted a mechanic: *"Evidence of leak on starboard brakes."* A little while later, the mechanic allegedly texted back, *"Removed evidence."*

I hope it was a joke. I suspect it was. Australians like a good laugh.

When something is wrong, most of us over age twelve are pretty good at "removing the evidence." As adults, we have learned to put our feelings aside and do what is required or expected of us. In the language of the street, we all learn how to suck it up. That is simply part of being grown-up. It sounds worse than it is. There are in fact many times in life when we really do need to dry our eyes and just do the right thing – to act like responsible adults, in other words. This behavior is – quite literally in this case – the opposite of being *childish*. We show up for work on Monday. Even though we are tired and would prefer a bubble bath, we visit our sick friend in the hospital. We show the flag at a funeral.

Few of us ever *want* to do those things, but we do them anyway. We sincerely *"want to want"* to do them. But sometimes, in the words of Leonard Cohen, you just need to "put your hat on your headache and dance." Obviously, this "hat" does not fit everyone – but may God and all the angels protect every one of us from ever giving our hearts to someone who refuses to wear it when we really need them to.

This is where the Moon enters the equations.

Maybe we get too good at all that sucking up. Maybe we become so inured to it that we hardly notice that we are doing it anymore. Maybe we don't take care of ourselves. We are bone-tired, or sad, or feeling empty, but, like that Australian airline mechanic, we *remove the evidence.* We dwell on the tasks we face rather than how we feel. We stop monitoring our own well-being.

As a result of that neglect, over time we might actually suffer illness – that, or some kind of creeping psychic malaise begins to take permanent root in us. One tragedy is that this psychospiritual disorder often masquerades as *maturity* and *adult responsibility.* We may be praised and congratulated for it.

Being human is always a balancing act – and in all of this, we are balancing the Moon (*self-care*) against Saturn (*acting like a mature adult.*) It is almost always a complicated negotiation, fraught with tricky judgment calls about where our duties and our boundaries need to duke it out. There are times to cry and there are times not to cry. Some of us naturally tilt one way or the other; that is just human diversity. *But for each one of us, during Moon times, something in our body, mind, or spirit is calling out for attention.* We need to heed that message, or we pay a big price down the road.

In such times, "removing the evidence" is a huge mistake.

THE SECRET OF HAPPINESS

As we learned back in chapter three, taking care of the Moon amounts to nothing less than the secret of happiness. Anyone making a consistently strong response to his or her Moon experiences a general sense of well-being. Anyone who tunes out those lunar messages might be productive and apparently sane, but she or he will not smile very often.

The late, great Noel Tyl described the natal Moon as a person's *reigning need*, which is about as good a two-word summary as we could ever find. It follows from his words that if we take good care of the Moon, we will have a satisfied subjective sense that *our needs have been met.* We are content and at peace.

Understanding *some* of those needs does not require any astrological knowledge at all. We all need food. We all need shelter. Those kinds of generic requirements are definitely lunar terrain; they are just not very specific to individuals. Anyone who is hungry and cold is probably not going to feel very happy.

Where the Moon begins to become more actively relevant lies higher in our hierarchy of needs than simply staying warm, dry, and nourished.

During times of lunar stimulation, those more personal, more idiosyncratic, needs begin to tug at you. Your inner child needs some attention.

T.G.I.F.

If you want to learn about the Moon, here is a productive technique: *watch what people do on the weekend.* One woman cannot wait to go shopping. Meanwhile, her husband wants to spend both Saturday and Sunday watching football games. Someone else curls up quietly with the poetry of Alfred Lord Tennyson. Another person plants a row of camelias.

In every case, we might use that wonderfully evocative word: *recreation.* But what are these people actually "re-creating?" What are they *restoring* that was sucked out of them between Monday and Friday? What are they *actually accomplishing inwardly* while shopping or planting a garden?

The first answers that come to mind form the subtitle of this book: *healing, regeneration, and recovery.* In astrological terms, these men and women are *re-establishing rapport with their Moons.* Instead of "removing the evidence," they are listening to their hearts, and *whimsically and spontaneously* doing what their hearts guide them to do. They are thereby returning themselves to a condition of happiness – a condition of *Hóhzó*, as the Navajo would say, a condition of harmony with all Creation.

- Shopping? *Maybe that woman has the Moon in the second house.*
- Football? *Maybe her husband has a fifth house Sagittarian Moon.*
- A quiet afternoon with Tennyson? *A Gemini Moon conjunct Saturn in the twelfth house?*
- Planting camelias? *Maybe the Moon is in Taurus in the fourth house.*

All of those images are about the *natal* Moon, which always offers the core, cradle-to-grave, message about the nature of our reigning needs. But in this chapter we are more concerned with transits, progressions, and solar arcs. Using those techniques mechanically, we might "predict" that those camelias would go into the ground when that Taurus Moon in the fourth house *gets stimulated* – or perhaps when that person's Moon is *progressing through Taurus.*

Taking a more evolutionary attitude, we might phrase it differently. We might make a suggestion to that client. "How's about planting some camelias this weekend? It would do you a world of good."

And they do, and it does.

SIR EDMUND HILLARY

His time of birth is Dirty Data, but what is certain is that Edmund Hillary and his *sherpa* companion, Tenzing Norgay, were the first human beings to stand on top of Mount Everest – *which, on the face of it, was a completely crazy, irrational thing to do.* Many had already died trying. The morning they were to set out from their camp for their final assault on the summit, Hillary saw that *his boots had frozen solid outside their tent that night.* Undaunted, he spent two hours thawing them out over a cook stove, put them on, and they made it to the peak.

But why?

Afterwards, no fine words were spoken – no "one small step for man, one giant step for mankind." Instead, to the first person Hillary saw on his descent, he intoned, "Well, George, we knocked the bastard off."

For great mountaineering quotes, you can't beat Hillary's predecessor, George Mallory. When he was asked why *he* wanted to climb Everest, he replied, "*Because it's there.*" Stirring words – but unfortunately, Mallory died miserably, 800 feet short of the summit, twenty-nine years before Sir Edmund made it.

Adding insult to injury, Mallory's memorable quote is often mis-attributed to Hillary.

Now, can you imagine anything less comfortable than climbing a freezing cold mountain five and half miles tall? Why did Edmund Hillary want to "knock the bastard off" in the first place? *Why did the thought of doing that make him happy?*

The best available birth time for Sir Edmund Hillary puts his Moon at about twenty-two degrees of Aries. We may not be sure of the exact degree, but we can be confident that we are right about the sign. *And what makes an Aries Moon happy?* The answer can take many forms, but they all come down to activities that *press one's competitive limits.* They all come down to things that "normal people" would probably view as simply stressful, wondering why anyone would bother with doing them.

Here, with Edmund Hillary, we see a situation in which the more universal Moon needs of comfort and nourishment were actually *overridden by the demands of his individuality.*

It is often that way with the Moon.

What *triggered* his mountain-climbing behavior at that particular time? His Aries Moon was, of course, lying latently in his psyche, cradle to grave, awaiting transits, progressions, or solar arcs for it to spring into action. When Hillary climbed Everest, there was a Saturn-Neptune conjunction in the heavens in Libra, *directly opposite the probable position of his Aries Moon.*

Those major, slow transits had plenty of time to develop "depth and complexity of meaning." The more immediate trigger was, of all things, *transiting Venus,* which was in a conjunction with his Aries Moon when he and Tenzing Norgay reached the summit.

It was time for Sir Edmund Hillary to do something nice for himself.

WHIMSY

Note that one might make the case that risking one's life – and certainly sacrificing one's creature comforts – in order to climb the tallest mountain in the world qualifies as an irrational act. That is a characterization, not a criticism. We might say the same for watching football games all weekend or disappearing into a book of poetry.

People experience lunar healing, regeneration, and recovery in many different ways, but all of them have one feature in common: in each case, they have *heeded the whimsies of their hearts.* That is how the Moon offers up, not only its "evidence," but also its remedies. That is how we listen to it, and thus energize and restore wellbeing in ourselves. In a word, the Moon does not *think*; it is not rational, nor should it be.

Anyone so constipated with logic, reason, and order that he or she cannot surrender to such whimsies from time to time has lost the thread that leads to joy in life. They have lost what is probably the central key to healing, regeneration, and recovery.

It comes down to the ability simply to feel. Earlier in the book, I quoted the seminal psychological thinker, Abraham H. Maslow. He said, *"It isn't normal to know what we want. It is a rare and difficult psychological achievement."*

We could quibble with Dr. Maslow. If we are hungry, we want something to eat. If we are feeling amorous, we want someone to love. We are very probably correct in those assessments of our issue and its cure. But just a little while ago, you read this line: *Where the Moon begins to become more actively relevant lies higher in our hierarchy of needs than simply staying warm, dry, and nourished.*

It is there at that higher, more individuated level, that Abraham Maslow's words strike home. What if that husband watching football games should have been quietly reading Tennyson – or planting camelias? The games will not work. He only thought that they would, probably because someone told him so.

YOU'RE NOT AS HAPPY AS YOU THINK YOU ARE . . .

When the natal Moon is stimulated by any significant transits, progression, or solar arcs, a good place to start our reflections lies in remembering that nothing in astrology ever happens without a good reason. Ultimately, everything that unfolds in your chart represents an *evolutionary need* arising in your consciousness. The Moon's job is to keep you nourished in body, mind, and spirit, so when it is triggered, there is either something wrong in those areas, or something that is *about to go wrong* unless you take immediate steps to heal, to remedy, or to satisfy it.

In other words, you may *think* that you are happy, but in reality you have either just "removed the evidence" of some emergent need, or it has simply not yet risen above the threshold of detectability.

In any case, your inner adult has hushed your inner child, and it is time to remedy that situation before it becomes a full-blown problem.

The only issue with phrasing a lunar event in such terms is that the words make it seem as if you are guilty of a lapse in self-care – that you have failed to listen to your heart. A more accurate understanding, at least at the outset of any major Moon time, is that it *signals a need to avoid falling into that kind of mistake.* It is not that you have already made it – rather, it is that you are standing on the brink of that possibility.

You can get it right; you can succeed. It is simply time to assess your-self emotionally – time to relax and *feel what you are really feeling*. Take your eyes *off* the prize for a change. Surrender. Don't make a fetish out of being strong, responsible, or so unremittingly "adult."

That is how you listen to the Moon.

All of these principles are universal. They apply to everyone. Where it gets specific starts with your knowing the sign and house of your natal Moon. That is where we encounter your *reigning needs* – and any response to lunar stimulus that is going to work needs to address them. Edmund Hillary needed an Arian adventure. A woman with a Piscean Moon in the ninth house might need a *spiritual pilgrimage* or a *meditation retreat*. A man with a Virgo Moon might feel better after *mowing the lawn* or *helping a child build a telescope*.

The next step in the analytic process is to look at the specific nature of the transit, progression, or solar arc that is stimulating the Moon. What moving planet are we talking about? In what sign and house does it fall? What aspect is it making to the natal Moon? All that will offer insight into where the doors through which we must pass might now be opening.

It quickly grows complicated – and thus tailor-made to fit the person in question.

Maybe someone has a Capricorn Moon in the twelfth house. One of her reigning needs is for *some uncontested hours alone* from time to time. Maybe Saturn transits through an opposition to her natal Moon from Cancer and the sixth house . . . and the plot thickens.

If she gets this transit right, she *asks for some help with her responsibili-ties* so that she can claim the quiet time that she needs – remember, the sixth house is about "servants." That is a funny word to use here, but the bottom line is that *friends serve each other*, and do so with open hearts if they are asked. She asks for support; she gets it. A friend steps up to the plate and relieves her of her duties for long enough that her emergent Moon-need for some quiet time can be met.

If she gets this Saturn transit to her Moon wrong, she *muscles through* her need for that time alone, pushing "the evidence" aside because of the perceived weight of her responsibilities and her commitment to fulfilling them.

She has made a spiritual mistake – and even worse, *the mistake has successfully masqueraded as a virtue.* The result? She feels sad – but she probably "removes the evidence" of her sadness from her mind, and stoically soldiers on through the mud, wind, and rain.

In the wrong direction.

THE MOON IN MOTION

There are three ways that Mother Nature moves the Moon around your chart – by transit, by progression, and by solar arc.

The *transiting* Moon is a very interesting beast, but I do not get much practical use out of it with my clients. As we saw in the previous chapter, it simply moves too fast to develop depth of meaning. Give it twenty-seven days, and the transiting Moon will have done everything that it ever possibly could do in your chart. If you live to be ninety years old, the transiting Moon will make every conceivable aspect in your chart about twelve hundred times. Even using generous orbs, the Moon transits through any aspect in about one single day. You can feel it when it is happening – but it simply never has time to develop the kind of thematic depth that I am looking for with my clients.

It is true that I don't get much practical use out of the transiting Moon *with my clients.* I sure get a lot of use out of it myself however. Most of the significant decisions in my life are timed by my "looking for a good Moon," avoiding the Void of Course Moon, and so on. In those ways, the transiting Moon plays a critical role in tactical astrology.

You can learn how to use it that way yourself in chapter four of *The Book of the Moon.* It is a fairly simple technique and it can smooth the feathers of reality for you.

The transiting Moon is interesting and helpful and even powerful in certain ways – but none of them have much to do with the deeper kinds of astrology we are exploring in these four volumes.

That leaves us with the *solar arc* Moon, moving along at the stately pace of about one degree per year – and thus a major player. And finally the star of the show, the workhorse of evolutionary astrology: the *progressed* Moon.

On average, the Moon progresses about one degree per month, although that figure varies widely. Given a six-degree orb, the progressed Moon remains actively engaged in an aspect for about six months going in and six months coming out again – a convenient year, centered on the date of exactitude. There is nothing graven in stone about that orb; it is just a good starting place. Naturally, the more precise the aspect becomes, the more powerfully it operates.

In all that I am about to write, I am thinking primarily of the progressed Moon, although the same principles will apply to the transiting Moon – just in a far less significant way. They also apply to the solar arc Moon, although because it moves so much more slowly, you will have to wait a lot longer to use them.

One beautiful thing about the progressed Moon is that it is almost always doing something interesting. I never ignore it. Everyone feels it deeply. Just talking about it usually helps me to establish a sense of emotional rapport with a client.

WHERE YOUR HEART IS

The position of the progressed Moon holds a mirror before your heart. It indicates where your heart is at any given time. No matter what is happening, it reflects how you are probably feeling about it. Outwardly, a person might be faced with a Saturn-pattern of *intensified duty*. Maybe, for example, she is moving to a different city.

With her progressed Moon in Capricorn or Virgo, her attitude is one of *focus* and *engagement*. She is tired, but, even though she might not be quick to admit it, she is actually pretty happy.

With her progressed Moon in Pisces, she *struggles to get herself out of bed* to face all the packing and the paperwork.

- By *sign*, the progressed Moon defines an *attitude* that currently flavors all of your perceptions and experiences.
- By *house*, the progressed Moon spotlights an area of current *emotional concern* or engagement.

In our "Building Blocks" chapter – up next – we will sketch out the Moon's passage through each house and sign in cookbook fashion. In this chapter, I want to offer you a method for considering any *aspects* which the Moon might form – and again, I am thinking primarily of the progressed Moon. To translate into the realm of the *transiting* Moon, just turn this into "how you will be feeling on Tuesday" – with the knowledge that the mood will pass by Wednesday. It is minor stuff, in other words. Translating into the realm of the *solar arc* Moon, much of what I write here will work without major modification – just remember that solar arcs, being of the nature of the Sun, tend to be quite active and biographical, even though the Moon generally has a more subjective orientation. Things tend to *happen visibly* with solar arcs.

Let's just not lose sight of the fact that sometimes it is the *invisible,* inner events that truly define the soul's journey. That realm is classic lunar territory.

We will begin our meditations on the moving Moon with a truly ancient astrological idea: *the Moon is the Great Mother.* When the Moon forms an aspect to a planet, it is as if the Great Mother Herself has said to that planet, *come sit on my lap and tell me where it hurts . . .*

Unless we have "removed the evidence" from our consciousness, the planet which the Moon is contacting *probably does hurt.* Some of the soul-needs it represents have not been met; it is starving for some attention and some nourishment. The trouble is that, unless we are little children, we probably have suppressed at least some of the pain. We are vulnerable to missing the message. We have probably become "adult" – which is to say, we have toughened up, at least to some extent. We have learned to live with the fact that some of our needs must always go unmet – that we do not always get what we want, that the universe does not exist to please us.

We have dried our eyes and learned to suck it up, "like grown-ups."

All that is a necessary part of life, at least once we get beyond puberty. Anyone who has not internalized those lessons quickly becomes an "impossible" person – self-indulgent, demanding, and unrealistic: a *prima donna,* along with whatever the equivalent male term might be. *But Mother Moon balances Father Saturn.* She is the other side of the equation. And when the spotlight is on her, lunar values must guide us back to the middle.

Great Mother (speaking gently): Come sit on my lap. How are you doing, my child? Is there anything I might do for you? Are you happy?

You (stoically): I'm just fine, thank you. How are you today?

Great Mother (beguilingly): So everything is fine with you? Close your eyes and feel. There is *nothing* you need or want? Everything is . . . *perfect?*

You (gazing into those soulful, infinite eyes): *Well . . .*

Great Mother: Nothing hurts . . .?

You: (breaking into incoherent, copious sobbing)

From Saturn's perspective, that sobbing is an indication of weakness. We have let ourselves collapse into a ball of emotions. From the Moon's point of view, *we have been brave and strong enough to allow suppressed feelings to come to the surface.* We have done the opposite of "removing the evidence"– instead, we have welcomed it. *We have allowed ourselves to become aware of an area of our lives that needs some tender loving care.*

In the process, we have headed off, not just a wave of sorrow, but rather a *lifestyle* of chronic, unnamed emptiness.

We have listened to our hearts.

Each planet and sensitive point in your chart can be understood as an evolutionary need. Everyone must learn to live with loss and resistance and misfortune. That's life – but problems arise when we forget the price we have paid for that appearance of strength, when we simply take this diet of thin soup to be the nature of adult reality. The Moon comes along and *awakens us to the hurt* – and points to the possibility that maybe we can heal it, maybe a door that once was closed is now open.

Maybe healing, regeneration, and recovery are on the horizon.

Each planet is of course in a sign and a house and enmeshed in a network of aspects. All of that astrological context is what gives them their unique individuality. Here, in just a few words, I want to give you a starting point for your meditations as the Moon forms aspects to the planets in your natal chart.

Remember: much of what follows is most vividly relevant when we are looking at the progressed Moon. In rough terms, it will remain within the orbs of an aspect for a year or so – enough time for a mood to give direction to a healing.

- When the Moon forms an aspect to the Sun, *give your poor ego a break.* You have a right to get what you want sometimes. You have a right to be selfish from time to time.

- When the Moon forms an aspect to the Moon, err in the direction of *self-indulgence*. Give yourself what you need. If you are tired, sleep. If you are hungry, eat.
- When the Moon forms an aspect to the Ascendant, *boldly start something new*. Break some new ground. You are done with some part of your old life. It has served its purpose. There is nothing more that you need to learn from it. Let it go.
- When the Moon forms an aspect to Mercury, *speak up*, and do it from your heart. No one will know what you are feeling unless you express it. No one will give you what you need unless you ask for it.
- When the Moon forms an aspect to Venus, *ask for a hug*. Address any feelings of loneliness. Relax into beauty. Soak in a tub. Gaze at a rose. Listen to music.
- When the Moon forms an aspect to Mars, if you are angry or resentful about something, *express it*. Don't hold it in. Sometimes we just need to blow out the emotional cobwebs. Go for it.
- When the Moon forms an aspect to Jupiter, you need something to go well. *You need a victory.* And neither of those good things will happen unless you are willing boldly to place a bet on yourself.
- When the Moon forms an aspect to Saturn, you need *some time alone*. You need to have a serious, constructive talk with someone you love. You are tired of an old way of behaving and ready to move to your next developmental stage.
- When the Moon forms an aspect to Uranus, knock down some walls and *claim more freedom in your life*. You have changed on the inside – make sure those changes are visible on the outside too. And if anyone disapproves . . . well, *that's kind of amusing, isn't it?*
- When the Moon forms an aspect to Neptune, your hunger for some spirit-time needs to be honored. *You need to refresh your connection with the Infinite.*
- When the Moon forms an aspect to Pluto, delve into psychologically-charged material. *You are ready to face something you were not ready to face before.* The mood of a psychoanalyst – or perhaps of a shaman – is upon you. Trust it.
- When the Moon forms an aspect to the nodal axis, *your feelings are being exaggerated and distorted by unresolved issues of a karmic nature.*

Follow them down into your psyche – but be wary of projecting them onto present-day situations and relationships.

PROGRESSED LUNAR PHASE

The phases of the Moon are technically not only about the Moon itself. They are linked to the Sun too. Since they are generated by the geometrical relationship between the two bodies, they would not exist without the Sun.

With the Moon advancing by progression at about *one degree per month* and the Sun by about *one degree per year*, watching them traverse the zodiac is a bit like watching the turtle chase the snail around the race-track. The period between successive alignments of the progressed Sun and the progressed Moon is nearly thirty years long – twenty-nine years, six months, and about eleven days, to be exact.

Depending on the initial geometry of your chart, you are guaranteed to experience such *a progressed New Moon* sometime before your thirtieth birthday, then like clockwork every three decades or so after that first one.

In *The Book of the Moon*, I explore progressed lunar phase in deep detail. It is a big, hugely important, subject, and one that does not generally get enough attention among astrologers. Here, because the scope of this book is wide, I only have space to telegraph the core ideas which underlie how the cycle of progressed lunar phases unfolds.

These words and images will give you a taste of it – and if it tastes good, please read *The Book of the Moon*.

- When the Moon is in *New* phase (which is to say, when it is between 0 degrees and 45 degrees ahead of the Sun) . . . something radically fresh and unprecedented is taking root in your life. To get it right, your only hope is to follow your heart. That is because your head doesn't really get it quite yet. Faith is rewarded, while letting either fear or even reason take over can only leave you stranded in the remains of a life that you have outgrown.
- When the Moon is in *Waxing Crescent* phase (which is to say, when it is between 45 degrees and 90 degrees ahead of the Sun) . . . we begin to see the concrete manifestation of what you started at the New Moon, but "we ain't seen nothing yet." The curtain has only risen six inches – and all we know is that the play has something to do with "people wearing shoes." Still, anticipation is mounting.

We expect the play to be a good one. Keep the faith; keep going, trusting the building wave of energy. You're famous – but not too many people know that about you yet.

- When the Moon is in *First Quarter* phase (which is to say, when it is between 90 degrees and 135 degrees ahead of the Sun) . . . it's too late to stop now. You are committed. The battle is joined. Forces that might oppose you begin to notice you for the first time. Sometimes you've got to fight to be free – but choose your battles carefully. Compromise what can be compromised, and fight like mad for what cannot be compromised. Just don't go down in self-righteous flames of glory. Winning is better, even if you have to make a few deals.

- When the Moon is in *Waxing Gibbous* phase (which is to say, when it is between 135 degrees and 180 degrees ahead of the Sun) . . . the momentum of your vision is strong, even unstoppable. Power is sexy. Drawn to your energy, *allies appear* with good ideas and fresh resources. Go ahead and form *symbiotic partnerships* with them – but be wary of losing sight of your original vision in the flurry of other people's energies and enthusiasms.

- When the Moon is in *Full phase* (which is to say, when it is between 180 degrees and 225 degrees ahead of the Sun) . . . what you planted as a seed back in the New Moon phase is now in full flower. Behold your creation. If you want to understand the exact nature of your karma, observe your life exactly as it is now. Everything is on the table, warts and all. There is often a strange feeling of anticlimax in this phase. William Butler Yeats said of it that "the soul trembles into stillness." You are taking stock, and wondering about the future, which now looms in a very different way.

- When the Moon is in *Waning Gibbous* phase (which is to say, when it is between 225 degrees and 270 degrees ahead of the Sun) . . . you are finishing what you started, even though your heart has begun to lose some of its previous level of engagement with everything you have created. You feel older. You feel a pull to move on to something different – but those doors are not yet opened. Your life is tied up with other people's lives now. You are caught in a web of old promises. You are invited to help other people, often *playing a role in their own significant transitions* – endings, divorces, spiritual crises, even deaths. It is not about you at this point.

- When the Moon reaches *Last Quarter* phase (which is to say, when it is between 270 degrees and 315 degrees ahead of the Sun) . . . *it is a time of release and completion.* Often it marks a period in which *forgiveness has ripened*, both of yourself and of others. Memory is curated, rendered clearer and more truthful than it was at the time it was originally laid down. Learning is digested. Look at old photographs of yourself, marvel, and get chills – and truly understand your life-story for the first time.

- When the Moon is in *Waning Crescent* phase (which is to say, when it is between 315 degrees and 360 degrees ahead of the Sun) . . . old material structures are falling away. Let them go. Attachment only leads to pain now. The veil between this world and the next one becomes thin. Psychic experiences abound. Meanwhile, *a new vision* is slowly taking shape in your heart. It is still in a nascent state, more akin to a feeling than to an idea or a concrete plan. Sit with that energy; immerse yourself in its vibration. (You will soon be acting on it as the Moon begins its new cycle . . .)

THE PROGRESSED MOON OUT OF BOUNDS

When the Moon (or any other planet) is described as being *Out of Bounds*, that simply means that it is further north or south in the sky than the highest or lowest point that the Sun can ever reach. Earth's equator, projected onto the sky, is called the *celestial equator*. Planets are usually above it or below it. In astronomy, that quality of "latitude" in the heavens is called *declination*. On the winter solstice (here in the northern hemisphere) when the noonday Sun hangs low in the sky, it is at a (slightly variable) southerly declination of 23 degrees 26 minutes – that means that it is that far below the celestial equator, which explains why the winter Sun rises so late, hangs so low at noon, and sets so early.

Any planet even further to the south would be defined as Out of Bounds. All of them except for Saturn and Neptune can do that.

And the Moon can do that too.

Reverse all of that astronomy for the summer solstice. It is the same, only backwards. At that moment, in the northern hemisphere, the Sun is 23 degrees 26 minutes north of the celestial equator – way up high in the sky, in other words.

Again, the figure of 23 degrees 26 minutes varies a bit year to year, but not by very much.

The term "Out of Bounds," by the way, comes from a hard-to-find book called *Declinations: The Other Dimension* by an astrologer named Kt (say KAY TEE) Boeher who worked some decades ago. I never met her and I know very little about her, except that she left her mark in the world in the form of a very useful piece of new astrological vocabulary.

The astronomy of declination quickly becomes complex. I did my best to explain it scientifically in *The Book of the Moon* – so, once again, I refer you there if you would like to pursue the subject in a more rigorous fashion. While I am at it, let me also draw your attention to Tony Howard of Astrology University, who has done groundbreaking work on Out of Bounds planets. So far, his material exists in the form of recorded talks. Many of us are hoping that he will find time to write a book about it one day.

For our strictly lunar purposes, suffice it to say that half of the human population is immune to ever experiencing an Out of Bounds Moon, either natally or by progression. But for those who do, it is an event of monumental impact.

Here is a way of thinking about it.

Start by drawing an equal sign between the Sun and the Equator.

Add what we know about the astrological Sun: it is your *ego* and your *identity*. The Sun is directly connected to *who you think you are* – and probably who everyone else thinks you are too. It is the shoes you get into and the hat you put on your head when you step out into the world on Monday morning.

Now add that the Moon is the heart and the soul of your life.

Now ask the following question: *what does it feel like when your heart and your soul are no longer aligned with those shoes and that hat?*

Not good!

With an Out of Bounds lunar progression, the issue becomes one of following your heart into a kind of psychic wilderness. It is a scary process, but one that can regenerate your life. Much that has supported your sense of identity – we might even say your sanity – is either no longer there or no longer working very well. A psychological rug has been pulled out from underneath you.

Let me scare myself silly for the sake of astrological science. *What if suddenly no one cared at all about astrology? Nobody wanted a session with me. Nobody read my books. My website was ignored.*

I've been doing this work for fifty years. It is a huge part of my identity. What if that rug were pulled out from underneath me? *What if my identity simply did not work for me – or for anyone else – anymore?*

If you can enter that spooky fantasy with me, you can begin to grasp the way an Out of Bounds Moon feels. While, at the material level, we often do see *identity-supporting structures falling away*, there is also an inward sense of *losing you*r *engagement* with that identity.

It is rare, but possible, that the Out of Bounds Moon experience is purely internal – that you simply realize that you are *no longer identified with your previous identity.* It just doesn't work for you any longer, even though the old structures of your life might still persist. But usually, because of synchronicity, we see outward endings as well.

With the Moon progressing Out of Bounds . . .

- A woman who has held the same job for many years experiences the collapse of the entire industry which employs her. *Who is she now?*
- A man who has been married for twenty-nine years hears his wife ask him for a divorce. *Who is he now?*
- A government falls; anarchy reigns. A professor flees with his family, escaping as a refugee to a country where he does not even speak the language. *Who is he now?*

These are all true stories, but they are only the outward synchronistic trappings of an inward event whose actual nature is rather different. In each case, the deeper truth is that the existing structure of these people's lives *had served its purpose,* had become stale, predictable, and mechanical.

Did they realize this? Was this their feeling state? Not necessarily – but it is the psychic and spiritual reality.

The ones who figure that part out do better in the long run than the ones who do not. The reality is that an Out of Bounds progressed Moon can be good luck masquerading as bad luck.

- A woman retires and moves to Florida. She wistfully says goodbye to an old neighborhood and her old friends – and looks forward to some fresh air in her new life.

- A man who has been taking care of his sickly, dependent mother for seventeen years sees her die peacefully in her bed at the age of ninety-seven. It is poignant, but he is now free to leave New Jersey and move to his beloved Arizona.
- The band breaks up. The ageing rock star no longer needs to pretend to be younger than he is. But he has no clear idea of what he will do next.

Re-inventing oneself can be an energizing opportunity, even if some good things have to fall away to clear the path. Like most times of a transition, an Out of Bounds progressed Moon calls for faith, creativity, and openness to unexpected inspiration.

TWO BORING LECTURES

As we pursue a deeper understanding of the Moon slipping Out of Bounds by progression, the best way I know to get there is to subject you to a pair of really boring rants. For mercy's sake, I will keep them brief. You have heard both of them enough times that you could cover these bases yourself. There is only one single point of interest in them, and that is that *while everybody will nod sleepily and agree with both of these sermons, they absolutely contradict each other.*

Life is full of paradoxes. Here comes a big one . . .

Boring Lecture Number One: Character counts. Adults keep their promises. They show up when they say they will show up. They do what they say they are going to do. They have made their stand in this world. You can count on them. They can resist temptation. Their appetites do not control them. They live their values. Fear does not make their decisions for them. They follow through. You can trust their word.

Boring Lecture Number Two: Life is change, so never say never. No one can say what he or she will become tomorrow. You have to follow your heart, and go with the flow of what is happening in the moment, always ready to adapt and always eager to learn. You have to follow your bliss. Consistency boils down ultimately to your right to be just as stupid next year as you were last year. Never make consistency a goal. You cannot step into the same river twice. Always let your soul be your pilot.

Good moral counsel in both cases – but just try following both sermons at once. Obviously these two homilies are pointing in opposite philosophical directions. People tend to pick the position that fits with whatever they feel like doing anyway. Here is the point – and how, taken together, these two ways of facing life illuminate the meaning of an Out of Bounds progressed Moon.

- The first lecture reflects the values of the *Sun* – the core values to which you must be true if your life is going to make any moral sense at all. That is the "Equator" of your life: the centerline of your identity, your dignity, and your sanity.
- The second lecture is about the *Moon* – and following the Moon, as we have seen, is always the secret of happiness. The Moon does not aim for consistency. It aims for attunement to the realities of the present moment.

When the Moon progresses Out of Bounds, the right course is indeed to let your soul be your pilot. You are experiencing a kind of death-and-rebirth: a *mini-reincarnation*. You have to trust the process, even though it will carry you deep into existential *terra incognita*.

Martin Luther trusted his Out of Bounds process, way back in 1517. He was a devout Roman Catholic priest – and appalled by the corruption of the church, particularly the selling of "indulgences" – a money-making practice which treated God as a corrupt judge, open to bribery. *Sex outside of your marriage? That'll be fifty dollars and we'll make it right, no problem. Murder? . . . hmmmm . . . we can take care of it, but that one is going to cost you . . .*

Martin Luther smelled a theological rat – but he struggled with the balance between the clear moral issue on one hand, and, on the other hand, his vows of loyalty to the Holy Church. When his Moon finally went Out of Bounds, it all exploded, He nailed the Ninety-Five Theses to the church door at Wittenburg – and unwittingly triggered the Protestant Reformation.

Luther also got himself excommunicated in the process – definitely a blemish on your *curriculum vitae* if you are a Roman Catholic priest. When his Moon returned in bounds, he had a job again. He was a Protestant minister.

That is how the progressed Moon Out of Bounds works. Trust your heart, and follow it into the existential wilderness. Don't wait for the rug to be pulled out from underneath you. Just step right off it – you are tired of it anyway. Have faith. You will land on your feet. But it is time to re-invent your identity.

ENTERING CANCER

Sooner or later, given enough time, every planet will enter Cancer by transit, progression, or solar arc. With the faster planets, you can count on that happening for you personally, often many times. With a slow planet – Pluto, for example – it will not happen in the lifetime of anyone now on the Earth. That is because Pluto's next Cancer ingress does not occur until August 14, 2157.

In the next chapter, we will look at each planet individually in terms of the specific meaning of its passage through Cancer. In the remaining pages of this chapter, my aim is to wrestle with understanding the basic principles that underlie the more formulaic planet-by-planet material we will catalog in the next chapter.

One critical piece of the puzzle is that as we contemplate a planet entering Cancer, we must also take into account the fact that it is very probably simultaneously leaving Gemini. While that is certainly an excellent guess, it will not always be true. That's because a planet moving in retrograde fashion could enter Cancer *via* the back door – from Leo, in other words.

Mostly, the flow is from Gemini into Cancer, and much of what we explore here reflects that more common situation.

Any planet – even a rather inward-looking one such as Neptune – takes on a more curious, outward, extroverted flavor when it is conditioned by Gemini. It has reached a stage in its journey in which *paying attention to new, surprising information* is an enormous evolutionary stimulus. If that Gemini passage was successful, that planet is now charged with fresh experience. As it crosses into Cancer, it needs to *reflect upon that Geminian experience and begin to digest it* – to integrate it, and to work with it in a quieter, emotionally-connected, healing way.

It has been a long while since Neptune entered Cancer, by the way. The last time it crossed that cusp was 1901-1902. The next time it touches Cancer will be July 3, 2065. Always these kinds of outer planet transits leave their fingerprints on history, but that is not the subject that we are exploring. Instead, let's think about the *personal meaning* of such a sea-change. Neptune, at least at its best, always reflects some manner of *transcendent spiritual interest.* When Neptune is conditioned by Gemini, a person might, for one example, feel guided to r*ead metaphysical literature* or to *seek spiritual teachers* – that is all pure Gemini. Then, as Neptune crosses into Cancer, the *underlying motivating values* animating the planet shift. Now, it is time to *reflect, feel,* and *digest* what he or she learned during the Gemini period. "Head knowledge" must cook in the alchemical cauldron of our deeper consciousness, and so turn into heart knowledge.

Let's go beyond Neptune. To put this Gemini-to-Cancer transition on the map in a way that relates to *any* planet crossing this cusp, think of a vacation trip to another continent. Such a journey is a big adventure, highly stimulating, even educational – there's the Gemini signature. With planets moving into Cancer, if I were to plan my ideal trip, I would punctuate travel days full of sights, sounds, and tastes *with days in which I remained quietly in one place* – "Cancer days," so to speak. That would give me time to reflect and digest. Without such islands of quiet, my cup would quickly run over. All of those cities and museums would blur, and little would have any lasting meaning for me. When I think of a vacation-from-hell, I envision a new hotel room every night, lots of strangers, an endless sensory onslaught – ten European capitals in twelve days, for example. Saigon to Wuhan via Lhasa and Kyoto, all before the Moon begins to wane.

Crazy-making, right?

Well, for me at least. If you have ten planets in Gemini, maybe such dense, relentless experience feels less daunting to you – but even if you are very Geminian, don't plan such an extravaganza when the sky is lit up by planets transiting through Cancer – and especially not if you have major Cancerian progressions or solar arcs currently happening in your chart.

Such relentless chaos would make even you feel crazy at such a time.

Simply said, a planet enters Cancer and it *needs time to reflect.* It needs quiet time. Experience itself can often be nothing but a distraction – but experience that we have *digested* . . . that is wisdom. That is healing, regeneration, and recovery in action.

And that is what Cancer is all about.

18

MOON TIMES,
CANCER TIMES:
THE BUILDING BLOCKS

By transit, the Moon will hit every one of your astrological houses be-tween Monday noon and Tuesday noon. Think about it: just like the Sun, the Moon rises once every day. That means that it has made the complete circuit of all the houses before it comes up again the next day.

You can feel it. You can see it in action – that is, if you feel like bothering with it. My prayer would be that you have better things to do with your life. The effects of such lunar transits are real, but trivial. The Moon only takes a month to complete a full tour of all the zodiacal signs. That is so quick that it falls beneath the threshold of what merits an astrologer's attention, at least when we are doing evolutionary astrology and trying to look at the big picture.

What I am about to cover in this chapter has some relevance to the transiting Moon, but it is really more attuned to the slower, more thematic, passage of the Moon around the chart by progression or by solar arc.

As we saw earlier, on average, by progression, the Moon takes a little over two years to get through a sign. Houses vary in width, so it is harder to put a figure on it, but it averages about the same length of time. *One degree per month* is the simple rule of thumb about the progressed Moon's motion – and it is a useful figure to know as you lie in bed playing astrology if you are not able to sleep. Beyond those wee hours reflections, your best bet is to use a computer or an ephemeris and look up the specifics. The progressed Moon's speed is slippery, and guessing at its position can get you into trouble in a professional or other high-stakes situation.

With the solar arc Moon, our one-degree-per-year principle works pretty well, especially when you are young. But as you get older, the drift between reality and our one-degree-per-year principle can get you into trouble too.

Once again, you really have to look it up.

The Moon Moving Through The Twelve Houses

THE MOON ENTERING THE FIRST HOUSE

The Challenge: I must master the art of getting anything new off on the right foot. I am starting something fresh. I am hungry to see some brand new possibilities and novel circumstances arising in my life. The trouble is that since this is truly a new start, I really do not know what I am doing – and yet I know that the choices I make now will set the tone for the whole cycle ahead, so I also need to be careful not to make any mistakes. That is my dilemma: I do not know what I am doing, but I can't afford to make any mistakes. Impossible? Yes, logically – but it is really a familiar situation. Whenever I begin a new venture in any kind of fresh territory, simple inexperience is part of the picture. How can I know what I am doing when I have never done it before? And yet beginnings often set the tone for what is to come, which leads me to . . .

How To Get It Right: I resolve to follow my heart. Something deep and intuitive inside of me *feels* the direction I must take and the new values which must guide me. If I trust my guts, I will set the wheels turning in a good way. I affirm that I have faith and that I have audacity – that "the Force is with me." I am also willing to be called self-centered – and that is because I am "centering" myself in a new way.

Making A Mess Of It: If I dither, that dithering will lock in as part of my character. That bad habit will be hard to break. If, in my insecurity, I stick to tried and true values and methods – things that have worked for me in the past – all I am doing is resolving that the future will be a clone of the past. The theme song of my life will be "second verse, same as the first." The real point is that I am ready for a new verse and maybe a whole new tune.

THE MOON ENTERING SECOND THE HOUSE

The Challenge: What I started "on a wing and a prayer"– on faith, in other words – now faces a *solvable* crisis. I am aware of daunting obstacles. Feelings of insecurity and the fear of impending failure are nipping at me. Retreat tempts me. Can I follow through on what I have started? Can I make it real? Can I make my dream work sustainably in the real world?

How To Get It Right: I resolve to use these feelings of insecurity and doubt as windows through which I can see my situation objectively. There are concrete reasons that I am experiencing these emotions of doubt. What do I need to change in order to feel that I am on solid ground? What *new resources* would cure me of these feelings? Is it money? Are they new tools? Is it the right allies? Knowledge? Education? *I trust these feelings to lead me to the facts* – and I resolve not to mistake feelings for facts. I can do this. I can "cash out" my vision. With the right resources, I can still make it happen.

Making A Mess Of It: If I misinterpret my emotional state as the actual nature of reality, I will get scared and try to bail out. I can snatch defeat from the jaws of victory. I will be tempted to try to cut my losses and move back to some previous set of circumstances which, in truth, I have outgrown. I can become paralyzed. I can define myself as a victim or a loser or a failure. I can thereby condemn myself to underachievement.

THE MOON ENTERING THE THIRD HOUSE

The Challenge: Unexpected data is always the most valuable kind. What is it that I do not know? What are the questions I have not even thought to ask? What am I missing? To carry my vision forward, I need a better understanding of where I am. Some of my most fundamental assumptions about my present circumstances are wrong – but which ones? When things that I do not expect loom before me, *can I even see them?*

How To Get It Right: I resolve to adopt a beginner's mind – I am just starting down an undiscovered road. I trust my curiosity. I learn more by listening than by talking. I read. I watch. I engage with media. I converse with interesting people and listen carefully to what they are telling me. I can learn something from almost anyone I meet. I connect the dots. I expect omens, signs and synchronicities to guide me – and by expecting them, I look for them, and by looking for them, I see them.

Making A Mess Of It: If my ego gets in my way now, I will defend my errors as if they were brilliant insights. I will fall in love with the sound of my own voice. I will listen to no one. Faced with life-saving messages, I will hit the delete button. Offered Warp Drive, I will harness up the trusty old ox cart – all in the Holy Name of my always having been "right all along."

THE MOON ENTERING THE FOURTH HOUSE

The Challenge: The secret of eternal happiness lies in my willingness to renew my dialog with my own soul. That time has come. My inner self is calling out for attention. It has fresh marching orders for me. Can I withdraw enough from the relentless demands of my outward life to make time to *feel what I have become* – not *what I was yesterday*, but what I have actually *become?*

How To Get It Right: I resolve to let feelings which I cannot under-stand or interpret rise up inside of me uncensored. I will create space and time in my life that is conducive to my attuning to my own heart. I will cul-tivate *soulfulness* in my life – and one of the ways I will succeed at that is by spending quiet, quality time with people whom I love. I will avoid excessive outward distraction. "Don't just do something, sit there" will be my mantra.

Making A Mess Of It: If I fail in this, I miss a whispered message from my own soul – a message that is trying to redirect my life away from a path that is beginning to verge on meaninglessness and toward one that could fill me with a sense of having been guided by angels. If I waste this time by just rearranging my pre-existing circumstances, I will have only rearranged the furniture in a house in which I no longer want to live.

THE MOON ENTERING THE FIFTH HOUSE

The Challenge: There are many components to spiritual health. One of them is simply taking joy in each moment of life. Without joy, I can become hardened and tough – I may be strong, but for what reason? Right now, I am too strong – or, better said, my hide has gotten too thick for my own good. I need to soften and relax. I resolve to recover my child-like sense of open-hearted wonder and playfulness.

How To Get It Right: I will make time for some play. I will not always reflexively do the responsible thing. I will honor my need for pleasure and release. While I make space for the pagan appetites of my body without shame, I will balance those pleasures with pleasures of the mind, heart, and soul – creativity, the arts, even the joys of meditation. In a sense, I am having a "second childhood"– which is to say that images of my next developmental stage are arising from my unconscious mind. This process works the same way as it does for children – the ones who let themselves dream of becoming astronauts might grow up and become happy airline pilots.

Making A Mess Of It: If I miss the point of this evolutionary step, I become stuck in the present – which quickly metamorphoses into being "stuck in the past." I may be strong and sane, able to handle what comes along, but I will have lost the evolutionary spark of the unpredictable, the creative, and the possibility of fundamental breakthroughs. I become mechanical. I have left no room for miracles, joy, and serendipity in my life.

THE MOON ENTERING THE SIXTH HOUSE

The Challenge: Preparing myself morally and spiritually for a rebirth and an empowerment. Not "beating myself up" – but actively and honestly taking responsibility for my weaknesses and character flaws. I make a fearless catalog of them. Seeing myself clearly. I accept that no problem is ever solved until it is recognized, and in spiritual matters, that I am my own problem. I discern truly helpful guides and mentors – while avoiding self-appointed gurus and psychologists.

How To Get It Right: I resolve to look into the honest mirror of my circumstances. What is not working in my life and what part have my own character flaws played in the failure? It is not that everything in my life is awful – the question is only, how can I make things even better? In order to accomplish those healing steps, it is of enormous benefit to me to have a person or two in my life to whom I can look up – mentors from whom I can draw inspiration and a practical sense of what steps I need to take. If I look for them, the laws of synchronicity guarantee that I will find them.

Making A Mess Of It: If I fail here, I feel burdened by duties and responsibilities that are simply draining me. My life is defined by other people's "orders." I blame these people for my circumstances rather than seeing my own part in creating the situation. Under the pressure of this kind of creeping hopelessness, I can feel trapped and defeated – feelings which might metamorphose into physical illness.

THE MOON ENTERING THE SEVENTH HOUSE

The Challenge: It is time for my soul to become visible – and there are two parts to that process. One is intimate and one is public. For a long time, I have been in the psychological "underworld," doing inner work and soul-recovery. Now I need to begin to express some of that wisdom in the community around me. I am ready to emerge more publicly. To succeed in doing that, I need some help – and some help from soul-friends is on the way. That is the intimate part of the equation. These soul-friends might take the form of new comrades or romantic interests, but they might also appear as an old trusted soul-friend revealing a new face.

How To Get It Right: I resolve to be open to being seen as I really am. I resolve to be receptive to being touched and even changed by people who come into my life now, letting them impact me in both practical and psychological ways. I will be discerning about who I trust – and I will learn more about how to trust. I am mindful of a kind of "aura of readiness" that has descended upon me, and which other people can see. It creates expectations in them toward me. I pass willingly through doors of empowerment as they open before me.

Making A Mess Of It: If I fail here, I experience a kind of psychic "stillbirth." I miss the boat, in other words. Important people appear in my life, and I turn away from them, thus missing significant opportunities for transformation. Doors open and I stare at them until they close again. I keep getting on with the past and I fail to create the more vibrant future which was available to me.

THE MOON ENTERING THE EIGHTH HOUSE

The Challenge: I always celebrate the process of personal growth, but the reality is that I have now become strong enough, wise enough, and mature enough that material which has been held in my unconscious mind is ready to surface. That will start to happen automatically. Facing it is not always easy, but I draw strength from an eternal truth: as I heal my wounds, I establish a foundation for greater wellbeing in the future. In my relationships, I am now ready to reveal much more of myself, and thus to go deeper with another human being than I have ever gone before.

How To Get It Right: I resolve to remember that there are many truly positive states of consciousness which are not characterized by jump-for-joy happiness. I recognize that if I get this process right, some strangely inexplicable moods will come upon me. Some will be difficult. If I follow them down into the dark, I am rewarded with a higher degree of sanity in my life. Having someone I trust to whom I can talk about these processes is an incalculable treasure. Such people are likely to appear now. I am integrating my sexuality with actual emotional and spiritual intimacy – and I willingly admit the gap that existed between them in the past.

Making A Mess Of It: If I miss this healing opportunity, I only experience a lingering bad mood and a dark attitude. I understand neither of them; I only project them outward onto the people in my life and the circumstances I face. After a while, they pass, leaving my soul simply feeling tired – and probably leaving me some interpersonal messes to clean up.

THE MOON ENTERING THE NINTH HOUSE

The Challenge: The deep inner work I have just completed has shifted the foundations of my perception. That means that my understanding of life now needs to play catch-up. Can I re-define reality in a way that reflects the wisdom I have earned? Can I recognize and weed out used-up beliefs I have had in the past which were in fact only the results of socialization, rationalization, and walls of defense? I need to stretch my boundaries and take a bigger view of everything, including my personal possibilities.

How To Get It Right: I resolve to seek broader education in some sense of that word – and it may not be academic. I will follow my heart, choosing to learn only what I feel drawn to learn, trusting my curiosity. It helps me now to break up my routines and habitual patterns by doing new things. Traveling can help me blow out the cobwebs. I need a fresh perspective on my life. Perhaps I gain some of it through philosophical or metaphysical study. Certainly I can acquire it by placing myself in unfamiliar situations – and watching myself adapt to them.

Making A Mess Of It: If I turn away from this evolutionary necessity, I slip into defending an outworn understanding of life, arguing for values which are no longer serving me, and mistaking delusional opinions for reality. I can become "preachy" in a way that reveals an underlying insecurity about my own sermons.

THE MOON ENTERING THE TENTH HOUSE

The Challenge: My mission is calling me. A happy convergence of readiness in myself and a need for me in the community is emerging. Can I make a gift of myself to the world? In phrasing it that way, I recognize that "the world" does not necessarily spell fame and fortune – it only indicates that I am ready to touch the lives of at least a few people whom I do not know in a personal way, offering something of myself to them in a fashion that feels good to me and helps them too. I am now "ripe" for this calling. My relationship to community and my role there is being triggered into rapid evolution, as if I am graduating to a new level of usefulness.

How To Get It Right: I resolve to be willing to put myself out there, stepping up to the podium somehow and making my presence felt beyond the realm of my immediate personal relationships. To succeed, I need to *focus* my mission and my message, cutting it down to the kinds of essentials that can actually penetrate the thick walls of the collective mind. I realize that no one is automatically interested in me; I must develop a skill set that *makes me interesting* to the people I am destined to help. I accept the paradox that I need to *earn the right to serve*.

Making A Mess Of It: If I miss this opportunity, I still find myself pulled into more public or social situations, but in a way that feels empty, pointless, or simply exhausting to me. If that were to happen, the underlying reason would be that my role in the community has almost no connection to the realities of my own soul.

THE MOON ENTERING THE ELEVENTH HOUSE

The Challenge: I must accept the fact that I am a pawn in a far larger game – a game which, in many cases, I do not even understand, or need to understand. I am being used by a higher intelligence; I am impacting people's lives now without knowing that I am doing it. All I have to do is to be myself, and be willing to mingle with people whom I do not know. Much that I have endeavored to create is coming to fruition now; I must see it through, even though inwardly I am already moving on to other possibilities – possibilities which are still unformed in the physical world, but which will coalesce as the Moon comes around to the Ascendant in a few years.

How To Get It Right: I resolve to be available to people whom I do not know in a personal way – strangers and mere acquaintances. I resolve to complete what I have started, to follow through, knowing that in so doing, I will be scattering seeds of wisdom here and there, touching the lives of many strangers and "bit players" in my life. Humility, faith, and surrender to a Higher Will keep me happy during this period.

Making A Mess Of It: If I fail here, there are two possibilities. The first one is that my restlessness and discontent translate into a wasteful false start of some sort. I feel like I need to take a new direction; the problem is that I do not yet know exactly what it is, so I hare off without a real vision. The second face of failure is that I find myself overextended with social responsibilities which mean nothing to me. I feel that my life is defined by the customs of the herd rather than by my own spirit.

THE MOON ENTERING THE TWELFTH HOUSE

The Challenge: Much of the life that I have been living has served its purpose. I am molting a personality, just as a bird might molt its feathers. Structures which have defined my identity are falling away, along with my sense of emotional engagement with them. The challenge I face is purely one of trusting this process of release as it plays out, and not letting fear or insecurity trick me into holding desperately onto the past – or compulsively creating a false start in my life in an attempt to cover my present nakedness and uncertainty.

How To Get It Right: I resolve to listen to my better angels. They are whispering in my ears now. "Have patience" is one of the things they are telling me. Because their voices are very soft, I can only hear them if I make myself very quiet too. That quiet might look like meditation. It might look like a spiritual retreat. It might simply look like me spending more time by myself, listening to my own heart. The one thing it always resembles is *faith*.

Making A Mess Of It: If I blow this passage, I slip into some manner of escapism as I unconsciously try to blunt the psychic sensitivity which is arising in me. I am likely to make some kind of major blunder in my life – and, if that is what happens, what is really going on is that I acted on a "half-baked" vision . . . one that would have worked fine if I had "left it in the oven" until the Moon came around to the Ascendant once again.

The Moon Moving Through The Twelve Signs

When the Moon progresses into Scorpio while it is in your fifth house, those intense Scorpionic values and motivations inform your creative life and your pathways to joy – that is the territory of the fifth house. If it progresses into Scorpio while in your tenth house, you are invited to bring those same Scorpionic attitudes to bear on the role you are playing in the larger community – tenth house existential terrain.

THE MOON PASSING THROUGH ARIES

The Right Attitude: To accomplish what I need to accomplish now, I need to be brave, bold, and relentless. I will not be stopped. I resolve to be auda-cious. I will not be intimidated. I have a right to assert myself and to claim what I need. I can think strategically; I do not need to win every battle. I just need to win the war – and win it in a way that reflects my core values and does not cause me shame.

What My Energy Now Attracts: Enemies, rivals, competitors, and wor-thy opponents appear, as do daunting, frightening circumstances. I am open to feeling scared, but I refuse to panic. I will stand my ground. I will be clear and direct in my self-expression. Challenges arise – and I rise to meet them. Opportunities for adventure abound, and if I am willing to take some risks, I am rewarded for it.

How Squandering My Energy Looks: Perhaps I simply fold up and run away in panic. I let myself be cowed or intimidated. I fail to defend myself or to defend something or someone I love. A mood of quiet resentment rots inside of me. Alternatively, I give myself over to rage. I am needlessly destructive, but I aim it at safe, innocent, or pointless targets. I am bloody-minded. I kick the dog; I slam doors. Everything feels like an emergency.

THE MOON PASSING THROUGH TAURUS

The Right Attitude: To accomplish what I need to accomplish at this point, I need first to calm down, get centered, and let my body tell me what I truly want to do. Only when every molecule of my being is calmly aligned with my heart and soul can I achieve the sustainable focus I now need. I have time – and I must use it patiently, not "by just waiting," but rather by actively attuning myself to the still, small voice within.

What My Energy Now Attracts: Opportunities for peace and quiet open up before me. The only question is, do I recognize them and value them sufficiently? They are not simply a chance for a rest – they are opportunities to silently realign my life with my soul. Experiences in Mother Nature present themselves. Animals may touch my life, reminding me of my own inner animal. People whose presence relaxes me appear on the scene – artists, bodyworkers, people who look more comfortable in bluejeans than in business suits.

How Squandering My Energy Looks: Perhaps I stick stubbornly to outworn plans that, in truth, no longer enchant or engage me. Perhaps I force myself into the *prison of consistency,* afraid to change direction, even when my heart is begging for it. Perhaps I confuse material security with inner peace – and then I pay too high a price for it.

THE MOON PASSING THROUGH GEMINI

The Right Attitude: To accomplish what I need to accomplish now, above all else, I need updated information. My understanding of what is happening in my life is flawed. If I keep my eyes, ears, and mind open I can correct those misimpressions and wrong assumptions. I have a right to ask any questions that enter my mind. For the sake of getting smarter, I am willing to look dumb. I engage actively in conversation and I listen carefully and critically to what I hear.

What My Energy Now Attracts: Everything in my life is sped up now. I resolve to surf the waves of experience no matter how wild the ride might get. Messages arrive. Omens and signs are abundant, if only I look for them. Anything that surprises me is particularly significant – I resolve to notice it. Books fall off shelves. "Random" channel-surfing yields mission-critical information. Situations crystallize in which, to succeed, I must multitask.

How Squandering My Energy Looks: Perhaps I simply talk too much – and if I become aware of doing that, I must ask myself what I am avoiding hearing. I wrap myself in a lather of petty distractions and entertainments in order to defend myself against actually learning what I need to learn. I rationalize. I argue pointlessly, even with myself. Meanwhile, the voice in my head sounds as if it has overdosed on caffeine.

THE MOON PASSING THROUGH CANCER

The Right Attitude: To accomplish what I need to accomplish now, I need to be gentle with myself, even self-indulgent. Deep down, I hurt more than I realize I do. It is a healing time for me, and only when I have recognized the need for that and have treated myself patiently and lovingly for a while, can I come to the realizations that will aim me in the right direction in the next chapters of my life. For a while, I aim to produce inner results rather than outward ones.

What My Energy Now Attracts: Healers of mind and body appear. They may be friends or professionals, or both. Opportunities simply to be quiet present themselves. Domestic circumstances shift in more welcoming ways. People appear whom I am in a position to help and support, and in helping them, I am healing something inside of myself. Cats want to sit in my lap.

How Squandering My Energy Looks: Instead of actively seeking experiences that can effectively address the hurt places inside of me, I merely whine and feel sorry for myself. I would rather play the victim and assign blame than actually heal. I exaggerate the needs and demands of other people, and martyr myself with unnecessary or excessive care giving. I attract "vampires" – human beings who suck the energy right out of me.

THE MOON PASSING THROUGH LEO

The Right Attitude: To accomplish what I need to accomplish now, I need to "dance as if no one is watching." I need to get over my residual fears of vulnerability, along with any fear of making a fool of myself, and simply express myself. I aim for looseness, lack of self-consciousness, and spontaneity. I give outward expression to my imagination, my vision, and my tastes.

What My Energy Now Attracts: Stages and spotlights crystalize before me – at least in some broad sense of those words. Eyes turn to me. Chances to speak up appear. I attract attention. Opportunities for creative work present themselves. For reasons I do not understand, suddenly everyone looks at me expectantly. My turn to shine has arrived.

How Squandering My Energy Looks: Instead of spontaneous, sincere self-expression, I self-consciously play to the crowd, seeking applause or approval. I am trying to *look* cool, sexy, important, spiritual, wise, or rich. I am like a rock star who likes his sunglasses more than playing his guitar.

THE MOON PASSING THROUGH VIRGO

The Right Attitude: To accomplish what I need to accomplish now, I must face the fact that necessary skills are missing in my repertoire. No problem – all I have to do is to roll up my sleeves, burn the midnight oil, and acquire them. I affirm to myself that I can learn to do anything. An attitude of humility helps, both in terms of recognizing my own (correctable) shortcomings – and also because being humble allows me to recognize the teachers who have the skills I need to learn and to enlist their help in doing so.

What My Energy Now Attracts: Situations of pressing responsibility emerge as my circumstances evolve. Facing them, I feel some degree of cluelessness or incompetence. Those self-critical impressions are quite accurate, but they are only meant as goads toward practical learning. The problems are soluble. I attract guides, role models, and mentors – the only question is, do I recognize them and let them teach me what I need to learn?

How Squandering My Energy Looks: Perhaps I pointlessly dissipate my vitality in worry. Maybe I get flustered. Maybe I become too hard on myself, feeling overwhelmed or as if I have already failed. If I fall into that trap, I probably aim some of it in outward directions, criticizing other people – or falling into an attitude that nothing is ever good enough.

THE MOON PASSING THROUGH LIBRA

The Right Attitude: To accomplish what I need to accomplish now, my first step is simply to take a breath and let it out again. I need to regroup and reorient myself. Calming down is an essential beginning in my current process of taking stock of where I really am in my life. As I reframe my direction and my priorities, it is helpful for me to *expect paradox* now – which means that whenever I feel that something is "perfectly clear," it probably means that I am missing the other half of the puzzle. If I look for that other half, I will find it. If I do not even imagine it to be there, I will never see – and it will come back to haunt me later.

What My Energy Now Attracts: Ambiguous situations arise – situations in which "every story has two sides." People appear in my life now who have points of view very different from my own. They are precious allies, if I can listen to them and take in the validity of what they are saying, even if I do not agree with it completely. They see what I do not see. Beauty, both in the form of art and of nature, crystallizes before my eyes. As I focus on it and let it mesmerize me, I relax and open up – and as I experience those moments of aesthetic trance, I come almost as if by magic to the realizations that will guide me to where I need to go.

How Squandering My Energy Looks: Maybe I dither, halting between courses, then nervously pick a direction out of insecurity rather than inspiration. Maybe I waste time in trivial social interactions. Maybe I become vain, trying to create an appearance that will open doors for me – and it might even work, except the doors which open will not be the right ones.

THE MOON PASSING THROUGH SCORPIO

The Right Attitude: To accomplish what I need to accomplish now, there are some unsettling truths about my emotional, subjective reality which I need to face. I have to be fiercely honest with myself about how I feel and what I actually want and need – and much of that is probably in contrast to what I am "supposed" to be feeling or what I might say "if I were a nice person." I have internalized some alien values – values which originated in other people's attitudes, probably in my early days. They are a virus which I need to cure if I am going to see my way clear to where happiness actually lies for me personally.

What My Energy Now Attracts: Intense conversations, both with others and with myself, unfold spontaneously now. Powerful moods, which might seem uncharacteristic of my usual nature, sweep up out of nowhere, and sweep me along with them. I am drawn to anything taboo or mysterious, and those kinds of experiences all seem to find their way to me unbidden as if by magnetism.

How Squandering My Energy Looks: I succumb to a monumental rotten mood; I indulge in it, rather than using it as an initial clue in a process of honest self-investigation. I sexualize and complicate relationships, at least in my own mind, that should not be sexualized or otherwise complicated. I create outward drama that is more about my own unresolved issues than I realize.

THE MOON PASSING THROUGH SAGITTARIUS

The Right Attitude: To accomplish what I need to accomplish now, I need to throw a monkey wrench into meshing gears of my daily life. I need something fresh and unprecedented to happen. In these brief lifetimes of ours, boredom must be a cardinal sin – there is so much to learn and see and experience, so why waste time on endless repetition? I am sometimes guilty of slipping into boredom's clutches – and I am going to fix that. I resolve to pack a decade's worth of experience into the next year or two. And if anyone wants to call me irresponsible, I will escape their tedious clutches before they get to the second "e" in the word.

What My Energy Now Attracts: Opportunities for new experiences. A chance to learn things that have always fascinated me, but into which I have never before had the time or the opportunity to delve. The open road looms – travel opportunities arise, along with contact with people from different cultures and walks of life. I am ready for some fresh air, and the laws of synchronicity guarantee that a breath of it is heading my way. I had better make sure that my window is wide open and that I am breathing deeply when it arrives.

How Squandering My Energy Looks: Perhaps I slip into a self-righteous defence of my *status quo* – and everyone (except me) can see that, a) I am being defensive, and b) no one has attacked me. It is just a battle I am waging with myself, in other words. No one ever wins one of those.

THE MOON PASSING THROUGH CAPRICORN

The Right Attitude: To accomplish what I need to accomplish now, I need to accept the fact that I am being called to do something dauntingly difficult. It is now or never. My first step is simply to acknowledge that fact and to affirm that the mountain that looms before me is in fact the one that I need to climb. I can do it too. I have been preparing for this moment for years. I have crossed into a new hemisphere in my life – I am now experienced, empowered, and mature enough to ascend to that peak. I just need to remember that the journey of a thousand miles starts with a single step.

What My Energy Now Attracts: Serious challenges requiring sustained self-discipline and long-term commitment come into focus before me. They may involve "great works" of an obvious nature – a professional *tour de force*, for example, or some other serious step, such as committing to a marriage or having a child or learning to play Chopin Études on the grand piano. Whatever the great work is, success at it demands everything I've got. It is possible that these challenges may be of a more inward nature – a meditation practice or undertaking Jungian analysis, for example.

How Squandering My Energy Looks: Perhaps, if I fail to control myself enough to climb the mountain I need to climb, I lapse into trying to control everybody else. In that endeavor I will surely fail – but not before I have thoroughly annoyed everyone I know. I will offer breathing lessons whenever I deem anyone requires them. I will experience myself as uptight, tense, and probably lonely, and I will not be alone in that assessment.

THE MOON PASSING THROUGH AQUARIUS

The Right Attitude: To accomplish what I need to accomplish now, I need to free myself from the need for anyone's approval. In parallel fashion, I must free myself of any concern about their baleful or worried judgments of me. My heart is trying to lead me down a road no one has seen before – I need to listen to it and block out everything else. That is where my path is leading me, and following it is how I can restore a higher kind of richness to my life. If, as I follow it, other people do not clap their hands, no matter. I am not a dancing monkey looking for them to throw me treats. I am free and this is my life, not anyone else's.

What My Energy Now Attracts: Doorways open to untraveled pathways. Rebels whisper encouragement in my ears. People who have forged their own pathways appear in my life, offering both friendship and inspiration. A fork appears in the road ahead of me – and one of the pathways is the famous "road less travelled." That is the road I need to take and which my heart wants me to follow.

How Squandering My Energy Looks: Perhaps, in order to avoid trouble or criticism, I choose the road *more* travelled. Perhaps I choose it simply to avoid upsetting or worrying someone else. Here's the tricky part: that wrong road, by definition, looks fine to almost everyone else, as if I would be a fool not to choose it. If I make that mistake, I will be congratulated for making "the smart choice." Inwardly, I sense that I have somehow betrayed myself. I begin to feel as if I were a character in a movie that was really starting to bore me.

THE MOON PASSING THROUGH PISCES

The Right Attitude: To accomplish what I need to accomplish now, I need a fresh vision for my life. My old one was fine, but it has played out. Realizing that – simply admitting the existence of that need to myself – is the first step. It is a big one too, because in even letting myself ask for a fresh vision, I am acknowledging that my present situation has grown stale. Opening to that fresh vision is easy – the only requirement is that I make time to sit quietly in an attitude of spiritual receptivity. Ask and ye shall receive, it is as simple as that – but first I must humbly ask.

What My Energy Now Attracts: Opportunities for spiritual growth and experience come to a focus in my circumstances. People with deep inner lives make contact with me – and their simple presence inspires and uplifts me. A chance to be alone with myself, experiencing quiet soul-time, presents itself. Psychic experiences, inexplicable events, small miracles – all conspire to convince me that there are realms beyond this one that we experience with our five senses. Emissaries of those realms are reaching out to me now.

How Squandering My Energy Looks: Perhaps I attempt to withdraw from my state of heightened sensitivity, not knowing what to do with it or how to handle it. I can numb it with food, or drugs, or alcohol – or television, or the Internet, or even by just working too hard. If I am successful in turning it off, the joke is on me: I have turned off the source of a fresh vision that would have inspired me for the rest of my days.

PLANETS ENTERING CANCER OR
ASPECTING THE MOON

Sooner or later, for all of us, planets will enter Cancer, signaling a healing time. Unless we die when we are very young, that is certainly true of all the faster transits, along with Jupiter and Saturn, and, very likely, Uranus as well.

With the transits of Neptune and Pluto and the whole family of solar arcs and progressions, having them enter Cancer is less certain. By solar arc, for example, the youngest members of my Pluto-in-Leo generation will have to wait until nearly the year 2300 before Pluto enters Cancer. My prediction is that there's not enough Botox in the world for any of them to make it. By transit, the next time Pluto enters Cancer is August 14, 2157 – for most of us, witnessing that glorious day is quite actuarially optimistic as well.

For the sake of completeness, I want to cover all of the possibilities here, even ones that are likely not to have direct relevance to anyone living today.

As we saw in the previous chapter, most of the time a planet enters Cancer from Gemini – the exception being a planet that happens to retrograde into Cancer from Leo. In what I write here, you'll often detect the underlying sense of flow out of Gemini and into Cancer.

On a Saturday night, Venus in Gemini may be dreaming of meeting new and interesting people, while Venus in Cancer is praying that there will be no loudly extroverted strangers at the party . . .

As planets form aspects to the Moon via transits, progressions, or solar arcs, the resultant emotional and existential synchronicities overlap considerably with what happens when those same planets pass through the sign Cancer. As we have emphasized through this series of books, all aspects are ultimately about integration. *Inviting the Moon to integrate with a planet is rather similar to having that same planet become suffused with the values and motivations of Cancer.* In what follows, we will focus on those points of overlap.

Naturally, if Mercury enters Cancer in the *eighth* house, that is different from Mercury entering Cancer in the *tenth* house. Similarly, Mercury forming a sextile to a Scorpio Moon cannot be equated with it forming an opposition to an Aquarian Moon.

As ever, the astrological angel lies in the details.

Take what follows the same way I am hoping you will take all of the similar thumbnail sketches throughout these thousand pages – as a solid starting point for some creative, individual thought that includes the larger astrological context.

THE SUN ENTERING CANCER – OR
ASPECTING THE MOON

What Needs Healing: My attunement to my own psychic and archetypal roots. My relationship to the "still, small voice within." My home. My family. My deepest soul connections.

How To Fix It: First, I simply need some quiet time – some shelter from the endless storm. I need to put some walls between me and the world for a while. Maybe the walls are physical, or maybe they are electronic or digital. Maybe they are psychic walls. However I accomplish that fortification, it is necessary because my deep self is trying to contact me. I need peace and quiet for that to happen. That contact might happen through dreams – and to dream, I need sleep, so I must now prioritize bedtime as well. I recognize that primary relationships require time – and that sometimes that might look like just sitting quietly together, and thus getting ourselves in synchrony energetically. I generously offer that gift of time to the ones I love. I ask for that gift myself.

The Price of Pretending That Everything Is Fine: Logic and strategy run away with me; I may be effective and productive – but I have let myself become mechanical. I go through the motions, as predictable as an empty elevator. My soul grows tired.

THE MOON ENTERING CANCER – OR
ASPECTING THE MOON

What Needs Healing: My ability to monitor my own condition. My ability positively to identify my own needs and how to meet them, as distinct from my merely complaining. My capacity to recognize loneliness, exhaustion, or any kind of hunger in myself, rather than simply pressing on stoically.

How To Fix It: First, I must open my heart compassionately toward myself. I must ask myself in a spirit of honesty how I am actually feeling. I must let myself cry, if that is what comes up – even if I cannot identify the source of the tears. Once I have laid that emotional foundation, I resolve to ask for what I need.

The Price of Pretending That Everything Is Fine: I put a shell between my heart and the people around me. Perhaps I even echo that self-protection with a parallel wall between my own conscious mind and my true inner state. Instead of caring for myself, I care for everyone else – whether or not they need it or benefit from it.

MERCURY ENTERING CANCER – OR ASPECTING THE MOON

What Needs Healing: My way of thinking and strategizing about how I take care of myself and other people, starting with myself, needs some attention. As I improve my own techniques of self-care, my skills and sensitivities regarding others will be swept along by the same wave.

How To Fix It: First, I resolve to set aside my unremittingly "adult" attitude – my commitment to always being strong – and actually do a better job of noticing my own hurts and needs. I will become aware of thought-patterns that rationalize away my awareness of my own pain. I sensitize myself to any repressive or judgmental language arising in my head; I will no longer harden myself with that kind of misguided inner pep talk. As I take these steps, I become aware of greater gentleness, compassion, and forgiveness in my attitudes toward other people and in how I express myself to them.

The Price of Pretending That Everything Is Fine: I fail to notice opportunities to comfort and soothe myself – my own stoic attitude blinds me to them. I hurt people verbally without knowing it or intending it, as I lash them with the same linguistic whip I am using to lash myself.

VENUS ENTERING CANCER – OR ASPECTING THE MOON

What Needs Healing: My closest relationships need some tender loving care now. This does not necessarily mean that they are in trouble – only that the time is right for some mindful maintenance, heading off potential estrangements or misunderstandings in the future before they can take root in the present.

How To Fix It: First, I resolve to simply *be there* with people I love, listening and appreciating them. Peaceful time spent together is enough. No psychodrama or difficult negotiations are required. Two people listening to music together, two people sitting in silence watching a perfect sunset slowly unfold – this is the medicine that I now need.

The Price of Pretending That Everything Is Fine: Conditions are created that invite the possibility of my drifting away from relationships upon which much of my actual happiness rests. A slow attrition in the quality of such connections is given a head start.

MARS ENTERING CANCER – OR ASPECTING THE MOON

What Needs Healing: My inner battering ram is now feeling battered. The fierceness of life, my endless struggle of it, the implicit competitiveness of it all – I can deal with it. I *have* been dealing with it, and I will continue to deal with it. But right now, I need to recognize that it is time to retreat, regroup, and do some soul-maintenance. My inner warrior is exhausted. A little break in the action can fix those leaks before they become a serious problem, with unfortunate consequences for my health and my attitude.

How To Fix It: First, I resolve to look for breaks in the action – chances to grab a moment to lick my wounds, relieve some pressure, and still not lose the ground that I have gained. Those moments exist – the only question is whether I recognize them, or keep pressing onward mechanically and mindlessly, toward a point of exhaustion.

The Price of Pretending That Everything Is Fine: I miss a chance for rest and recuperation, and I probably do not actually gain very much in exchange for losing it. Later, when I really do need to be sharper, my energy fails me because I missed the chance to "fuel up" when I had it.

JUPITER ENTERING CANCER – OR ASPECTING THE MOON

What Needs Healing: My faith in life needs a boost – or to say it less dramatically, my ability to maintain a positive attitude could use some support and encouragement. I need to see possibilities rather than looming limitations or obstacles. And those possibilities need to reflect more sensitivity toward my soul, and perhaps less focus on gaining outward victories.

How To Fix It: First, I can derive enormous healing benefits now simply from a good laugh – humor is powerful medicine. At this point, I need an inward victory more than I need outward kudos. I can jump-start this healing process by simply doing something nice for myself – giving myself a present, getting a massage, taking some time off.

The Price of Pretending That Everything Is Fine: I can maintain a certain posture of bravado in the face of my various challenges and energy drains, but keeping up those appearances comes at a higher price than it seems: these missed opportunities for soul-restoration will come back to haunt me sooner or later.

SATURN ENTERING CANCER – OR ASPECTING THE MOON

What Needs Healing: My dignity and self-respect could use a booster shot. This positive development arises from real accomplishment rather than from simply patting myself on the back or giving myself a pep talk. Solitude is not the same thing as loneliness; right now, solitude helps me to think and feel more clearly about who I have become, how I have changed, and how my needs are evolving with the passage of time.

How To Fix It: First, I need to do something that makes me feel proud of myself – and probably that accomplishment is something I do not so much "want to do" as "want to have done." Cleaning the house is a small example; there are certainly larger ones – still, we all know how we feel as we *contemplate* house cleaning, as opposed to the good feelings that arise when we have *actually finished* the job. Quiet time alone is powerful medicine now. I resolve to claim some for myself.

The Price of Pretending That Everything Is Fine: I soldier on, mistaking my emotional starvation for maturity and realism. I confuse self-sacrifice with the two-way street of actual love.

URANUS ENTERING CANCER – OR ASPECTING THE MOON

What Needs Healing: My sense of freedom and autonomy in life. My sense that I am living a life that I myself have chosen, and that I am not someone else's property. My right to simply and spontaneously be myself and to follow my own path. My ability to maintain my own independent integrity in the face of other people's judgments, criticism, or even their well-meaning – and probably wrong – advice.

How To Fix It: First, I need to get clear about what I am actually feeling, as distinct from what I have been taught to imagine that I feel. I need to be sure that the needs and desires I am expressing derive directly from my own soul rather than from what I have been trained to *believe that I wanted*. If I am on track with that healing, a reliable confirmation is that other people will worry about me and want to "correct" my feelings. When I am right, they will think I am wrong.

The Price of Pretending That Everything Is Fine: I become emotionally dissociated from my own life; I feel alienated, irrelevant, and distant, even if I look as if everything is copacetic. I cruise along vacantly, and punctuate it with episodes of crankiness and pointless contrariness.

NEPTUNE ENTERING CANCER – OR ASPECTING THE MOON

What Needs Healing: My relationship with my own soul. That sounds dire, but it does not mean that I have become estranged from my spiritual nature – only that I am being called to attend to the inner plane, where some gifts await me. The Great Mystery is summoning me into the inner sanctum because it has a message for me. If I have fallen into the trap of taking this world too seriously, as if it were all there is, then I need to heal that rift between myself and everything that lies beyond the realm of simple appearances.

How To Fix It: First, I need to act in a way that supports my being able to pay some quiet, extended attention to my inner life. I need to make time for peace and quiet. It might help me to read something inspirational or metaphysical, just to help establish a mood of receptivity to the higher realms. Meditation and prayer are really the heart of the matter, so long as the techniques I use are more gentle than rigidly disciplined.

The Price of Pretending That Everything Is Fine: The temptation to shut down my emotional sensitivities becomes compellingly powerful; I slip into behaviors that distract me from my own inner state. My feelings become heightened in intensity – but also ungrounded and prone to delusion, fear, and errors of judgment.

PLUTO ENTERING CANCER – OR
ASPECTING THE MOON

What Needs Healing: The parts of myself that are brokenhearted. The parts of myself that have been lied to, abused, or humiliated. The parts of myself that have done things of which I am not proud. Much of that radioactive material has been locked in my unconscious mind, held behind the repressive mechanism. It is currently beginning to erupt. I have paid too high a psychological price for that repression; I do not need to pay it any longer.

How To Fix It: First, I resolve to feel whatever I feel. No emotion, however edgy, is taboo. Whatever I feel, I resolve to follow it down into the dark and thereby recover the parts of my own soul that have been stolen from me. The help of another psychologically-savvy human being or two can be precious now – these burdens might be too weighty for me to carry them all by myself. I look for people worthy of being the trusted bearers of my secrets.

The Price of Pretending That Everything Is Fine: Material looms up out of the psychic depths inside of me and grabs the steering wheel of my life. Unwittingly, I project my pain onto innocent people, hurting them or fearing them in ways that have little to do with who they actually are. I confuse my wounded past with my potentially healing present – and thereby create a present which only echoes the wounds of the past.

19

CELESTIAL NAVIGATION II: PLUTO AND MARS TIMES, SCORPIO TIMES

When Pluto or Mars loom on the edge of your astrological radar screen, or when any slow-moving planets enter Scorpio or the eighth house, some astrologers might suggest that your life is about to turn into a scary movie. Those kinds of cringeworthy – not to mention useless – predictions are not rare. Still, it would be naïve of me to offer glib assurances to the contrary – such times can indeed *sometimes* prove frightening. The problem is not so much that an ominous view of what happens when the Scorpio clan comes to town is totally wrong – it is just that it is incomplete. Specifically, it leaves out all the good stuff.

Such an interpretation of this family of symbols also leaves out some serious magic: if you *aim consciously* for the higher ground, that choice has the effect of insulating you against some of the darker possibilities.

One uncomfortable, but inescapable, fact is that when dreadful things do happen to people, the Scorpio clan is often lit up. I do not want to sweep that reality under the carpet. We just have to be careful not to turn the statement around and assume that whenever Mars, Pluto, the eighth house, or Scorpio are activated, that trouble is inevitable.

Trouble is only one of the possibilities.

THE DEEPER REALITY

When these symbols are triggered, the time has come to face material that most of us would rather not face. That much is sure. Beyond that, we enter a realm where, while freedom and personal responsibility are not magic bullets, they remain powerful forces – even potentially life-saving ones.

These Scorpionic processes of healing, regeneration, and recovery signal times when we are finally ready to face wounded places in the psyche *which we were not ready to face earlier in our lives.* Dealing with them is difficult, but we can do it – and if we succeed, we realize that we have been paying a terrible price for *not* dealing with them all along. We had simply become inured to a *status quo* in which energy had been chronically sucked out of us. It was as if we were a business that had been bleeding its profits to a Mafia protection racket for so long we had forgotten all about prosperity. Escape that criminal activity, and it turns out that you are actually a lot richer than you had ever imagined – except that here, your wealth lies in energy, not in your bank account.

THE THREE FACES OF THE SCORPIO CLAN

When these Scorpionic symbols step into the spotlight, we can discern three possibilities: *we can learn what we need to learn the easy way, the hard way, or not at all.* Before I go any further in explaining these three perspectives, I want to underscore the fact that real life is more complicated than what I am about to write. For one thing, there is a lot of blur among these three possibilities. Beyond that blur, there is also a *moral* danger in the words that follow. I want to spell out that danger so that we can studiously avoid falling prey to it.

Everything starts with one simple insight: *if we "get a Scorpio clan event right," there is less chance of our experiencing disaster.* As ever, consciousness influences how the energies manifest. That is a bedrock astrological principle. *The moral danger is that, with a little misinterpretation and oversimplification, in thinking this way, an astrologer could easily slip into "blaming the victim."* Loudly and clearly: when people get sick or lose a loved one or their house burns down, that is not necessarily a sign that they "were afraid to deal with something." Karma works in mysterious ways. No simple formula, such as "just be spiritual and nothing bad will ever happen to you" can explain everything.

To keep our work honest, let's never forget that fact.

With all that said, in my experience it is helpful to distinguish three possible existential expressions of transits, progressions, and solar arcs involving the Scorpio clan. One of them can be defined as optimal, and I would encourage us all to aim for that higher ground – but not burden ourselves with pointless, and probably groundless, guilt if we experience painful biographical developments during such a time.

Our three possibilities are:

- *Dealing consciously* with Scorpionic issues *before* they manifest biographically.
- *Learning the lessons the hard way* by living them out – but still learning what we need to learn.
- *Not learning anything at all*; instead acting it all out, or simply staying stuck in repetitive wounding patterns.

To illustrate how these three possibilities play out in real life, I want to present three short case studies. Each one reflects how consciousness interacts with these archetypal fields of possibility. Only the final one represents unmitigated spiritual disaster.

DEALING CONSCIOUSLY . . . JOHN LENNON

In 1970, John Lennon entered Primal Scream Therapy with Arthur Janov, who had just published a popular book by that same title. Briefly, in this style of therapy, patients re-enter traumatic situations remembered from their childhoods and by *screaming in pain without inhibition,* they release the pent-up energies that were trapped in their unconscious minds and in their physical bodies.

That, by the way, is almost the definition of a Scorpionic process. We do not have to literally scream during such a time– but anyone who is afraid of strong emotions will not do well with these healing processes. They are not simply about insight; they are about *energetic release.*

As a youngster, John Lennon had experienced his mother's accidental death, along with what he felt was his abandonment by his father. Before his mother was killed, he had been put in the psychologically devastating position of being asked to choose between his parents. No child is likely to come through such abusive, nightmarish experience free of scar tissue.

Beatlemania, while it made John Lennon famous and fabulously wealthy, was also not the kind of experience guaranteed to create groundedness in anyone. He was, in other words, a deeply wounded soul, and thus a good candidate for cathartic Scorpionic work.

After Primal Scream therapy, Lennon said, *"I just know myself better, that's all. I can handle myself better. That Janov thing, the primal scream and so on, it does affect you, because you recognize yourself in there . . . I no longer have any need for drugs, the Maharishi or the Beatles. I am myself and I know why."*

What was going on astrologically when John Lennon made this journey into the dark? Solar arc Pluto was conjuncting his natal Venus, while solar arc Venus aligned with his Mars. Meanwhile, Pluto was transiting back and forth over his natal Neptune.

The Scorpio can was center stage, in other words. That meant that he was ready for this process, in other words. Synchronicity created the circumstances that opened the healing, regenerative door for him – and he had grace and courage enough to pass through it and recover something of himself.

In this regard, John Lennon illustrates our first possibility: *dealing consciously with Scorpionic issues before they manifest biographically.*

LEARNING THE HARD WAY – BUT STILL LEARNING . . . RAM DASS

On February 19, 1997, spiritual teacher, Ram Dass, experienced a stroke that left him significantly paralyzed. At that time, solar arc Pluto was only a quarter-degree away from an exact trine to his natal Saturn – and the specific nature of his Saturn, as we will see in a moment, is our interpretive key here.

Meanwhile, both transiting Jupiter and transiting Uranus were entering his eighth house – more Scorpio clan symbolism.

Of the event, Ram Dass said, "The stroke was giving me lessons, and I realized that was grace – fierce grace."

Natally, Ram Dass had a Pluto-Saturn opposition, with Saturn in Capricorn in his seventh house. Thus, he was born with a *blockage* (Saturn) to his *ability to trust other people* (seventh house.) On top of it, he was an Aries with a Sun-Uranus conjunction – a very independent individual. As a result of the stroke, Ram Dass lost much of his physical mobility. He had no choice but to *become reliant on other people.* In other words, with that stroke *Pluto offered Ram Dass an opportunity to face one of his most elemental evolutionary issues.*

He learned what he needed to learn about trust and interdependency, even if it was learned in a very hard way.

Could Ram Dass have avoided the stroke if he had faced his issues around trust and interdependency earlier and in a more conscious way?

Were I to say that, I would feel judgmental, arrogant, and inappropriate. *Might* it be true? Yes, I think it might be. In not going any further than that, I am not trying to be diplomatic. I am just telling the truth as I see it, which is that I do not know. This story provides a good illustration of what I meant earlier when I wrote about *moral danger* – how, with a little misinterpretation and oversimplification, an astrologer could slip into "blaming the victim."

The bottom line – on which we can rely without any doubt – is that Ram Dass seems genuinely to have learned what he needed to learn from his stroke. He did not fail his Pluto test. He shows us that we can accomplish this healing by *living it out* as well as by *thinking it out.* The latter may be the more comfortable path, but in the end, either way we can learn the lesson. With my clients, when I see the Scorpio clan looming on the horizon, I naturally try to nudge them in the direction of "dealing consciously" with this material – but I never lose respect for that more "embodied" way of getting to the same healing bottom line. I've done it that way, and I bet you've done it too.

NOT LEARNING ANYTHING AT ALL . . . JEFFREY DAHMER

(A quick note: I very nearly did not use the following example, simply because it is so sickening. But "sickening" realities are part of life and the astrological window through which we reflect on them is the Scorpionic clan. To be a good astrologer is to deal honestly with human existence, even in its more difficult manifestations, so please bear with me.)

Jeffrey Dahmer was a sadistic serial killer "famous" for cannibalism, among other barbarities. Over a period of thirteen years, he murdered about seventeen men. Google him if you have the stomach for this kind of thing and want to know more.

Dahmer committed his first murder on June 18, 1978. Within a period of just *three days* on either side of that exact date, *transiting Mars had squared his natal Sun, made a trine to his Jupiter, and finally aligned with his natal Pluto*. Meanwhile, and more importantly, *transiting Pluto was stationing near his Ascendant*. That Pluto transit over his Ascendant is the big thematic marker, while the Mars transits illustrate the *theme-triggering* effects of the faster planets.

Dahmer's thirteen-year murder spree coincided nearly exactly with the passage of transiting Pluto through his first house.

Did he learn anything? We have no evidence of that at all. It appears that Dahmer was simply "acting out" the poisonous hatreds in his own psyche.

What kind of karma must a human being have in order to harbor such bitter, twisted rage? That is a bigger subject than I want to tackle here. Suffice to say that Jeffrey Dahmer had a Piscean south lunar node, so it was ruled by Neptune and by Jupiter. His Neptune was in Scorpio in the first house, while his Jupiter was squared by an Arian Mars. *In prior lifetimes, he had been scarred by violence and probably by madness too.*

Reflecting the *specifically karmic origins* of his misconduct, on the day of his first murder, his *solar arc south node aligned with his natal Mars, while Pluto made a conjunction by solar arc with his north node*. Both aspects were accurate within about half a degree.

His karmic wave was breaking.

Could Dahmer have instead used this influx of Scorpionic energy to generate conscious self-awareness rather than death and pain and horror? Could he have learned and grown – and possibly, instead of committing murder, have voiced the most horrific primal scream in human history?

I cannot answer those questions. But here is what I do know: that whenever I sit with a client, I need to maintain that kind of faith in the resiliency of the human soul – that, or I should find a different kind of work. When the Scorpio clan comes calling, healing, regeneration, and recovery require that kind of spiritual and psychological resiliency. If we have lived in a reasonably conscious way, we have been preparing for this moment for a lifetime – or maybe two. We are ready. That resiliency is waiting, and so is the courage.

THE NUTS AND BOLTS

In this Scorpionic branch of the Water Family, we have the eighth zodiacal sign and the corresponding eighth house, plus both an ancient and a modern planetary ruler. Each symbol is different, but each one can be activated by transits, progressions, or solar arcs. And each one can manifest, as we have just seen, as . . .

- Simple direct learning
- Learning by experience
- Or failing to learn at all

That is a lot of symbolic balls and a lot of possibilities to juggle. Let's see if we can sort them out in an orderly way.

SCORPIO

The sign Scorpio, at least at its best, symbolizes the *motivation* to deal with difficult material. Its mood is one of fascination with anything *psychologically charged* or even *taboo*. It represents the part of the human psyche which *assigns high value* to digging beneath the surface appearance of things, of simply *investigating*, especially in the context of uncomfortable areas. Scorpio is *suspicious* in the way a good psychologist or detective is suspicious.

When a planet enters Scorpio, those kinds of *emotional and attitudinal agendas* begin to motivate its behavior. Whatever the planet's intrinsic nature, it suddenly seems to be saying "give me some truth."

- Ambitious Jupiter, for example, begins to wonder exactly *why* it has the particular ambitions it has.
- Austere Saturn *questions the origins* of its self-sacrificial motivation to "do without." Why is it willing to live that way?
- Spiritual Neptune dares to *doubt and question its religion.*
- Competitive Mars wonders *what it is fighting for.*
- Sweet Venus punctures the balloon of *runaway romantic projection.*

For any planet, Scorpio times are times for self-inquiry. They often involve pressing against walls of psychological resistance. It is time for us to learn things that we do not want to know.

If we get any kind of Scorpio ingress wrong, then whatever psychic toxins we harbor rise up and infect that moving planet with a poisonous, bloody-minded attitude. Jupiter lives to destroy those who would dare compete with it. Saturn delights in self-denial and masochism – and tries to inflict them on others. Neptune stages an Inquisition. Mars just wants to kill something, while Venus goes on believing that "he will leave his wife" or that "she really loves me, deep down, despite everything."

THE EIGHTH HOUSE

In the *eighth house*, we observe *actions* and *behaviors* connected with these same Scorpionic "taboo" areas. As ever, when we move from sign-theory to house-theory, we switch from *motives* to *actions*, from *ideas* to *facts*, from *infinite possibility* to *making clear choices and burning bridges behind us*.

When the eighth house is stimulated by transits, progressions, or solar arcs . . .

- Sometimes *deaths* occur at close emotional range.
- The revealing psychological processes associated specifically with the *coupling* sexuality often arise – "true love never runs smooth," and all of that. When a couple moves from "just dating" to "getting serious," they have entered the eighth house. The truly *evolutionary work* of intimacy begins.
- *Weird experiences* that reveal the interpenetration of other dimensions with our own can happen: ghosts and hauntings, sorcery, healings, apparitions – all can present themselves.
- It is not unusual to see a person experiencing eighth house stimulus enter *deep psychotherapy*, or seek serious *psychic or astrological readings*, or simply have a profoundly life-altering conversation or two.

Again, with houses, it is all about actions and behaviors, and *making the biographical choices* which define the ultimate shapes of our outward lives – in this case, by welcoming greater depth, seriousness, and a sense of life's transitoriness into our circumstances.

MARS AND PLUTO: CO-RULERS OF SCORPIO

Completing our quick survey of the Scorpionic clan, we finally come to Mars and Pluto – the traditional ruler of Scorpio and the modern one, respectively. As with the other two signs that currently have dual rulerships – Aquarius and Pisces – this question is charged with passionate controversy among astrologers, often pitting the traditionalists against modern psychological astrologers.

Which planet is the *real* ruler of Scorpio?

To me, the *natural association* between each one of these planets and Scorpio is self-evident – if we ring the Scorpio bell, both Mars and Pluto start vibrating. If we run Scorpionic principles up the flagpole, both Mars and Pluto salute. It is not that Mars and Pluto are fighting over which one of them "rules" Scorpio. It is really more that they both *like* Scorpio – and neither one of them feels any more competitive than you do when you and someone else are both friends with the same person. That's Mars and Pluto and the waltz they do with Scorpio. No jealousy; just a three-way shared connection.

MARS

We explored Mars in detail in *The Book of Fire*. For the sake of completeness, let me quickly recapitulate the main points here.

- Mars, like Scorpio, is *passionate*. In Mars times, passions run high. Good news or bad? Obviously passion can lead to bad judgment calls. But what would life be without any passion at all? In Mars times, opportunities to *restore your passionate engagement* with existence arise. It is time to claim them and thus to reinvigorate yourself.

- Mars is *warrior-energy*. In Mars times, you may have to defend yourself, or defend something or someone you love. Let's take a moment to pity people who have nothing so precious in their lives that they would not die for it if they had to.

- Mars is *sexy*. In a Mars time, you are invited to boldly claim that part of your being, to put yourself out there erotically in an unabashed, pagan sort of way. It is no time to be shy or prim. Sexually, Mars *initiates*.

- Mars carries *anger*. Expressing that emotion can be dangerous – but not as dangerous as holding it inside yourself, unexpressed. Always be wary of anger's tendency to *exaggerate* and *grandstand*, but know that during Mars times harbored anger needs to come to the surface.
- Mars is *adventurous*. When it arrives in a sensitive zone, the open road calls. Unknown territory beckons. Take risks. It is time to heed the wild urge to just roll the dice and see what happens.
- Mars is *prone to accidents* – and the best way to avoid them is to make sure that you are not harboring unresolved resentment or anger. Those kinds of tensions are often the culprits which underlie the sorts of errors that lead to physical mishaps. A practical bottom line, however, is that, during a Mars time, it is helpful not to climb up shaky ladders or to attempt any money-saving Do It Yourself electrical repairs.
- During a Mars period, you are invited to choose between being *Hunter* or being *Prey* – go for Hunter!

PLUTO

The transits and solar arcs of Pluto can transform your life. The process can even be joyful and liberating. But sometimes they accomplish that transformation in the same way that nuclear warfare might lead to an enthusiasm for urban renewal. *Everything blows up* and we have a chance to start over again. Everything collapses, and then maybe – *maybe* – we can rise, phoenix-like, from our own ashes.

Plutonian periods can actually be quieter. That can be a disappointment to hyperventilated astrologers who already had you nailed to a cross, dead of a disfiguring disease, or baked in a witch's oven. As I indicated earlier, I do not want to whitewash the hard realities of life. In speaking of Pluto, I especially want to avoid the kind of magical thinking in which we believe that we can control the onslaught of the universe with our good attitude alone. We cannot control the universe – but I do believe that we can *influence* it. I do believe that if we *understand what our souls are trying to face* during a Plutonian time – if we bravely embrace that inner work – we can significantly lessen our risk of experiencing some kind of Plutonian nightmare.

We can prove those hyperventilated astrologers wrong.

Hard things – and grossly unfair things – happen in this world. They are not Pluto's fault, but they are definitely Plutonian categories of experience. There is no way to speak honestly and accurately about the transits and solar arcs of Pluto without using strong imagery. Pluto is not so much "the planet of evil" as the planet that gives us the ability to *deal with evil*. Dreadful things do happen – and sometimes they happen because of people's bloody-minded intentions or behaviors.

Our question here is about how we heal from contact with life's darkness. How do we regenerate ourselves and recover after such bitter experiences?

POSSIBLE RESPONSES TO PLUTONIAN STIMULUS

Here are a few variations on the same story. All of them are probably tales that you have heard before, and maybe some that you have lived yourself. The ways of darkness are drearily familiar. It is the higher ground that shines like a golden city.

Our starting point is what was once simply called "the work of the devil." It is still an excellent metaphor. Specifically, a little girl is abused sexually by her uncle.

We may not believe in the devil, but to many of us, such an event is at least the very essence of evil.

Enter astrology: *very probably, when the sexual abuse is happening, the child is experiencing some kind of Plutonian stimulus.* Parents beware – that is one obvious take-away. Parenting always requires vigilance, but if your child is experiencing a Plutonian event, while it does not mean that he or she will be abused, err in the direction of caution, even over-protection, during that specific period.

Much later, in her adult life, another Plutonian period looms on the horizon of the girl's birthchart. As a result of her childhood trauma, she has had a long history of dysfunctional sexual and romantic relationships. With Pluto back in the spotlight, it is now potentially time for her to heal from those wounds. *In classic Plutonian fashion, she is now ready to face something she would not have been ready to face just a year or two before.* Pluto's arrival signals that kind of preparedness. The time is ripe for healing and recovery. She is now strong enough – maybe *barely* strong enough – but that is all that is required.

How does she respond? What happens?

Here is where our story becomes multifaceted. Once again, we see those three roads we explored earlier: dealing consciously with the wound, dealing with it by living it out, or simply not learning anything at all and repeating the old wounding pattern.

- In one version of the story – one that parallels John Lennon's encounter with Primal Scream therapy – our protagonist goes into psychotherapy. The repressed memories of the sexual abuse surface. She has skillful support in the form of a good therapist . . . and perhaps a decent, sensitive man appears in her life as well. She "descends into hell" – healing these kinds of wounds is always tough – but she rises up, healed and strong and vibrant, and reclaims her faith in her body-heart connection, along with her sexual dignity.

- In another version of the story – one that parallels our anecdote about Ram Dass – the woman *becomes involved with a man who is the psychic clone of her twisted uncle.* They become lovers – she is vulnerable to that kind of distorted male energy because of the specific way that her boundaries were violated and poisoned when she was a child. The man encourages her to watch dehumanizing pornography. He wonders aloud if "her friend JoAnn might like to join them in bed one evening." *After a while, she becomes thoroughly disgusted with him and the whole situation.* She recognizes that she has made a self-destructive choice in letting this loser even get near her, let alone having sex with him. *She wonders why she ever did that.* She is willing to take responsibility for her behavior – but she delves more deeply into it than simply feeling stupid or ashamed. Her disgust triggers in her a desire to get to the bottom of her issues. She seeks help, and she finds it. This second storyline now converges with our first one – she has learned what she needed to learn, even if she "learned it the hard way." Even when we ultimately get it right, Pluto times can be raw like that. No shame!

- In a third version of the story – one that parallels our description of Jeffrey Dahmer – she *marries* the sleazebag. She has learned nothing at all, obviously. She is now a tragic figure. But our critical insight here – one that runs through the heart of Pluto theory – is that she is simply *reenacting her initial wound.* That which is not healed tends to be repeated.

THE REMARKABLE SUCCESS OF EVIL
IN THIS WORLD

In the old days, theologians put a lot of juice into their narrative about God versus the Devil. When I was young, I had a taste of it thrust upon me. Due to some complex Plutonian circumstances, I spent a couple of my teenage years in a conservative Missouri Synod Lutheran school – a situation where I often found myself in trouble due to "doctrinal differences" with the headmaster. I think all of this was actually an echo of some nasty karma of mine involving the Holy Inquisition. Here's an example of my narrowly escaping "the rack" while enrolled in that parochial school – and I probably only survived because it was 1965, not 1492.

> *Me*: God is omnipotent, right? All powerful. He can do anything, right?
> *Headmaster:* Oh yes. Praise God.
> *Me*: So how come there's still a devil? How come God hasn't won? *That's a pretty damned impressive performance on Satan's part, considering the alleged competition . . .*

You can imagine the headmaster's reaction. Still, my question was a fair one. For obvious reasons, the more shallow Christian theologians have always tended to dodge it. These are deeper waters than I want to swim in with you now – I'll spare you a sermon, in other words – and instead cut to a very practical perspective, one that neatly illuminates the enormous, metastasizing success of true darkness in the human world.

It all starts with a simple, sad image:

A little boy is hit hard by his abusive father. In this image, I'm not talking about "correction." I am talking about full-on, flagrant child abuse. I am talking about a parent losing it and really hurting his kid.

Two scenarios follow thirty years later for that little boy:

- He is heading for a stress-related heart attack because of job pressures. His boss is impossible, demanding, and abusive. Our subject should look for another job, but he "feels that he cannot." *Once again, he feels trapped in an abusive situation, with no escape.*
- He has sworn to himself that he will never hit his own child. *But he loses his temper one night and clobbers the boy.*

The wound his father dealt him – *and his adaptation to it* – underlies his horrible work situation. That part is fairly transparent – he is still the victim, so to speak. *But also hits his own child,* even though he has solemnly promised himself that he would never do to his son what his father did to him. He learned his father's act too. This *doubling effect* has always been evil's secret weapon. When we are abused, we learn two things: *how to be abused and also how to abuse others.* This is how the darkness metastasizes. Thinking about this satanic alchemy provides one of life's more sobering meditations.

Before we all get the blues, let me immediately apply the remedy: *any positive response to a Scorpionic event breaks that chain of metastasizing evil.* That abused child, maybe with Pluto aspecting his fourth house Saturn, comes to understand what a pipsqueak his father really was, and how his father was himself a victim of his own father's abuse, and his father before him, and so on in the dizzying chain of misery. Under Plutonian stimulus, our protagonist releases that pent-up energy. Maybe it happens in psychotherapy. Maybe it happens in a trusted relationship. However he does it, *he breaks the chain.*

In severing that link to the poisonous past, he has obviously helped himself. He quits that deadening job – or he never accepted in the first place. He disciplines his son without resorting to violence. The benefits of his conscious response to Pluto transiting his Saturn are clear and obvious.

What he does not see – and perhaps does not even *need* to see – is how this wounding, nightmarish chain might be a thousand years long. Because of the reality of reincarnation, he may even have *been* an earlier link or two in it.

And he has broken it.

I always like to blow the trumpet for this point with my clients. There is something truly heroic about a strong response to Scorpionic realities.

EULOGY FOR A FRIEND

What follows is a true story, and a painful one. It ends sadly, but I tell it because we can use it as an alchemist would, turning lead to gold. Woven into the tale are life-saving insights into how Plutonian healing actually works, even though in this specific situation, events unfolded in a darker way. I want to start by spelling out the bottom line, then flesh it out in human terms with the actual tale.

We never cure Pluto problems with insight and understanding alone. They can only be healed by *cathartic emotional release.*

In North Carolina, many years ago, I had a friend and client whom I will call Kate. She had been through medical school, graduated as a physician, then gone on to become a clinical psychiatrist with a large practice. Despite her rigorous academic and medical training, she had retained enough open-mindedness to visit an astrologer. We hit it off, and a friendly, collegial relationship soon developed. I would refer people to her when they asked me to recommend a medically-oriented mental health professional.

Kate experienced Pluto making a hard aspect to her Moon. Strong, stormy energies that she did not fully understand were rising up out of her unconscious mind, right on schedule. She got scared. When suicidal thoughts started crossing her mind, because of her values, her training, and her culture, she checked herself trustingly into the psychiatric wing of the local hospital. Three weeks later, when she was released, she came to sit with me. Kate was as mad as hell. She felt – correctly, I believe – that the Plutonian spiritual crisis she had experienced, however awful it had been, had also *potentially contained the seeds of release and transformation.* She had checked herself into the psych ward in hopes of finding a safe place to do that inner work – a place where she would be guided by wise, caring souls, while being securely protected from her own darker impulses.

Instead they had drugged her into passive stability for three weeks. When she had "calmed down," they released her.

She felt that she had been robbed of an experience that her soul needed. In her view, which I shared, a kind of *unproductive escapism* had been forced on her. She felt that the psychiatrists into whose care she had placed herself were – and these were her exact words – *afraid of strong emotions.*

Pluto's gifts can be difficult to receive, but they can be precious and liberating. Accepting them, even if it hurts, can be part of a process of healing, regeneration, and recovery – for example, learning a truly dark secret in one's family history or discovering a partner's infidelity. No one enjoys such realizations, but how many people would say that they would have preferred never to have found out? Perhaps a few would say that – but none of them are Scorpionic people. Scorpionic people, by definition, always *want to know.*

An old line comes to mind: *the truth will set you free, but first it will make you miserable.*

Back to my story: two or three years later, my friend Kate committed suicide. One can never know what might have been, but my feeling was that, *had she been supported in doing her Plutonian work during that crisis, she would still be alive today.*

Psychiatric medicine is a complicated territory and I am no more qualified to issue pronouncements about it than I am to pontificate about biochemistry or particle physics. But there are some drums I will beat until the day I die.

- One is that the mind and the brain are not the same thing.
- A second is that what arises in our consciousness always arises for a spiritual purpose; there is something we need to learn from it, not simply something that we need to be "gotten through."
- A third is that a spiritual crisis, while it can be horrifying, can also be a healing crisis.

Barbara Schermer was an astrologer whose work I really liked. She passed away in 2014, leaving us too early, but not before gifting us with a fine, helpful book called *Astrology Alive: A Guide to Experiential Astrology and the Healing Arts.* I once attended a lecture of hers about Pluto in which she feelingly explored the same points that underlie the sad story I have just told. Echoing Kate, Barbara Schermer said that "no one can do well during a Pluto transit if he or she is afraid of strong emotions".

OLD WOUNDS

Dark experiences create wounding memories. As metaphysical astrologers, we realize that some of those wounds actually predate our present birth. No matter how ancient they might be, those wounds lie inside us, as fresh as newly-cut daisies, ready to grab the helm and steer us straight for the reefs. They are time-bombs, ticking away – and during Scorpionic times, the clock strikes zero.

What kind of Loch Ness monster then surfaces from the psychic depths? Sometimes painful memories arise. We might remember wounding *facts*, typically ones that had been softened by rationalization and denial, or even clinically repressed. I have often seen difficult *prior-life memories* surface at such times too. That kind of literal remembering can be part of the process.

But the heart of the matter is that these wounds are encoded and stored in the psyche in the form of emotions.

These experiences have poisoned our hearts, not simply our thinking. What did it *feel like* to be beaten as a child? What kind of *emotional adaptation* did I make to that reality? Or what if I was really tortured to death in the name of Jesus in a prior life? What did *that* feel like? *And how does that toxic hurt live on in my present life?*

It is the memories of the heart, not the memories of the mind, that survive the trauma of death and rebirth – or the lesser trauma of psychological repression.

That is where the toxins are stored in the psyche. And that is where they must be healed – not by insight alone, but by *catharsis*. That is why Barbara Schermer was right when she said that no one can do well during a Pluto transit if he or she is afraid of strong emotions.

And I believe that being robbed of that catharsis is why my friend Kate ended her life.

THE GRAND PRIZE

You are lying awake in your bed at 4:00 in the morning, dwelling on some trivial disagreement or insult you endured that afternoon. In the language of the Buddha, you are "punishing yourself for someone else's sin."

And you even know you are doing that. We all do it from time to time.

You make a decision: *I just won't think about it any more.* I need some sleep. And naturally two minutes later you are thinking about it again.

All of your mental discipline – all of the concentration skills that got you through algebra in high school, all the focus that lets you figure out your taxes – *none of it is strong enough medicine to hold the memory of that one trivial ego-bruise out of your head for two minutes.*

Compare and contrast: that poor little girl who was sexually abused has perhaps "forgotten about it" by the time she is in her teens – but of course "forgotten about it" is not quite the right wording. The trauma of the abuse is *repressed*, locked away in her unconscious mind *where it still wields a baleful influence upon her emerging sexuality.* There are many possibilities there. All of them are sad. Does she become promiscuous? Or unnaturally terrified of physical touch?

The point I am underscoring is that, at least in one version of the story, *she does not remember the abuse.* And without the slightest awareness of making any effort, she holds the traumatic memory out of her consciousness.

A trivial insult renders us insomniac against our own will at 4:00 in the morning, while a life-shattering violation is forbidden access to the conscious mind.

The juxtaposition of those two observations is what finally brings us to our Grand Prize – and why I can genuinely encourage my clients to greet Scorpionic times with enthusiasm rather than with fear.

As we compare these two scenarios, we are faced with a stark realization about *exactly how much psychic energy is locked up in a repression.* We are not aware of the price we are paying – repression is, after all, an unconscious reflex – but the cost is enormous. What batteries are drained that way? Where does that energy come from? The answer is *the budget.* As a human being, you only have so much juice, so much life-force. With repression bleeding out its daily *mordida,* you are simply *diminished.* An extravagant price is paid in terms of your creativity, your libido, your ability to concentrate, your spiritual life, even your effective intelligence.

Balancing that terrible cost is a sobering realization: *repression is a necessary psychic function.* We all have experiences so overwhelmingly dreadful and so simply confusing that we cannot integrate them *at the time we are having them.* What is a five-year-old child to make, for example, of her uncles' intrusion on the boundaries of her soul? Of the evidence of his sexual arousal? It is fair to say that we *survive* because of repression – survive, and potentially live to become stronger and wiser.

When that burgeoning strength and wisdom reaches critical mass – when we are perhaps *ready to deal directly with the unconscious material . . .* well, welcome to Scorpionic times.

My imagery has been dramatic here. Not everyone has been abused in the horrible ways I have been describing. We all carry some hurt and shame though – that is part of being human, and it probably has a lot to do with why we have taken birth in the first place.

For some of you who have been through the kinds of horrors I have recounted here, these pages have perhaps been rough going. My apologies for that – my hope is that these books can be helpful for people learning to counsel other human beings, and such realities are part of what we must be prepared to face in the counseling room.

There is no guarantee that anyone will do well with Plutonian times. As we have seen, one possibility is that we learn nothing at all – and then we typically just "act out" the wound again, repeating it or passing it on to someone else.

There is, as ever, a soul-guarantee that we *can* do well with these times. If we succeed, the repression – or rationalization or denial – is undone. We may have actually needed it for a long while, but we do not need it any longer. That enormous flux of energy that has been tied up in holding the black tide out of the conscious mind is now free to flow.

What will happen with it? What will you do with that new vitality?

Whatever you please – it is your energy.

Revivification of body, mind, and spirit is the unsung Grand Prize available to anyone who responds bravely, even heroically, to Scorpionic stimulus.

When it comes to healing, regeneration, and recovery, this family of astrological symbols – so often represented ominously – is actually a magic elixir.

20

PLUTO AND MARS TIMES, SCORPIO TIMES: THE BUILDING BLOCKS

These two edgy planets, each one with a bad reputation among many astrologers, are both part of the Water Family. That means that once you cut them down to their cores, they too are part of the healing and regenerative processes that keep us alive. The way they do that is not always comfortable, but let's not let the discomfort blind us to their higher purpose. You can think of Mars and Pluto the same way you think of the one friend who will tell you the things that you *need* to hear even if you do not *want* to hear them.

Our main purpose in this chapter is to look at Mars and Pluto in motion sign by sign and house by house. But first let's quickly review how they move, and add a few more dimensions which we did not cover in the previous chapter.

In the sky, Mars takes 687 days to swing around the zodiac and return to a specific starting point – say, a certain star or a certain sensitive degree in your chart. That way of looking at its orbital cycle is called the *sidereal* period. 687 days works out to two years, minus about six weeks. Since the Sun is moving too, the time between successive conjunctions of Mars and the Sun is a little longer. That is called its *synodic* period, and it runs about two years, one month, plus about nineteen days.

As Mars nears its opposition to the Sun, it slows down, stops, and turns retrograde. It does the same thing, only backwards, after the opposition – making another station and turning direct. The length of time that Mars is retrograde is variable, running two or three months depending on its distance from the Sun at the time – remember, when a planet is further from the Sun, its speedometer reads lower.

Bottom line, while Mars's *average* speed runs about half a degree per day, it can be moving faster or slower – or even effectively at a full stop – depending on where it is in its orbital cycle.

Translating all of that into *progressions*, days naturally become years. To have a *progressed* Mars return after a full cycle, in other words, you would need to live almost seven centuries. On average, Mars will progress through a full degree every two years or so – but if you were born near a station, it will take a lot longer. For example, Mars makes a station and turns retrograde on October 30, 2022. A little girl born that day will have to wait until she is in her early seventies before her progressed Mars turns direct – and during those seven decades, it will have moved only seventeen degrees.

The practical heart of the matter is that for both the transits and the progressions of Mars, check your computer.

Solar arcs are always easier to think about – one degree per year, plus or minus a tiny fraction. Just as with the rest of the planets, you can calculate Mars' solar arcs in your head, and be pretty close.

Moving on to consider the motions of Scorpio's modern ruler, Pluto, is like moving from thinking about teenage fashions to thinking about the evolution of galaxies. Pluto's orbital period is 248.5 years. Currently, as I write in 2020, Pluto is slowing down. After its quick twelve year run through Scorpio, it took only thirteen years to get through Sagittarius. Capricorn takes sixteen years. It enters Aquarius in January 2024 and remains there until January 2044, after a twenty-year passage.

As Pluto continues to slow down, its run through Pisces will require twenty-three years, and Aries will need thirty-one. Then, in 2095, Pluto reaches aphelion in slow-boat Taurus and spends thirty-four years there.

Thinking about Pluto's cycle this way puts us in the position of gnats thinking about continental drift. The changes happen so slowly that it is a challenge to relate to them emotionally. But I think we can, with a little bit of imagination.

We have seen all along how slower astrological events have time to develop depth and complexity of meaning. Over centuries, we can see that while Pluto is in Taurus, its transits take *about three times longer* than they do when it is in Scorpio. *Does that spell three times more depth and complexity of meaning?* Were people simply deeper back then? Or were their psychological processes just happening more slowly? My guess is that, because of human diversity, both then and now, both ideas contain a kernel of truth.

I often joke with clients that in my personal experience, Pluto's transits "take twice as long as they need to." Thinking about Pluto in Taurus gives me perspective on that one. If you had to go through a period of "intensified personal growth," would you prefer to get through it as quickly as possible? Or would you choose to spread it out over a longer period? I guess it's like watching people getting into the water at the beach in May before the ocean has warmed up – some prefer the sudden plunge and some like to go inch by torturous inch.

Pluto's last passage through Taurus ran from about 1851 to 1884. How were people different then? Deeper and more reflective? Both Freud and Jung were born with Pluto in Taurus – that is a point worth considering.

Wrestling with that question could spin us off into an entirely different book, so I think I will just plant that seed and move on.

One interesting effect of Pluto's passage through Aquarius will be its impact upon the "Boomer" generation. Many of them will experience a rather rare astrological event: *an opposition of transiting Pluto to natal Pluto.* On average, that opposition happens at age 124, and so for obvious reasons historical astrologers have not paid it much attention. Those "baby boomers" all have Pluto in Leo, so they have been positioned to experience the faster half of Pluto's cycle, as it accelerated through Virgo and Libra, peaked in Scorpio and started slowing down in Sagittarius and Capricorn. I will experience Pluto opposite Pluto myself just a few weeks after my 84th birthday. If I am still around and still have all my marbles, I promise I will give you a report.

With more people living into their eighties and nineties, this is that rarest of astrological realities: relatively virgin territory.

Now that we have a sense of their rhythms, let's look at Mars and Pluto as they pass through each of the signs and houses, one at a time. By the way, in *The Book of Fire*, we explored Mars passing through *aspects* with each of the planets rather than its passage through the individual signs and houses, so all of the Mars material here is new. And of course this is our first look at Pluto.

PLUTO PASSING THROUGH THE TWELVE SIGNS

When Pluto transits into a new sign, it is of course doing the same thing for everyone on the planet earth at that same moment. But if Pluto enters Aquarius in your personal sixth house, those Plutonian/Aquarian values and motivations impact your work and your responsibilities. If it enters Aquarius in your seventh house, you are invited to bring those attitudes to bear on your intimate life.

When Pluto passes through Aries, we are all invited to heal the soul-sickness created by *anger, resentment, and the effects of violenc*e – whether that means violence we ourselves have perpetrated or violence done to us. If we fail to heal, then we become hurtful and cruel, perhaps to others, or perhaps to ourselves.

Similar effects come into play when Pluto forms aspects to Mars.

When Pluto passes through Taurus, we are all invited to heal the soul-sickness created by *estrangement from instinct* and alienation from our physical bodies. The price we have paid for *materialism* in all its myriad forms presses at us. If we fail to heal, then we become lazy, greedy, and impervious to change.

Similar effects come into play when Pluto forms aspects to Venus.

When Pluto passes through Gemini, we are all invited to heal the soul-sickness created by *distraction, chaos, chronic overstimulation, and the sheer speed of events*, along with the loss of perspective they engender. If we fail to heal, then we become *hypnotized by our senses* and forget the ultimate reasons behind why we are here.

Similar effects come into play when Pluto forms aspects to Mercury.

When Pluto passes through Cancer, we are all invited to heal the soul-sickness created by *dysfunction in our families* and the pressure of the roles that we are conscripted into playing there. Ancestral patterns of damage and delusion come to the surface. If we fail to heal, then we become the embodiment of our ancestral wounds.

Similar effects come into play when Pluto forms aspects to the Moon.

When Pluto passes through Leo, we are all invited to heal the soul-sickness created by the *egocentric need to be the center of attention.* The inner tyrant comes to the surface. The spoiled child rises up. If we fail to heal, then we become autocratic and self-important, as if the world revolves around us.

Similar effects come into play when Pluto forms aspects to the Sun.

When Pluto passes through Virgo, we are all invited to heal the soul-sickness created by *shame, self-doubt, and humiliations* in this life or in previous ones. We have an opportunity to reflect on the damage we have sustained from *bad mentors* and negative role models – or simply from the lack of positive guidance. If we fail to heal, then we become self-destructive and self-limiting.

Similar effects come into play when Pluto forms aspects to Mercury.

When Pluto passes through Libra, we are all invited to heal the soul-sickness created by breaches of human trust – *lies, betrayals, abandonment,* and *failed relationships.* If we fail to heal, then we become lonely and isolated. We become tragic romantics.

Similar effects come into play when Pluto forms aspects to Venus.

When Pluto passes through Scorpio, we are all invited to heal the soul-sickness created by the *misuse or misdirection of sexual energy,* interpersonal *power struggles,* or *dramas around death and dying,* both in this life or other lifetimes. If we fail to heal, then we become bitter, pessimistic and dark.

Similar effects come into play when Pluto forms aspects to its own position, or to Mars.

When Pluto passes through Sagittarius, we are all invited to heal the soul-sickness created by *bad religion* and distorting belief-systems. The toxic effects of *ethnic, gender, and cross-cultural prejudice* come to the surface. If we fail to heal, then we become dogmatic, xenophobic, and inclined to dehumanize those who are different from ourselves.

Similar effects come into play when Pluto forms aspects to Jupiter.

When Pluto passes through Capricorn, we are all invited to heal the soul-sickness created by blind adherence to the *norms and values of the past.* The karma of a selfish "me first" attitude surfaces, countered by the potential realization of the dignity that comes from serving one's community. If we fail to heal, then we become autocratic, selfish, and insensitive to the suffering of others.

Similar effects come into play when Pluto forms aspects to Saturn.

When Pluto passes through Aquarius, we are all invited to heal the soul-sickness created by the *cold dissociation* that comes from a shocking, overwhelming pace of change or cultural disruption, along with *social alienation,* both in this lifetime and in previous ones. If we fail to heal, then we become frozen emotionally, cut off from our own hearts, distant from what makes us human.

Similar effects come into play when Pluto forms aspects to Saturn or Uranus.

When Pluto passes through Pisces, we are all invited to heal the soul-sickness created by escapism in all its many forms – *physical addictions, compulsive pleasures, religious delusion, living in fantasy.* If we fail to heal, then we become passive, indulging in our own weakness, sleeping and dreaming our lives away.

Similar effects come into play when Pluto forms aspects to Jupiter or Neptune.

As Pluto Passes Through the Twelve Houses . . .

PLUTO ENTERING THE FIRST HOUSE

The Evolutionary Aim: I resolve to become more real, more direct, and more authentic in how I present myself in the world. People will interpret those changes as my becoming more intense and perhaps more confrontive. I resolve to be comfortable with their judgments and not allow them to sway me. How people read me does not concern me as much as truth concerns me.

The Path to Soul-Recovery: Transparent honesty is the heart of the matter, but I will not lose track of kindness and therefore sometimes I will choose to keep my mouth shut. But I will not lie. Gradually I will weed out all the relationships in my life that simply require too much walking-on-eggshells diplomacy. I will be especially vigilant in eliminating relationships in which I am punished for truthfulness or directness.

The Cost of Failure: I become mean, using psychological insight – real or invented – as a way of punishing other people and keeping them safely at arm's length. Fear and denial underlie all my behavior.

PLUTO ENTERING THE SECOND HOUSE

The Evolutionary Aim: I resolve to convince myself that letting myself be more honest, direct, and truthful is something I have now learned how to do gracefully. I can, in other words, do it without leaving a trail of blood behind me. I have the right skills. I aim to recognize that the social relationships that are actually important to me spiritually are with people who cope with my taking this evolutionary step. Meanwhile, I will do what I need to do in order to make sure that I have the material resources that are necessary for my journey and which are rightfully mine. I will fight those battles if I have to and I will win.

The Path to Soul-Recovery: Step by step, I risk increasing levels of truthfulness and clarity with the people around me. I learn, sometimes as a result of errors, the skills that empower me as a truthsayer. I am not afraid of those errors; I learn from making them. I give myself the tools I need to support these evolutionary processes. Perhaps I invest in psychotherapy or deep astrological counsel. Perhaps I simply need money in order to take the next steps on my journey. If so, I claim it.

The Cost of Failure: A feeling of falseness enters my life, as if I am playing a part in someone else's movie. I feel insecure, as if my phony status is always on the edge of being revealed. I undercut my future by unwittingly positioning myself in impossible practical situations. Perhaps I make bad financial decisions which trigger wasteful dramas in my life.

PLUTO ENTERING THE THIRD HOUSE

The Evolutionary Aim: I resolve to develop the sorts of precise communication skills which allow a flow of deeper truth to pass effectively between myself and the world. Perhaps this resolution is supported by education.

My style of speech becomes more direct and my thinking more penetrating. I may even be accused of being suspicious – and I know that does not mean that I am wrong about what I see. I realize that this improvement is a two-way street, with equal emphasis on me bettering myself as one who can *hear* difficult truths without becoming defensive.

The Path to Soul-Recovery: I take the risk of saying what I see, even if saying it makes me feel uncomfortable and even if I am unsure about how my truths will be received. I am willing to ask the right questions, even if I fear that I might not like the answers. I listen to criticism with an open mind, discerning what is useful in it – while weeding out other people's projections and personal judgments. Those judgments are their business, not mine.

The Cost of Failure: Sarcasm, anger and bitterness infect my speech. I say hurtful things that I don't even mean just for effect, and I am not sure why I am doing it. I value impact over truth. Dark thoughts haunt me.

PLUTO ENTERING THE FOURTH HOUSE

The Evolutionary Aim: I resolve to dive deeply into understanding how I was shaped, impacted, and limited by my family when I was growing up. I can do this without condemning anyone; the process is only about truth and discernment. I wrestle with the ancestral shadow. I am ready to see what really happened to me, to my parents, to their parents, and so on.

The Path to Soul-Recovery: The sorts of inquiries, values, and perspectives that are typically part of the psychotherapeutic process are what illuminate my path now. I may not need to be "in psychotherapy" in the formal sense of the term, but I make a similarly fearless inquiry into my memories of growing up – and into the forces which shaped my parents, their parents, and their parent's parents. I recognize that I am healing an ancestral wound. If I have photographs of my grandparents, I use them to look deeply into their eyes, asking them penetrating questions – and hearing their answers..

The Cost of Failure: I come to embody the ancestral shadow. I become its puppet, mechanically repeating a dysfunctional family myth. As a result, increasingly I experience a depressing sense of my life being controlled and diminished by "fate."

PLUTO ENTERING THE FIFTH HOUSE

The Evolutionary Aim: I resolve to bash through any walls that lie between me and experiencing unabashed animal joy at being alive. I will be honest with myself about the nature of my own true desires of flesh, mind, and spirit. I will act on them without any inhibition, except for one: a promise not to damage anyone else in the process. Simultaneously, I resolve to weed out unconscious compulsions to avoid dealing with my own wounds by numbing them with "pleasures" I might use in escapist, avoiding ways – eating instead of crying, for one illustration.

The Path to Soul-Recovery: Experiences of pagan ecstasy and release nourish me now. I cut through any social scripts I have internalized about *pretending* to be happy – I will not fake it. I know when my soul feels alive and when it doesn't. I know what kinds of experiences trigger both of those feelings. I will not settle for less than reaching the higher ground. I keep company with people who are catalysts for joy. I claim my natural creativity.

The Cost of Failure: I simply grow tired of my life. I might not use those words, but I feel that soul- tiredness in my bones as I go through whatever motions other people require of me. I find solace in oblivion.

PLUTO ENTERING THE SIXTH HOUSE

The Evolutionary Aim: I resolve to be of genuine use to a few other people and to do that by offering them gifts which spring directly from my grow-ing storehouse of wisdom. Those people feel good receiving these gifts and I feel good giving them. My focus is on doing work that actually matters – that makes a difference in other people's lives – and which expresses the fruits of the healing efforts I have made on my own psyche. I will not sim-ply "serve." Instead, I will make a gift of myself – of insights and powers which stem directly from my soul.

The Path to Soul-Recovery: The human world is always full of suffer-ing and need; there is never a shortage of either of them. Therefore I am rich in opportunities to be of service. All I have to do is to keep my eyes open for them. The laws of synchronicity guarantee that they will appear. Meanwhile, helpful teachers and mentors arrive in my own life. I will rec-ognize them by the steadiness of their gaze. I will soak up the wisdom that radiates from them.

The Cost of Failure: I feel lost and useless, caught up in responsibilities that are slowly sucking the life out of me and giving me nothing in return. This soul-sickness can turn into physical illnesses and complaints – conditions which outwardly mirror my inward distaste for the current realities of my life.

PLUTO ENTERING THE SEVENTH HOUSE

The Evolutionary Aim: I resolve to give anyone who professes to love me the chance actually to know me. I will, in other words, be fully, nakedly, present in my important relationships, even if that means falling short of other people's expectations or projected requirements. I resolve to be transparent about what I feel and who I have become – and if who I really am doesn't work for someone else, then maybe we are both in the wrong relationship. If that is true, I am not afraid to see it and admit it.

The Path to Soul-Recovery: I will actively work on deepening my connections to other people and making them more genuinely authentic. I will struggle toward increasing levels of emotional presence and its corresponding vulnerabilities. I resolve to do my half of the work, and not take the cheap exit ramp of doing nothing and then blaming everyone but myself. Honesty is my path now, and sometimes it is a steep and rocky one. I accept that, I resolve to face any losses it entails, and I begin walking it.

The Cost of Failure: Intimate dramas arise – dramas characterized by two people projecting their own issues onto each other, hurling psychiatric diagnoses over the wall they have built between themselves as if they were sticks of dynamite, neither of them really seeing nor hearing the other one.

PLUTO ENTERING THE EIGHTH HOUSE

The Evolutionary Aim: I resolve to stimulate my evolutionary hunger, instilling in myself a deeper sense of urgency and a renewed fire in my belly regarding my spiritual path. Perhaps the medicine I need to accomplish that is a freshened realization of the brevity of my life. Perhaps circumstances arise to remind me of that fact – deaths occurring in my circle, for example. My motto from now on is "nothing but the truth." I do not have time for anything less; I realize that anything less than truthfulness is foolish waste. I resolve that this urgency will be vividly reflected in my most intimate relationships.

The Path to Soul-Recovery: No path is so efficacious for me now as a deep meditation upon how short life is, along with reflections on the inevitability of death. Such reflections are not morbid or depressing for me; instead they are stimulating, driving me to live each moment more fully. Through synchronicity, there is a heightened possibility that pivotal deaths – or brushes with my own death – might figure in my experience during this period.

The Cost of Failure: A bleak mood of defeat and despair takes hold of me. Everything feels futile. Life feels empty, yet I cling to it in fear and insecurity. I create intimate dramas which are animated by my own unresolved issues projected onto others.

PLUTO ENTERING THE NINTH HOUSE

The Evolutionary Aim: I resolve to question the basis of everything that I believe. I am willing to see what beliefs can stand their ground – and which ones cannot. I am not afraid of hard questions about my moral values, my religious tenets, or my philosophy of life. I recognize that anything which cannot survive such questioning is delusional, and thus is not helping me forward on the path toward real wisdom. I resolve to face whatever fears prevent me from literally traveling to physical places my soul is hungry to see. I face down anything which stands between me and receiving the empowering knowledge I took birth in order to learn.

The Path to Soul-Recovery: Wide experience that carries me outside the framework of what is familiar to me works evolutionary magic now. I need shock and surprise; I need a fresh context for my life. I resolve to travel if I can; I resolve to learn things in areas I have never before explored, but which have always fascinated me. I will stretch my horizons; I will break up my routines. It is time to blow out my mental dust willies.

The Cost of Failure: I drown in the stiff, predictable world of my own pre-existing opinions and habitual routines. I preach and I pontificate, quite unaware that those behaviors reveal my own underlying sense of insecurity around the beliefs which I am professing. I slip into being afraid of change and a xenophobic terror of anything – or anyone – I have not seen before.

PLUTO ENTERING THE TENTH HOUSE

The Evolutionary Aim: I resolve to be responsive to a need which is presently arising in my community. I realize that I have recently evolved to a point where I can satisfy that need – and I recognize that these personal maturations have triggered a moral *requirement* of service in me. It is simply right and natural that I accept such a role; I know it and so do many other people. One dimension of that community need is for me to function as a truthsayer – one who looks the devil in the eye on behalf of the community. I resolve to fill those shoes. I will create meaning in my life by serving something larger and more important than myself.

The Path to Soul-Recovery: There is dignity and a sense of spiritual maturity in accepting the burden of service. There is even joy in it, and certainly a sense of meaning. I resolve to do what I can for the larger circle of people around me, and I am grateful for the personal gifts offering such service brings me, even if by all appearances much is being asked of me.

The Cost of Failure: A feeling of pointless, existential meaninglessness poisons my attitude toward my life. I also seem to drift into the crosshairs of collective projection – that means that, reflecting and confirming my dark emotional state, I may become a target of vilification or a victim of some injustice.

PLUTO ENTERING THE ELEVENTH HOUSE

The Evolutionary Aim: I resolve to have an honest conversation with myself about the true nature of my desires, intentions, and developmental direction for this lifetime. I reflect honestly on how I am doing in terms of fulfilling them. Which of my aims and priorities are actually authentic – and which ones are simply artefacts of my social conditioning, my family's dreams for me, and simple cultural training? *What kind of person am I actually in the process of becoming?* What am I actually doing about fulfilling my true soul-intentions – and how am I squandering my time? As I reflect upon that second question, I resolve particularly to scrutinize my network of social obligations, looking for entanglements that serve no higher purpose at all, and only serve to drain my batteries.

The Path to Soul-Recovery: I actively seek the company of groups of people whose aims and values are resonant with my own. I recognize that the process of my becoming the person whom I actually want to become is inseparable from having their support. I recognize these people by their honesty, their directness, and their openness to speaking psychospiritual language.

The Cost of Failure: I fritter away precious time dealing with interpersonal dramas, along with the sorts of endlessly draining, fruitless human politics that infect dysfunctional organizations, clans, and crowds. Their monkey business becomes my business.

PLUTO ENTERING THE TWELFTH HOUSE

The Evolutionary Aim: I resolve to recognize that my next steps on the spiritual path are inseparable from psychological work – and by that I essentially mean dealing honestly and humbly with my own woundedness. Psychotherapy is a possibility, but there are many ways to do that kind of healing – deep astrological work comes to mind, as do soul-retrieval, past life regressions, and so on. The underlying point is that I am being held back in my spiritual journey by the emotional weight of countless hurts and unresolved interpersonal dramas. I do not need to work through each one of them one at a time, but rather to realize that they are summed in my heart as one bad feeling which I need to release in some kind of *catharsis* – perhaps in a primal scream.

The Path to Soul-Recovery: I realize that there is no weightless angelic part of me that can somehow break off from my humanity and float up to heaven. Hurts must be healed, or they will simply hold me back. I resolve squarely to face my anger and resentments, my moral failures, my human hungers, and all of my rationalizations. I resolve to achieve the *grace of forgiveness*, both of myself and of others – and to do it honestly, which often means *slowly*. If forgiveness happens too fast, it is probably only spiritual posturing, and not truly authentic.

The Cost of Failure: I feel cut off from life's mysteries, cut off from contact with the transcendent and the divine. I feel lost in a cold, material, existential universe that runs on madly without any real purpose at all. Whining fugues of self-pity are stuck on Repeat in my head.

Mars Passing Through The Twelve Signs

A sign, as ever, provides motives and needs, while a house is where we visibly carry out our efforts. For Taurus, for example, groundedness, peace, and reason top the agenda. If Mars enters Taurus while in your personal third house, much will rest on the words you find to express the desires that you are feeling and experiencing. If it enters Taurus while in your twelfth house, no words will be necessary at all.

MARS ENTERING ARIES

The Present Evolutionary Challenge: Can I steady my nerves in the face of fear and intimidation? Can I conquer the panic reflex? Can I effectively protect myself and those whom I love? Can I recognize transitory opportunities and seize them before they vanish?

The Synchronistic Correlates: Stressful, even scary situations arise. Rivals, competitors, bullies, and antagonists appear.

What's Worth Fighting For: Standing up for myself and those I love. My honor and dignity. My right to thrive.

What's Not: The petty offences of people who really do not matter to me. Trying to win arguments with people who will never change and never listen. My right to bang my head against a wall.

MARS ENTERING TAURUS

The Present Evolutionary Challenge: In prioritizing my own peace of mind, can I cut through to what is truly essential and let go of the rest? Can I care for my physical body in such a way that I feel strong enough to have a sense of relative safety, both from antagonists and from disease?

The Synchronistic Correlates: Opportunities for physical exercise and exertion. Opportunities to get sweaty. Opportunities to experience the centering effects of silence and the natural world. A chance to win the peace.

What's Worth Fighting For: My health and the health of those whom I love, both physical and mental. The basic things that really, fundamentally, count towards happiness in life – a peaceful home, loving family, quiet time, and a chance to feed my spiritual life.

What's Not: The illusions of safety created by mere material security. The extra dollar, the extra lock on the door, the extra burglar alarm. The agreement and support of fools.

MARS ENTERING GEMINI

The Present Evolutionary Challenge: Can I develop my voice into an instrument that can effectively protect and promote the people, places, and things that matter to me? Can I beguile and persuade when it comes to promoting ideas that are worth defending? Can I argue passionately without losing my emotional balance, without seeming unnecessarily strident, and without sacrificing clarity?

The Synchronistic Correlates: Conversations arise that require forceful, effective responses from me. Critical information is available too, but only if I dig for it. Shocks and surprises come flying out of nowhere.

What's Worth Fighting For: Arguments over things that truly matter. My right to be heard, even if people disagree with me. Being taken seriously. Access to personally important information.

What's Not: Symbolic arguments in which the apparent subject of disagreement is a stand-in for something that both people are actually afraid to talk about.

MARS ENTERING CANCER

The Present Evolutionary Challenge: Can I identify anything in my life that is so fundamentally connected to the roots of what I am that I would willingly die for it? Often the answer lies with my soul-clan – but sometimes what is worth defending is the land under my feet or even a sacred idea or principle of some sort. Can I claim that strength? Can I defend what must be defended? Can I protect – fiercely if necessary – my right to secure my own health and wellbeing?

The Synchronistic Correlates: Challenges to the welfare of something that is central to my identity – something that I am bound to defend by all the laws of the universe and the laws which govern the human soul. Situations appear in which, in order to sustain my own health, I need to show my teeth.

What's Worth Fighting For: People and places that I expect to love for the rest of my days on earth. My own right to be well and happy.

What's Not: Boundaries which are really more about defending my ego against growth than anything truly connected to the wellbeing of my soul. Always staying "safely unthreatened" is not the purpose of my life.

MARS ENTERING LEO

The Present Evolutionary Challenge: Can I overcome fearful, nervous self-consciousness enough to really let loose and express myself without inhibition – and can I do that skillfully enough that other people willingly offer me their undivided attention? (Can I, in other words, resolve an ancient paradox – can I find the sweet spot between crude, uncontrolled, self-indulgent spontaneity, on one hand, and an effective sense of "theater" on the other?)

The Synchronistic Correlates: Chances to speak up. Chances to perform or to be in the spotlight. Circumstances where all eyes turn to me. Something dramatic needs to be said, and said well – deep down, I know that I am the one whose voice must be heard, or a needful truth will go unspoken.

What's Worth Fighting For: My right to give outward expression to my inner life – to express what I deem sacred, beautiful, and worth living for. Expanding my ability to face being vulnerable and to improve my skills in so doing.

What's Not: Mere showmanship. Getting attention for its own sake. Just taking up space and other people's time. Feeling as if I do not exist unless I am being applauded. Looking cool.

MARS ENTERING VIRGO

The Present Evolutionary Challenge: Can I assert true mastery and skill in a field that is actually meaningful to me? Can I thereby *demonstrate* that I should be taken seriously in such a way that everyone simply assumes my mastery to be reality from then on? Can I assert my skills in a way that makes a difference in another person's life – perhaps a person in real crisis? Can I *compete* effectively, if competition is necessary?

The Synchronistic Correlates: Stressful, challenging, do-or-die situations in which I either boldly take charge and turn a bad situation around – or wish I had done that, realizing that a reflexive lack of confidence held me back from succeeding. As hockey Hall of Famer, Wayne Gretzky said, "We miss 100% of the shots we don't take."

What's Worth Fighting For: Social recognition for the skillsets I actually possess, but which might be underestimated by other people. Excellence. The effective deployment of my talents, techniques, and training in ways that fill me with the good feeling of a job well done – and fully appreciated.

What's Not: Nitpicking arguments over trivial details that do not really matter in the big picture. Crippling worry over what might possibly go wrong. Endless preparation. Stressing over how to prevent failures that probably will not happen and regarding which I could probably improvise solutions even if they did.

MARS ENTERING LIBRA

The Present Evolutionary Challenge: Can I do the edgy but necessary conflict-resolution work that keeping relationships healthy always requires? Can I negotiate effectively in order to see that my real needs are met, while maintaining respectful, open minded awareness of the needs of my partners and friends? Can I keep my eye on the prize – which is the ultimate well-being for all concerned – even if I am feeling bloody-minded or resentful?

The Synchronistic Correlates: Underlying interpersonal issues which have been lying latent are triggered into active manifestation by unforeseen emerging circumstances. Stresses arise, revealing the fault lines. The firecracker has been there all along – but now something lights the fuse.

What's Worth Fighting For: Keeping love alive and, above all, real. Helping relationships to last even though everyone is always changing and old contracts need to be re-negotiated in the light of what we have both become.

What's Not: Winning arguments that are no more than sniping sublimations of underlying tensions and frustrations that go unspoken and unrevealed. The dubious satisfaction which comes from making someone else look wrong. Zingers that leave other people devastated and me simply looking witty – and mean.

MARS ENTERING SCORPIO

The Present Evolutionary Challenge: Anger always exaggerates, and passion always distorts our perceptions. Add that seeing any truth denied or avoided can make me passionately angry. Putting two and two together, can I be sufficiently mindful of *my own reactions* that I can remain constructively focused on mutual long-term benefits rather than creating a "righteous war" that everyone loses?

The Synchronistic Correlates: Rationalizations unravel. Lies are exposed. Truth comes out. Drama reigns. "One thing leads to another . . . push comes to shove."

What's Worth Fighting For: Clearing the air. An end to stiffness, phoniness, and pretending that everything is fine when it really is not. Honest resolutions which ultimately work toward everyone's ultimate good.

What's Not: Landing verbal blows which leave other people humiliated, destroyed emotionally – or hellbent on vengeance. Sneak attacks. Using genuine psychological insight as a death-ray instead of as a medicine.

MARS ENTERING SAGITTARIUS

The Present Evolutionary Challenge: Can I break out of my safe comfort zone and boldly do what I have never done before? Can I break up the routines of thought, attitude and behavior that threaten to turn me into a robot? Can I escape my own predictability?

The Synchronistic Correlates: Opportunities for some fresh air to blow through the windows of my life – a chance to travel, to learn, and to experience stimuli that I had never before seen or imagined. Challenges to my existing beliefs and understandings.

What's Worth Fighting For: My right to be wiser tomorrow than I am today. My right to stretch my horizons. My right to bust out of any existential prisons, whether others have created them for me or I have created them for myself.

What's Not: My opinions. If others agree with me, that is fine – and ditto if they do not. If I need to make someone else hew to my party line, that probably means that I myself am insecure about it. If I win such an argument, my prize is only my right to be just as clueless tomorrow as I was yesterday.

MARS ENTERING CAPRICORN

The Present Evolutionary Challenge: Can I admit that a mountain which I must climb lies before me – or will my fear of climbing it blind me to its existence and the way it is summoning me? Simply said, I must bite the bullet and do something difficult now. It is a victory that would give me a lot more joy as I looked back on it than it would afford me while I was banging my head against the wall and actually doing it. Can I be strong and resolute enough to make that effort? Can I do what must be done?

The Synchronistic Correlates: The moment of truth arises. It is now or never – and "never" is truly an attractive option, just a bad one. I can, in other words, walk away from this chance to become more than I've ever been, or ever imagined that I could be. But I can also do better than that. I can roll the dice, believe in myself, steel myself, and start climbing.

What's Worth Fighting For: Excellence. Accomplishment. The dignity and self-respect that come from challenging my own previous limits. The positive soul-feedback that arises from accomplishing Great Works in some meaningful category of life.

What's Not: Running other people's lives for them, controlling – or trying to control – everyone's behavior except my own. Getting angry at cats because they do not "herd" well.

MARS ENTERING AQUARIUS

The Present Evolutionary Challenge: Can I defend my right to follow my own stars? Can I be true to myself even if in so doing, I elicit criticism, worry, and misunderstanding? The question is not simply one of my "knowing myself". More precisely, the question centers on my strategic ability to *protect* my right to live my own life. It is a warrior's question, not one for a psychologist or a philosopher.

The Synchronistic Correlates: Tyrants, critics, and self-appointed psychiatrists loom, all of them offering me reams of bad advice, even if it is often well-intended. I thank them for affording me this excellent opportunity to ignore them and to do what I actually want to do anyway.

What's Worth Fighting For: My right to navigate by my own good instincts, knowing how short life is and how foolishly wasteful it is to let anyone else make my decisions for me. My right to master the highest of *karate* moves – simply walking away from a battle that I recognize I do not actually need to fight.

What's Not: Arguing with fools. Arguing with people who are simply not capable of relating to my motives and higher values. Reaching compromises that leave everyone feeling ripped off and unsatisfied.

MARS ENTERING PISCES

The Present Evolutionary Challenge: Can I hold my awareness one-pointed and steady in the face of a significant – and unsettling – expansion of my psychic sensitivity? Can I surf those edgy waves without letting fear trigger a reflexive withdrawal? Can I recognize conflictual human situations in which I can actually *win by losing*? Can my soul rather than my ego be the commander of my inner army, helping me to realize that sometimes there is simply no need to defend myself?

The Synchronistic Correlates: Opportunities for significant spiritual breakthrough which present themselves as *optional* risks and adventures. It takes courage for me to accept them, in other words. I must recognize these opportunities and engage with them voluntarily. Situations crystallize before me in which surrendering leads to victory, while "winning" leads to defeat and loss. I can, for example, successfully fight to keep something I would be better off without.

What's Worth Fighting For: Above all, my own spiritual growth. It is wise for me to claim such evolutionary opportunities even if in order to do so, I might appear to be selfish or too aggressive. I fiercely defend my right to live out my soul's own journey. I can burn bridges behind me.

What's Not: Trying to impress others with my level of spiritual attainment. Winning battles that do not matter; winning for the sake of pride. Defending my right to escape from life; defending my own numbness.

As Mars Passes Through The Twelve Houses . . .

MARS ENTERING THE FIRST HOUSE

Where I Must Now Assert Myself: For the sake of my continued soul growth, a time has crystalized before me in which I need to act decisively and unilaterally, probably without support and probably in the face of resistance, in order to press for some essential changes in my circumstances. I will actively *lead* my own life rather than allowing it to "happen" to me.

The Skills I Need In Order To Win: I will be firm and direct; I will not be intimidated. I resolve to remain cool under pressure. I will use just enough force to get what I need, and no more force than that. I will be the hunter rather than the prey. I can be dangerous if I have to be.

The Face of Overreach: If I use this energy in an unskillful or unconsciously reflexive way, I will either behave cruelly, letting myself be motivated by unreflective anger – or I will simmer with unexpressed resentment and frustration, creating dangerous levels of explosive tension in my psyche and my body.

MARS ENTERING THE SECOND HOUSE

Where I Must Now Assert Myself: For the sake of my continued soul growth, I resolve to behave in a way that ultimately enhances my courage and my self-confidence. I will be stronger when this is over than I am as it begins. I will validate my warrior nature in my own mind and in the minds of people who are watching me. I will take risks. I aim for victory. There may be material objects – tools, clothing, even financial resources – I must acquire in order to have a practical basis for the confidence that I require at this crossroads.

The Skills I Need In Order To Win: Above all, I must make a fearless, unashamed assessment of my actual strategic position in terms of my strength and my liabilities. If I am going to succeed, what resources, material or personal, do I now lack and must find? How do I go about acquiring them? Bravado alone will not see me through this challenge. I need to establish a *basis* for victory.

The Face of Overreach: If I use this energy in an unskillful or unconsciously reflexive way, I may bluster. I may rail against life's unfairness. I may cry out for justice, even though no one is listening and no one cares anyway. In the end, I will either give up – or embark upon a lost cause with no realistic hope of success, arranging to go down in flames of glory.

MARS ENTERING THE THIRD HOUSE

Where I Must Now Assert Myself: For the sake of my continued soul growth, I need to get something off my chest. There are words which need to be said – and heard. I have a right to speak passionately; that passion is deep and sincere, and it is one facet of the truth which I must now articulate. Another possibility is that I might need to apologize for my own part in a misunderstanding – and it does take a lot of courage to apologize. Either way, I insist upon being heard.

The Skills I Need In Order To Win: My most effective tactic now is to simply open my mouth and announce that I have something important to say. Once I have done that, the die is cast – and from that moment on, I have faith that I can improvise the rest of my speech.

The Face of Overreach: If I use this energy in an unskillful or unconsciously reflexive way, I simply sound strident and angry, as if I have "my knickers in a knot" – as if I am merely *whining* in a way that no one wants to hear or to take seriously.

MARS ENTERING THE FOURTH HOUSE

Where I Must Now Assert Myself: For the sake of my continued soul growth, I resolve to claim some quiet, reflective time for myself. At this crossroads, I have a right to turn away from other people's demands and to create a chance for me to hear the whispers of my own soul. I can defend my home against intrusion – and "home" in this sense can mean any one of three possibilities: "home base" within me, my physical dwelling, or my family.

The Skills I Need In Order To Win: Above all, the skill of sensitivity toward myself: an awareness of my tiredness, or my feelings of being lost, or in need of inner guidance. I also need a warrior's sense of do-or-die loyalty toward my own people. I recognize a precious treasure – that there are people in my life so valuable to me that I would give my life for them.

The Face of Overreach: If I use this energy in an unskillful or unconsciously reflexive way, I swallow resentments, humiliations, and rage in the name of keeping the peace or avoiding retaliation and punishment. That poison then leaks out from me in the form of my abusing the people closest to me.

MARS ENTERING THE FIFTH HOUSE

Where I Must Now Assert Myself: For the sake of my continued soul growth, I need to step boldly onto the stage of life. It is time for me really to *perform*, to show people what I have to offer, and to do it with dash and *brio*. I must be brave and self-possessed enough to face an audience, whether it is composed of three people, three hundred people, or three billion people. It is time to show them what I've got.

The Skills I Need In Order To Win: Comedian George Burns once said, "Sincerity is everything. If you can fake that, you have it made." Well, I am not going to fake anything – but I do need to develop certain theatrical skills of self-projection – skills which allow me to effectively convey my inner states to people who are watching me, and to elicit from them a kind of emotional identification with me. If I have to practice in front of a mirror to attain those skills, so be it. Preparation and self-awareness are not incompatible with sincerity.

The Face of Overreach: If I use this energy in an unskillful or unconsciously reflexive way, I try to substitute bombast, fireworks, and drama for actual content. Most people soon figure out that kind of trickery, and my audience soon loses interest in me. To ease the pain of that rejection, I then enter into a self-abusive relationship with some pleasure.

MARS ENTERING THE SIXTH HOUSE

Where I Must Now Assert Myself: For the sake of my continued soul growth, I must forcefully assert my right to be of genuine service to others and then internalize the resultant boost in my sense of my own worth which comes from seeing the results of my helping them. I have much to offer; the problem is that too few people know that. I need to announce loudly and clearly that "I can do that . . ." I also need to reach out effectively to those who are my natural mentors, asking for their help, guidance, and their blessing.

The Skills I Need In Order To Win: The ability to recognize a fit between what I have to offer and emergent needs in the people who now present themselves to me. I see their need and I step competently into the role of helper. I also recognize those who can help me put some polish on the innate skills with which I was born.

The Face of Overreach: If I use this energy in an unskillful or unconsciously reflexive way, I experience stress that is related to the weight of my various duties and responsibilities. The apparent source of that stress is probably obvious – impossible tasks, incompetent management – but its true source is that I should have graduated from that situation long ago.

MARS ENTERING THE SEVENTH HOUSE

Where I Must Now Assert Myself: For the sake of my continued soul growth, I will learn to make the exact nature of my needs and desires clear in the context of my primary relationships. I accept that I cannot get everything I want – but I do resolve to negotiate in a direct, forceful, and honest way, and to make sure that my position is accurately understood. I will not only set boundaries – I will defend them forcefully if necessary.

The Skills I Need In Order To Win: Enough self-confidence and sense of my own legitimacy that I can project an atmosphere in which I am naturally taken seriously. No one can dismiss me. If I feel the need to make threats or issue ultimatums, I resolve to carry them out. Warrior-fashion, I will be true to my word.

The Face of Overreach: If I use this energy in an unskillful or unconsciously reflexive way, old angers – even ones with no connection to my present friends or partners – vent themselves on innocent targets, weakening the critical bonds of trust and good will upon which all intimate negotiations ultimately depend.

MARS ENTERING THE EIGHTH HOUSE

Where I Must Now Assert Myself: For the sake of my continued soul growth, I will bravely dive into some psychologically-charged material which I have never before faced squarely. I will look honestly at parts of my life which are fraught with shame or embarrassment, and I resolve to understand what wounding experiences in this life or other lifetimes led me to those dark dungeons of stuckness.

The Skills I Need In Order To Win: I recognize, above all else, that inner work requires enormous courage. I will claim it and go forward. I will especially attend honestly to the hidden, and perhaps unwelcome, messages that are woven into the unvarnished realities of my actual sexual history. I will do that with an open heart, free of defensiveness. My only devotion is to finding the whole truth. I can do this work alone; no one else needs to know about it unless I choose to share it with someone I would trust with my life.

The Face of Overreach: If I use this energy in an unskillful or unconsciously reflexive way, I erect walls of rationalization between myself and truths which could ultimately liberate me. I blame others; I displace potential self-insight into psychiatric analysis of other people – and I then convert that analysis into blame and condemnation of them, all in order to avoid my own healing.

MARS ENTERING THE NINTH HOUSE

Where I Must Now Assert Myself: For the sake of my continued soul growth, I need some adventure in my life. I need to break the stranglehold of everything that is familiar and habitual, and thus see my life in a fresh light. I am hungry for the open road, both literally and philosophically. I will claim, aggressively if necessary, my right to spread my wings and fly. No one can stop me.

The Skills I Need In Order To Win: Above all, I resolve to question the actual origin and spiritual legitimacy of the moral strictures which have constrained my life. Many of them are reflective of natural law, and I will continue to honor them – but I will do that because I have chosen to do so, not because I have been so trained and conditioned. I fear no questions, however heretical they may sound – true faith can stand up to honest doubts without collapsing.

The Face of Overreach: If I use this energy in an unskillful or unconsciously reflexive way, I preach, pontificate, bluster and argue. I even harangue people who agree with me, driving them to shut me out – which I then misinterpret as their infuriating disagreement, goading me to further argument. People cross the street to avoid me, even people who are on my side.

MARS ENTERING THE TENTH HOUSE

Where I Must Now Assert Myself: For the sake of my continued soul growth, I surrender to the reality that the time has come for me to bear some kind of visible fruit in my community. I claim my rightful place as one who influences the shape of the times in which I find myself living. I am not powerless to have an impact on history – even if it is very local history. My strength gives strength to others, even to those whom I do not know personally.

The Skills I Need In Order To Win: How can I carry myself in the public world in a way that conveys a sense of self-assurance, effectiveness and confidence to people who barely know me? I must now correctly recognize my calling and audaciously rise to it. I can stand up for something. I can lead if the winds blow me in that direction. Being seen publicly does not intimidate me. I can move naturally and spontaneously even when people are watching me.

The Face of Overreach: If I use this energy in an unskillful or unconsciously reflexive way, I will attract enemies and antagonists. I will either find myself enmeshed in pointless conflicts, or cast in the role of the designated victim.

MARS ENTERING THE ELEVENTH HOUSE

Where I Must Now Assert Myself: For the sake of my continued soul growth, I must now undertake two tasks which loom before me. The first is to fearlessly weed out my social circle, reducing or eliminating my involvement with people who only drain my time and energy. The second is to fill that vacuum with my natural soul-tribe and then to take my rightful place in it.

The Skills I Need In Order To Win: Above all, a clear sense of my own true priorities in life. It is only in the light of that kind of clarity about myself that I can correctly discern who in my circle is helping me attain those aims and who is only distracting me from reaching them. Once that understanding is crystalized in my mind, I need to act decisively in cutting social ties that no longer serve my higher purposes.

The Face of Overreach: If I use this energy in an unskillful or unconsciously reflexive way, I then find myself swept up in group dramas or group calamities which actually have nothing to teach me and which serve no purpose other than wasting my time.

MARS ENTERING THE TWELFTH HOUSE

Where I Must Assert Myself: For the sake of my continued soul growth, I choose simply to leave this world behind for a while. I resolve to disentangle myself from society and my more trivial relationships for a while, even in the face of protests. I heed that inner call. I seek a vision and a spiritual breakthrough. I resolve that nothing will prevent me from finding it. I can do all of this on my own; most external advice is only a distraction for me now.

The Skills I Need In Order To Win: Enough spiritual self-possession that I can walk away from everything that supports my worldly identity without feeling that I have lost my mind. Centeredness that transcends my "name, rank, and serial number." The courage to face weird or unsettling meditation experiences without losing my equilibrium.

The Face of Overreach: If I use this energy in an unskillful or unconsciously reflexive way, I become frightened of my own inner states and I then seek to avoid them or to turn them off. I can accomplish that by cultivating endless distraction, by simple escapism, or by creating unnecessary drama around loss, tragedy, or the natural endings of things.

ENTERING SCORPIO

WHEN THE SUN ENTERS SCORPIO . . . healing experiences arise when you allow your nature and your identity to become more intense and psychological. Your social circle is likely to contract as a result – and you need to balance that contraction with fewer relationships characterized by greater depth and honesty. Be wary of isolating yourself and just slipping into a dark mood.

WHEN THE MOON ENTERS SCORPIO . . . healing experiences arise when you allow your mood to become "suspicious" – which is to say, eager to penetrate beneath the surface appearances of things. Charged material looms up out the unconscious mind. It is all grist for the mill; you need to be aware of it, even if you do not like it. Be wary of loss of perspective. Never forget that laughter and humor are powerful medicines when it comes to keeping your balance.

WHEN MERCURY ENTERS SCORPIO . . . healing experiences arise when you allow your interests and curiosities to turn toward darker, more taboo subjects. Let that happen. You are hungry for truly honest conversations with people who look you straight in the eye. Just be wary of hurting people with truths that they are simply not ready to hear.

WHEN VENUS ENTERS SCORPIO . . . healing experiences arise when you allow your relationships to be tested. It is truth time, and your true friends are the ones who appreciate that sense of honest connection, and offer more of the same back to you. Be wary of impatience – in matters of psychological truth, people have their own pace and rhythm. You can lose worthy connections by seeming impatient or disrespectful of their right to set their own boundaries and schedules.

WHEN MARS ENTERS SCORPIO . . . healing experiences arise when you allow your passions to come to the surface. Those feelings need to be recognized, received, and honored by you – but not given entirely free reign. Don't unwittingly hurt people under the holy banner of "just being honest." Be wary of self-righteousness. Be wary of your inner lynch mob and your inner judge and jury. Keep one eye on compassion and forgiveness.

WHEN JUPITER ENTERS SCORPIO . . . healing experiences arise when you allow your dreams and ambitions to take on a more insistent tone, one that underscores and makes clear what you truly desire – as distinct from what you were trained to believe that you wanted. It is truth-time regarding your actual aims and ambitions in life. The realization of exactly what will truly make you happy might startle you now. Be wary of winning at all costs. Seek only victories that are worthy of you.

WHEN SATURN ENTERS SCORPIO . . . healing experiences arise when you allow your need for solitude to come forth. The need for some time to yourself will increase at first – but then you will realize that it is not simply solitude that you want, but rather the absence from your life of certain people who only drain your energy. Simply said, you have outgrown them. It is a time of hard, but necessary, choices. Be wary of the kinds of psychological judgmentalness that can only leave you cold and alone – and preoccupied with being "right."

WHEN URANUS ENTERS SCORPIO . . . healing experiences arise when you allow your hunger, needs, and desires to be liberated from the conventional moral strictures of society. Be wary of throwing out the baby with the bathwater – some of those strictures are indeed prim and false, and you will be better off without them constraining you, while others reflect natural law – and no one gets away with breaking those deeper laws of mind and spirit for very long.

WHEN NEPTUNE ENTERS SCORPIO . . . healing experiences arise when you allow your spirituality to fuse with your psychological self. Hard questions come up regarding your beliefs or any religious feelings you might have. Do not be afraid of those questions – any faith worth having can stand up to truth. Be wary of taking cheap refuge in cynicism. Be wary of sexual escapism.

WHEN PLUTO ENTERS SCORPIO . . . healing experiences arise when you allow your truth-and-lies detector to swallow some steroids, as it probably is doing right now. You penetrate illusions, even cherished ones. You can smell a lie from a mile away – and a rationalization from across town. Be wary of judging people who are simply not as strong as you. Above all, be wary of confusing truth with simply taking a dark view of everything and everyone.

21

CELESTIAL NAVIGATION III: NEPTUNE AND JUPITER TIMES, PISCES TIMES

Neptune and Jupiter are very different creatures, but they are forever linked through their common rulership of Pisces. If one single principle ties them together, here it is: when either one of them steps into the spotlight by transit or by solar arc, there is one attitude that will see you through: *faith*. Sometimes that is all we have.

The miracle is that faith is often enough.

I am tempted to write that "by faith, I don't mean religion." But actually religion can be part of it too. The astrological symbols for religion are Sagittarius and the ninth house. Jupiter rules them both – *but Neptune doesn't*. Right there we have an insight into one of the main differences between these two planets. They both hold "faith" in common, but they come by it in radically different ways. With Jupiter, we can indeed draw strength from *belief-systems* – that is where "religion," at least the broadest sense of the word, actually does in fact play a role in these healing processes. With Neptune, faith comes from something more akin to surrendering to the *direct experience* of the transcendent.

Neptune, in other words, is a mystic, while Jupiter is more like a philosopher or a theologian.

Or a very wise clown – and we will soon get to that part.

But once again, it is ultimately faith that animates both of these planets, even if they get to it differently. With either one of them, sometimes you just have to close your eyes and jump.

That is what faith often looks like.

Back in chapter five, I tried to address a common question I have often heard from my students. They can easily see Neptune's connection with Pisces, but Jupiter's connection often strikes them as more elusive. There are many technical points that could be made here, but let me quickly repeat the one that, for me at least, best cuts right to the heart of the matter. Just think of all the Pisceans you know, and try dividing them up into the "Neptunian" and "Jupitarian" ones. You will probably find that it is easy to do. In that "fishy" population, there are dreamy, mystical, sensitive types – and lots of big-hearted, funny, generous party animals.

Neptune might sit in meditation and genuinely feel unity with all of life, while Jupiter gives you a big, sincere hug – along with the shirt off his back, if you need one.

Neptune might feel unity with all of life, but Jupiter does a better job of expressing a sense of unguarded, whole-hearted acceptance *of you personally.*

Let's get to know these two planets as separate individuals, starting with Neptune.

A PRIMER ON THE TRANSITS AND SOLAR ARCS OF NEPTUNE

Neptune is the *planet of visions.* Since everything in astrology happens purposefully, when Neptune comes along, that means that *you need a vision.* Such a vision, as we will see, is not to be confused with any kind of plan or strategy. It is far more magical than that. Receiving such a vision is more akin to angels whispering in your ear than it is to plotting an itinerary. And if angels are whispering to you that way, you would be a fool not to listen to them.

But how do we listen to angels? They speak in very soft tones. To hear them, you have to be very, very quiet . . .

STAND STILL LIKE THE HUMMINGBIRD

"Don't just do something – sit there!" When we are faced with a Neptunian time, that inversion of the usual exhortation is the best advice in the world. Henry Miller, the brilliant, naughty, writer from the middle of last century, titled one of his collections of essays, *Stand Still Like the Hummingbird*. That lovely phrase – reflecting patience without torpor – is the very essence of a conscious response to a Neptunian event.

During such a time, something extraordinary is trying to happen. In a nutshell, *your consciousness is expanding*. Remember our Hindu proverb? *When the pickpocket meets the saint, he sees pockets*. When Neptune knocks on your door, you are becoming less like the pickpocket and more like the saint. You may not resemble either one of them very much, but they define the poles of the Neptunian evolutionary spectrum. That is the spectrum along which your upward travel is now accelerating – or at least trying to accelerate.

The Neptunian vision that is starting to crystalize in you is not entirely metaphysical in orientation. It also contains some purely practical elements. Biographically, it will eventually aim you in a new direction. But that practical material is like a footnote on page 497 of the book of your vision – it is significant, but totally secondary. During a period of Neptunian stimulus, the heart of what is happening to you is essentially *mystical*. Unlike "more practical matters," what you attain now, you can keep for eternity. You can take it with you when you exit this world. There is in fact no force in the universe that can ever steal it from you. Call it wisdom. Call it a step in the direction of enlightenment. Humans have been making up names for it for a very long time. However we label this condition, we know it when we see it. We can all recognize that kind of inner luminosity in others when we are fortunate enough to encounter such souls. Perhaps we can even recognize glimmerings of it in ourselves.

Pick a lowlife politician. Then pick your favorite spiritual teacher. If they played chess, who would win? Would you want to stake your life on that prediction? But the politician's eyes, while perhaps intelligent, are also feral, while the teacher's eyes suggest spaciousness, acceptance, and compassion. The difference between that politician and that spiritual teacher reflects the exact difference that you can make in yourself, at least if you respond well and consciously to a Neptunian transit or solar arc.

And that treasure can accompany you into your next incarnation.

A HAPPY ENVIRONMENTAL ENGINEER

I am picturing a woman in her forties. She is drawing a sample of water from an aquifer, bringing it back to her laboratory, putting it in a centrifuge, sorting out its levels of chemical contamination, comparing them with standards established by Congress. She is an environmental engineer, with a master's degree in chemistry. She has been in that professional field for twenty-two years. The work feels meaningful to her; she has the feeling that she is on the right course with her life – that she is doing what she was born to do, and helping the world in a practical way in the process.

Her guardian angels agree. She is exactly where she is supposed to be.

Now imagine that we approached this environmental engineer with our crystal ball when she was nine years old. We say, "Want to see what you are going to be when you grow up?" At age nine, becoming an environmental engineer has never crossed her mind. She anticipates a future either as a movie star or a princess, or maybe both. She is, after all, only nine years old.

We pull the silk scarf off the crystal ball and the truth is revealed. The little girl beholds her future self, clipboard in hand. She is a little round in the middle, with a sensible haircut, wearing glasses, drawing that sample of water from the aquifer.

The girl runs from the room with tears in her eyes.

But in her forties, she loves her job. She loves her life.

We could fairly say that at age nine she *does not* grasp the meaningfulness of the future that lies before her. But we cut closer to the Neptunian heart of the matter if we phrase it a little bit differently.

The child *cannot* grasp that future.

Saying that she "does not" grasp it implies that perhaps we could explain it to her, and then she *would* understand it. For example, I imagine that you often don't understand something about the inner working of your computer. Then someone explains it to you, and you do understand it. But no matter how carefully we explained the joys of being an environmental engineer to her, the nine-year-old still *could not* understand her future path. It would still depress her. That is because *she is not yet sufficiently conscious of herself to grasp it.* That insight is beyond her capabilities.

Right there in those few words lies the real magic of a Neptunian event. *Consciousness itself is expanding.* The change is not about information. It is about the foundation upon which all information – and all understanding – rests.

Remember that footnote on page 497 of the book of your vision? That the vision that is arising in you contains some practical guidance? *To receive that guidance, you must become wiser.* You must become a more evolved being. The "little girl" must "grow up."

And that is exactly what is trying to happen.

Like that nine-year-old girl, it is not that you *do not* know what you are doing. It is that you *cannot* know it – at least until you make a spiritual breakthrough.

So don't just do something – sit there. Stand still like a hummingbird.

PSYCHIC SIDE EFFECTS

"Hearing angels whisper" is as good a Neptunian metaphor as any. Where does inspiration come from? How does it actually arise? We can all relate to the cartoon character with the lightbulb lighting over his head. *But how can we explain it?*

One point is sure: the universal reality of people receiving "flashes of insight" proves beyond any reasonable doubt the existence of a larger framework of consciousness – something upon which our conscious minds float like corks in the sea. *During times of Neptunian stimulation, the veil between the conscious mind and that larger framework of awareness grows permeable and transparent.*

That is how the inspiration gets in.

The trouble is that other things can get in too. The open window that wafts the scent of springtime into your bedroom also lets in the flies and gnats. That is the nature of an open window. It does not discriminate. During a Neptunian time, your levels of psychic sensitivity open up. That is why you can get on the same wavelength as those angels and thus hear their messages. That psychic attunement is really what Neptune is all about.

But you will also be assailed by flies and gnats in the form of all of the ambient psychic noise around you – geopolitical tensions, your sullen co-worker with relationship blues, the bad vibes coming off that angry neo-Nazi in the car next to yours at the red light.

No problem? Possibly – with some quiet time and some spiritual self-care, you can purify those psychic viruses. That is how you keep your "immune response" strong. Remember: if you respond well to Neptune, you are on an evolutionary fast track. You are making a breakthrough. Your "powers" are increasing rapidly – no need to worry about a few flies and gnats.

But if, during a Neptunian episode, you do not take good spiritual care of yourself – if you do not take time to "stand still like the humming-bird" – then those flies and gnats start buzzing in your ears. They begin to drive you crazy. You become desperate to be rid of them.

And you *can* be rid of them – in more ways than one. There is the higher path, as we have been describing it: meditation, quiet time, inner work. But there are lower paths as well. To travel them, all you have to do is *figure out a way to turn off your advancing psychic sensitivity*. It is not difficult.

- You can arrange to stay hyper-busy, making sure that you are constantly distracted.
- You can arrange to be too exhausted to feel anything.
- You can drink too much, drug too much.
- You can disappear into video games or the Internet.
- You can succumb to various compulsions, sexual, financial, experiential – whatever.

The list of ways we can escape from life is long and familiar – and so is the list of people who have squandered Neptunian periods in exactly those ways.

Turning off one's psychic sensors works fine – at least in the immediate sense. You no longer hear the flies and gnats. The trouble is that you no longer hear the voices of the angels either. No new vision arises. *That means that since there is no new calendar for the coming year, you map it using last year's calendar.* Deadening repetition is the result. After Neptune moves on, maybe you "sober up." The period of that Neptunian stimulus recedes in your mind the way a dream does. You barely remember that period of a year or two. Your memory of it is gauzy, half blacked out. And you probably have no idea of the opportunity you squandered.

All you know is that you feel as if you are about to start your tenth year as a sophomore in high school.

It is better to "stand still like the hummingbird," to try to become more like your favorite spiritual teacher and less like that feral politician, and to wait patiently for those angels to whisper in your ear . . .

A QUICK PRIMER ON THE TRANSITS AND SOLAR ARCS OF JUPITER

In chapter twenty-one of *The Book of Fire*, we explored the transits and solar arcs of Jupiter. Rather than re-writing that material here, or just pasting it word-for-word into this volume, I refer you back to those pages. For now, as a refresher, let's just quickly review a few basic insights into what happens when this planet steps to center stage in your chart.

- Jupiter can be seen as *Santa Claus*. Like Santa, he will often bring you what you want, but be careful what you ask him for. Kids get bamboozled into believing some expensive toy will guarantee them eternal happiness. In an ecstasy of anticipation, they open the present under the Christmas tree – and ninety minutes later, that toy is pushed aside and the kid is in a grumpy mood. Don't be like that! In a Jupiter time, ponder your desires, challenging them before you energize them.

- *All that glitters is not gold* – that cliché reflects the cautionary side of any Jupiter time. So does, "Be careful what you pray for – you might get it."

- But *gold does, in fact, glitter* . . . thinking big is appropriate now. What you really need and what will actually benefit your soul is always "a step up" in a Jupiter time. Don't be shy. Don't be afraid to think big.

- *"If you know what's good for you . . ."* That line smacks of gangsters issuing threats. Strip the line of its *Mafia* overtones and it becomes the single most pivotal Jupiter question. Do you actually *know* what would be good for you? The trouble is that people usually believe that they automatically have the answer. They imagine, for example, that "if only they had a few million dollars," happiness would arise without further effort. We are *socialized* into having false-flag desires that are not good for us. In a Jupiter time, you need to sort that out or you will waste the opportunity.

- *You need a victory now.* Nothing astrological ever happens without reflecting an evolutionary need. When Jupiter comes along, *you need something to go right.* You need to be the architect of an encouraging event or a breakthrough in your life.
- To claim that victory, you need to be *bold* and *audacious.* You need to bet on yourself. Your mantra must be, *roll the dice . . . I feel lucky.*
- *How have you been settling for too little?* To "know what is good for you," you must recognize that you have outgrown some previous limitations. They may have once been relevant and realistic, even helpful, but they are not that way any longer. *You are better than that now.* You are capable of reaching higher.
- *Act as if you deserve more, and you will get it.* Think boldly. Jupiter the King of the Gods does not want to see any small-potatoes bets on the table.

Those eight perspectives are the heart of the matter when Jupiter comes knocking. To take it one step further, here is a three-tiered model of possible responses to a Jupiter stimulus. This section is taken directly from *The Book of Fire,* with only a few changes here and there. It bears repetition in this context too.

THREE LEVELS OF RESPONSE TO JUPITER

Looking at the effects of transiting or solar arc Jupiter, we can distinguish three possibilities. One is truly lucky, one of them is the opposite – and one of them is a subject astrologers typically like to avoid: that is that sometimes Jupiter *seems to do nothing at all.*

Level One: Armed with hard-won self-knowledge and grounded faith in the notion that we are ready to move onward to greater victories and higher levels of self-actualization, we are aware of what is actually good for us. We move boldly and decisively to claim it, remembering always that Lord Jupiter does not like to see small bets on the table. We make a genuinely triumphant breakthrough, both inwardly and existentially. Synchronistically, reality responds to our wise and audacious heart with a big dose of what the world calls good fortune. We indeed "get lucky."

Level Two: Bamboozled by the world into mistaking glitter for gold, we set our sights on seizing a mirage. The "mirage" is actually real enough in the physical sense – but when we attempt to dine on it, it turns to saccharine vapor in our mouths. As U2 put it in their song *Stuck in a Moment*, "You can't get enough of what you don't really need." Remember that kid on Christmas morning, with that longed-for piece of plastic pushed aside? Perhaps a lesson is learned – it is fair to ask ourselves, is there ever really any such thing as a mistake? And yet, the pressing question is, what might have happened if we had used that Jupiter energy with more wisdom and genuine self-awareness . . .?

Level Three: This is the one astrologers often don't like to talk about: the client complains that "nothing happened" – that those bright Jupiter promises we made fizzled down to zero. The primary point I would underscore here is that astrology never fails; it is astrologers who fail. In this case, there is a good chance that the astrologer fell into the *materialist fallacy* – that is, the idea that astrological events must always be materially visible. The reality is that such events can sometimes operate purely on internal and intrapsychic planes. In the case of the apparently failed Jupiter transit, here's what very likely happened: *the client was self-aware enough not to be beguiled by mere glitter – but not bold or audacious enough to actively claim the victory he or she needed and deserved.* That is why "nothing happened." The bad door was closed, but so was the good one. And "what happened" happened on the inward plane alone.

JUPITER, NEPTUNE, AND LOSS

Astrologers often associate Neptune with the possibility of losses, but it is rare to see them connect loss with a Jupiter transit. That connection is real, however – it is not unusual to see reversals and defeats arise during Jupiter-dominated periods. This of course not only runs counter to popular astrological lore, but also to much of what I have written here so far myself. No one would think "choosing glitter over gold" was a positive development – but it is not quite the same as loss.

I mean, you can *keep* all that glitter if you want to.

There are some deep mystical waters here and we will soon fathom them. But let's start out simply by getting our toes wet.

LOSING THAT (FILL IN THE BLANK) WAS THE BEST THING THAT EVER HAPPENED TO ME

When a Jupiter transit or solar arc correlates with loss or an apparent reversal of fortunes, often *in retrospect* we see it as a blessing in disguise. At the time we experienced the loss, we did not interpret it positively at all – only later, looking back, did we see the Divine Hand in it.

Perhaps during a Jupiter transit through an aspect to your natal Venus, someone "steals your partner." You are miserably heartbroken, sitting in a dive bar, drinking straight bourbon and listening to baleful, old Patsy Cline tunes. Down the road, you meet someone new *and find yourself far happier than you had been in the previous relationship.* You have had time to reflect upon how "steal-able" your former partner was, and what that indicated about his or her moral qualities. *Time has given you perspective.* Casually, in a conversation with a friend, you hear yourself saying the words, "losing that faithless slimeball of a turkey was the best thing that ever happened to me."

Jupiter conjuncts your Midheaven by solar arc. Instead of the promotion an astrologer might have promised, you wind up getting fired as the result of a hostile corporate buy-out. Suddenly you have no income. A big part of your identity is shattered. You are stressed and horrified at life's unfairness and your personal misfortune, not to mention having been ripped off by that worthless astrologer. The future looms with nightmarish uncertainty. What will happen to you? Will you become a homeless person?

Three months later, you have found another position. Your professional satisfaction – and maybe even your income – are up by half. You guessed it: a short while later, you find yourself telling a friend that "losing that sweat-shop job was the best thing that ever happened to me".

Jupiter often works exactly that way. At the outset of this chapter, I used the word *faith*. We can use it again as we reflect on the gifts that are often hidden in events that do not go the way that we wanted them to go. *If Jupiter brings you loss, try to have faith.* Try to see that there might be a blessing hidden in it. That is good advice – especially when we come to appreciate its practical twist. With this kind of Jupiter event, once you get a few miles down the road, you are in fact likely to see that loss in a positive light.

So why be miserable now? With faith on your side, maybe you can start being happy today – even when Dumbo and Bimbo are off merrily fornicating somewhere, or when your being fired means that some foreign zillionaire is enjoying an extra helping of caviar while you worry about feeding your kids.

Stay with Dumbo and Bimbo for a moment. At first reading, that line probably made you chuckle. It is more important than it sounds – and it illuminates one of Jupiter's most effective tools when it comes to keeping the faith: *humor.* Laughing at loss and misfortune is an old human gambit for dealing with life's reversals. Near the outset of this chapter, we referenced Jupiter as the *wise clown.* Just think of the healing power of humor, and you have grasped a major remedy in Jupiter's arsenal of medicines.

NEVER FORGET THAT JUPITER RULES PISCES

I banged that drum at the outset of this chapter, and I want to bang it again now. Pisces is of course the last sign of the zodiac. As such, it has a natural correlation with *endings,* and thus sometimes with *losses.* Modern astrologers, blinded as they often are by Jupiter's obvious link to Sagittarius, are better at remembering *Neptune's* Piscean connection than they are with Jupiter.

Even more evident in modern practice is the belief that the twelfth house – with its natural correlation with Pisces – spells bad news. When I was young, I learned to call it the "House of Troubles." While I would never want to put an automatic jinx on any astrological symbol, it does make sense that the final house – like Pisces, the final sign – would have a natural resonance with things falling apart.

On a lark, I just Googled a distinctly out-of-fashion term which I heard a few times when I was a young astrologer: *Sorrowing Pisces.* The search brought me directly to a facsimile edition of a 1904 book by one Coulson Turnbull, entitled *The Divine Language of Celestial Correspondences.* Here is a quote from it:

> *The life of the Pisces persons is one constant battle: the overcoming of obstacles, the meeting of tremendous disappointments, the* Via Crucia, *indeed the Gethsemane before the supreme and heavenly crucifixion of the sensate body, the dark before the light . . .*

It makes you really not want to be a Pisces, doesn't it?

Astrologers today tend not to take such a dim view of the sign, which is obviously a healthy development. I shudder to reflect on how many sensitive Piscean souls were pushed over the edge into clinical depression while reading the dire words of our Mr. Turnbull.

Still, Pisces is indeed the last sign of the zodiac . . . thus invoking the last days, apocalypse, decay and death. The connection with *finality* is hard to avoid.

At a practical level, we see in this symbolism of endings and unravelings a crystal-clear astrological justification for our observation that Jupiter events can coincide with losses. *All we need to do is to remember that Jupiter rules Pisces,* and everything falls into place. That happens in a way that leads me to wonder how astrologers could have ever slipped into the Jupiter-as-Santa-Claus fantasy. To make this dimension of Jupiter click in a more humanistic way, we just have to get past Coulson Turnbull's narrow view that loss is always a tragedy. Many times it isn't. Sometimes we even see benefits right away. Other times they might take a while to sink in.

Think of the death of a beloved ninety-eight-year-old relative. We are sad to lose her – but, because we love her, we are also happy to see her released from the cage that her physical body had become.

But is "happy" really the right word?

Maybe not exactly, but it might be the best word we can find.

Whatever that feeling is, let's call it another face of Jupiter.

MYSTICS DON'T DATE VERY MUCH

Moving on from Jupiter to Neptune and its own connection with loss, let's start by thinking about *the common association between celibacy and a formal commitment to the spiritual path.* The vows of a monk or a nun have often included sexual abstinence. Sex itself is just a starting point as we reflect on a far broader Neptunian theme – and that is that the whole spectrum of spiritual practice really boils down to one simple ideal: *non-attachment.* We get attached to our bodies, our egos, our fabled importance, our money, our looks . . . and every such attachment slows down our progress up the Neptunian mountain.

Still, even today, there are not many yogis in Himalayan caves listed on Match.com. In a loving sexual bond, we naturally *get attached to each other.*

Is that kind of love an impediment to our evolution? For many of us, such shared affection and support is actually quite the opposite: it might in fact help us to *get over ourselves,* and thus actually serve the evolutionary process.

With Neptune in the seventh or eighth house, or in aspect to Venus, perhaps sex *is* your spiritual path.

Thinking about the monastic vow of celibacy is not really our central point; it is just a way of entering the larger question. *The point is that Neptunian mysticism and non-attachment are inseparable concepts.* Sex is just one particularly popular form of attachment. Reflecting on losing our attachment to our sexuality – even abstractly – is a fiercely Neptunian form of meditation. Who would you then be? *How deeply has your gender sunk into your identity?*

The wisest human I ever knowingly met was Khenpo Karthar Rinpoche, a Buddhist *lama.* During the talk he offered, he taught for a couple of hours while sitting on a meditation cushion positioned on a prayer rug. When we came back from the break, he said, "If I returned and saw someone attacking this prayer rug with a knife, I would be angry. It is *my* rug . . ."

He then pointed out that the rug actually belonged to someone else. He had never seen it before today and would probably never see it again. With a stricken look on his face, Khenpo Karthar said, *"Two hours and I am already attached to a rug . . ."*

Again, that is probably the wisest human being I've ever met.

The journey is long.

Mysticism and celibacy is just one thread in the larger tapestry of spiritual practices centered on achieving a state of non-attachment. Mystics have often taken *vows of poverty* too. They often intentionally obscure their physical attractiveness – shaved heads, dull clothing, faces mostly covered: vanity is just one attachment to be defeated. They *fast,* thus defeating their attachment to food. They practice silence and isolation. They sleep on hard mattresses under thin blankets.

Allied with conscious intent, such practices of non-attachment have produced genuine saints. These methods work, in other words. But in and of themselves, they are nothing – only *behaviors,* that is all.

"Giving things up" can be nothing but simple masochism – nothing but pointless, purposeless, self-punishment. Such asceticism can reflect shame and self-loathing, a degradation of the human spirit, not something that uplifts it. That mere *behavior* of non-attachment can actually hold a soul back in its evolution.

Worse, this unspeakable crime has often been perpetrated on innocent souls "in the name of God."

It is enough to make you believe in Satan.

NEPTUNE AND NON-ATTACHMENT

We come to delicate crossroads. During a Neptunian transit or solar arc, *might you need to give something up?* The question, as you are perhaps beginning to see, is a slippery one. There are healthy forms of "giving things up," and unhealthy ones too. Let's start with a simple answer: *probably.* Probably you will have to give something up.

Along comes Neptune, and you need a fresh vision for your life. As we saw earlier, angels are whispering in your ear. To hear their voices, you need to "stand still like the hummingbird." *What will you give up in order to create space for that listening silence in yourself?* You are probably attached to the general buzz of your life, or at least entangled in it.

Some of that buzz needs to go.

During your Neptune transit, do you surrender your role on the committee? Do you relinquish the presidency of the local astrological society?

Note that we are not *judging* those entanglements negatively. Nobody is using a word such as "sin" or anything even close to it. We are miles away from that kind of shaming. We are only recognizing that in order to respond well and consciously to Neptunian stimulus, *you have to simplify your life.* You have to make some space. That inevitably means letting something go, even something honorable, desirable, and good. That is how we hear angels when they whisper. That is how we welcome them. A fresh vision is trying to arise out of the depths of your consciousness. It is as if you are *molting a personality,* taking off the "tight shoes" of everything you are habituated to being.

You need to make space within the structural institutions of your life for that new start. Entanglements must fall away – and they typically do, even without your intending it, often propelled by the eternal laws of synchronicity. Things happen that set you free.

Here once again we see the common Piscean threads which bind Neptune to Jupiter. Your sense of identity boils down to a narrative in your head, supported by a set of relationships, responsibilities, and other external manifestations: perhaps a job, a primary relationship, family, and so on.

When any of those structures dissolve, the path of wisdom during a Neptunian time is to just let them go.

The Neptunian psychological process of release may not be as simple as Jupiter's "losing that *(whatever)* was the best thing that ever happened to me." With Neptune, it often has a closer kinship to the way we felt when our beloved ninety-eight-year-old relative passed away: poignant, complicated – and necessary.

Remember the word I invoked at the beginning of this chapter? The word that runs through this Piscean clan like blood runs through your veins?

The word was *faith*.

Sometimes faith is all you have. The good news is that, when either Jupiter or Neptune come calling, that faith is poised to grow and deepen.

FORGIVENESS

As I invoke the sacred word "forgiveness," I feel a need to immediately present my Plutonian credentials – I want, in other words, to be as honest about it as I can be, even if in doing so I might seem hard or critical. *In my view, an awful lot of what flies under the banner of forgiveness is actually nothing but denial, suppression, and avoidance.* Religion, along with much popular spiritual philosophy, pressures us to be forgiving – and shames us if we are slow to move in that direction.

The main result is that many of us learn how to fake it.

My attitude is that no one should ever *strive* for forgiveness. I am aware of how counter-intuitive that statement probably sounds. Here is why I express it that way: I feel that true forgiveness only comes at the end of a long, emotionally-fraught process – a process that probably includes feeling rage, despair, even hatred. Those are obviously not virtuous emotions, but they are at least honest ones.

You probably recognize the voice of the Scorpio clan in the forgoing words. As we have seen, those symbols also play an essential role in the processes of healing, regeneration, and recovery. Without that kind of Scorpionic honesty, we waste our time trying to solve non-existent problems, while carefully avoiding any awareness of our real ones. We might even *fake forgiveness*, perhaps without even being aware that we are doing it.

As we reflect on Jupiter and Neptune, rather than thinking of forgiveness as a virtue toward which we should strive, it is more helpful to frame it as a *grace* – a gift that arises naturally at the end of a long, profoundly Scorpionic process. As I speak of endings, the astrological mind naturally turns to the last sign – to the Pisces clan, in other words. *That tells us that the final capping grace of forgiveness resides in the realm of Jupiter, Neptune, the twelfth house, and the sign of the Fishes.*

Back in the fifth grade, you had a boyfriend. Your relationship was as chaste as Jesus, Mary, and Joseph, but it represented a source of pride for you. It symbolized your emerging social sophistication and hinted at your prospects for attaining adult status. Your boyfriend was a cutie too, and so his choosing you above all others also enhanced your social position.

Along came evil Sabina to steal him away. Word was that she kissed with her tongue sticking out. Eeew. There were rumors of even worse things she might do. In your eleven-year-old mind, she quickly became *Sabina the Whore*. Maybe you were not even exactly sure what that word meant, but you knew it was bad and so was she.

Years slipped by. By then, Sabina had moved away. You graduated from high school and went on with your life. Maybe you got married.

Before you know it, here comes your twentieth high school reunion. There you are in the banquet hall faced with a lot of semi-familiar faces. Who walks in but Sabina?

As soon as you recognize her, words form by reflex in your mind: *"the whore . . ."*

Immediately you laugh at yourself. You get up and approach her. You say your name. She recognizes you. In that moment, each of you remembers the ancient drama and the poisonous animosity – and the sleepless nights – it created way back then in the fifth grade.

You each let all of that go a long, long time ago. You hug Sabina and she hugs you back. You don't even need to talk about it.

That is forgiveness.

Such forgiveness requires no effort at all. It is the *result of efforts that you have already made.* That is the *Piscean grace* that comes at the end of a long Scorpionic process.

. . . a process of healing, regeneration, and recovery that begins with attuning to our hearts in the Cancer clan, proceeds through wrestling with our hearts in the Scorpio clan, and culminates in transcendence and spiritual liberation with transits, progressions, or solar arcs involving the Fishes.

ENTERING PISCES

Depending on the geometry of your chart, there are planets that will enter Pisces at some point and some that never will, simply because life is too short for them to get there. My own Neptune, for example, will cross into Pisces by solar arc on August 28, 2084, a few months after my 135th birthday.

If I'm around then, I will have a party in Tahiti. You're invited. In fact, I'll fly you there.

Transiting Mercury, meanwhile, has entered Pisces about seventy times since I was born – and since we are talking about a transit, it did the same thing for everybody at exactly the same times – transits happen in the sky we all share. But Pisces is on my fourth house cusp, so the meaning of the transit was different for me than it was for most other people. It always had a more interior or domestic flavor.

By *progression,* in my personal chart, it happens that the Sun, Mercury, Venus, and Mars have all entered Pisces in my lifetime. The situation is a little unusual – most people would never have had that much Piscean experience. It was that way for me simply because those planets were all in Sagittarius, Capricorn, or Aquarius when I was born. They didn't have far to go to get into Pisces, in other words.

If, on the other hand, you were born with those planets all in Cancer or Leo, they will never get that far – unless you live to be bizarrely ancient enough to frighten little children, they will never reach Pisces.

If that does happen, maybe you can promise us all a party in Tahiti too.

When – and if – a planet enters Pisces by transit, progression or solar arc, it senses *intimations of the psychic vastness that surrounds it.* The planet becomes fascinated by the call of that spaciousness, pulled by it, eager to heed it.

Some people will frame this call in religious or spiritual terms, while others might use different language. To them, it might feel like a need for quiet time, or a pull toward immersing oneself in creativity and imagination.

On the dark side of the spectrum, some will experience it as a desire for oblivion or even the extinction of consciousness.

A planet entering Pisces, in other words, can manifest in many different ways – but always underlying it is *the strange gravity of those vast realms of mind that lie beyond the tight, restrictive frontiers of normal consciousness.* Mars might feel the need to *fight* for such experiences, while Jupiter feels it *deserves* them and Venus feels the need to *share* them.

Each planet retains its own intrinsic nature, in other words – but it also finds itself mesmerized by the mantra of *beyond, beyond, beyond . . . and beyond that too.*

22

NEPTUNE AND JUPITER TIMES, PISCES TIMES: THE BUILDING BLOCKS

One of the joys of working with Jupiter is its convenient habit of spending about one year in each sign. You hardly need an ephemeris or a computer to work with it. Lying in bed with insomnia, you can link Jupiter's transiting position to various glorious victories and notorious pratfalls in your life. "Six years ago . . . let's see, that'd be six *signs* ago . . ."

All of that is simply because it takes Jupiter twelve years to orbit the Sun. As we saw back in chapter sixteen, the exact figure is actually 11.862 years – which falls just seven weeks short of an even dozen.

As we saw back in chapter sixteen, Jupiter's transits are powerful, especially when it is near a station and thus moving slowly. By progression, Jupiter is too slow to be worth your attention – and of course Jupiter's solar arcs run at the usual pace of about one degree per year.

In the thumbnail sketches which follow, we will consider Jupiter as it passes through each of the signs and houses. When it enters any of them by transit, it will stay there for about a year – although that figure varies more with the houses since they are not all the same width. In any case, that lets us know that Jupiter has long enough to develop some real psychic momentum, but the passage is brief enough that the mind can easily encompass it.

By solar arc, Jupiter will be in that new sign or house for something closer to three decades, so it represents a major change in the patterns of your life.

Leonard Nimoy – Mr. Spock of *Star Trek* fame – experienced solar arc Jupiter aligning with his Midheaven in April 1963. His biggest breakthrough actually came a little later. *Star Trek* did not air until 1966, but that means that Jupiter was only three degrees or so into his tenth house at that point – still within reasonable orbs of a conjunction with his Midheaven. Earlier, and right as Jupiter was hitting his Midheaven, Nimoy went from playing bit parts to more prestigious appearances on many of the big TV shows of that period – *Perry Mason, Combat, The Outer Limits, The Virginian, The Man From U.N.C.L.E.* . . .

In classic fashion, Jupiter opened *doorways to opportunity* for him.

Meanwhile, Nimoy's co-star, William Shatner, was also experiencing Jupiter's influence. When *Star Trek* first aired, transiting Jupiter was less than a month from making the first in a series of three trine aspects to his natal Sun, while solar arc Jupiter was trining his very "Captain Kirk" north node of the Moon in Aries.

Playing the part of a starship commander was probably good practice for him spiritually, as well as a professional gold mine for a young actor.

In *The Book of Fire,* we reflected on Jupiter contacting each of the other planets by aspect. For a more complete perspective, you might want to review that material. In that volume, we also offered "cookbook" paragraphs about Jupiter's journey through the twelve astrological houses. For the sake of completeness and easy reference, we will include that same house-ingress material again here, with just a few tweaks and literary repentances on my part.

Do keep perspective though – if you live a normal span of years, Jupiter will *transit* through each of your twelve houses perhaps seven times, but you would have to live a third of a millennium for it to enter each house by solar arc. Much of what follows will, in other words, be of more practical use to you in thinking of Jupiter's transits through the houses.

Our thumbnail sketches of Jupiter's passage through each sign are new material, not covered in any previous volume.

Neptune, meanwhile, moves at a much more languorous pace than Jupiter, taking about 165 years to make a single circuit of the zodiac. That works out to any Neptune transit through a sign lasting about fourteen years, with minor variations. Neptune's solar arcs move at the usual pace – and I would suggest that you ignore its progressions entirely since they are so slow.

After we are finished with Jupiter, we will explore Neptune sign by sign and house by house in the same cookbook fashion.

All of that Neptunian material is new here in *The Book of Water*.

JUPITER PASSING THROUGH THE TWELVE HOUSES

When Jupiter moves out of the twelfth house and into the first house . . . the transition signals a major green light in your evolutionary journey. It is time to bet big, especially if you are betting on yourself. The wind is in your sails and The Force is With You. If you drop your morning toast off the table, it will now land butter-side up almost every time. Angels are watching over you, not to mention your toast. Entering contests – literally – is actually a good idea now. The odds of winning are markedly improved – but your luck will be even better if you "enter contests" in areas of your existing life that are ripe for improvement. Dare to hope for a better tomorrow. That hope is what triggers the magic. It is time to take chances in areas where you are actively, personally engaged, such as your home, your profession, your relationships and so forth. I cannot help but be vague – that is because while the other eleven houses tend to refer to specific areas of life, the first house operates in a more generalized way. It is really about any area in which choice and volition play a part. Ultimately, this Jupiter event is about developing faith in the magical, life-shaping power of your *will* and *intentions*. Every arena of life provides an effective laboratory for that kind of evolutionary work. Dare to believe in yourself – and then put your money where your mouth is.

When Jupiter moves out of the first house and into the second house . . . the focus of activity shifts to the *resource base* necessary for the support and continuation of whatever intentions you set moving while Jupiter was in the first house. Classically, the second house is about *money*, and finding ways to cash out your dreams might be part of what is happening now. Do you need to ask someone for financial help? Do you need to be bold enough to take out a loan? Those are definite possibilities. But the second house is not only about money – there are many other kinds of *resources* in the world. They can take the form of *skills* you need to acquire or strategic *alliances* you need to create. In all cases, the key is to *ask for what you need.* You're building confidence in yourself now – but it is helpful not to frame confidence in narrowly psychological terms. Jupiter in the second house is not as much about "giving yourself a big hug" as it is about providing your- self with *concrete, objective reasons* to have faith in your dream.

When Jupiter moves out of the second house and into the third house . . . your voice needs to be heard. You really do have something important to say; you are a fountain of good ideas. Have faith in that! Hold your head high and speak up. If you are a shy person, join a discussion group or take part in a theatrical performance or join Toastmasters – during this period, it is imperative not to let shyness control you. For your journey through life to continue unfolding on its natural path, you must now realize that you have been underestimating your intelligence, your level of articulation, and the helpful relevance of your ideas. Is it time to write a letter to the editor or to start that book you have always wanted to write? There's al- ways an element of *learning* connected with the third house. With Jupiter there, precious educational opportunities arise. These are characterized by the right teachers showing up, armed with the right teachings – which is to say the teachings that are most relevant to putting some polish on your own thoughts. This is typically a *busy* time, one that might make you feel like a billiard ball bouncing around a pool table. Underlying the chaos, the universe is communicating unexpected information to you via omens, repeated messages, and synchronicities. Pay attention! There is something you need to learn if you are going to move forward successfully from here.

When Jupiter moves out of the third house and into the fourth house . . . the time has come to slow down and take stock of *who you have become.* If you quiet yourself enough to do that, you will probably like what you discover. You are better than you thought you were. That is true in many categories of life – and each one of those breakthroughs is a natural side effect of the work you have been doing on yourself. Beware, though – if you fail to slow down and take stock, you will not realize what you have accomplished. You won't claim the prize that you have earned. More is at stake here than the possibility of missing a chance to pat yourself on the back: *your dreams and intentions in life need to be placed on a more ambitious foundation.* Right now, you are like the seed of a beautiful flower germinating invisibly under the ground. Water that seed! In order to experience the quiet that is necessary at this phase of your journey, you may need to make some changes in your domestic situation. You might, for example, need to move to a more pleasant home. You might need to rethink some of your family responsibilities in a way that leaves you more inward time. As ever with Jupiter, it is a good time to bet on yourself. Ask for anything you need in order to better hear the still small voice within, and there is an excellent chance that blessing will come your way.

When Jupiter moves out of the fourth house and into the fifth house . . . the seed you planted in the fourth house is ready to blossom into a beautiful flower. This is a time of *creative self-expression* – and probably a time of being recognized and appreciated for it. For any of that to happen, you need to take the risk of stepping out onto the stage of life. Face those butterflies in your stomach and put yourself out there in front of people. Inwardly you will probably feel vulnerable. Don't worry – outwardly you will probably look a lot more confident than you feel. For all of us, life can sometimes be a battering experience. Our ability to continue to hope and to have faith is often challenged. During this period of your life, opportunities arise for you to *renew your basic animal joy*. From the evolutionary point of view, it is imperative now that you *have a really good time*. That statement might sound lightweight – until you reflect on the accumulated impact of all the disappointments and hard things you have experienced in your life. This is not about whining; it is about the *art of recovering* from all of that disappointment and heartbreak. Now is the time to practice that art. So celebrate! Dance! Spend some money on yourself. Why do you think God gave you that *Visa* card?

When Jupiter moves out of the fifth house and into the sixth house . . . the focus shifts to an increase in your workload and an inflation of your responsibilities. Until we reflect deeply on those words, such a prophecy naturally sounds gloomy. The key is to realize that work and responsibility do not necessarily equate with misery – although of course sometimes they do. What makes the difference? The dull slog of "doing what must be done" rarely brings anyone much joy, especially when we feel that we could train an intelligent chimpanzee to do the same job. But what about doing *work that actually matters* to you? What about being *really good at something* that gives you true pleasure and fulfillment – and probably adds something wonderful to another person's life in the bargain? Your evolutionary effort now lies in realizing that you have been underestimating your capacity for *joyful competence*. Here's an illustration: since you are reading this book, I know that you are interested in astrology. Some of the most fun you will ever have is surfing the waves of an intense astrological consultation with a deeply engaged client. Is it time for you to "hang out your shingle" as an astrologer? Not all of us need to become professional astrologers, but that scenario illustrates the central point: *there are forms of work and responsibility which are worthy of you and which can give you a lot of joy.* All the laws of synchronicity suggest that exactly those sorts of opportunities now lie before you. What if you don't see them? Then instead look for mentors, role models, and teachers who are ahead of you on that road. Follow in their footsteps; those footsteps will soon be your own.

When Jupiter moves out of the sixth house and into the seventh house . . . help and support are on the way. Even though the seventh house is conventionally framed as the house of marriage, we need to cast our nets more widely. How much, for example, do you value your treasured friendships? Those people are precious seventh house gifts too. Jupiter entering the seventh house can bring you new friends. It can also bring you *catalytic allies* in your creative or professional life. None of this is to say that romantic or intimate developments are unlikely at this time; they are common under this kind of Jupiter influence as well. Maybe you will "meet someone." What if you are already in a good relationship? Jupiter's question then becomes how can you make that existing relationship even better? To lift these statements above mere fortune-telling, we have to add an active ingredient: a recognition that, *in your intimate life, it is time to stop settling for too little.* To find these precious soul-friends, you need to elevate your vision. How have you shortchanged yourself in terms of the people you have attracted into your life – or in terms of the existing "contracts" with them? You have come to a time when you need some help; the help is there somewhere right before your eyes. Look *up* toward a higher kind of love, and you will find it.

When Jupiter moves out of the seventh house and into the eighth house . . . opportunities arise that, while emotionally daunting, can lay the foundation for many satisfying developments down the road. Facing your own woundedness and the systems of reflexive defense that have grown up around it can put a knot in your stomach and a lump in your throat. Anyone who has done psychological work knows exactly what I'm talking about. But once accomplished, that kind of inner healing liberates us from looping patterns of self-limiting or self-destructive behavior. It is a fast track to deeper aliveness. Opportunities to do exactly that kind of healing are abundant now. Pivotal conversations happen, counselors appear, secrets are revealed. Try to accept these fierce treasures gratefully, even if they hurt at the time. Often the triggers for such breakthroughs involve sexual energy, the impact of sexual soulmates, and the unique, soul-revealing, intimacy of such bonds. Sometimes the cathartic dramas involve someone passing through that mysterious doorway we call death. It sounds strange to think of death as a gift – but someone sharing their end-of-life experience with you can be a treasure that you will hold precious for the rest of your own time on earth.

When Jupiter moves out of the eighth house and into the ninth house . . . at the simplest and most concrete level, this event alerts you to an impending *travel opportunity.* We can also predict the appearance of opportunities to *expand your horizons* in other ways: classes, lectures, conversations with people who have something exotic and valuable to teach you. A lofty philosophical note makes itself heard in your life. At a deeper level, you are harvesting the fruit of the inner work you have already done while Jupiter was passing through the eighth house. *The underlying point is that the saner you become, the more clearly you see reality and the more boldly you participate in it.* You have made some significant breakthroughs over the past year or two; these breakthroughs have "cleaned your windows." Your understanding of life is less distorted. In a sense, your intellect is now trying to catch up with what your deeper psyche has *already* learned. You are rewriting your philosophy of life in a way that reflects your hard-won wisdom. To add some fresh air to this valuable process, it is helpful for you to experience an outward change of scenery, along with some unfamiliar educational input. All of that simply serves the purpose of breaking up stubborn patterns in your existing mental and existential routines.

When Jupiter moves out of the ninth house and into the tenth house . . . it is time for the inner efforts you have been making to translate into an improvement in your worldly status and circumstances. Career is the classic focus of the tenth house, and it is common for professional opportunities to open up at this time: new jobs, increases in pay, promotions, and so on. But the scope of the symbolism is broader: Jupiter passing through the tenth house also refers to elevations in your *status in your community* – your general reputation and how you look to people who do not actually know you personally. At the deepest level, it is about your mission calling you – and little in this world is as good for the dignity of a human soul as doing work that you know really truly matters. As always with Jupiter, the underlying evolutionary question is, how have you been underestimating yourself? It is time to apply that kind of thinking to your role in the world – to actively make a bid for more recognition and recompense. You need a chance to show the world the full extent of your capabilities. Look for it and it will be there, and that positive feedback is regenerative for you. Synchronistically, worldly doors open now – the laws of the universe guarantee that. Here is what they do not guarantee: that you recognize these doors and march through them with your head held high.

When Jupiter moves out of the tenth house and into the eleventh house . . . the focus is on *updating* your *priorities* and *goals* in life. You have probably achieved a position of some strength in your community. Chances are that, at least from an exterior point of view, things are looking pretty decent for you now, maybe even enviable. Weirdly, underlying those appearances, there is an insidious sense of tedium. *Is this all there is?* The time has come to look ahead and reflect upon a fresh and more enlivening set of long-term dreams and ambitions – ones worthy of the person you have actually become. It is time to think big and to plan accordingly. This is not about impressing other people; it is about recognizing that you are capable of impressing yourself – of doing more than you have ever done before. Speculate freely about that possibility; let your imagination conjure up a future you would be grateful and proud to live. As you do that, look around you: you will find *allies*, people who can be helpful to you. *Network* with them; you will find that their goals and their strengths are convergent with your own. It is a time of *social synergy*. Traditionally, the eleventh house was called the house of friends. It is more accurate to think of it as a house of networking and alliances. The key here is realizing that in order to recognize these relationships, you must first have framed a direction in life that inspires you. *Without clear goals, how can you possibly recognize the people who might help you achieve them?*

When Jupiter moves out of the eleventh house and into the twelfth house . . . what the wisest part of you truly desires at this point is a quiet mountaintop, away from the craziness of the world – a place where you can reflect and listen to the "still, small voice within." You are actually preparing the ground for a colorful, life-changing new start when Jupiter crosses your Ascendant. You are probably not thinking in those terms at the moment. No worry; if you take this opportunity to reflect, then the right doors will open for you when the time comes. Doors will open in any case. How are you going to know which doors are the right ones for you? The answer brings us back to you sitting on that "quiet mountaintop," attuning yourself to inspiration. If you have made time to receive the vision that is pressing at you, your actions and decisions as Jupiter crosses your Ascendant will be the right ones for you. Because of the laws of synchronicity, opportunities for this kind of precious quiet time away from the buzz of your life crystallize before you now. They may come into your life packaged as contact with spiritual teachings or teachers – or they may be as simple as a friend offering you the use of a cabin somewhere far from the madding crowd. Whatever form the gift takes, *angels are trying to whisper in your ears.* Take time to listen. Those angels love you and they are a lot smarter than you. It takes a real fool to ignore them.

JUPITER PASSING THROUGH THE TWELVE SIGNS

When Jupiter transits into a new sign, it is of course doing the same thing for everyone on Earth at that same moment. But if Jupiter enters Aries in your personal sixth house, those values and motivations impact your work and your responsibilities in the world. If it enters Aries in your seventh house, you are invited to bring those attitudes to bear on your intimate life.

JUPITER ENTERING ARIES

The Values That Guide Me To A Wise Victory: As a Spiritual Warrior, I choose my battles consciously. I am not afraid to walk away from pointless ones. Once chosen, I aim to win them. I use just enough force, and no more than that.

A Winning Attitude: I can do this. I deserve this. I have a right to this. I would rather die trying than to not try at all.

If It Is Glitter, Not Gold: My ego needed the kind of boost that comes, not so much from winning as from defeating someone else. The prize I have won pleases my pride, but not my soul.

The Missed Opportunity: I let my main chance slip by. I hesitated, and the moment was lost. I watched as others claimed a victory that should have been my own.

JUPITER ENTERING TAURUS

The Values That Guide Me To A Wise Victory: As I reflect upon this crossroads, I realize that what I must rightly prioritize now is my peace of mind – that is more important than anything else. Simplicity leads to calm and a feeling of security. Happiness is wanting what I have, rather than having everything that I want.

A Winning Attitude: I do not care if I impress anyone. My serenity does not derive from appearances or from material success beyond what I actually need. I don't sweat the small stuff. I listen to my body. I meet its needs and I heed its requests.

If It Is Glitter, Not Gold: My victories and successes are all of a worldly, material nature. Their emptiness is revealed in the fact that they do not lead to serenity or to peace.

The Missed Opportunity: Preoccupation with the endless onslaught of practical issues blinds me to a chance to drop some useless complications from my life and thereby achieve inner peace.

JUPITER ENTERING GEMINI

The Values That Guide Me To A Wise Victory: As I study the existential landscape that lies before me, I realize that I simply do not have enough information to navigate it. There is so much that I do not know – and so many unimagined opportunities hidden only by my own ignorance. I let simple curiosity and my hunger to learn guide me into this rich informational matrix. I trust my fascinations.

A Winning Attitude: I am not dumb, but I am ignorant – and ignorance is 100% curable. My mind is open to possibilities. I am a beginner, and proud of it.

If It Is Glitter, Not Gold: My prideful need to be seen as the expert might enthrall an audience, but it teaches me nothing that I did not already know.

The Missed Opportunity: I fail to see the one critical clue or missing piece of information that could have turned a golden key in the door to my best future.

JUPITER ENTERING CANCER

The Values That Guide Me To A Wise Victory: As I think about the many possible paths that lie open to me, I realize that wisdom is begging me to turn inward and to listen to my own heart. I also realize that happiness is an inner state, not an outer one. I recognize that of all the possible outer conditions I might create, the ones that are most directly supportive of happiness are about home, family, and the people I love.

A Winning Attitude: I know what is good for me and I am willing to bet the house on getting it – and that means claiming some quiet time, both alone and with a few special people. Love thrives on peaceful shared silences. I resolve not to starve my loved ones for attention.

If It Is Glitter, Not Gold: My ego intervenes and I focus on "looking wise and benevolent" rather than truly being present. I demand that family "keep up appearances" rather than my actually listening to them. I put energy into "house" rather than "home."

The Missed Opportunity: I hide inside my shell rather than sharing my life with the people I love. Instead of sitting quietly together by fire waiting for the right words to well up from the psychic depths, we watch a distracting movie full of car chases and special effects.

JUPITER ENTERING LEO

The Values That Guide Me To A Wise Victory: As I study the existential landscape that lies before me, I realize that it is now my turn to step out bravely onto the stage of life and show everyone what I've got. I am willing to take that chance. I am willing to risk being that vulnerable – and to trust that what I have to give will be appreciated.

A Winning Attitude: I am ready. I am good at what I do. I have faith in my ability to improvise in the moment, even with "people looking." There's no one here but us humans . . .

If It Is Glitter, Not Gold: My deep-down insecurity takes over, and I focus on eliciting awe-struck worship rather than on authentic self-revelation. Even if I receive applause, it feels like sawdust in my mouth – empty and meaningless, as if "my hair" got the praise rather than my soul.

The Missed Opportunity: I succumb to hesitation and self-consciousness, letting a chance to shine pass me by. I keep a gift that should have been generously given.

JUPITER ENTERING VIRGO

The Values That Guide Me To A Wise Victory: As I reflect upon this crossroads, I realize that skills which I have been developing for years are now flowering. They are "near enough to perfect" that it is time for me to offer them confidently to anyone who needs them. I have matured; I am ready – and others are ready for me, needing to receive my competent support.

A Winning Attitude: I am very good at what I do. My skill-levels are extraordinary and I am near the height of my power. There is genuine joy in service; the time has come for my competence to be appreciated and recognized.

If It Is Glitter, Not Gold: My dignity rests on the false basis of the exercise of skills and execution of responsibilities which have little or no connection to who I really am. I am good at something which I personally do not value or take very seriously.

The Missed Opportunity: I let a chance go by to be recognized for what I am good at doing, or I miss an opportunity to make a breakthrough step in my capabilities – I fail, for example, to sit with a teacher or mentor who could have been a powerful catalyst for me.

JUPITER ENTERING LIBRA

The Values That Guide Me To A Wise Victory: As I consider the forks in the road ahead, I realize any kind of black-and-white thinking now would be a mistake. I strive for balance, sometimes between opposite paths that seem hard to reconcile. I value a sense of paradox and I am tolerant of life's moral and practical ambiguities. I look for worthy partners in whatever undertakings I face – people with whom I am proud to associate *Winning Attitude*: I can deal well with complexity. *Wise compromises* are a characteristic of the path to the higher ground for me now. Meanwhile, I resist the comforting temptations of any kind of dogmatic certainty. I can think for myself, but I also listen to helpful advice. Two heads are wiser than one.

If It Is Glitter, Not Gold: I sacrifice too much of my truth on the altar of appearances. In surrendering my autonomy, I create a false and unstable peace. I put a new coat of paint on a fallen-down house. I am photographed with "cool people."

The Missed Opportunity: I dither; I try to turn left and right at the same time. I smile when my heart is frowning – or crying. I wasted my time arranging to be photographed with those "cool people".

JUPITER ENTERING SCORPIO

The Values That Guide Me To A Wise Victory: As I contemplate the existential landscape that lies before me, I recognize that what now serves me best is penetrating honesty and bold directness. There are no guarantees, but if ever the simple truth were going to trigger a breakthrough, now is the moment for it.

A Winning Attitude: I put my clearest truth on the table and I accept whatever results might follow. I have faith; I am optimistic – but I am strong enough to play whatever hand is dealt me. In the end, the only person with whom I live is myself. I will keep my conscience clear.

If It Is Glitter, Not Gold: Mere drama can be the Fool's Gold version of truthfulness and reality. Shakespeare said it best: "It is a tale told by an idiot, full of sound and fury, signifying nothing."

The Missed Opportunity: I silenced myself when I should have spoken. I was diplomatic when I should have been direct. I was nice when I should have been fierce and had a right to be angry.

JUPITER ENTERING SAGITTARIUS

The Values That Guide Me To A Wise Victory: As I choose among the many possible paths that are open to me now, I keep in mind that this chapter of my life is not about getting myself tangled up in trivialities and minutia. My life is now, above all, a *quest for meaning*. Among all paths, I choose the one that is the most bold and audacious. I smell an adventure.

A Winning Attitude: I live in the ever-present knowledge that life is short and that every moment is precious and will never return. I scoff at the silliness of "practicality" as a response to fragile realities of human existence. I seize opportunity when it presents itself.

If It Is Glitter, Not Gold: Sunglasses do not make a rock star. Spiritual wealth is not counted in a bank. Robes turn no one into a guru. Ego inflates; I trip over my own pride, creating a blunder of over-extension.

The Missed Opportunity: Caution takes over. I fear insecurity or failure or practical reversals to the point that I let a chance to pass through a magical doorway go to waste.

JUPITER ENTERING CAPRICORN

The Values That Guide Me To A Wise Victory: As I reflect upon the possibilities built into this moment of time, I recognize that the right pathway for me now is the one that leads straight up the steepest mountain in the range that lies before me. Difficulty does not intimidate me; it attracts me.

A Winning Attitude: I can do anything – at least anything my soul-path requires of me – if I stick to it in a spirit of self-discipline, dedication, and devotion. With that attitude, even what seems impossible yields to me over time. "Undaunted" is my middle name.

If It Is Glitter, Not Gold: I seek success as it was defined for me by other people. I get to the peak of the wrong mountain. I may be praised, envied, and respected for it, but deep down inside, I know it was never really my mountain.

The Missed Opportunity: I pall at the foot of the mountain I am to climb, losing heart as I contemplate the distant peak. I create reasons why this could not possibly be *my* mountain. I find a minor little hill and I climb that instead.

JUPITER ENTERING AQUARIUS

The Values That Guide Me To A Wise Victory: As I consider the forks in the road ahead, I realize that the right one for me to take now might very well be a path that everyone is warning me against or which they simply do not value or take very seriously. Worse, there may be an unspoken consensus that I am not worthy or capable enough to succeed at what I choose to do. Thinking for myself, independently of anyone else's praise or blame, is my North Star at this crossroads.

A Winning Attitude: I trust my own judgment even if others do not support it. I am not afraid to define victory and success in my own way. What other people think of me does not greatly concern me.

If It Is Glitter, Not Gold: My "freedom and independence" are wasted in pointless idiosyncrasies – quirkish rebellions, shocking views designed only for effect, even silly glasses or cartoonish outfits.

The Missed Opportunity: I allow other people's lack of faith or imagination to blunt my faith in my own genius. I come up with a brilliant idea, then I look at the skeptical faces around me and I say, "Nawwww . . ."

JUPITER ENTERING PISCES

The Values That Guide Me To A Wise Victory: As I think about the many possible paths that are open to me now, I make the wisest choices when I focus on two realities. First, my guiding principle is that ultimately nothing is more central to my well-being than taking good care of my spiritual life. Second, I recognize that I am ready to graduate to a new and higher level of spiritual practice. I have outgrown the old ones.

A Winning Attitude: I am on my way to Enlightenment. The road ahead may still be long, but I am on it. It is working. I can do it. I am worthy of this path and I am ready to follow it further up the mystical mountain.

If It Is Glitter, Not Gold: Ego itself never gets enlightened, any more than a lobster can become a ballerina. Instead of opening to the luminosity beneath it, I pump energy into the spiritual aspects of my personality – my impressive metaphysical fluency, my flawless yoga postures, the length of my meditations.

The Missed Opportunity: I sleep through it. A chance for a spiritual breakthrough slips through my fingers because I did not have enough faith in myself that I could do it and that it was the right time for it to happen.

Neptune Passing Through The Twelve Signs

Given Neptune's long orbit, some of these sign-passages will happen before and after your time on Earth, but not while you are here. In the interests of completeness, I include all twelve of them.

NEPTUNE ENTERING ARIES

The Emerging Archetype: The Spiritual Warrior

My Most Skillful Current Method of Soul Growth: Facing challenges. It is now time for me to face people and situations which frighten me. Within reason, I need to take some risks. Looking death in the eye. Spiritual adventures call me.

Synchronistic Correlates: The demon we call fear stands between me and a soul breakthrough. Opportunities arise for sudden enlightenment experiences. The doorway to spiritual adventures opens before me. Rivals or antagonists appear – they are, simultaneously, a) obstacles on my path, and b) my path.

Lost and Wasted: I am seduced by blood-myths, martyrdom, and glorious lost causes. I seek redemption in self-destructive behaviors. I become drunk on the poisonous elixir of anger, and mistake it for righteous spiritual indignation.

NEPTUNE ENTERING TAURUS

The Emerging Archetype: The Earth Mother or Earth Father.

My Most Skillful Current Method of Soul Growth: Promoting calmness of mind. Silencing the endless chatter of my inner dialog. The time has come to Integrate normal everyday life with higher mindfulness. Body-centered paths present themselves to me: Yoga, *Tai Chi*, and Sacred Dance. Listening to music. Mantra and chant. Sitting silently in nature. Mystical communion with animals.

Synchronistic Correlates: Opportunities to be in quiet places are now offered to me. Contacts with Earth-centered forms of spiritual practice crystalize before my eyes – Native American, Taoist or Celtic paths, for example. Animals appear as signs and guides. Music lifts me up.

Lost and Wasted: I become lost in materialistic delusions. I confuse outward conditions with inward states. I give too much power to material forms, giving away my spiritual power to crystals, crosses, meditation cushions, or psychoactive chemicals, forgetting that the true source of that power does not lie in the physical realm.

NEPTUNE ENTERING GEMINI

The Emerging Archetype: The Spiritual Teacher

My Most Skillful Current Method of Soul Growth: Above all, metaphysical learning accelerates my current evolutionary passages. I devote myself to sacred teachings, trying to approach them as a beginner, without pretense. I accept that my understanding itself requires correction. With this humble posture solidly established, I can then learn by teaching. Faced with spiritual need in others, I say things that I did not know that I knew. Higher beings help me find the words.

Synchronistic Correlates: The spiritual and metaphysical literature of the world falls off shelves and lands on my feet. Omens and signs abound. Teachers appear. Their words have a fresh impact on me, shaking me out of previous certainties.

Lost and Wasted: I talk about spirituality rather than experiencing it. I mistake thoughts for direct contact with higher levels of reality. The Zen tradition teaches that religion is like a finger pointing at the Moon. I stare at the finger.

NEPTUNE ENTERING CANCER

The Emerging Archetype: The Great Mother; The Healer

My Most Skillful Current Method of Soul Growth: The time has come for me to open the heart chakra. Meditating on kindness, I now send love along with sincere wishes for healing to all beings – including the ones closest to me, and especially the ones who drive me crazy. Contemplations arise that put tears in my eyes. In traditional terms, meditation on the "feminine" face of the Divine: the All-Accepting Mother.

Synchronistic Correlates: Opportunities to be gentle, kind, and forgiving abound. Wounded people or wounded creatures appear. Soulful experiences. I encounter people who immediately feel like family. A chance arises to be quiet, contained, and protected in a safe, sacred place.

Lost and Wasted: I become afraid of my own sensitivity and seek to shield it from the harshness of the world. I become so effective at such self-protection that I become immune to compassion – which is to say that I do not experience the suffering of other beings.

NEPTUNE ENTERING LEO

The Emerging Archetype: The Hierophant

My Most Skillful Current Method of Soul Growth: Accepting the social mantle of some degree of spiritual authority, all the while scrupulously avoiding the pitfalls that accompany any such title. Inspiring others effectively. Staying humble about it.

Synchronistic Correlates: I have reached a stage in my inner journey in which a responsibility arises to offer encouragement, guidance, and inspiration to others. People look to me for it, and doors open for me to offer a gift to the community in the form of my own example.

Lost and Wasted: I start thinking I look good in that funny hat they always offer the priestly class. I may have advanced spiritually, but I now find myself disoriented in an evolutionary *cul-de-sac* created by my own pride.

NEPTUNE ENTERING VIRGO

The Emerging Archetype: The Servant of Humanity

My Most Skillful Current Method of Soul Growth: It is now time to make other people's needs more important to me than my own needs. Using service as a path toward getting over myself – and using service as a way of further disrupting the stranglehold of ego on my larger consciousness.

Synchronistic Correlates: Opportunities to be genuinely helpful to others appear. Teachers show up at exactly the right moment, along with chances for me to teach others some spiritual lessons by example rather than by words. Humbling circumstances now provide me with a clear mirror of my true condition; handled wisely, these are precious occasions of effective, efficient growth rather than sources of shame.

Lost and Wasted: I find myself serving other people in a way that feels mechanical, as if the best of what I am remains invisible, irrelevant to the role that I am playing. I could fall prey now to an unworthy teacher.

NEPTUNE ENTERING LIBRA

The Emerging Archetype: The Soul Mate; The Sacred Artist

My Most Skillful Current Method of Soul Growth: Allowing interdependency to now arise between myself and someone who, while different from me, is on a similar plane of spiritual evolution. Comparing notes; corroborating our spiritual experiences. Finding serenity and balance in my spirit through the contemplation – and perhaps the creation – of beauty.

Synchronistic Correlates: Encounters with spiritual equals crystallize before me, along with encounters with spiritual friends. Experiences of soul-recognition dawn. Transcendent rapture is now triggered by immersion of my senses in beauty or by losing myself in any visionary or creative process.

Lost and Wasted: I dissipate my energy in romantic fantasy; I fall into the delusion that my own spiritual experience is dependent upon someone else triggering it. I become self-indulgent and hyper-sensitive, seeking numbness and mistaking it for peace.

NEPTUNE ENTERING SCORPIO

The Emerging Archetype: The Shaman

My Most Skillful Current Method of Soul Growth: Facing my own psychological woundedness, whether the wounds are from this lifetime or from previous ones. I have now come to a point where two realities interact – and one of them sounds bad while the other sounds good. The first is that my unresolved hurt places are blocking my evolution. The second is that I am ready to heal them and thereby unleash a spiritual breakthrough.

Synchronistic Correlates: Tense situations now arise, charged with psychological drama. If I am mindful of my reactions and the part I play in creating these situations, they offer keys to understanding and healing my wounds. Confrontive teachers appear before me. As I advance in the healing processes, I notice certain mysterious powers beginning to jell in me . . . others begin to notice them too.

Lost and Wasted: I am emotionally drained by crazy interpersonal situations that defy resolution and which seem inescapable. I am hungry for something which I might mistake for sex – and then pursue it as if sex were what it actually was.

NEPTUNE ENTERING SAGITTARIUS

The Emerging Archetype: The Seeker

My Most Skillful Current Method of Soul Growth: Now is the time to stretch my philosophical horizons, immersing myself in religions, cultures, or worldviews that were previously alien to me. I need to blow out the metaphysical tumbleweeds, ask myself hard questions, and seek fresh perspectives. At this present crossroads, I am not afraid to test my philosophical premises against reality. Positive thinking? Visualizing wealth or abundance? I check them out – I see if they work for me, or not.

Synchronistic Correlates: Opportunities for me to travel or experience other cultures appear now. Pilgrimage is possible – the sacrament of the Sacred Journey. Encounters with perspectives that challenge my root assumptions and create fresh aliveness in me arise spontaneously now. A chance for true mind training presents itself.

Lost and Wasted: I make a religion out of not learning anything. I slip into some sort of lazy Fundamentalism in which defending and justifying my pre-existing opinions becomes more pressing to me than actually ever exposing myself to anything fresh and helpful.

NEPTUNE ENTERING CAPRICORN

The Emerging Archetype: The Elder; The Wizard

My Most Skillful Current Method of Soul Growth: If I am wise, I now willingly face the test of solitary spiritual self-discipline. I get serious about my commitment to some kind of daily, structured evolutionary practice. I make sure that my higher Will has dominion over all of my appetites – a process which generally involves periods of some kind of abstinence or self-denial.

Synchronistic Correlates: The chance to be alone arises, along with the corresponding chance to distinguish solitude from loneliness. I experience encounters with demanding teachers and teachings. Fierce temptations crystallize before me – and if I can resist them, I pass the test and I become immune to them forever.

Lost and Wasted: I make a virtue out of pointless misery and "doing without", as if they were inherently holy. Alternatively, I slip into materialistic denial of the existence of higher dimensions or of any ultimate meaning in life. My inner Scrooge slowly takes over.

NEPTUNE ENTERING AQUARIUS

The Emerging Archetype: The Sacred Heretic

My Most Skillful Current Method of Soul Growth: I am now facing the radical need to think for myself in spiritual matters. Questioning religion; doubting the teachings I have received is currently evolutionary rocket fuel for me. I commit to the truth, the whole truth, and nothing but the truth. Success with any of this now depends upon my learning to tolerate other people who might be thinking that I "must not be a very spiritual person" or that I "have fallen away from grace."

Synchronistic Correlates: Unsettling experiences can arise now as, for example, when spiritual teachers are exposed in hypocrisy or serious moral error. Inescapable new understandings dawn in me – understandings which lead me to question what I had always believed to be the truth. The choice arises between being truly spiritual and being *thought of* as spiritual.

Lost and Wasted: I go through the motions of reciting old beliefs that I have actually outgrown. As I do that, I become increasingly distant and detached. Feelings of isolation and meaninglessness rumble beneath my surface social appearance.

NEPTUNE ENTERING PISCES

The Emerging Archetype: The Mystic

My Most Skillful Current Method of Soul Growth: I realize that I have now arrived at a point of breakthrough. The work is really done at this point; I only need to get out of my own way, open my mind, and let go of the belief that there is anything else I need to earn, accomplish or resolve. Can I now surrender without reservation to the love of the Infinite?

Synchronistic Correlates: Opportunities to simply "be" arise in my life. Floods of numinous feeling now enter my mind, sweeping me along. Psychic experiences and premonitions come unbidden. Devotional feelings rise up from my heart, putting tears in my eyes. I witness things that I cannot understand, and which I do not need to understand.

Lost and Wasted: I get frightened of what is happening to me, and I do my best to turn away from this psychic opening. I deny it; I find ways to ground myself and numb myself. I slip into a kind of ghostly half-life.

Neptune Passing Through The Twelve Houses

NEPTUNE ENTERING THE FIRST HOUSE

For the sake of my soul, the action I must now take is . . . unilateral and might even appear to other people to be an act of selfishness on my part. Sometimes ego is the tool that my soul must use. Now is such a time. I resolve to claim the experiences that support my journey, even if in order to do that, I fail to live up to the expectations and projected requirements of certain people around me.

To help me with this evolutionary step, the universe presents me with . . . forks in the road on my soul's rising journey. On one hand, I can walk away from my expected and accustomed role and climb alone to the spiritual mountain top. That is the right choice. Down the other fork, little changes except that I have now put my spiritual life in a little box, while leaving the rest of my outward life in another box – a box held in other people's hands.

If I misuse or misunderstand this energy, the negative appearances which arise are . . . a sense that I have missed the boat. I feel lost and uninspired, as if I were walking in my sleep. I probably "hang on a cross" that other people have erected for me. I may blunder into believing in some mirage, perhaps even a glamourous one, but one that offers no nutrition to my soul.

NEPTUNE ENTERING THE SECOND HOUSE

For the sake of my soul, the action I must now take is . . . quite possibly the very concrete action of investing money in my spiritual journey. Is there something I presently need – some object, some experience – the lack of which is holding me back in my inner work? Money is not really the issue; that is only the outward appearance. The real issue is a question of how much I value myself and how preciously I hold the opportunity of this incarnation.

To help me with this evolutionary step, the universe presents me with . . . a chance to graduate to the next evolutionary stage. The door is open; the only questions are how much I value myself and therefore how clearly I assess what methods and practices have now become appropriate to me at this evolutionary crossroads. If I doubt myself, I remain a spiritual PhD candidate mistaking myself for a high school student. I under-extend myself spiritually.

If I misuse or misunderstand this energy, the negative appearances which arise are . . . evolutionary stagnation because I did not believe in myself enough to secure the experiences, teachings, and tools which I actually needed.

NEPTUNE ENTERING THE THIRD HOUSE

For the sake of my soul, the action I must now take is . . . easy to say, and hard to do: I need to simply keep my eyes open. I resolve to try to look at the world in a way that is free of consensual social conditioning. As I do that, I begin to "see things" (hear things, even smell things) that are "not there" according to most people. The very foundation of my perceptual faculties is shifting in an expanded and far more mystical direction. To support me in this process of awakening, it enhances my equilibrium to read metaphysics and to experience contact with true spiritual teachers.

To help me with this evolutionary step, the universe presents me with . . . opportunities to sit with spiritual mentors. Perceptions that must be "believed to be seen." Spooky experiences. Omens. Divine guidance. Books and teachings that are custom designed to trigger breakthroughs for me.

If I misuse or misunderstand this energy, the negative appearances which arise are . . . simply confusing. Chaotic, even delusional, thoughts enter my mind. I mistake wishes and fears for reality. My speech becomes difficult for others to follow.

NEPTUNE ENTERING THE FOURTH HOUSE

For the sake of my soul, the action I must now take is . . . to withdraw somewhat from the world's dramas, dilemmas, and entertainments and instead find some quiet havens. A safe, quiet *place* is a great help too. That is because I am very attuned now to the ambient energies underneath my feet and under any roof that is over my head. I can draw comfort and energy from my soul-family – both the visible and the invisible one – but my stability can be disrupted by familial disharmony.

To help me with this evolutionary step, the universe presents me with . . . little pockets of peace if only I am astute enough to look for them and to recognize them. Input about my family, especially related to my ancestors and the land from which they came, presents itself to me. I feel the presence of my ancestors, as if they are guiding me now, or concerned for me. Experiences in magical places are offered to me, whether or not they are officially recognized as sacred in any formal religious sense.

If I misuse or misunderstand this energy, the negative appearances which arise are . . . connected with my being turned into a kind of ghost, mostly as a result of succumbing to the pressures of familial roles and expectations. I slip into sleepy daydreams.

NEPTUNE ENTERING THE FIFTH HOUSE

For the sake of my soul, the action I must now take is . . . inseparable from my achieving ecstatic states. Joy is now the catalyst that I need for a major spiritual breakthrough. As I learn to surrender to this flow of happy energy, I abandon myself to the universe . . . I experience faith in the marrow of my bones . . . I become "like a little child," without fear or the need to control anything. Playful creative expression helps me now – trance-dancing, losing myself in rhythm, letting inspiration guide me.

To help me with this evolutionary step, the universe presents me with . . . chances simply to *play*. People come into my life who trigger joy and creativity in me – they are my *playmates*, and quite probably old soul-connections too. Opportunities to loosen up and to forget myself appear out of nowhere.

If I misuse or misunderstand this energy, the negative appearances which arise are . . . my slipping into torpor and succumbing to a hunger for oblivion. The mere satisfaction of my animal appetites can tempt and distort me, without any connection to mindful spiritual ecstasy.

NEPTUNE ENTERING THE SIXTH HOUSE

For the sake of my soul, the action I must now take is . . . to commit myself to regularity and self-discipline in any spiritual practices toward which I am drawn. Everything boils down to *disciplined repetition* as I turn methods of soul-growth into routines which I now begin to practice by reflex. I am harnessing the power of *habit* as my greatest spiritual ally. Meanwhile, I seek worthy, effective teachers. Once I have found them, I surrender to them.

To help me with this evolutionary step, the universe presents me with . . . the opportunity to turn good spiritual hygiene into a habitual pattern of daily behavior. I meet people who inspire me, and in whose footsteps I can follow: spiritual teachers and role models arise in my path and they act as powerful catalysts to my evolution. Opportunities to be of service to others appear. Such service helps me to loosen the grasp of ego on my consciousness, and thus supports me in generating full receptivity to these teachers.

If I misuse or misunderstand this energy, the negative appearances which arise are . . . that I find myself dissolving into duties and responsibilities, losing the thread of my own path as I become overwhelmed by the exaggerated needs and demands of others.

NEPTUNE ENTERING THE SEVENTH HOUSE

For the sake of my soul, the action I must now take is . . . to make authentic connections with true kindred spirits whom I feel see my soul when they look into my eyes. I trust that I can tell when that kind of mind-link is happening – and I promise myself that I will acknowledge when it is *not* happening and walk away. Relationships with a true spiritual basis allow an integration of soul and personality; that integration is my aim now, and I cannot accomplish it alone.

To help me with this evolutionary step, the universe presents me with . . . a few people with whom I can sit in silence and feel deeply connected without any need for words, or touch, or any kind of shared distraction. I quickly recognize these people; they seem inexplicably familiar to me. Weird psychic experiences arise spontaneously between us: we phone each other at the same moment, say the same word at the same time, meet for lunch and find ourselves dressed in shirts of the same color.

If I misuse or misunderstand this energy, the negative appearances which arise are . . . intimate delusions. I trust the wrong people. I am seduced, at least in some sense of the word, and it may not be sexual. I fall in love with a projection of my own mind, mistaking it for the reality of another person. I become involved with someone who is given to addiction or escapism, or simply one who is a lot weaker than me.

NEPTUNE ENTERING THE EIGHTH HOUSE

For the sake of my soul, the action I must now take is . . . to charge myself with renewed *chi* or *prana* or *life-force* – or whatever we might call it. My next evolutionary steps require that kind of energetic boost. I accomplish this essential spiritual refueling by interfacing my consciousness with strong energies of various sorts. These energies might be sexual in a *Tantric* sense – but they can also be experiences with sacred objects or sacred places, or storms, or crashing waves. However I interface with such sources of *prana*, I must now learn to open my energy-body to the primal forces that animate the universe and enter into symbiosis with them.

To help me with this evolutionary step, the universe presents me with . . . experiences that give me goosebumps. I may have contact with occult powers or occult initiations. An experience of sacred sexuality is a possibility. I may encounter shamanic work or training. I find myself animated by forces that I do not understand; I learn to trust them and partner myself with them.

If I misuse or misunderstand this energy, the negative appearances which arise are . . . linked to delusional projections from my desire-body. I place my faith in mirages. Gradually they drain me of life-force, all the while promising to increase it. I gradually become increasingly moody and inclined toward depressive states.

NEPTUNE ENTERING THE NINTH HOUSE

For the sake of my soul, the action I must now take is . . . to blow out my spiritual and philosophical cobwebs. Thinking deeply about life's big, persistent questions is one of the main engines that drive anyone's spiritual evolution, and right now I need fresh grist for that precise thought-mill. That grist might come from some kind of unfamiliar metaphysical training, but by far the most effective method for me gaining it now lies in *pilgrimage* – a journey undertaken to a place that feels sacred to me. Contact with the exotic opens my heart and my mind in new ways. Something holy is out there waiting for me to show up.

To help me with this evolutionary step, the universe presents me with . . . a chance for philosophical and spiritual renewal: new teachings, fresh language, the presence of magic. The open road looms before me, reviving me, bringing my attention to focus on the present moment, which is where the magic is always located.

If I misuse or misunderstand this energy, the negative appearances which arise are . . . a vulnerability to getting tangled up in ungrounded theories, faiths, and beliefs. Letting religion stand between me and the reality of my actual experience. "Faith" becomes the enemy of truth. Using religion as a defense mechanism against actual growth.

NEPTUNE ENTERING THE TENTH HOUSE

For the sake of my soul, the action I must now take is . . . humbly to accept that because I have been given rich spiritual gifts in the form of the guidance that I have already received, both from visible teachers and from invisible ones, that the time has now come for me to find a way to pass those gifts on. I need to play what we might call a "priestly" role in my community, all the while being wary of ego's slippery slope – and I resolve to remember that not all "priests" wear the obvious uniforms. I need the *role*, not the funny hat.

To help me with this evolutionary step, the universe presents me with . . . two doorways through which I need to pass. The first is people whom I do not know deeply and yet who I can see would benefit from some kind of spiritual input from me. The second is public situations which genuinely need my help – space for what I have to offer opens up in the community, in other words. I recognize "the call" and I rise to it.

If I misuse or misunderstand this energy, the negative appearances which arise are . . . feeling as if I am drifting through my life without any real purpose, leaving me feeling like a ghost. Working in a professional situation that has no real point and in which I feel as if my soul is unknown and unseen. Worse, succumbing to spiritual self-importance, slipping into becoming some kind of self-appointed guru, psychologist, or spokesperson for God.

NEPTUNE ENTERING THE ELEVENTH HOUSE

For the sake of my soul, the action I must now take is . . . two-fold. First, it is imperative that I find and ally myself with my spiritual clan – my congregation, my *sangha*, my pagan tribe, whatever I might call it. I need their psychic support, and they need mine. Secondly, it is time for me to recalculate the priorities which underlie my direction in life. Distractions are eclipsing the directional needs of my soul, and that must stop. Life is too short for me to allow that kind of seduction to happen.

To help me with this evolutionary step, the universe presents me with . . . chances to meet groups of people who are kindred souls. If I am an evolutionary astrologer, the perfect class appears. If I am a yogi, ditto. If I practice a religion, I find the perfect congregation of believers. If I recognize these opportunities and I respond wisely, I am initiated into my natural tribe, and deeply energized by it.

If I misuse or misunderstand this energy, the negative appearances which arise are . . . that my vitality is leached away in pointless, draining social interactions which teach me nothing at all and only trivialize my life. Perhaps I am sucked into a cult – or just into a group of deluded, clueless, addicted, superficial, or escapist people.

NEPTUNE ENTERING THE TWELFTH HOUSE

For the sake of my soul, the action I must now take is . . . to recognize that I am now standing on the brink of a significant breakthrough in the evolution of my consciousness, but that the process is delicate, not guaranteed to be successful, and must be nurtured. Finding quiet, solitary time is pivotal now. I have everything I need; it is all already inside of me. For that reason, I will not be distracted by external things – even ones that seem certifiably spiritual or holy. I resolve to use this time with a serious internal spiritual intention, and to support that intention with a deep immersion in mostly solitary metaphysical processes.

To help me with this evolutionary step, the universe presents me with . . . a vividly pressing sense of the transparency of this physical world. Psychic experiences are abundant. Contact arises with inspiring, advanced souls. The right books appear at the right time. Miracles happen.

If I misuse or misunderstand this energy, the negative appearances which arise are . . . that I become overwhelmed by my own sensitivity and so turn away from it. I cling to the way I used to be as a way of avoiding what I need to become.

ENTERING PISCES – OR FORMING AN ASPECT WITH NEPTUNE

In the thumbnail sketches which follow, I want to focus on the core changes which unfold in the orientation of any planet as it crosses out of Aquarius and into Pisces. As ever in these simple guidelines, my words are intended to reflect an essential transformation stripped of its larger astrological context. A solar Gemini might react differently to such an event than would a solar Taurus. These sketches are starting points, that is all.

In planning these ten paragraphs, I realized that they are a good fit with each of these same planets forming an aspect with Neptune, so I am including that perspective too. Jupiter aspects are worth seeing through these lenses too, but the fit is not quite as compelling for me, so I have elected not to mention them.

WHEN THE SUN ENTERS PISCES – OR FORMS AN ASPECT WITH NEPTUNE . . . your fundamental nature and your social identity become softer and more fluid. You are less "identified with your identity." You laugh more, hug more, tie yourself in mental knots less. You are drawn in a more spiritual direction. All of these things *need* to happen, so your best course is just to trust them and flow with them. Other dimensions of the universe interact with the one in which we live in our physical bodies – that is one reason why life does not always need to make sense. Just be wary of drifting into fantasyland. Your inner life is your North Star. Keep your eyes on it and you will not get lost.

WHEN THE MOON ENTERS PISCES – OR FORMS AN ASPECT WITH NEPTUNE . . . the trickle of connection between your emotional body and your psychic sensitivity becomes a torrent. You can surf this evolutionary wave successfully – but to handle it without becoming inundated by the unresolved emotions of everyone around you, you need to create pockets of quiet time for renewal and regeneration, away from other human beings. Trust your instincts. Make your home a temple.

WHEN MERCURY ENTERS PISCES – OR FORMS AN ASPECT WITH NEPTUNE . . . it is as if you have been thinking "reasonably" in three dimensions, but now suddenly you are thinking in four. Your eyes, ears, and even your nose are now reacting to stimuli of a higher order. It is unsettling until you get accustomed to it. You know things that you have no rational way of knowing. Your dreams become more vivid – and harder to sort out from "reality." Your creativity goes through the roof.

WHEN VENUS ENTERS PISCES – OR FORMS AN ASPECT WITH NEPTUNE . . . you become more tender and sentimental, eager to feel more actively connected to the people you love. Boundaries dissolve – which can be a good thing or a bad one, depending on how you harness the energy. You have a right to be discriminating. Don't be a doormat – you can still say no if you want to. But gazing into the eyes of a soul-friend and seeing that soul gazing back at you is high octane fuel for your journey now.

WHEN MARS ENTERS PISCES – OR FORMS AN ASPECT WITH NEPTUNE . . . bold, adventurous actions taken in service of your spiritual evolution are indicated. Perhaps for example you go on a vision quest – or maybe you simply "make yourself" go sit with a spiritual teacher or get yourself to that meditation class. Be decisive and let your inner "spiritual warrior" take the helm – and remember that there is no time to waste. No one gets out of here alive. Act as if you know that.

WHEN JUPITER ENTERS PISCES – OR FORMS AN ASPECT WITH NEPTUNE . . . above all, believe in the worth of the spiritual work that *you have already done* in this lifetime. Believe the fact that because of it, you are right now at this moment worthy of a higher state of being. Believe that you deserve a shot at claiming that prize – and be willing to invest in yourself concretely to that end. What are the specific evolutionary catalysts that could trigger a higher state for you? Trips? Teachers? A sabbatical? Ask for what you need. Be willing to pay for it if you have to. Do not underestimate your readiness for a breakthrough. Do not miss this chance. Everything is impermanent – this door will not remain open forever.

WHEN SATURN ENTERS PISCES – OR FORMS AN AS-
PECT WITH NEPTUNE . . . you have come to a steep and rocky place
on the spiritual mountain you are climbing. Obstacles ripen and appear –
and you are ripe to conquer them. Committed, disciplined, relentless effort
undertaken willingly now yields extraordinary results – but not overnight.
Patience and relentlessness are rewarded as the months go by. This is more
of a time for making lifelong spiritual vows than a time for "amazing weekend workshops." Solitude is a sacrament. Silence is a psychedelic.

WHEN URANUS ENTERS PISCES – OR FORMS AN AS-
PECT WITH NEPTUNE . . . honor your inner heretic. The honest reality of your direct experience of the transcendent is a thousand times more
valuable than all of your philosophy, religious beliefs, and metaphysical
training – most of which derived from the experience of other people anyway. Expect weird and unpredictable events, both in psychic terms and in
your outward life. Your guardian angels are not exactly guarding you now –
but they are laying out a trail of breadcrumbs for you to follow into a deep
dark forest of mystery.

WHEN NEPTUNE ENTERS PISCES – OR FORMS AN AS-
PECT WITH NEPTUNE . . . the ground on which you *thought* you were
standing turns into transparent dream-stuff – or, more accurately, you realize that it has always been that way. This is a pulse of pure mysticism. It is
not just about insights or "powers," although acquiring them may be part
of the experience too. In essence, everything is now about awareness itself.
You are becoming mindful of the luminosity that is your true nature. Your
ego is dissolving, and you are becoming identified with that luminosity.

WHEN PLUTO ENTERS PISCES – OR FORMS AN ASPECT
WITH NEPTUNE . . . light enters dark places in your psyche. Visualize
a high Teacher – Jesus, Buddha, Mohammed, whoever – and ask yourself
how such a lofty being would now view your hurts, your anger, your shame,
your darkness. Let that potent mixture of absolute *psychological honesty,*
absolute *forgiveness,* and *radical acceptance* pervade your mind the way the
perfume of fresh roses pervades a room.

23

THE BIOPSYCHIC SCRIPT

There is a small class of transits, progressions, and solar arcs whose calculation does not require a computer or an ephemeris. All you have to know is someone's age and you've got the answer. Each one of these configurations is about the relationship of a moving planet to the place where it started – where it lies in your natal chart, in other words. In *The Book of Earth*, we explored one of these cycles in great detail: *Saturn Returns*. Every twenty-nine and a half years, Saturn is back where it started, as surely as the minute-hand of a clock comes back home after sixty minutes.

That clock metaphor, by the way, is really the easiest way to understand all of these cyclical rhythms. They all work that same way, and for the same reason we just saw with that minute hand. We are looking at cycles of fixed lengths, and it does not matter if it is the minute hand of a clock or a planet orbiting the Sun. Either way, they all get back home at a predictable time.

In *The Book of Air*, we reflected on a second example of this kind of cycle. Uranus completes an orbit of the Sun once every eighty-four years. Adding the Uranian cycle to Saturn's cycle, we introduced new detail into the picture of the human ageing process. At roughly age twenty-one – a quarter of the way around the chart – Uranus reaches its *Waxing Square* relative to its natal position. It is as if you checked that minute hand on the clock *after only fifteen minutes had passed*. At forty-two, we have the *Uranian Opposition*. At sixty-three, the *Waning Square* – and finally, at eighty-four, the *Uranian Return*. Apart from the timing of the Uranian Return itself, those numbers flex slightly because of the way that planets speed up and slow down in their orbits. With Uranus, the timing we gave for the squares and the opposition might be off a couple of years, but they are approximately right.

Here, in *The Book of Water,* we complete our picture of how we all "grow up." This *biopsychic script* underlies the life-saga of every human being who has ever existed. Because the orbit of every planet operates in this kind of cyclical fashion, we can generate an extremely complex picture if we want to – but maybe it is too complex. As ever with astrology, some judicious editing is critical. There are many planetary cycles. A few represent profoundly important age-related changes in our perspective on life, while some are relatively trivial.

- In this chapter, I want to introduce several of these cycles – even some of which are relatively secondary in significance, but still worth understanding.
- I will devote the entirety of the next chapter to exploring the cycle of *progressed Lunar Returns.* Those events take their place alongside Saturn Returns and the four-pointed Uranian cycle to form the Holy Trinity of our biopsychic script.

It is *those three astrological cycles which universally underlie everyone's processes of physical, psychological, and spiritual maturation.* They are like the blank pages of life – but those pages are numbered for all of us in a very specific sequence – a sequence ultimately of questions, not of answers.

Before we complete our "holy trinity" with the Moon in chapter twenty-four, let's consider some other pieces of the puzzle. Like most of astrology's technical details, the more of them that you can handle *without losing your holistic, intuitive engagement with the interpretive process,* the better.

My suggestion is that in learning to grasp the biopsychic script, that you first internalize the cycles of Saturn, Uranus, and the Moon, then take a moment to assess yourself. If you can go a little further without a wrinkled brow, add the configurations which I present in this chapter. As you will soon see, they are all compelling and powerful, but just not quite as pivotal as the returns of Saturn and the progressed Moon, and the four-pointed Uranian cycle.

LET'S NOT IGNORE WHAT'S OBVIOUS

As an astrologer endowed with a dollop of common sense, here is a way to keep perspective on the biopsychic script: *no matter what is going on in their charts, we would all hesitate to predict "major professional breakthroughs" for people in their nineties or "finding true love" for six-year-olds.*

We understand, almost without having to think about it, that all possibilities in human psychology and experience are very much overshadowed by a person's age. With specific knowledge of the three main cyclical planetary patterns, we take our instincts about the obvious realities of human life and look at them through a microscope rather than through those old glasses you wore twelve years ago. Add a few more factors which we are about to introduce, and you go from *new* glasses straight to X-ray vision.

INSIGNIFICANT CYCLES

There are some planetary cycles that can be safely ignored. We could, for example, talk about the *synodic cycles* – back to a conjunction with the Sun – of Mercury (116 days), Venus (584 days), and Mars (780 days) – but those cycles move too quickly to develop much depth and complexity of meaning. I am getting near my own 225th synodic Mercury Return, for example. To tell you the truth, I can't remember what the 117th one meant to me.

We all love our *solar returns*, of course, and usually make a big deal of them. We call them *birthdays*. But after a while, birthdays tend to blur too. Like those synodic returns, they are just too numerous to give you that big "biopsychic script" view of life's symphonic development over decades of change and growth. By the way, astrologers often set up "solar return charts" – charts erected for the exact instant the Sun completes its annual cycle. They are powerful and fascinating. My friend and colleague in Paris, Lynn Bell, wrote a wonderful book about them called *Cycles of Light*. I recommend it.

JUPITER RETURNS

I do pay serious attention to *Jupiter returns*. They happen like clockwork every twelve years and they can be relied upon to open up *doorways to opportunity*. I view them as secondary players in the biopsychic script – good to know about, but just not quite as critical as our big three.

Bill Gates – the bazillionaire founder of Microsoft – was born on October 28, 1955. According to Wikipedia, he wrote his first computer program when he was thirteen years old. He turned thirteen at the end of 1968 – and experienced a triple-hit Jupiter Return between October 1967 and May 1968. That timing is close, but not quite exact. I cannot help but wonder what "doorways to opportunity" were opening for Bill Gates just a few months before he actually wrote code for the first time. What books fell in his lap? What did he see on television that got him thinking . . .?

On June 8, 2001, *Harry Potter* author, J.K. Rowling experienced a Jupiter Return. She was already on top of the world, but her cake was soon to be frosted: the film version of her first book, *Harry Potter and the Philosopher's Stone*, was released on November 16, 2001, mightily reinforcing her popularity, not to mention presumably her bank account. Here's something that probably felt even more like a truly meaningful triumph for her. J.K. Rowling had had a hard life in the intimate department, but on December 26, 2001, *she remarried.* Marrying a second time has been called "the triumph of hope over experience." Fair enough – but sometimes hope can win. My impression is that Ms. Rowling did well the second time. In classic fashion, her Jupiter return opened a doorway of opportunity for her – in this case an intimate one.

On a bleaker note, Adolph Hitler experienced his own Jupiter Return on January 23, 1925. He had been sentenced to five years in prison, but on December 24, 1924, after serving only one year – *and only one month before his exact Jupiter return* – the Bavarian Supreme Court pardoned him. Hitler was released from jail – and immediately published *Mein Kampf* to enormous success, and the whole Nazi nightmare began. Lucky Adolph. Obviously he must have *felt lucky*, as Jupiter took him from being a prisoner to being a political pop star.

SOLAR ARC CYCLES

By *solar arc*, every one of the planets and Angles forms a *semi-sextile* aspect to its natal position at around age thirty. They all move at about one degree per year, so by around one's thirtieth birthday, they have each advanced thirty degrees. That semi-sextile lines up reasonably well with the first Saturn Return, and adds another note – a jarring one – to our sudden exit from an epoch we all imagined would last forever: our *youth.*

Similarly, all solar arcs hit a *semi-square* at about age forty-five, marking another edgy piece in the puzzle of *midlife*.

Every solar arc hits a *sextile* to its own natal position when we are approximately sixty years old – and that is the first *major* aspect to form in the solar arc cycle. This sextile heralds an *unexpected pulse of energy* which often impacts people around their second Saturn Returns . . . and which then leads directly into the profoundly important – and iconoclastic – time of the Waning Uranian Square. As we explored in *The Book of Earth*, it is then that we make the choices that determine whether we will become a wild man or wild woman, free and alive in our old age – or just boring and bored.

It is important to be careful about the timing of this *Grand Sextile*. By the time we are sixty, our simple one-degree-per-year formula with solar arcs has probably begun to drift away from reality enough to get you into trouble. You can easily be off by a year or so if you "do it in your head." It is better to check your computer.

Age ninety (or so) brings a massive *solar arc square*, neatly correlating with the obvious challenges that arise with advancing years.

You can further fill in that solar arc perspective with *quintiles* and *noviles* and *septiles* too, if you want. Their effects are real – but, as ever, much of the craft of astrology lies in knowing what to leave out. We only have so much time with a client and so many "gigabytes of information" in our heads. As ever, editorial choices must be made.

THE PLUTO SQUARE

Still thinking of age-linked astrological events, there is one such cycle that nearly rises in my mind to the same level of drama as the cycles of Saturn, Uranus, and the Moon. That is the *Pluto Square* – the time when transiting Pluto squares its natal position. Here is a taste of how significant that period can be: *at that time, we have a shot at getting to the very heart of the matter in terms of our psychological healing.* At the Pluto Square, the *root issue* that underlies all of our other issues is revealed, for good or for ill – for good if we face it, and for ill if we instead act it out.

At what age do we reach this Plutonian crossroads? That is where we run into problems. The answer lies all over the map, oscillating from generation to generation. That means that while the Pluto Square is an authentic life-changer and therefore deserves a place in the biopsychic script, it is also sort of a *floating point* on the calendar. Unlike the Saturn Return, for example, we cannot know it is happening simply because a person is fifty-nine years old.

The seminal British author, Jane Austen, for example, was born with Pluto in Capricorn, so the planet was beginning to slow down – remember, Pluto reaches its slowest speed in Taurus, just three signs later. For Jane Austen, Pluto reached the square to its birth position when she would have been seventy-one years old – that was thirty years after she had died.

Carl Jung made it to his Pluto Square, but he was seventy-eight years old.

On the other hand, I was born in 1949, with Pluto speeding up because it had swung around to Leo. That meant that I hit my own Pluto square much earlier than Jane Austen or Carl Jung. I was only a baby – just forty years old.

Most of my "Boomer" generation reflects that timing, give or take a little bit.

That Pluto Square was an important passage for me, by the way – a chance to deal with some of my own root issues and attachments. That much is true for everybody. What varies is only the *nature* of our issues and attachments. Those impediments are of course unique to each one of us, and have a lot to do with the Moon's south node – but the sign Pluto occupied when we were born does at least give us a broad generational insight. Each "Pluto tribe" brings certain signature Shadow pieces into the world, collectively. Specifically, for all of us Pluto-in-Leo types, part of our generational Shadow is the desire to be seen as some kind of "rock star." With Pluto ruling my chart as well as my lunar south node, I shared that spiritual disorder with the rest of my generation, but perhaps I "enjoyed" an extra helping of it. Worse, having a bit of a public profile, I was in a good position to feed the addiction if I wanted to.

Here's what I wrote about the dark side of Pluto in Leo back in chapter ten:

> The Price of Failure: *I live a fake life. I keep one eye on the audience at all times, adjusting my behaviors according to their reactions. I live for reviews. I hunger after some golden city on the hill, which does not actually exist, and so I never get there. I cannot walk past a mirror without checking myself out.*

During the time of my own Pluto Square, I experienced many tempting opportunities to cash in on what was then the big "New Age" marketplace. I found myself writing an astrology column for a famous glamour magazine. I had rock star friends and celebrity endorsements. If I had been willing to sell my soul, I probably could've become one of those wealthy Los Angeles self-help gurus.

In my soul, I knew that I had to quickly do something to solidify my credentials as the Prince of Darkness, so I wrote *Stalking Anubis*, my murder mystery about an evil guru. The book poked fun at New Age gullibility, and nicely shut that door for me.

When you get to your own Pluto Square – or when you look back on it – you might go to chapter ten and review your own generational "Price of Failure" based on the natal sign of your Pluto.

Ain't nobody immune.

People born in, say, 1986, with Pluto in Scorpio, will hit their Pluto Square in 2027, at age forty-one or so. Will they be *"defined by a dark or tragic interpretation of human existence, with their negativity repelling people, especially younger ones?"*

People born in, say, 1997, with Pluto in Sagittarius, hit their squares when they are about fifty years old. Will they *"become fearful and judgmental regarding any people or ideas that diverge too far from their narrow comfort zone? Will they feel compelled to make converts to their own view of things – and thus unwittingly reveal their underlying insecurity about that view?"*

Children being born today as I write these words in summer 2020, and beyond, will be experiencing their Pluto Squares at ever-greater ages, as Pluto slows down in its orbit. People born in 2086, for example, will be around ninety years old when they finally get to it. Thinking of the babies born today, dealing with the shadow-side of Pluto in Capricorn, some will heal the ancient wounds, while some will pay the price of failure, having to admit, *"I effectively become a slave. I may not look that way; I may appear to be successful or prosperous, even righteous. But in my heart I am faced with the reality of living a life for which other people wrote the script. There is no sweetness in my tiredness at the end of a day, and no real sense of accomplishment."*

Always, with Pluto, *we have to affirm the human capacity to heal.* No one has to be defined by the Shadow. It is just that no one escapes its clutches unless they are willing to wrestle with it honestly, humbly, and bravely.

When you reach your Pluto Square, you have a good shot at succeeding in that healing and regenerative process. You are face-to-face with the heart of the matter psychologically and spiritually.

Just remember that our astrological insights into your own Shadow are not only about the sign Pluto occupied when you were born. That is a good starting place – but Pluto's house position is just as important, and then from there we would need to get into the whole territory of nodal analysis which we explored in *Yesterday's Sky*.

THE NEPTUNE SQUARE

I always pay attention to the *Neptune Square*, when transiting Neptune forms a square to natal Neptune. This event often marks a serious *spiritual crisis*. Who am I really? Does my life have any purpose? Pressingly, *how many of my spiritual beliefs or alleged sources of meaning in my life have no connection to the authentic realities of my actual experience?* How much of my faith is only a comforting lie?

The Neptune Square always reminds me of a line from *The Promised Land*, one of Bruce Springsteen's anthemic songs: *Gonna be a twister to blow everything down that ain't got the faith to stand its ground*. The point is that sometimes you *need* a spiritual crisis or a crisis of faith. *They keep your faith honest*. The last place you want to be when you realize that your "religion" has failed you and has actually been phony all along is your death bed.

At the Neptune Square:
- People leave churches that are not speaking authentically to their hearts.
- Atheists wake up.
- Scientists get helpful, mind-blowing astrological readings.
- Romantic bubbles burst.
- Cynics are brought to their knees by the honest pain in their own hearts.
- Empty marriages collapse.
- Miracles happen to people who don't believe in miracles.
- Miracles fail to happen to people who believe that miracles will always rescue them from their own folly.

For Bruce Springsteen, his own "twister" hit in 1990 and 1991 as transiting Neptune made a square to its natal position. After experiencing phenomenal, even fanatical, levels of success, he unexpectedly made a controversial move. Right on the doorstep of his Neptune Square, In late 1989, he suddenly dissolved the E Street Band. He changed his musical style, releasing a couple of "more positive" albums made with Los Angeles session musicians rather than with his old friends and bandmates.

Neither album did very well. Springsteen's identity – both personally and musically – had been based on angst, hunger, and pain. He had *turned that hurt into art*, and thus had become a kind of "high priest" who was probably healing other hurt souls through his cathartic performances.

In 1980, the New Jersey State Assembly decided to honor Springsteen by introducing a resolution to make his signature tune, *Born to Run*, the "unofficial rock theme of our state's youth." Here are some lyrics capturing Springsteen's alchemical genius for turning pain into art – but probably not exactly embodying the tone the State Assembly wanted to convey about young people from New Jersey. They really should have listened to the song before issuing their resolution.

> *Oh baby, this town rips the bones from your back,*
> *it's a death trap, it's a suicide rap.*
> *We gotta get out while we're young,*
> *'cause tramps like us, baby, we were born to run.*

Speaking of the creative use Bruce Springsteen made of his troubled relationship with his father, he once said, "What would I conceivably have written about without him? I mean, you can imagine that if everything had gone great between us, we would have had disaster. *I would have written just happy songs – and I tried it in the early '90s and it didn't work; the public didn't like it.*" Remember: the early 1990s marked Bruce Springsteen's Neptune Square. A question seemingly pressed at him then: *who would I be if I were not defined by my own pain?*

Had the "religion" of being a lost soul in a muscle car begun to fail him? He had once sung a line straight from his heart: *"All the redemption I can offer, girl, is beneath this dirty hood."* Were those words simply becoming less true for him? Were they becoming an empty posture?

Was it time for Bruce Springsteen to *shed a personality*, Neptune-fashion?

Neptune is naturally more subtle than Pluto. As Bruce left his band, moved west, and began to risk making a different kind of music, you really have to look beneath the surface events and think about what they meant at a more soulful level. Neptune's transits are always ultimately about the two-step we do with our own egos – and it is difficult to imagine more ego-adrenaline than being a rock star, especially back in that giddy period. In worldly terms, Bruce was a monumentally lucky guy. But spiritually he faced a challenge that very few of us could even imagine. How many of us ever hear 30,000 people chanting our name? What strength must we discover in ourselves if we are to walk away from all that? What solace can we find to balance that kind of loss?

Topping it off, poor Bruce even has Pluto in "rock star" Leo – and you may remember what we wrote about that placement just a few paragraphs ago.

How did Springsteen react to his Neptune Square? I think it is fair to say that he rose to it. *He dissolved his band and walked away from a social context of friendships that had defined him – and increasingly probably trapped him – since his adolescence. He abandoned a style of musical composition and performance that had made him famous and wealthy.*

In essence, Springsteen walked away from his own ego. He knew that it just wasn't working for him anymore. On the face of it, everything looked like he was making a terrible mistake.

The "loss face" of Neptune we explored earlier was vividly present – and he apparently even embraced it.

As is so often the case with Neptune, appearance and reality were at odds. *I think it is fair to say that, had Bruce Springsteen not let go of his ego-structure during that Neptunian time, he would have run the risk of becoming a caricature of himself* – that mortal risk for ageing rock stars. Springsteen surfed his spiritual crisis. He got out of his own way – and was rewarded with Neptune's classic gift: *a life-renewing vision.* By 1994, just on the other side of his Neptune Square, he had won an Academy Award, plus four Grammys, for his song about HIV-AIDS, *Streets of Philadelphia.* Here are its opening lines. Think of what we have been exploring about the Neptune Square as you read them.

I was bruised and battered,
I couldn't tell what I felt.
I was unrecognizable to myself.
I saw my reflection in a window,
I didn't know my own face.

As they say, you can't make this stuff up. Astrology works, even in the lives of people who don't believe in it. I have no idea if Bruce Springsteen has any knowledge of astrology or any interest in it. I assume not or his interest would likely have gotten some media coverage. Still, he demonstrates something which I like to underscore: that no one really *needs* astrology. We can live well and consciously without it, guided by our own hearts.

I do wish I could have done a reading for him back in 1990 though – I think it would have given him comfort in a scary time, along with some encouragement that he was on the right track. Like the rest of us, at his Neptune Square, *he needed a spiritual crisis.* And he got one, and he seemingly used it well.

Astrology, employed consciously, sometimes works like an angel appearing at the foot of your bed in the darkest hour, saying, "it's going to be alright."

PERSPECTIVE ON ASPECTS OTHER THAN CONJUNCTIONS

A quick technical sidebar: you may have noticed that I have put major emphasis on Saturn Returns and Lunar Returns – *conjunctions*, in other words – while with Uranus I include *squares* and *oppositions*, and how with Neptune and Pluto, everything is focused exclusively on squares. (Nobody has to worry about Neptune or Pluto *Returns* – life is not long enough for us to experience them.)

But what about Saturn's squares and oppositions? What about the Moon's?

Those are fair questions, and those aspects are indeed relevant to the broader maturational processes reflected in our biopsychic script. They just operate at a less pivotal level. The problem is familiar: astrology produces an overwhelming flood of data. Half of our craft lies in making good judgments about what symbolism to use and what to ignore. However we look at it, this information-avalanche compels us to throw away three-quarters of what we might potentially use. We just have to be mindful enough to throw away the less pressing configurations, while identifying and keeping the ones that actually reveal the heart of the story.

In that editorial process, other astrologers might make different judgments than I do. That is fine – I would never pretend that there was only "one right way" to do astrology. But this is a good moment for me to echo a point I made at the outset of this chapter, *when it comes to understanding the biopsychic script, I recommend that you start with Saturn Returns, the four major Uranian aspects, and progressed Lunar Returns.* Those three cycles lay the foundation. They are the skeleton upon which everything else hangs.

Once you've grasped them, go ahead and add more layers – but only if you can do that and still keep your integrative intuition engaged. I would recommend adding, in this order, Pluto Squares, Jupiter Returns, and then Neptune Squares. Beyond that, if you still have heart-energy to spare, bring in those solar arc events, starting with the Grand Sextile.

Now that we have explored some of the secondary elements in the human lifecycle, let's finally add the third leg of the main tripod upon which the entire system hangs. Let's take a deep look at the mysteries of the progressed Moon and its cycle of Returns.

24

THE CYCLE OF PROGRESSED LUNAR RETURNS

The ever-mysterious Moon is forever tantalizing us, forever lying just beyond the grasp of our understanding. That is as it should be since the Moon is one of the astrological factors which shoots its tendrils into a far wider framework of reality than we ever learned about in school. As the lead member of the Water Family, the Moon always seeks the lowest level – sinking down, down, down into the very roots of the human mind, where consciousness and cosmos begin to become indistinguishable from each other. The Moon is as present, protean, and in-your-face as a bad mood on Monday morning – but at the same time, it is always connected to something higher and vaster . . . something that is at once inside us and yet also beyond us.

Staying in harmony with that transcendent vastness, letting it guide us, is nothing less than the secret of happiness. That is the pivotal role that the Moon plays in all our processes of healing, regeneration, and recovery.

In the end, if we are not happy, it is fair to say that we are not healed.

Luna is always with us – but rarely is hearing its messages so mission-critical to our soul's homeward journey as when the progressed Moon returns to its starting point. At those junctures, our hearts are rebooted in new and unexpected ways.

Understanding these Lunar Returns and weaving them into the warp and weft of the biopsychic script is the purpose of this chapter. Adding Lunar Returns to the cycles of Saturn and Uranus, and perhaps spicing them with some of the material explored in the previous chapter, completes our picture of how humans pass through time – and how time changes us all.

Let's take another look into the crystal-clear mirror of the rhythms of the heavens.

GOD'S FABLED SENSE OF HUMOR

Among the many pieces of compelling evidence that the Mind Behind the Universe gets the joke – or maybe *created* the joke – is the way it compelled Saturn and the Moon to dance together. Two more distinct planets would be hard to imagine, yet their cycles are similar in length – twenty-nine years for Saturn and twenty-seven for the Moon. That means that while they are not the same length, they are close enough to be forever entangled.

Just like two people who were not born to be dance partners, Saturn and the Moon are forever putting their feet down on either side of the downbeat, one ahead, one laid back. That means that as they dance they are constantly stepping on each other's toes.

The Moon is heart and soul. It *feels* rather than thinks. It moves by *instinct,* trusts whimsy, and does not require the universe to make any logical sense at all. Saturn, on the other hand, is all reason, logic, and calculation. The Moon gives primacy to its subjective emotional reactions, while Saturn – ever-objective – is concerned strictly with *what is* rather than how we might happen to feel about it.

Tell Saturn how you feel about something, and it would look at you cockeyed, obviously wondering why you bothered to report something so irrelevant to the task at hand.

Saturn is always alert to what might go wrong and what Plan B might look like, while the Moon is more likely to "trust God."

Say two plus two equals four and Saturn nods approvingly, while the Moon gets a wistful, faraway look in its eye, as if it knows something about those numbers which it could never explain to Saturn.

Let's make the Moon look dumb for a moment – and don't worry, we will soon do the same for Saturn.

- Saturn says "Sweetheart, the budget looks pretty tight this month, let's economize." The Moon responds, "But you said we could try that new French restaurant." Saturn says, "Honey, it's really expensive. If we eat there we won't be able to pay our electric bill." The Moon says, *"You never care about my feelings. I told you, I want to eat at that restaurant."*

Now let's make Saturn look just as dumb:
- The Moon says, "Darling, I just have a bad feeling about that guy. I don't think you should trust him." Saturn says, "But he's been great so far – plus he is a major investor in my project. Why don't you trust him? What's he ever done to you?" The Moon says, *"I don't know . . . I just have a bad feeling about him, that's all."* Two years later, "that guy" absconds with all the funds and moves to Uruguay under an assumed name. Saturn should have listened to the Moon.

Saturn and the Moon as dance partners? Yes indeed – and, if you have been thinking about what I've written here so far, you probably see something else too: despite stepping on each others' toes, *Saturn and the Moon really need each other.* It's a marriage made in heaven – just not in the way people usually intend that phrase.

As we have seen consistently in all four of the Element Families, *it is not about harmony, it is about interdependency.*

METAPHYSICS 101

The Moon, by *progression*, moves a little faster than Saturn does by *transit*. Like clockwork, we all get to our first progressed Lunar Return at age twenty-seven years and four months.

The timing of Saturn Returns is slightly trickier. Being transits, they involve retrogradation. Because of that, more often than not a person's Saturn Return embraces, not one, but three exact conjunctions, all happening within less than a year. All three of these hits cluster around the date that Saturn gets back to its starting point of its solar orbit – which happens twenty-nine years, six months, after our first breath. That of course happens like clockwork – the retrograde motions are just an optical illusion created by the fact that we are watching from the Earth, which is a moving point itself.

The bottom line is that the Moon arrives home about twenty-six-months before Saturn does. And that gap brings us straight to the heart of the matter: *Lunar inspiration must precede Saturnian manifestation.*

Those six words are the essence of everything we need to understand.

With a little bit of translation, those words also represent the most fundamental principle of metaphysics. Philosophical language varies, but metaphysical thinkers have always posited the existence of a *mental plane* underlying the physical plane. In some traditions, that mental plane goes by an even more evocative name: the *causal plane* – and that is because it "causes" everything that ever happens in the material world.

Saturn may rule our three-dimensional, time-bound, realm, but behind it – *or underneath it, or beyond it, or inside it* – is an inner, subtle realm represented by the Moon. Things must first happen there before anything *that we can see* ever happens.

And remember, the Moon *progresses* just a little faster than Saturn *transits*. It must first establish an *underlying energetic foundation* in that invisible "metaphysical" realm before things can precipitate out into the realm of atoms and molecules – the place we currently call home, and which some people actually mistake for reality. The point is that physical manifestation always comes later. That is why Saturn is slower than the Moon. Examples abound:

- A woman visualizes "the perfect parking space" in a crowded downtown area. Five minutes later, she finds it.
- A man with leukemia visualizes white blood cells riding to his rescue; he survives – while someone "who doesn't believe in that stuff" dies.
- A kid playing Parcheesi sees "snake eyes" just before she rolls the dice. One second later, she rolls a pair of ones: *snake eyes.*
- A good psychic "sees cancer in a woman's aura," warns her – and the woman immediately makes lifestyle changes. *The cancer never manifests.* No conventional doctor would see what had just happened – despite "cancer in her aura," she would have gotten a clean bill of health in a physical examination. (Everyone agrees that with cancer, it's "best to catch it early." Because that psychic tuned in on the Moon-plane, she *really* caught it early.)

- J.K. Rowling, stuck on a train, gets an idea for a series of novels about a school for young wizards, thinking that might be fun to write about someday . . .

MAGIC

We all appreciate a good attitude for obvious reasons. Under the world's present mythic regime with its misplaced faith in notions of randomness and runaway materialism, we are given little idea of the practical, even *occult*, power wielded by such a good attitude. That magical, reality-shaping, power belongs to the Moon, not to Saturn.

Contemporary astrologers usually agree that Saturn is more "realistic" than the Moon. Little do they know that it is so often actually the Moon that is pulling the strings that give shape to reality, manipulating the synchronicity grid, working lunar magic. The Moon wields that wand while hidden "behind the scenes" of this world, operating deep on the causal plane.

In the light of all of that, let me repeat a line from earlier: *we get to our first progressed Lunar Return about twenty-six-months before we get to our first Saturn Return.* The Moon comes first, then Saturn follows. Here is what that means in terms of the biopsychic script, as we begin to understand the role of the first progressed Lunar Return

- We must *feel* the shape of a personally meaningful path through mid-life before we can spell it out logically or strategically. It is the soul-instincts of the Moon which establish the *visionary, transrational foundation* for our middle years. They answer the most basic questions about the *right values* that will guide us in relative happiness through the labyrinth of hard choices which characterize everyone's middle passage.

At a less visible, even less purely psychological level, the Moon also pulls the magical strings of what we are taught to label "luck" or "chance." With its dominion over the causal plane, the Moon *creates underlying energetic structures* around which all of the so-called wild cards of life coalesce. Our plain-language word "attitude" hardly does proper justice to this lunar superpower.

- At progressed Lunar Returns, the Moon's sorcery prepares and manipulates the energetic stage, attracting circumstances which support us in successfully *doing something* when Saturn finally drags its languorous carcass into the spotlight and soaks up all the applause – half of which rightfully belonged to the Moon.

I am being mean to poor Saturn with that last line. I am doing that as a kind of Affirmative Action program to make up for a thousand years of astrologers not giving the Moon enough credit for its pivotal role in the processes which underlie everything that we are actually able to manifest in life.

A QUICK REVIEW OF THE SATURN CYCLE

Here in one short sentence is the practical application of everything we have said so far: *Successful Lunar Returns set the stage for successful Saturn Returns.* That principle is fundamental and inviolable. We cannot understand one kind of Return without understanding the other. Saturn and the Moon are in a *symbiotic relationship,* even though they look goofy when they try to dance together.

The Moon, by its nature, is the more subtle of the two. Because of that, we can understand the purpose of the three Lunar Returns more clearly if we see them reflected in Saturn's more visible light. To that end, let's quickly review the meaning of Saturn Returns. What exactly is it that the Lunar Returns are preparing us for? I explored Saturn Returns in detail in chapter twenty-three of *The Book of Earth.* Here is much of that theory again, summarized in eight quick bullets:

- We can look at human life as comprising three distinct ages, each with a distinct evolutionary purpose: *youth, midlife,* and *elderhood.*
- The first Saturn Return, at age twenty-nine, marks the *end of youth and the beginning of midlife.*
- The second Saturn Return, at age fifty-nine, marks the *end of midlife and the beginning of elderhood.*
- In a symbolic sense, the third Saturn Return, at age eighty-eight, simply marks the end of life. Many of us pass away before getting there. Those who experience the third Saturn Return enter a mysterious realm in which the veil between this world and the next grows thin. Death is their constant companion – maybe feared,

maybe even treasured as a wise counselor, but ever-present in any case.

- The purpose of the first *Saturn cycle* – the first thirty years or so of life – lies in *dreaming*. We are trying to *receive a vision* that will guide us meaningfully through the rest of our journey. Failure during the first Saturn cycle manifests as youth squandered on simple, blind appetite – or, perhaps even worse, on "practicality."

- The purpose of the second *Saturn cycle* – the next thirty years or so of life – lies in *making the dream real*. Doing something about it. Making a meaningful stand in the world. Failure during the second Saturn cycle manifests as a life of *time-serving drudgery*, with no larger purpose or overriding sense of meaning in anything we do at all.

- The purpose of the third *Saturn cycle* – the third thirty years or so of life – lies in playing the role of the *Elder*, generously passing on the fruits of our experience to those who come after us. Failure during the third cycle of Saturn manifests as an old person simply becoming an "old fart" – and if you need that term defined, be careful: you are probably in danger of becoming one.

- The purpose of the fourth *Saturn cycle* – the time past age eighty-eight – lies in entering a state of *mystical wizardry*, making peace with your non-material nature, preparing to execute that human masterpiece: *a peaceful, conscious death.*

That's three hundred words or so – and it probably gives us enough of an understanding of the Saturn cycle that we can grasp how Lunar Returns prepare us *emotionally* and *psychically* for each one of these steps along the way.

The point, as we will soon see, is that there are a lot of good ways to be young, a person in midlife, or to be old. *Of all of those good pathways, which one is right for you?* That is a question for the human heart – one which the Moon must answer, in other words.

Once the Moon's plan is in hand, Saturn just makes the coffee.

THE FIRST PROGRESSED LUNAR RETURN

Picture two women, Susie and Cilla. Both are in their forties. Both are happy with their lives. Both appear to be sane and fulfilled, and they each experience themselves that way. Each one feels about as comfortable in life as we humans can get. Each one feels that she has found her natural place in the world. Their guardian angels would agree. Susie and Cilla have complaints and worries, of course – again, they are human. But given the realities of life, for each of these women in midlife, we can affirm that what they are experiencing is as good as it gets. They are both doing fine.

- Cilla is a pediatric physician working in a public hospital in an underserved part of the city. She has been in a stable relationship since her late twenties. She has a spoiled cat whom she loves. She's a vegetarian and prefers herbal tea over coffee. The last time she had an alcoholic drink was one glass of champagne with four friends last New Year's Eve. It is now the middle of March. She phones her ageing parents every Sunday afternoon, and takes a yoga class every Thursday evening.

- Susie is a wilder soul. She is currently a bartender in Key West, Florida. She likes tending bar because that kind of work gives her a lot of freedom. "It's a *job*, not my life," she says. She's been married a couple of times, but neither of the marriages took. She is still friends with her ex's and she even sleeps with one of them from time to time. Right now, she is squirrelling away money as fast as she can because she plans to quit her bartending job and have an open-ended adventure in South America starting sometime next year – or at least as soon as she has enough cash saved up to quit her job and go.

Unless the horizons of our imaginations are far too narrow for our own good, we instinctively bless and honor these two imaginary women. Each one has made her own choices and created a pattern of experience in her middle years that works well for her. Each woman has listened to her heart and followed its counsel – which is to say that *each one has paid attention to her Moon.*

Underlying all the choices implicit in both of their lives, we see that classic lunar signature: *pure whimsy.* On the face of it, Cilla, being the more practical one, might not seem to be nearly as whimsical a creature as Susie – but ultimately who is to say that it is "more logical" to be a doctor than to be a bartender? Who is to say that "reason declares" that a stable relationship is superior to the life of a single person?

Susie will certainly pack more varied experience into her life than will Cilla – and who is to say that her choice is not closer to life's ultimate purpose?

Or that it is not?

You probably already see where this is going astrologically:
- Cilla's natal Moon lies in Capricorn in her tenth house.
- Susie's natal Moon lies in Sagittarius in her fifth house.

As we learned back in chapter three, *taking care of the Moon is the secret of happiness*. Each of these women has heeded the *transrational message* of her Moon – and each one of them came to a turning point in that regard at her first Lunar Return, which sealed the deal. In so doing, each woman has created *a midlife worth living*.

But Cilla's life would make Susie miserable, and *vice versa*.

As we will soon explore in detail, Cilla and Susie, just like you and me, each reached a definitive crossroads at her first progressed Lunar Return. Each woman then, at age twenty-seven, faced the same possibility: *that her heart would whisper in her ear, offering her precious, transrational guidance about the path of meaning, purpose, and happiness that lay ahead for her.* Each one could heed the message – or ignore it, and simply be swept along in the floodtide of "practical advice" that rains down on us all.

Both Susie and Cilla got it right. Not everyone does. But these two women both chose paths of healing, regeneration, and recovery. In so doing, they did not need to understand the rhyme or reason underlying the healing. They did not require insights. All they needed to do was to surrender to their own hearts.

Susie and Cilla both serve as good examples – and the fact they made *such different choices* is what brings us past mere theory and into the realm of real wisdom.

LET'S GO TO HIGH SCHOOL: THE FIRST
PROGRESSED LUNAR RETURN.

At the first progressed lunar return, we are twenty-seven years old. Hopefully, we have reached a level of maturity by then in which we can let our hearts speak to us about the right shape of the next three decades of our lives. The questions the first progressed Lunar Return raises are profound and lie miles beyond the range of mere logic or reason.

- What is the correct ratio of work to adventure for me? Which one of the two is rightfully more important?
- What about my inner life versus my outward productivity?
- Am I suited to long-term partnership or am I better off single? Either answer is fine, but I do need to choose one or the other.
- In love, what about the eternal question of passion – with all its difficulties – versus peaceful companionship? Which path works best for me?
- What about having kids? Is that right for me – or not?
- What about where I should live? Where is my natural home?
- In what should I believe? What values might give meaning to my life?

Only the heart can answer questions such as those. The answers transcend reason and must arise directly from the interior world. They are utterly personal and individual. We might say that we "must consult our souls" for advice and guidance in these matters – and pity anyone who tries to find answers with a calculator, religious dogma, or some online app.

Fair enough – but the way we say all of that astrologically is simply that *we must ask our Moons.* Because of the eternal laws of synchronicity, circumstances – often involving major forks in the road of life – arise at the first progressed Lunar Return. These *times of critical choice* trigger such reflections, perhaps revealing our hearts to us.

It behooves us to listen.

TIMING

By progression, the Moon conjuncts its natal position precisely only on one single day, but naturally the first Lunar Return embraces a longer period of time. How long? The most pressing parts of the passage occur when the progressed Moon is within five or six degrees of the exact alignment with its natal position. Given the Moon's average speed of about one degree per month, that boils down to a period of about a year or so, centered on the exact conjunction, and running about six months on either side of it.

Another way of looking at it, which also works well, is to reflect on the *entire period of the Moon's passage through its natal sign.* That runs two, or maybe nearly three years, depending on how fast the Moon is going.

The timing is not rocket science; the *interpretation* is.

In any case, a couple of years after the progressed Lunar Return, like clockwork, along comes the Saturn Return. That event marks a time to make *concrete, binding, choices and commitments*, and probably to close some doors behind us – maybe burn some bridges too. Those choices will naturally reflect the nature of your natal Saturn – *but they had better have been inspired by the whimsical values of the Moon as well.*

That complex, cooperative synthesis of these "two dancers" is pretty close to the heart of the art of ageing meaningfully, happily, and gracefully.

Fail in it, and you may be productive and outwardly successful, Saturn-fashion – but happiness will elude you. Happiness is the gift of the Moon, not of Saturn.

Here is the short version: at the progressed Lunar Return, *you feel it* and at the Saturn Return you need to *do something about it.*

TIME FOR COLLEGE

By calling all that I have just presented the "high school" version of the first Lunar Return, I do not mean to diminish it. All that I said is really how it works – with one significant tweak: while the actual periods of the progressed Lunar and Saturn Returns do operate as I have just described them, the process is actually far less localized in time.

And this is where we "go to college." The courses will be a little more demanding, but they will also zero in on the truth a lot more precisely.

- *We have an ongoing, ever-present relationship with our Moons and our Saturns. It is not as if either one of them turns on or turns off with the relevant progression or transit.* They are *always* doing that awkward dance with each other.

This point is especially clear when we look at the lives of highly self-actualized people. With every one of them, we can always discern the same biographical pattern: at several points in their lives, they threw caution to the wind and *surrendered to the irrational*. They did what pleased them without running the plan past the Reason Police.

To the people around them, they might have even seemed to have gone completely bonkers, as if they had become *lunatics* – and I hope you can delight in that revealingly lunar word as much as I do.

The transrational experiences of the heart that were gleaned during that "lunatic" period – *even if it did not coincide specifically with a progressed Lunar Return* – were then fed into Saturn's more sober data-crunching machinery. At that point, something serious – some Saturnian *Great Work* – is accepted, *based on the Moon's inspiration*.

Our "college" insight here is that, once again, this alchemical interaction of lunar *inspiration* and Saturnian *perspiration* must happen *throughout life*. We will see its mark over and over again, and not just at the two Returns.

Those Returns only signal *critical crescendos* in a psychic process which must remain ongoing.

Again, as you contemplate the biography of any self-actualized, truly individuated human being, you will see the fingerprint of this archetypal evolutionary structure as clearly as a loud burp at a quiet funeral. If you look for it, you cannot miss it. This dance between the Moon and Saturn is an elemental part of the inner workings, cradle to grave, of your birthchart, not just of certain transits and progressions.

That said, at the first progressed Lunar Return, *specific realizations and events arise that contain the seed-knowledge of how you can arrange to be happy in midlife*. At that time, something pivotal to your future is taking shape *on the causal plane*.

At the first Saturn Return, *you have an opportunity to wheel and deal with reality*, trying to strike a practical bargain about how to make that happiness crystallize here on the physical plane.

Let me give you an example.

BABA RAM DASS

Beloved spiritual teacher, Ram Dass, left this physical world on the Winter Solstice of 2019. He was eighty-eight years old – in his third Saturn Return, standing on the threshold of that fourth Saturn cycle where we all look death straight in the eye.

Many of us have been touched by him. For those few who might not know his story, here it is in quick summary. As a young man, Ram Dass was Richard Alpert. He earned his PhD in psychology and quickly became a professor at Harvard University. In 1958, he was awarded a tenure track position at that prestigious institution, right as he was hitting that magical age of twenty-seven: his first progressed Lunar Return.

By 1961, at his first Saturn Return, he was working with Timothy Leary doing research on the possible therapeutic uses of psychedelic drugs, such as LSD – which were not yet illegal, let alone widely known or controversial. In short order, psychedelic research grew notorious. Ram Dass – who was still Dr. Richard Alpert – was fired from Harvard. In 1967, he traveled to India, where he met his guru, Neem Karoli Baba. The guru gave him the name, Ram Dass, which means Servant of God.

From then on, Ram Dass became a countercultural icon, publishing many books and traveling around the world to teach, all the while remaining devoted to his guru, who died in September 1973.

In February 1997, Ram Dass suffered a stroke which left him significantly weakened and partly paralyzed. His work continued, but leaving his home in Hawaii became increasingly impractical and travel was soon given up entirely.

Ram Dass took birth in Boston, Massachusetts on April 6, 1931 at 10:40 AM-EST. Here's his chart.

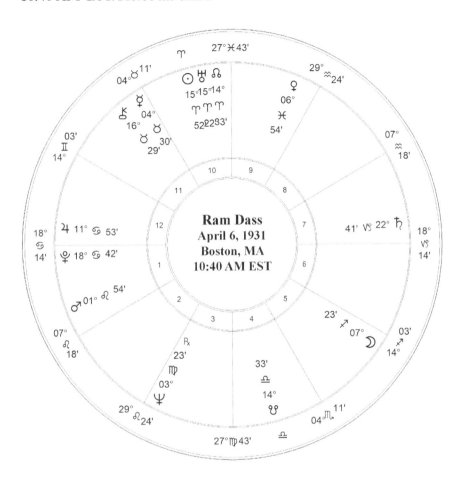

At a mechanical level, astrology always works. The danger lies in being seduced by the way it simply and reliably mirrors *what you already know* about reality right back at you. If you succumb to that party trick, you might be dazzled into missing the deeper messages a chart can provide.

In thinking of Ram Dass's lunar and Saturn cycles, let's start at that mechanical level – and run the risk of letting astrology tell us what we knew before we ate breakfast this morning.

Then I promise we will dig deeper.

When Ram Dass hit his first progressed Lunar Return, one of the events with which it correlated was that he got on the tenure track at Harvard – a fact which we mentioned a moment ago. The astrological symbolism is absolutely transparent: his Moon is in Sagittarius – a sign commonly related to *universities* and *higher education*.

Click.

The fifth house position of his natal Moon is related to *children*. He was of course *teaching undergraduates* – "children," at least in the broad sense of the world. More pointedly, around that same time, he published his first academic book, which was entitled *Identification and Child Rearing*.

Click again.

The fifth house, where his natal Moon lies, is also commonly called the *house of love affairs*. I am not sure what was going on in Ram Dass's life in the romantic department – but we do know that he fathered a child when he was twenty-four, something about which he only learned many years later. This event does suggest that at least no one was going to mistake him for a virgin.

Bingo, bingo, bingo, in other words.

All of this is what I mean by the chart "working mechanically."

The fact that everything lines up between his life and the symbols is a good sign, even though it contains not a scrap of new information or insight. It does tell us that Ram Dass was at least somewhat in tune with his Moon at this critical juncture – which implies that he was putting himself in a good position for happiness in midlife, not to mention preparing the inner ground for a strong Saturn Return.

We will soon have some deeper things to say about his Sagittarian fifth house Moon.

Moving on to Saturn, while still continuing to do astrology in a rote way . . .

When a conventional astrologer sees Saturn in the seventh house, we often hear baleful predictions about bad relationships. That dark view might be augmented – at least in the mind of such a fatalistic astrologer – by Saturn's many "unfortunate aspects": specifically, an opposition to Pluto and a square to his Sun-Uranus conjunction in Aries.

A simplistic view of "Richard Alpert's" life quickly corroborates that gloomy perspective on relationships – and do remember that the seventh house is about relationships *in general,* not only romantic ones. After a very promising professional start, the young professor, Dr. Richard Alpert, *"got involved with drugs because of that scoundrel, Timothy Leary, who destroyed him."* Quoting Wikipedia, "After returning from a visiting professorship at the University of California, Berkeley, in 1961, Alpert devoted himself to joining Leary in experimentation with and intensive research to the potentially therapeutic effects of hallucinogenic drugs . . ."

Saturn's timing: in Spring, 1960, transiting Saturn stationed just four degrees short of the conjunction. On January 27, 1961, Ram Dass had his one and only precise Saturn Return, but the planet was back within half a degree of exactitude in late September 1961, as Ram Dass returned to the east coast and "met his fate.".

Bingo, once again. Saturn – in the form of Timothy Leary – "struck" right on schedule.

Let's see if we can go any deeper.

Biographical events around the Lunar and Saturn Returns are significant and symbolic, but, as always they trigger underlying evolutionary intentions which unfold over a lifetime. A little while ago, I wrote that this dance between the Moon and Saturn is an ongoing process. Its gears turn and churn constantly, cradle to grave, in your birthchart, not just during these Lunar and Saturn Returns, which only represent peaks in the larger scheme of things.

Was Ram Dass's involvement with psychedelic drugs and Timothy Leary really his "downfall?" It certainly *looked* that way at the time. Here's a rhetorical question: *what do you figure his parents thought?"*

And yet, with even a penny's worth of hindsight, we can see it all so much more clearly. Those "irrational" events were pivotal moments in Ram Dass's journey. Without them, he could not have become what he came here to become. Ram Dass participated in an eternal human sacrament: *a strong, transrational, response to the Moon laid the foundation for a strong practical response to Saturn.* And we can observe this interdependency in action throughout his whole life, not just narrowly focused at the Lunar and Saturn Returns.

Remember our bartender, Susie, from a few pages ago? It was not a random choice to give her a fifth house Sagittarian Moon. Ram Dass had one too. He was not the same person as Susie – but he had some of that same "damn the torpedoes" energy we saw in our portrayal of her. *Like Susie, Ram Dass was willing to take chances.* Sagittarian-fashion, he framed his life as an adventure and as a learning experience rather than as a task.

That lunar attitude served him well in the long run – even if it cost him the chance to someday become the esteemed and eminently respectable – and totally forgotten – "Dr Richard Alpert, *professor emeritus*, of Harvard University."

There are deep waters in the fifth house, but it is ultimately about *reclaiming joy.* To Ram Dass – and to our imaginary Susie – saying that "life is a party," while far from presenting a complete cosmology, would ring a louder bell in their hearts than saying that "life boils down to duties and responsibilities."

That is where it gets really interesting: that last line – that "life is a list of duties and responsibilities" – *could come straight from the pursed lips of Saturn in Capricorn.*

And there it is – Saturn in Capricorn – powerfully placed near Ram Dass's Descendant, and squaring his Sun, to boot. Could "Richard Alpert" have sacrificed his life on an altar of endless duty? His Sagittarian heart might have bristled at the thought, but the astrological answer to our question is certainly yes.

Did he sacrifice his life that way? *Well, yes and no and not exactly . . .* The point is that the duties and life of service which he actually did ultimately accept *reflected his individuality.*

For most of his life, he was after all Ram Dass – the *Servant* of God.

Add one more insight and we can fully appreciate the dance of the two Returns: *that Ram Dass would not have succeeded in achieving that lofty expression of his Saturn were it not for his initial strong response to his natal Moon.* To be serious, he first had to be wild. To devote himself to his proper mission, he first had to master the art of the jailbreak. To become Ram Dass, he first had to be fired from Harvard.

His Moon and his Saturn were utterly different in tone, but he integrated them.

There are more details to glean from Ram Dass's progressed Lunar Return, and more broadly from the interplay of his Moon and his Saturn throughout his life. Sagittarius is often linked to *foreign experience* and the soul-triggering impact of *culture shock*. You could call it a "gypsy" Moon in the folk sense of that word – no reference to the *Roma* people. *Concretely, Ram Dass's wandering Sagittarian instincts led him to India and to Eastern religion.* Had he not had contact with those two leavening, alien cultural realities, can we even begin to imagine his life flowering the way it did? Without India, would Ram Dass have learned about meditation? Would his name ever have even become "Ram Dass?"

Those are all the clear fingerprints of his Sagittarian Moon, and they are found throughout his life. It is helpful to remember that Ram Dass was well-past these two Returns and already in his middle thirties when he first traveled to India. His natal Moon did not require a Lunar Return for it to work, feeding his Saturn with whimsical inspiration. That happened for him cradle to grave.

With all that said, let's move on to look more deeply at Ram Dass's Saturn, there in its own sign Capricorn, sitting only four degrees above his Descendant. It is a powerhouse planet in every way. We all have Saturn in our charts, but Ram Dass got the Rolls Royce version. It was strengthened by two conditions: being in the sign it ruled and by being "angular," which is to say conjunct the horizon.

Start by remembering that, at the deepest evolutionary levels of understanding, the seventh house always symbolizes people *without whom we cannot become what we need to become.* They are the *catalysts* of our souls. Add that Saturn, especially when it lies in Capricorn, reflects *elders.*

Timothy Leary had a massive impact on Ram Dass's life – and Leary was born in 1920. That made him about eleven years older – and eleven years looks like a significant age difference when you are in your late twenties. *Leary's impact on Ram Dass was, in other words, clearly foreshadowed in Ram Dass's birthchart.*

And, as we saw, their relationship began in earnest right on schedule at Ram Dass's Saturn Return.

Probably even more importantly, while in India Ram Dass met his guru, and trusted him, *and that ongoing spiritual bond with a much older man utterly transformed his life* – again, even turning him, literally, from Richard Alpert to Baba Ram Dass.

Neem Karoli Baba is a mysterious figure in many ways, but the best guess is that he was born sometime around the year 1900 – approximately one full Saturn cycle before Ram Dass. Clearly, he reflects the younger man's seventh house Saturn in Capricorn.

The same wild Sagittarian Moon which led Ram Dass to Timothy Leary led him to Neem Karoli Baba – and if he had not trusted those whimsies, would he have found his pathway home?

It is tempting to explore the various transits, progressions and solar arcs that were in play at various points in Ram Dass's adventurous, generous life, but that would carry us too far afield. Our main take-away here is that, for him – and for the rest of us – the dialog of Saturn and the Moon is ongoing, and at the first Lunar and Saturn Returns, an opportunity to cement their synergistic partnership arises.

- If we get that Moon-Saturn partnership right, a subjective feeling that we are *being guided by higher forces* is firmly cemented into our lives and our consciousnesses. Our resultant course through life's long middle reflects that dynamic partnership with a higher power.

And if we are too timid – *or too rational* – to trust the Moon, poor Saturn becomes all machinery and no inspiration. Our car may be shiny, but it has no driver, no fuel, and no destination.

Let's move on and reflect upon the *second* Returns of these two planets. Three decades have now passed. That is a lot of water under the bridge. Maybe we have learned something in the process.

Maybe we have earned more than a few wrinkles and gray hair.

Maybe life has been generous with us, at least spiritually. Maybe it is time to pass some of those gifts along to the ones who are about to inherit the stage.

ENTERING THE CYCLE OF THE ELDER

The late fifties are a strange period of life for most people. Despite our predictable jokes and complaints about ageing, the majority of us do not yet really feel "old" precisely – but it is definitely beginning to sink in that *we have more life behind us than what remains ahead of us.*

- For people who never listened well to their Moons, the fifties must be an awful time, plagued with the realization that something precious – yet something which they cannot quite define – has slipped through their fingers.
- For people who have heeded the Moon's guidance, warm feelings of a well-lived life – one that has had genuine meaning for them – begin to *mellow their appetites* and put *the look of tempered wisdom in their eyes.*

Astrologically, as the progressed Moon and transiting Saturn finish their second swing around the birthchart, Saturn has now lagged an *additional* twenty-six-months behind the Moon. That is why the second progressed Lunar Return occurs when we are about fifty-five, while the second Saturn Return does not hit until about four years later – at around age fifty-nine. During those four years, we all feel sort of "east of the Sun and west of the Moon," caught in the middle of a complex psychospiritual transition. This four-year period takes that long because it needs to, and not simply for astronomical reasons. The psychological and spiritual adjustments it represents completely alter our view of life, and they require some time to sink into our bones.

- At the second progressed Lunar Return, we experience *a secret, inner initiation* into Elderhood. Others might see some of its outward expressions, but no one can understand its true meaning except, possibly, ourselves.
- At the second Saturn Return, we come to the *outward, visible initiation* into Elderhood. It is time to begin to *enact* what we have realized, and not just at the progressed Lunar Return, but rather throughout our lives so far. We now show our spiritual cards, for better or for worse.

As we saw in *The Book of Earth,* even if we ourselves would rather ignore it, our friends generally guarantee that our second Saturn Return enjoys a high level of visibility. On our sixtieth birthdays – slightly behind schedule, in other words – they inevitably throw a party. Nominally, it is held "in our honor" – but the festivities typically involve calling us grandpa or grandma, while offering dead flowers, geriatric medications, rubber pants, plus a phony Viagra prescription.

Hopefully, the years have now tempered us enough to take it all in good humor. But our friends' message is clear: in their eyes, we are now officially "old."

Often it does not actually feel that way to us.

Most of us still have some life left in our bones at that point. Further augmenting the weirdness, the whole "turning sixty" thing invariably feels anticlimactic. The reality is that our second Saturn Return – which is what actually correlates with this process of initiation – is now many months behind us.

So, at our second Saturn Return:

- We have already been through the transition, and . . .
- Our friends have it all wrong anyway.

Earlier in this chapter, we summarized the Saturn cycle. If you are fuzzy about the second Saturn Return, it would be helpful to go back and have a peek at that page – or even better, to review that chapter in *The Book of Earth*.

Now let's look at specifically how the second *progressed* Lunar Return weaves the web of *secret inner processes* which underlie the epochal and *eminently visible* passages reflected four years later in the second Saturn Return.

TWO IMAGINARY ELDERS

In my next couple of stories, let's imagine that you and I are buddies. One day, I tell you that I have a feeling that I need to introduce you to a friend – actually a serious *mentor* of mine. She is an older, very private, woman. I cherish her; she is someone who I sometimes think might possibly even be fully enlightened. At any rate, I feel that it might be important for you to meet her. I also express trepidation about making the introduction because not everyone feels comfortable with her.

I warn you that she is sort of . . . *intense.*

With that scenario, we have actually set up a pair of tales. I am going to tell this story two times, each one involving a different wise woman. They are both "wizards" in the ancient sense of the word – both masters of the third Saturn cycle – but as distinct from each other as a panther and a poodle.

WIZARD NUMERO UNO

We arrive at the home of my friend – her name is Priscilla – exactly on schedule, just one minute before noon. Given her precise nature, I would not want to be late. She lives far from town in a little house which you cannot see from the road. A bit of a hermit, she lives there alone. She is in her eighties.

As she answers the door, I introduce you. Without smiling, Priscilla looks you steadily in the eye for slightly longer than seems appropriate, as if she is taking her time to size you up. After a few strange moments, she nods her head once, as if she has come to an accepting conclusion about you. Still locked in eye-contact, she shakes your hand and formally welcomes you to her home.

You have the distinct sense that your introduction might have gone otherwise.

You look around the room. Earth tones dominate. Heavy curtains conceal the windows. It is as if she lives in a library. Books are everywhere. There is no television or computer monitor visible.

The vibrations of her living room put you in a different century, long, long ago.

Priscilla offers us tea. There is no honey. We sit down with our mugs and we talk about life. Her language is precise and she speaks in full paragraphs. When it is your turn to speak, she listens carefully – *and six times she quotes your exact words ten or fifteen minutes later.*

The sheer waste and frivolity that are apparently the guiding stars by which most of humanity navigates life are a common thread in our conversation – and yet Priscilla seems more sad for them than judgmental.

We discuss Jung and Krishnamurti. We reflect on Buddhist notions of the emptiness of all phenomena and the impermanence of life. She refers to past lives as casually as many of us would refer to last summer.

After a couple of hours, we sense that it is time for us to go. Priscilla shakes your hand again. Once more, she looks deeply into your eyes for a little longer than is necessary. This time her gaze is softer. It seems that you have passed a test.

It feels inexplicably weird to be as proud of her approval as you are.

She thanks me for bringing you to visit. She invites us back any time. You get the impression that Priscilla does not say that to everyone.

As we get in my car and drive away, I ask you, somewhat nervously, what you thought of Priscilla. You thank me profusely for the experience. You agree that you might just have been in the presence of an enlightened being. You know that Priscilla's presence sunk down into your soul like a stone falling into a deep well. You sense that you will remember and cherish this day for the rest of your life.

But three minutes later, I crack a stupid joke, and you laugh at it more loudly than it deserves – and you follow-up with a silly remark of your own. After two hours with Priscilla, we both need some comic relief. I had warned you that she was intense.

Our time with Priscilla was precious, but now that it is over, we both could use a laugh.

WIZARD NUMERO DOS

We arrive at noon at the door of my second friend, Susan, who is also in her eighties. I am nervous, wondering if it was smart for me to bring you here. I never know how she is going to behave. Susan can be what the world might call "inappropriate," especially for an older woman such as herself. Inwardly, I am praying that she does not do anything that offends you. She'll say whatever enters her mind. I've seen her pretty drunk once or twice too – not ever mean, but loud and inclined to say things out loud which other people might only be brave enough to think.

Several times, I've seen her flirting with people forty years younger than herself, seemingly without much reference to anyone's gender.

Ever tricky, just in case Susan behaves badly, I have done my best to make *you* feel responsible for our being there, even though deep down I know it's "my fault."

Knock, knock, and Susan answers. She is wearing a tee-shirt emblazoned with a logo unflattering to the current Administration. I introduce you to her. Susan looks you straight in the eye, *and the sheer intelligence of her gaze hits you like a laser beam.* Politely, you put out your hand to shake. She brushes it aside, and instead she gives you a warm smile and a quick hug, and welcomes you expansively to her home.

We sit down at Susan's kitchen table as the clock strikes noon. Unbidden, she pours each of us a shot of tequila, straight up. Soon it feels as if we are all old friends. We talk about life. With a twinkle in her eye and some salty language, Susan conveys a compelling stew of insight, humor, forgiveness, metaphysical assumptions, a penetrating perspective – and, above all, *a profound disrespect for spiritual pretense of any sort.*

You get the feeling that if she were to meet the Pope, she would be respectful – but she would call him Francis. And that the Pope would like her.

Maybe the subject drifts into sex. She is not shy about it at all – in fact, even though she is in her eighties, there is still something unabashedly sexy about her. *Apropos* of our conversation, she recounts the tale of a lurid affair she had when she was young. And she recounts what she *learned* from it. Her story is matter of fact, undefended, totally naughty, and yet self-accepting – but also wistful about the pain she caused herself and others.

You get the feeling that Susan's life is an open book. This is a woman without the slightest need for secrets. She would like you to like her, but she is not going to play any games to earn your affection. Giving that affection – or not – is up to you.

Susan loves life and is not afraid of it. She sees how serious it is and, at the same time, how *funny* – and somehow those simultaneous, contradictory, perspectives have found a point of unbroken unity in her consciousness. Her very being conveys that unity and does so without ever preaching about it.

A couple of hours later, it is time for us to go. After warm goodbye hugs at Susan's door, we head for my car. We are both slightly tipsy from the tequila. I ask you what you thought of my friend. You thank me for the experience. *You agree that you might just have been in the presence of an enlightened being. You know that Susan's presence sunk down into your soul like a stone falling into a deep well. You sense that you will remember and cherish this day for the rest of your life.*

Familiar words – but Susan and Priscilla are certainly two very different kinds of Elder. Yet each one is a genuine wise woman. Each one is a gift to anyone fortunate enough to be in her presence.

If they met, would Susan and Priscilla get along? Probably, even though their paths are so distinct. Each one of them is secure in her own identity and generous in her interpretations of other people's paths.

The point is, there are a lot of different ways to be an Elder.

As we saw, Priscilla and Susan are both in their eighties.

Five well-lived decades have wrought an evolutionary miracle in Cilla, our pediatric physician, and another miracle in Susie, who was once our happy-go-lucky bartender from Key West, Florida.

PRISCILLA'S SECOND LUNAR RETURN

With her natal Moon in Capricorn and the tenth house, Priscilla always sensed that retirement was just not on the radar screen for her. During her second Lunar Return as she turned fifty-five, her career as a pediatric physician was still vibrant and active. In conversation, friends might casually refer to a future time "when she retires," presuming that it would happen sometime in the next ten years or so.

The statement would always seem a little off base to Priscilla, although she understood its common-sense reality well enough. She knew that retirement – in the sense of withdrawing from her community to play golf and watch television – would never make her happy. Being a *Healer* (Moon) had always been her *Mission* (tenth house). Getting older would not change that. Capricorn had manifested as *responsibility* and *competence* – but now, at her second Lunar Return, it felt as if some new kind of butterfly was trying to emerge from that Capricornian chrysalis.

Capricorn, like Saturn, represents the archetype of the Elder – and even though Priscilla had possessed a Capricorn Moon since she was "little Cilla," her face was now beginning to catch up with her soul.

Could her *life* catch up with her soul too?

At her second Lunar Return, Priscilla, like the rest of us, experienced a secret inner initiation into elderhood. The word "secret" might imply midnight meetings and code words, but that is not what it is about. "Secret" here just means that these changes are happening inside of us, where no one else is likely to have any direct awareness of them.

The Moon is a powerful alchemical cauldron, but for it to brew those magical elixirs successfully, the lid needs to fit tightly. It is usually best, in other words, if we do not talk about it too much.

Priscilla takes her work as a doctor seriously. She is proud of it – but she is also beginning to *feel a little tired of it* as well. That's a critical line. Many of us reach our middle fifties and a certain *weariness* settles into our bones.

This weariness marks a major fork in the road.

If we take the wrong path, we misread that fatigue as a natural side effect of our getting older. It is not – it is a sign that we are weary, not of life, but rather *of the way we have been living*. We are ready to begin to imagine new possibilities. The source of these visionary possibilities is the Moon, which is to say that they are not the result of logical deduction or any kind of conventional problem-solving. Instead, they arise from a matrix of inspiration, reflection, dreams, fantasies, and *patience* – a matrix which has now ripened.

In her fifties, Priscilla continued her medical career, but she also began a study of "Jung and Krishnamurti." She had always been a healer – she is a doctor, so even the taxman would agree with that assessment. But now the Capricorn Elder begins to constellate within her in a fresh way, leading her to lay down a fresh *attitudinal, energetic foundation* upon which a brand new definition of what it means to be a healer in her community can rise.

Elders tend more toward healing souls than to healing bodies.

Maybe Priscilla begins a study of evolutionary astrology – that is only one illustration, one of many thousands of good possibilities. But being an evolutionary astrologer could potentially provide her with a new vehicle for the expression of her healing intentions and her Elder-wisdom, and so suggesting it works well here as a way of concretizing our thinking.

Maybe no one at the hospital where she works has any idea that Priscilla is pursuing these kinds of philosophical interests. For her, Jung, Krishnamurti, and evolutionary astrology are all, as we saw, part of a *secret initiation*. The alchemical cauldron is bubbling away – with the lid on tightly, as it should be.

Come Priscilla's second *Saturn* Return, she may still be a few years away from retiring from her medical career – but she accepts money for an astrological consultation for the first time. Or she offers a living room class about Jungian Perspectives on Jiddu Krishnamurti. Her maturational steps forward in life now begin to "get real" in other words – although angels would laugh at my use of the word "real" here. To them, what was happening invisibly during Priscilla's second Lunar Return was every bit as real as these outward events. In fact, to the angels, it was *more* real since it was unfolding on the causal plane, which is where every existential "fact" ultimately sends down its roots.

STAYING HAPPY

How to be happy as we get older? The world always tries to frighten us about the ageing process, as if it were "all downhill from here." It really does not have to be that way, but it is true that the *basis of happiness* is shifting. We seek a different treasure and we need a different map in order to be able to find it. As we learned in *The Book of Earth,* much of the secret of happiness after the second Saturn Return lies in our finding some *avenue of appreciated generosity* toward people younger than ourselves. From then on, as Elders, we are in a *symbiotic relationship* with everyone under sixty – they benefit from the relationship, and so do we.

At the second Lunar Return, we sense the *possibility* of that avenue opening up. *We set the mood of our elderhood.* We begin to fumble toward it through the fog of all that we have created in midlife, guided only by heart, soul, and instinct. We do not yet have anything like a specific plan, nor do we need one. The process is more emotional and intuitive than rational. That is the nature of the Moon.

Critically, at the second Lunar Return, we also find that some of our compulsive midlife drives are beginning incrementally to lose their hold on us, making way for the opening of a new set of motivational avenues. We still probably like sex and money and power and looking good – all the usual monkey business – but just not quite as *compellingly* as we did ten years earlier.

A space is opening up in us for something new.

Try explaining marriage to a bright ten-year-old. You quickly hit the limits of his or her understanding – limits that only the passage of time can shatter. Something very similar happens for all of us at the second Lunar Return . . . a younger person might genuinely understand our descriptive words about the transitions – but not like she or he will understand them when they arrive at that stage themselves. Old people are not necessarily wiser than younger ones - but for all of us, unless we cancel ourselves out with laziness or addiction, wisdom deepens with time.

DON'T FORGET THE BARTENDER

What about Susan? How did she navigate the passage from bartender to a wild wizard woman? I won't parse out her story in the same way I just did with Priscilla. The principles are exactly the same; it is only the tone of the lunar process that differs.

Susan, at fifty-five, was under significant social pressure to "grow up" and "to start acting her age."

She blithely ignored it, clicked her heels, and went out dancing instead.

RAM DASS AND ELDERHOOD

Ram Dass experienced his second Lunar Return on January 31, 1986. Remembering that this event is, at its root, a "secret" initiation, much of the actual evolutionary changes that occur remain invisible. In our astrological zeal to "make predictions," we need to be careful never to lose that critical perspective: with the Moon, *it is what is happening inside us* that needs to occupy center stage. Outward material events are secondary. It is not that "nothing happens" at the second Lunar Return – that is not true at all. It is only that we need to be careful of being seduced by appearances, and thus missing the deeper layers of meaning.

With that caution in mind, let's reflect on Ram Dass and the events in his life which mirror this lunar initiation. In 1986, at his second Lunar Return, he was instrumental in founding the Dying Center, first in New Mexico, then in California. This hospice was the first residential facility in the United States where people with terminal conditions could come to try to die as consciously as they could, blessed with mindful spiritual support around them. To be fair, I imagine that many more conventional hospices over the years have also offered spiritual support to the dying. In America, the majority of them would naturally use Judeo-Christian metaphors, which might seem jarring to the kinds of people drawn to Ram Dass.

What did founding the Dying Center *mean* for the emerging elder in Ram Dass? That is the question that brings us directly to the heart of his second Lunar Return. As ever, that Lunar Return is about changes in the *tonality of our being*, and not narrowly about any of our "doings." Those "doings" are only shadows cast in the material world by the real action, which is happening on the causal plane.

Ram Dass's Moon is, as we saw earlier, in Sagittarius and the fifth house. Here's a simple formula, cut straight from conventional astrological boilerplate: Sagittarius is about *journeys* and the fifth house is about *joy*.

Can death be a joyful journey?

That line is easy to say – in fact you could probably train a parrot to say it. A parrot – or some phony guru with dollar signs in his eyes.

But to *truly feel* that death can be a joyful journey – to truly experience that possibility in your heart – can be seen as a pinnacle spiritual accomplishment for anyone born with a Sagittarian Moon in the fifth house. Few attain that level of commitment to living life as an adventure right to the last drop. Few attain that purity of faith.

Did Ram Dass himself attain it? That was certainly one of his evolutionary goals in life – his chart guarantees that. My answering such a question would be pretentious. *But I know that it was his question to answer.* And because of the eternal laws of mind and spirit, it was at least *possible* that his answer could be yes.

If *you* were to lie there dying, how much would you value the simple radiant presence of someone who had climbed that high on the spiritual mountain? Might their faith give you faith? Might some of their wisdom be contagious? Reaching that spiritual pinnacle was *the invisible, secret, goal* of Ram Dass's soul at his second Lunar Return. That was *the kind of Elder* he was striving to become.

And, oh, by the way – as this inner secret initiation was happening, he opened "the first residential facility in the United States where people with terminal conditions could come to try to die as consciously as they could, with mindful spiritual support around them."

With the Moon, the real action always unfolds on the causal plane. The material plane may register a few ripples on the surface, but it sharpens our astrological eye to remember that those events are only minor side-effects.

THE THIRD LUNAR RETURN

The Moon progresses back to its natal position for a third time when we are about eighty-two years old. By then, many of us have already left our physical bodies behind and gone beyond the reach of astrology. Even if we are still breathing, by any standard we are now widely viewed as *old*, even if we still have twenty years of life left in us.

Meanwhile, our third Saturn Return is still quite far away – that twenty-six-month difference between the two cycles has now grown to a lag of over six years. We'll be eighty-eight by the time that third Saturn

Return finally happens. Assuming that we survive, those six years will pass quickly, at least at a subjective level. Time goes by more and more rapidly as we age. Ask anyone in his or her eighties, and they are likely to tell you the same thing – *the past thirty years just whipped by. It seems like just yesterday I was in my fifties.*

We reflected on this change in our relationship to time itself in *The Book of Earth*. It is quite pivotal in understanding how we actually experience these later stages of the biopsychic script. Intuitively, the central principle is not hard to grasp: tell a teenager that he or she needs to "wait for an hour" and you know what kind of attitude you are likely to encounter. In contrast, imagine you are a business person in midlife on a trip. You just heard over the airport P.A. that your flight is delayed for an hour. You sigh and go back to your book.

You're older now; an hour is no longer a very long time.

For our purposes, the major effect of this *age-bending-time* phenomenon is that, even if we are destined to become a centenarian, at our third Lunar Return, we understand that *death is just around the corner.* However many years we might have left in this world, we sense that they will pass in the blink of an eye.

There is no honest way of thinking about the third Lunar Return that fails to include the psychospiritual impact of that reality.

To many younger people, those words probably sound depressing. It is not really that way at all. Older people – especially more conscious ones – tend to have a more accepting attitude toward death, and less fear about it. After all, they have been living with its presence for a long time. Some of them would even welcome death – and we must be careful never to confuse that acceptance with "clinical depression".

For the wiser ones, it can feel more like their ticket home.

FEELING MY AGE

In strategizing about how to write this next section of the book, I just had a funny experience. Sharing it suddenly seems like a better choice than my original plan. My intention had been to start exploring a new dimension of the third Lunar Return – *how as we get older, we tend to feel "left behind" by the rapid changes of society.* In trying to think about what word-pictures

I might paint in order to convey that idea, I had hit upon a possible approach: I wanted to illustrate how ageing often excludes us from the "conversation" of contemporary culture. I thought I might do that by constructing a sentence in the opaque language of contemporary teenage slang. I would then use that sentence to point out how, to the ears of an older person, the teenager's coded sentence might as well be written in Urdu.

Personally, I don't actually know any of that slang, so I figured I would just do a Google search for it. I did that – and sure enough, I learned some new words, along with some old words with new meanings. But as I did that search, I hit upon two realizations that completely scuttled my plan.

- The first realization was that, Google as I might, I would almost undoubtedly make a perfect ass of myself by getting the sentence wrong. Young people reading it would roll their eyes and probably feel compelled to say those dreaded words, *"OK, Boomer . . ."* And they would be right – I can't speak their language any more than I would expect any of them to be able to "speak fluent Hippie" without sounding ridiculous the way I can. Hey, I was there . . .

- The second realization I came to before abandoning my original approach was that the idea of constructing such a sentence *simply bored the pants off me.* Why learn a language that would only make me look dumb and artificial? *And why bother to learn a language that will be forgotten and replaced in five years, perhaps far less?*

My own third Lunar Return is still a decade away, but I can feel it coming. As I extrapolate forward from what I have just written, I realize that *I am a creature of my own time in the world and that my time is passing.*

I imagine that whatever feelings I just described, I will feel them ten times more deeply at my third Lunar Return. Again, let me underscore how difficult it is to make these honest points without them sounding depressing.

They aren't depressing, not at all.

Whatever our age, there is a kind of acceptance of reality *as it is* which is hardwired into every single one of these biopsychic script events – and a good rule of thumb with every one of them is that you cannot really understand them in a full, integrative, accepting way until you arrive at that age yourself.

The *evolutions of attitude* that happen around the third lunar Return do not reflect disinterest in the world, nor are they directly linked to the approach of death – although death is always in the background as we enter the fourth cycle of life. Instead, they are connected to our *changed relationship to time* – the way it simply zooms by as we get older. *As the years pass faster and faster, everything that is transitory begins to seem even more transitory.* Styles, jokes, customs, the code-speak of each generation, the pop stars *du jour*, world leaders, headline events – even things that used to seem eternal – all melt away in the rearview mirror.

Back in those far-flung hippie days when I was "a longhaired freak" playing bass in a rock band, we used to say, "rock and roll will never die."

Right.

Now I know better.

Now I know that everything dies.

To understand the third Lunar Return, take all the ideas that I have just expressed and try to reframe them in your mind as joyful and liberating.

Try to see them as a source of serenity rather than sadness or alienation.

That is the heart of the third Lunar Return.

GETTING IT WRONG

Some old folks just don't get it. Age itself is not guaranteed to teach us anything. I know people in their teens who are already wiser than people in their nineties. You probably do too. Consciousness is never generated by an unconscious process, such as simply getting older. Some people just get old with not much to show for it except wrinkles and thinning hair – and something inside them gives up the ghost at this third Lunar crossroads. I expect that such lost souls tend not to live very much longer. They have no reason to, except maybe fear. And fear is no friend of longevity.

It is tempting to pontificate that "young people cannot possibly understand any of this", but that is not really true. I guarantee that there are some young folks reading these words right now and understanding everything I am writing perfectly well.

Just add reincarnation to the equations and the mystery is lessened: those young people *have all been old before.* At some deep interior level, we all have a memory so long that it would give us vertigo even to think about it. The principles which underlie the cycle of Lunar and Saturn Returns are all archetypal

– and archetypes are the inheritance of every human being, no matter his or her age. That is why I firmly believe that there are young astrologers who can understand all of this, *and thus help clients who are older than themselves.*

Those young ones can understand everything that I am writing now – just not like they *will* understand it in the marrow of their bones when they hit their eighties.

If you are wise today, doesn't it make sense to believe that you might be even wiser in ten years – or fifty years?

And isn't the opposite thought a depressing dead-end, which fortunately, collapses under the slightest scrutiny?

ACCEPTANCE

There is a high spiritual art to simply letting things be what they are.

Countering that absolute acceptance of reality is another impulse: *we humans like to control everything.*

Much of that controlling drive is actually linked to our survival – and we are all great fans of survival. We naturally, and quite reasonably, want to control our food supply, the temperatures to which we are exposed, the purity of the water we drink. We want to control our children in a way that protects them from danger. We worry about money. We take vitamins, eat organic vegetables. Some of us buy guns.

If we can just figure out a way to control everything, maybe we can live forever . . .

It is a futile fantasy of course, but a nearly universal one – *until the third Lunar Return.* Once again, the ultimate psychospiritual foundation of this developmental stage in the biopsychic script is the knowledge of our impending and utterly inescapable exit from this physical plane. *Accept death, and you can accept practically anything.* There is an incalculable power built into that kind of surrendering. And it is a power which becomes vastly more available to us around age eighty-two, as the Moon progresses to its third conjunction with the place it occupied at our birth, so very long ago.

Conventionally, we are exhorted to *respect our elders.* If we truly grasp the message of the last few pages, we can see that our "respecting" them is hardly the point – it is more that we would be fools to miss a chance to sit at their feet.

That statement applies strictly to true elders. Old farts, on the other hand – well, let us at least strive to be kind to them. We might say that they have suffered enough, but actually their self-imposed suffering is not yet quite done. No need to punish them for their judgmentalness, their bitterness, or their obsession with getting on with the past. The consciousness they have created for themselves is its own punishment.

They can at least take comfort in the idea of reincarnation.

KRISHNAMURTI

In his early adolescence, Jiddu Krishnamurti fell in with English Theosophists. That happened way back in the colonial India of a century ago, back when "the Sun never set on the British empire".

To their credit, these Theosophists recognized a great soul in young Krishnamurti.

To their eternal discredit, they attempted to turn him into something that he did want to become – a Messiah for all humanity.

There is controversy around the time, and even the date, of Krishnamurti's birth. There is, however, a B-rated chart in Astrodatabank which I find plausible. It shows an Aquarian Ascendant and a wildly Out of Bounds Moon in Sagittarius, along with a Sun-Uranus opposition. Any single one of those highly independent factors would be enough to suggest that Krishnamurti would experience impatience with anyone else trying to live his life for him. Taken together, they form an indelible astrological statement of radical individuality and an equally radical penchant for honesty.

Krishnamurti rebelled against all attempts to frame him as "The Coming World Teacher." I understand that he once simply declared that "the Age of Gurus is dead". He walked away from all of that "spiritual" *fru-fru*, and simply chose to be himself. He certainly did not want to become a guru, although he was – and still is – often revered in that light by many people.

Krishnamurti died at age ninety, just two years after his third Saturn Return, which brings us to the end of the cycle of astrological events we are exploring in these pages – but it is something he said at his third Lunar Return which I now want to put in the spotlight. With these words, he demonstrated the pinnacle of *absolute acceptance of life as it is*, concentrating his wisdom down into one absolutely psychedelic phrase – and once again, these are words we could train a parrot to say, but which only a true Elder could feel and truly project.

Jiddu Krishnamurti experienced his third Lunar Return on March 30, 1977. That same year, he gave a talk in California. New Zealand-born spiritual teacher, Jim Dreaver, who was in attendance, later wrote, "Part way through this particular talk, Krishnamurti suddenly paused, leaned forward and said, almost conspiratorially, *'Do you want to know what my secret is?'*"

Krishnamurti rarely spoke in personal terms, Dreaver recalls. "Almost as though we were one body we sat up. I could see people all around me lean forward, their ears straining and their mouths slowly opening in hushed anticipation".

Then Krishnamurti, "in a soft, almost shy voice", said:

"You see, I don't mind what happens."

It's the singer, not the song. Krishnmurti, master of the third Lunar Return, had learned its deepest, most challenging lesson: *a radical, absolute acceptance of whatever actually happens.*

I wish that we all could have been there to receive the psychic pulse of that wisdom as it emanated from him in that moment.

I don't mind what happens.

Krishnmurti no longer needed to control the uncontrollable. He had given up that neurosis. He had liberated himself from that impediment to joy. A twelve-year-old could possibly learn that same lesson. Such a twelve-year-old could probably walk on water and heal lepers too.

How amazing it is that as we enter our eighties, an "astro-biological" force comes into play to support us in glimpsing that same wisdom. Glimpse it, and you will laugh at the feeble irrelevance even of death itself.

And probably just in time.

You will not mind what happens, even if that means that you die.

You will know that life can heal us of anything, even our deepest fears – that we can all regenerate and recover, even from our deepest madness.

25

THE ASCENDANT

Every astrologer knows about the Ascendant – it is universally understood to be a key element of the whole system. Still, there is a slippery question regarding how exactly to define it. The term Ascendant actually has three different meanings – meanings which interlock rather than contradict each other. Keeping the distinctions among them clear can save us some confusion.

- I might, for one concrete example, simply say that poet and musician Leonard Cohen *had Virgo rising*. No astrologer would bat an eye. Simple: Virgo was his Ascendant sign.
- Equally, I might say that Cohen had *27° 58' of Virgo rising* – in other words, much of Virgo actually fell in his twelfth house, while only the last couple of degrees of the sign remained on the eastern horizon. The rest of Virgo had already risen. A few more minutes and Libra would have been Cohen's Ascendant.
- Thirdly, I might say that Leonard Cohen had Mercury *in* his Ascendant – which is to say, Mercury was in his first house, even though the planet was not in Virgo at all, but rather in the middle of Libra.

All three of these usages of the term Ascendant are accurate and legitimate, and none are rare among practicing astrologers. But as you can see, these three definitions are all somewhat different. As we will soon see, the latter one – that Cohen had Mercury *in his Ascendant* – is actually the most practical of the three. In it, we essentially draw an equal sign between the Ascendant and the first house.

Fair enough; their meanings are effectively equivalent.

HOW YOU DAWN ON PEOPLE

Had I ever had the chance to do a reading for Leonard Cohen, I might have said that *Virgo was dawning over Montreal* at the instant that he took his first breath, exactly as the Sun dawns every morning. That is a quick, clear *physical* definition of the Ascendant.

(Leonard Cohen was in fact actually born right at dawn, with the Sun conjunct his Ascendant too, but I want to keep everything simpler for our initial purposes here.)

After telling Leonard Cohen that Virgo was dawning when he was born, I would have then added that therefore *he himself dawns on people in a Virgo way*. Those simple words provide a quick, clear *astrological* definition of the Ascendant. In a nutshell, it represents how we present ourselves to the world. It is about our *vibrations*, or to be a little more formal in my language, it is about our *affect*.

We might simply call the Ascendant your *style*.

In my first book, *The Inner Sky*, I defined the Ascendant as the *mask* we wear. That is a pretty good metaphor – it should be, since I stole it from the finest of sources: Carl Gustav Jung. His word was *persona*, which is just the old Greek word for mask.

Wearing such a "mask" does not really mean that we are hiding anything in a malicious or sneaky way. It is just a reflection of the fact that we all are required to create a simplified, streamlined, and highly edited, version of ourselves in order for us to deal functionally with everyday life.

That is what the Ascendant is about – or at least part of what it is about. We will go deeper in a little while.

So far, all of this reflects the first of our three possible definitions of the Ascendant – the sign that was rising in the east at one's birth. But Leonard Cohen also had Mercury in his first house – Mercury was *in* his Ascendant by our third definition. That alerts us to the fact that much of his style or affect could not be explained by Virgo alone. *He also dawned on people in a Mercurial way,* coming across as verbal, curious – and perhaps easily bored, unless things of interest were actively happening.

Going further, his Mercury was in *artsy, relationship-oriented* Libra – not picky, technical Virgo. Cohen was, after all, a poet and a lyricist. All of those qualities would be revealed spontaneously in his affect too. The point is that the Mercury signature in his outward social expression was unmistakably obvious – Mercury was as much a part of Cohen's Ascendant as was Virgo.

I mentioned that Cohen was born at sunrise. Therefore the Sun, as well as Mercury, was part of his style. He came across as a *solar* individual. Generally that implies at least some degree of *charisma,* even qualities of leadership, and perhaps of selfishness. The sun has *gravity;* so do solar people. All of that was certainly true of Leonard Cohen. I am concentrating more on his first house Mercury here though – *the reason I am doing that is because it helps us underscore how it is possible for a second sign to become part of someone's Ascendant complex.* Mercury was *in* Cohen's Ascendant – but it was in Libra, which added Libran dimensions to his style.

What about our second definition of the Ascendant – that Leonard Cohen had 27° 58' of Virgo rising? That is useful information too, but more for technical reasons. In essence, that degree divides his twelfth house from his first house. A planet could thus be in Virgo, but have nothing at all to do with his Ascendant. Cohen, for example, had a tight conjunction of Venus and Neptune in just under thirteen degrees of Virgo. Unlike his Libran Mercury, they were not "in his Ascendant." They were already fifteen degrees up in the Montreal sky, solidly in his twelfth house – losses, endings, and wistful spirituality.

That explains a lot about why Leonard Cohen was forever saying goodbye to people he loved.

A NOTE FROM ME TO YOU

Given the natural association between the Ascendant and the first house, this chapter should have rightfully appeared in *The Book of Fire,* right at the outset of this series. Why didn't it? The short version is simply that I forgot. In that first book, we looked carefully at the triad of Aries and Mars and the first house, but I did not take time to dive very deeply into the Ascendant itself.

All along throughout these four books, my intention has been to try to unlock some of the underlying mysteries that bind a sign, a house, and a planet (or two) into a single *clan* – and then to cast some light on how that clan fits into its larger element *family*.

Astrology, like the animal kingdom, can be overwhelmingly complicated. Biologists have avoided at least a few headaches by thinking in orderly taxonomical fashion about *phylum, genus, and species.* In these four volumes, my aim has been to attempt something similar in astrological terms.

Along the way, the Ascendant sort of disappeared from my thinking. That oversight happened simply because the Ascendant is certainly not a planet, nor exactly simply a sign, nor exactly a house.

But it is certainly very important.

In *The Inner Sky*, for example, I wrote about the "primal triad" of Sun, Moon, and Ascendant, framing the Ascendant as one of the three most significant symbols in all of astrology. I suggested that there was no better place to begin an astrological analysis than with unraveling that critical triad of symbols.

THE MAGIC FORMULA

In *The Inner Sky*, I proposed a simple, foundational formula to get a birth-chart interpretation solidly off the launching pad. We start by turning each sign into an archetype – Aries could be "the Warrior" and Gemini could be "the Teacher," for example. The formula then becomes that you *are* (insert the Sun's sign archetype) *with the soul of* (insert the Moon's sign archetype) *wearing the mask of* (insert the Ascendant's sign archetype).

- Ram Dass, for example, becomes the *pioneer* with the soul of a *gypsy* wearing the mask of the *healer*.
- Marilyn Monroe is the *storyteller* with the soul of the *exile* wearing the mask of the *queen*.
- Winston Churchill becomes the *philosopher* with the soul of a *king* wearing the mask of the *servant*.

Every sign has a darker, weaker side too. We can create bad archetypes for each one of them and merrily apply the same formula. With history's designated bad guys, it can be pretty transparent:

- Hitler becomes the *materialist* with the soul of a *tyrant* wearing the mask of the *snob.*
- Heidi Fleiss, the infamous "Hollywood Madame," becomes the *schemer* with the soul of the *reckless fool* wearing the mask of the *criminal.*
- Peter Sutcliffe, the "Yorkshire Ripper," emerges as the *trickster* with the soul of the *invisible man* wearing the mask of the *seducer.*

We can also apply these negative archetypes in a more intimate, and certainly more helpful way – not to shame anyone, but to crystallize shadow information in a cautionary fashion. While I, for one example, prefer to think of myself in noble terms as the *elder* with the soul of a *pioneer* wearing the mask of the *shaman,* it is possible that at times my partner Michelle sees me in less flattering terms. To her, on a bad day, I might appear to be the *curmudgeon* with the soul of the *bully* wearing the mask of the *evil sorcerer.*

Beauty is always in the eye of the beholder.

This simple Sun-Moon-Ascendant formula still works quite well, especially for people beginning to learn astrology. It pulls a lot of information together into one single, manageable sentence, and thus helps us to stave off our ancient enemy: getting so overwhelmed by the complexity of the symbolism that our intuition disengages.

Here's a Table of these archetypes, both the high ones and the low ones. I encourage you to add to it as you please. It practically begs for a creative response.

Sign	High Archetypes	Low Archetypes
Aries	Warrior; Survivor; Daredevil ; Pioneed; Hero	Bully; Reckless Fool; Walking Emergency; Hothead
Taurus	Silent One; Earth Spirit; Wood-Elf; Totem Animal *(pick a creature)*	Subborn Mule; Banker; Materialist; Lazybones; Lounge Lizard
Gemini	Witness; Storyteller; Communicator; Messenger; Teacher	Chatterbox; Eternal Adolescent; Trickster; Scatterbrain; Liar

Cancer	Healer; Caregiver; Dream-weaver; Psychotherapist	Smothering Mother; Crybaby; Invisible Man/Woman; Whiner
Leo	King/Queen; Performer; Clown; Child; Aristocrat	Autocrat; Megalomaniac; Spoiled Brat; Prima Donna
Virgo	Servant; Critic; Analyst; Mentor; Perfectionist; Craftsperson	Martyr; Drudge; Whiner; Fault-finder; Nitpicker; Failure
Libra	Lover; Artist; Diplomat; Peacemaker; Counselor; Friend	Flirt; Fence-sitter; Snob; Clinging Vine; Codependent
Scorpio	Shaman; Psychoanalyst; Detective; Hypnotist; Truth-teller	Seducer; Introder; Back-stabber; Wicked Witch/Evil Sorcerer
Sagittarius	Gypsy; Scholar; Philosopher; Pilgrim; Optimist; King or Queen	Guileless Fool; Overbearing Jerk; Fanatic; Know-It-All
Capricorn	Parent; Prime Minister; Hermit; Elder; Strategist; Solid Rock	Tyrant; Curmudgeon; Schemer; Power-Tripper; Control Freak
Aquarius	Exile; Genius; Scientist; Rebel; Truthsayer; Revolutionary	Misfit; Kook; Sociapath; Crimial; Iceberg
Pisces	Mystic; Dreamer; Poet; Seer; Visionary	Addict; Lost Soul; Helpless One; Escapist; Flake

In any case, all of this spotlights how significant I believe the Ascendant to be. When it comes to looking at the human personality through the lens of the birthchart, in my mind, the Ascendant is one of the "big three" – hence my term, *the primal triad*. Just add the lunar nodes, and you've got the essence of the whole system of evolutionary astrology.

Remember our third definition of the Ascendant, which includes any planets in the first house – those would be relevant to our understanding as well. Throughout all four of these books, you will find cookbook paragraphs about the meaning of each planet when it is in the first house. To fully understand the Ascendant, just add that information too.

MASKS

Calling the Ascendant "the mask" is evocative, but there is a problem with one of the implications of the word: *a mask hides a face*. Hiding is not really the purpose of the Ascendant at all. We are not actually trying to *hide* anything behind it. What we are doing is more like *filtering* or *editing ourselves* as a way of adapting to the realities of social interaction. Maybe you are introduced to a stranger. *Pro forma*, she politely inquires, "How are you today?"

Your line of course is, "Fine, thank you. How are you?"

She is probably fine too.

But maybe the truth is that you have actually been a little depressed for a few days, and you are not quite sure why. Maybe your back aches. Maybe you are worried about your kids or money or all the bad news on television.

Your line in the script is still "fine, thank you."

How long would it take for you to give that stranger an honest answer? *And why would you bother?* Your relationship is not that intimate. It does not require the kind of honesty that requires effort, time, and vulnerability – the kind of honesty we expect with dear friends or in healthy partnerships. In social situations, simply saying "fine, thank you" is perfectly appropriate. Further, a truly honest answer would bore both of you to death. You wish each other well – but you do not actually care about each other that much in a personal way. If I assert that "99% of human relationships are superficial", it sounds awful, as if I am condemning us all to an eternity of chit-chat.

That is not what I mean at all. I just mean that to function sanely and comfortably in the social world, we all need to do some serious editing. *We need to filter out most of what we actually are.* How intimate do you want to be with the check-out person in the grocery store when she asks you how you are doing today? Or the cop who stops you for driving a little too fast?

Bless our social filters – we need them. That is the Ascendant in action. Make a strong response to it, and you won't be telling your deepest secrets to the Fed Ex delivery guy who just knocked on your door with a package.

Screw it up, and you will.

STAINED GLASS

Stained glass filters the light that shines through it, and thus provides my single favorite metaphor for the Ascendent. Unlike a mask, *stained glass does not hide anything at all*. Light still gets through – but in an "edited" form.

The stained glass metaphor works right down to a truly granular level of detail. Blue stained glass is blue because it blocks all the wavelengths of light except for the blue ones. Shine a flashlight through blue glass and only blue light comes through. The original white light is a mixture of all the colors of the rainbow – but that blue glass blocks out the red and the green and the yellow.

What happens if you now shine a *red* light through that same blue glass? You will see *violet*. Shine a yellow light through it – what happens? *Green* appears. In other words, to know what color you are going to see, you need to know two things:

- First, the color of the stained glass.
- And second, the color of the light that you are shining through it.

The Ascendant works in precisely that same fashion. This means that to know how someone is actually going to "dawn on you," you need to know more than her Ascendant. You also need to know what kind of light is shining through it – *you need to know the rest of her chart,* in other words. Put a Virgo Ascendant on a Gemini with a Pisces Moon and you will see something very different than *that same Ascendant* on a Capricorn with the Moon in Taurus.

Sigmund Freud had Scorpio rising. So, very probably, did Napoleon. But Freud had a seventh house Taurus Sun and a Gemini Moon in the eighth house – that meant that the light shining through his intense Scorpio "stained glass" had an *interpersonal* and *psychological* tone.

Napoleon, meanwhile, was very probably a tenth house Leo with a Capricorn Moon – and thus not cut out for a career as a psychotherapist. Rather than inviting someone to intimacy and the sharing of secrets, as we see with Sigmund Freud, Napoleon's Scorpio Ascendant transmitted the Leo and Capricorn colors of *authority* and *domination* – and added a threatening note to them.

I hope that it is obvious that I am keeping my examples of Freud and Napoleon as simple as possible. They both naturally had Mars, and Venus, and Mercury, and the rest of the planets in their charts – all of that was part of the light shining through their stained glass too. But you get the idea: start by thinking of all of the possibilities inherent in the sign of the Scorpion, then imagine meeting Sigmund Freud – and compare that experience to what it might have felt like to meet Napoleon Bonaparte.

Wearing 'the mask of the Scorpion" can, in other words, have more than one meaning.

How do we sort it out? The answer, as we contemplate anyone's Ascendant, is always to remember to ask ourselves the same question: *what color is the light that is shining through it?*

THE LIGHT OF THE SOUL SHINES THROUGH EVERY GESTURE

Let's go back for a moment to our familiar ritual exchange: "how are you, fine thank you." The words naturally epitomize the superficiality of any conventional social interaction – but lurking behind them, we detect something a lot more inspiring.

You are introduced to someone and you both say your predictable lines – and *immediately you hate the rascal.* What is going on? If he were a rattlesnake, he would have just rattled.

Try this: *there was something about the way he said "fine, thank you" that just instantly rubbed you the wrong way.* Two quick observations:
  • I am aware of how completely crazy that last line sounds.
  • I am completely confident that you know exactly what I mean and that you have had precisely that same instantaneous experience of judgment countless times.

Obviously, it was not really the man's *words* that alarmed you. They are the same words that everyone says. It was something far more primordial. *What was transmitted to you in those first seconds of your interaction?* Remember: the Ascendant is like stained glass: *it colors the light of the soul as it translates itself into the world of social interaction.*

That is what I mean when I say that "the light of the soul shines through every gesture." Whatever it was that shone through the stained glass of that man's Ascendant repelled you, and that transmission took less than a second. Of course we could tell the same story in a happy way. Sometimes you meet someone and by the time you get to "fine, thank you", you already feel connected.

The overriding point is that we all make fairly instantaneous assessments of other people. Something elemental comes through even in the most superficial of interactions. *No one can hide his or her vibrations.* Once again, the light of the soul shines through every gesture.

People like to say that you can't judge a book by its cover. *But with other human beings we often can – and we often do.*

And we are often pretty good at it.

All of this is part of understanding how the Ascendant actually works. It is not simply about chit-chat. It is the "stained glass" through which souls make initial contact with each other. It is the medium that conveys the mystery of "love at first sight" – not to mention the mystery of instant antipathy.

The Ascendant may be "superficial" – but so is your skin. And you would be hard-pressed without your skin. Calling the Ascendant superficial just means that it is on the surface. *Like skin, it is the membrane that separates consciousness from cosmos.*

And the membrane is permeable. Information flows through it in both directions.

BECOMING WHAT YOU ARE HERE TO BE

Get your act together – that is an old slang exhortation from a couple of generations ago. I suspect that younger people do not use it anymore, but most of us can still understand the meaning of the phrase. It means *get yourself organized. Do something. Become what you are supposed to be. Get your show on the road. Do what you are supposed to do.* Instead of saying "get your act together," a humanistic psychologist might speak more loftily of *self-actualization* – which actually means approximately the same thing.

Oprah Winfrey popularized the phrase, *be your best self,* and that line is cut from the same cloth as well.

All of those common sayings bring us directly to the higher octave of the Ascendant. It is there that we can potentially find answers to one of life's most pressingly eternal questions: *where exactly do I put my foot next?*

If we always have a good answer to that one, we will always know what we are doing. We will always *have our act together.* We will be self-actualized, or at least moving along the path toward it.

Houses, as we have seen throughout this series, are active and behavioral. They are about what we actually *do* – the choices we make and the stands we take in this world. The Ascendant, as we have seen, is essentially identical in meaning to the first house, so it too is similarly active. It too is about how we *manifest our souls through our specific behaviors.*

But exactly which behaviors are the right ones for you personally? *Of all of the different people whom you could possibly be, which one is the right one?* Which of those many potential *personas* – all of which might be legitimate – best serves you on your spiritual path?

Those are the central *evolutionary* questions with the Ascendant – and the ones which bring us beyond merely describing your social style, and instead move us squarely into developmental, counseling territory.

AT THE COCKTAIL PARTY

Fifty people, all turned out in their finest attire, all milling about on their feet, all engaged in the usual yack, yack, yack. Brie, crackers, and chardonnay. Posturing, flirting, and name-dropping.

You get the picture.

Maybe that is not your natural habitat, nor is it mine – but it is actually a wonderful place to study Ascendants. *They are the masks we all wear when our attendance is required at the great cocktail party of the world.*

Perhaps you notice a woman across the room. As soon as you recognize her, you quickly pivot in order to avoid her eyes. You met her at the last gathering of this group and you are not eager to repeat the experience. It was not that you actively disliked her or that she did anything offensive. She was simply *tedious,* that's all.

When you first met her, you said the fateful words, "How are you?" *And twenty minutes later, she finally finished telling you how she was.* Her report included details regarding her feelings about the unfairness of her electric bill, her views on the weather, and a detailed description of how it is sometimes difficult for her to fall asleep at night.

When you spot her across the room, you understandably turn quickly away – *but you are not quite fast enough.* She sees you pivot. She understands that you wanted to avoid contact. Her feelings are naturally hurt. *You are not the only person who has turned away from her.* It is a pattern. In the poor woman's mind, self-pitying words form: *"I don't know why no one seems to like me. When I meet them, I try my best to be open . . ."*

Well, "open" is the problem, lady. Someone asks you how you are and what you are really supposed to say is "fine, thank you." She doesn't understand that.

The dubious "joys of superficiality" are not the point. There is of course no particular joy in superficiality. *The point is that the generation of human intimacy is a delicate dance.* It is an art. Unless we are talking about love – or hate – at first sight, people generally take a while deciding how they are going to relate to each other. Even when "the light of the soul shines through every gesture," *and we like what we see in another person*, there is still always some give-and-take before we even decide whether to talk about maybe having lunch together someday. As the process unfolds, there is much social choreography – and handling that choreography gracefully and comfortably is purely Ascendant territory.

"How are you" and "fine, thank you" are nothing but time-fillers as something far more ancient and subtle passes between people's eyes and souls.

The poor, awkward woman in my anecdote is *making a weak response to her Ascendant*, whatever sign it might be. She has failed to "have her act together." She lacks what the French would call *savoir faire* – which literally translates as "knowing what to do." To the French, *savoir faire* signifies pretty much what the word *poise* means to English speakers.

This awkward woman is tedious because she bores you by rattling on too much about personal things – things that do not interest you simply because *she herself* does not yet interest you.

If she were a friend, it would be different. Friends *do* interest you. They have earned that. They have done the dance with you.

What is this woman's Ascendant? Which sign might give too much detail that way? Virgo is an obvious candidate – and possibly she has Virgo rising. *But having Virgo rising does not mean that you are destined to spend your life boring other people at cocktail parties.* With that Ascendant, that is not "how you get your act together." Virgo, as we explored in *The Book of Earth*, does in fact attend to detail – but that does not necessarily mean cataloging every detail out loud.

Were I to counsel this woman, I might praise her ability to *notice details* about other people and to *remember* them. With a Virgo Ascendant, I would emphasize that the path of self-actualization for her lies very much in the domain of finding *a meaningful form of service*. Figuring out ways to be *helpful* to others is good for her, socially as well as spiritually. I would encourage her to *capitalize on her ability to listen carefully and to remember what she hears*. She can connect the dots behind whatever information people offer about themselves, and she can use that knowledge to offer meaningful, effective support. *By focusing on other people's needs rather than on her own insecurities*, she can learn to make herself useful. People will like her for that – and she will be supporting herself in the very act of supporting them.

This is one way that she can "get her act together." This is how she can self-actualize. That is what Virgo rising looks like when it has *savoir faire* – when it "knows what to do".

SHY VERSUS QUIET

We might describe a person as *shy*. Everyone understands the meaning of that word – the poor man simply feels self-conscious and uncomfortable in social situations, so he probably avoids them whenever possible. If his attendance is required, perhaps he clams up, then over-compensates, then clams up again.

Shyness is not a pleasant condition to have or to watch. But being human means existing in a network of social relationships, whether we like it or not. If we are shy, that means that much of daily life is rendered painful.

Meanwhile, we might describe a second person as *quiet*. Note how, while the words shy and quiet overlap significantly, no one will ever confuse them. A quiet person is *an introvert who is easy and self-accepting about being that way* – while a shy person is an introvert who is clumsy and self-conscious about it.

In either case, we might imagine that we are looking at someone with Cancer rising. And the sign Cancer represents *a spectrum of possibilities for our social expression ranging from shyness up to quiet*. In counseling someone with a Cancer Ascendant, we do not merely aim to *characterize* their social behavior, pigeon-holing them in some static description of inescapable awkwardness in groups. Instead, we aim to *heal and help*. In talking to a shy person, we point to a path that leads to becoming *a self-accepting quiet person*. We help them move up the spectrum – and thus "to get their act together."

We try to teach such a person how to be quiet without exactly being shy about it.

THE RULER OF THE ASCENDANT

Long ago, astrologers noticed that whatever planet ruled the ascending sign would play an exaggerated role in a person's life. They came to call that planet *the ruler of the chart*. It is still a useful term, but let's aim to be more precise about it. If you have Virgo rising, then Mercury is the ruler of your chart – but that does not necessarily mean that Mercury is the most powerful planet in your astrological make-up. It may be a *candidate* for that honor, but ruling the Ascendant does not exactly seal the deal. We can understand the role played by the "chart ruler" with considerably more precision if we see it in the light of what we have just been exploring about the Ascendant in general.

Start by remembering that the Ascendant is about how we *express ourselves behaviorally*. No one can hide his or her rising sign – it is always obvious, almost by definition. *The planet that happens to rule the Ascendant partakes of that same exaggeratedly active, behavioral quality.* For that reason, it always aims the spotlight at *where the person's life is happening* – what "theaters of behavior" are chronically emphasized in his or her biography.

- Ruler of the Ascendant in the tenth house? *Lots of a career or mission focus.*
- In Cancer? *Nurturing activities* and *domestic motivations* are constantly evident in the shape of the biography.
- Ascendant ruler in the fifth house? *Creativity, love affairs – or maybe the focus is on kids.*

That quality of *underscoring behavioral activation* is probably the main reason that our astrological ancestors called the planet that ruled the Ascendant the "ruler of the chart." Simply said, like the Ascendant itself, it *shows*. You cannot hide it. If our main astrological concern is with outward existential descriptions and characterizations of the visible shape of a life, that chart-ruling planet can be relied upon to provide pivotal clues. There is more to know about that planet though. Looking at it from a higher level, the Ascendant offers insight into our best *path of self-actualization* – how to get our act together. Cancer rising? *Be quiet, not shy.* Virgo rising? *Get good at something that helps other people.* Sagittarius? *Travel, live the adventure.* Aquarius? *Be yourself no matter what anyone says.* The planet which rules the Ascendant rings exactly those same bells, *adding further helpful advice about specific biographical directions that are likely to be fruitful.*

Virgo rising? As we have seen, that means that you need to get good at something that helps other people. *So where is Mercury and how can it help you succeed in making that happen?* Maybe Mercury is in the sixth house – *seek your mentors.* They will help you to self-actualize, and without them, it will be much more difficult to do that. Mercury in Scorpio? *Study the more penetrating forms of psychology.* Claim your voice as a truthsayer.

Double it up: what if that same chart-ruling Scorpionic Mercury lies, once again, in the sixth house? Put two and two together: *look for mentors who can help you learn about those penetrating forms of psychology.*

Leonard Cohen had Virgo rising, as we saw at the outset of this chapter. That meant that Mercury ruled his chart, from Libra and the first house. It was powerfully placed, in other words – no surprise, considering the mark he left on the world with his voice.

Libra reflected Cohen's *artistry* and the first house added the need for *independent, autonomous behavior.* As chart-ruler, Mercury itself meant that for Cohen to self-actualize, he would need to *find his voice.* But his true voice would be *romantic* and *artistic* – those are specifically Libran energies. And to find it, he would have to make *unilateral decisions* which others would sometimes interpret as *selfish* – there's the signature of the first house.

Read Leonard Cohen's biography and you will see plenty of exactly those kinds of behaviors. His artistry is self-event. He was arguably the most eloquent voice of his generation. But what about his mixture of Libran *romanticism* and first house *autonomy* – even selfishness? Did they manifest in his life too? His song, *Bird on a Wire*, contains this highly autobiographical couplet:

> *If I, if I have been unkind*
> *I hope that you can just let it go by.*
> *If I, if I have been untrue*
> *I hope you know it was never to you.*

To be in an intimate relationship with Leonard Cohen would obviously not have been a path for the faint-hearted or the conventional. Yet by following his own Ascendant path of self-actualization, he graced the world with lyrics of such luminosity that I suspect they will be remembered alongside the poetry of Yeats and Wordsworth. I can imagine that a thousand years from now people will still be saying *there is a crack in everything. That's how the light gets in* – and have no idea where the words originated, just as today people might say, "All that glitters is not gold," and have no idea that they are quoting William Shakespeare.

I think it is fair to say that Leonard Cohen got his act together.

Let's go through the Ascendant sign by sign in cookbook fashion. As ever, please remember to take these notes only as your launching pad.

If there happens to be a planet "in the Ascendant" – in the first house, in other words – remember to give it equal weight. Even better, try to integrate the planet with the rising sign itself.

And don't forget about the planet (or planets) that rules the Ascendant. If you need some help in interpreting that planet, you can always look it up in terms of its sign and its house somewhere in these four volumes. That will give you a good starting place – and remember to add *specifically self-actualizing* dimensions to your interpretation of that chart-ruling planet.

THE ARIES ASCENDANT

The Path To Self-Actualization: In order to fulfill my specific evolutionary goals in this life, I resolve to push through any fears or intimidations that stand between me and the experiences I aim to have. I am learning how to be *effectively assertive* in skillful ways. I am on the path of the Warrior, which means that my real battle is always with my own fear. When I fully get my act together, I will play a protective role toward people, ideas, or things that I love and which deserve to be defended.

The Stained Glass Through Which the Light of My Soul Shines: I am complex, but in what people see when they look at me, there is a distinct spin in the direction of my appearing honest, avid, and eager to cut to the chase. People might impute aggression or competitiveness to me, even if I am not actually feeling any of those things.

When I Am Merely Wearing A Mask: If I slip into posturing and posing, I can take on an air of *bravado.* I can hide my own insecurities and fears behind my ability to be intimidating to other peoples. I can come across as "the bull in the china shop."

What I Look Like When I Am Lost: If I have failed to follow the thread of my own natural path, then I seem chronically tense and nervous, coming across with "a chip on my shoulder." I create conflict and drama where none is necessary. I startle easily. My social reflex is to argue and negate everything I hear. I alienate people.

THE TAURUS ASCENDANT

The Path To Self-Actualization: In order to fulfill my specific evolutionary goals in this life, I resolve to start by simply trying to take it easy. I need to calm down and get centered. I will make a priority of staying grounded, natural and straightforward, no matter what happens. I want to be comfortable materially, but I affirm that more of that comfort comes from living simply and "being here now" than from money and all of the complex distractions it can buy. I pay careful attention to the needs and appetites of my body. I value relationships with people who love me as I actually am rather than as what they plan for me to become.

The Stained Glass Through Which the Light of My Soul Shines: I am complex, but in what people see, there is a distinct spin in the direction of disarming naturalness, apparent simplicity, and an earthy lack of airs or pretense. People feel easy around me unless they are the sorts of posers who want me to see them through the lens of their fancy titles, connections, and stylish hairdos.

When I Am Merely Wearing A Mask: If I slip into posturing and posing myself, I can take on an air of stubborn rigidity, as if I were set in my ways – and committed irrevocably to remaining that way. I can seem pedantic and judgmental, out of kilter with the times.

What I Look Like When I Am Lost: If I have failed to follow the thread of my natural path, then I come across as materialistic, crass, and narrow-minded, insensitive to any of life's subtleties or nuances of meaning. I can be a boor.

THE GEMINI ASCENDANT

The Path To Self-Actualization: In order to fulfill my specific evolutionary goals in this life, I resolve to commit to a path of endless learning and the exploration of my intelligence. I will let simple curiosity guide me. I cherish open-mindedness in myself and in others. I like to be surprised – and if I am wrong, I sincerely appreciate being proven wrong since that is one way that I keep on learning. I resolve, on the basis of this ever-expanding base of knowledge, to claim the full power of my voice, whether it is spoken or written.

The Stained Glass Through Which the Light of My Soul Shines: I am complex, but in what people see, there is a distinct spin in the direction of my seeming energetic, open to experience and engaged in a spirit of fascination with everything that happens around me. People will often interpret these qualities in me as "youthfulness," regardless of my age. I speak easily, but my presence also seems to invite conversation. People want to talk with me.

When I Am Merely Wearing A Mask: If I slip into posturing and posing, I can take on an air of pedantry, as if I have a compelling need simply to be heard – at length. I hide my heart behind a flood of words. I overestimate the patience of my audience. I speak of things which everyone already knows as if they were great revelations.

What I Look Like When I Am Lost: If I have failed to follow the thread of my natural path, then I come across as simply flaky, long-winded, and tedious. I flit from interest to interest, never focusing on one particular thing or achieving anything of consequence. I seem to be all tactics, but never with any apparent sense of strategy nor any long-term aim.

THE CANCER ASCENDANT

The Path To Self-Actualization: In order to fulfill my specific evolutionary goals in this life, I resolve to claim my full power and destiny as a healer of souls, minds, and/or bodies. I will not be afraid to seek the teachings I need in order to achieve that aim, nor will I succumb to the temptation to withdraw from the pain and horror of the world. Instead I will find a way to actively address it. To sustain myself on this path of caring engagement, I seek the support of my soul-family and I prioritize keeping our bond active and strong.

The Stained Glass Through Which the Light of My Soul Shines: I am complex, but in what people see, there is a distinct spin in the direction of kindness and caring. People are drawn to express their hurts to me. I listen well. I radiate sensitivity. Perceptive people will also sense that I am cautious and self-protective.

When I Am Merely Wearing A Mask: If I slip into posturing and posing, I can take on an air of withdrawn, cautious distance, as if I were content to remain essentially invisible. I can use caring behavior toward others as a way of hiding my real needs and feelings. It is easy to trick people into talking about themselves, and that means that I need to reveal nothing about my own needs or feelings.

What I Look Like When I Am Lost: If I have failed to follow the thread of my natural path, then I come across as guarded and inclined toward emotional self-isolation. I become self-conscious and self-protective to the point of defensiveness. My nurturing energy is misdirected toward myself, with none left over for other people, which leads to an exaggerated, even hypochondriacal, attention to my own complaints of body and soul.

THE LEO ASCENDANT

The Path To Self-Actualization: In order to fulfill my specific evolutionary goals in this life, I resolve simply to shine. I will overcome my self-consciousness, step out onto the stage of life, and express myself, heart and soul, without inhibition. I resolve to become tempered, confident, and skillful when all eyes are on me. I recognize that such self-expression, if it is to be successful, requires that I develop certain performance skills – and that means effort, experience, and training. Sincerity is essential, but sincerity alone is not sufficient. Actors say that you should only make your audience happy once, not twice – happy when you step into the spotlight, but not happy when you finally leave it.

The Stained Glass Through Which the Light of My Soul Shines: I am complex, but in what people see, there is a distinct spin in the direction of the *appearance* of confidence, authority, and wellbeing – even if I am not actually always feeling that way. I wear the mask of the King or the Queen, which makes truly getting to know me seem much easier than it actually is.

When I Am Merely Wearing A Mask: If I slip into posturing and posing, I can take on an air of presumption, even of superiority, as if I were "entitled" somehow. I can hide behind a role that I have learned how to play. My fear of truly vulnerable and honest self-revelation can lead me to "create a character" and spend my life playing that part.

What I Look Like When I Am Lost: If I have failed to follow the thread of my natural path, then I come across as autocratic and demanding. I issue proclamations which wise people ignore, while fools believe them. Soon I am surrounded by adoring fools.

THE VIRGO ASCENDANT

The Path To Self-Actualization: In order to fulfill my specific evolutionary goals in this life, I resolve to prioritize learning a set of skills which are helpful to other people and which give me a sense of joy, accomplishment, and dignity when I offer them. These skills might take the form of "a job"– but they are not necessarily something for which I would be paid. Finding a path of meaningful service – work that matters – is really the heart of the matter, not simply money. I will strive to become genuinely indispensable.

The Stained Glass Through Which the Light of My Soul Shines: I am complex, but in what people see, there is a distinct spin in the direction of seriousness, competence, and the desire to be of use to others. I radiate discernment, alertness to errors and flaws, and a desire to improve everything I touch.

When I Am Merely Wearing A Mask: If I slip into posturing and posing, I can take on an air of fussiness, even worried agitation. I can become compulsively supportive of others in ways that reflect only an exaggerated sense of duty rather than offering a genuine gift of myself. I can edge toward martyrdom and self-sacrifice.

What I Look Like When I Am Lost: If I have failed to follow the thread of my natural path, then I come across as perpetually nervous and worried. I talk compulsively. My reflexive attitude becomes one of criticism – of always seeing what is wrong with everything. I seem to send out a message to others that they can dismiss me, use me, and generally treat me presumptuously.

THE LIBRA ASCENDANT

The Path To Self-Actualization: In order to fulfill my specific evolutionary goals in this life, I resolve to seek alliances with people who balance me emotionally, spiritually, and practically. I recognize that I cannot do what I am here to do all by myself. I build effective interpersonal skills and meaningful, productive partnerships. I present myself amiably and attractively. I can be sufficiently diplomatic to get along with people who are very different from me, but who might still play essential supporting roles in my journey.

The Stained Glass Through Which the Light of My Soul Shines: I am complex, but in what people see, there is a distinct spin in the direction of them greeting me as pleasant, reasonable company – someone who is on their side. Not everyone will fall in love with me, but generally, people will like me. A deeper way to say the same thing is that people will tend to *overestimate the amount of common ground that we share.* In my social relationships, that is fine – it's why most people think I am all right. In intimacy, I need to make sure that I am meeting my partners in the middle – not three-quarters of the way over toward their position.

When I Am Merely Wearing A Mask: If I slip into posturing and posing, I can take on an air of exaggerated "niceness" which creates a note of falseness in my interactions. I may be the only one who notices it, but the effect is that I can feel lonely in a crowd of people, even ones who feel as if they know me and like me. The reality is that they do not actually have a clear sense of who I am, they only believe that they do.

What I Look Like When I Am Lost: If I have failed to follow the thread of my natural path, then I come across merely as a social butterfly, engaged in a range of relationships which serve no real purpose at all. I might become overly concerned with my appearance, both physically and socially, slipping into superficiality, name-dropping, or mere vanity.

THE SCORPIO ASCENDANT

The Path To Self-Actualization: In order to fulfill my specific evolutionary goals in this life, I resolve never to apologize for my intensity or for my honesty, nor to allow polite collective customs which only serve to avoid and deny the truth to rob me of my natural voice. I do not need to force my perceptions on anyone – but if someone presses me in the direction of pretending to be more shallow than I am, I resolve to simply walk away. I avoid lying unless lies are really the only way to avoid a serious body count.

The Stained Glass Through Which the Light of My Soul Shines: I am complex, but in what people see, there is a distinct spin in the direction of my weaving a sort of "truth zone" around me. People are welcome to step into it and to be real, or to avoid me if they prefer – but once in the zone, we pursue emotional and psychological reality relentlessly. As a result, I will hear many secrets and many confessions in the course of this lifetime.

When I Am Merely Wearing A Mask: If I slip into posturing and posing, I can take on an air of forced, theatrical intensity. I can enjoy shocking people. I can act for dramatic effect rather than for the sake of simply putting human psychological reality on the table.

What I Look Like When I Am Lost: If I have failed to follow the thread of my natural path, then I come across as moody, dark, and brooding. My reflexes become negative and critical. I might slip into a kind of psychological sadism, hurting people with my insights. A pessimistic, dismissive view of life radiates from me, while I slip into cynicism about any possibility of human decency or altruism.

THE SAGITTARIUS ASCENDANT

The Path To Self-Actualization: In order to fulfill my specific evolutionary goals in this life, I resolve to embrace my life as an endless quest and an unfolding adventure, constantly stretching my horizons intellectually, culturally, and spiritually. I will spend my life learning. I will travel. I will absorb fresh perspectives from people who come from different walks of life or different cultures. I will stand up for my principles and I will express them out loud. And I will dance until I am ninety years old.

The Stained Glass Through Which the Light of My Soul Shines: I am complex, but in what people see, there is a distinct spin in the direction of big-hearted openness to life. I look like I am fun, even perhaps inclined to be a little wild. There is also an element of something philosophical in my aura, as if people can tell with one look that I will always put my principles ahead of any mere practical advantage. I am colorful, and I embrace that quality. People who do not like it can walk away.

When I Am Merely Wearing A Mask: If I slip into posturing and posing, I can take on a self-righteous air. I can come across as a *know-it-all.*

In social situations, I can take up more energetic space than most people would think is appropriate, unwittingly demanding attention in ways that strain people's patience.

What I Look Like When I Am Lost: If I have failed to follow the thread of my natural path, then I come across in a crashing and banging way, seemingly oblivious to other people's legitimate needs or rightful boundaries. I can seem narrow-minded in a preachy, judgmental way, as if I am God's appointed messenger and it is "my way or the highway".

THE CAPRICORN ASCENDANT

The Path To Self-Actualization: In order to fulfill my specific evolutionary goals in this life, I resolve to define a prize worthy of attaining and then to keep my eye on it, pursuing it relentlessly. I value excellence and accomplishment over notions of living a balanced life. I am willing to make sacrifices and to discipline myself in order to create some kind of great work. Effort does not daunt me. I can work alone if I need to. I am a self-starter.

The Stained Glass Through Which the Light of My Soul Shines: I am complex, but in what people see, there is a distinct spin in the direction of focused seriousness of purpose. I am not always "strictly business" – I can be funny and entertaining too. But I radiate integrity, along with the aura of being the sort of person who can actually get things done in an effective, practical, efficient way. In my outward style, an appearance of self-sufficiency is exaggerated beyond what I really feel inside. I need people more than I seem to need them.

When I Am Merely Wearing A Mask: If I slip into posturing and posing, I can be officious and controlling. I might offer too much unsolicited advice or correction, assuming a kind of authority over others which they have not in fact granted me. I radiate an attitude that seems to suggest that I believe that the universe exists mainly to annoy me.

What I Look Like When I Am Lost: If I have failed to follow the thread of my natural path, then I come across with an air of priggish judgmentalness. I can be awkward socially. I labor under the weight of my grievous responsibilities, but turn away from help or from opportunities to release my burdens.

THE AQUARIUS ASCENDANT

The Path To Self-Actualization: In order to fulfill my specific evolutionary goals in this life, I resolve to follow my own independent instincts no matter where they lead me. I accept the fact that in this lifetime I am destined to travel "the road less traveled." I am happy if people like me and accept me, but I do not need anyone's approval – and I willingly recognize that, if I am true to myself, there will be those who judge me, mock me, or worry about me. It is not that I do not care about that – it is that I resolve never to allow such pressures to affect my direction in life. If anyone wants to think that I am weird, that is their business, not mine.

The Stained Glass Through Which the Light of My Soul Shines: I am complex, but in what people see, there is a distinct spin in the direction of my being my own person and following my own counsel. I radiate free-thinking independence. From a conventional perspective, there is something unusual about my energy and social presentation. I may even seem strange to more conventional people – and such assessments do not bother me. What they think of me is not really my concern.

When I Am Merely Wearing A Mask: If I slip into posturing and posing, I can take on an air of exaggerated, even theatrical, idiosyncrasy, as if I am *trying* to shock or unsettle people. Instead of being free, I merely seem silly or contrary. Another possibility is that I adjust superficially to what is expected of me, and simply seem distant and disengaged – and probably I feel that way too.

What I Look Like When I Am Lost: If I have failed to follow the thread of my natural path, then I might actually come across as "normal and appropriate," to the point that I go unnoticed – but if anyone feels moved to get closer to me, he or she quickly senses a kind of emotional absence in me, as if my soul were lurking behind a thick wall of distorting, translucent glass.

THE PISCES ASCENDANT

The Path To Self-Actualization: In order to fulfill my specific evolutionary goals in this life, I resolve to prioritize exploring consciousness and expanding my awareness of my inner world. That may take the appearance of following some kind of overt spiritual path – but just as easily, it could mean maximizing my creative life. There is more than one way to explore deep consciousness, in other words. I resolve always to put the life and wellbeing of my soul ahead of all other practical or material concerns. I will walk that talk until the day I die – and when my death comes, unlike most people, I will be ready for it. I will know that I am only going home.

The Stained Glass Through Which the Light of My Soul Shines: I am complex, but in what people see, there is a distinct spin in the direction of warmth, caring, and sensitivity. I can play many roles, fit into many diverse social situations. There is a fluidity about my outward character. People who feel that they know me well will often describe me in different ways, but all will agree that I am kind, and a little mysterious.

When I Am Merely Wearing A Mask: If I slip into posturing and posing, I can assume the air of "the master actor." That means that I am able to play any role, but that I am uncertain about which one is my authentic self. Like a chameleon, I can take on the coloration of my social surroundings, blending in without a ripple, shrouded in a fog of pleasant vagueness.

What I Look Like When I Am Lost: If I have failed to follow the thread of my natural path, then I come across as drifting and rudderless. I seem to be a sensitive person who is overwhelmed by life, resigned to hoping that nothing bad happens to me, but powerless to do anything about it. I slip into fantasyland, never missing an opportunity to "absent myself" from direct, active engagement with anything or anybody.

26

OUR MAP TO THE
GOLDEN CITY

Astrology's star is currently rising everywhere, especially among young-er people. An article in *The Atlantic* in January 2018, trumpeted *The New Age of Astrology*, and added, "In a stressful, data-driven era, many young people find comfort and insight in the zodiac – *even if they don't exactly believe in it.*"

Well, we astrologers have been damned with faint praise before. May-be we should take encouragement wherever we can find it, despite the zinger in that final phrase – which, by the way, insults young people at least as much as it insults astrologers.

Thank you anyway, *The Atlantic*.

An article in the October 28, 2019 issue of *The New Yorker* magazine was entitled, *Astrology in the Age of Uncertainty*. There we read, "Millennials who see no contradiction between using astrology and believing in science are fueling a resurgence of the practice."

The faintness of the praise there in *The New Yorker* piece is slightly more masked – the snarky implication being that there is *of course* a con-tradiction between astrology and science, if only we have brains enough to look for it.

OK, magazines. Two can play this game. It's my turn to be snarky.

Immediately both of these magazine headlines make me think of the prophetic words of Max Planck, who is often seen as the father of quantum mechanics: *A scientific truth does not triumph by convincing its opponents and making them see the light, but rather because its opponents eventually die and a new generation grows up that is familiar with it.*

Sweet revenge, right? Once the young people are on your side, then time is on your side too. Might astrology be heading for a *golden city*, at least once our ignorant critics have all bitten the dust? I fervently hope so – but here in my own grandfather years, I also hope to influence our choice of routes to that golden city. Some will work better than others. I am hopeful about our eventual arrival there – and a little worried too. Astrology's current upsurge in popularity might prove to be transitory. I think it is an *opportunity to be seized* rather than a helping of dumb luck to be enjoyed while we have it.

According to a 2009 Harris poll, 26% of Americans "believe in astrology." (I am not sure what the figures are in other countries, but I suspect that number is fairly representative.) Flip the figures: another way to say exactly the same thing is that *about three-quarters of the population disbelieves in astrology* – often loudly and militantly, often while wearing the crown of academic or spiritual authority.

That is the hostile reality of the environment in which all living astrologers have grown up. We have all needed to adapt to it, starting with how we were dismissed in grammar school science class. No one becomes an astrologer today unless all of that negativity is like water off a duck's back. That is why, as a group, astrologers are so highly Uranian: *only people who have been inclined to question authority and doubt the dominant paradigm could possibly choose to pursue astrology in a serious way.*

And yet here I am, trying to tell them what to do. It would be easier to herd cats – or to preach socialism on Wall Street, or polyamory in the convent.

That anti-astrology antagonism is softening now. Our "poll numbers" are on the upswing. Maybe that will help. It is easy to rhapsodize about a future in which a young person choosing to pursue astrology as a career causes no one to bat an eye, not even a high school guidance counsellor. I do think that would be a better, wiser, kinder world – and of course simply bringing the estimable benefits of astrological insight to a wider swath of humanity is as righteous as wishing for more organic vegetables in every supermarket.

Thinking about our possible route to that golden city, the big question in my mind is, will we astrologers use this present opportunity actually to create that astrology-positive future – or will we miss the opportunity, pander to the crowd, make a few dollars, and allow this little boost in our fashionability to turn out to be as transitory as yesterday's Tweet?

That question brings me right back to me being in my grandfather years and wanting to use whatever wisdom I have acquired to help us steer us past the various slippery slopes which lie before us.

The subtitle of this book is "Healing, Regeneration, and Recovery" – and, to me, those three words lie at the heart of any kind of astrology that is worth practicing or preserving. No one has ever been healed, regenerated, or helped in recovery by being told that he or she is doomed – or even that he or she has no choices.

Nobody has ever really been helped very much simply by being described either. Presumably they are already familiar with themselves.

We astrologers are capable of so much more than that. If we do this work right, we are *actively helpful*. When we are at our best, healing souls is the heart of our craft and always our conscious intention. That is a promise that we can make to our clients – and one which we can keep, provided that we use our skills wisely and keep our eye on the true prize.

Earlier in these pages, I quoted a 1904 book which informed anyone born in the month following February 18 that her life would be "one constant battle: the overcoming of obstacles, the meeting of tremendous disappointments . . ."

I shudder to think of the impact of such a toxic prediction upon a sensitive, impressionable Piscean soul, especially a young one. Fortunately, that kind of extreme darkness and negativity is mostly out of fashion in the world of contemporary astrology – but rigid predictions and dead-end "character delineations" are still alive and well, and almost as dangerous as they ever were. For example, on a lark, I just Googled my own Sun sign, Capricorn. I was immediately whisked directly to the website of *Cosmopolitan* magazine, where I gleaned the following (slightly abridged) insights into myself: *ambitious* (read: workaholic), *realistic* (read: pessimistic), *sensitive* (read: touchy), *disciplined* (read: uptight).

I lacked the moral courage to click on, "What are Capricorns like sexually?" I am not sure I could have faced it. I am sure that if I had clicked it, my Scorpio Ascendant and my Aries Moon would have been inclined toward *jihad*.

That kind of *half-witted wittiness* has always been a pop astrology staple. I am resigned to that reality. My fear is that pandering to fools, while profitable, is probably not the optimal route to our golden city.

We can all laugh at this kind of embarrassing, glamour magazine astrology, and also quickly see how spectacularly it flunks every reality check. But what if astrologers deliver essentially the same poisons in fancier intellectual garb? I don't want to hurt anyone or to waste my time on any personal wars, so I will not name names here. Instead, to protect the guilty, I will write fancifully, lampooning a fictional modern astrological interpretation of a natal Moon in Scorpio squared by Pluto, based on my impressions from several sources. In the following words, I am fantasizing about an allegedly serious astrology text, perhaps written by an astrologer with academic letters after his or her name.

> *SCORPIO MOON IN THE FOURTH HOUSE: The underlying psychological complexes which explain your tendencies toward depressive ideation and your chronic inability to experience trust in a partner (or to be trustworthy yourself) have their origin in your unresolved relationship with your mother, who failed properly to form the essential maternal-infant pair-bond with you – an unfortunate circumstance which resulted from her own unresolved depressive issues and her ambivalence toward motherhood, all of which was further complicated by her emotional rejection of your father, which in turn derived from her earlier rejection of her own father, who very likely abused her. In unconscious loyalty to your mother, you too are inclined to hide your authentic self behind a sexualized persona . . .*

And blah, blah, blah. This hypothetical reading of the Moon configuration could possibly even be true – although naturally many other interpretations exist as well. Even if these stylized, academically intimidating, words were accurate, the problem is that they lead nowhere – they *describe*, but they do not *help*. There is no healing in them. *They are diagnostic, but not prescriptive.* They may be the words of a Seer, but they are not the words of a Healer.

They are like the mechanic saying, "Yeah, you're right – your car won't start," then walking away.

Has anyone ever been healed by a diagnosis? Has mere diagnosis ever triggered regeneration or recovery in anyone?

My point is that astrology is capable of so much more. My prayer for the future of our craft is that we claim its full healing potential rather than simply holding a depressing – or embarrassing – mirror before people's foibles, shortcomings, and wounds, even if what we see in the mirror is accurate.

How tragic it would be if, on the edge of this golden public relations opportunity, we failed to move astrology beyond description and into prescription?

I call my own style of astrology "evolutionary" mostly for the simple reason that it recognizes that people are capable of change and growth. In the system I have been presenting over these past four volumes, we try to fan the flames of *intentional self-improvement* rather than quenching them with deadening pigeon-hole "descriptions" – such as *Cosmopolitan's* insulting view of Capricorn or my parody of that gloomy psychological astrologer.

Illustrating the higher ground, here is a condensed version of what you read earlier in *The Book of Water* regarding a natal Scorpio Moon. As you think about these next few lines, imagine that the person reading them is someone whose particular "mother issues" that psychological astrologer just described with uncanny accuracy. Compare the effect of those dead-end words with the potentially healing – and hopeful – impact of the following language:

> *I resolve to be true to my own heart no matter where it leads me. I will let myself feel anything and everything, no matter how dark or taboo it might be, so long as it rises up naturally within me . . . I am skillful at looking beneath the surface of other people's behavior. I can see the true story behind their "official" story . . . I can handle it when people express strong emotions . . . To be happy, I need a feeling of authenticity and realness in my primary relationships. I need to feel connected to other people in a naked, heart-to-heart kind of way . . . One secret of happiness for me is the realization that I am not required to be happy all the time.*

The earlier paragraph of "psychological astrology" leaves the client feeling *nailed,* while this second one offers a sense of *authentic direction* and *possibility.* Rather than focusing on a wounding past, it describes a healing path forward into the future.

That is one difference between prescription versus mere description.

I think it is as clear as a window pane that a person is much more likely to be helped, encouraged, and guided by that evolutionary language than he or she would ever be simply by being placed in a box with a psychiatric label.

Let me quickly add that the psychological astrologer's analysis *can potentially be part of the evolutionary astrologer's presentation.* In fact, if presented with less rigidity, it should be. The problem with that analysis is not so much that it is wrong; the problem is that it is *hopeless.* It leads nowhere except to a bleak landscape of depressing insight. Evolutionary astrology, in other words, does not refute psychological astrology – it includes it, adds to it, loosens it up, and ultimately goes beyond it.

If you read our first, admittedly somewhat cartoonish, "psychological" interpretation and immediately follow it with the second evolutionary one, you have something that reflects the power of the whole integrated system. Diagnosis alone helps no one, but *diagnosis and prescription* – that is evolutionary astrology. That is the path to healing, regeneration, and recovery.

Evolutionary astrology is the synthesis of twentieth century psychological astrology and ancient metaphysics – not to mention simple hope, and faith in the human potential for transformation.

To be clear, I am miles from saying that to get to our golden city, we all need to become evolutionary astrologers. I would never want to be that rigid or to express such a diminished respect for the diversity of our astrological traditions. What I am saying is only that I believe that this more open-ended, supportive *philosophy* is where our future lies. People today do not want to be signed, sealed, and delivered by their astrologers. They want to be helped. They want their autonomy to be honored, enhanced, and respected. They want their own power to be recognized, not dismissed or ignored.

While I am at it, let me take a shot at another sacred cow in current astrological practice: *making predictions.* As soon as we claim to see anyone's future – even if it is a cheery one – we have unwittingly endorsed the view that we are all just marionettes dangling from strings held by the planets. When they twitch, we twitch. And that is a sad illusion. We are actually far more powerful than that. *The choices we make* influence the shapes of our lives – to me, that is really just common sense.

In evolutionary astrology, we do not predict the future; we *create* the future. We can predict the *questions* that people will be facing at any given time. Within the limits of our wisdom, we can even suggest answers – and also warn people about life's tempting pitfalls. *But we can never know what is going to happen.*

Sometimes, by using common sense and the laws of probability, we can make an accurate guess, that's all. What happens for example when an unscrupulous clerk who has been stealing money out of the cash register experiences transiting Saturn hitting his Ascendant? Getting busted for thievery is a lot more likely than winning a trip to Paris.

An astrologer who predicted that the clerk would get caught is likely to be proven correct.

But might there be another possibility? Might that clerk have developed a *guilty conscience* and begun slipping bills back *into* that cash register – and maybe living on thin soup in order to afford to do it? That could also be a response to Saturn hitting the Ascendant, and obviously a far loftier one. If an astrologer suggested something like that second possibility – even not knowing specifically about the thievery – *and if the client listened, and was inspired to change his behavior* . . . well, that is the kind of soul-healing astrology that I am advocating here.

Bottom line, if we are transparent about its inherently *probabilistic nature*, prediction is a legitimate use of astrology. We just have to be clear with our clients that in making predictions, we are like economists or meteorologists presenting "educated guesses" – there is a 30% chance of rain showers today, *and 90% chance you are going to be caught with your hand in the till. And a 10% chance of a moral renaissance.*

Fair enough. We can do that.

We astrologers get into trouble when we make predictive claims without those kinds of caveats. We may often be right, but in the end, such claims will always blow up in our faces. And our wrong predictions get a lot of press. Remember, 74% of the people out there think we are self-deluded at best, or charlatans at worst. Let's not play into their hands by purporting to do something at which we often fail. Just this month, a prominent Internet astrologer scored the following headline in the prestigious *New York Times* – "Will Coronavirus Kill Astrology?" She had predicted on CBS television in front of who knows how many people "that 2020 would be a great year, and it will be a prosperous year." And of course, with the Covid-19 pandemic, quite the opposite has happened – spectacularly. Hence our latest moment of infamy in the *New York Times*.

The jackals are always circling.

My point is not to beat up this astrologer for getting a prediction wrong. My point is that *astrology beats itself up* when we make any kind of attractive promise that we cannot actually fulfill, such as claiming that we can foresee the future. Such posturing inevitably catches up with us – and yet, like a moth to the flame, we soon make more predictions. The public expects it – and until we wake up to the fact that we are healers, not omniscient gods, we will continue to live up to our own bad press.

I am obviously partisan to evolutionary astrology practised in the technical ways that I teach it – a timed Ascendant, Placidus houses, the Mean lunar nodes, attention to declination and lunar phase, and so on.

But my point here is far larger.

I see no reason why, for example, a Hellenistic astrologer using Whole Sign houses and ignoring everything except the seven classical planets could not update his or her language to include more room for evolutionary possibility, along with positing *a future which does not yet exist* simply because we have not yet created it. The same would go for Vedic astrology, Cosmobiology, the Uranian system – or even Sun sign columns. "What's Up for Taurus this Month" can potentially be framed in more open-ended language. Such a columnist can write in the language of personal responsibility and respect for each person's own life-shaping creative power. I tried that myself when I did the Sun Sign column for *Elle* magazine many years ago – and, OK, they eventually fired me. I lost a nice paycheck, but at least I kept my dignity.

My deeper point is that these issues are philosophical and moral, not technical. It is not about the school of thought to which we subscribe astrologically. It is about whether or not we value free will and its constant companion: personal responsibility.

As we partner with our clients to help them create futures they desire – and to warn them of glitzy ones they would be better off avoiding – we are not only offering genuine help, we are also using astrology in a way that is consistent with the way the universe actually works. We can be helpful *and be right* at the same time.

It is a sweet combination – and one that might allow our craft to succeed at becoming a lasting part of the mainstream human future. It might lead us to the golden city. And it would be an astrology unerringly centered on processes of healing, regeneration, and recovery.

If astrology's true star rises in the world, society might very well find itself swallowing some unexpected medicine – a sacred, and rather psychedelic, medicine at that.

- Just the observed fact that a map of the sky at the instant of your birth can speak so directly to your soul implies an interconnectedness between ourselves and nature that goes beyond even mystical environmentalism in the scope of its implications.

- Jupiter – half a billion miles away – comes to the degree of the zodiac that was overhead when you were born. You get a promotion. What does that imply about the actual fabric of reality? What does that indicate about how things actually work in this universe? What does that mean about "cosmic oneness"?

- The fact that your birthchart not only describes you, but also illuminates a path of happiness and meaning for you, tells us – *what exactly?* Can it mean anything other than the fact that "something up there loves you and is helping you?" That there is some larger purpose to your life? That you are *connected to a soul-nurturing cosmos* in ways few people today recognize? That the universe itself seems to be an *incubator of consciousness?*

- A baby takes his first breath. Maybe his chart describes a soulmate *who has not yet even been born.* Decades later, they meet. That second chart was prophesied in the first one, *before the second chart even existed.* Try reconciling that observed fact with any notion of a random universe.

- Sky and mind, mind and sky: like two mirrors facing each other. Let that idea sink in and chew on it – and then think of trying to explain it to your high school physics teacher. Might you feel like an astronaut trying to explain that the Earth is actually round to a Neanderthal? That is what we mean by "paradigm shift".

- A corporation has a chart. A relationship has a chart. Even a *question* has a chart. And there are no physical bodies involved. *Those charts still work.* Even if we create a materialistic understanding of how astrology functions, that understanding founders on these non-material observations. Perhaps the universe is more like an idea than a clock. That is another face of "paradigm shift."

We live in an enchanted universe and it lives inside of us. If we experience the impact of conscious, choice-centered astrology – *and if we think about the implications of what we are experiencing* – the ground shifts beneath our feet. We are luminous creatures on a mysterious, meaningful journey, not cogs in some mindless revenue-generating machine.

Given the present madness of the world, does that not all sound as if it might spell healing, regeneration, and recovery on a societal scale?

Astrology's star is indeed rising, and it is currently surfing other waves of cultural change. We hear about a *postmodern world*. We hear about *late-stage capitalism*. Every day we are assailed with another story of impending apocalypse, and any one of them might come true – but no story of endings can exist without a story of new beginnings.

We present-day astrologers are part of an ancient lineage. The past continues to live on inside us. Can we help create tomorrow too? Astrology is robust; its star may rise and fall, but its flame has never died, nor will it. *And yet we now find ourselves faced with an opportunity to offer our healing gift to a wider audience.* Synchronistically, that opportunity comes at a time when the world itself badly needs regeneration and recovery – it needs *a new myth of itself.*

I pray that we astrologers are skillful in the way we navigate this crossroads.

May generosity of spirit rather than personal ambition be our North Star, and may respect for the life-shaping power of human consciousness be the firm foundation upon which we stand.

Amen – and onward we march into the fog and the mysteries.

I want to thank all of you for giving me the chance to live this blessed life. Your support and enthusiasm have helped me to heal, to regenerate, and to recover more times than I can count.

Thank you for that. Be well, be merry, and blessed be.

– Steven Forrest
Borrego Springs, California
June 2020

27

AFTERWORD: LOOSE ENDS – AND THE FORREST CENTER FOR EVOLUTIONARY ASTROLOGY

Conspicuously absent from these four volumes is that absolutely critical ground upon which evolutionary astrology rests – *the nodes of the Moon, their rulers, and their aspects*. Emphatically, no one can do evolutionary astrology without that knowledge. It illuminates the specific issues left over from prior lifetimes – issues which reincarnated along with us in order that we might resolve them this time around.

I left that critical material out of these four books simply because I had already recorded it all in sign-by-sign, house-by-house, aspect-by-aspect, detail in my 2008 book, *Yesterday's Sky: Astrology and Reincarnation*.

To do evolutionary astrology as I practice it, you need that knowledge.

I also ignored Chiron. That may have been a mistake – I do often use it in my practice, partly because Chiron's effects are real, and partly because it is popular and people often ask about it. Still, I often wonder about the other Centaur objects, of which there are many. Why use Chiron and ignore Pholus, for example?

All of that leads quickly to my decision to skip the asteroids. Ceres? Pallas? Juno? Vesta? Those are usually cited as the "big four." But Hygiea is now known to be more massive than Juno . . . and then there are thousands more.

I had to set a boundary somewhere and decided to limit the scope of this project to the ten planets which most astrologers currently recognize as planets-in-full. There went Chiron, along with the rest of these smaller astronomical bodies.

I have misgivings about leaving out the newly-discovered planet, Eris. After all, it is the size of Pluto. I take it seriously, and I have no doubt that Eris will eventually be viewed as the equal of Pluto in its impact on our lives. I left Eris out simply because, unlike the rest of what I have written in this series, I do not at this point have the same depth of client experience with it as I do with the other planets. I wanted the material in these books to be bullet-proof and reliable, and I did not feel that I could live up to that standard quite yet with Eris.

So: I left a lot of material out, despite the length of this Elements project. I should add that one of my literary goals in writing this series was to see to it that when all was said and done, you would still outweigh these four books.

Speaking of which, you may have noticed that each one has gotten a little bit heavier than its predecessor. That is easy to explain. With Fire and Earth, we were still in the simpler world of signs with single rulers. Air gave us the dual rulership of Aquarius – four planets to explore rather than three. And here with Water, we had to add a fifth planet, since both Scorpio and Pisces are each ruled by two planets.

Along with Saturn and Pluto currently transiting through Capricorn (where my Sun, Jupiter, and Mercury lie), my Moon has been progressing through my twelfth house throughout much of this whole Elements project. Saturn and Pluto meant a lot of hard work and soul-searching, but I knew that such a lunar progression meant that much would naturally be falling away in my life at the same time in order to make space for a new start – one that I could not yet envision. Specifically, in order to make time to write, I have had to let go of many of my teaching programs. Sure enough, into the vacuum came an opportunity to entirely restructure my Apprenticeship Programs, which leads me to exciting news. I am currently in the process of helping to create The Forrest Center for Evolutionary Astrology, which we hope to launch around the time this final volume in the Elements series first appears in print.

All along, the most persistent problem with my teaching programs has been the need to have relative beginners sitting beside students who already had developed professional astrological practices. My teaching situation always reflected the dilemma of "the little red schoolhouse," in other words.

Somehow, the classes always worked, consistently drawing between fifty and eighty students for each program. But the price was my having to toggle my gaze between sometimes-puzzled faces on the beginners and the politely suppressed yawns of the people who had heard me tell that same story a dozen times.

Along came two people, both of them major blessings in my life. One of them is Jeff Parrett – who wrote the Introduction to The Book of Fire and helped fund me writing it. Jeff had retired a few years before, relatively young and merrily flush, from a successful career in the burgeoning Internet Technology world here in California. He has been generous financially with our FCEA project, but equally helpfully, he understands business structures, tax laws, and many other mission-critical things for making the school a reality.

And he believes in it with the kind of energy only a good Sagittarian can emanate.

My other blessing is Dr. Catie Cadge. She is a tenured professor of art history at Anza College, with many years of experience with online teaching. She understands both the technology and the human interface of that modern form of pedagogy – how to keep students engaged, how to monitor their progress, and so on.

Jeff and Catie are also both fine astrologers, who have both been long-time students of mine.

Our aim with the Forrest Center for Evolutionary Astrology is to solve the little red schoolhouse problem. We will replace it with a more structured, step-by-step program of instruction. Without going into too much detail, let me just say that the FCEA will be a hybrid program, with both online and "live" components. In broad terms, beginning students will learn the basic material online – in other words, I will never again have to recite, "there are twelve signs in the zodiac . . ."

My own active teaching will move up a notch from there, taking the form of a mixture of webinars and actual physical meetings – and I anticipate that the latter will echo the shape of my old Apprenticeship Programs, except that everyone will arrive in the room already knowing that there are, in fact, twelve signs in the zodiac.

If you want to learn more about the programs we offer at the FCEA, please have a look at our website: https://forrestastrology.center

Meanwhile, my own website – www.forrestastrology.com – run by the able Tony Howard, is full of books and articles that I have written, along with floods of recorded lectures and instructional videos. Some of them are free, some help me pay my bills. All together, what is available on that website represents a vast astrological library, *which looks like it was hit by a tornado*. A complete education in evolutionary astrology as I practice it is available to anyone there. The trouble is that you might find a third grade class coming right after a post-doctoral seminar – and to understand that seminar you actually needed an eleventh grade class, which you had not gotten to yet, mostly because you did not know that it was there.

You get the picture: chaos reigns.

One of our fundamental mandates with the FCEA is simply to *organize* that material in step-by-step fashion. We want to take the hand of a beginner and hold it right through getting his or her astrological PhD.

We are also aware that some people who join the program will not be kindergarteners at all. There will be ways for more advanced students – and certainly ones who have been part of my Apprenticeship Programs – to place out of the more elementary material.

There will be much more information to come about the Forrest Center for Evolutionary Astrology. These four Elements books will be some of its most fundamental textbooks – which is one reason why I have had to hurry up and get them written.

At this point – actually on the very day that my Moon progresses out of the twelfth house and into my Ascendant – I simply want to formally announce the school.

So: thank you to Jeff Parrett and Catie Cadge, and everyone else who has supported me in creating this legacy.

My gratitude is beyond my capacity to express it.

LEARN ASTROLOGY WITH STEVEN FORREST

Interested in learning more about Steven's unique approach to astrology? For a listing of lectures and workshops that are available in a variety of audio and video formats online for instant viewing and download, visit https://www.forrestastrology.com/store.

Better yet, join the many successful students who have completed Steven's Astrological Apprenticeship Program, where he teaches both the specific techniques of interpretation and the style of presentation that have made him one of the most successful and influential astrologers in the world.

Steven takes great joy in passing on the teachings and strategies that have worked for him over the years through his Apprenticeship Program, and in 2018 was honored with the prestigious Regulus Award for his years of dedication in the field.

The Apprenticeship Program presents students with a rare opportunity to learn astrology in a supportive environment of like-minded individuals, who together create a feeling of community and connection, leading to bonds that last throughout life. Some come to the program to train professionally, while others come for personal or spiritual enrichment.

Learn more at www.forrestastrology.com.

Printed in Great Britain
by Amazon

48709519R00312